Learning Greek in Western Europe,
1396–1529

Learning Greek in Western Europe, 1396–1529
Grammars, Lexica, and Classroom Texts

Paul Botley

American Philosophical Society
Philadelphia · 2010

> TRANSACTIONS
> of the
> AMERICAN PHILOSOPHICAL SOCIETY
> Held at Philadelphia
> For Promoting Useful Knowledge
> Volume 100, Part 2

Copyright © 2010 by the American Philosophical Society for its *Transactions* series, Volume 100. All rights reserved.

ISBN-13: 978-1-60618-002-0

US ISSN: 0065-9746

Library of Congress Cataloging-in-Publication Data

Botley, Paul.
  Learning Greek in Western Europe, 1396-1529 : grammars, lexica, and classroom texts / Paul Botley.
    p. cm.—(Transactions of the American Philosophical Society held at Philadelphia for promoting useful knowledge ; v. 100, pt. 5)
  Includes bibliographical references and index.
  ISBN 978-1-60618-002-0
  1. Greek language—Study and teaching—Europe—History—To 1500. 2. Greek language—Study and teaching—Europe—History—16th century. 3. Greek philology—Study and teaching—Europe—History—To 1500. 4. Greek philology—Study and teaching—Europe—History—16th century. 5. Greek language—Grammar, Historical. 6. Greek language—Lexicology, Historical. I. Title.

PA240.E85B67 2010
488.007104'09024—dc22   2010021467

Contents

Abbreviations	vii
Acknowledgments	ix
Preface	xi
Chapter 1: Greek Grammars	1
Ancient and Byzantine Greek Grammatical Works	3
Greek Grammars in Western Europe, 1396–1529	6
Manuel Calecas, 1391–1396?	6
Manuel Chrysoloras, by 1406	7
George Scholarios, ca. 1430	12
Matthaeus Camariotes, by 1490	13
Theodore Gaza, 1461–1462	14
Constantine Lascaris, 1463–1466	26
Johann Reuchlin, 1479–1481	31
Aldus Manutius, 1480s	33
Conrad Celtis, 1491	33
Demetrius Chalcondyles, 1493	34
Urbano Bolzanio, 1497	36
Georg Simler, 1512	40
Ottomar Nachtgall, 1517	42
Joannes Oecolampadius, 1518	44
Philip Melanchthon, 1518	45
Adrien Amerot, 1520	47
Jean Chéradame, 1521	48
Jacobus Ceporinus, 1522	49
Sanctes Pagninus, 1525	50
Johann Winther of Andernach, 1527	51
Johann Metzler, 1529	52

vi   Contents

Chapter 2: Greek Lexica — 55
  Ancient and Byzantine Greek Lexica — 55
  The Suda Lexicon — 55
  Julius Pollux — 58
  The *Etymologicum magnum* — 58
  Valerius Harpocration — 59
  Phrynichus — 60
  Stephanus of Byzantium — 60
  Hesychius — 61
  Greek Lexica in Western Europe, 1396–1529 — 61

Chapter 3: Student Texts — 71
  Elementary Pamphlets — 72
  The Greek Scriptures — 75
  Greek Translations of Latin Texts — 76
  The *Aurea verba* and Pseudo-Phocylides — 77
  Aesop — 79
  Homer — 80
  Lucian — 85
  Aristophanes — 88
  Xenophon — 91
  Demosthenes — 93
  Isocrates — 96
  Plutarch — 97
  Plato — 99
  Hesiod — 100
  Theocritus — 102
  Euripides — 104
  Sophocles — 106
  Pindar — 108
  Apollonius of Rhodes — 109
  Pseudo-Orpheus — 110
  Quintus of Smyrna — 111

Epilogue — 115

Appendix 1: Printed Texts for Students of Greek, 1471–1529 — 119

Appendix 2: Printed Greek Lexica, 1478–1529 — 155

Notes — 163

Bibliography — 233

Index — 259

Abbreviations

The abbreviations used for classical works and authors are those used in the third edition of the *Oxford Classical Dictionary*. Abbreviations for journal titles are to be found in *L'année philologique*. In addition, the following abbreviations are used in this work:

BAV   Bibliotheca Apostolica Vaticana

BL   British Library, London

BLC   British Library Public Catalogue (http://blpc.bl.uk)

EE   Allen, P. S., H. M. Allen, and H. W. Garrod, eds. *Opus Epistolarum Des. Erasmi Roterodami*. 12 vols. Oxford: Clarendon Press, 1906–58

ISTC *The Illustrated Incunabula Short Title Catalogue*. Primary Source Media, in association with the British Library. CD-ROM. VBIA Ver. 1.5

OCD   Hornblower, S., and A. Spawforth, eds. *The Oxford Classical Dictionary*. 3rd ed., rev. Oxford: Oxford University Press, 2003

PBN   Bibliothèque nationale, Paris

PG   Migne, J.-P., ed. *Patrologiae cursus completus: Series graeca*. 161 vols. Paris: Migne, 1857–66

PL   Migne, J.-P., ed. *Patrologiae cursus completus: Series latina*. 221 vols. Paris: Migne, 1844–90

RGK   Gamillscheg, E., and D. Harlfinger. *Repertorium der griechischen Kopisten 800–1600*. 3 vols. Vienna: Verlag der Österreichischen Akademie der Wissenschaften, 1981–97

Early printed Greek grammars or lexica are detailed in appendices 1 and 2. In the footnotes of this book, works in these appendices are identified by appendix number and item number. Thus Melanchthon's grammar of 1527 is appendix 1, no. 165. All texts quoted in this book have been repunctuated, and all translations are my own.

Acknowledgments

This book owes its existence to three institutions. Much of the research on which it is founded was completed while I was Munby Fellow at the University Library, Cambridge. Most of the writing was made possible by a fellowship at the Institute of Greece, Rome, and the Classical Tradition at the University of Bristol. The resulting text was scrutinized and mended at the Warburg Institute in London during my time as one of the editors of the correspondence of Joseph Scaliger. Friends and colleagues at all these places were generous with their time, but I am particularly grateful to Anthony Ossa-Richardson, Eugenia Russell, and David Speranzi for their corrections to my text.

My other debts are to the dead. In a work such as this, I am very aware of what I owe to earlier generations of careful scholarship. My gratitude for what they have enabled me to know can only be registered baldly in this note. I also owe a great deal to the pioneering scholars studied here, who have passed on to me some of what they gave to their own students. From them I learned that the cardinal virtues of the scholar are *diligentia* and *industria*. I cannot have noticed everything of relevance to my subject in the following pages, and it is impossible that what I have set down here is free from error. But whatever the faults of this book, I have, I hope, used both.

Paul Botley
London, 2010

Preface

This book attempts to assemble scattered pieces of evidence in order to construct a more complete image of student activity than any that has previously appeared. It emerged from my earlier study of Latin translations of Greek texts produced during the same period.[1] I found that the history of the translation of many Greek texts was tied up with the history of Greek instruction in the classrooms of the period. More broadly, I became aware that while these translators were at work, the expectations and assumptions of their readers were being altered by the expansion of Greek studies. Before turning to specific translations, it seemed necessary to establish their context by examining the diffusion of elementary Greek studies in Western Europe during the same period. What began as a preliminary study has now grown into a book.

This book is an attempt to answer a question that I first asked at the very beginning of my research: how did students learn Greek in Renaissance Europe? While an answer to this question was of interest to scholars working in a number of different fields, few attempts had been made to provide an answer appropriate to the varied interests of those who asked it. Many related questions have been answered over the years by scholars, and one of the functions of this book is to bring together some of the detailed scholarship that has accumulated on Greek studies in Renaissance Europe. My aim has been to digest the results of these sophisticated researches into the diffusion of Greek texts to produce something that might be of use to a broader scholarly community. For this reason, all passages of Latin and Greek quoted in the text have been provided with a translation. I have tried to summarize and draw attention to the latest research in the field. I have also attempted to state what we do not know. Such statements are always dangerous, but it is important to make the effort. One of the purposes of surveys such as this is to tell us where to look next.

This book aims to supply convenient summaries of the distribution, virtues, and limitations of the tools of Renaissance Greek scholarship. To this end, it examines three types of text. Chapter 1 studies Greek grammatical works, Chapter 2 looks at Greek dictionaries, and Chapter 3 surveys some of the Greek texts used by students of the language in the early stages of their instruction. These chapters are divided into carefully focused sections in order to accommodate readers who prefer to concentrate on the fortunes of writers or works of particular interest to them. Not everyone who is interested in Sophocles is interested in Simler. I am aware that these summaries often make for rather dense reading, but they could have been lightened only by omitting pertinent material.

Greek grammars of the fifteenth century have been only partially investigated. The aim of the first chapter is to place what we know about the production and diffusion of these early grammars into some chronological order. It is for this reason that the following pages are so full of precise dates. For the period after 1471, this chapter is largely founded upon bibliographical research. Since Greek grammars are among the earliest Greek texts printed, most previous bibliographical work has been produced by scholars interested in the early history of Greek printing.[2] All students of early Greek printing are indebted to the great surveys of Renouard and Legrand.[3] Yet there has been little systematic work on Greek grammars in this period by those who are interested in the evolution of Greek studies in the universities and schools of Western Europe.[4] The bibliography of early printed Greek grammars appended to this study is intended to lay the foundations for a clearer understanding of this evolution. While it is substantial, it is probably incomplete. It should allow new items to be quickly contextualized, and it may also do something to lay to rest some of the bibliographical ghosts that still appear in the secondary literature from time to time.

The Greek dictionaries of the period are in many ways far less problematic. These substantial works have usually survived in significant numbers in the libraries of Europe. A detailed description of these dictionaries has been appended to this work because it seems that no such survey has appeared before. It also serves another purpose. While the existence of these dictionaries is well established, the shifting combinations of minor lexical works in their appendices have not been charted before. In this appendix, these supplementary texts are documented for the first time in some detail.

This survey of early Greek grammatical works led to the rediscovery of many of the brief Greek texts that were used to introduce Latin readers to the Greek language. Some of these texts, long banished from classical curricula, have received little attention from literary historians, despite the fact that they were regularly used in the classroom by generations of students. The third chapter of this book provides the first survey of the elementary texts commonly used by students of Greek during the period under investigation. All authors who were studied or lectured on at some time during this period are included here. This survey is itself extracted from a broader survey that I am now compiling of the fortunes of all Greek authors during the period. It is also derived from the works of modern textual critics. These critics are usually more interested in what Demosthenes actually wrote than in what Renaissance readers of Demosthenes read, and they tend to be interested in his fifteenth-century manuscripts only insofar as they contribute to this end. More often than not, I have found that I am interested in just that part of the manuscript tradition that textual scholars have worked hardest to eliminate. In short, I have read many prefaces to modern editions of Greek texts, and modern studies of Greek manuscript traditions, in search of information that they were not primarily intended to provide. Happily, this situation is changing, and the obscure backwaters of these traditions are now attracting the attention of able scholars.

Finally, the boundaries of this work require some explanation. The teaching of Leonzio Pilato in Italy in the 1350s and 1360s represents something of a false dawn for Greek studies in the West, and this survey accordingly begins in 1396, the year in which the influential grammarian and teacher Manuel Chrysoloras arrived in Italy. The terminus of 1529 derives, in part, from the work of two scholars. First, the year 1530 saw the publication of Nicolas Clénard's *Institutiones in linguam graecam* and 1531 that of his *Meditationes*. Clénard's work came to dominate Greek teaching in

Catholic Europe for the rest of the century, and the diffusion of his work has already been well documented.[5] Second, Guillaume Budé's *Commentarii linguae graecae* emerged in 1529, a work that put Greek lexicography on a new foundation.[6]

More important, this terminus was chosen because it defines a period that saw the transition from manuscript to print. This is essential if the advance of Greek studies into Northern Europe is to be understood. A history of Greek studies in the fifteenth century would be largely a history of their fortunes in Italy, and it would concern itself primarily with manuscript material. Greek flourished in Italy without the printing press, while north of the Alps it was almost entirely dependent upon it. The following pages attempt to strike a balance between discussion of manuscript and discussion of printed sources.

Chapter 1

Greek Grammars

The period surveyed in this book covers the emergence and decline of the Byzantine educational tradition in the West. Nowhere is this more apparent than in the production and diffusion of Greek grammars. The majority of the Greek grammars of the fifteenth century, and all of the most influential ones, were written by Greek scholars in Greek. Until the last days of the Greek Empire, Constantinople continued to produce native scholars of eminence. The fall of the city in 1453 brought many of these to teach in the West, but the East created few teachers to succeed them. Crete under Venetian rule produced a number of prolific scribes but a rather smaller number of teachers of the language. In southern Italy, the situation was little better. Greek was, it seems, taught at the Monastery of San Niccolò di Casole, near Otranto, for much of the century. This monastery appears to have had a remarkable library: it was here that Bessarion discovered a manuscript of the *Posthomerica* of Quintus,[1] and Janus Lascaris found Colluthus's *De raptu Helenae* in Corigliano nearby.[2] According to the Calabrian scholar Galateo of Lecce, writing around the end of the century, the monastery of San Niccolò had been a center for Greek studies: "Quicumque graecis litteris operam dare cupiebat, iis maxima parte victus, praeceptor, domicilium sine aliqua mercede donabatur. Sic res graeca, quae cotidie retrolabitur, sustentabatur"[3] (Whoever wanted to study Greek received most of their keep, a teacher, and a lodging at no cost. Thus the Greek world, which daily declines, was sustained). In 1480 the Turks sacked the monastery and took Otranto. The destruction of San Niccolò marked the end of one of the last important outposts of the native Greek educational tradition in southern Italy. With the death of Constantine Lascaris in 1501, the famous Greek school of Sicily in Messina also fell into obscurity. Despite the prominent position of several Greek exiles, throughout the second half of the fifteenth century, the tuition of Western scholars by native Greek speakers was in decline.

This decline coincided with a growing confidence among Latin teachers of Greek. In the 1470s and 1480s, when Johann Reuchlin or Aldus Manutius wrote on Greek grammar, they did so in Greek. The first Greek grammar of consequence to be composed in Latin was that of Urbano Bolzanio, published in Venice in 1497. At Venice in 1504, Scipione Forteguerri, with one eye on the rival Greek school of Demetrius Chalcondyles in Milan, pronounced upon the advantages of native Greek teachers over Italian ones. He says that the Greeks know their own literature better than the Latins, and the Latins know theirs better than the Greeks; but the Latins can learn the literature of the Greeks better than the Greeks can learn that of the Latins.[4] At the end of the fifteenth century, the native Greek accent was still much admired by Western students. Benedetto Giovio, for example, had studied Greek by himself, but he went to Chalcondyles in order to perfect his accent.[5] Forteguerri's response to the argument that it is better to learn pronunciation from a native Greek is not very convincing: he turns to a passage from Quintilian about how too much attention to Greek can infect your Latin.[6] A more decisive riposte to the claims of the native accent was being prepared in Venice, where the Byzantine pronunciation of ancient Greek was first questioned in the circle around Aldus Manutius in the early years of the sixteenth century.[7] The emergence of new ideas about pronunciation coincided with the end of the predominance of the Byzantine exiles in Greek instruction.

During the fifteenth century, Greek grammar meant the works of Chrysoloras, Gaza, or Lascaris. These grammars were written entirely in Greek, and they offered the student the sort of immersion in the language that was considered proper for the acquisition of the ancient languages. Latin textbooks, after all, were not written in the vernaculars. Nevertheless, the fact that they were in Greek did make these textbooks very hard work for the beginner. Their difficulties were mitigated because the Byzantine East and the Latin West had inherited a common grammatical tradition from antiquity: a thorough training in this grammar had always been a fundamental part of their respective curricula. Nevertheless, Western students of the language remained heavily dependent upon their Greek teachers for the exposition of the most basic texts at this early stage in their learning. It is worth remembering that the first Greek texts construed by these early Western students were their grammars of the language, and the first Greek words learnt by Latinists during the fifteenth century were the Greek names of grammatical forms and constructions.

It is hoped that the descriptions of the grammars and their users that follow will throw some light on the shifting perspectives of Greek teachers and their students during this period. By and large, we do not hear very much of the difficulties of learning the language. For teachers, dwelling on these difficulties was likely to deter potential students; keen students were not likely to want to publicize their difficulties; and mature scholars tended to forget that they ever had them. No doubt some disenchanted students once owned those Greek books that are carefully annotated on their first pages and largely untouched thereafter. One moment of pain is worth recording here. In 1511, Angelo Colocci wrote to Scipione Forteguerri:

Avvisandovi che tornando da esi questi mesi passati, io mi renduto al greco, dal quale mere gia disperato, ut scitis; et in summa con grandissima celerita ho passati li circumflexi e li εἰς -μι, che gia dubitava de legereli come si havesse havto [*sic*] ad superar l'Alpe.[8]

[Let me tell you that, turning from these things in these last months, I have gone back to Greek, a subject that, as you know, I had entirely given up on. And, in short, with the greatest speed, I got through the contracted verbs and the verbs in -μι, which I had been as reluctant to read as if I had had to cross the Alps.]

Then as now the full majesty of the Greek verb was a daunting obstacle. The only Greek work printed in Northern Europe in the fifteenth century was a pamphlet produced in Deventer around 1488.[9] This work consists of eighteen leaves that present unadorned the entire conjugation of the verb τύπτω. It is likely that the young Erasmus struggled with this uncompromising volume. It is impossible to know how many emerged as Greek scholars from their reading of such a pamphlet, but the mystique of the language could only be enhanced by such monuments to its difficulties.

Because so few descriptions survive of what went on in the classroom, we are forced to deduce what we can from the grammars themselves. We do have a description of the methods of one student in Florence in 1493, which may serve to illustrate the ways students used these books. Girolamo Amaseo wrote to his brother about his methods of learning Greek:

> Hunc autem ordinem servavi: Constantinum omnem primo pernotavi, ut perciperem quo progressu uteretur in erudiendis tyrunculis. Et vix Guarinus mihi explicarat declinationes graecas et coniugationes, cum libellum mira dispositione ex Constantino, excerptis quibusdam necessariis, confeci, quem tibi ad percipiendum nominum et verborum inflexionem spero fore non inutilem; ut ubi ego quindecim diebus, tu octo ad summum, si tibi non defeceris, eum memoriae commendaveris. Hunc autem cum videris, non displicebit: sex enim chartulis non solum inflexiones, sed brevi, quantum tyroni necessitas est, partium orationum voculas praelibamus et variam perplexamque verborum coniugationem absolvimus.[10]
>
> [I have followed this method. First, I made notes on Constantine Lascaris's whole grammar, so that I might see what order he uses in teaching beginners. And hardly had Guarino explained to me the Greek declensions and conjugations than I had made a very well-organized little book of certain important extracts from Lascaris. I hope that this little book will be useful to you for learning the endings of the nouns and verbs: if you are diligent you will commit to memory what took me fifteen days in no more than eight. You will be pleased when you see this: in six short leaves I have sampled not only the endings but briefly, as much as a beginner needs, the words of the parts of speech, and I have written out the varied and complex conjugation of the verbs.]

The grammar of Lascaris that Girolamo reduced to six leaves was itself only a bare summary of Greek grammar.[11] In an attempt to lighten the burden on their students, the Greek grammarians of Renaissance Europe experimented with different ways of defining and presenting the essential elements of the language. These experiments, and a debate on the proper use of such summaries, are described in this chapter.

ANCIENT AND BYZANTINE GREEK GRAMMATICAL WORKS

No elementary Greek grammar survives from antiquity. All that we now have relates to either the teaching of ancient Greek to Greek-speaking students, or to the study of grammatical ideas by erudite Greek-speaking scholars. For centuries, Byzantine scholars had mined the extensive and complex Greek grammatical works of antiquity for brief expositions of difficult points. These summaries and excerpts made by the Byzantine scholars are one reason that the early grammarians have come down to us in such a fragmentary state. These grammarians were not forgotten during the Renaissance, but the requirements of Western students were different from those of their Greek counterparts, and elementary grammars were produced to meet these needs. Before turning to the Greek grammarians of the fifteenth and sixteenth centuries, it is as well to look at the fortunes of the works of two of these ancient grammarians, Apollonius Dyscolus and his son, Aelius Herodian. While some of what follows throws some light on the Renaissance fortunes of these authors, they are discussed here primarily because they were used by the grammarians of the Renaissance in the compilation of their own grammars.

An interest in Apollonius among Western scholars can be traced back to the 1420s. In 1423, Giovanni Aurispa brought a manuscript of "Apollonius grammaticus" to Italy.[12] Francesco Filelfo, a friend of all things Greek, said that, while he lived in Constantinople in the 1420s, he searched in vain for the grammatical works of Apollonius and Herodian.[13] Filelfo may, in fact, have looked for the works attributed to Apollonius in his copy of the Suda lexicon.[14] There he would have found that twenty works were attributed to this legendarily difficult grammarian. Of these, today we have only four: three of these are the so-called *scripta minora* on pronouns, adverbs, and conjunctions; the fourth, a longer work on syntax, is in four books. It seems that by Filelfo's day only these works were extant, but on his return to Italy he continued his search for others. In 1441, he asked Pietro Pierleoni for Apollonius.[15] In 1456, in Milan, he followed up another promising lead: he had heard that the Greek scribe and scholar Andronicus Callistus had a manuscript of Apollonius and wrote to Callistus asking for the work.[16] This manuscript probably contained nothing new to Filelfo: Callistus seems to have owned a manuscript of Apollonius, now in Paris, that has the four extant treatises.[17] Callistus, however, perhaps conscious of the rarity of the work, was reluctant to send Filelfo his copy. When in 1461, Filelfo persuaded Palla Strozzi, Callistus's patron, to lend him a copy of Apollonius's work on syntax, he returned it promptly a few months later, commenting archly on his reliability in such matters.[18] In fact, the early 1460s seem to have been a period of increased interest in the work of Apollonius: besides Callistus and Filelfo's copies, we know that the tireless grammarian and teacher Constantine Lascaris copied two manuscripts of Apollonius in Milan around this time and seems to have used another.[19]

Other indications of the works of Apollonius in the period are rare, although it is possible that some of the surviving notices of "Apollonius" refer to the grammarian and not to the author of the *Argonautica*.[20] Angelo Poliziano borrowed a copy of the grammarian from the private library of the Medici in 1481 in connection with his Greek course at the Florentine *Studio*.[21] The surviving works were first printed in 1495, in a beautifully printed edition that acquired a reputation for formidable difficulty.[22] A reprint was not called for until 1515, and Apollonius's work seems often to have inspired more awe than understanding. In 1517, Richard Pace wrote in his dialogue *De fructu qui ex doctrina percipitur*, "'Et siquid interim amplius hac in re intelligere cupis, lege Apollonium grammaticum . . .' 'Dii meliora,' inquit Rhetorica, 'mallem me in Timaeum Platonis relegares. Huicne sphingi vis me allegare? Nam is in grammatica, aenigmata plane scribere videtur'"[23] ("'And if you want to know any more on this subject, read Apollonius the grammarian . . .' 'Good God,' says Rhetoric, 'I had rather you exiled me to Plato's *Timaeus*. Do you want to send me off to this sphinx? For in grammatical matters, he seems clearly to write riddles'"). Apollonius seems to have been rarely used, even among Greek scholars. He often receives an honorable mention by Renaissance grammarians, but only Theodore Gaza seems to have made much use of his work for his grammar, and as we shall see, parts of Gaza's work attracted the same accusations of obscurity as those of Apollonius.[24]

The situation with another of the great grammarians of antiquity, Aelius Herodian, is rather more complicated. Confusion arises from the fact that Herodian's vast work on accentuation, the *Prosodia Catholica*, survives only in epitomes and extracts. Some scribes seem to have succumbed to a temptation to attribute to the great grammarian a number of anonymous *opuscula* on the subject of accentuation. Modern scholarship has still not entirely disentangled these threads, but it is clear that much of what remains of Herodian's great work has been transmitted in two distinct epitomes. The first epitome was perhaps made by the sixth century Aristotelian commentator Joannes Philoponus and it circulated under his name. It appears to have had little diffusion in the Renaissance.[25] The second epitome is attributed wrongly to Arcadius of Antiocheia or, with more probability, to Theodosius of Alexandria.[26] Constantine Lascaris copied what is today the oldest surviving manuscript of this Theodosian epitome. He made this copy from a lost παλαιὰ βίβλος that he found in the monastery of San Salvatore in Messina about 1480.[27] Lascaris certainly made good use of his discovery. In 1482 he produced a work on the accentuation of verbs, which he dedicated to the vice-regent of Sicily, Jacobo Ximenes Muriel. This work is actually Lascaris's summary of the epitome of Herodian's sixteenth book.[28] This work was followed a few years later by another longer work on accentuation, also drawn from the Theodosian epitome, which he subscribed in Messina in November 1488.[29]

The works of other Byzantine grammarians will be touched upon later in this chapter. One late Byzantine grammarian, Manuel Moschopoulos, proved particularly popular during the fifteenth century. Of the numerous works of Moschopoulos, his grammar, *Erotemata*, is of interest here.[30] It was the grammar of choice in the last decades of Byzantium: a single scribe, George Baiophoros, is known to have produced seven copies of the work in Constantinople in the 1420s and 1430s.[31] The first Westerner known to have made use of the work was Giovanni Tortelli, who used this grammar when he was studying Greek in Constantinople between 1435 and 1437.[32] Even dedicated students like Tortelli might have found the work daunting. Moschopoulos's grammar divides the Greek noun into no fewer than fifty-six declensions, a classification that went back at least as far as late antiquity and the work of Theodosius of Alexandria. His declensions are distinguished on the basis of the gender of the noun and the termination of the nominative singular. Moschopoulos's division of the Greek verb into thirteen conjugations is even more ancient, and can be traced back to Dionysius Thrax in the second century BC.[33] Whatever its merits, the sheer number of available manuscripts of Moschopoulos's work ensured it a significant diffusion in fifteenth-century Italy, and several of these early owners can be identified. A copy of the grammar, dated 1404 and apparently one of the earliest copies to reach Italy, belonged to Niccolò Niccoli in Florence.[34] The Venetian Francesco Barbaro owned a copy.[35] Cristoforo Garatone, a student of Guarino Veronese and papal representative in Constantinople, acquired one of Baiophoros's copies between 1433 and 1446, and this copy was probably in the Vatican Library when it was cataloged in 1455.[36] A copy made by Peter the Cretan may have been connected with the school of Vittorino da Feltre in Mantua.[37] Palla Strozzi donated a copy of Moschopoulos's grammar to the monastery of S. Justina in Padua, while Angelo Poliziano was using the work in Florence in the late 1480s.[38] Another of Baiophoros's copies appears to have passed through the hands of Constantine Lascaris, and by the time of his death in 1501, Lascaris owned two other copies of Moschopoulos's grammar: a manuscript now in Madrid and the *editio princeps* of the work, printed in Milan about 1493.[39] Johann Reuchlin acquired a manuscript of the work, apparently the first copy to reach Germany.[40] In France, George Hermonymus made a copy around 1501 for Guillaume Budé.[41] Ultimately, however, Moschopoulos's work proved too demanding for

Western students, and throughout the fifteenth century, grammarians and teachers searched for ways to abbreviate and simplify its contents.

Greek Grammars in Western Europe, 1396–1529

The practical grammarian had two conflicting aims: he needed to describe all the features of the language that his students might meet, and he needed to abbreviate this information so that it could be learned. The Greek grammarians of Renaissance Europe adopted different approaches to this situation. What follows is intended to provide a description of all Greek grammatical works used in Western Europe during this period. It excludes all pamphlets that deal only with the elements of Greek orthography, details of which are to be found in Appendix 1. It also excludes all those who compiled tables or summaries from the works of other grammarians. Thus the popular tables of teachers such as Richard Croke and Girolamo Aleandro are not to be found here, although their works too are detailed in the appendix.

Manuel Calecas, 1391–1396?

The Greek grammar of Manuel Calecas is the first Greek grammar that can be said with certainty to have been studied in Western Europe in the period under investigation. In the last years of the fourteenth century or the first years of the fifteenth, the Florentine Chancellor Coluccio Salutati studied Greek with the help of this grammar. Salutati may have used Calecas's work because there was no other grammar available to him, or he may have preferred it to the other grammars that were available to him. The question cannot yet be answered because neither Calecas's grammar nor that of his fellow teacher Manuel Chrysoloras is securely dated. In this matter, only two termini can be found. The first comes from letters dated from February to March 1396 in which Salutati professes his ignorance of Greek.[42] The second comes from the date of Salutati's death, May 1406. At some time between these two dates, Salutati struggled with the fragmentary manuscript of the work that is now in Paris.[43]

Calecas probably compiled his grammar between 1391 and 1396.[44] During this period, Calecas was teaching in Constantinople and learning Latin. We can be fairly confident that Salutati's acquaintance with Calecas's grammar owed something to Jacopo Angeli da Scarperia. Angeli set out for Constantinople in 1395, arriving in the city in the autumn. There, he took Greek lessons from Manuel Chrysoloras and was introduced by Chrysoloras to Calecas. Salutati wrote to Angeli in March 1396 to ask him to bring Greek manuscripts back to Florence.[45] Angeli and Chrysoloras arrived back in Florence no later than February 1397. While in Italy, Angeli continued his correspondence with Calecas and attempted to secure Greek manuscripts through him.[46] We do not know who taught Salutati with this grammar. Calecas himself was in Italy from about 1401 to 1403, but he did not, as far as we know, visit Florence.[47] The portion of Calecas's grammar in Salutati's manuscript was not written by Salutati. It is in an unpracticed Greek hand, and we may guess that it was copied by an Italian student of the language.[48] This is followed by a copy, in Salutati's hand, of a short treatise by Manuel Chrysoloras on the Greek breathings. Salutati probably received this treatise, which is considered in more detail in the following section, in 1397 or 1398. Salutati's use of Calecas's grammar may be plausibly located between 1396 and 1398.

Calecas's grammar makes a number of simplifications that seem to be directed at the needs of Western students. Most striking is that he reduces the number of declensions of the Greek noun from the fifty-six expounded by Moschopoulos to just five, the same number as the Latin noun. The first declension has all the imparisyllabic nouns; the remaining declensions have the parisyllabic nouns.[49] Calecas defines the same thirteen verb conjugations that had been in use since at least the time of Dionysius Thrax in the second century BC: six barytone conjugations, three contracted conjugations, and four conjugations in -μι. Like Dionysius, he related the first three conjugations in -μι to the three contracted conjugations, and the fourth conjugation in -μι to the sixth barytone conjugation.[50] Salutati seems never to have progressed very far with his Greek studies, and after this inauspicious start, Calecas's grammar failed to make much of an impression in Italy. Today only a handful of copies survive.[51] It is, however, worth observing that it is the only Greek grammar that can be shown to have been used in Florence between 1396 and 1406. Since no copy of Chrysoloras's grammar has yet been connected with any of his Florentine students, it is possible that they used Calecas's work. Two later teachers are known to have possessed copies of this rare work. Pietro da Montagnana owned a manuscript of Calecas's grammar, which he bequeathed to the monastery of San Giovanni in Verdara in Padua in 1478, and Giovanni Calfurnio owned a manuscript of Calecas's grammar at his death in 1503.[52]

Manuel Chrysoloras, by 1406

Manuel Chrysoloras was responsible for what was by far the most popular Greek grammar used in fifteenth-century Italy. The date of the composition of this important grammar, however, remains uncertain. Chrysoloras first taught Greek on Italian soil in 1390, when the Florentine Roberto de' Rossi took some lessons from him in Venice.[53] Though Chrysoloras returned to Constantinople soon afterward, he was drawn back to Italy in 1396 by the prospect of a teaching position in Florence, and he taught in the city from 1397 to 1400. Cammelli believed that the *Erotemata* were composed in Italy in 1397 or 1398.[54] Pertusi believed that they were composed in Constantinople before 1397.[55] The earliest dated manuscript of Chrysoloras's work was bought by his student Guarino Veronese in Constantinople on March 1, 1406.[56]

Salutati's manuscript of Calecas's grammar also contains a copy of a short grammatical work of Chrysoloras. The history of this work is worth exploring because it may throw some light on the dates of the grammars of Calecas and Chrysoloras. It begins around 1397, when Salutati sent to Chrysoloras a letter requesting some guidance on the subject of the Greek breathings. In 1397 or 1398, Chrysoloras, in Florence, responded with a letter and a short treatise, both in Greek, on the subject of the breathings.[57] This treatise was apparently written by Chrysoloras specifically for Salutati. Salutati himself subsequently copied it into his manuscript of Calecas from Chrysoloras's lost autograph.[58] The treatise is usually found appended to copies of the *Erotemata*, but it is not known when the treatise was first appended to the grammar. Neither is it known whether the grammar was extant when the treatise was composed. The treatise may have been an expansion of the brief notes on the breathings that Chrysoloras had already included in his grammar. If the grammar was composed after the treatise, Chrysoloras chose not to insert the discussion in its proper place in the

Erotemata, perhaps in the belief that it dealt with the breathings in more detail than was appropriate for an elementary student text.

If the grammar had been complete before 1400, we might have expected to find it among the books of Chrysoloras's Florentine students. These included Antonio Corbinelli, who left his Greek books to the Badia Fiorentina in 1425, but I know of no copy of the grammar among Corbinelli's books. Chrysoloras also taught Palla Strozzi. A list of Strozzi's books in 1431 included among the Greek manuscripts "Grammaticha et sermones Demostenis," and among the Latin manuscripts is a volume "Ebreorum latinorum grecorumque grammaticha," but neither can be shown to contain Chrysoloras's work.[59] Neither do any of Chrysoloras's other students—Leonardo Bruni, Pier Paolo Vergerio, and Jacopo Angeli—mention a Greek grammar. A letter of Pier Candido Decembrio refers to a copy of the *Erotemata* written by his father, Uberto.[60] After leaving Florence, Chrysoloras taught Uberto Decembrio in Lombardy, so it is likely that he made this copy between 1400 and 1403.[61] This would make it the earliest known manuscript of the work, but if it survives, it has not been identified. The fact remains that the only Greek grammar that Coluccio Salutati can be shown to have used is that of Manuel Calecas. Before his arrival in Italy, Chrysoloras does not seem to have been a grammarian. It would have been natural for him to take to Italy the classroom texts current in his day, which probably included Moschopoulos's *Erotemata* and may have included the recently composed grammar of Calecas.

Chrysoloras's grammar was called *Erotemata*, "Questions," because it was presented as a series of questions asked by the master of his pupil. This question-and-answer method was part of a long classroom tradition—Donatus's *Ars minor*, familiar to students in the middle ages and the Renaissance, made use of it—but the technique was particularly influential among the later Byzantine grammarians.[62] The author of the anonymous preface to the *editio princeps* of the epitome of Chrysoloras's grammar believed that "hoc opusculum magis ad latinorum utilitatem quam ipsorum graecorum necessitatem composuit"[63] (he composed this little work more for the use of the Latins than for the needs of the Greeks), and it seems not to have been used with native Greek students. Western students did not need a detailed map of the entire language in order to take their first steps. They did not need an account of all possible inflexions but general statements of broad application. To put the matter in Western terms, they needed an *Ars minor*, not Priscian.

Chrysoloras's important contribution was to simplify the medieval and classical grammatical legacy for his Western students.[64] From at least the time of Theodosius of Alexandria in the fourth century AD until the fifteenth century, the Greek noun had been customarily divided into fifty-six paradigms.[65] Roger Bacon had already criticized this arrangement in the thirteenth century.[66] Chrysoloras reduced these fifty-six noun paradigms to just ten: four parisyllabic declensions, one imparisyllabic declension, and five contracted declensions. This treatment of the nouns proved very influential and was largely followed by his successors.[67] Chrysoloras did not change the thirteen verb conjugations that the Byzantine grammarians had inherited from Dionysius Thrax and that had been retained by Calecas: he detailed six barytone conjugations, three contracted conjugations, and four conjugations in -μι.[68] Like his predecessors, he related the first three conjugations in -μι to the three contracted conjugations, and the fourth conjugation in -μι to the sixth barytone conjugation.[69] The popularity of this grammar was due to Chrysoloras's rationalization of the complex tradition that had come down to the Byzantines.[70]

By 1418, Chrysoloras's student, Guarino Veronese, had composed two of the most widely used grammatical works of the fifteenth century. Guarino's Latin grammar the *Regulae grammaticales* is first mentioned in a letter of his dated January 19, 1418.[71] By this date, he had also abbreviated and translated Chrysoloras's *Erotemata*.[72] Guarino's epitome omits the short work on the breathings, discussed previously; he eliminates Chrysoloras's discussion of the syllable and the word; and he curtails the rules of pronunciation. Guarino retained Chrysoloras's division of the noun declensions and verb conjugations.[73] In this form, the *Erotemata* were regularly used in the classroom. In 1459, Guarino's son, Battista, wrote of students of Greek,

> Habeant regulas quas parentis nostri praeceptor Manuel Chrysoloras summatim collegit, vel quas parens ipse noster compendii amantissimus ex illis contraxit; et inter docendum admoneantur maxime verborum tempora generali quadam praeceptione derivare; et ea quae apud illos ἀνώμαλα verba sunt tamquam ungues calleant. Sic enim facillime (quod in ea lingua utilissimum est) nomen a verbo et verborum tempora etiam prima fronte discernent. Hoc autem et frequenti et diligenti praeceptoris interrogatione consequentur.[74]
>
> [Let them have the rules that our father's teacher, Manuel Chrysoloras, collected together, or those rules that our father himself, a great lover of *compendia*, extracted from Chrysoloras. And during teaching, let them be told to derive the tenses of the verbs from some general principle; and let them know thoroughly the verbs that the Greeks call *anomala* [i.e., irregular]. For in this way they will easily distinguish even at first glance (which is very useful in that language) a noun from a verb and the tenses of the verb. They will learn this by the constant and careful questioning of their teacher.]

The use of this epitome as a classroom text at Guarino's school ensured that in this form it was widely diffused.[75]

Chrysoloras's was the grammar that instructed all of the great Greek scholars of the first half, and most of those of the second half, of the fifteenth century. Zomino (or Sozomeno) of Pistoia made two manuscripts based on Chrysoloras's work. The first of these, a copy of the full text of Chrysoloras with some revisions and variants, is assigned to the final years of Zomino's first period in Florence, from 1415 to 1417.[76] The other, which draws on his first copy and on a copy of Guarino's epitome, is associated with Zomino's teaching activity in Florence in the 1420s.[77] According to Vespasiano da Bisticci, in Florence Zomino taught, among others, Matteo Palmieri, Pandolfo Pandolfini, Bartolomeo Strozzi, and Francesco Vettori.[78] All these must thus have been taught from Chrysoloras's grammar. Pietro da Montagnana seems to have used Chrysoloras to teach Greek in Padua in the 1450s. We have seen that he owned a copy of the grammar of Manuel Calecas, but Guarino's epitome seems to have been more important for his teaching.[79] He made a copy of Guarino's Latin compendium of Chrysoloras with some modifications and reorganization,[80] he owned another manuscript that had a copy of the Greek text of the epitome,[81] and he wrote a copy of the Greek epitome with an interlinear Latin version and marginalia.[82] Pietro's successor in Padua, Demetrius Chalcondyles, also used Chrysoloras from the beginning of his teaching there in 1463.[83] Three copies of Chrysoloras's work can certainly be linked to Constantine Lascaris and may relate to his teaching in Milan before the publication of his own grammar, that is, between 1458 and 1463. Of these, one shows signs that it was used by one of

Lascaris's pupils in Milan, Giorgio Valla.[84] The scribe Joannes Scutariota, who seems to have worked in Florence throughout his life, made at least two copies of Chrysoloras.[85] Joannes Rhosos made a copy in Bologna, perhaps in the 1460s.[86] Cristoforo Persona added Guarino's epitome to a Greek–Latin lexicon.[87]

Pontico Virunio was using Chrysoloras when he began to lecture on Greek in Reggio in December 1500. The following year he edited the Greek text of Guarino's epitome.[88] He says it is small but sufficient "modo praeceptor sit copiosus" (as long as the teacher is eloquent). Short is also easy, he believed: "Nam quanto brevius, tanto citius disces, et summe proficies incredibili temporis brevitate" (For the shorter it is the quicker you will learn, and you will be very proficient in an unbelievably short time). Virunio recommended that the student master this little work before moving on to the much more demanding grammar of Urbano Bolzanio recently printed in Venice.[89] Later, in 1510, Virunio took on some of the work of this "copiosus praeceptor" when he added a Latin commentary to another Greek edition of Guarino's epitome of Chrysoloras's grammar.[90] This commentary seems to record some of what went on in Virunio's own expositions of Chrysoloras.

The place of Chrysoloras's grammar among the earliest products of the Greek presses testifies to the success of this formula. It was, in Guarino's epitome, the first complete Greek work ever printed.[91] It was the first Greek book printed in Florence.[92] In 1507, it became the first Greek grammar printed in France. This French Chrysoloras was edited by François Tissard and dedicated to the archbishop of Toulouse, John of Orléans, then only fifteen years old.[93] Tissard writes that he had studied under Battista Guarino in Ferrara, under Filippo Beroaldo in Bologna, and under Giovanni Calfurnio in Padua. All these scholars knew Greek, but Tissard says that he learned his Greek from one Demetrius of Sparta.[94] The Paris edition of 1507 is of the full text of Chrysoloras's grammar. If Tissard had it set from a printed copy, then it must have been from one of the two Florentine editions printed between 1496 and 1500, the only editions of the full text before 1507.[95]

When the Italian Girolamo Aleandro arrived in Paris to teach Greek, he found them very attached to their editions of Chrysoloras. Writing to Aldus Manutius in July 1508, he said, "[I parigiani] volenno che io li instituisse con quelle *Erotemate*; io li ho praeposto quelle vostre [di Lascaris] per essere et melior via et per etc [*sic*]"[96] (The Parisians want me to teach them with those *Erotemata*; I have suggested to them that Lascaris of yours because it is better and because etc.). Aleandro did not feel the need to list the advantages of the Aldine Lascaris to its publisher. It was a much finer piece of printing, it had a Latin translation, and it was supplied with a collection of student texts. It was also an expensive book, even before the costs of getting it to Paris had been added. This last factor probably accounts for much of the loyalty of the Parisians to the unpolished products of their first Greek press. Chrysoloras seems to have remained in favor because, when the first edition had sold out in 1512, the work was reprinted in Paris.[97] Aleandro, still in Paris, seems to have decided to lecture on the grammar of Theodore Gaza in 1511, and the editing of Chrysoloras was assigned to one of Aleandro's pupils, François Vatable, then only nineteen. By the time Gourmont reprinted this edition in 1516, his Paris press had also printed editions of the grammars of Gaza and Urbano but still no edition of Lascaris.[98] Jean Chéradame edited Chrysoloras for Gourmont perhaps around 1524, and a new translation was printed in Paris in 1534 by Dominicus Sylvius.[99]

Aldus did not publish an edition of Chrysoloras's grammar until 1512, by which time he had printed an edition of Urbano's Greek grammar in Latin and was on his third edition of the parallel text of Lascaris. According to the preface of this edition, Marcus Musurus had encouraged Aldus to print a new edition of Chrysoloras's grammar.[100] Musurus was teaching Greek in Venice at the time and was in a good position to know what he could teach and what students would buy. The late date of the first Aldine Chrysoloras might be assigned to a feeling that the market for Chrysoloras's work had already been satisfied by other printers: Chrysoloras had been printed a dozen times before 1512. Furthermore, Aldus's educational contacts—of whom, more later—were very likely satisfied with the editions of Lascaris that he had been issuing and had no wish to accommodate themselves to a new grammar. As we have seen, Aleandro in 1508 had a personal preference for Lascaris's work over that of Chrysoloras. However, in 1512 Aldus may have felt that he was issuing a definitive edition of the venerable grammarian. The Aldine edition of Chrysoloras was the first to be supplemented by extracts from the grammatical works of Chalcondyles and Gaza. Like the fine edition of Gaza's grammar printed in 1495, this Chrysoloras was printed in Greek only. Moreover, a number of copies of this Aldine edition of Chrysoloras's grammar survive on vellum, to my knowledge the only printed Greek grammar from this period to have received this honor.[101] By 1512, Chrysoloras had become, in a manner of speaking, a classic.

The Aldine edition of 1512 seems to represent the high-water mark of Chrysoloras's grammar. That year it was printed in Venice, Paris, and Tübingen. In 1513, Demetrius Ducas left the Aldine Press for Spain to participate in the work on the great polyglot Bible that was under way in Alcalá in Spain.[102] He seems to have taken with him a copy of the Aldine Chrysoloras, and the following year he supervised a reprint of the work in Alcalá. This is the first Greek grammar—and probably the first Greek book—to be printed in Spain; it is also the first Latin translation of the full text of Chrysoloras.[103] But elsewhere the grammar was being replaced. In Paris in 1511, Aleandro turned to Gaza for his Greek classes, and in Cambridge in the same year Erasmus, too, decided to change from Chrysoloras to Gaza. In Louvain, the Greek press of Thierry Martens printed many editions of Gaza, and he printed an edition of the grammars of Lascaris and Amerot, but he never printed Chrysoloras.

In Germany, Chrysoloras's reign was very brief. At the height of the grammar's popularity in Italy, Greek was rarely studied in Germany, and by the time Greek was becoming common there, the work had been superseded. Some early copies did make their way there. A manuscript made in Italy by Demetrius Sgouropoulos was the property of Joannes Tröster, a canon of Regensburg, in 1470,[104] and this copy was later owned by Willibald Pirckheimer.[105] A copy survives that seems to have belonged to Rudolf Agricola's younger brother Hendrik.[106] Chrysoloras was first printed in Greek in Tübingen in 1512, in an edition addressed to Johann Reuchlin by Georg Simler. Reuchlin was still using Chrysoloras, perhaps in this very edition, in his lessons ten years later.[107] Chrysoloras's grammar was printed in Strasbourg in December 1516, and Ottomar Nachtgall taught from it there in the winter of 1516–17. A few months later, Nachtgall produced his *Progymnasmata*, a textbook of Greek grammar that drew heavily upon Chrysoloras. However, by the time Nachtgall came to expand and rewrite this work in 1521, he had transferred his allegiances to Gaza's work. It was from this book, not from Chrysoloras, that Greek was taught in Strasbourg until at least 1523.[108]

By now the tide was running fast against Chrysoloras's grammar. Melchior Volmar found fault with it in 1525:

> Equidem Manuelem Chrysoloram inter graecos iudicavi semper (quantum ego in hanc partem graece scripta intelligere possum, atque adeo magistra rerum experientia didici) praeter caeteros maxime idoneum esse, qui linguae suae ipse principia nobis daret . . . Sed erat tamen etiam in illo ipso Chrysolora quod desyderarem: nempe formationes quas vocant verborum, a primo themate per singula tempora declinationes illas, deductionesque adolescentulis penitus pernoscendas, et exacte promptissimeque tenendas. Quas etsi in universum haudquaquam neglexerit, tamen si respectum agas eorum quos erudiendos, ac primo veluti lacte educandos susceperis, benignius paulo proculdubio de illis fuerat praecipiendum.[109]
>
> [Among the Greeks (as far as I can understand things written in Greek on this subject and have learnt by experience that teaches these matters), I have always thought Manuel Chrysoloras more suitable than others to give us the elements of his language . . . But yet there was something lacking even in Chrysoloras himself, namely what they call the formations of the verbs, those inflexions of the verb stem for each tense, and the variations that must be thoroughly learned by young students and remembered accurately and ready for use. Even though Chrysoloras did not neglect these things altogether, yet as regards those who must be instructed and as it were weaned, he should certainly have taught those things rather more gently.]

Volmar's reservations about Chrysoloras's grammar concern his treatment of the verbs. Aldus, of course, had already noticed this weakness in 1512 and attempted to remedy it.[110] A new translation of the epitome by Alban Thorer, printed in Basle in 1528, managed to attract the criticisms of another grammarian, Johann Winther of Andernach.[111] For the rest of the sixteenth century, Chrysoloras was hardly used in Northern Europe. Most of the last editions of his grammar came from Venice: at least thirteen editions of the full text or of Guarino's epitome were printed there between 1531 and 1550. The last edition ever printed was published in Venice in 1564.[112]

George Scholarios, ca. 1430

George Scholarios is best known as the first patriarch of Constantinople under Ottoman rule. Less well known is that he produced a Greek grammar for his students in the city. Scholarios's grammar, the only fifteenth-century Greek grammar to have received the attentions of a modern editor, is in two parts: the first part is an accidence, the second part a lexicon.[113] Very few manuscripts include the lexicon, and only the grammar proper is considered here. This exists in three distinct drafts. The first, extant in Scholarios's autograph, was compiled around 1430, when its author was about twenty-five years old.[114] The second, also an autograph, was produced sometime before 1439, when he revised and expanded the grammar and added more examples.[115] A third variant on the grammar emerged as a result of the discussions at the council of Ferrara-Florence in 1439. One of the obstacles to the successful union of the Eastern and Western churches was the interpretation of the procession of the Holy Spirit as enunciated in the creed. This aspect of the debate turned on the precise significance of the Greek preposition διά. Scholarios had been in favor of the union of the churches while he attended the council, and the first draft of his grammar favored the Western interpretation of the preposition. However, on his return to Constantinople, he came to lead the antiunion party, and he rewrote this element of his grammar in the light of this political and religious conversion.[116] These different drafts simplify the process of establishing the relationships among surviving manuscripts of the grammar. Of the thirteen surviving manuscripts of this grammar, two are autograph and one has been corrected and revised by the author.[117] As a consequence, we know more about the evolution of the grammar than of any other surveyed in this chapter.

Scholarios used the same noun declensions as Chrysoloras, but he arranged them for the student under each of the three genders. This was a return to the practice of Manuel Moschopoulos. His verb scheme is the same as that used by Dionysius Thrax and Chrysoloras: thirteen conjugations, six barytone, three contracted, and four in -μι.[118] Following these predecessors, he, too, related the first three conjugations in -μι to the three contracted conjugations, and the fourth conjugation in -μι to the sixth barytone conjugation.[119] This grammar was used in Scholarios's school with both Greek and Italian students. One surviving manuscript was apparently made by Scholarios's nephew and pupil, Theodore Sophianos.[120] We know that during his time in Constantinople, from 1435 to 1437, Giovanni Tortelli studied, or was taught from, Scholarios's grammar.[121] The grammar also had an interesting history in *quattrocento* Italy. The earliest autograph copy, now in Padua, is Scholarios's first draft that he produced for the Greek nobleman Manuel Sebastopulos about 1430.[122] It seems that this manuscript subsequently came into the possession of Palla Strozzi.[123] A likely intermediary for this acquisition was the Greek Andronicus Callistus. In 1449, he himself made a copy of Scholarios's grammar, which passed through the hands of Giorgio Valla on its way to the Vatican Library.[124] We know that Callistus was with Strozzi in Padua by 1461 and may have been there since 1459. He stayed with Strozzi until the latter's death in May 1462. It was in Padua that Scholarios's grammar found its most enthusiastic Western student, Pietro da Montagnana, who acquired Scholarios's first autograph copy. Pietro not only annotated this manuscript but also produced a translation of the work at the head of a collection of student texts.[125] Pietro's copy of the Greek text probably formed part of his donation to San Giovanni in Verdara in Padua in 1477 and 1478; his Latin text was certainly donated.

Two more manuscripts are worth noticing. The first was copied in Florence around 1470 by Andronicus Galiziotes for the Sicilian Ludovico Saccano and left by Saccano to the cathedral library in Messina around 1480.[126] The second is Scholarios's second autograph copy, a later draft that he also made for Sebastopoulos sometime between 1430 and 1439.[127] This manuscript, which formed the basis for the modern edition of the grammar, may have been the copy that belonged to the library of Johann Reuchlin.[128] It seems to have been among Reuchlin's books that the scholar and teacher Johann Cuno consulted the work in the late fifteenth or early sixteenth century, the first known use of the work in Northern Europe.[129]

MATTHAEUS CAMARIOTES, BY 1490

Matthaeus Camariotes was born in Thessalonica and moved to Constantinople in the years immediately before the fall of the city. After studying there with Scholarios, he survived the sack of the city to return to search for his family.[130] By 1466, he was back in his native Thessalonica. It appears that some time after this date he settled in Italy: by 1484, Giorgio Valla could speak of him as his teacher, "praeceptor ille optimus."[131]

He died in 1490. A manuscript of Proclus copied by Camariotes, apparently in the 1480s, belonged to Marsilio Ficino. It may have been acquired by Ficino on Camariotes' death, and this possibility lends some support to the hypothesis that he died in Italy.[132]

Camariotes seems to have worked as a teacher of grammar and rhetoric in the East. In this capacity, he is responsible for a surviving compendium from Hermogenes and for a brief summary of the *Progymnasmata* ascribed to Aphthonius.[133] It is for his work as a grammarian that he appears in the present book. He is the author of an unpublished Greek grammar, which survives in just two manuscripts. One, from the seventeenth century, is now on Mount Athos. The other, in Oxford, is in Camariotes' own small hand, rubricated by the author.[134] The observations here are based on an examination of this autograph. Because his grammar seems to have been intended to teach the language to native Greek speakers, it is likely to have been completed before he moved to Italy. It is plausibly dated after Scholarios's grammar but before that of Theodore Gaza.

The grammar is entitled εἰσαγωγὴ εἰς τὴν γραμματικήν. It is entirely in Greek and appears not to have been made with Western students in mind. In his presentation of the elements of the language, Camariotes seems to have been entirely uninfluenced by the grammars made by his compatriots for their Western students. Camariotes did make some attempt to rationalize the complex tradition passed down to the fifteenth century via the grammar of Manuel Moschopoulos. Camariotes' verb scheme is similar to that of Chrysoloras and Scholarios. He defines thirteen conjugations: six barytone, three contracted, and four in -μι. Like Chrysoloras, Camariotes states that the three circumflex verbs are derived from the sixth barytone conjugation by contraction.[135] His noun scheme is more innovative. He distinguishes his declensions—which he does not number—on the basis of the termination of the nominative singular, but unlike Moschopoulos and Scholarios, he does not divide them by gender: nouns of different genders with the same terminations are considered together. He separates the contracted from the uncontracted nouns.[136] This rationalization still leaves the declensions rather complex.

Theodore Gaza, 1461–1462

Theodore Gaza, better known for his influential translations of Aristotle, is the author of an important Greek grammar. Gaza seems to have arrived in Italy from Constantinople in 1440, when he was between twenty-five and thirty years old.[137] He landed in Sicily in 1440 and travelled on to Pisa.[138] By October 1440, he was in Pavia;[139] by 1442, he was in Milan.[140] In 1443, he moved on again to Mantua, where he probably taught Greek to Vittorino da Feltre. After Vittorino's death in 1446, at the invitation of Giovanni Aurispa, he moved to Ferrara, where he taught Greek to a number of students.[141] To this period his speech *De literis graecis* has been assigned, which seems to indicate that his ideas about teaching were maturing in Ferrara.[142] That his reputation as a teacher was growing is indicated by the fact that in 1447 he was offered a position at the Florentine Studio, an offer that he declined.[143] It has been proposed that Gaza's grammar was compiled in connection with his teaching in Ferrara, that is, from 1446 to 1449, and Gaza's latest biographer has repeated this suggestion.[144] The date is plausible, and there is a piece of evidence to support it. In 1540, Johann Walder stated that he had compiled his edition of the first two books of Gaza's grammar using a copy that had belonged to Battista Guarino and that this copy had been written while Gaza was teaching in Ferrara.[145] Battista was twelve when Gaza began his teaching in that city.

It is unfortunate that the manuscript used by Walder has not come to light. Everything else that is known about the grammar suggests that it was produced later. Battista Guarino was certainly well placed to acquire one of the very earliest copies of the work, but we have seen that he was using Chrysoloras's *Erotemata* with his students in 1459.[146] Some light is thrown on the production of the work by Gaza's fellow grammarian Constantine Lascaris. Lascaris knew Gaza: he addresses him one surviving letter, perhaps to be assigned to 1462, when Lascaris was teaching Greek privately in Milan.[147] Lascaris praises Gaza's grammar in the preface to his *De nomine et verbo* and in his different postscripts to this work. These notices do not provide any secure termini. Although this work of Lascaris was certainly complete by 1468, the preface and postscripts could have been written some time after the composition of the work itself. A more useful notice comes from Lascaris's preface to his own Greek grammar, in which he asserts that Gaza composed his grammar in Rome.[148]

Gaza was in Rome on several occasions. He decided to move from Ferrara to Rome at the end of 1449; in November, he wrote to Giovanni Tortelli from Grottaferrata, just outside Rome, where he was staying to avoid the plague that was rife in the city.[149] In Rome, besides his well-known activities as a translator, he also taught Greek. After the death of Nicholas V in March 1455, Gaza moved to Naples; he was certainly there by November 1455.[150] In Naples he continued to translate and taught Greek to Pontano and Panormita. His movements between 1458 and 1461 are uncertain. By the spring of 1462, he was in Policastro in Calabria, and he may have remained there for the rest of the year.[151] He seems to have spent some months in Rome in 1463, perhaps coinciding with Bessarion's appointment as patriarch of Constantinople, before he retired to the monastery of San Giovanni a Piro in Calabria. He may have been in San Giovanni by November 1463.[152] He seems to have spent some years there: new statutes for this monastery were completed on October 7, 1466, apparently under Gaza's care.[153] Subsequently he moved back to Rome, where we find him in September 1467.[154] He seems to have remained in Rome until at least 1474.[155] In 1475 or 1476, he died in Calabria. Thus it appears that Gaza was in Rome from 1450 to 1455, in 1463, and again from 1467 until at least 1474.

This information must be controlled by the earliest notice of Gaza's grammar. Michael Apostolis mentions this grammar in his attack on Gaza, and Andronicus Callistus also refers to it in his defense of his cousin. This defense was complete by May 1462, when Bessarion congratulated him on it.[156] The next notice also comes from Callistus. In an undated letter, Callistus wrote to Demetrius Chalcondyles that he was using Gaza's grammar with his students in Bologna. Callistus began teaching in Bologna in 1462, probably after the death of his patron Palla Strozzi in May.[157] His letter to Chalcondyles can be located between October 13, 1463, and August 28, 1466.[158] Chalcondyles was teaching Greek in Padua using Chrysoloras's grammar at the time, and Callistus judged that this information would be of interest to his fellow teacher. Callistus himself seems to have taken a keen interest in grammatical matters: he owned the grammatical works of Apollonius Dyscolus and George Scholarios and corresponded with Filelfo about Greek grammar.[159] Since Gaza's grammar was certainly known by May 1462, we are able to exclude Gaza's last period in Rome from

1467. The years from 1450 to 1455, when he worked in Rome for Nicholas V, would thus seem to be the most likely time for the preparation of his grammar and perhaps for its publication.

At Ferrara, Gaza no doubt grew in confidence as a teacher. It is likely that it was there that he became aware of the limitations of Chrysoloras's grammar and began to supply some of its defects himself. However, Gaza's grammar—at least in its fourth and last book—presupposes access to the ancient and Byzantine grammarians from which it is drawn. These ancient works were likely to be far more easily available in the Rome of Nicholas V than in Ferrara in the 1440s.[160] Yet if he had published it before 1456, then it is surprising that we hear nothing of it until 1462. It is plausible that Gaza ordered and reworked his grammatical notes into a grammar during his time in southern Italy and published this grammar for the benefit of a wider audience in Rome. The year of his return to Rome, 1463, may not have been a happy one. In the same year that Lascaris was elected to teach Greek in Milan and Chalcondyles was elected to the new chair of Greek in Padua, Gaza wrote to Panormita from Rome explaining that he has had to sell his manuscripts to make ends meet.[161] Perhaps he also raised money by taking students for Greek lessons. The year 1462 coincides with the first records of the grammar from Apostolis and Callistus and is consistent with the dated manuscripts. As far as I am aware, no scribe who produced a copy of Gaza's grammar is known to have been active before 1455. Had Gaza published his grammar under the patronage of Nicholas V, we might have expected a copy to have found its way into the papal library and into the catalog of its contents compiled in 1455: as it is, the first clearly identifiable copy of Gaza's grammar to find its way into the Vatican was Callistus's own copy, which entered the library between 1475 and 1481.[162]

The surviving manuscripts support the contention that Gaza's grammar was published in the early 1460s. In the eighteenth century, Humphrey Hody wrote that an autograph copy of the grammar was to be found in Nuremberg, but modern paleographers have not identified such a manuscript, and we may doubt the accuracy of this notice.[163] Among the oldest manuscripts of Gaza's grammar must be placed one in the hand of Constantine Lascaris, which contains book four and excerpts from book three.[164] Johannes Regiomontanus, who studied Greek in Italy in the 1460s, owned and annotated what appears to be an early copy of the grammar.[165] The earliest dated subscription to a manuscript of Gaza's grammar was added to a copy made by the prolific and well-documented scribe Joannes Rhosos on February 1, 1467.[166] Another copy of approximately the same date was written by Francesco Vitali.[167] Immanuel Rhusotas, whose earliest recorded scribal activity goes back to 1465, made three copies of Gaza's grammar.[168] Besides the manuscript detailed above, Rhosos made at least six more copies of Gaza's grammar. He finished a copy in Rome in 1479 that was bought by King Edward IV's representative in Rome, John Shirwood.[169] A copy survives from Gaza's own hand, apparently made while its author was in Rome in the early 1470s.[170] Whenever Gaza published his grammar, it is certain that manuscripts multiplied rapidly in the 1460s and 1470s.

Gaza's grammar was arranged in four books of increasing difficulty.[171] The first book is a simple accidence. It deals with the Greek letters, the article, the declensions of the noun, the conjugations of the verb, the participles, pronouns, prepositions, adverbs, and conjunctions. It says nothing of pronunciation or of accentuation. Gaza divides the Greek noun into five declensions: four parisyllabic and one imparisyllabic.

In the fifth declension, that of the imparisyllabic nouns, he includes the contracted nouns, of which he distinguishes eight forms. He exchanges what had been the third and fourth declensions in Chrysoloras so that the Attic declension becomes his fourth declension. He does not explain why he has done this, but he is likely to have reasoned that the rarest parisyllabic declension should be the last considered. Many later grammarians followed his lead in this matter.[172] For the contracted nouns, Gaza's treatment also differs from that of his predecessors.

Gaza's most striking innovation was to reduce the number of the verb conjugations from thirteen to just five. He distinguished four barytone conjugations instead of the more usual six. The verbs in -μι, usually presented as four conjugations, are defined as a single fifth conjugation with four variants. The contracted verbs, defined as three more conjugations by Chrysoloras, are presented by Gaza as variants within his third conjugation of the barytone verbs. The student is presented with full paradigms of τύπτω and τίθημι and encouraged to view all other verbs as variations on these two grand themes. The clarity and simplicity of Gaza's verb scheme is a great pedagogical advantage.

The second book of the grammar covered the same material as the first book and in the same order, but in much greater detail. This, too, was a useful device for the teacher: it enabled Gaza to be thorough and still to graduate the difficulty of his grammar. This book deals very briefly with accentuation, a matter that Gaza postpones until book three. He gathers under different headings those features the noun declensions have in common with one another, and details those that are distinctive. He follows the same procedure for the verb conjugations. As a rule, he avoids mentioning dialectal variants. The third book dealt with accentuation, orthography, and prosody, the fourth with syntax. This fourth book is the most extensive treatment of Greek syntax produced in the fifteenth century and, as we shall see, it soon acquired a reputation for obscurity.

It has been demonstrated that this fourth book is founded partly on the works of Apollonius Dyscolus and Maximus Planudes on syntax, and particularly on the work of Michael Syncellus.[173] It is unlikely to be a coincidence that the work of Syncellus was a matter for discussion among Gaza's circle in the years between 1456 and 1461. In a lost letter to Filelfo, Callistus cited the work of Syncellus in support of the phrase "νοὸς βάρος." In March 1456, Filelfo wrote to Callistus in Pavia, explaining that he regarded it as a Latinism and criticizing the work of Syncellus in this matter; Filelfo repeated his criticism of Syncellus in a letter in May of the same year.[174] In fact, Filelfo does not seem to have had a copy of Syncellus's work to hand in 1456: in January 1461, he wrote to Palla Strozzi in Padua requesting a copy of a manuscript of this author, which Callistus owned.[175] We have already noticed Callistus's copy of Apollonius, and it is tempting to speculate that Callistus's manuscript of Syncellus passed to Gaza in the early 1460s. A manuscript of Syncellus that seems to have belonged to Gaza passed to Poliziano and finally entered the library of San Marco in 1497.[176]

We may also follow the diffusion of Gaza's grammar though its students. Callistus's students in Bologna included Giorgio Merula and Argino da Basseto;[177] Antonio de Lebrixa was in Bologna while Callistus was teaching there and may have studied under him;[178] the Englishman William Selling graduated Doctor of Divinity in Bologna on March 22, 1466, new style, and may also have studied Greek under Callistus.[179] All these students are thus likely to have been taught using Gaza's grammar.

Callistus taught Alfonsus Dursos, and Dursos is known to have made a copy of Gaza's grammar.[180] The scribe George Trivizias made three copies of the complete grammar between its publication around 1462 and his death in 1485, one of which was subsequently used by Petrus Bravus of Verona in Padua.[181] Another of Trivizias's copies came into the possession of Lazzaro Bonamico, apparently in the early years of the sixteenth century.[182]

Gaza's grammar seems to have been adopted by another influential Greek teacher, Demetrius Chalcondyles. We have seen that in 1463 Chalcondyles was teaching from Chrysoloras's grammar in Padua, and that by 1466 he knew that Callistus was using Gaza's grammar in Bologna. Chalcondyles may have followed Callistus's lead and adopted Gaza's grammar. Callistus had already prepared the ground for Gaza's grammar in Florence. Callistus moved from Bologna to Rome sometime in 1466; he remained there for five years before moving to Florence in August 1471. In Florence he numbered Angelo Poliziano and Bartolomeo Fonzio among his pupils;[183] it may have been in Florence that he taught Giorgio Valla.[184] Callistus left Florence in March 1475; Chalcondyles, whose own grammatical work is considered later, took up a chair there in September.[185]

Chalcondyles is known to have made a copy of Gaza's grammar.[186] If he did use the grammar in Florence in the 1480s, he would have used it with Johann Reuchlin, Thomas Linacre, and William Grocyn.[187] However, he may have reserved Gaza's work for the more advanced students whom he preferred to teach. Certainly, Chrysoloras, in Guarino's epitome, was the only work of Greek grammar to be printed in Florence during Chalcondyles' time there.[188] There is some evidence for the use of Gaza's grammar in Florence in the 1470s. Poliziano used it to teach Greek to the young Piero de'Medici from 1475 to May 1479. In September 1478, the six-year-old Piero proudly informed his father that he knew "quasi tucto il primo libro di Theodoro a mente" (nearly all of the first book of Gaza by heart).[189] Poliziano certainly used Gaza in connection with his lectures on Homer in the late 1480s.[190] Circumstantial evidence connects Chalcondyles with another manuscript of Gaza's work in Florence. Bernardo Nerli was a close friend of Chalcondyles: in November 1486 he stood as godfather to Chalcondyles' first son, who was given the name Theophilus-Tryphon.[191] In 1488, in the preface to the Florentine *editio princeps* of Homer, Nerli calls Chalcondyles his teacher. Nerli signed his own copy of Gaza's grammar on February 15, 1485, and in his manuscript the work is preceded by the verse epitaph for Gaza that Chalcondyles composed in Florence.[192]

When Andronicus Callistus left Florence in 1475, he traveled north to Milan. We know that he took his library with him because he became involved in a dispute over duties to pay on these books as he passed through Cremona. In Milan he formed a plan to leave for Northern Europe. He sold his books—six cases of manuscripts—to Bonaccorso Pisano, formerly his student in Pavia. Bonaccorso, together with his partner Francesco della Torre, would in the late 1470s begin an ambitious program of Greek printing in Milan, perhaps based on the books they acquired from Callistus in 1475. When in 1476 Francesco della Torre wrote to Lorenzo de' Medici to explain the circumstances in which he had purchased Callistus's books, he said that Callistus had decided to leave Milan to travel north with a "signore della Morea."[193] When next we hear of Callistus, he is in London writing to France on behalf of George Hermonymus of Sparta. It seems reasonable to suppose that the "signore" and George are the same person and that Callistus left Milan in his company. This supposition is of relevance here because the tradition of using Gaza's grammar in Northern Europe can be traced back to Hermonymus.

Callistus's own copy of Gaza's grammar, which entered the Vatican Library between 1475 and 1481, had been copied by Hermonymus.[194] In 1479 Hermonymus, now in Paris, sent a copy of the first book of the grammar to Johann Reuchlin.[195] Hermonymus reproduced this first book in Greek at least six times and the second book at least once. One of the copies of the first book was owned by Jacques Toussain, who taught from Gaza's grammar and provided a translation of the third book.[196] The grammar was used by Guillaume Budé in Paris, and it seems likely that he used a manuscript made by his teacher Hermonymus.[197] Until Hermonymus started multiplying copies of individual books, Gaza's grammar had tended to circulate as a whole.[198] The popularity of the grammar in Northern Europe over the following decades was due in part to the fact that its graduated books could be isolated in this way.

Gaza's grammar may have reached England from the continent, or it may have come directly from Italy. Cornelio Vitelli might well have brought the grammar to England. The Italian appears to have reached England in 1484, and the scribe Joannes Serbopoulos's first dated copy of Gaza was made in England in November 1484.[199] Vitelli appears to have left England early in 1487; he taught in Louvain from February 1487 until January the following year; late in 1489 or early in 1490, he returned to England. It may not be a coincidence that in October 1489 Serbopoulos finished another copy of Gaza's grammar in Reading.[200] From autumn 1490, Vitelli was again in Oxford, this time at Exeter College. After he left Oxford in the summer of 1492, we hear little more of him, but Serbopoulos continued to produce copies of Gaza's grammar: his third dated manuscript of the work was completed in Reading in October 1494.[201] The Greek made his first dated manuscript of Gaza's grammar before Grocyn or Linacre left for Italy, and he made one more before Grocyn's return. That is to say, the tradition of using Gaza's grammar was not brought to England by Grocyn or Linacre. It is also worth noting that Serbopoulos's last dated manuscript of Gaza immediately preceded the publication in Venice of the *editio princeps*. As will be seen, a number of copies of the printed edition were acquired by Englishmen.

Two influential Greek scholars associated with the Aldine Press are known to have used Gaza's grammar. Marcus Musurus taught from it, probably in the first decade of the sixteenth century, and an annotated copy that belonged to Scipione Forteguerri survives.[202] Aldus Manutius's *editio princeps* of Gaza's grammar was a particularly fine piece of printing. This book, his only edition of the grammar, received its colophon on Christmas Day 1495.[203] It was supplemented by the work of Apollonius Dyscolus, another grammarian with a formidable reputation, and by a little work supposedly culled from Herodian, *De numeris*. In 1517, Richard Pace, who had studied Greek in Padua, Bologna, and Ferrara in the early years of the century, thought well of this edition of Gaza: "Iste [Apollonius Dyscolus] et Theodorus Gaza coniuncti sunt a chalcographis in uno codice sed Theodorus, et merito, est praepositus, ut clarior, apertior, et omnibus utilior"[204] (The printers have combined Apollonius and Theodore Gaza in one volume, but Gaza is rightly placed first because he is clearer, more accessible, and more useful to everyone). This combination of texts made the edition a far more serious grammar than the work of Lascaris that Aldus had printed in the same year. It had no Latin translation, and it was significantly more expensive than Lascaris's grammar:

in the Aldine catalogs of 1498 and 1503, the volume is for sale for one Venetian ducat.[205] At this price, it was also more expensive than Urbano's fine grammar, which he printed in 1497.[206] As might be expected of such an edition, it sold far more slowly than the other Aldine grammars: it was still on sale in 1513, by which time Aldus was advertising his third edition of Lascaris and had sold out of Urbano's grammar.[207]

If it sold slowly, it also managed to find some careful owners: more copies of this edition survive than of any other early Greek grammar. One hundred sixty-two extant copies have been cataloged.[208] Its survival must owe something to the fact that it is beautifully printed in a large Greek font on large paper. A number of these early owners are known. A copy was presented by Aldus to Antonius Vicens a few weeks after its completion in 1496.[209] Copies annotated by Marcus Musurus and Scipione Forteguerri are extant.[210] Giovanni Calfurnio, a teacher in Padua, owned a manuscript copy of the grammar and also acquired a copy of Aldus's edition.[211] In November 1500, another teacher, Daniel Clario of Ragusa, asked Aldus for "volumina Theodori et Constantini quae petieram"[212] (the volumes of Theodore and Constantine that I had asked for). This request must be for copies of the Aldine Gaza and the first Aldine Lascaris of 1494 and 1495. Hernan Nuñez de Guzman bought his copy in Bologna, probably between 1500 and 1505 for one-and-a-half gold pieces.[213] A copy in the university library in Cambridge may once have belonged to Henry Bullock. Bullock was in Erasmus's Greek class in Cambridge in 1512, a class in which Gaza's grammar was certainly used.[214] Cuthbert Tunstall donated his own copy of the edition to Cambridge University Library in 1528.[215] Johann Cuno's notebook has extracts from the grammar, and he is very likely to have taught with Gaza.[216] Cuno went to Basle in 1510 and taught there the sons of Johann Amorbach. This may be related to another copy of the Aldine Gaza that declares on its title page, "Sum Amorbachiorum" (I belong to the Amorbachs).[217] Another of Cuno's pupils, Beatus Rhenanus, went on to produce a Latin translation of the first book in 1516.[218]

Gaza's grammar came to be widely regarded as a difficult work, an impression fostered by its association in the Aldine edition with Apollonius. As such, it was not often considered an appropriate text for beginners. Gaza's work was repackaged as an elementary grammar in Northern Europe. Denys Lefèvre seems to have been the first to teach Greek with Gaza's grammar at the University of Paris, not long after 1504.[219] We have already seen that on his arrival in Paris, Aleandro was asked to teach from Chrysoloras's grammar, printed there in 1507.[220] He preferred instead to send for copies of the Aldine Lascaris for his lessons. Subsequently, he must have realized that larger classes of students could not be sustained by importing large and expensive grammars from Venice. Sometime in 1511, Aleandro turned to the first book of Gaza's grammar as the basis for his lectures. This slim volume was printed by Gourmont, the first time any portion of the text had been printed since the Aldine of 1495.[221] It is not a remarkable example of the printer's art: Gourmont's first Greek font had the accents cast separately from the letters and they often float uncomfortably above them. These were not fine collector's pieces like the first Aldine Gaza, and as a consequence, far fewer copies survive. Nevertheless, the Aleandro-Gourmont edition of Gaza was an important development for Greek studies in Northern Europe. Students could now buy the first installment of a Greek course cheaply and see how they progressed with it.

The availability of cheap texts of the first book of Gaza's grammar seems to have induced Erasmus to adopt it. He had been using Chrysoloras with his pupils in

England, and it seems probable that he had been using Gourmont's edition of 1507. In October 1511, he wrote that a change might make his lectures more popular: "Hactenus praelegimus Chrysolorae Grammaticen, sed paucis; fortassis frequentiori auditorio Theodori Grammaticam auspicabimur"[222] (Previously I have lectured on Chrysoloras's grammar, but to few students; perhaps I shall make a start on Gaza's grammar with a larger audience). Larger numbers of students were more profitable to the private teacher, and students were more likely to take up the language if the essential textbooks were not prohibitively expensive. Erasmus made the decision to switch to Gaza's grammar in England. Perhaps England, having no firmly established tradition of Greek teaching, was better placed to take up the more modern grammar of Gaza. Certainly in 1516 Fox's statutes of Corpus Christi College recommended that students at the college be taught Greek with Gaza.[223] Erasmus had a high opinion of Gaza in 1511. That year he wrote for his English students, "Inter graecos optime de grammatica conscripsit Theodorus Gaza, proxime Constantinus"[224] (Among the Greeks, Theodore Gaza wrote best about grammar, followed by Constantine Lascaris). It is worth noticing that Erasmus's order of merit—Gaza first, then Lascaris—is the same as Aleandro's. As we saw above, in 1501 Erasmus had not expressed any preferences. His decision to change to Gaza's grammar was not founded on any sudden realization of its excellence but on the availability of cheap printed texts of the first book from Paris.

Erasmus is only the most prominent example of the influence of Aleandro's teaching in Paris. Perhaps eighteen months after the edition of Gaza, Aleandro saw to the printing of a supplementary work.[225] In the preface to his *Tabulae*, Aleandro writes, "Tabellas hasce . . . recognovi, ad normamque Theodoreae grammatice, quam vobis enarraturi sumus, redegi"[226] (I have revised these tables and rearranged them in accordance with Gaza's grammar, which I am about to lecture on). Aleandro saw these tables as an accompaniment to his lectures. This pamphlet consists of only four leaves, of which the first holds the title page and Aleandro's introduction. It consists of a table of the Greek alphabet and its various divisions, followed by Aleandro's notes on pronunciation, accentuation, and syllables. These are elementary matters about which Gaza's first book has nothing to say. The disjunction between the new pronunciation expounded in Aleandro's *Tabulae* and the Byzantine pronunciation assumed in Gaza's third book may account for the fact that it was the last book of the grammar to be translated.

Aleandro's teaching model came to be used throughout the universities of Northern Europe in the first decades of the sixteenth century. His *Tabulae* were frequently reprinted in Northern Europe in the second and third decades of the sixteenth century. Rutger Rescius studied under Aleandro in Paris before he moved to Louvain. He worked as a corrector for Martens's new Greek press in 1516 and very likely oversaw the production of two new works there.[227] In March 1516, Gaza's grammar was reprinted in Louvain, and Aleandro's *Tabulae* were reprinted together with a small collection of grammatical notes and texts in the same month. Rescius, writing in this edition, says, "Tabellas quasdam rudes graecarum literarum rudibus ad Theodori Gazae grammatices formam conscripsi, easque auditoribus meis hyeme superiori dictavi, ex quibus cum non nihil sese profecisse sentirent, me invitum diuque repugnantem, tandem in manus hominum dare coegerunt"[228] (I compiled some unpolished tables, adapted to the form of Gaza's grammar, for those who are unskilled in Greek, and last winter I dictated them to my pupils. They felt that they profited from these, and although I was unwilling and resisted for a long time, they finally compelled me to publish them). This throws some light on the use of Gaza for Greek teaching in Louvain in the winter of 1515–16. About 1525, in Etten near Breda, Christopher Rianus used the first book of Gaza's grammar, Aleandro's *Tabulae*, and Lucian in his lessons.[229] Aleandro had taught with just this combination of texts.

No sooner had Gaza been established in the classroom than the need was felt to have him in Latin as well as Greek. Erasmus contributed further to Gaza's popularity when he translated the first book of his grammar into Latin in 1516.[230] This version was dedicated to a distinguished teacher of Greek, Joannes Caesarius. Caesarius had been travelling in Italy at the same time as Erasmus in 1509.[231] On his return, around 1510, he established himself as a private teacher in Cologne. At Cologne he taught Greek to Henricus Glareanus,[232] he taught Hermann, the count of Neuenahr,[233] he taught Croke's successor in Leipzig, Petrus Mosellanus,[234] and he was teaching there when Croke matriculated at the university in 1515.[235] Erasmus's version presumably had its origins in his own experiences as a teacher of Greek. In the preface to his translation, Erasmus condemns those teachers who discourage their students by introducing them to the *arcana* of their subject before they teach them the elements: "Nimirum rudem discipulum odio suo retundunt et alienant, quem allici inescarique potius oportuit commoda brevitate, luce, ordine, simplicitate aliisque id genus illecebris"[236] (No wonder then that they blunt and discourage the inexperienced student with their offensive behavior, whom it is necessary to attract and entice with appropriate brevity, clarity, order, simplicity, and other such lures). Brevity, orderliness, and simplicity are the qualities that Erasmus values in this first book of Gaza. Erasmus supplied his translation to allow the student of Greek easier access to this elementary text. In order to make Gaza's first book even easier for the beginner, he added subheadings and marginalia.[237] He corrected a number of errors that, he said, had crept into the text, and he removed some unnecessary repetitions of verb forms. After Erasmus's treatment, Gaza's first book was an even better manual than it had been before. Still, Erasmus was not, as is sometimes stated, the initiator of the change to Gaza's grammar; and if he had not translated it, its popularity was such that someone else would have done so. Beatus Rhenanus describes in November 1516 how he had himself completed a translation of Gaza's first book when a visiting friend pointed out to him that Erasmus's version had already reached print. This friend produced for Rhenanus a copy of what must have been the Louvain edition of July 1516 for him to read.[238]

The year 1516 was an important one for Gaza's grammar. The fourth book, *De constructione*, had been printed for the first time since 1495 as a supplement to Chrysoloras in 1512.[239] In 1516, Richard Croke translated it. He would certainly have used it during his time in Paris. Aleandro had returned to Paris from Orléans and resumed his teaching in June 1511.[240] At the end of July, Croke attended Aleandro's lecture on Ausonius.[241] Croke subsequently worked with Erasmus and Gourmont on the printing of *The Praise of Folly*.[242] Thereafter he moved to Louvain, in March 1515 he matriculated at Cologne,[243] and shortly afterward he moved to Leipzig.[244] In the spring of 1516, he published in Leipzig a miscellany of elementary grammatical texts drawn from, among others, Aleandro, Gaza, and Urbano.[245] On December 31, 1516, Croke signed his dedicatory preface to his version of Gaza's fourth book, addressed to Albert, bishop of Magdeburg.[246] He says that he has made this version "ut hec

Theodori praecepta . . . a nostris hominibus intelligantur" (so that these precepts of Theodorus . . . might be understood by us Latins). This preface contains a notice of another contemporary attempt to translate the fourth book. Thomas More had written to Croke that a translation of the fourth book by Gervasius Amoenus had been completed and published.[247] Since More's letter arrived after the printer had begun his work, says Croke, he allowed publication to continue; he also states that he has received More's encouragement to translate the first three books. Once it was printed, he sent a copy of his translation to Reuchlin. In 1517, he returned to England and began to teach Greek at Cambridge, presumably on the basis of Gaza's grammar, although by 1520 he had composed a brief work of his own.[248]

Over the next few years, a complete Latin text of Gaza emerged. In fact, as the experiences of Rhenanus and Croke show, there was something of a race to translate it. Erasmus's version of Gaza's second book seems to have been conceived when he arrived in Louvain in July 1517. There he became familiar with Rescius, whose Greek course has been described previously. Erasmus's version of the second book finally reached print in 1518.[249] Like the translation of the first book, it, too, was dedicated to Joannes Caesarius. By 1518, only the third book remained untranslated. This remaining book was translated into Latin sometime before October 1521 by Jacques Toussain.[250] By this date, Jean Vatel had pieced together a complete parallel text from the versions of Erasmus, Toussain, and Croke.[251] Vatel stated that his reason for making this complete Latin text was to produce a volume in imitation of the successful Aldine edition of Lascaris.[252] In 1523, another Greek–Latin edition of Gaza's grammar was printed in Basle. In the preface to this edition, Valentine Curio says that the translation he prints follows Erasmus closely for the first two books: "In tertio vero et quarto interim Conradii Heresbachii, uti ille auditoribus suis forte ad verbum enarrabat, interim Iacobi Tusani atque Croci hominum eruditorum interpretationem, veluti centones nectentes consarcinavimus"[253] (In the third and fourth book, we have pieced together like centos the translation of learned men, sometimes that of Conrad Heresbach as he explained it word by word to his students, sometimes that of Jacques Toussain and Croke). Like Vatel, Curio also states that the Latin translation is needed for those who want to learn Greek without a teacher.

Gaza's grammar was not without its problems or its critics. Constantine Lascaris, while full of praise for Gaza's grammar, was first to voice a reservation, which was often repeated: "ὁ σοφὸς Θεόδωρος κάλλιστα καὶ ἐλλογιμώτατα τὸ τέταρτον τῆς ἑαυτοῦ γραμματικῆς συνέθηκε πάνυ τοῖς λογίοις ἐπωφελές, εἰ καὶ δύσκολον τυγχάνει καὶ δηλίου κολυμβητοῦ δεόμενον διὰ τὴν ἀπειρίαν τῆς τέχνης· καὶ τ' ἄλλα πάντα ἀναγκαῖα τὰς σκιὰς τῶν παλαιῶν περιέχοντα"[254] (The wise Theodore most skillfully and eloquently put together the fourth book of his grammar, very useful to the learned, containing everything necessary and the shades of the ancients, albeit it is difficult and needs a "Delian diver" because of the vastness of the field). In the preface to his edition of 1495, Aldus had called Gaza the chief of the grammarians, "ceterorum grammaticorum facile princeps,"[255] but he, too, thought that his readers needed to be advised to persevere in the face of this forbidding volume: "Non sum nescius, studiose lector, hanc Apollonii Theodoriqve grammaticen visum iri tibi primo duriusculam atque insuavem, deinde, cum eam accurate relegeris, et facilem et iocundam"[256] (I am aware, studious reader, that this grammar of Apollonius and Theodore will seem to you at first rather difficult and unpleasant; and then, when you reread it carefully, it will seem both easy and enjoyable). When Croke said that he hoped that his version would make Gaza easier for the student, he repeats Lascaris's reservation, "etsi greci aliqui δηλίου κολυμβητοῦ suum Theodorum egere affirment"²⁵⁷ (even though some Greeks say that their Theodore needs a "Delian diver"). According to Vatel, Croke's version was not a success:

> In quarto ut Ricardus Crocus, homo alioque non spernendus, satis nobis non faceret, in causa fragmenta quaedam fuere stilum referentia sive Erasmi, sive Coppi, aut alterius cuiuspiam huius farinae. Nam legisse et haec Crocus ipse videbatur, pugnabat in multis tamen. Quamobrem in illius luto haesi, interdum in his, atque id magis, ut ansam aliis exhiberem Theodoricae eruendae lectionis.²⁵⁸
>
> [In the fourth book, Richard Croke, a man otherwise to be taken seriously, has not satisfied us. The reason for this is that certain passages mimic the style of Erasmus or Cop or some other writer of this sort. For though Croke himself seemed to have read these, yet he struggled against them in many places. For this reason, I was sometimes stuck in the mud here or there, and the more so that I might provide others with a means of digging out Theodore's meaning.]

Perhaps Croke should not be blamed for his difficulties in the notoriously difficult fourth book. Vatel attempted to reestablish Gaza's text. To this end, he obtained "exemplaria"—apparently manuscripts, not printed copies—of Gaza's grammar from Henricus Glareanus, Pierre Danès, Mustellius, and others; he set particular store by a manuscript or annotated edition of Gaza that belonged to Agostino Giustiniani.²⁵⁹

During the 1520s, a consensus grew that Gaza was too difficult for students. In 1523, Curio describes the difficulty of Gaza's grammar:

> Theodorus Gaza . . . libros quattuor de institutione grammatica posteritati reliquit, quibus vir ille rem grammaticam in universum miro ordinis compendio complexus est, atqui sic arcta brevitate, ut non rudibus, sed eruditis prorsus scripsisse haec videatur. Nam cum ubique fere obscuriusculus sit, tum locos quosdam habet, praesertim in posterioribus libris, vixdum ab eruditissimis intellectos, et qui iuxta proverbium Oedipum aliquando requirant coniectorem.²⁶⁰
>
> [Theodore Gaza . . . left four books on grammar to posterity, in which that man gathered all grammar into a remarkably orderly compendium, and it is so compressed that it might seem to have been written not for beginners but for scholars. For while it is somewhat difficult almost everywhere, it has some places, especially in the later books, which are hardly understood by the most learned, and which (as the proverb has it) sometimes need an Oedipus to solve them.]

In order to mitigate its difficulties, the examples from ancient authors that Gaza cites were given a reference and a Latin translation by Heresbach.²⁶¹ The problem of its extreme compression, however, remained. In 1524, Glareanus—whose manuscript of Gaza's grammar Vatel had consulted for his edition of 1523—echoed Curio's sentiment. In the preface to his edition of Urbano's grammar he wrote, "Theodorus ipse non tam discipulis ea quam praeceptoribus scripsisse videtur; qui viam commonstravit compendiosam sane, sed quam non facile quivis apprehenderit, saltem rudiusculus et harum rerum imperitior, nisi ductore quodam atque commonstratore"²⁶² (Theodore himself might seem to have written these things not so much for students as for teachers. He has shown them a road that is certainly short but that not everyone—at least not those inexperienced and unskilled in these matters—will easily follow without a guide and someone to show them the way). Melchior Volmar, the champion of Demetrius Chalcondyles' grammar, added to the growing chorus in 1525 when he wrote that even the first book is too unforgiving for beginners:

> Nam Theodori Gazae, viri citra controversiam doctissimi et aliorum grammaticorum facile principis, graviores sunt institutiones quam ut huic aetati recte convenire possint, tum nimis in arctum coegit compendium primi libri. De quarto quid attinet dicere? In quo non solum ea quae de suo Gaza nobis ingenio attulit, sed illa etiam quae ex Apollonii Difficilis et aliorum quorundam libris non parum multa descripsit, dum brevis esse laborat, aut potius de industria sic obscuravit, ut non immerito a graecis ipsis ac eiusdem ordinis hominibus iactatum sit δηλίου κολυμβητοῦ δεόμενον.[263]
>
> [For the grammar of Theodore Gaza, undeniably a very learned man and certainly the greatest of the Greek grammarians, is too harsh to be appropriate to this age, and he has too narrowly compressed the summary that is his first book. What can be said of the fourth book? In which while striving for brevity, he has deliberately obscured not only those things that he brought to us from his own resources but also the many things that he drew from the works of Apollonius Dyscolus and other grammarians, so that the Greeks themselves and men of the same profession rightly claim that he needs a "Delian diver."]

Most damning is Volmar's claim that to understand Gaza's grammar you need already to know what he professes to teach: "Quodque mirum nobis maxime videri debet, ut quum grammaticae praeceptiones in hoc sint institutae, ut ad intelligentiam authorum in primis conferant, has Theodori non nisi ex illorum lectione et multa et varia, denique accurata singulorum nec oscitante observatione sis intellecturus"[264] (And what should seem most remarkable to us is that, although grammars are composed primarily to enable us to understand the authors, you will not understand Gaza's without wide and varied reading in those authors and accurate and careful study of the details). Guillaume Budé said that he knew nothing so famous, or so obscure, as the fourth book of Gaza's grammar.[265] Ludovicus Vives wrote in *De ratione studii puerilis* that Gaza's fourth book was difficult and obscure.[266] There was one last attempt to save Gaza from such accusations. In 1527 Ercole Girlando translated the grammar again:

> Cum superioribus diebus Theodori Gaze summi philosophi de re grammatica quatuor doctissimos libros a nonnullis in latinum sermonem versos perlegerem, eos inveni hac interpretatione multo obscuriores factos. In his enim multa fuerunt praetermissa, quae omnino ad percipienda Theodori sensa necessaria erant; multa rursus addita, quae tamen superflua, nihil afferebant commodi studiosis; multa praeterea perplexe dicta; multa obscurius interpretata, quam ut vel doctissimus possit intelligere.[267]
>
> [When I recently read through the four books of the grammar of the great thinker Theodore Gaza, which have been translated by several people into Latin, I found them made much more difficult by this translation. For these translations omitted many things that were essential for understanding Gaza's meaning; they added many superfluities that did nothing to help the student; they said many things besides in a complicated way; and many were too obscurely rendered for even a very learned man to be able to understand them.]

This enthusiasm was not enough to maintain Gaza's work in the classrooms of Europe. The famous fourth book did, however, manage to attract a commentary in the eighteenth century, and the whole grammar was reprinted in Venice as late as 1807.[268]

Constantine Lascaris, 1463–1466

Constantine Lascaris was the most prolific Greek grammarian of the fifteenth century. He taught Greek in Milan and Messina for more than forty years. In his youth he had studied under Joannes Argyropoulos in Constantinople. He was nineteen years old when the city fell to the Turks in 1453 and he was captured. We know little of his life during the years from 1453 to 1458, other than that he found himself in Rhodes and Fera between 1455 and 1457. We know much more about his studies after he arrived in Milan in 1458. His personal library survives largely intact in Madrid. He was in the habit of writing informative, even conversational, subscriptions to many of his manuscripts, and these throw some light on his interests and teaching methods. We are also fortunate that he supplied informative prologues and postscripts to his grammatical works.[269]

Such Greek teaching as was available in Milan in the early 1450s was probably informal for we have no record of it. Francesco Filelfo, the man best placed to form a judgment, did not think highly of it. He wrote to the Florentine Donato Acciaiuoli in 1451 with a criticism of contemporary Greek textbooks: "Accepi esse apud vos quosdam priscos de arte grammatica libros, quorum velim nomina ad me scribas. Nam quibus hoc tempore in publicis ludis graeci utuntur libris pleni sunt ineptiarum, ac plane tales ut ad dediscendum sint quam ad discendum longe magis accommodati"[270] (I understand that you have certain books of the ancient grammarians. Would you write to me with their names? For the books that the Greeks are presently using in the public schools are full of absurdities and are clearly such as are much better for unlearning than for learning). In these circumstances, we might have thought that Filelfo would welcome the arrival of a scholar of Lascaris's abilities in the city. Certainly, Lascaris worked hard to provide better textbooks. He seems to have come to Milan late in 1458, and he taught Greek privately there for four years.[271] The earliest dated work of Lascaris, a little treatise on the pronouns and their dialectal variants, was produced in 1460.[272] Two years later, still as a private teacher, he published another short work on poetic tropes and figures, Περὶ τρόπων καὶ σχημάτων ποιητικῶν, a treatise that he addressed to his pupils in Milan.[273] Lascaris's influential summary of Greek grammar, Ἐπιτομὴ τῶν ὀκτὼ τοῦ λόγου μερῶν, was published in Milan in 1463.[274]

The year of its publication was a significant one for Greek studies in Milan. Lascaris found himself at the center of a confrontation brought on by the internal politics of the University of Milan. The Greek teacher Demetrio Castreno, a protégé of Filelfo, had arrived in Milan shortly before Lascaris in 1458.[275] Like Lascaris, Castreno had been teaching Greek privately in the city. With Filelfo's support, Castreno was elected to the chair of Greek at Milan on October 9, 1462.[276] It is not clear that he ever took up this post, however, for on December 14, 1462, a petition was addressed to Francesco Sforza, signed by forty-seven of the great and good in Milan, which supported Lascaris's candidacy for this same post. Lascaris was elected to the position on July 24, 1463.[277] The unlucky Castreno seems to have paid the price for his champion's unpopularity.

Some of the names on this petition are worth noting because they supply some indication of the intellectual circles in which Lascaris moved in Milan.[278] It was signed by the eminent scholar Pier Candido Decembrio, whose father had studied Greek with Manuel Chrysoloras, and who had already made versions of Homer,

Plato, and Appian.[279] It was signed by Lampugnino Birago, who subsequently translated the history of Dionysius of Halicarnassus and several works of Plutarch.[280] It was signed by Leodrisio Crivelli, who had fallen out with Filelfo late in 1461 or in 1462, and who was to translate over the coming months a text enthusiastically expounded by Lascaris in Milan, the *Orphic Argonautica*.[281] The name of Bartolomeo of Sulmona also appears on this petition. Bartolomeo had written a Latin grammar in Milan during the years between 1457 and 1463, a period covering most of Lascaris's career in the city.[282] He had also been a vocal critic of Filelfo's long verse panegyric, the *Sforziad*.[283] Lascaris wrote an extant letter to Bartolomeo in which he sharply criticized Filelfo's knowledge of Greek.[284] The petition was also signed by Bartolomeo Calco, Filippo Feruffini, and Bonino Mombrizio. Calco had already studied Greek under Gregorio Tifernas in Milan in the summer of 1456.[285] Feruffini had previously enjoyed good relations with Filelfo, and Filippo knew enough Greek in 1451 to receive a letter in that language from him.[286] Mombrizio, as will be seen, would soon translate Lascaris's new grammar. It was at the request of these three scholars that Lascaris wrote his extended treatment of the Greek noun, Περὶ ὀνόματος, which he published in Milan in 1463. Lascaris's earlier *Compendium* of Greek grammar was also expanded for their benefit.[287]

Lascaris's grammar appears to have dominated teaching in Milan during the last decades of the fifteenth century. Giorgio Valla would have used it when he studied with Lascaris in Milan between 1462 and 1465.[288] Lascaris himself made a presentation copy for the Duke of Milan's ten-year-old daughter Ippolyta Sforza, an apt pupil.[289] To the years between 1463 and Lascaris's departure for Naples in 1465 belongs Bonino Mombrizio's Latin verse translation of Lascaris's *Compendium*, a work that he, too, dedicated to Ippolyta Sforza.[290] In June 1465, Lascaris was summoned to Naples by King Ferdinand of Aragon, perhaps as tutor to Ippolyta Sforza.[291] His tenure of this post is uncertain: no extant document attests to this position, and some that might have been expected to mention it do not. He certainly taught Greek in Naples, but his Neapolitan students were not as able or as enthusiastic as his Milanese ones: in Milan they had asked him to expand his *Compendium*; in Naples they asked him to shorten it again.[292]

For reasons that remain unclear, his stay in Naples was to prove brief: in 1466 he moved to Messina and in February 1468 he officially took up one of the chairs of Greek there.[293] He taught at the Greek school of the Basilian monastery of San Salvatore until his death in 1501.[294] It was in Messina in 1468 that he completed his exposition of the Greek verb, Περὶ ῥήματος, a companion to the work on the noun that he had begun to compile in Milan. On completion, these two works were joined together as the second book of Lascaris's grammar. The following year, the grammar was expanded again. Now, while the *Compendium* remained the first book, a new work, Περὶ συντάξεως, emerged as the second book, while Περὶ ὀνόματος καὶ ῥήματος became the third book.[295] The following year, he composed a short explanation of the iota subscript. With this work, his collection of teaching texts seems to have been complete.

Like Chrysoloras, Lascaris's *Compendium* divided the Greek noun into ten declensions. The first four of these are parisyllabic, the fifth is imparisyllabic. He defines a further five contracted declensions as subdivisions of the fifth declension and follows Chrysoloras's scheme with only slight modifications.[296] Lascaris also taught a total of thirteen verb conjugations: he first defines six barytone conjugations; he then derives three contracted conjugations from the sixth barytone conjugation; finally, he expounds four verb conjugations in -μι. He relates the first three of these conjugations in -μι to the three contracted declensions and the fourth to the sixth barytone conjugation.[297] Martínez-Manzano believes that a manuscript now in Madrid and never printed preserves a late revision of the entire grammar, prepared by Lascaris.[298] Here, the first book, a revision of the *Compendium*, goes under the title Μεθοδικὸν τῆς κλίσεως τῶν ὀκτὼ μερῶν τοῦ λόγου. The most striking feature of this text of the grammar is that Lascaris defines only four barytone conjugations for the verb instead of the six he inherited from Chrysoloras, giving him a total of eleven conjugations.[299] It is unlikely to be a coincidence that the same number of conjugations is also found in the summary of Theodosius's summary of Herodian that Lascaris made in Messina in 1488.[300] Lascaris taught his students with the first *Compendium*, which had the standard thirteen conjugations.[301] None of the printed texts of Lascaris's grammar reproduce this innovation, and consequently this attempt to simplify the forbidding Greek verb was neither published nor imitated.

Lascaris was a great *epitomator*. The first surviving work of his is a short compendium on the pronouns, which he published in Milan in 1460. He made a biographical dictionary, which he compiled largely from the Suda lexicon.[302] He collected extracts from Plutarch and *sententiae* from Diogenes Laertius.[303] He published a list of the ancient Greek authors of Sicily and another of the writers of Calabria.[304] His extracts from Herodian have already been noticed.[305] In Naples and perhaps again in Messina, he further trimmed the summary of Greek accidence that he had produced in Milan.[306] Lascaris's opinions regarding the use and abuse of *compendia* appear from the preface he wrote in Messina for his revised edition of his grammatical works.[307] Lascaris's comprehensive knowledge of the surviving Greek grammarians informs a description of the history of grammatical writing in terms of brevity or fullness. The ancient world, he says, produced a very substantial body of writing on Greek grammar: "Οἱ γὰρ παλαιότατοι εὐτυχίας οὔσης τῷ γένει ἐπιμελέστατα περὶ γραμματικῆς ἔγραψαν· ἵνα μὴ μιᾷ βίβλῳ τὸ πᾶν αὐτῆς παραδοῖεν"[308] (The ancient grammarians, while fortune favored the Greek race, wrote with great care about grammar, so that all of it might not be passed down within the confines of a single volume). This statement hints that the very bulk of these treatments was a factor in their destruction. Subsequently, he continues, grammatical writing fell into decline: "Οἱ δὲ πολλῷ μετ᾽ αὐτοὺς τὰ ἐκείνων συντέμνοντες συνέστειλαν, οἷα Θεοδόσιος καὶ Χοιροβοσκὸς καὶ ἄλλοι· ὧν τὰ ἐρωτήματα Μοσχόπουλος καὶ οἱ ἐπ᾽ αὐτοῦ βραχύναντες διὰ τὴν δυστυχίαν τοῦ γένους τὰ παλαιὰ ἐπεκάλυψαν"[309] (Those who came long after them, men such as Theodosios, Choeroboscos, and others, abbreviated them, cutting them short; Moschopoulos and his contemporaries, abbreviating these *Erotemata* because of the misfortune of the Greek race, covered up the ancient works). And, he continues, even Moschopoulos's abbreviation of the ancient grammarians came in time to appear rather too long to Byzantine students. Lascaris paints a picture of the Greek grammatical heritage being squeezed to accommodate the declining learning of the Greek world until it was in danger of disappearing altogether.

Nevertheless, if such summaries were responsible for the loss of much of the earlier grammatical works, this preface also shows that Lascaris was happy to use epitomes with students of the Greek language: "Τουτὶ δὲ δι᾽ ἐπιτομῶν διαφόρων τὸ καλὸν ἐφυτεύθη· ὧν τὸ στενὸν ἥ τε ζῶσα φωνὴ ἀνεπλήρωσεν, ἥ τε τῶν ἀκουόντων σπουδή"[310] (This good result was produced by means of different epitomes, the narrowness of which was filled out by the explanation of the teacher and by the enthusiasm of the students). Not all such *compendia* are valuable. Thus far I have been quoting from Lascaris's preface to his grammar, a text that did not reach print during the Renaissance. In the first Aldine edition of Lascaris's complete grammar, the third book, *De nomine et verbo*, is followed by an interesting postscript.[311] Here, Lascaris acknowledges the contribution of other grammarians and alludes to a misguided attempt to shorten Chrysoloras's *Erotemata*: "ὁ σοφὸς Μανουῆλος ὁ Χρυσολωρᾶς, ὁ φυτεύσας καὶ διδάξας ἐν Ἰταλίᾳ τὰ ἑλληνικά, οὗ τὸ βιβλίον οὐκ οἶδ' ὅπως τινὲς τῶν ἀμαθῶν συστείλαντες διέφθειραν..."[312] (the learned Manuel Chrysoloras, who planted and taught Greek culture in Italy, whose book some ignorant people somehow managed to ruin by abbreviating it...). The reference appears to be to Guarino Veronese's popular summary of Chrysoloras's work.[313] In the preface, the suggestion that he had a low opinion of this summary is confirmed by his observation that, when he arrived in Milan to teach Greek, he found there no abbreviated grammar that he was prepared to use: "Μηδεμίαν τε ἐπιτομὴν χρησίμην εὑρὼν ἀφ' ὧν ἔτυχον νομίσας παλαιῶν γραμματικῶν ἐπιτομὰς πολλῶν συνέταξα τοῖς μαθηταῖς χαριζόμενος πολλοῖς οὖσι καὶ λογίοις"[314] (Finding no useful epitome, from the works of the ancients grammarians that I happened to have, I composed epitomes of many things for my students, who were numerous and learned). Still, students do need to start somewhere: "Ἐπεὶ δὲ ἡ ἡμετέρα πρακτικὴ γραμματικὴ ποικίλη τε τυγχάνει καὶ δύσκολος καὶ οἷόν τι πέλαγος ἀχανές, οὐ δεῖ τοὺς ἀκροατὰς μόναις ἀρκεῖσθαι ταῖς ἐπιτομαῖς ὥσπερ σκιαγραφίαις οὔσαις, ἀλλὰ μεθ' αὐτὰς [sic] ἀναγινώσκειν πάντα τὰ παλαιὰ Ἐρωτήματα."[315] (Since then it happens that our actual grammar is complex and difficult and like some vast ocean, it is not necessary for the students to be satisfied with the epitomes alone (which are like rough sketches), but after them to read all the ancient *Erotemata*). The bulk of even the surviving Greek grammatical works is such that it would daunt the beginner in the language. His epitomes provide these students with their entrance to the language, but they should ultimately turn to the sources from which he has compiled them. In the preface he defends the use of such compendia:

Καὶ ἀεὶ δι' ἐπιτομῶν ἐδίδαξα ἔν τε Μεδιολάνῳ καὶ Νεαπόλει καὶ Μεσσήνῃ τῆς Σικελίας, πολλοὺς ὠφελήσας Γραικοὺς καὶ Λατίνους. Ταῦτά τοι οὐδὲν ἀπεικὸς ἀπ' ἐπιτομῶν ἄρξασθαι, οὔτ' αὐτῶν ὀλιγωρεῖν χρὴ οὔτε διασύρειν, ὅπερ τινὲς εὐήθεις ποιοῦσι. Πλούσιοι γὰρ καὶ πένητες, παῖδες, νέοι, ἄνδρες, γέροντες, Ἕλληνες καὶ Λατῖνοι, δι' αὐτῶν παιδεύονται. Ἄμεινόν τε ὀλιγομαθεῖς γενέσθαι ἢ ἀμαθεῖς. Ἀπὸ γὰρ μικρῶν ἀρχῶν ἐπὶ τὰ μείζω ἀναχθῆναι οἷόν τε· ὅπερ εἰ οἱ ἐν τῇ Ἑλλάδι ὄντες λόγιοι ἐποίουν, ἀληθῶς πολλοὺς εὐφυεῖς ὄντας ἐπαίδευον. Νῦν δὲ τὰ μὲν μακρὰ ὀνοῦντες, τῶν δ' ἐπιτομῶν καταφρονοῦντες, ἄγευστοι λόγων πάντῃ διατελοῦσι. Διὸ παραινῶ πάντας τοὺς τῶν λόγων ἐραστάς, οἵας ἂν εἶεν ἡλικίας, εὐποροῦντας λογίου καθηγητοῦ ἀπ' ἐπιτομῶν ἄρξασθαι οἵων ἂν τύχοιεν καὶ γραμματικῆς ἀπογεύσασθαι, μεθ' ἧς ἡδὺ τὸ ἀκούειν καὶ ἀναγινώσκειν.[316]

[And I have always taught with epitomes at Milan, Naples, and Messina, helping many Greeks and Latins. There is nothing inappropriate in beginning with epitomes, neither is it necessary to despise or disparage them, as some foolish people do. For rich and poor, boys, adolescents, adults, and old men, Greeks and Latins, are taught with them. It is better to be imperfectly knowledgeable than perfectly ignorant. For it is possible to advance from small beginnings to greater things. If the learned men of Hellas had done this, they would certainly have produced many well-educated men. And now, delighting in lengthy works and spurning epitomes, they remain entirely ignorant of literature. For this reason I advise all lovers of literature, however old they may be, who have a learned teacher, to start with such epitomes as they can find and to get a taste of grammar: it is a pleasant thing to listen and read with her help.]

This sounds rather as though Lascaris has in mind some particular Greek teacher or teachers currently working in the East. It is not likely that he was thinking of the Greek grammar of George Scholarios because this grammar is not very large. Lascaris had access to Scholarios's grammar in the cathedral library in Messina, and he mentions Scholarios without prejudice in the postscript to his *De nomine et verbo*.[317] This disagreement over methods of teaching Greek seems otherwise unnoticed.

The later popularity of his grammar owed something to the number of prominent scholars who passed through his school and ultimately came to teach the language themselves along the same lines as their master. Lascaris's *Compendium* of Greek grammar was first printed in Milan in 1476 in Greek only, long after his departure.[318] By 1480, it had been provided with a Latin translation by Giovanni Crastoni, and a parallel Greek–Latin text was issued in Milan in that year.[319] The next edition was in Vicenza in Greek and Latin in 1489.[320] At Florence, Angelo Poliziano transcribed passages from *De nomine et verbo* in 1484, and he used Lascaris in his commentary on the *Odyssey* later in the decade.[321] In 1493, the student Girolamo Amaseo seems to have used the *Compendium* in private in Florence before moving on to lectures on Gaza's grammar.[322] The widespread use of Lascaris's text as a first student grammar was confirmed by the decision of Aldus Manutius to make it one of the first texts to come from his new Venetian press.

A number of factors informed Aldus's choice of Lascaris. First was the contemporary demand for the work. Aldus writes in the preface, "Nullae enim extabant impressae venales et petebantur a nobis frequenter"[323] (There were no printed copies for sale, and I was often asked for them). Aldus's edition was the fourth printing of Lascaris's work and the first in Venice. A second factor that influenced Aldus's decision to print Lascaris was that he had recently received a manuscript of the text that had been revised by the author's own hand. Pietro Bembo and Angelo Gabrieli, having decided to learn Greek under Lascaris, set out for Sicily in 1492, arriving in Messina in May.[324] By August 1494, they were in Venice with a manuscript of Lascaris's grammar.[325] Although Aldus boasted of this manuscript in his preface, the Aldine Press did not make much use of it, preferring to base its edition on a copy of the *Compendium* printed in 1480 or 1489. The manuscript brought from Messina contained more of Lascaris's grammatical works than just the *Compendium*, but only that work was printed. This first Aldine grammar received its colophon in March 1495 and was for sale in Venice from the Press in 1498 for four *marcelli*.[326] Aldus's first grammar had to be a beginner's text so that it would sell in numbers and quickly. With these considerations in mind, it was given a Latin translation.[327] The translation printed besides the *Compendium* seems to have been a light revision of Crastoni's. Its status as a beginner's grammar was reinforced by the addition of a number of basic Greek texts in prose and verse, the so-called Aldine Appendix.[328] It was not until around 1502 that the complete text of Lascaris's grammar was printed, together with a number of Lascaris's brief grammatical treatises. It went on sale in Venice for three *lire*.[329] The translations of these books of the grammar and the treatises were presumably in-house productions.

Lascaris's grammar had a checkered career in Northern Europe. It was probably for some years the most widely used grammar in Poland: one hundred copies were ordered from Aldus for Krakow in December 1505, an order—if it was fulfilled—that would have greatly advanced Greek studies in Poland.[330] In More's *Utopia*, written in 1515 and 1516, Lascaris's work was the only Greek grammar that Raphael Hythlodaeus took with him to the island. The compliment is mixed, however, because Hythlodaeus implies that he would have preferred to have given the Utopians a copy of Gaza's grammar.[331] Lascaris was not very well received in Paris. When Girolamo Aleandro arrived in the city to teach Greek in 1508, he promptly ordered copies of the Aldine Lascaris for his students, despite the fact that Chrysoloras's grammar had just been printed there, and despite the urging of several unnamed Parisians.[332] Parisian resistance to Lascaris seems to have continued, and Aleandro subsequently decided to use a Parisian edition of Gaza's grammar for his lessons.[333] There appears to be no reason why Gourmont's Parisian press could not have printed Lascaris's work: it did print the grammars of Chrysoloras, Gaza, and Urbano while Aleandro was there but did not print Lascaris at all before 1530. In 1525, Gourmont even reprinted the long-neglected grammar of Demetrius Chalcondyles.[334] The editor of this edition, Melchior Volmar, had very clear ideas about the relative merits of the Byzantine grammarians. Of Lascaris's work, he wrote, "Tantum effecit e regione graeci sermonis vulgaris et ad verbum pene dixerim inepta tralatio ista ut huic adhaerentes lectorem pariter et authorem cum magno ipsorum dispendio auditores fastidiant"[335] (He uses such obscure words from demotic Greek and has that literal, even clumsy, translation, so that those students who use this grammar despise both the lecturer and the author of the work, to the great loss of all concerned). Lascaris's grammar went through a respectable number of reprints in the first half of the sixteenth century, and like Chrysoloras's grammar, it fell from grace in the second half of the century. It did, however, survive long enough to leave its mark on Nikolaos Sophianos's influential grammar of contemporary Greek,[336] and it was briefly revived in the first decades of the nineteenth century by several editions printed in Venice.[337]

JOHANN REUCHLIN, 1479–1481

A single notice survives of a grammatical work composed by Johann Reuchlin. This notice is part of a brief account of his career that appears in the preface to his work *De rudimentis hebraicis*, published in 1506.[338] This preface, and the records of the universities he attended, allows a picture of his movements to be constructed. His advanced education began with Priscian in Paris in 1472, when he was eighteen years old. The following year we have our first notice of his Greek studies: in Paris, he tells us, he studied under some of the pupils of Gregorio Tifernas.[339] He continued his studies at the University of Basle, where he matriculated for the bachelor's degree in September 1474. He remained in Basle until 1477, and during his time in the city, he studied Greek under the Byzantine Andronicus Contoblacas.[340] Having received his master's degree in Basle in 1477, he moved back to Paris to study law. While in Paris, he studied Greek under George Hermonymus, whose movements are discussed elsewhere.[341] In January 1479, Reuchlin matriculated as a law student at the University of Orléans. In 1506, he noted with some satisfaction that he had paid for his legal training by taking on students for Greek lessons. The following comment, which has earned him his place here among the grammarians, seems to refer to this period in Orléans: "Simul enim et didici latinorum iura et docui graecorum praecepta, de quibus tunc artem grammaticam graece conscripsi cui titulus extabat Μικροπαιδεία, id est *Micropaedia*. Eam anno post Pictonibus Galliae Aquitanis publice legi atque illic in iure civili cathedram merui"[342] (For at the same time I learned the laws of the Latins and taught the rules of the Greeks. It was then that I wrote a Greek grammar in Greek entitled Μικροπαιδεία, that is, *Micropaedia*. The following year, at Poitiers in Aquitaine, I lectured publicly on this grammar, and there I obtained a chair in civil law). Reuchlin was licensed in Poitiers in June 1481, so his Greek teaching and the composition of his grammar must be located in the years between 1479 and 1481.

It seems that, immediately after his matriculation at Orléans, he wrote a letter to his former teacher Hermonymus in Paris. This letter is lost, but Hermonymus's reply is extant.[343] He writes that he is sending Reuchlin a copy of the first book of Gaza's grammar, informs him that a Greek lexicon he asked after is available to buy, and says that, although he cannot sell him the manuscript of the Greek fables he has asked for, he does have other copies that he can send. If these texts were for Reuchlin's own use, then his studies cannot have been very far advanced. Neither Contoblacas nor Hermonymus had any great reputation as teachers of Greek, but if after some years under their guidance he had got no further than the first book of Gaza's grammar, he must have been a dull pupil indeed. It is more likely that the books he ordered from Hermonymus were intended for use with his own students. The first book of Gaza's grammar may thus have been the text from which he began to teach in Orléans, and Gaza's work may have provided a basis for Reuchlin's *Micropaedia*. The name of this lost grammar does not suggest a very ambitious work. Nevertheless, it appears to have been the first work of Greek grammar to be written by a non-Greek since Roger Bacon's work in the thirteenth century.[344]

Reuchlin moved to the University of Tübingen at the end of 1481. In the spring of 1482, he went to Florence and then to Rome, where he attended Argyropoulos's lectures on Thucydides. According to one surviving account, Argyropoulos asked Reuchlin to read aloud and then translate a passage from the historian, an exercise that he performed very creditably.[345] By 1488, Reuchlin's confidence with the language was such that he was prepared to publish his first translation of a Greek text.[346] We know that Reuchlin was teaching Greek in Heidelberg in the last years of the fifteenth century and that Johann Cuno and Jodocus Gallus Rubeaquensis were among his pupils.[347] Reuchlin's own grammar, *Micropaedia*, has not come to light, but at least one grammatical work of Reuchlin's does survive: his brief exposition in Latin of the differences between the Greek dialects.[348]

We also have evidence of Reuchlin's acquaintance with other grammarians. He owned a manuscript of Lascaris's work;[349] he owned a copy of Bonaccorso's 1480 edition of Lascaris's *Compendium*, a volume that he gave to the young Philip Melanchthon in March 1509;[350] he also owned a copy of Scholarios's grammar, a relatively rare work.[351] Georg Simler's grammatical work, considered later, was printed in Tübingen in March 1512, and part of this work was addressed by Simler to his former teacher, Reuchlin. It included an edition of Chrysoloras's *Erotemata* in Guarino's epitome, in Greek only. While Richard Croke was teaching Greek in Leipzig, he sent a copy of his translation of book four of Gaza's grammar to Reuchlin in Stuttgart in 1516.[352] Nevertheless, the only grammar that we know for certain that Reuchlin used in his classes is that of Chrysoloras. In February 1522, he wrote to Michael Hummelberg that he had been teaching with this grammar, perhaps from the text printed in Simler's edition.

ALDUS MANUTIUS, 1480S

Aldus Manutius tutored the young princes of Carpi, Alberto and Leonello Pio, from about 1483 to 1489. In a letter to their mother, Caterina, probably written in 1487, Aldus talks of some of his works, including several items related to the teaching of Greek. Of these, his *De accentibus et latinis et graecis opusculum* did not reach print, although its contents may have eventually emerged elsewhere.[353] Another work that he mentions, the *Libellus graecus tamquam isagogicus*, may ultimately have evolved into the so-called Aldine Greek appendix, a collection of elementary texts, which is discussed later.[354] In 1493, in the preface to his Latin grammar, he talks first of his *Institutiones graecae*, a Greek grammar that he seems to have compiled sometime in the 1480s.[355]

Aldus's Greek grammar was eventually published in 1515, some months after the death of its author. An autograph manuscript survives, which shows alterations in Aldus's hand, and it is possible that by 1515 the work had become very different from the one that he began many years earlier.[356] According to Marcus Musurus's preface to the posthumous edition, Aldus did not feel that the grammar was complete at his death in February 1515. He entrusted his manuscript of the work to Musurus, who edited it for publication as a tribute to the great printer in November 1515. This was the first and only edition of the grammar, and Aldus has many finer monuments.

The work defines the ten standard declensions of the noun: four parisyllabic, one imparisyllabic, and five contracted.[357] He reveals a debt to Gaza's grammar in his decision to reverse the order of the third and fourth declensions.[358] Most of the nouns he chooses as paradigms were standard, but he does choose "bookseller," ὁ βιβλιοπώλης, to illustrate the first of his ten declensions.[359] When he expounds the declensions of the pronouns he uses "Plato" to illustrate the first person, "Aristotle" for the second, and "Aldus" for the third.[360] The verbs are divided into the usual thirteen conjugations: six barytone, three contracted, and four in -μι.[361] The most striking feature of this portion of the grammar—which takes up over two thirds of the book—is the space Aldus devotes to setting out the paradigms of the verbs: each verb conjugation is produced in full. As we have seen, Aldus seems to have found fault with Chrysoloras's brief treatment of the verb in his 1512 edition of that grammar.[362] Aldus's own grammar certainly provided the student with a handy reference guide to the conjugations, but the simplifications of grammars such as Gaza's were less daunting to the beginner. The timing of the publication of Aldus's work was also unfortunate: by 1515, grammatical manuals in Latin were becoming more usual in the classroom than ones in Greek. Whatever its merits, it is the only surviving grammar produced in Greek by a Western student of the language.

CONRAD CELTIS, 1491

The wandering German poet Conrad Celtis went to Italy only once. In the summer of 1487, he traveled first to Venice, then to Padua; he moved on to Ferrara to study with Battista Guarino, and then to Bologna, where he studied with Filippo Beroaldo; next he went to Florence and Rome before returning north via Venice in 1489.[363] After two years in Poland, he returned to Germany. It was probably in Italy that he acquired what Greek he had. He had a copy of Lascaris's grammar, and perhaps some other texts. From these he compiled a booklet of Greek morphology. This short work provided tables of the declensions of nouns and the conjugation of verbs.[364] For all its limitations, it seems to merit the title, more usually bestowed on Urbano Bolzanio's grammar, of the first Greek grammar to be written in Latin since Roger Bacon produced his grammar in the thirteenth century.[365]

A grammar of sorts was certainly in existence by 1491. That year, Joannes de Pisnicze asked Celtis for a copy, and Heinrich von Bünau wanted the grammar urgently in the last months of 1495.[366] Celtis introduced the abbot Johannes Trithemius to Greek in 1494, and we may guess that this was the grammar used.[367] In October 1497, Celtis left Ingolstadt for Vienna, where he taught Greek and interpreted Homer for his students.[368] In May 1498 Johann Schlecta thanked Celtis for sending him *praecepta graeca*, which must refer to another copy of this work.[369] The grammar survives today in just two manuscripts, both of which must be located in this Viennese context. One surviving copy of the grammar has the title "Institutio grammaticae graecae a chunrado protucio celte, Viennae tradita."[370] The other was made by Johann Rosenperger in 1500.[371]

It was probably Rosenperger's copy of the grammar, together with copies of some ancient colloquies and vocabularies copied by Celtis in Sponheim in 1495, that he sent to Aldus in 1504 to be printed. Aldus returned this unsolicited manuscript to its owner in September. In an accompanying letter he explained politely, "Institutiones graecas et dictionarium remittimus, quia multa iam impressa habentur quibus erudiantur qui graecas literas discere concupiscunt"[372] (We are returning the Greek grammar and the dictionary, for there are already many of these available in print for those who want to learn Greek). A note on the Rosenperger manuscript had asked Aldus to expend a great deal of editorial labor on this work in order to make it fit for publication. Celtis asked him to provide a prefatory letter directed to European students of Greek. He asked him to include an alphabet, a list of abbreviations, and notes on pronunciation as they appeared at the end of the first edition of Lascaris—that is to say, as they appeared in the first Aldine Appendix of 1495.[373] He asked Aldus to supply a section on defective verbs. Finally, he asked him to edit the volume as necessary and to add the accents that he had not included in his work. Celtis was not a man easily embarrassed.

Demetrius Chalcondyles, 1493

Demetrius Chalcondyles, an Athenian by birth, was responsible for the last Greek grammar of the period written in Greek. Chalcondyles' early career is obscure. It is possible that he was the Demetrius who taught Greek to Giovanni Antonio Campano in Perugia around 1452.[374] If so, he probably used Chrysoloras's grammar, for there were few alternatives available at the time. In October 1463 he was elected as the first occupant of the new chair of Greek in Padua.[375] At Padua, one of his pupils, Hartmann Schedel, recorded that he taught *Erotemata* in 1463.[376] Only three works went under this name in quattrocento Italy: the grammars of Manuel Moschopoulos, of Manuel

Chrysoloras, and of Chalcondyles himself. Chalcondyles' interest in the grammatical work of Moschopoulos is demonstrated by the fact that he was responsible for the first printed edition of Moschopoulos's grammar thirty years later. Chalcondyles remained in Padua until at least 1469, and he may have stayed until 1475. In September of that year, he took up the chair in Florence, which had been recently vacated by Andronicus Callistus. Callistus had ensured that Chalcondyles was made aware of Gaza's new grammar between 1463 and 1466, and Chalcondyles may well have used Gaza's work during his time in Florence.[377]

Chalcondyles' own grammar seems to have been a product of his vigorous old age. He moved to Milan in 1491 at the age of sixty-eight. There he edited the first printed edition of the Suda lexicon at the age of seventy-six.[378] He fathered his tenth child, Ptolemy, the following year, and he was still lecturing at the age of eighty. In Milan, Chalcondyles oversaw the *editio princeps* of the works of Isocrates in 1493. His Greek grammar, together with the first printed texts of Moschopoulos's *Erotemata* and the work of Gregory Pardus of Corinth on the dialects, seems to have come from the Milanese press in the same year.[379] Like Chrysoloras, Chalcondyles taught ten noun declensions: four parisyllabic and one imparisyllabic, followed by five contracted declensions. He did, however, follow Gaza in exchanging the positions of the third and fourth declensions, so that the Attic declension is his fourth.[380] Like Chrysoloras, Chalcondyles defines thirteen verb conjugations: six barytone conjugations, three contracted conjugations, and four verbs in -μι.

It may be guessed that Chalcondyles used his grammar in his teaching in Milan, but there is little evidence for its use. Perhaps this was because Chalcondyles chose not to teach the language to beginners in Milan. A prospective student, Girolamo Amaseo, wrote in 1493 that he had asked Niccolò Leonico Tomeo for advice: "Is suadebat Mediolanum esse eundum, sed id dissuasit: asserit enim Demetrium non libenter tradere prima elementa et minutias"[381] (He tried to persuade me that I should go to Milan, but this consideration deterred me: for he claimed that Demetrius did not like to teach the rudiments and minutiae of the language). Baldassare Castiglione, who would later find fame with his *Libro del cortegiano*, was sent to study Greek under Chalcondyles in Milan in 1494. Baldassare, then sixteen years old and presumably no tyro, seems to have used his master's grammatical work.[382] Hernan Nuñez de Guzman acquired a copy, apparently in Milan in the early years of the sixteenth century;[383] and Guillaume Budé owned and annotated a copy now in Paris.[384] However, Chalcondyles' grammar seems not to have made much impression on contemporaries. At Messina, Constantine Lascaris acquired and annotated a copy of the *editio princeps*, the only Greek grammar besides Lascaris's own to be printed in Milan during his lifetime.[385] In his copy, Lascaris annotated the work of Gregory of Corinth but not that of Chalcondyles.

One element of the work did enjoy a wider circulation. Chalcondyles' treatment of the formation of the verb tenses was often reprinted as a supplement to Chrysoloras' grammar: as we have seen, the weakness of Chrysoloras in this area had been observed by contemporaries.[386] Chalcondyles' work was first used in this way in the Aldine edition of Chrysoloras of 1512.[387] This was the text that Demetrius Ducas took with him to Spain in 1513. It was reprinted in Alcalá the following year with a Latin interlinear translation of Chalcondyles on the tenses.[388] This was the first time any part of his grammar was translated, and no Latin translation of the whole work was ever made.

In 1516, Erasmus recorded his rather low opinion of Chalcondyles' abilities as a grammarian, but this seems to be because he believed that some of the infelicities of Gaza's grammar were due to Chalcondyles, an unlikely charge.[389] Erasmus shows no other signs of any acquaintance with Chalcondyles' grammar. Chalcondyles' grammar was not reprinted for over thirty years. In 1525, however, it found a vocal advocate in Melchior Volmar, who made use of an exemplar supplied by Pierre Danès.[390]

Urbano Bolzanio, 1497

Urbano Bolzanio traveled widely in Greece, Asia Minor, Egypt, and the Greek islands before studying under Constantine Lascaris in Messina around 1484.[391] He moved to Florence in 1484 and stayed in the city until 1489, during which period he taught Greek to Giovanni de' Medici, the future Pope Leo X.[392] From 1490, he taught in Venice, where he numbered the great Greek scholar Scipione Forteguerri among his students. He taught Niccolò Leonico Tomeo, who subsequently lectured with distinction on Aristotle in Padua.[393] Daniel Renier, who later received the dedication of the Aldine Thucydides, learned Greek with Urbano.[394] Albertus Castrifrancanus, who delivered Urbano's funeral oration in 1524, was a pupil.[395] He taught Marcus Musurus, Giovanni Antonio Flaminio,[396] Marcantonio Sabellico, and Gasparo Contarini.[397] This is a very impressive list of students.

Urbano's Greek grammar was first advertised by Aldus in his preface to the *Cornucopiae* of August 1496.[398] The grammar was produced, according to its own preface, at Aldus's request and with his encouragement.[399] When it was printed, in January 1497, Aldus dedicated it to Giovanni Francesco Pico, then approaching his thirtieth year, with the recommendation that he use it for his own Greek studies. A medal was printed in honor of Urbano shortly after, and the closed book that appears on the reverse may be intended to represent his grammar.[400] Looking back on the first edition fourteen years later, Urbano said of its editing, "Aldus . . . nostras de inflexione nominum ac verborum annotationes latino atque interim graeco sermone compositas hinc inde collegit, moxque in eam quam hactenus vidistis formam haud mediocri redegit labore. Demum . . . editionem maturavit"[401] (Aldus . . . collected together my notes on the inflection of the noun and verb that I had written in Latin and sometimes in Greek. Next, after great effort, he revised them into that form that you have seen. Then he brought out the edition). The word Urbano uses here, *maturare*, may hint that he thought Aldus's procedure rather too hurried. Urbano was a painstaking scholar: fourteen years later, in 1512, he published a revision of this grammar, and even then he says that Pierio Valeriano's requests for the grammar caused him to bring it out more quickly than he would have liked.[402] Nor did even this revision content him. In 1523, he completed a final revision of the work, one that would not reach print for another twenty years.

Urbano's grammar is written in Latin, the first full treatment of Greek grammar to be composed in the language. This decision seems to have been made to make the work more accessible to beginners. When it came to the verb conjugations, Urbano did not innovate. Like Chrysoloras, he defined thirteen verb conjugations: six barytone, three circumflex, and four in -μι. He writes that the middle tenses of the verb are usually introduced by grammarians with the actives and with the passives, where the forms are shared: "Sed quia hic ordo, licet eruditioribus perspicuus habeatur, rudibus tamen ac literas grecas discere modo aggredientibus confusionem quandam ac prope desperationem inducere solet, ausus sum, Theodorum imitatus, eo relicto ordine, verba media seorsum ab activis et passivis declinare"⁴⁰³ (But since this arrangement, although it might be clear to the more learned, usually brings on a certain confusion and near desperation in the inexperienced and in those beginning to learn Greek, I have dared, in imitation of Theodore Gaza, to abandon that arrangement and to decline the middle tenses of the verbs separately from the active and passive tenses). The Italian grammarian also defined ten noun declensions: four parisyllabic and one imparisyllabic, followed by five contracted declensions. Urbano followed the lead of his teacher Lascaris in modifying Chrysoloras's scheme for the fifth contracted declension.⁴⁰⁴ Like Aldus and Chalcondyles, he followed Gaza's lead by making the Attic declension his fourth declension.⁴⁰⁵ Writing on the fifth declension, Urbano says,

> Quoniam huius quintae declinationis multae ac variae sunt terminationes tam in masculinis quam in aliis, ab re non erit aliquanto altius ea repetere quae ad eius cognitionem necessaria sunt. Non tamen generales regulas [et] uniuscuiusque terminationes ponere intendimus, sicut Herodianus fecit et qui eum secuti sunt, ne ob regularum inculcationem fastidio rudes lectores afficiantur, sed ea duntaxat sine quibus non facile intelligi possit quo modo unumquodque nomen sit declinandum.⁴⁰⁶
> [Since the endings of this fifth declension, in the masculine and in the other genders, are many and varied, it is worth revisiting more thoroughly those things that are required for knowledge of it. However, I do not mean to set out the general rules and the endings of every noun, as Herodian and his followers did, lest inexperienced readers be bored by the inculcation of the rules, but only those rules without which the correct way to decline each noun cannot be easily understood.]

This, too, is a welcome concession to the capacities of his readers. However, when he comes to describe the contracted declensions, he writes, "Nec quisque miretur si etiam in his declinationibus plura ponentur quam ab aliis iunioribus tradita sunt, quoniam non solum ea quae frequenti habentur in usu scribere statui, sed etiam quae apud poetas reperiuntur"⁴⁰⁷ (And let no one be surprised if in these declensions more forms will be shown than have been given to young students by other grammarians, for I have decided to record not only the forms that are in common use but also those that are found in the poets). Later, Urbano would come to believe that it was a mistake to burden the beginner with a mass of dialectal variants, and this important but unwieldy body of information was relegated to the deeper recesses of the grammar. Despite his concern for those new to the language, the arcana of Urbano's work are not for the fainthearted.

Scholars regarded Urbano's grammar highly. In 1501, in the preface to his edition of Guarino's epitome of Chrysoloras, Pontico Virunio praised it in extravagant terms.⁴⁰⁸ Melanchthon said that he thought it better than his own grammar.⁴⁰⁹ In July 1501, Erasmus complained to James Tutor that he could not get hold of a copy of either Lascaris's or Urbano's grammars: "Grammaticen graecam summo studio vestigavi, ut emptam tibi mitterem, sed iam utraque divendita fuerat, et Constantini quae dicitur, quaeque Urbani."⁴¹⁰ (I have looked very hard for a Greek grammar, so that I might buy one and send it to you, but the grammar attributed to Constantine and Urbano's grammar have both sold out). It is very likely that Aldus had by this time sold out of Lascaris's grammar because he reprinted it about 1502 and no one had reprinted it in the interval.⁴¹¹ Urbano's grammar, however, appeared for sale in the second Aldine catalog of June 1503.⁴¹² Erasmus indicates no preference, and at this stage in his Greek studies, he may have had none: in 1501 poor northern students had to take what they could get. Commercially the grammar was only a modest success. In the Aldine catalog of 1498 the grammars of Urbano and Lascaris are for sale at the same price. By the time of the second catalog of 1503, Urbano's grammar was significantly cheaper. Perhaps the Aldine Press encountered problems finding buyers for a nonstandard grammar, however competent. Lascaris's grammar had been reprinted by Aldus in the interim. Remaining copies of Urbano's grammar must have sold out before November 1513, since it does not appear in the third Aldine catalog.

The fact that copies of Urbano's work were no longer available led to two new editions in 1512. In Paris, a straightforward copy of the Aldine *editio princeps* was printed. The timing of this edition seems to have been unfortunate, for the same year a revised edition was printed in Venice.⁴¹³ When he revised his grammar for the edition of 1512, Urbano wrote,

Quum per aliquot postea annos fere omnes Italiae insignes urbes animi gratia circuirem, animadverteremque multos qui non nihil scriptis nostris invigilassent ad frugem brevi compendio pervenisse, animum induxi ut primum me in ocium recepissem ea iterum et ad clariorem excudere lucernam, addere, detrahere, invertere, ac velut invitatis hospitibus coenam parare, demumque operam dare ut in publicum sic elucubrata quam primum prodirent.⁴¹⁴

[When for some years afterward I was visiting almost all the great cities of Italy for my soul's sake, and I noticed that many who had spent some time on my grammar had benefited from a short summary of it, I decided that as soon as I had leisure I would reshape it with more care; that I would add, remove, and transpose material, and prepare a meal as if for invited guests; and that finally I would ensure that the work thus laboriously composed be published as soon as possible.]

It seems Urbano had come across students of his grammar who had compiled extracts for their own convenience. The urge to make a compendium is a very plausible reaction to the dense collection of material that Urbano compiled for his first grammar. The observation that his students found it helpful to rearrange his grammar led him to do so himself. He continues, "Grammaticorum igitur copiam ingentem ex omni propemodum Europa collegi; moxque omnis eos perlegi sane quam accurate, habitoque delectu rerum annotatu dignarum duos composui libellos, quorum alter introducendis consulet adulescentibus, alter penitissima quaeque grammatices arcana provectis iam ad interiora viris demonstrabit"⁴¹⁵ (I gathered a great supply of grammars from nearly all of Europe; and I soon read them all with great care, and having made a collection of noteworthy matters, I composed two short books. The first will guide younger students in the elements; the second will show to men who have advanced further all the most deeply hidden parts of Greek grammar). The revised text, then, consisted of two books. The first and shortest was an accidence intended for beginners. The second book developed the material introduced in the first in more depth and was directed at scholars. Urbano removed the dialectal variants from his introduction to the Greek noun and supplied summary tables of the article and the ten declensions. His treatment of the verb was compressed in accordance with similar principles. The second book dealt with everything in more detail and paid particular attention to dialectal variants.⁴¹⁶ This revision was not dedicated to anyone, and it was, in fact, rare in the fifteenth century for Greek grammars to be so dedicated. A postscript to the Venice edition shows that Urbano's nephew, Pierio Valeriano, had asked for it to be dedicated to Giovanni Francesco della Rovere but that this request apparently arrived too late for Urbano to oblige.[417] The lack of a dedication is consistent with Valeriano's later description of his uncle's indifference to worldly advancement.[418]

This revised text was printed again in Basle by Valentine Curio in 1524. Glareanus says that he was about to lecture on Homer in Basle when he discovered that many of his students lacked a grammar. This may have been a convenient fiction: Gaza's grammar had been printed in Greek and Latin by Curio toward the end of 1523. Glareanus says in his preface that he considered many grammars and finally chose Urbano's grammar over Gaza's. Gaza's work is, he admits, the more learned of the two, but he insists that it is not so appropriate for beginners.[419] Urbano satisfies a number of criteria: "Nobis qui latine didicimus, non facilior alia videtur via graeca discentibus quam analogia graecorum ad latina, deinde ut exemplis pateant commodis quae proposita sunt, denique ut simplicissima sint quae traduntur. Quae quidem Urbanus hic noster adamussim observavit"[420] (To us who have learned in Latin, there would seem to be no other easier way for learners than by the analogy of Greek to Latin; then that those things that are propounded should be explained with appropriate examples; and finally that the things that are passed on should be very simple. These considerations our Urbano has observed very carefully). Glareanus goes on to say that Urbano's work does not overburden the beginner with variants drawn from the dialects as some teachers do:

> Porro vehementer errare mihi videntur, qui nostra aetate grammatica docere conantur. Quippe qui simul atque initio quae communis sunt linguae docuerunt, continuo subiungunt quae Aeolica, quae Ionica, quae Dorica, fortassis etiam (si diis placet) quae Sarmatica, quae Indica. Obtundere hoc est, non docere.[421]
>
> [Moreover, those who try to teach grammar nowadays seem to me to make a great mistake: those who from the beginning have taught the common dialect add immediately the variants from Aeolic, Ionic, Doric, perhaps even (if it pleases the gods) from Sarmatian and Indian. This is not to teach students Greek but to pound them with it.]

As we have seen, and as Glareanus notes, neither Gaza nor Urbano are guilty of this crime. In the Basle reprint of 1530, the editor, Curio, restates the preference of Urbano to Gaza and points out again that Urbano does not bother the beginner with dialectal variants. As shown above, Urbano only gradually came to see that these variants deterred the inexperienced student.

In 1523, at the age of eighty-one, Urbano completed a final revision of his grammar. This time he arranged the work into nine books. As he explains in his preface to Benedetto Accolti, the wish to alleviate the *taedium* of his students seems to have informed the new edition: "Casu autem erat in promptu opus illud meum . . . a me nuper quam accuratissime potui castigatum et ordine meliorem digestum; silva quippe illa prioris alteriusque editionis, quae in libros duos tantum congesta tedium afferre poterat, in plures nunc fasciculos distributa"[422] (It happened that my grammar was ready . . . recently corrected as carefully as I could and put in better order, inasmuch as the tangled work of the first and second editions, which when presented in only two books could bore students, has now been arranged into many brief chapters). This final revision divided the grammar further and, consequently, made it much easier for the student to navigate. In a further prefatory note, Urbano expanded with great confidence on the rationale behind the reorganized edition. He foresaw three types of reader for his grammar:

> Unum quidem eorum qui graece adhuc nihil didicissent ipsaque tantum linguae huius quaererent tirocinia. Haec prioribus libris—primo, secundo, et tertio—ita complexi sumus ut unusquisque quantumlibet rudis eorum lectione multum proficere se cognosceret. Alterum vero eorum qui primis iam essent elementis imbuti, octo quippe orationis partes agnoscerent, sed nondum exactam rerum grammaticalium rationem progressumque percepissent. Pro his quattuor libros—quartum, quintum, sextum, septimum—adieci in quibus tota fere linguarum graecarum litteratura declaratur perplexitatesque illae demum explicantur quae tota aetate mea (cum librorum tum erudientium defectu) magna ex parte incognitae fuerunt. Tertium demum genus erat eorum qui aliquid omnino profecissent, sed tam vastum mare sulcantibus pleraeque (ut ita dicam) subaquaneae cautes occursabant in quas impingerent; quae rectam omnium itinerum semitam impedirent, eas libro octavo planas et pervias reddidimus. Nono vero reliquas orationi[s] partes ad erudita ingenia facientibus tum mea tum antiquorum scriptorum industria complanatas in medium protulimus.[423]
>
> [The first type comprised those who had not yet learned any Greek and who sought only the first elements of the language. I have embraced these elements in the first three books in such a way that anyone, however inexperienced, will recognize that he has benefited greatly from reading them. The second type comprised those who had absorbed the first elements, inasmuch as they knew the eight parts of speech but had not yet understood the precise theory and practice of grammatical matters. For these students, I have added books four to seven, in which nearly all of Greek literature is expounded, and in which those difficulties are finally explained that were largely unknown during my lifetime due to a lack of books and learned men. The third type was made up of those who had certainly learned something, but for those sailing (so to speak) over such a vast ocean many submerged rocks were waiting on which they might strike; those things that might obstruct them in their travels I have made level and easy in the eighth book. In the ninth book, for those who aspire to be learned, I have revealed the remaining parts of speech made smooth by my efforts and by those of ancient writers.]

Books I through III of the posthumous edition contain the material from the first book of the second edition. The remaining books largely reproduce the material from the second book of the second edition in much the same order but more clearly divided and better signposted. This revision was entrusted by Urbano's pupil Daniel Renier to the printer Giovanni da Trino, who had printed the revised grammar in Venice in 1512. Unfortunately Da Trino died, and since Urbano also died in April 1524, the final revision remained unpublished until 1545. Urbano's grammar went through a respectable number of editions in the sixteenth century, with the last edition printed in Venice in 1585.[424] Urbano's was the last grammar of the period to be written by an Italian.

GEORG SIMLER, 1512

In 1512 the first Greek grammar to be printed in Germany came off the presses of Thomas Anshelm in Tübingen. This was part of a substantial volume put together by Georg Simler with the encouragement of some of his colleagues at the university there.[425] The first and longest part of the work was a grammatical treatise that confined itself largely to Latin grammar. The second part of the work dealt specifically with Greek. Simler dedicated this Greek portion of the edition to Johann Reuchlin.

It began with a work of some five leaves dealing with the Greek letters, their pronunciation, and the most common Greek abbreviations. This contained nothing new: in one form or another, such introductions had been circulating in Western Europe for many years. It was followed by Guarino Veronese's abbreviation of the *Erotemata* of Manuel Chrysoloras, in Greek and Latin. In 1512 this was the most substantial Greek work yet printed in Germany. It was supplemented by Simler's own *Isagogicum in literas graecanicas*, a modestly conceived set of notes intended to extend and explain the information available in the epitome of Chrysoloras. It is this *Isagogicum* that earns Simler his place here among the grammarians.[426]

Besides the abbreviated Chrysoloras, Simler seems to have owned or had access to a wide range of grammatical works. He knew Gaza's grammar and Apollonius Dyscolus, almost certainly from the Aldine *editio princeps* of these works of 1495.[427] He knew not only Lascaris's grammar but also his work on the iota subscript, a combination of texts that had been printed only twice by 1512: in Venice around 1502 and in Ferrara in 1510.[428] He knew the works of pseudo-Cyril and Ammonius on the differences between similar words, which suggests that he saw either the Aldine lexicon of 1497 or its descendant printed in Ferrara in 1510.[429] Finally, he also knew Urbano Bolzanio's grammar, for which the only available printed edition was the Aldine *editio princeps* of 1497.[430] In an aside, he alludes to some other books: "Sed in hac re non stemus: exigit enim volumina ne dicam volumen, et Κήπους Ἀδώνιδος et *Magnum etymologicum*. Curiosis et qui iam prope consenuerunt in literis graecanicis commendo inextrabilia thematum involucra"[431] (But let us not linger on this matter, for it needs not one book but books, both the *Gardens of Adonis* and the *Etymologicum magnum*. For those who are curious, and those who have spent their life on Greek, I recommend the hopelessly tangled and involved works on these matters). This is reference to the learned grammatical miscellany known as the *Thesaurus cornucopiae*, and to the substantial Greek lexicon, the *Etymologicum magnum*.[432] The former was printed by Aldus in 1496, and the latter was being sold through Aldus by 1502. All the books used by Simler were available in Aldine editions, and if Simler did not own them himself, he is likely to have been able to use them in Reuchlin's library. Simler had studied under Reuchlin; he helped bring his famous *Rudimenta Hebraica* to publication in 1506, and the following year he produced a commentary on one of Reuchlin's Latin comedies.[433] Aldus had sent Reuchlin a copy of the *Etymologicum magnum* in 1502.[434]

The passing comment of Simler on these books is characteristic of his approach throughout the *Isagogicum*. Compared to the terse rulebooks of some of the grammarians, he adopts a refreshingly conversational tone. He often writes that he is cutting his explanations short, or that he is simplifying a complex situation, and he frequently refers his students to more advanced works of Greek grammar. Discussing some of the possible variants in the fifth Greek declensions, for example, he terminates his discussion: "Crases, synaereses et linguas nostro non possumus adnectere commentariolo. Est enim multiplex tractatio, varietatesque gustandam proponimus, graecitatem non examussim discutiendam; nec in unum possunt omnia libellum contrudi: ansam praebuisse studiosis nunc contenti sumus"[435] (We cannot deal with cases of crasis, synaeresis, and the dialects in our little commentary. For it is a complicated business, and we have set about sampling its variety, not analyzing Greek precisely. Not everything can be squeezed into one little book. Here we have contented ourselves with providing a foothold for students). He goes on to provide his readers with a long list of Greek grammarians for further reading. Simler cites at least as many Latin authors in this work as he does Greek ones. He points out parallels with Latin where he thinks them useful. Discussing the Greek numbers, he writes that the Greek ending -κοντα is just like the Latin ending -ginta, and that -κοντος is equivalent to the Latin -gesimus.[436] While discussing one of the noun declensions he comments, "Ex hoc ordine declinatur apud latinos genesis. Ex his puto quemlibet elicere posse quantum literae graecae latinis ancillentur, ad promovendum sermonis romani pomerium"[437] (In this declension, "genesis" is declined by Latin writers. From this I think that anyone can deduce how much Greek helps Latin in extending the boundaries of Roman speech). Simler's importance does not lie in the excellence of his work on Greek: when Conrad Peutinger received a copy of the work from Anshelm in 1512, his response was more polite than enthusiastic.[438] Nevertheless, Simler's efforts to make elementary Greek learning accessible to his Latin students do seem to have found an echo in the work of his own pupil Melanchthon.

Ottomar Nachtgall, 1517

Ottomar Nachtgall, born in Strasbourg around 1478 or 1480, is better known for his works on music than for his Greek teaching.[439] He taught music in Vienna before 1510[440] and studied Greek in Paris under Aleandro at some date between 1511 and 1513.[441] In 1514, he returned to Strasbourg, where he was appointed organist at St. Thomas in March 1515. Later that year, he dedicated his *Musicae institutiones* to Symphorian Pollio and Johann Rudolfinger, ministers of Strasbourg cathedral.[442]

Before Nachtgall's return from Paris, students of Greek in Strasbourg had been taught from Gaza's grammar by Conrad Melissopolitanus.[443] By 1515, Nachtgall had taken on this role himself. In that year, he oversaw a long series of student texts from the Greek press in Strasbourg. These included a parallel Greek–Latin text of Lucian, two works of Isocrates, a collection of gnomic verse, and a volume of short Greek prayers. This last volume, intended for beginners, included his own notes on Greek orthography.[444] In October, a collection of grammatical tables was printed in Strasbourg, and in December the following year, the full text of Chrysoloras was printed by Knoblouch.[445]

In the spring of 1517, Nachtgall adopted the Latin name Luscinius, a humanist rite of passage, and published his first original grammatical work from Knoblouch's press, the *Progymnasmata graecanicae literaturae*.[446] He dedicated this pamphlet of fourteen leaves to the Strasbourg teacher Hieronymus Gebweiler, and he noted in this dedication that he had received encouragement from Johann Guida, Baltasar Bisner, Stephan Widersdorf, and Stephan Dieler.[447] From this preface we learn that he had been lecturing in Strasbourg on Chrysoloras's grammar during the winter of 1516–17, and the *Progymnasmata* would appear to be intended as a companion to further lectures on this grammar. He names in this preface some of his students: Gregorius Viggrammius, Joannes de Andelou, Erasmus Egkirch, Martin Ergersheim, Philippus Valerianus, Georgius Anellus, and Joannes Chelius.[448] This work, which he says that he compiled in a few days, goes further than the orthographical notes of 1515. It aims, he says, to summarize the rudiments of the language in a brief and memorable form.[449] He admits that he cannot deal adequately with the Greek verb in such a short work, and that to learn the verb is a laborious task.⁴⁵⁰ Still, he insists, his summary has value as an overview:

> Nemo enim negat in discenda cosmographia multo esse conducibilius primo universum orbis ambitum sub oculos ponere, quam vicatim (ut ita dicam) promovendo, ex paludibus, planicie, clivis et convallibus tantae machinae rationem colligere. Itaque primo typo et quasi per transennam nostram, amice lector, omnes merces ipsas contempleris licebit. Prominent enim ex ea omnes graecitatis coniugationes . . .⁴⁵¹
>
> [Nobody denies that the geography of the world is much more easily learned by setting the whole globe before one's eyes at the beginning, than it is by piecing together the system of this great mechanism from its individual marshes, plains, hills, and valleys—advancing, as it were, village by village. And so, dear reader, in its original form and as if viewed through our lattice, you will be able to consider all the wares. For all the Greek conjugations stand out from these . . .]

The metaphor of the shop-front lattice is repeated in the preface, presumably composed afterward, in which he wrote of his pamphlet "omnia hic velut per transennam primo spectandum obtulimus" (here I have set out everything as if displayed for a preliminary inspection behind a lattice).⁴⁵²

Nachtgall took a trip to Italy in 1518, returning to Germany in May, and he visited Rome in 1519.⁴⁵³ In Rome, he noted with approval the Greek press established by Pope Leo X but found little else to praise.⁴⁵⁴ In the spring of 1520, his position as organist at Strasbourg was taken from him, and the following years were difficult ones for him.⁴⁵⁵ In 1521 he published two works of Greek grammar. The first of these, the *Elementale introductorium*, a small volume of forty leaves, was printed in January.⁴⁵⁶ It reproduced the introductory material of the first *Progymnasmata* of 1517, reprinted Aleandro's popular *Tabulae*, and dealt with the noun declensions and verb conjugations in some detail.⁴⁵⁷ At several points in his discussion of the nouns and verbs in his *Progymnasmata* of 1517, 1521, and 1523, Nachtgall refers the reader to supplementary tables that are not in the grammar.⁴⁵⁸ His references to these tables are indicated in the margins by the traditional pointing hand, a piece of type commonly used to pick out something noteworthy in the text. Here, however, the finger points away from the text, beyond the book. If such tables had been printed in Strasbourg, we might have expected one to survive, bound with a copy of the grammar. It seems that Nachtgall had his students copy out the tables of the declensions and conjugations at this point.

It is clear from the *Elementale introductorium* that between 1517 and 1521 Nachtgall had transferred his loyalties from the grammar of Chrysoloras to that of Gaza. The most obvious consequence of this is that the Attic declension, which formed Nachtgall's third in 1517, had become his fourth declension by 1521.⁴⁵⁹ A more ambitious grammar, apparently published in the spring of 1521, has a title similar to that of the first pamphlet, *Progymnasmata graecae literaturae*. It does, however, contain a greatly expanded work, running to 115 pages. It contains several asides in which Nachtgall attacks specific readings in the Vulgate translation of the Bible, and the *superstitiosi interpretes* who defend them.⁴⁶⁰ As befits a musician, the passages he criticizes are those that were often sung during services.

There are two features of this work that merit particular notice. First, it announces on the title page the addition of an *Auctarium*, "quo docetur qua ratione citra praeceptoris operam graece discere possis" (in which is taught how you may learn Greek without a tutor), an appendix directed specifically at students wanting to learn Greek on their own. This was not an entirely new departure for Nachtgall. In 1515, in the preface to his Lucian, he wrote, "Visus sum mihi operae precium facturus, si deorum Luciani Samosatensis dialogos . . . graecolatinos fieri curarem, quo graecitatis adhuc rudes, quasi ex mutis (ut aiunt) magistris, graeci aliquando evadere possent"[461] (I thought it would be useful if I edited the *Dialogues of the Gods* by Lucian of Samosata in Greek and Latin, so that those who have not yet learned Greek could, as it were from dumb teachers, become Greeks hereafter). In 1521, however, he is very specific about directing his efforts at such students: "Quandoquidem ubere ingeniorum proventu, hoc felicissimo saeculo, complures videas αὐτοδιδάκτους ad utriusque linguae egregiam peritiam eluctatos, operae precium mihi videor facturus si caeteris qua ratione consimilia audeant aggrediar pro virili commonstrare"[462] (Since you can see, in this fortunate age with its rich crop of talent, very many self-taught scholars who have managed to gain great knowledge of both languages, I think that I shall be doing something worthwhile if I attempt, as best I can, to show others how they can achieve very similar results). It is possible that, when Nachtgall was deprived of his ecclesiastical position, he also lost his right to teach Greek publicly in the city. If so, this appendix constitutes Nachtgall's response to the Church authorities. Self-taught scholars, whose access to the scriptural texts was unmediated by authorized teachers, could certainly undermine the role of the Church in the interpretation of the Scriptures. The second unusual feature of the revised grammar is that it has a long preface, addressed to Johann Botzheim, defending Greek studies against its detractors. The title given to this letter on the title page of the grammar is worth quoting in full: "Nuncupatoria epistola de utilitate graecarum literarum et praefracta cervice quorundam mataeologorum qui iis contemptis, ac in publicis concionibus theonino dente laceratis, falso sibi scientiae opinionem induerunt"[463] (A dedicatory letter on the usefulness of Greek and on the stiff necks of certain fools who, having condemned it and savaged it in public assemblies with their critical teeth, falsely dress themselves in the opinion of knowledge). This letter takes up no fewer than twenty-six pages, in which Erasmus, Reuchlin, Melanchthon, and Oecolampadius are all praised.[464] Despite his sympathy for some of the reformers' positions, Nachtgall never broke away from the Roman Church. Clearly, however, his Greek teaching had aroused some vocal opposition.

Nachtgall left Strasbourg for Augsburg after the publication of this book.[465] After his departure, in 1523, his *Progymnasmata* were reprinted for the second and final time in Strasbourg. The *Auctarium* remains in this reprint, but the provocative prefatory letter has been removed without comment and no prefatory letter has been composed to take its place. Nachtgall may have continued to teach Greek privately, but he published no more works on Greek grammar.

JOANNES OECOLAMPADIUS, 1518

Joannes Oecolampadius entered the University of Heidelberg at the end of the fifteenth century. He subsequently studied Greek in Tübingen, where he met Philip Melanchthon, and he studied the language in Stuttgart under Johann Reuchlin between 1513 and 1515. In 1515 he moved to Basle, where he worked as a corrector at Froben's press. His *Graecae literaturae dragmata* were first printed in Basle in 1518, an edition that has now become very rare. Oecolampadius's prefatory letter dedicates the work to Hartmann Hallwiler, whose uncle held a post at the city's cathedral.[466] The date of this letter, August 31, 1518, indicates that the printing of Oecolampadius's grammar postdates that of Melanchthon's by some months. Oecolampadius's work was, however, composed earlier because Melanchthon commends it in the preface to his own grammar.[467] It is likely to be much earlier because, in his preface, Oecolampadius writes that Petrus Scybenardus encouraged him to write the work in Heidelberg.[468] Once it had come off the press in Basle, the author sent a signed copy to Willibald Pirckheimer in Nuremberg.[469]

The grammar compresses its material into a slim volume. In a brief preface, Oecolampadius writes, "Laborem nostrum, amice lector, post tot grammaticos supervacaneum ne credas. Nam etsi angustiori quodam libello et incultiori, in rem tamen tuam et clarius et fidelius plaeraque hic congesta sunt"[470] (Do not believe, kind reader, that our work is superfluous after so many other grammars. For even if everything has been collected here in a rather slender and unpolished little book, still it has been done for your benefit with clarity and fidelity). The work is divided into three parts. This first deals with orthography. Despite its compression, this section still fills about thirty-seven pages, and it makes for a rather daunting start to the grammar. It covers pronunciation, abbreviations, numbers, accents, breathings, and iota subscripts, this last specifically drawn from Lascaris's work on the subject.[471] The second part is a straightforward accidence, founded largely on Chrysoloras.[472] It defines ten declensions of the noun, five uncontracted and five contracted.[473] Oecolampadius follows Gaza and his imitators by making the Attic declension his fourth.[474] It defines thirteen conjugations of the verb: six Barytone conjugations, three circumflex conjugations, and four in -μι.[475] The third part deals with syntax, very narrowly conceived. The work was reprinted by Andreas Cratander in 1521 in Basle and in Paris in 1522.[476] By November 1522, Oecolampadius was back in Basle, working as a corrector at the press of Cratander. Cratander reprinted the grammar in Basle in 1523. Its compression may have provoked some complaints. In the preface to the Basle edition of 1523 Cratander writes, "Quaeruntur aliqui de difficultate huius grammatices, quae quidem graecae linguae amplissimam vim paucissimis comprehendit; et tam clare ut non pauci, qui modo inter eruditos habentur quod graece sciunt, huic ferant acceptum"[477] (Some complain of the difficulty of this grammar, which does indeed comprehend the very great force of the Greek language in very few words; and it does this so clearly that many who are held learned simply because they know Greek are indebted to it). It was subsequently reprinted in Paris in 1528 and in Basle in 1535 and 1546.[478]

Philip Melanchthon, 1518

In March 1509, Johann Reuchlin presented the twelve-year-old Melanchthon with a printed edition of Lascaris's *Compendium* of Greek grammar.[479] At the time, Melanchthon seems to have been studying under Georg Simler in Pforzheim, and he followed his teacher to Tübingen around 1510.[480] In May 1518, he saw the first edition of his influential Greek grammar through the presses of Thomas Anshelm in Hagenau.[481] It was dedicated to Bernhard Maurus, apparently one of his students.[482] This edition seems to have sold out by August 1520, when a second, revised edition was published by the same printer. From the preface to this revised work, it appears that

Melanchthon had originally composed his Greek grammar for use with the young students he taught privately. By 1520, he writes in this later preface, he would have been happy to allow his grammar to disappear altogether, but the printers had urged him to publish it. For his own classes, he says, he would have been content to use the works of Urbano Bolzanio and of his fellow German, Oecolampadius.[483] Urbano's work had been in print since 1497, and a revision had been published in 1512. Oecolampadius's work has been printed just four months after Melanchthon's first appeared.[484] Three months after the publication of Melanchthon's grammar, at the age of eighteen, he was appointed professor of Greek at the new University of Wittenberg.[485] Melanchthon's grammar was immediately popular: there were eleven editions between 1518 and 1529, all except one of them printed in Germany.[486]

The most striking element of Melanchthon's grammar is the great care he takes to accommodate the work to the capacities of his students. This grammar is addressed to the adult teacher of younger students as much as to the students themselves. The students it envisages are German schoolboys: throughout the volumes, the pupils are always referred to as *pueri*. When explaining the Greek article, he advises that knowledge of the German article is the best way to learn how to use it.[487] It is this conception of his audience that informs his solicitous attitude toward their difficulties. Other grammarians tend to summarize and abbreviate, compressing the difficulties into the smallest possible space. Melanchthon's grammar is not particularly short, and like his master Simler, he is happy to lighten the way with conversational asides. He saw that it was not so much the length of a grammar that would deter the student but the amount of it the student was expected to commit to memory. When some point of grammar is difficult, or when the quantity of material to be memorized is daunting, he says so. As he said in the preface, an intelligent and attractive piece of writing, "nihil ambitioni, nihil pompae datum. Hic unus est operi genius, ut prosit"[488] (Ambition and display have no place here. The guiding spirit of this work is that it should benefit the reader).

Discussing the Greek accents, a perennial difficulty, he supplies some rules, while observing that, among the Greeks, the accents are learned more by use than by recourse to such rules.[489] He repeats this judgment a little later in his rule on accentuation,[490] and it is consistent with his stance in the preface.[491] When he comes to the variety of comparative and superlative adjectives, he writes, "In regulam grammaticam omnia cogi nequeunt"[492] (Not everything can be reduced to a grammatical rule). This skepticism as to the value of rules is an unusual and rather comforting trait in a grammarian.

Melanchthon makes the most of the fact that students of Greek will already know a good deal of Latin. Sometimes the complexity of Greek is presented as a virtue: when he points out that Greek has dual forms as well as singular and plural, he writes, "Vincit ... latinum sermonem duali numero graeca copia"[493] (The abundance of Greek surpasses that of Latin in the dual). More often, the similarities between Latin and Greek are stressed so that students' new knowledge can be built on what they already know. Melanchthon defines the usual ten declensions of the noun.[494] He points out that his first Greek declension corresponds to the first declension of Latin nouns,[495] that the third Greek declension corresponds to the second Latin,[496] and that the fifth declension has similarities with the third Latin declension.[497] He follows Gaza in making the Attic declension his fourth, and he illustrates this declension with the proper noun Ἀνδρόγεως, noting that students will have already encountered it a number of times in the *Aeneid*.⁴⁹⁸ When he reaches the Greek verb, he apologizes for the length of his description of the functions of the aorist tense: "Longius forsan immoror huic disputationi quam ferat τὸ αὐτοσχεδιάζειν. Sed visum est precium operae id, quia scio his nonnunquam labyrinthis temporum graecorum pueros turbari, praesertim re latinis ignota"⁴⁹⁹ (Perhaps I have stayed longer over this discussion than is appropriate for these hurried notes. But it seemed worth making the effort because I know that boys sometimes have difficulties in the mazes of the Greek tenses, especially in a matter that is not known from Latin). When he comes to the inflections of the verb, he attempts to make the material more manageable. He defines the usual thirteen conjugations: six simple, three contracted, and four in -μι. He provides a full paradigm of τύπτω and explains its elements in some detail.⁵⁰⁰ He deals very quickly with the contracted conjugations, referring his reader to the paradigms laid out in full in Guarino's abbreviation of Chrysoloras, and he sets out fully only one of the usual four conjugations of the verbs in -μι, "ne pueri paradigmatum turba sese obrui horreant"⁵⁰¹ (so that boys are not afraid of being overwhelmed by the crowd of paradigms).

For all its virtues, Melanchthon's grammar was rarely printed outside Germany and had little influence outside her borders. This was partly because it went under the name of one of the most prominent advocates of the reformed religion, and as such, it could hardly be used with Roman Catholic students. It was also because Melanchthon had chosen to write a very Protestant grammar. He often illustrated his points in the grammar with examples from the Scriptures, and sometimes commented on or corrected the Vulgate translation.⁵⁰² Melanchthon intended that his Greek grammar should provide his young students with the linguistic tools that would enable them to challenge the ancient authorities.

Adrien Amerot, 1520

Adrien Amerot de Guenneville was born in Soissons. He studied Greek with Aleandro in Paris sometime between 1511 and 1513. In November 1513 he matriculated at the University of Louvain. He seems to have remained in touch with his former teacher, for in a letter of May 1515, he asked Aleandro about the accentuation of Greek as it is expounded in the third book of Gaza's grammar. He graduated with a master's degree at Louvain in 1516.⁵⁰³ At Louvain he taught Greek privately. His grammar, the first Greek grammar written by a Frenchman, seems to have been compiled by at least 1518, when Nicolaus of 's -Hertogenbosch and Paschasius Berselius encouraged him to publish it.⁵⁰⁴ Thierry Martens printed this, the *Compendium graecae grammatices*, in Louvain in 1520, and the author dedicated it to Antoine de la Marck, archdeacon of Brabant. He represented his grammar as a summary, drawn partly "e prolixis graecorum commentariis" (from extensive Greek commentaries) and partly from his own reading of Greek authors. He refers to the grammars of Chrysoloras, Gaza, and Urbano.⁵⁰⁵ In his preface he wrote,

> Operae precium me facturum ratus si, dimissis graecorum sinuosis anfractibus, institutionis graecae methodum planam, brevem et expeditam monstrarem cupidae graecarum literarum iuventuti. Quandoquidem nihil aeque discentem adiuvat, nihil tam illustrat ingenium ac firmat, quam ab omnibus superfluis expurgata lectionis synceritas, et amica memoriae luculenta brevitas.⁵⁰⁶

[I thought I would be doing something worthwhile if, having banished the tortuous digressions of the Greeks, I should show the plain, short, and quick method of Greek instruction to young men who want to learn Greek. Sometimes nothing so helps the learner, nothing clarifies and strengthens his ability more, than a clear reading purged of everything irrelevant, and a lucid brevity that helps the memory.]

In fact, this preface is full of concern for the overburdened student, who, he says, spends years over what may be learned in months. This is partly due to the sheer number of rules they are expected to master, the "molesta et gravis moles preceptorum," which crushes and suffocates their natural abilities. These students, he believes, get lost in the detail of the language. To other problems that they face, "studiosorum desperatio comes adiungitur, dum immensam inutilium preceptionum congeriem sibi propositam vident, ex qua tamen ne ipsam quidem artis integritatem consequi possint"[507] (the students' desperation accompanies them, as they see placed before them a vast collection of useless rules—but one that does not allow them to achieve real perfection in the language). Many able students are put off Greek by this sort of presentation, he says. Still more are lost to the subject by ignorant teachers: "Ut nulla lingua difficilior est quam graeca si indiligentem ac somnolentum nanciscatur interpretem, ita nulla facilior si arte neque παρὰ κωφοῦ διδασκάλου, [id est] a muto magistro, doceatur"[508] (Just as no language is more difficult than Greek if it has a lazy and dozy interpreter, so no language is easier if it is taught skillfully and not by a mute teacher.) Amerot claims that, properly taught, a student of average talents should be able to master Greek grammar in just three months, a claim calculated to endear his work to young men in a hurry.[509]

Despite these cares, Amerot's grammar is not, in general, much clearer than its rivals'. It retains the ten noun declensions and thirteen verb conjugations that had been standard since Chrysoloras's day. It does have one striking mnemonic device. At the beginning of the section on the Greek verbs is an attractive woodcut page, designed to fold out from the grammar.[510] This shows a tree whose roots and branches represent the subdivisions of the Greek verb. The six roots, for example, represent the six barytone conjugations. This presentation is not without precedent: printers had previously used space and ornamental type to present the text in more memorable ways. Still, this was the most unusual example to date and one consistent with Amerot's emphasis on easing the burdens that Greek imposed on the memories of his students.

Amerot's grammar was not subsequently reprinted, but two portions of it were felt to be sufficiently useful summaries of their material to warrant reissue. An extract from this grammar that dealt with the Greek numbers, *De notis arithmeticis*, reappeared in the dictionary printed in Paris in 1530 by Morrhius and in subsequent editions of the dictionary.[511] Another section of this grammar, a digression on the Greek dialects, was extracted from the larger grammar and printed separately in 1530.[512]

JEAN CHÉRADAME, 1521

Jean Chéradame seems to have begun teaching Greek in Paris around 1517.[513] His work on Greek grammar, *Grammatica isagogica*, was first printed in Paris by Gilles de Gourmont in August 1521.[514] He dedicates it to the bishop of Tournai, Louis Guilliard, and it contains dedicatory verses from Georgius Hopylius, Matthaeus Caradasius, Joannes Ligarius, and Antonius Ligarius. In a postscript, Chéradame acknowledges the help of Hopylius and Jacques Toussain.[515] This collection of acknowledgments frames a slender, highly abbreviated grammar.

This grammar follows Gaza with no innovations. Chéradame divides the noun into five declensions: four parisyllabic and one imparisyllabic. Like Gaza, the Attic declension is his fourth.[516] In the fifth declension, he includes the contracted nouns, of which he distinguishes eight forms.[517] Writing on the verb, he distinguishes four barytone conjugations. The verbs in -μι are defined as a single fifth conjugation,[518] while the contracted verbs are presented as variants within his third conjugation of the barytone verbs.[519]

Chéradame's grammar should not be confused with a Greek work printed at least twice by Gourmont under Chéradame's name and the title *Introductio sane quam utilis graecarum musarum adyta compendio ingredi cupientibus*. The first edition of this introduction may be located in 1523, and another seems to have been printed in 1527.[520] This pamphlet, dedicated to the priest Adam Pluyette, has just six leaves, which contain notes on the alphabet, accents, pronunciation, and the definite article.

Chéradame edited two other well-established grammars for Gourmont. His edition of the complete text of Chrysoloras's grammar emerged about 1524 and was dedicated to two abbots: Guillaume, abbot of Sainte Geneviève, and Charles Boucher, abbot of Saint Magloire.[521] In 1526 he oversaw the publication of the Greek text of Gaza's grammar.[522] His own grammar was never reprinted, but one element of his work did have a brief afterlife in print. In the dedicatory preface to the grammar, Chéradame announced his plan for a new Greek dictionary, a work that finally emerged from Gourmont's press in April 1523.[523] A short work on the Greek numbers was extracted from the grammar and printed in this dictionary with a dedication from Chéradame to Jean Odoard. From this source it was reprinted in the Basle dictionaries of 1524 and 1525.[524]

Jacobus Ceporinus, 1522

Jakob Wiesendanger was born in 1500 in Dinhard, not far from Winterthur. He completed his earliest studies in Cologne and then enrolled at Vienna in the winter of 1518–19. In Vienna, he took students for Greek lessons, among whom was Georg Rithaimer. He also began to use the name *Ceporus*, from the Greek κηπουρός, "gardener." He moved on to study Greek and Hebrew under Reuchlin in Ingolstadt, and by the winter of 1520, he was in Basle. In Basle, it seems that the name *Ceporinus* began to be used.[525]

Ceporinus appears in this book for his *Compendium graecae grammaticae*, first printed in Basle by Valentine Curio in June 1522.[526] Copies of this work must have been disposed of very quickly indeed, for it was reprinted by Curio just six months later, this time with Hesiod's *Works and Days* and some Greek epigrams appended.[527] It may have owed its popularity to its brevity: Curio announced that it was intended for those who do not have time for the more advanced grammars of Urbano Bolzanio or Theodore Gaza.[528] Ceporinus's grammatical work is a compressed summary of Greek grammar in nine chapters, organized around the parts of speech. He defines only four declensions for the nouns: three parisyllabic and the fourth imparisyllabic.[529]

He omits the so-called Attic declension, discussing its forms among the dialectal variants of his third declension. He defines just eight conjugations for the verbs, relegating the contracted verbs to an appendix.[530] After the death of the author, Ulrich Zwingli praised Ceporinus's grammar in general and his treatment of the dialects in particular.[531] This slender volume was an elementary text, a factor that has contributed to the near-complete disappearance of the earliest editions. That it was dedicated to the reformer Zwingli is likely to have ensured that this edition did not enter Catholic classrooms.

In February 1525, Ceporinus was named professor of Greek and Hebrew in Zurich, but his lectures were cut short by his death in December at the age of twenty-six.[532] His short life had been very productive. In 1523, he had been responsible for an edition of the Greek text of Dionysius Periegetes, Aratus, and Proclus in Basle.[533] In 1524, he corrected the Greek text of the New Testament for the same press.[534] In Zurich, Froschauer printed the author's revision of his grammar posthumously in 1526, probably the first Greek book printed in the city.[535] His edition of Pindar's *Odes* also emerged in Basle the same year, with a fulsome tribute from Zwingli. This revised text of his grammar—with the dedication to Zwingli judiciously excised—was reprinted in Paris in 1529, and there were numerous reprints of the grammar throughout the sixteenth century. It was still being used with students in Zurich in the eighteenth century.[536]

Sanctes Pagninus, 1525

Sanctes Pagninus, better known for his important work on the Hebrew scriptures, published two works for students of Greek grammar in 1525. The first of these, his *Isagoge*, is a very substantial volume of 1,160 pages.[537] Its great size is due to the fact that it combines a dictionary and grammar in one volume. This edition was divided into two parts by the printer. This must have been done for ease of binding, since the division serves no structural purpose and the two parts are foliated consecutively. The whole work is divided into seven books of very unequal length.

The first book, of just seventeen pages, introduces the student to the alphabet, pronunciation, the accents and breathings, and the Greek article. In this respect, it covers much the same ground, and in much the same way, as many of the elementary pamphlets that were becoming increasingly popular. The real work for the student begins in the second book, the longest of the grammar, which deals with the noun. It defines ten declensions of the noun: the first four are parisyllabic, the fifth is imparisyllabic, and the last five are contracted. Pagninus retains Chrysoloras's order of the declensions, although he notes that Gaza makes the Attic declension his fourth.[538] It is in this book that the most unusual feature of Pagninus's grammar first appears. He follows the discussion of the forms of each of the first five declensions with an alphabetical list of nouns that belong to that declension. These five vocabularies, lexica in miniature, take up the bulk of the second book, filling 484 of its 544 pages. He passes quickly over the five contracted declensions, and the third book, eight short pages on the pronouns, ends the first part of the grammar.

The second part begins with the fourth book on the verb. As might be expected, this is nearly as long as the book on the noun. Pagninus defines the usual thirteen conjugations of the verb: six barytone, three contracted, and four in -μι. He supplies a separate lexicon for each of the six barytone conjugations, and another for the verbs in -μι. In total, of the 526 pages of this book, 467 are given over to the lexica. The remaining books are very brief, dealing with the participles, prepositions, conjunctions, and adverbs. Pagninus deals with the last three categories in alphabetical order, too, but this is less remarkable, since earlier grammarians had done likewise. In the preface to the work, Pagninus promised his readers a Greek dictionary. To judge from the contents of his Greek grammar, he must already have begun to compile this work. Moreover, the entries in the vocabularies of his grammar often cite their sources, a practice not yet fashionable among contemporary lexicographers. Most often, Pagninus's references are to the Greek scriptures or to Homer, although other authors also appear.

The *Isagoge* is a large, expensively produced work of reference, in small, closely printed type. Pagninus's second grammatical work offers a less daunting prospect to the student. The book, which he called the *Enchiridion*, is a summary of his larger work.[539] It is undated, but it appears to have been printed not long after the first. This slim volume contains a combination of simple texts and an accidence. After a discussion of the alphabet, the reader is faced with a number of Greek prayers, all of which are first transliterated into Latin letters and then translated into Latin. The longer passages of Greek are broken down into more manageable parts. Then the grammatical discussion begins, divided into fifty-four short chapters. After the grammar, there are more short Greek texts, although there are no more transliterations.

Pagninus's work is unusual for two reasons. The first is that both his Greek grammars are ostentatiously orthodox. We have already met the Protestant grammars of Nachtgall, Oecolampadius, Melanchthon, and Ceporinus. Pagninus was here producing a work to reclaim Greek studies for Rome. Both of his works were printed in the papal enclave of Avignon. Pagninus dedicated the *Isagoge* to François de Clermont, cardinal archbishop of Auch and papal legate to Avignon.[540] It received the protection of a privilege from the short-lived German pope, Hadrian VI, on March 11, 1523, and it is the only Greek grammar of the period to have received a papal privilege.[541] Hadrian seems to have wanted to reclaim the study of the biblical languages from the Reformers. He had been in Spain from 1515 until his election as Pope in 1522. There he had worked closely with Cardinal Ximenes, sponsor of the Complutensian Polyglot Bible, as regent after the death of Ferdinand of Aragon.[542] As a cardinal, Hadrian had encouraged Erasmus to translate the Old Testament as he had translated the New.[543] Pagninus's first work, a Hebrew vocabulary, emerged under Hadrian's auspices in Rome in 1523. The more modest *Enchiridion* was dedicated to a lesser ecclesiastical dignitary, the bishop John Nicholas.

Johann Winther of Andernach, 1527

Johann Winther, better known for his translations of Greek medical works, was responsible for a single short grammatical work, the *Syntaxis graeca*.[544] The preface to this work, dated from the house of Nicolas Bérault, informs us that it was composed in 1526 while Andernach was teaching Latin and Greek in Liège.[545] At the beginning of 1527, when he was about twenty-two years of age, he traveled from Liège to Paris, where his grammatical work was printed by Gilles de Gourmont in April 1527.[546] It was dedicated to Antoine de la Marck, who was abbot of Beaulieu in the

Ardennes, canon of St. Lambertus in Liège, and archdeacon of Brabant.[547] Winther writes that very few had treated Greek syntax in Latin, and that the Greeks who had written on syntax—Apollonius and Gaza—wrote in such a way "ut vix pauci ad plenum intellexerint"[548] (that hardly anyone understands them completely). The truth of this remark has already been demonstrated.[549]

Winther's work is addressed to *pueri*. His experience of teaching, or of learning, Greek seems to be one of large lecture halls filled with younger students. He does not believe that they were well served by their lecturers. Writing on the Greek article, one of the finer points of the language and one that he feels such teachers have neglected, he comments as follows:

> Solet etiam hodie professorum vulgus, haud scio quomodo, huiusmodi rerum velut quisquiliarum nullam habere rationem, dum hoc solum spectant: quantum iuventus audiat, non item quam bene quid intelligat. Ecquid, per Musas quaeso, in omni studiorum genere pernitiosius atque tumultuaria illa autorum lectio, quae facit ut non minora (quemadmodum μεγαλοφρονοῦσιν ἐκείνοις videtur) sed potiora interim aut nescimus aut certe negligamus. Quod cum miseri adolescentes non intelligant, saepe vix Aesopo trito aut decem duntaxat Homeri paginis lectitatis ad professionem erumpunt.[550]
>
> [For some reason, today's crowd of teachers usually do not treat this matter, as if it were trivial, considering only how much Greek the students hear, not how well they understand it. By the Muses, is there anything more damaging in any field of study than to rush through authors in lectures? It ensures that we do not know, or simply pass over, not just the lesser points (as if they were supremely confident in them) but even the more important ones. Since the poor students do not understand the lectures, they often leave to look for a job having scarcely read well-thumbed Aesop or ten short pages of Homer.]

Greek, it seems, was well enough established in the curricula for lectures on the subject to have become rather perfunctory. His words suggest a man disillusioned with teaching as a career. Even as he wrote, he may already have found another use for his talents. At the end of his work, he writes, "Habes, optime lector, de octo orationis partibus breviter. De figuris illis poeticis ... nonnulla tractarem, nisi alio nunc me ventus avocaret. Facturus tamen sum in alio opere, quod haud ita multo post tibi communicabimus"[551] (You have, reader, my brief exposition of grammar. I would have treated the poetic figures of speech had the wind not called me away to another task. This I shall perform in another work, which we shall share with you soon). The following year, he began the first of many translations from the Greek physicians, which earned him his lasting reputation among scholars. He never published another grammatical work.

JOHANN METZLER, 1529

Johann Metzler studied under Urbano Bolzanio and Richard Croke.[552] He seems to have taught Greek in Vratislava from at least 1527.[553] His brief grammatical work *Primae grammatices graecae partis rudimenta* was printed in Hagenau in July 1529.[554] Joachim Camerarius supplied Greek verses for the title page. Metzler addressed it from his home in Vratislava to his fellow teachers there, Joannes Rullus and Andreas Winckler, so we may guess that it formed part of the course in that city.

He makes an apology for publishing yet another grammar when there are already so many available:

> Nec dubito quin sub nomine et tutela vestra excudenda typis tradita tanquam vestra sitis defensuri meque vindicaturi ab impudentia et temeritate quod rudimenta grammatices vulgare audeam, cuius tot institutiones a viris doctis conscriptae circumferuntur ut numero pene aequare discipulos videantur.[555]
>
> [I am sure that you will defend works printed under your name and protection as if they were your own and that you will vindicate me from the charge of presumption and temerity because I dare to publish an elementary grammar when so many such manuals written by learned men are circulating that there seem to be almost as many of them as there are students.]

By 1529, there were certainly a large number of grammars and of editions competing for the attentions of students and teachers. Metzler's own work is no more than an accidence, as he himself explains in his preface, intended to provide students with the basic elements of the language. For more profound knowledge, he advises his students to turn to the grammars of Urbano and Gaza.

Metzler's teachers, Urbano and Croke, valued Gaza's grammar highly, although Urbano's grammar did not take up Gaza's most striking innovations. Metzler follows Gaza's arrangement of the nouns, perhaps attracted by its simplicity, and defines just five declensions. The first four of these are parisyllabic and, like Gaza, he makes the Attic declension his fourth. The fifth declension includes all the imparisyllabic nouns, and it is here that he comments on the limitations of his grammar:

> Quinta declinatio ... omnia complectitur, et tam varia habet terminationes obliquorumque formationes ut compendio indicari pueris nequeat. Quare eis consulo, ne de his initio sint solliciti, quaerant interim ex praeceptoribus et lexico. Nam quae passim traduntur regulae non nisi a provectioribus intelliguntur. Immo certam eius cognitionem non nisi ex frequenti autorum lectione cognosces.[556]
>
> [The fifth declension includes everything and has such varied endings and forms of the oblique cases that it cannot be shown to boys in summary form. For this reason, I advise them, in order that they should not be worried about these matters at the beginning, that for the time being they consult teachers and a dictionary. For the rules that are usually taught are understood only by more advanced students. In fact, you will come to sure knowledge of this declension only from great familiarity with Greek writers.]

Like Gaza, he defines eight varieties of contracted nouns. Metzler displays a certain weariness with the grammarians' debates over the number of the declensions: he says that the reader can label these varieties as declensions if he so wishes, but the important thing to remember is that they are derived from the fifth, imparisyllabic, declension.[557] When it comes to the verb, he echoes Ceporinus and says that there are only eight conjugations: four in -ω and four in -μι.[558] He deals with three varieties of the contracted verb, but he chooses not to call these varieties conjugations.

Metzler's grammar had some small success, for it was subsequently reprinted several times, as was a revision of the work made by Antonius Niger in the middle of the century.[559]

Chapter 2

Greek Lexica

Ancient and Byzantine Greek Lexica

A number of classical lexica—variously epitomized or conflated by Byzantine users—were imported from the East in the fifteenth century: the works of Harpocration, Phrynichus, Pollux, Hesychius, and Stephanus, and the larger compilations of the *Etymologicum magnum* and the Suda lexicon. These were, of course, entirely in Greek and tended naturally to concentrate on the more obscure terms and usages. Despite their difficulties for the Latin scholar, they were eagerly sought. In 1396, the year before Manuel Chrysoloras's arrival in Florence, Coluccio Salutati wrote to Jacopo Angeli, who was then in Constantinople, to encourage him in his search for Greek manuscripts: "Platonica velim cuncta tecum portes et vocabulorum auctores quot haberi possunt, ex quibus pendet omnis huius perceptionis difficultas"[1] (Please bring all the works of Plato with you and as many dictionaries as are available: every problem of understanding depends on these dictionaries). He realized that Greek texts themselves were of little use without the tools to unlock their meaning, and he doubtless remembered the story that Petrarch had cherished a Greek manuscript of Homer he could not read.[2] Before considering the use and development of Greek dictionaries in Renaissance Europe, it is as well to discuss the availability of the remnants of ancient lexicography. These works are discussed here in something approaching the order in which they became available in the West.

The Suda Lexicon

The Suda lexicon is a treasure trove of miscellaneous information about ancient writers and their works. The value of its biographical sketches was recognized in Western Europe in the thirteenth century by Robert Grosseteste, who selected and translated over seventy articles. Grosseteste's manuscript of the lexicon survived, and William Grocyn subsequently owned a copy of the Suda that had been made from it.[3] In Italy, the fortunes of the Suda in the fifteenth century can be traced back to Guarino Veronese, whose manuscript of the lexicon was probably acquired on his way back from Constantinople in 1408. His was perhaps the first copy to reach quattrocento Italy.[4] Guarino's manuscript, now lost, was probably the exemplar for an another early copy of the lexicon. This was apparently made in Mantua in 1422 by Peter of Crete, a scribe who is known to have worked for Vittorino da Feltre.[5] Francesco Filelfo brought another copy of the Suda lexicon to Italy in 1427, and his familiarity with the work is apparent throughout his correspondence. It may have been from this manuscript that Filelfo translated the article *De sacerdotio Iesu Christi*.[6]

The Suda seems to have taken a little longer to find its way to Rome. Cristoforo Garatone acquired another copy, apparently in Constantinople, sometime between 1433 and 1446, and this copy was probably in the Vatican Library by 1455.[7] One copy of the lexicon can be placed during the pontificate of Nicholas V, made by Demetrius Xanthopulus and dated February 14, 1454.[8] The work certainly aroused some interest during this period, for Lauro Quirini translated *De fide christiana* from the Suda and dedicated it to Nicholas.[9] Michael Apostolis contributed to two copies, the first probably, and the second certainly, in Crete: he collaborated with George Calophrenas to produce one and with Michael Lygizos to produce the other.[10] A copy of the Suda, made by George Gregoropoulos sometime in the second half of the fifteenth century, would also appear to have been transcribed in Crete.[11] Giovanni Aurispa possessed part of the lexicon at his death in 1459;[12] Lilio Tifernas finished a copy in Città di Castello in December 1463;[13] Bessarion had a copy in his library by 1468 and two by the time of his death in 1472;[14] and Poliziano made use of an unidentified manuscript of the work in Florence in the late 1480s.[15]

We have some details of the fortunes of another manuscript. Constantine Lascaris owned an early thirteenth-century copy of the Suda. He recognized its value as a source of biographical information and extracted a biographical guide from the lexicon, apparently around 1463 while he was in Milan.[16] When Francesco Faraone edited Dictys Cretensis for publication in Messina in 1498, he asked Lascaris if he could find the work extant in Greek. Lascaris could not, but he was able to tell Faraone what the Suda had to say on the subject of Dictys.[17] Lascaris may have introduced his students to the work. In September 1495, about a year after they had returned from Lascaris's school in Messina, Pietro Bembo wrote to his fellow student Angelo Gabrieli, "Sudae τὰ ὑπολείποντα valde opto ut describi mandes ex eo libro quem scis"[18] (I would very much like you to arrange for the transcription of the rest of the Suda from that manuscript that you know). Lascaris seems to have attached particular value to his manuscript of the work, for in his will he made it the subject of a very specific bequest to the monastery of San Salvatore in Messina.[19]

The first printed edition of the Suda was edited by Demetrius Chalcondyles, who paid twenty-five ducats, a large sum, for the exemplar from which it was printed in 1499.[20] The extent of Chalcondyles' editorial work is unclear: he states that he used several manuscripts for the edition, and it is known that he inserted some words from the lexicon of Zonaras and some from Paulus Aegineta.[21] We know a great deal about the early history of this edition. The contract between the financial backers and the printers survives, signed on April 13, 1499. From this we learn that eight hundred copies were to be printed and that Taddeo Ugoleto of Parma was to receive two complimentary copies.[22] The edition was to be caught up in the revolutions in Milan: French troops took possession of the city in September, and printing was finally completed under the French occupation in the middle of November.[23] According to the prefatory dialogue, the price was to be three ducats, an expensive book but still a fraction of the price paid by Chalcondyles for the manuscript exemplar.[24]

At some time over the following weeks, Joannes Angelus Scinzenzeler and Joannes de Romano acquired a portion of this edition, presumably in their capacity as booksellers. By February 1500, Ludovico Sforza had recovered Milan, and on March 21, he received the surrender of the French garrison in Novara.[25] Two days later, Chalcondyles' petition for the recovery of these books received the attention of the duke in Novara.[26] It is remarkable that Chalcondyles could command the duke's attention—or at least his signature—on such a matter at such a time. We do not know the outcome of this litigation, but Ludovico's favor is unlikely to have benefited Chalcondyles. The duke quickly retreated to Ferrara, where he was to be found on March 28.[27] On April 8, 1500, the French retook Milan, seized the duke, and sent him to France.[28] Chalcondyles was eventually recalled to Milan in March 1501 by Georges d'Amboise, the legate of Louis XII in the city.[29]

At some time in the succeeding months, the remainder of the Milanese Suda edition came into the possession of Aldus Manutius in Venice. The exact date of the transaction is unclear. In 1502, Reuchlin seems to have believed that Aldus could supply him with a copy, for in a letter from August 18, 1502, Aldus replied that he could not;[30] in November 1502, Reuchlin wrote to Aldus again, requesting "Suidam ut polliceris" (Suidas, as you promised).[31] This exchange may indicate that Aldus was at this time in the process of acquiring the remainder of the Milan edition.[32] A letter of Aldus to Reuchlin of December 24, 1502, seems to indicate that Aldus had finally fulfilled the order.[33] Whenever and however he obtained them, the volumes appeared in his catalog of June 1503, at which time he was selling them for three-and-a-half ducats apiece.[34] A suggestive coincidence of dates is worth noting here: the Aldine Sophocles was completed in the second half of August 1502, and in October, Chalcondyles began to lecture on this text in Milan.[35] These are the very months in which Aldus seems to have been attempting to acquire the remainder of the Suda edition: Chalcondyles may have exchanged his copies of the lexicon for copies of Sophocles, which he could sell to his students. Aldus had cultivated the network of scholarly contacts necessary to sell expensive and learned volumes such as the Suda.

Another edition of the Suda was projected a few years later. Sometime between 1510 and 1520, Gershom Soncino wrote to Pontico Virunio for advice on whether to print a new edition of the lexicon.[36] Despite Virunio's enthusiastic reply, the edition never appeared. Aldus may have beaten Soncino to it: he was advertising a new edition in his catalog of November 1513, although the new Aldine edition, based on a different and more complete manuscript, did not receive its colophon until February 1514.[37] Perhaps Soncino was wise to abandon his edition: despite Aldus's contacts, it seems that it had taken him the best part of twelve years to find homes for the remainder of the edition, which he had bought in 1502 or 1503.

In his Adage, "Festina lente," Erasmus tells of someone who refused to lend his rare manuscript of the Suda for fear of losing the scholarly advantages it lent him. Erasmus himself owned a copy of the work by 1516, probably a printed edition, and probably the second Aldine edition: it is cited frequently in his *Annotations* on the New Testament published in that year.[38] Erasmus's copy has not been located, but the copies of the *editio princeps* owned and annotated by Scipione Forteguerri and Janus Lascaris have survived.[39] Willibald Pirckheimer's copy, decorated by Albrecht Dürer, has come down to us,[40] as has that of Hernan Nuñez de Guzman.[41]

JULIUS POLLUX

The *Onomasticon* of Julius Pollux was composed during the reign of the emperor Commodus. It survives only in an abridgement and is arranged in ten books ordered by topic rather than alphabetically. There is abundant evidence for its diffusion in fifteenth-century Italy. Giovanni Aurispa is the first Westerner known to have had a manuscript in the fifteenth century: he brought the text back from the East in 1423,[42] and Ambrogio Traversari acquired a manuscript from him soon after his return to Italy.[43] In 1428, Francesco Filelfo lent Aurispa a manuscript that he subsequently spent years attempting to retrieve.[44] Guarino Veronese owned a manuscript at his death in 1460.[45]

In the second half of the century, copies multiplied, but the work remained confined to Italy. George Trivizias and Joannes Rhosos collaborated on a manuscript of Pollux, and Trivizias made two other copies himself.[46] Around 1456, during his travels after the fall of Constantinople, Constantine Lascaris acquired a fourteenth-century manuscript in Rhodes.[47] He took this manuscript with him to Milan in 1458, and on to Naples and Messina in 1465–66. Giorgio Merula acquired a copy in Ferrara from Nardo Palmieri in 1462.[48] Bessarion and, through his bequest, the Republic of Venice owned a copy.[49] Theodore Gaza cited Pollux in his work on the Greek calendar, published in Rome in 1470.[50] Angelo Poliziano cites Pollux twice in his marginalia to his version of the fifth book of the *Iliad*, which was made between about 1472 and 1475.[51] The young Poliziano may have had his attention drawn to these passages by his teacher at the time, Andronicus Callistus. Ermolao Barbaro owned a Greek manuscript of Pollux.[52]

In 1498 a Venetian printing company obtained a license to print Pollux, but the privilege was never exercised.[53] The *editio princeps* was the Aldine of April 1502, which Aldus dedicated to Elia Capriolo of Brescia.[54] In an undated letter, Daniel Clario of Ragusa asked Aldus for a Greek lexicon for one "Helius poeta," apparently a simple request for a copy of the Aldine dictionary. It would be pleasant to think that this dedication of his latest lexicon was part of a grand gesture on Aldus's behalf, but it is hard to imagine why Capriolo would be called a poet. Aldus sent Reuchlin a copy of this newly printed volume in August 1502.[55] Willibald Pirckheimer, always an avid collector of Aldus's editions, had his own copy decorated by Albrecht Dürer.[56] Henricus Urbanus, writing on behalf of the Cistercians in Georgenthal, asked Aldus for a copy in November 1505, although it is not clear that Aldus fulfilled this order.[57] Erasmus consulted Pollux in connection with his edition of the New Testament in 1516 and probably saw a copy some years earlier.[58] It was reprinted by the Juntine Press in 1520.

THE *ETYMOLOGICUM MAGNUM*

Several copies of the twelfth-century Byzantine compilation known as the *Etymologicum magnum* circulated in quattrocento Italy. Early in the century, two copies were available in Florence: one was in the library of Niccolò Niccoli;[59] the other belonged to the monk and translator Ambrogio Traversari.[60] A thirteenth-century manuscript of the work belonged to Carlo Marsuppini, who died in 1453. This manuscript was subsequently owned by Angelo Poliziano, who used a definition from the *Etymologicum magnum* in the marginalia to his translation of the third book of the *Iliad*, presented in 1472; he made more use of the work for his commentary on the *Odyssey* in the late 1480s.[61] Poliziano's manuscript entered the library of San Marco in Florence in 1497, apparently bought from the lexicographer Guarino of Favera.[62]

In October 1466, Francesco Filelfo wrote to Joannes Argyropoulos from Milan to ask if there was a copy of the *Etymologicum magnum* in Florence.[63] In fact, in 1466, two manuscripts were produced: George Calofrenas made one in Crete for Filelfo, while another was written in Milan.[64] Bessarion, naturally, was in possession of a copy by 1468.[65] Other copies are less securely dated. We know that Janus Lascaris acquired a copy from Corigliano in Puglia.[66] Another was to be found in San Giovanni in Verdara in Padua.[67] Alessandro Benedetti, a physician who traveled extensively in the Greek-speaking East between 1475 and 1490, acquired a copy. He established himself at the university in Padua on his return and died in Venice in 1512.[68]

The *Etymologicum magnum* was first printed in Venice by Zacharias Callierges in 1499.[69] This edition was subsequently acquired by Aldus Manutius, who was selling copies for two ducats and three lire in 1503.[70] It sold even more slowly than the Suda: it was still for sale in the Aldine catalog of November 1513 and was not reprinted until 1549.[71] A number of early owners can be identified: Aldus sent Johann Reuchlin a copy in August 1502,[72] and Giovanni Calfurnio acquired a copy before his death in 1503.[73] Henricus Urbanus, writing on behalf of the Cistercians of Georgenthal, asked Aldus for this edition in November 1505.[74] Beatus Rhenanus owned a copy,[75] and Willibald Pirckheimer had a copy decorated by Albrecht Dürer.[76] Nuñez de Guzman bought his copy in Bologna, apparently between 1500 and 1505, for two and a half ducats.[77] Erasmus certainly consulted, and probably owned, a copy.[78] Cuthbert Tunstall donated his copy in 1528 to Cambridge University Library, where it remains today,[79] and Guillaume Budé's annotated copy survives in Paris.[80]

Valerius Harpocration

The second-century lexicon of Valerius Harpocration details words and phrases drawn largely, but not exclusively, from the Greek orators. It appears not to have been widely available in Italy in the first half of the fifteenth century. Francesco Filelfo certainly owned a manuscript by 1444,[81] and another copy was in the Vatican Library by 1455.[82] After 1466, Constantine Lascaris made a copy for his own use at his school in Messina, and in one of his characteristic subscriptions he noted that ἐχρῆτο ἀεὶ ὡς κηπιδίῳ γραμματικῆς[83] (he used it constantly as a little garden of grammar). Demetrius Damilas added a copy to a manuscript of Gaza's grammar,[84] while the monk Hilarion made a manuscript of Harpocration in 1496.[85]

At least three copies can be connected specifically with Florence. Michael Apostolis made a copy, apparently in the 1450s or 1460s, which was subsequently annotated by Lauro Quirini.[86] In 1492, Janus Lascaris brought a manuscript of Harpocration back to Florence from his journey to the eastern Mediterranean.[87] The scribe Caesar Strategos added Harpocration to a manuscript of Procopius's *De aedificiis* in Florence at the end of the fifteenth century.[88]

Venice had several manuscript copies by the end of the century. Bessarion had at least one by 1468, and this formed part of his donation to the republic on his death in 1472.[89] A manuscript of the minor Attic orators and Harpocration was made by

Marcus Musurus.[90] George Moschus, a corrector at the Aldine Press and brother of the better-known Demetrius, made a copy.[91] Venice also hosted the first printed text of Harpocration, from the Aldine Press, in 1503.[92] No new edition was called for until the second Aldine of 1527, so it may have taken the press more than twenty years to sell all the copies of its first printing.[93]

Phrynichus

In the ninth century, the patriarch Photius recorded his observations on the Σοφιστικὴ προπαρασκευή, an immense lexicographical work in thirty-seven books, compiled by the strict Atticist Phrynichus. He notes that although Phrynichus is learned, he is so verbose that the work could be reduced to one fifth of its size without any detriment to its substance.[94] The work that Photius saw has been almost entirely lost: a brief epitome, which survives in a single manuscript, was not edited until the twentieth century.[95] Instead we have another lexical work from the same author, the so-called *Eclogues*. This work, too, survives only in an abridgement, and we must hope that we are missing only the redundant verbiage noticed by the patriarch.

Numerous manuscripts of the *Eclogues* are extant from the fourteenth and fifteenth centuries, but it is not easy to attach names to them.[96] A copy was certainly in Bessarion's library by 1468 and was part of his bequest to the Republic of Venice in 1472.[97] A copy now in the Vatican seems to have been made by George Trivizias between 1461 and 1485.[98] Joannes Rhosos made a manuscript in Venice, which he completed in June 1491.[99] In 1501, Aldus's associate Scipio Forteguerri made a copy, but the Aldine Press showed little interest in printing the work.[100] In fact, it was not printed until 1517 when Zacharias Callierges edited it for publication in Rome.[101] It was used in the compilation of the Greek dictionary of Guarino of Favera, printed in Rome in 1523.[102] The following year, the Aldine Press finally remedied its earlier neglect: its Greek dictionary of 1524 included a copy of Callierges' edition among its lexical appendices.[103]

Stephanus of Byzantium

Stephanus of Byzantium composed his *Ethnica* in sixty books in the sixth century. Like so many of the lexicographers, this work, too, survives only in an epitome. Stephanus lists place names, and the adjectives derived from them, in alphabetical order. His work seems to have resurfaced in the West later than most of the other lexical works surveyed here. Bessarion did not have a copy of Stephanus in his library, so we may suppose that it only came to light after his death in 1472. It was certainly available by 1485, for George Trivizias, who died that year, made a copy of the work.[104] Thereafter, copies multiplied rapidly. Michael Souliardos made three in Florence, one undated, one in 1487, and another in 1496.[105] In 1491, Janus Lascaris came across one in the substantial library of the Paduan professor Giovanni Calfurnio, and Joannes Rhosos made a copy of Calfurnio's manuscript dated March 31, 1492.[106] Another manuscript, written by Thomas Dydimus Feltrinus de Zanetellis, belonged to the library of Ermolao Barbaro, that is, before the death of Ermolao in 1493.[107] Demetrius Moschus also made two copies, apparently in the last decade of the fifteenth century.[108]

Stephanus was first printed by Aldus in January 1502 and dedicated to Giovanni Taberio, who was then teaching Greek in Brescia.[109] From Aldus's preface to Stephanus, we learn that Taberio had already bought textbooks from the Aldine Press:

> Cum itaque tu istic summa laude et graece et latine publice quam plurimos doceas, scripserisque ad me superioribus diebus ut quosdam graecos libros, quod esset eis opus discipulis tuis, ad te mitterem; et tunc illos misi libenter, et nunc Stephanum, qui de urbibus scripsit, damus libentissime.[110]
> [And so since you teach Greek and Latin publicly there to a very large audience and to great acclaim, and wrote to me recently asking me to send you certain Greek books because your pupils needed them, not only was I happy to send them then, but now, too, I am very happy to give you Stephanus, who wrote about cities.]

Stephanus's work would appear to be of only marginal value to the student, but the direction given to it by Aldus in the preface suggests that he was eager to maximize its appeal to the educational market. The Aldine text was reprinted by the Giunta in Florence in 1521.

Hesychius

Hesychius, an Alexandrian lexicographer, probably lived in the fifth century after Christ. His lexicon of rare words survives in an abridgement, and the history of this work in the fifteenth century is that of the single surviving manuscript known to us. This was made around 1430.[111] We do not know its fortunes during the rest of the century, although Francesco Filelfo cites the work in a letter of 1476.[112] It was the printer's copy for the *editio princeps* of 1514, and it carries the annotations of its first editor in Venice, Marcus Musurus.[113] In the preface to this edition, Aldus says that he obtained the manuscript from Jacopo Bardellone, to whom the book is dedicated. It seems to have entered the Marciana between 1734 and 1740.[114] It is possible that Thomas More owned or consulted the edition of 1514.[115] Erasmus probably owned a copy of this edition: he does not cite Hesychius in the first edition of his annotations on the New Testament in 1516, but he does cite him in the second edition of 1519.[116] Willibald Pirckheimer's fine library contained a copy.[117] The Aldine edition was popular enough to be reprinted in Florence in 1520 and in Hagenau in 1521.

Greek Lexica in Western Europe, 1396–1529

The complex Greek lexica of late antiquity and Byzantium were of limited use to the student beginning to learn the language. These works had been compiled to polish the Atticism of Greek writers or to explain allusions in the classical authors. Western students of the language needed bilingual dictionaries if they were to make any progress without a teacher. At the beginning of the fifteenth century, however, there were very few Greek–Latin dictionaries available in the West that sought to provide the student with elementary vocabulary. In these circumstances, texts available in both languages assumed an important role as latent dictionaries. Traversari describes his own program of Greek studies, and his own solution, in a letter:

Psalterium habui grecum mihi per religionis institutionem admodum familiare. Id igitur cum latino conferre incepi, atque notare singula tum verba tum nomina et reliquas orationis partes, quidquid singula significarent mandare memoriae, ac vim verborum omnium tenere quantum fas erat . . . Transivi deinceps ad Evangelia, Epistulas Pauli Actusque Apostolorum . . . Habent enim satis magnam verborum copiam suntque omnia translata fideliter ac diligenter nec inconcinne. Postmodum vero et gentilium libros videre volui eosque haud facile intellexi.[118]

[I had a Greek Psalter with which I was quite familiar from my religious studies. So I started to compare it with a Latin version, to mark individual verbs, nouns, and other parts of speech, to commit to memory the meaning of each one, and to grasp the force of all the words as far as possible . . . Then I moved on to the Gospels, the letters of Paul, and the Acts of the Apostles . . . For they have quite a large stock of words, and have all been translated faithfully and carefully and not inelegantly. Afterwards I wanted to see profane books, and I understood them with difficulty.]

In the fifteenth century, if Western students wanted elementary Greek lexica, they had to make them for themselves. Consequently, the first texts used by students of Greek were those with readily available Latin translations. Traversari used the vulgate Latin translation of the Psalms to unlock the Greek text and to construct a vocabulary.

In 1459, Battista Guarino also said that students should compile their own vocabularies from their reading of Greek authors:

Hoc imprimis servent ut in ea lingua vocabulorum varietatem et copiam (quibus ea maxime abundat) non tam memoria quam et scriptis colligant; atque eo promptiora erunt si in ordinem redacta fuerint. Ex hac enim scribendi assiduitate menti magis imprimuntur, et accentus (quorum sermo ille plenus est) penitus notantur; aut si forte (ut est memoria labilis) effluxerint, habebunt semper quo tanquam in thesaurum se recipiant.[119]

[It is particularly important that they gather together the many and varied words of that language (it is well supplied with them), committing them to writing rather than simply to memory. And the words will be more quickly found if they arrange them in order. Through this constant attention to writing, they are more easily remembered; the accents, which are very common in that language, are carefully noted; and if they should forget (the memory is prone to stumble), they will always have something to return to, as if to a storehouse.]

These word lists, *in ordinem redacta*, would accompany these students during their earliest readings. Over sixty years later, in the preface to Oecolampadius's Greek grammar, Cratander attributes the success of some in learning Greek to a similar plan: "Principio cognitis articulis, inflexionem nominum atque verborum didicerunt generalem, eamque non admodum anxie. Deinde latina facta cum graecis aliquot menses contulerunt propter copiam vocum acquirendam. Postremo repositi ad grammatica, [sic] libellum hunc ab initio perlegerunt accuratissime"[120] (At the beginning, when they had learned the articles, they learned the general pattern of the inflections of the nouns and verbs, and that none too carefully. Then they compared Latin translations with Greek texts for a few months to acquire a good vocabulary. Finally, they returned to grammatical matters and read this little book carefully from the beginning). With the single exception of the *Isagoge* of Sanctes Pagninus, none of the grammars printed before 1530 had rudimentary lexica attached. Instead, they were often supplemented by a number of simple Greek texts from which students were expected to extract their vocabularies.

There are few lexica of intermediate vocabularies in this period. One of the most modern looking—a collection of vocabularies, each organized around a theme—was in fact among the most ancient and was not widely used by students. Marsilio Ficino made a copy of these vocabularies, perhaps while he was learning Greek between 1456 and 1462.[121] During his time in Constantinople, from 1435 to 1437, Giovanni Tortelli compiled a vocabulary of contemporary Greek, apparently intended for the use of Western travelers in Greek-speaking lands.[122] Nearly a century later, in 1527, Stefano da Sabio compiled an unusual vocabulary that he said would allow Italians to learn demotic and classical Greek and enable Greeks to learn Latin.[123] Such vocabularies were rare. As a rule, Greek dictionaries were substantial volumes, reference tools that, for all their faults, attempted to be comprehensive.

The origins of the earliest Greek–Latin lexica in use in the West in the fifteenth century are still unclear. There are few copies that can be assigned with any confidence to the first decades of the fifteenth century. In 1425, Francesco Barbaro wrote to Antonio Corbinelli to ask for one such work for Pietro Miani, who was then learning Greek in his old age.[124] Whatever this manuscript might have been, one Greek–Latin lexicon—usually attributed in the fifteenth century to Cyril of Alexandria—certainly belonged to Francesco Barbaro by the time of his death in 1454.[125] It is, however, unlikely that this lexicon came into Miani's possession in 1425, since it began to circulate in Italy only in the 1430s. Nicolaus Cusanus brought his eighth-century manuscript of pseudo-Cyril's dictionary with him to the Council of Basle, which began in 1431.[126] In the same year, another manuscript was produced, signed by a scribe who called himself Michael the Notary. It contains the lexicon together with a number of elementary texts, a combination that suggests that it was used by a student of the language.[127] Cardinal Giovanni of Ragusa, who participated in the Council of Basle, may have copied his own manuscript of pseudo-Cyril from Cusanus's manuscript.[128] In the second half of the century, numerous copies were made. Of these, we may notice here that Janus Pannonius copied a manuscript of pseudo-Cyril in Ferrara about 1450 while he was learning Greek,[129] that Giorgio Merula owned a copy that was certainly in existence by 1472,[130] that Francesco da Castiglione owned a copy,[131] that Cristoforo Persona appears to have had a copy,[132] and that Phanourios Karabelos made a copy for Michael Ialinas in Italy in 1489.[133]

In the early decades of the fifteenth century, scholars were obliged to make their own dictionaries. One such dictionary was compiled by Zomino of Pistoia in the course of his studies in the 1420s.[134] This autograph manuscript has a few prefatory leaves of rough grammatical notes followed by a Greek–Latin lexicon. Zomino seems to have adopted a procedure similar to that described by Battista Guarino in 1459. He took a blank paper manuscript and indexed it according to the first two letters of each word: for the letter beta, for example, he had ten divisions: βα, βδ, βε, βη, βι, βλ, βο, βρ, βυ, and βω. When he encountered a new Greek word in the course of his studies, he wrote it and its meaning in his manuscript under the appropriate subdivision. Consequently, after the first two letters, the words are not in alphabetical order. If he managed to fill up the space he had allotted for the subdivision in the manuscript, he continued the entry on a blank page at the end and added a note under the main entry referring the reader to the pages at the end of the manuscript. Another scholar, Giovanni Tortelli, also made his own Greek–Latin lexicon, probably while he was studying in Constantinople between 1435 and 1437.[135] The compilations of other scholars have yet to be identified. Vespasiano da Bisticci refers ambiguously to one project begun in Florence by Niccolò della Luna, perhaps in the 1430s or 1440s: "Vidi già composti dallui dua vocabolisti greci colla ispositione latina, che si vede era l'ordine da volere tradurre, come è detto"[136] (I have seen two Greek dictionaries that had been prepared by him with a Latin translation, which it seems he wanted to translate, as he said). Niccolò had been a pupil of Filelfo and Marsuppini and potentially had access to the Greek dictionaries in the well-stocked libraries of Florence. Works such as the Suda lexicon and the *Etymologicum magnum* contained a great deal of information of interest to Latin scholars, although such a translation need not have done much to help students of the Greek language. We know relatively little of Niccolò. Whatever his plans were, his early death seems to have put an end to them.[137]

Niccolò's project may have been contemporary with the compilation of an influential Greek–Latin lexicon, perhaps put into circulation around 1440.[138] A Greek–Latin lexicon, completed in Florence on September 13, 1441, by Cristoforo Benna, is the earliest dated copy of this work and provides evidence for its arrival in Florence.[139] Joannes Scutariota copied the Greek portion of a copy of this lexicon, which belonged to Giannozzo Manetti. Since Scutariota seems to have worked all his life in Florence, and since Manetti left the city in 1453, it would appear to predate that year.[140] Manetti had studied Greek with Traversari, but the monk may have been dead before this new lexicon reached Florence.[141] Scutariota made two other copies of this lexicon that have not been connected with Manetti.[142] Constantine Lascaris used the lexicon with his students in Milan: a copy in his hand, dated around 1464, was owned by his pupil Leodrisio Crivelli.[143] A copy dated 1470 was left to the library of the cathedral church in Messina by Ludovico Saccano on Saccano's death in 1480.[144] Michael Lygizos and Michael Apostolis both made copies, and Immanuel Rhusotas made two.[145]

Giovanni Crastoni was responsible for editing the first printed Greek–Latin lexicon. A native of Piacenza and a Carmelite monk, practically nothing is known of his early life. By the time Filelfo sent him a friendly letter in Greek in 1474, Crastoni was probably about fifty years old.[146] In Milan, he worked to bring to publication a collection of elementary Greek texts. The first of these seems to have been the Greek–Latin lexicon that he dedicated to Franciscus Ferrarius. This lexicon does not carry a date, but a copy that once belonged to Pietro da Montagnana was donated to the library of San Giovanni in Verdara in Padua on March 28, 1478.[147] Around 1480, a shorter work of Crastoni, a Latin–Greek dictionary, was printed by Bonaccorso, and the preface of Bonaccorso to this work tells us that Filelfo still thought well of Crastoni.[148] Although the two volumes make a natural pair, their different sizes make it clear that they were not intended to be bound together. Crastoni supplied the Latin translation alongside the grammar of Constantine Lascaris when it was reprinted by Bonaccorso in 1480 and prepared the text of a Greek–Latin edition of the Psalter in 1481.[149] He also wrote a Greek life of Alexander, of which only a Latin translation survives.[150] He seems still to have been in Milan in 1496 or 1497, when he helped to edit Terentianus Maurus, and he provided an epigram for Cruceius's translation of Callimachus's *Hymns*.[151] Thereafter, we hear no more of him.

Crastoni did not compile this influential Greek–Latin lexicon himself, although he did make a number of additions.[152] It is plausible that the manuscript or manuscripts from which the first edition of the Greek–Latin lexicon was printed had once belonged to Andronicus Callistus. Callistus's large collection of Greek manuscripts had been purchased by Bonaccorso and Giovanni Francesco della Torre in Milan in 1475.[153] No lexicon, however, has yet been identified as having been made or owned by Callistus.[154] There had been an attempt to bring together the dictionaries compiled around 1440 and that of pseudo-Cyril, which may be significant in this context. It has been observed that the early leaves of Crastoni's printed lexicon include glosses from pseudo-Cyril that soon fade out.[155] Constantine Lascaris's copy of the lexicon also has glosses from pseudo-Cyril on the first twenty-six leaves.[156] Another example of this conflated lexicon was written by George Hermonymus, the Greek who met Callistus in Milan in 1475 and accompanied him to London in 1476. Hermonymus's copy has also been expanded with glosses from the lexicon attributed to Cyril.[157]

According to Bonaccorso's preface to the first edition of Crastoni's Greek–Latin lexicon, the monk did a number of things to his source manuscript to prepare it for the press.[158] He ordered the words alphabetically. He supplied the genitive of nouns, which were presumably given only in the nominative in the glossary he used. He added the articles to these nouns to indicate their gender. For the verbs, he supplied the future tense, the pluperfect, and the middle. He also indicated whether verbs were active, passive, neuter, common, or deponent. Henri Estienne, writing in 1569, identified three problems with Crastoni's lexicon: its glosses of Greek words are too brief and sometimes lapse into Italian; it does not indicate the *constructio* of Greek words, that is, how they would be used in a sentence; and it does not record the Greek authors these meanings are derived from.[159] Scholars were slow to remedy these shortcomings.

For all its limitations, Crastoni's work remained at the heart of subsequent dictionaries for decades. Before 1497, there were two separate editions of Crastoni's Latin–Greek dictionary and two editions of his more substantial Greek–Latin dictionary. In 1497, Aldus Manutius united both types of lexica in a single volume, which he put on sale for one Venetian ducat.[160] He describes the edition in his prefatory letter as "duplex uno volumine dictionarium" (a double dictionary in a single volume), referring to its principal innovation: as well as a Greek–Latin lexicon, it also includes a long list of cross-references to enable the reader to find the Greek equivalents of Latin words. Manutius prefaces this part of the lexicon with a curious apology:

> Si quid tam in dictionario graeco quam in hoc indice frustra a te quaesitum fuerit, quia videlicet plurima desint, id aequo animo ferre debes; tum quia multo plures res esse quam vocabula non es nescius, tum etiam quoniam infinitas prope graecas dictiones in unum cogere est cuivis magis arduum quam vitium nomina recensere Virgilio fuerit.[161]
>
> [If there is anything in the Greek dictionary or in this index that you look for and cannot find—for there are many omissions—please do not be annoyed. For you know that there are many more things than words, and because to gather the near-infinite number of Greek words together in one volume is harder for anyone to accomplish than it was for Vergil to list the names of the vines.]

He goes on to quote Vergil's lines from the *Georgics* about counting the Libyan sands or the Ionian waves.[162] The Latin–Greek portion of this dictionary is not convenient to use. Beside each Latin word it lists the folio and line number where the Greek equivalent may be found. Moreover, the reader is instructed to number the folios by hand so that these cross-references can be used. Antonio Codro Urceo bought a copy of this Aldine lexicon of 1497, as he notes in a letter dated April 15, 1498. In this letter, he continues,

Vocabularium mihi ab Aldo missum vendidi statim, cum vidissem illud nihil ad meum. Tabula enim illa quae est in ultima parte libri derideretur a doctis viris. Eodem enim labore quo factum est charta prima vel secunda vel tertia potuisset scribi dictio illa graeca quae illo numero queritur. Differentias vocabulorum similium, vel pene similium, iam videram in libro qui erat Alexandri Strociae, et in meo notaveram.[163]

[I immediately sold the dictionary that Aldus sent me when I saw that it had nothing of interest to me. The index that is at the end of the book is mocked by learned men, for the same effort that recorded the first, second, or third page could as easily have supplied the Greek word that is sought in that place. The *Differences of like* (or nearly like) *words* I had already seen in a book of Alessandro Strozzi and copied into my book.]

At least this method of inverting the Greek–Latin dictionary produced an internal consistency within the dictionary, rather than a separate text that could, over time, diverge from its other half. It also effectively ended the life of the shorter Latin–Greek *vocabulista*, which was not printed again.

A dictionary printed in Ferrara in 1510 was the first to remedy this problem by printing the Greek words beside the Latin, but it did not do much to expand the scope of its Aldine exemplar.[164] It does have some revisions and additions that are indicated to the reader by marginal signs.[165] A dictionary published by Froben in Basle in 1524 omitted the Latin–Greek lexicon altogether and included a preface by Erasmus explaining the decision to the reader. He wrote that this section of the dictionary was a useless burden on the volume: "Nec tamen huius ullum usum video, nisi si quis meditetur graece scribere. Atqui ea facultas ex autoribus petenda est, quae ex dictionariis infeliciter peteretur"[166] (And yet I do not see any use for this, unless someone is thinking of writing in Greek. And that ability, which might be unhappily sought in dictionaries, should really be sought in the Greek authors). Erasmus was no doubt right to think that the desire to write Greek was unusual: he himself wrote very little Greek despite his command of the language. He goes on to record a conversation he once had with Aldus about the rationale behind the Latin–Greek section of the Aldine lexicon: "Aldus ipse quondam a me rogatus quur indice tam operoso pariter et odioso duxisset onerandum esse codicem, nihil aliud respondit quam hac difficultate deterritos fuisse aeditionis aemulos"[167] (I once asked Aldus himself why he thought that the book should be burdened with such an elaborate and annoying index. His only reply was that those who wanted to copy his edition had been put off by this very difficulty). This does sound like the sort of thing Aldus might say, and it might even be true. Unless the later printer preserved the pagination of the Aldine exemplar exactly, the index would have to be recompiled from scratch. A dictionary printed in Modena between 1499 and 1500 used a similar technique to provide a Latin–Greek index to the main Greek–Latin dictionary.[168]

Another innovation of the Aldine dictionary was to include a handful of brief lexical works after the dictionary. Aldus printed a work, which he attributed to Cyril, on words whose meanings change according to their accentuation.[169] This addition, together with the other supplements to the Aldine edition, were reprinted in Tricaelius's dictionary in Ferrara in 1510. This short work of pseudo-Cyril occasioned a comment from Pontico Virunio: "Cyrillum Aldus Baptizavit, cum non sit, de quo in vocabulariis nostris graecis multa scripsimus"[170] (Aldus baptized the work as Cyril's, although it may not be his. I have written a great deal on Cyril in my Greek vocabularies). Aldus printed another work for the first time, one attributed to the grammarian

Ammonius on distinctions between easily confused words.[171] The Aldine dictionary also included a brief account of military vocabulary and a couple of pages on the various meanings of ως and η. These lexical appendices became a matter of some rivalry in the second decade of the sixteenth century between the two great Greek presses of Basle and Paris. To explore this rivalry in detail, we must look at the first Greek dictionary printed in Northern Europe.

The production of the dictionary in 1512 seems to have severely stretched the resources of Gilles de Gourmont's Greek press in Paris. It was edited by Girolamo Aleandro, who wrote the preface on behalf of his editorial team to excuse the numerous printer's errors:

> Qui omnes oratum te velint, lector aequissime, ne istas impressorias labes sibi adscribas, quod te facturum non ambigerent, si quam misera sit in hac urbe graecae impressionis conditio cognosceres, quando, praeter impolitiam, tam parvo etiam numero characteres invenias, ut (quod mercatorum vel negligentia, vel avaritia facit) non solum unam alteramve literam inter cudendum aliquando omittere, sed et totum opus plusculos dies intermittere necesse fuerit.[172]
>
> [They all ask, most just reader, that you do not ascribe these printer's errors to them. Nor would they imagine that you would do so if you knew the wretched state of Greek printing in this city: since, besides a lack of skill, you can find so little Greek type (either through the negligence or the greed of the merchants) that it was not only necessary during printing to leave out the odd letter, but it was even necessary to stop work entirely for several days.]

Aleandro had come from the well-equipped printing house of Aldus Manutius in 1508, so his growing exasperation with conditions in Paris is understandable.[173] Since he had started to print Greek in 1507, Gourmont had been using a Greek font that had the accents and breathings cast separately from the letters. While this reduced the amount of type that the printer needed to buy, it created some practical difficulties in preparing the text. The first problem was scholarly: on the printed page, the relationship between the Greek letters and the accents they supported could appear tenuous. The second problem was economic: such a font reduced the number of lines that could be printed on each page. Aleandro had already apologized for this font to his readers in 1509.[174] By 1512, as the press began to look to bigger projects, it was becoming increasingly unsatisfactory. The bulk of the new dictionary was printed with this first font. This included the Greek–Latin dictionary, the lexical appendix of pseudo-Cyril, the brief word lists derived from Gaza's translations of Aristotle's works on animals and Theophrastus's works on plants, and the additional words adopted from the Ferrara dictionary of 1510. By the time these had all been printed, the new Greek font was ready, and it was used to print the remaining works: Ammonius's *De adfinium vocabulorum differentia*, the account of military terminology, and the meanings of ως and η. The Greek–Latin lexicon had been foliated and given line numbers down the center of the page between the two columns of text. This allowed the final element of the dictionary, a Latin–Greek lexicon, to supply cross-references to the more developed entries of the first lexicon after the simple Greek rendering. Aleandro's preface welcomes the new Greek type: "Sed iam omnia haec in melius rediguntur. Nam et accentus non ut antea temporarii literis perpetuo adhaerent et furtivae notae quotidie exscalpuntur"[175] (But now all these matters are improved. For, unlike before, the changing accents are now permanently joined to the letters, and the new type is being produced daily). The first dated use of Gourmont's new Greek font was in the edition of Chrysoloras, which received its colophon in May or July 1512.[176] The dictionary was completed in December of that year. To judge from the two states in which the title and final pages of the Paris dictionary are found, the edition was divided for sale between two shops in Paris.

Apart from the limited dictionary attached to the fifth volume of the Complutensian Polyglot Bible in 1515, no new bilingual dictionary was printed in Europe until Valentine Curio printed his dictionary in Basle in 1519. Froben had been meditating a lexicon since at least 1518 and had attempted to enlist Erasmus's help in the project. In October of that year, Erasmus suggested that Froben look to Johann Cuno's additions to the dictionary of Bruno Amorbach.[177] The title of this first Basle dictionary boasted of its improvements on the Ferrara dictionary of 1510. This edition led to something of a competition between the printers of Basle and Paris, partly provoked by the disparaging remarks of the editor of the Basle dictionary, Curio. In his preface, he wrote, "Lexicon hoc . . . dedimus, adauctum et illustratum locis ferme ter mille, aut forte pluribus, ultra Ferrariensem aeditionem, atque etiam Parrhisianam, quae tamen huius videtur simia, ut illa est Aldinae"[178] (We have published this lexicon, which is enlarged and clarified in three thousand places, maybe more, beyond the Ferrara edition and even the Paris edition, which, however, seems to have aped the Ferrara edition, just as that edition aped the Aldine). Curio marks his additions with inverted commas and his clarifications with asterisks. He also says that he has removed other material from the earlier dictionaries: "Resectae sunt historiae καὶ τῆς φύσεως ἐξηγήσεις, et alia eius generis taedia, quae intempestiva lectionis ostentatio ceu remoram infulcivit"[179] (I have cut the histories and the explanations of nature and other wearisome matters of this sort, inappropriately ostentatious material that had attached itself to the book like a sucking fish to a ship). This comment seems to refer to the additional matter printed with the Ferrara and Paris editions and to the appendices of the Paris edition that were derived from Gaza's translations of the natural works of Aristotle and Theophrastus.

This challenge did not pass unremarked by the Paris press, and the title of the next Parisian dictionary of 1521, printed by Petrus Vidovaeus, is also provocative: *Dictionarium graecum innumeris locis auctum ac locupletatum . . . cui vel assurgere, vel cedere iure debeant dictionaria alia omnia alicubi antehac excusa. . . .* (A Greek dictionary, expanded and enriched in countless places . . . to which all other dictionaries previously printed must properly either aspire or yield . . .). This dictionary went one better than Curio by including a short work of John Philoponus on the Greek dialects. As the title of the Paris edition has it, *Ioannis Grammatici libellus de differentiis linguarum, adulescentibus graecae linguae candidatis non utilis modo sed etiam necessarius, cum nullo alio lexico impressus* (The short work of John the Grammarian on the dialects, a work not only useful but necessary to young students of Greek, and not printed in any other dictionary). It was true that this work had not been printed in any other dictionary, but it had been printed twice by Aldus: in the *Thesaurus cornucopiae* of 1496 and again with the third Aldine Lascaris of 1512.[180] In a short postscript, Vidovaeus takes issue with Curio's edition:

> Hoc monendus es, paucula quidem nos adiecisse praeter aeditionem Basiliensem, quae qualis fuerit non profero, sed omnia, praesertim quae recens adiecta erant, reposuisse ex Hesychii,

Suidae, aliorum lectione, ut nesciam utri maiorem gratiam mereantur, qui vetera restituunt, an qui nova primi comminiscuntur.[181]

[You should know that I have added some small items not included in the Basle edition. Regarding that edition, I do not offer an opinion, but all its contents, especially those that were newly added, were repeated from Hesychius, Suidas, and others; so that I do not know who deserves more thanks, those who restored the old works or those who first came up with new things.]

The response from Curio in Basle emerged in a new dictionary of 1522, whose title ran, *Lexicon graecum iam secundum plus trium millium dictionum auctario locupletatum; ad hoc multis ante parum latine redditis elegantius ac magis apposite interpretatis . . .* (The second Greek lexicon, enriched by the addition of more than three thousand words. Moreover, many words previously glossed in a manner that was hardly Latin have now been translated with elegance and propriety . . .). It included a number of brief lexical works that had not appeared in the Paris edition: to the work of Joannes on the dialects, Curio now added Eustathius and Gregory of Corinth on the same subject and also included the brief works attributed to Herodian, Joannes, and Choeroboscos on enclitics. These, the title page noted, were *omnia iam recens adiecta* (all recently added), possibly a deliberate echo of Vidovaeus's words of the previous year. Curio also repeated some of his insulting language of 1519 when he referred in his preface to the "Parisienses sedulae nostrae industriae simiae" (Parisian apes of our careful labor). Curio acknowledges the contribution to this dictionary made by an unnamed Greek scholar. This scholar, he notes pointedly, supplied words that were not even in the Suda or Hesychius.

The reply of Paris emerged the following year from Gourmont's press, and this time, the dictionary went so far as to name its rival on its title page: *Lexicon graecum, caeteris omnibus aut in Italia, aut Gallia Germaniave antehac excusis multo locupletius, utpote supra ter mille additiones Basiliensi Lexico anno MDXII apud Curionem impresso adiectas, amplius quinque recentiorum additionum milibus auctum* (A Greek lexicon, much richer than all others printed before in Italy, France, or Germany, inasmuch as it has been expanded by five thousand additions over and above the three thousand additions made to the lexicon printed in Basle in 1522). These additions are all marked in the margin, much as they had been by Curio in 1519. To prove this edition's independence from the previous Basle edition, or perhaps to show that many of the Basle additions were trivial, another section has been added: "Additiones quae iam in Germania editae fuerunt" (Additions that have already been published in Germany). This dictionary has no fewer than six dedicatory letters, but no reference is made to the Basle edition. Instead, at the end of the volume, Gourmont prints his request, addressed to the provost of Paris, for some legal protection for his book. The request stresses the labors of correction, and the additional words added:

Et pource que s'il estoit permis a tous imprimeurs et librairies imprimer et vendre ledict livre avec lesdictes additions, ledict suppliant seroit en dangier de perdre ses fraiz et vacations. Ce consideré, vous plaise donner privilege audict suppliant, que nul aultre puisse imprimer ne vendre ledict livre avec lesdictes additions . . . sans le congé et permission dudict suppliant, sur peine de confiscation dudict livre et d'amende envers le Roy.

[And since if all printers and booksellers were allowed to print and sell the aforesaid book with the aforesaid additions, the aforesaid supplicant would be in danger of losing his money and time. This considered, may it please you to grant a privilege to the aforesaid supplicant that no one else may print or sell the aforesaid book with the aforesaid additions . . . without the leave and permission of the aforesaid supplicant, on pain of confiscation of the aforesaid book and compensation for the king.]

Finally, Gourmont prints the note that granted this request for a privilege of three years.

The next dictionary was printed in Basle in 1524, but Curio's name is not connected with it. Instead Erasmus, who acknowledges that his editorial role in the dictionary has been limited, makes an attempt to draw a line under the quarrel in his preface. He deprecates those who expand the dictionaries with words such as "'Ααρών. nomen proprium"; he wishes that Guillaume Budé, the great French scholar, had been able to contribute, and he acknowledges a debt to the editor of the previous Paris dictionary, Guillaume du Main.[182] This time, the Basle dictionary had been revised and expanded by the Dutchman Jacobus Ceratinus. Curio resurfaces as editor of the next Basle dictionary in 1525, but this time, he has nothing to say about Parisian dictionaries. A truce had broken out.

This rivalry resulted in the printing of a remarkable number of dictionaries. In the five years between 1519 and 1525, there were six substantial dictionaries printed in Basle and Paris and two more in Venice in 1524 and 1525. These large, expensive books must have been selling rapidly in order to justify such a rate of printing. With such a rich market at stake, perhaps it is not surprising that things became a little heated. In the middle of this great outpouring, the most scholarly lexicon of the period was very nearly buried. Guarino of Favera produced his own Greek-only dictionary in 1523. This work was compiled with great industry and skill using the full resources of the Vatican Library.[183] Its virtues warranted a reprint in Basle in 1538, one in Venice in 1712, and another in the same city as late as 1801, by which date its contemporaries had long been obsolete.[184] In the 1520s, however, most printers competed to satisfy a more lucrative market, producing Greek–Latin lexica for the students of the expanding schools of Northern Europe.

Chapter 3

Student Texts

It seems to have been usual for Greek students to spend the first part of their studies learning grammar alone, before moving on to a Greek author. In 1459, in his educational treatise *De ordine docendi et studendi*, Battista Guarino included in this work some guidelines for teachers of Greek. He sees a preliminary stage at which students would learn the basics of Greek grammar. Only when they had mastered these elements of the language would they be introduced to Greek authors: "Paulatim deinde ad scriptores progredientur, et ad eos primo qui in soluta oratione faciliores; ne, dum sententiarum pondere laborare coguntur, id quod in principiis maxime desideramus, regularum quas didicerunt confirmationem omittant. Ut igitur quisquam durissimus erit, ita postremus eis tradatur"[1] (Then gradually they proceed to the authors, and first to the more straightforward prose writers, so that they do not neglect to reinforce the rules that they have learned (which is what, in the beginning, we chiefly desire) because they are compelled to labor over weighty sentences. And so the hardest authors will be given to them last.) In Padua in 1463, Hartmann Schedel noted that Demetrius Chalcondyles first taught Chrysoloras and then Hesiod. After the initial phase of learning the elements of the grammar, the study of a specific text could begin.

The process of lecturing on a Greek text was one that continually recalled and reinforced the elements of the language. Girolamo Amaseo describes how Guarino of Favera expounded Greek texts to his class of sixteen students in Florence in 1493:

> Primo sententiam lectionis paucis et dilucide eleganterque colligit; post interpretationem primam, verborum et nominum inflexionem, si duriuscula est, reperit; etimologiam non tacet et figuras reliquas. Secundo eam ipsam lectionem percurrit et, ne quae prius dixerat obliviscamur, confirmat, examinatque nos omnes et, post ipsam statim lectionem, aliquis e numero nostro eam exponit. Cogimur declinare, nec displicet: omnia enim studia suam habent infanciam.[2]
>
> [First, he elegantly and lucidly expresses the meaning of the text in a few words. After the first translation, if the case of the verbs and nouns is a little difficult, he clarifies it. He does not neglect etymology or the other figures of speech. Second, he goes though the same text and, so that we do not forget what he has just said, he reinforces it, examines us all, and immediately after the reading of the text, one of us expounds it. We are required to decline the nouns, and this is not a chore: every study has its infancy.]

First was Guarino's translation of the text. In the exposition of the etymologies and the figures he is probably demonstrating the links between Greek and

Latin. Guarino's *prima interpretatio* may be compared with Philip Melanchthon's practice some years later. In 1527, in the preface to a Latin–Greek edition of Demosthenes, Melanchthon wrote, "Scis mihi, cum graecum autorem paulo obscuriorem scholae nostrae interpretor, morem esse simul convertendi eum in latinum sermonem, ut perpetuam sententiam propius conspectam graecae linguae tyrones citius adsequantur"[3] (You know that, when I lecture on one of the more difficult Greek authors to our school, my habit is to translate it into Latin at the same time, so that beginners in Greek might more quickly understand the continuous meaning of the text that is studied closely). In the following pages, I shall often say that a teacher "lectured" on a Greek text. It is something like this procedure that I understand by the word.

This chapter surveys the fortunes of the Greek authors regularly used in the classrooms of the period. It indicates which authors, and which parts of their work, were most often used with students. This survey does not include every Greek author ever used to learn Greek in the period: any available Greek author could potentially have been used to learn Greek, and many that are not detailed here were certainly used by some students somewhere. However, it does include all those texts that were regularly used in the classroom. I have attempted to place them in the order in which the prospective student was likely to have met them and in accordance with the frequency with which they were used in the classroom. This sequence should not, of course, be taken too seriously.

Elementary Pamphlets

Before considering the Greek authors used by students, it is as well to look first at the most common variety of printed Greek text. Explanations of the Greek alphabet and the most common ligatures were often prefaces to manuscript copies of grammars. However, it was the advent of printing that caused slender introductory pamphlets to become a phenomenon in their own right. In their time, these pamphlets were the cheapest and most common of all Greek texts, but today they are very rare. They were always ephemeral productions: because they could be so cheaply replaced, they were often discarded, and because they were too slender to warrant binding, they were far more likely to disintegrate with use. Most of those that have come down to us owe their survival to the fact that they were bound with more substantial works. In all probability, a number of editions of these early Greek pamphlets are lost: when entire editions of a Greek grammar are represented today by only a single copy, it is reasonable to suppose that more fragile products of the Greek presses have disappeared altogether. The confusions caused by this rarity are compounded by the uncertain status of many of the pamphlets that have survived. Some of these survivors, now found bound with elementary grammars from the same press, also circulated separately. Some that never circulated separately have subsequently been given their own bindings by shrewd booksellers and zealous librarians. It is hoped that the first appendix to the present book will do something to clarify this confusion.

We may distinguish three types of text found in these student pamphlets. Some were little more than alphabets that illustrated the most common ligatures and provided a few notes on pronunciation; some more ambitious products provided tables of the declensions of the nouns and the conjugations of the verbs; and some provided anthologies of short first-reading texts. These slender volumes were the cheapest books among the printer's stock. As such, they might be used to whet the appetites of potential customers for the more substantial and more expensive products of a single press. A pamphlet printed by Aldus Manutius in 1497, the *Brevissima introductio* to Greek letters, seems to have been prepared as a sample of the quality of the products of the press. It contains notes on the alphabet and a collection of prayers. In 1497, Aldus responded to a letter of Conrad Celtis with a gift of this short work.[4]

The earliest surviving pamphlet, printed in Milan about 1480, had a very specific role to play. It appears to have been envisaged as a supplement to the Greek–Latin lexicon printed by the same press perhaps two years earlier. Besides the Greek alphabet and diphthongs, its eight leaves have details of the augmentation and reduplication of Greek verbs, a work attributed to Sassuolo da Prato.[5] Although there is nothing here that is not available in contemporary grammars, it did enable the novice to use the lexicon to look up the Greek verbs he found in his texts. It extended the potential readership of the lexicon to those who had not mastered the grammar.

Printers in Germany used pamphlets to capitalize on contemporary enthusiasm for Greek, despite having only a small stock of Greek type. Pamphlets printed in Erfurt in 1501, the first Greek works printed in Germany, used a font that does not have accents, breathings, or iota subscripts.[6] The abbreviations and ligatures that they illustrate have been carved from a woodblock. We have seen that when Celtis sent Aldus his Greek grammar and vocabularies for printing in 1504, he asked him to add the accents to his text: "Quia in exemplari et aliis grecis codicibus quoscumque in Germania et Gallia reperi appositos non vidi sed nudas dictiones"[7] (Since in my exemplar and in all the other Greek manuscripts I have found in Germany and France, I have seen only bare letters without the accents added). The early German printers worked hard to make a small quantity of Greek type go a long way. The shortest surviving German pamphlet, also printed in Erfurt, contains only four leaves. The Greek font used has no ligatures, accents, breathings, or iota subscripts, but it compensates for the inadequacy of its type by the great care with which it is produced. Again, the abbreviations and ligatures are printed from a woodcut, and it is handsomely printed throughout in red and black with a full-page woodcut on the final page. We have seen that Gourmont's first Greek font of 1507 had the accents cast separately, a situation that continued until 1512.[8] In some parts of Germany the accents and breathings did not reach the letters until much later. A pamphlet of Greek prayers printed in Wittenberg in 1511, for example, does not have them.[9] When Richard Croke arrived in Leipzig in 1515, Valentine Schumann did not have any accented type for Croke's edition of Ausonius in October, nor for the Greek quotations in his *Encomium* printed in December. Schumann seems to have acquired the full font over the following months: he used it to print Croke's *Tables* in 1516.[10]

After the Milanese pamphlet of 1480, the next recorded pamphlet is also the first Greek text printed in Northern Europe.[11] Its eighteen leaves contain the entire conjugation of the verb τύπτω and nothing else. The full extent of the Greek verb, so baldly presented, must have been rather daunting to new students, although the prestige of the language probably benefited from perceptions of its difficulty. It is of interest because, while an exposition of the Greek alphabet or a collection of prayers may—and often did—stand alone, this pamphlet required other grammatical material to make it worthwhile. It implies the existence of a broader course of Greek studies. A few other coincidences are also suggestive. The printer of the pamphlet, Richard Paffraet, knew both Rudolf Agricola and his student, Alexander Hegius.[12] Hegius, of course, was the headmaster of Erasmus's school in Deventer. Although it was probably issued after Erasmus left Deventer in 1484, he did not move too far away, and he may well have acquired a copy: Erasmus's first Greek words appear in a letter of his dated to about 1489. Whatever this larger course might have been, we know nothing of it.

On February 28, 1495, the new Greek press of Aldus Manutius put the colophon on what was very likely its first Greek edition, the grammar of Constantine Lascaris. Just over a week later, on March 8, 1495, a collection of student texts in Greek and Latin was appended to this edition. This collection, the so-called Aldine Appendix, was to influence the shape of Greek studies for decades to come. It was the most widely distributed and most frequently reprinted student anthology of Greek texts. Despite the separate colophons, there is no evidence that the two works were intended to circulate separately.[13] This influential pamphlet contains a Greek alphabet and the diphthongs; it explains all the ligatures of the Aldine Greek font; it prints the Lord's Prayer, two prayers to the Virgin, the Creed, the prologue to John's Gospel, the *Aurea verba* attributed to Pythagoras, and the verses attributed to Phocylides, all alongside a literal Latin translation. The influence of the Greek font of the Aldine Press on subsequent Greek typography ensured that Aldus's presentation of the Greek ligatures would remain relevant for a very long time.

The Appendix was reprinted by the Aldine Press with subsequent editions of Lascaris and with Aldus's Latin grammar in 1501, 1502, 1508, 1512, 1514, and 1523.[14] At least two abbreviations of the Appendix were issued by the press: the first, already noticed, in 1497, and another in 1526.[15] It was reproduced many times in various forms by northern presses. Some of its material appeared in the Erfurt pamphlets of 1501 to 1505.[16] The Aldine text of 1497 was reprinted in Siena in 1505, the only Greek book printed in the city before 1530.[17] Much of it was reprinted with the Ferrara Lascaris of 1510.[18] It was repeated in the Paris copy of Aldus's Latin grammar in 1513,[19] and a series of pamphlets printed by Gourmont in Paris from about that date followed the format of printing notes on Greek orthography with Greek prayers. By 1530, many thousands of copies had been printed.

Another brief but popular work was composed by Girolamo Aleandro to supplement his lectures on Gaza in Paris.[20] As well as the alphabet, this also contained his own notes on pronunciation, a matter that is not treated in Gaza's first book. This procedure allowed Aleandro to isolate debates about the pronunciation of Greek from the grammar proper. The availability of such introductions to the first elements of orthography and pronunciation was assumed by Philip Melanchthon in his grammatical work. The Aldine Appendix had been printed in Tübingen in July 1512, and was likely to have been within the means of the fifteen-year-old Melanchthon when he arrived there in September.[21] Some years later, in his grammar of 1518, he ran briefly through the Greek alphabet and referred his readers to a similar pamphlet recently printed by Thomas Anshelm.[22] Over the following years, pamphlets of this sort proliferated, and by 1522 Melanchthon had replaced his specific notice with a general one: "Reliquae ad cognoscendas literas pertinent, require ex elementalibus libellis, qui iam ubique manibus puerorum teruntur"[23] (For the remaining things that are relevant to the letters, look in the elementary pamphlets, which are found everywhere thumbed by schoolboys). Melanchthon's grammar avoids all discussion of Greek pronunciation, and he used the pamphlets as a convenient way of sidestepping a debate that was of little relevance for beginners and that was becoming increasingly controversial.

THE GREEK SCRIPTURES

The contents of many of the elementary pamphlets illustrate a well-established teaching strategy. The language was approached through Greek texts that the pupils already knew by heart in their Latin translations: the Greek Scriptures and the liturgy. Enea Silvio Piccolomini wrote in a work addressed to the king of Bohemia: "Credimus te instructum esse ut Christianum decet, orationem scire dominicam, salutationem beatae virginis, Iohannis evangelium, symbolum fidei, collectas quoque plures, quae sint mortis peccata, quae sancti spiritus dona, quae magni praecepta dei, quae opera misericordiae..."[24] (We trust that you have been instructed as befits a Christian, that you know the Lord's prayer, the Hail Mary, the Gospel of John, the Creed, also several collects, the names of the mortal sins, the gifts of the Holy Spirit, the Ten Commandments, the Works of Mercy...). The Greek versions of many of these texts were regularly presented to students of the language. They had several advantages. The meaning of the Greek text was already familiar, and so the student could concentrate on its grammar. They could also pick up basic vocabulary quickly without needing to refer to a lexicon.

The use of Greek prayers as first readers has a long history. Roger Bacon in his grammar had used the Lord's Prayer, Hail Mary, Creed, Magnificat, and the Songs of Symeon and Zachariah as his first Greek texts.[25] The *Pater noster* and the *Ave Maria* were regularly appended to Chrysoloras's grammar in both its manuscript and printed forms. George Hermonymus prepared three copies of Chrysostom's Liturgy and four manuscripts of various Greek prayers for his students.[26] The first volume of the Aldine Christian poets included a Christian Homeric cento. The Greek text of this cento was provided with an interleaved Latin translation and in the center of the five gatherings that make up the work is another Greek–Latin text: "Ad annunciationem purissimae Dei genetricis."[27] It relates and magnifies the events of the Nativity and was apparently composed for the occasion. In the second volume of the Christian Poets, the Greek authors are similarly provided with a Latin version. The center pages of these four gatherings contain a collection of prayers in Greek and Latin. It seems that these Aldine prayers are the first Greek texts since antiquity to be composed as exercises for Western students.

A further advantage of the Greek Scriptures for the student was that they were widely available in a literal Latin translation. Ambrogio Traversari had already recommended this approach to the Greek language in his letter to Francesco Coppola.[28] According to Battista Guarino,

> Inveniuntur nonnunquam, praesertim in sacris libris, non nulli graece latineque exscripti ita ut ne una quidem syllaba interpretationis versiculus aut maior aut minor sit. Ii ad hanc rem sic optime conducent, ut quosdam ego cognoverim qui hac ratione ad maximam huius linguae noticiam absque praeceptore ullo pervenerint.[29]
>
> [Sometimes some books, particularly sacred books, are found written out in Greek and Latin in such a way that a verse of the translation is not longer or shorter than the original by even one syllable. These books serve this purpose so well that I have known some who have attained great knowledge of this language by this method without any teacher at all.]

At Bologna in 1459 Antonius Bentivolus wrote to Andrea Contrario to say that he needed Cicero, Homer, and a Greek Psalter for his studies.[30] In England, sometime before 1465, John Farley borrowed from the Grey Friars in Oxford a Greek manuscript of the Psalter that had once belonged to Robert Grosseteste. Transliterations in the margins of this manuscript suggest that he had compared it with a Latin Psalter in an attempt to teach himself some Greek.[31] In Germany, in 1495, the abbot Johannes Trithemius was using a Greek Psalter in his studies.[32] The Psalter was printed in Greek for the first time in Milan in 1481, a text that had a Latin version printed alongside.[33] The editor, Giovanni Crastoni, whose lexicon was discussed above, provided his own Latin translation of the Greek text. Crastoni anticipated that his edition would be used by students of the Greek language. In his preface, he points out that Vergil used Grecisms in his poetry, and he continues, "Feci hoc et ipse in hoc psalterio, non tamen ut graecis schematis uterer, sed ut graece discere volentibus morem gererem, verbum verbo reddidi"[34] (I have done this myself in this Psalter; but I have rendered word for word, not so that I might use Greek constructions, but so that I might oblige those wanting to learn Greek). Where his translation differs from the traditional texts he reproduces the Greek idiom closely in his version, and he follows even the word order of the Greek text. Despite the challenge to the accuracy of the Vulgate translation thrown down in his preface, Crastoni's version of the Psalter, the first new translation of any part of the Scriptures to be printed, seems to have gone unremarked because it was clearly a tool for the student of Greek rather than the student of theology.

By 1494, the Psalter had been printed in Greek three times, but the Greek New Testament was not printed until twenty years later in 1514.[35] The New Testament did, however, play its part in the teaching of Greek. Palla Strozzi proudly records that his fine manuscript of the Gospels in Greek once belonged to his teacher, Manuel Chrysoloras.[36] Giovanni Tortelli used the Greek Gospels in conjunction with the Vulgate translation in his Greek studies in Constantinople between 1435 and 1437.[37] Vittorino da Feltre acquired the Gospels in Greek for Cecilia Gonzaga when she was just seven years old.[38] Joannes Regiomontanus copied the New Testament as an exercise in the Greek language.[39] In France, Hermonymus produced only one copy of the Psalter for his students but no fewer than ten manuscripts of portions of the New Testament.[40] In England, in the last decades of the fifteenth century, Joannes Serbopoulos made four New Testament manuscripts.[41] In 1501, while learning Greek, Erasmus was looking for Greek texts of the Psalms and the Gospels.[42] The first edition of the New Testament in Greek, the Complutensian, comes equipped with a very brief introduction to Greek and a substantial Greek–Latin lexicon. Students did not end their Greek studies with the Scriptures; they began with them. That they were familiar texts was a great practical advantage, but they were also studied because they were precisely the sort of Greek most students wanted to know.

GREEK TRANSLATIONS OF LATIN TEXTS

If *collatio* of Greek texts with their Latin translations enabled the student to acquire vocabulary and basic syntax, then *ad verbum* Greek translations of Latin texts were potentially just as useful as Latin ones of Greek texts. Ambrogio Traversari saw this, and having promised to provide Greek instruction for Cardinal Cesarini, he made attempts to acquire a Greek–Latin Boethius for Cesarini's use.[43] Greeks could also make use of this strategy with Latin translations: a manuscript page survives that shows Bessarion using Cicero's translation of Plato's *Timaeus* to learn Latin.[44]

One Greek translation was certainly used by students of Greek. Theodore Gaza produced a version of Cicero's *De senectute*, a work that was often introduced to young Latin scholars in the original language.[45] Adolf Occo owned a copy of Gaza's version, George Hermonymus made at least two copies of it, and Constantine Lascaris made a further copy of it in Messina.[46] The Greek translation of *De senectute* was read and annotated by Pier Candido Decembrio and by Michael Marullus.[47] The particular significance of *De senectute* for students of Greek may lie in the fact that it contained Cicero's rendering of a passage from Xenophon's *Cyropaedia*.[48] Here, they could see how the great orator himself went about the task of translation.

Occo also owned a copy of another, more popular, Greek translation in his own hand.[49] Students of Latin would have come across the so-called *Disticha Catonis* as part of their elementary Latin instruction. As with the Greek Scriptures, it was their prior familiarity with the text that made Maximus Planudes's Greek version useful to beginners.[50] Gaza and Poliziano owned a manuscript of this version of the *Distichs*.[51] Hermonymus copied at least three manuscripts of the *Distichs*, one of which was owned by Guillaume Budé.[52] This Greek version was first printed in the Aldine Theocritus of 1496, a volume that also contained a collection of relatively simple Greek poetry for advancing students.[53] Thereafter, Planudes' text was reprinted many times. It was printed in Paris in 1512 as part of Aleandro's collection of student texts, *Gnomologia*; it was printed in Florence in 1515 as a supplement to the Juntine edition of Chrysoloras's grammar; it was printed in Strasbourg in 1515 in a collection of student texts.[54] By the late summer of 1514, it had been equipped with a slight commentary by Erasmus, and in this form the bilingual text was reprinted many times alongside a collection of elementary texts, which included the mimes attributed to Publilius Syrus and a Latin version of Isocrates' *Ad Demonicum*.[55] Greek translations, which had originally been made for the benefit of Byzantine students of the Latin language or to allow Greek scholars access to Latin thought, ultimately provided Western students of Greek with a number of their elementary texts.

THE *AUREA VERBA* AND PSEUDO-PHOCYLIDES

Many of the texts used by students will be familiar to modern students of classical literature, but two collections of didactic verse, staples of the Renaissance classroom, are less well known. The first and most popular collection, and one that students of Greek in the period could hardly avoid, was the so-called *Aurea verba*. These verses were usually attributed to Pythagoras, although an edition of the *Aurea verba* printed in Ferrara in 1510 assigns them to a Pythagorean, Philolaus of Croton.[56] The reason for this new attribution is not made clear, and both attributions look highly unlikely to modern eyes. This skepticism may have been alive in the fifteenth century, for when Constantine Lascaris composed his brief lives of Pythagoras and Philolaus, he made no mention of the ubiquitous *Aurea verba*.[57] The second collection of gnomic verses was nearly as popular in the same period. These verses were usually attributed to the Milesian Phocylides, whom the Suda places in the sixth century BC. Lascaris believed that the author of these verses was a contemporary of Theognis, but they are the work of a much later writer.[58] Pseudo-Phocylides seems to have been used with Latin students in southern Italy as early as the twelfth century: a tenth-century manuscript of the work has an interlinear Latin translation of that date.[59]

Both works were very widely used in fifteenth-century Italy, and they often appear together in the manuscripts. A modern student of the diffusion of these works lists over one hundred and fifty manuscripts of pseudo-Phocylides, of which fifty-eight are from the fifteenth century. She notices nearly two hundred manuscripts of the *Aurea verba*, of which seventy-nine are from the fifteenth century. Of these seventy-nine manuscripts, thirty-three also contain pseudo-Phocylides. Copies of both works are extant from the pens of many of the Greek scribes of the period: George Chrysococces, Joannes Scutariota, Michael Lygizos, Joannes Rhosos, Michael Apostolis, Antonio Damilas, Michael Souliardos, Petrus Hypselas, and Andreas Donos all made copies.[60] The most prominent native teachers of the language copied these collections of sententious verse: Joannes Argyropoulos copied the *Aurea verba*; Andronicus Callistus copied both collections; George Hermonymus made two copies of pseudo-Phocylides, one of which subsequently came into the hands of Guillaume Budé; Constantine Lascaris copied both collections; Demetrius Chalcondyles appended the *Aurea verba* to a copy of Chrysoloras's grammar that he had made; and Demetrius Moschus, around the end of the fifteenth century, copied both collections and added pseudo-Phocylides to a copy of Moschopoulos.[61]

Their Italian students also made numerous copies. Agostino Dati of Siena (d. 1478) is known to have translated the *Aurea verba* as an exercise.[62] In 1470, when he was about sixteen years old, Angelo Poliziano copied a portion of pseudo-Phocylides into a miscellany; Bartolomeo Zamberti made a copy in 1491 at the age of eighteen; Antonio Codro Urceo made two copies of both collections in the last years of the fifteenth century; Giorgio Valla copied pseudo-Phocylides; Francesco Vitali made a copy, apparently in Vicenza; and Adolf Occo had also made a copy before his death in 1503.[63] In Paris in 1512, Girolamo Aleandro announced his intention to lecture on a miscellany that included both collections.[64] In 1514, as a new Greek course based on Chrysoloras's grammar came off the presses in Alcalá, Juan Vergara became a fellow of Ximenes' college of San Ildefonso. In the same year, he made a copy of the *Aurea verba* with a Latin translation.[65] Since he was, at this date, an experienced Greek scholar, we may guess that his students benefited from this version in some way. The Latin version of Stefano Negri, first printed in Milan in 1521, may indicate the use of the work in his Greek teaching there.[66]

These collections were to students of Greek what the *Distichs of Cato* were to students of Latin. Their position among the elementary texts of the curriculum was firmly established by the Aldine Appendix of 1495. The Appendix was the *editio princeps* of the Greek text of both the *Aurea verba* and pseudo-Phocylides.[67] This handbook, discussed previously, supplied the student with literal prose translations of the texts. I know of twenty-nine Greek editions of the *Aurea verba*, and at least twenty-six editions of pseudo-Phocylides in Greek between 1495 and 1525. In this period, pseudo-Phocylides was never printed in Greek without the *Aurea verba*, and the latter were printed only once in Greek without pseudo-Phocylides. Almost all of these editions of the Greek text were printed alongside Latin versions.[68]

Their compression of ethical principles in memorable tags made them particularly appropriate for impressionable students, and both works inspired some interest beyond their use in Greek studies. An early Byzantine commentary on the *Aurea verba* by Hierocles was translated into Latin by Giovanni Aurispa around 1449 and dedicated to Pope Nicholas V in 1454.[69] Rinuccio Aretino's version of the *Aurea verba* seems to be the earliest we have, translated apparently in the early 1440s.[70] Bartolomeo Fonzio made another version, which he dedicated to the son of Pier Filippo Pandolfini in 1485. Fonzio characterizes his work as a morally improving text, not as an introduction to Greek.[71] Jacobus Questenberg made a parallel Greek–Latin presentation manuscript of the *Aurea verba*, apparently using his own translation, and dedicated it to Pope Alexander VI sometime between 1492 and 1502.[72] In contrast, pseudo-Phocylides inspired only one Latin treatment before 1530. The verse translation of Jacob Locher, completed around 1500, seems to have been made from the copy of the text attached to the first Aldine edition of Lascaris's grammar of 1495.[73] Locher had studied Greek under Celtis in Ingolstadt sometime between 1494 and 1497 and succeeded Celtis in Ingolstadt after his departure.[74]

Aesop

The medieval Latin curriculum retained some vestiges of the bilingual education of late antiquity. Some elements of this curriculum were adapted during the Renaissance to accommodate the new Greek learning. The use of Aesop's fables to teach Greek marks the revival of an ancient tradition. Quintilian had recommended that students of rhetoric should study composition by paraphrasing Aesop's fables.[75] A set of Latin fables attributed to Aesop were much used in the Middle Ages as elementary Latin reading texts. This Aesop had been so thoroughly Latinized that it was used to teach Latin grammar, and the fables, provided with an exegetical gloss, were one of the most widely used texts of the fifteenth and early sixteenth centuries. They were popular apprentice pieces, particularly for younger students of Greek, because their morality was orthodox and accessible and because Latin translations were widely available.

A number of scholars and students had provided the apparatus to enable Greek to be approached through Aesop. The fables appear to have been used at the school of Guarino Veronese, who even named his second son Esopo.[76] They also appear at the school of Vittorino da Feltre. Peter of Crete, a scribe known to have worked for Vittorino, made a Greek manuscript of Aesop.[77] Another manuscript from the 1430s has the fables as part of a student collection: it has a Latin–Greek lexicon of adverbs, the Greek letters, the verb εἰμί, the *Credo* and *Ave Maria*, the prologue to John's Gospel, and the Greek–Latin lexicon attributed to Cyril; it is followed by over two hundred fables of Aesop.[78] With the school of Guarino may be connected the versions of Lorenzo Valla, who translated thirty-three fables in Gaeta in 1438; and of Ermolao Barbaro the elder, whose version of thirty-three fables was dedicated to Ambrogio Traversari in 1422.[79] With Vittorino's school, two other early versions seem to be linked: that of Ognibene da Lonigo, who translated one hundred and twenty fables, probably in the 1420s; and of Gregorio Correr, who dedicated his version of fifty-nine fables between 1431 and 1433.[80] Rinuccio Aretino's version of one hundred fables was made in 1447, perhaps from a Greek manuscript he brought with him from the East in 1423.[81]

Three of these Latin translations—Ognibene's, Valla's, and Rinuccio's—reached print in the fifteenth century. Aesop was also among the first Greek texts to be printed. Bonaccorso Pisano printed his Greek Aesop alongside the *editio princeps* of the Latin translation of Rinuccio in Milan around 1478.[82] Bonaccorso's preface to Giovanni Francesco della Torre suggests that della Torre's children might find it a useful introduction to both Greek and Latin. The colophon to Bonaccorso's edition of Aesop returns, rather apologetically, to this readership: "Bonus Accursius Pisanus impressit, qui non doctorum hominum sed rudium ac puerorum gratia hunc laborem suscepit"[83] (Bonaccorso Pisano, who took up this task not for learned men but for the unpolished and for boys, printed this book). Poliziano is known to have used the Greek Aesop in his lessons with the young Piero de' Medici sometime between the summer of 1475 and May 1479.[84] Poliziano would, of course, have had no difficulty in laying his hands on a manuscript of Aesop during this period, but the appearance of Bonaccorso's edition was certainly very timely for Piero's education. It is probably Bonaccorso's edition that Bartolomeo Calco refers to in his letter to Giovanni Stefano da Castiglione of February 6, 1495. Calco, as we have seen, had signed the petition to appoint Constantine Lascaris to the chair of Greek in Milan in 1463, and Lascaris compiled his work on the Greek noun at his request.[85] Calco recommends the fables for their brevity and clarity.[86] This Aesop was reprinted in 1497 in Reggio, another edition emerged in Venice around 1498, while the Aldine edition of the Greek fabulists was issued in 1505.[87]

George Hermonymus seems once again to provide the essential link between the Italian schools of Greek and those of Northern Europe. We have seen that while Reuchlin was studying in Orléans in 1479, Hermonymus sent him a copy of Gaza's Greek grammar in his own hand, accompanied by a letter.[88] Reuchlin had obviously expressed an interest in one of Hermonymus's manuscripts. The Greek wrote back, "Fabulae quas in camera mea vidisti non sunt venales. Habeo tamen manu mea scriptas quae erunt ad beneplacitum tuum"[89] (The fables that you saw in my room are not for sale. However, I have some written in my own hand that are at your disposal). These fables, surely Aesop's, were probably for use with Reuchlin's students in Orléans. Whatever became of this request, by the 1490s, Aesop had certainly reached Germany. Joannes Trithemius made a copy in 1496 of the Greek–Latin text from Bonaccorso's edition as part of his efforts to learn Greek.[90] Adolf Occo was in possession of a Greek manuscript of Aesop at his death in 1503.[91] Matthias Theodoricus, perhaps a pupil of Reuchlin's, included Aesop among a number of elementary texts he copied in 1503 and 1504.[92]

Homer

In the first century, Quintilian had recommended that Greek studies begin with Homer, although by the fourth century, the young Saint Augustine found that the obligation to read Homer bred in him an antipathy to Greek studies.[93] In Quintilian's day, Latin readers might have read the translations of Homer made by Livius Andronicus, by Gnaeus Matius, by Attius Labeo, and by the emperor Claudius's freedman, Polybius; or they might have turned to the *Ilias latina*, an uneven summary of the *Iliad* in just over a thousand hexameters.[94] While the versions of Matius, Labeo, and Polybius have disappeared, the *Ilias latina* survived and multiplied in the Middle Ages to supply the Latin West with much of what it knew of the great poet. Often it was attributed to one Pindar of Thebes and presented as a translation; sometimes it was claimed that this Pindar had composed it for his son's education.[95] The short and simple *Ilias latina* had found its own small place in the Latin curriculum and still retained it in the fifteenth century. Like Aesop, on his return to the West, the Greek Homer could occupy a niche prepared for him by medieval Latin teachers.

In the fourteenth century, Homer was the first literary Greek text to attract serious attention. Our history of the poems in Western Europe begins in January 1354, when Petrarch was presented with a Greek codex of the *Iliad* in Milan.[96] The outlines of this story are well known. Between about 1358 and 1362, Leonzio Pilato, Petrarch's tutor, had already begun to make a Latin version of the *Iliad*. Petrarch and Boccaccio persuaded him to complete his translation of the *Iliad* and make a version of the *Odyssey*.[97] Before the end of the decade, Giovanni Malpaghini di Ravenna had made for Petrarch Latin manuscripts of the *Iliad* and the *Odyssey*.[98] Pilato's versions have attracted criticism for their poor Latinity and rigid adherence to the Greek original, but these very qualities made them a much more useful companion for someone attempting to learn Homer's language. Boccaccio acquired what Greek he had from Pilato's explication of Homer:

> Ipse ego fui qui primus ex latinis a Leontio Pylato in privato *Iliadem* audivi. Ipse insuper fui qui ut legerentur publice libri Homeri operatus sum; et esto non satis plene perceperim, percepi tamen quantum potui; nec dubium si permansisset homo ille vagus diutius penes nos quin plenius percepissem.[99]
>
> [I myself was the first of the Latins who heard the *Iliad* in private from Leonzio Pilato. What's more, it was I who ensured that there were public lectures on Homer; and although I did not learn enough, I learned as much as I could; and certainly if that restless man had remained with us longer, I would have learned more.]

Despite his enthusiasm for the poet, Petrarch seems never to have advanced very far with him in Greek, and Boccaccio may not have fared much better. But had they made more progress, further difficulties would have emerged: to know only Homer in Greek is a poor introduction to the less-exalted writers of the language. Following Petrarch's death in 1374, his Greek manuscript of the *Iliad* remained in Padua, apparently unread, until 1388. It then moved to Pavia, where it stayed until Janus Lascaris acquired it in 1499.[100]

Interest was rekindled in Florence in the 1390s by Coluccio Salutati. In 1392 Salutati attempted to persuade Antonio Loschi to rewrite Pilato's literal translation in hexameters.[101] This project might be compared with Salutati's own revision of Simon Atumano's Latin translation of Plutarch's essay *De cohibenda iracundia*, made at a time when Salutati knew little, if any, Greek.[102] It was not until the arrival of Manuel Chrysoloras in Florence, at Salutati's invitation, that Homer's Greek could be profitably reexamined. Chrysoloras has been connected with two manuscripts of the *Odyssey* and one of the *Iliad*.[103] His pupil Pier Paolo Vergerio had a manuscript of the *Odyssey* from his fellow student Palla Strozzi in the winter of 1400–1401, and with the help of Pilato's translation, he read a good deal of the *Odyssey* in Padua during this period.[104] Vergerio also produced a version that appears not to have survived.[105] Two other manuscripts are suggestive. The first is a revision of Pilato's translations written in a manuscript dated 1398.[106] It is tempting to associate this with Chrysoloras's teaching, if only because it is hard to come up with another context conducive to such a work. The second witness is a copy of Pilato's translation of the *Odyssey* written by Tedaldo della Casa, apparently in the first years of the fifteenth century.[107] Another pupil of

Chrysoloras, Leonardo Bruni, translated three Homeric speeches "oratorio more," but these were not published for nearly forty years.[108]

Homer soon entered classrooms outside Florence. About 1427, Guarino Veronese made versions, now lost, of parts of the *Iliad* and *Odyssey*.[109] We may guess that these two books played some part in the curriculum of his school. According to his son, Battista Guarino, writing in 1459, Homer should be the first poet for the student of Greek: only after Homer can the student attempt the other heroic poets, the tragedians, and the writers of comedy.[110] Vittorino da Feltre, who appears to have studied Greek with Theodore Gaza in Mantua between 1443 and his death in 1446, had a copy of Homer, a commentary, and a lexicon to unlock the works.[111] By 1446, Gaza himself, now in Ferrara, was lecturing on Homer,[112] and by 1448 Filelfo owned a manuscript of the *Iliad* and the *Battle of the Frogs and Mice*, copied by Gaza, which had a continuous interlinear Greek paraphrase.[113] In the second half of the century, Constantine Lascaris taught Homer to his students in Milan and Messina.[114] We may number Petrus Castellus of Paris among his northern students of Homer.[115] A manuscript of the *Odyssey*, perhaps made around 1460, has some interlinear Latin glosses and belonged to Pietro da Montagnana.[116] Antonio Codro Urceo was teaching Homer in his Greek classes in Bologna in the second half of the 1480s and the early 1490s.[117] Urbano Bolzanio owned a manuscript of Homer and taught the poems; a lost translation of, and commentary on, the poet was attributed to him.[118]

But to return to Florence, in 1427 Filelfo arrived back in Italy with a Greek manuscript of Homer, and in Florence during the years between 1429 and 1434 he lectured on the *Iliad*.[119] It may have been in Florence that he began a verse translation of the *Iliad* and *Odyssey*.[120] Giannozzo Manetti, who was a friend of Filelfo's in Florence, owned a manuscript of Pilato's *Iliad* translation and a Greek text of the same poem. This copy, made for him by Joannes Scutariota, has an interlinear gloss on book I and the beginning of book II.[121] Marsilio Ficino, believed to have been taught Greek by Francesco da Castiglione, translated the *Homeric Hymns* in his youth in Florence, presumably in the later 1450s. This version seems to have been made simply to practice his Greek and was not intended for publication.[122] Homer is not recorded among the works taught by Andronicus Callistus in Bologna in the 1460s, although Joannes Rhosos completed a copy of the *Iliad* in that city in May 1465 while Callistus was teaching there.[123] By 1471, Callistus was teaching in Florence, and Homer was certainly one of his texts.[124] Bartolomeo Fonzio, one of his pupils in Florence, produced a version of the first four books of the *Iliad*, apparently as part of his Greek studies.[125] Another of Callistus's pupils, Angelo Poliziano, translated books II–V of the *Iliad* into Latin hexameters during the Greek scholar's residence in the city.[126] After Callistus's departure in 1475, progress on this fine translation halted, but between 1475 and 1479, Poliziano required his young student Piero de' Medici to commit to memory passages from Homer.[127] The chair of Greek in Florence, vacated by Callistus, was soon taken up by another student of Homer, Demetrius Chalcondyles.[128] Given Chalcondyles' editorial work on the first printed text of Homer, it is likely that he taught the poet at some time during his sixteen-year stay in the city, but evidence that he did so has yet to emerge. There were, however, lectures on Homer in Florence during Chalcondyles' time in the city: in 1485, Poliziano read the prolusion to his lectures on Homer, and he lectured on the *Odyssey* and the *Iliad* in Florence between 1487 and 1489.[129] Chalcondyles is known to have lectured on the *Homeric Hymns* and the *Iliad* while he was in Milan in 1507 and 1508. In 1508, he was teaching his son Basilio the ninth book of the *Odyssey*.[130]

In 1489, Chalcondyles edited the first printed Greek text of Homer, a remarkable piece of printing that was dedicated to Piero de' Medici.[131] This huge book has survived in many copies. Willibald Pirckheimer owned a copy of the edition, which he had decorated by Albrecht Dürer.[132] At his death in 1503, the Paduan teacher Giovanni Calfurnio owned a copy.[133] In Venice, Vettor Fausto owned and annotated a copy of this edition, which is now in the Marciana.[134] Cuthbert Tunstall donated his own copy to the library of the University of Cambridge in 1528, where it remains today.[135] The remainder of the edition was eventually acquired by Aldus at some time between 1498 and 1503. By 1504, it had finally sold out, which means that it took sixteen years for all of the copies to find their first owners.[136]

In Florence around 1493, in a speech that detailed some of the benefits of Greek learning, Janus Lascaris publicly extolled Homer's virtues:

Homerus pater omnium et princeps et magister ante oculos tibi proponendus est. Ab hoc veluti ab oceano omnes fluvii et omnes eloquentiae fontes emanaverunt. Hic tibi volvendus est, hic perlegendus, in huius operibus erit evigilandum. Hic alet, hic augebit, hic tibi vires ac carmina reparabit.[137]

[You must set Homer, the father of everything, the lord and master, before your eyes. From him, as from an ocean, all the rivers and all the founts of eloquence have flowed. Him you must leaf through, him you must read over, for his works you must be ready to burn the midnight oil. He will nourish, he will increase, he will replenish your energies and your poetry.]

Homer was certainly taught at the Florentine *Studio* in 1493, although not, it would appear, by Lascaris. In April 1493, a young student, Girolamo Amaseo, pestered his brother for money to buy a copy of the *editio princeps* of Homer. We learn that he had been attending classes on Homer given by Guarino of Favera in Florence. We know from another source that Guarino was reading Eustathius's commentary on Homer with his student Carlo Antinori, and 1493 is a very plausible date for this.[138] The results of this work on Eustathius eventually appeared in the Aldine *Thesaurus cornucopiae* of 1496.[139] In the preface to this edition, Guarino wrote that this was compiled "ὅπως μὴ οἱ πρὸς τοὺς ποιητὰς καὶ τὸν Ὅμηρον μάλιστα σπουδάζοντες ὁσημέραι ἐρωτῶντες, ποῖον τοῦτο χρόνον τὸ ῥῆμα; μήτοι ἀόριστος πρῶτος, ἢ μέσος παρακείμενος, ἢ καὶ ὑπερουντέλικος; καὶ τ' ἄλλα ὡσαύτως, ἀεὶ ἐνοχλοῦντες τὰ τῶν διδασκάλων ὦτα περικόπτωσι"[140] (so that those busy with the poets and Homer in particular and asking every day, "What is the tense of this verb? Would it be the first aorist, or the middle perfect, or the pluperfect?" and other such things, forever making a nuisance of themselves, may not deafen the ears of their teachers). Amaseo's letter shows a brash young man, willing to bother Poliziano on his arrival in Florence, and very likely one of the loud students for whom Guarino made his compilation. Amaseo describes the texts on which Guarino lectured: "Legit mane *Odysseam* versus autem triginta; post prandium Aristophanem, versus saltem viginti; vicesima secunda hora *Iliadem*, versus quadraginta"[141] (He reads thirty lines of the *Odyssey* in the morning; after lunch, at least twenty lines of Aristophanes; and in the evening forty lines of the *Iliad*). The *Odyssey* is significantly shorter than the *Iliad*. If we assume that progress through the poems would pick up a little as the students improved their command of Homeric Greek, this rate would allow all of Homer to be covered in one year. This may be compared with the rate at which Scipione Forteguerri taught the *Odyssey* in Bologna in 1510, probably from the first Aldine edition of the works printed in 1504.[142] Forteguerri wrote to Angelo Colocci, "Lego qui privatamente a certi scholari forestieri, a requisitione di messer Paulo Bombasio, la *Odyssea* di Homero, e fo bon percosso adeo che va in ogni sei lezioni un libro"[143] (As requested by Paulo Bombasio, I am lecturing here privately to some foreign students on Homer's *Odyssey*, and I am making such good progress that we get through one book in six lessons). This would be about eighty lines every class. For comparison, Greek schoolboys in the eleventh century were required to learn between thirty and fifty lines of Homer by heart every day.[144]

Greek texts of Homer were, of course, harder to find in Northern Europe in the fifteenth century. Adolf Occo owned two manuscripts of Homer, one of which was partly copied by Constantine Lascaris,[145] and Rudolf Agricola was transcribing one in 1479.[146] When Janus Lascaris followed the French king to France in late 1495 or early in 1496, he took with him a copy of the printed text that he is known to have owned. Lascaris lent a copy of this edition to the French historian Paulus Aemilius.[147] It seems that Lascaris taught Homer to Guillaume Budé, for in the last years of the fifteenth century, Budé was reading and annotating his copy of the *editio princeps* of the poet.[148] In his annotations, Budé drew on two sets of scholia that were part of Bessarion's donation to Venice, a text he could presumably only have consulted through Lascaris.[149] In France, Erasmus borrowed a copy of Homer from Augustine Vincent, of which he was obliged to return a portion in September 1500. He wrote to its owner, "Ego quidem ita huius autoris ardeo amore, ut cum intelligere nequeam, aspectu tamen ipso recreer ac pascar"[150] (I so burn with love for this writer that even when I cannot understand him, I am restored and nourished by the very sight of his book.) A chance comment from a former pupil tells us that, at some point in his life, Erasmus taught from the *Odyssey*.[151] He certainly owned a copy of the first Aldine Homer, which he had received from Philip Melanchthon.[152]

Melanchthon—whose own copy of part of the first Aldine Homer also survives—did a great deal to bring Homer to Germany.[153] Conrad Celtis had preceded him, lecturing on Homer in Vienna sometime between 1497 and his death in 1508.[154] But Melanchthon lectured regularly and successfully on Homer from the time of his arrival in Wittenberg in 1518.[155] Homer appeared in Melanchthon's first Greek grammar of 1518: a short text, "Thersita," from the *Iliad*, and another from the *Homeric Hymns*.[156] From this date, German students who had previously traveled to France for their Greek could now find it in Germany. Thus in August 1517, the Swiss Heinrich Glareanus writes that he is attending lectures given by a native Greek speaker in Paris on the *Odyssey*; by 1520 he is reading the *Iliad* in Basle.[157] The same year, the first two books of the *Odyssey* were printed in Greek in Basle, a text intended to accompany Oecolampadius's Greek grammar and the Basle lexicon of 1519.[158] The printer Andreas Cratander explained, "Duos priores Ὀδυσσείας libros in forma portatili iam damus, ubi versus tanto interstitio seiuncti sunt, ut quicquid ex ore praeceptoris adnotatu dignum audieris, mox calamo excipere possis, id quod addiscentium memoriam maxime iuvat"[159] (We now offer the first two books of the *Odyssey* in a handy volume, in which the lines of verse are widely spaced so that you may write down anything noteworthy that the teacher says, a practice that greatly helps the memory of students). In Paris in April 1527, Johann Winther's grammar included the shorter *Homeric Hymn in Mercurium*, presumably following Melanchthon's lead.[160] However, despite growing interest, Homer was not printed in Greek in Northern Europe until 1523, when Martens printed the complete works in Louvain.[161] In October of the same year, two books of the *Iliad* were printed with Melchior Volmar's notes in Paris. This classroom edition was dedicated to Petrus Rossetus, who had taught Greek using these books of the *Iliad*.[162]

Homer's primacy was never seriously challenged in the classroom, but his difficulty for beginners was mitigated by the use of the pseudo-Homeric, mock-heroic *Battle of the Frogs and Mice* in their studies. In 1429, Carlo Marsuppini had made a verse translation of this poem, possibly the first Latin verse translation of a Greek poet made since antiquity.[163] Theodore Gaza produced a paraphrase of the poem between 1440 and 1448, a period during which he was teaching Greek to Italian students.[164] The young Elisio Calenzio produced a Latin verse imitation of the poem around 1448.[165] Manuscripts from the middle of the century place the work in an educational context: in 1449, Andronicus Callistus copied a manuscript that has George Scholarios's grammar, the *Aurea verba*, pseudo-Phocylides, the *Battle of the Frogs and Mice*, and Epictetus's *Encheiridion*.[166] In the 1460s, apparently in connection with his teaching in Padua, Demetrius Chalcondyles made a manuscript that contained Chrysoloras's grammar, Aesop's fables, and the pseudo-Homeric *Battle*.[167]

Around 1474 in Brescia, this little poem became the first Greek text from pagan antiquity to be printed. The Greek was printed with an interlinear Latin translation, alongside Marsuppini's translation in hexameters, to accommodate those who wanted to learn Greek and those who simply wanted a good translation of the work itself.[168] Another edition of the Greek text, with a Greek gloss, emerged in Venice in 1486,[169] and the text was printed again in the Florentine edition of the complete works in 1488. It was equally popular north of the Alps, becoming the second Greek text to be printed in France, as a part of Tissard's program of Greek studies.[170] Marsuppini's version was, in fact, printed at least seven times between 1474 and 1516.[171] Johann Reuchlin made a prose translation sometime between May 1486 and July 1495,[172] and between 1511 and 1513, the versions of two other northern translators emerged: those of Servatius Aedicollius and Thilonius Philymnus.[173] That this little work was not by Homer had certainly been suggested by 1515, and in 1518 Froben, while defending its educational value, acknowledged that it was not Homer's.[174] Nevertheless, Melanchthon, speaking on the usefulness of fables in 1526, could still say that Homer wrote his little mock epic "for the children whom he taught everywhere in Greece."[175]

LUCIAN

In the preface to the 1527 Antwerp edition of Erasmus's translations of Lucian, the editor Joannes Grapheus wrote, "Proinde cum iam totus mundus passim graecisset, non video (multorum etiam iudicio) quid ad eam linguam discendam magis conducat Luciano"[176] (And so since now everyone everywhere is going Greek, I do not see— and many agree with me—what contributes more to learning that language than Lucian). The place of Lucian in the new curricula owed much to the brevity of many of his works and to his straightforward Attic prose. Certainly, works of Lucian were among the first Greek works to be rendered into Latin, and many scholars met them at the start of their Greek studies. At the end of the fourteenth century, Chrysoloras brought a manuscript of Lucian to Italy, which played a part in his classes.[177] His Greek manuscript of Lucian soon gave rise to a copy, carefully made by a Latin student of Greek. This copy has an interlinear Latin gloss made by an anonymous pupil of Chrysoloras and is to date the only manuscript that has been shown to come from this famous classroom. A student of Greek, Bertoldo, otherwise unknown, translated Lucian's *Timon* and dedicated his version to Pellegrino Zambeccari. Since Zambeccari died in 1400, it is likely that it represents the first translation of Lucian ever made in the West.[178] It survives in two early copies, one of 1403 and another that belonged to Coluccio Salutati.[179] The first Latin translation of *Charon*, complete by 1403, was made from this manuscript, and Salutati owned a copy of this version, too.[180]

The other scholar connected to Lucian in the early years of the fifteenth century is Guarino Veronese.[181] He followed Chrysoloras back to Constantinople and, during his stay in the city between 1403 and 1408, translated three works of Lucian: *Calumnia*, *Muscae encomium*, and *Parasitus*.[182] This first work proved particularly popular and found at least eight translators in the period.[183] The second, *Muscae encomium*, attracted another anonymous version and a version by Nicolas Bérault.[184] Pontico Virunio's commentary on this Greek text may be connected with his teaching of the language in the early sixteenth century.[185] Another work seems to have been used in Ferrara: Celio Calcagnini held a chair of Greek and Latin in that city from 1507 or 1509, and Lucian's *Iudicium vocalium*, in Calcagnini's translation, was printed among the student texts appended to Lascaris's grammar in Ferrara in 1510.[186]

The complete Greek text appeared in print in Florence in 1496, a substantial folio printed in Greek capitals with accents.[187] A copy of this edition entered the extensive library of the Paduan teacher Giovanni Calfurnio sometime before his death in 1503.[188] Niccolò Leonico Tomeo, who taught for many years in Venice and Padua, owned and annotated a copy of this edition, as did Scipione Forteguerri.[189] Willibald Pirckheimer, a fortunate man, had his personal copy decorated by Albrecht Dürer.[190] The second printed edition, the Aldine, emerged in June 1503.[191] At two Venetian ducats, it was an expensive volume: it was twice the price of the Aldine lexicon, for example, or of Gaza's Greek grammar.[192] Nevertheless, it was this edition that was to play a large part in the subsequent fortunes of Lucian's works. This was the edition that Erasmus owned, and it was from this that he made his many versions.[193] It was probably also from this edition that he taught his students, one of whom, Giovanni Boerio, dedicated his translation of *Calumnia* to Prince Henry around 1506.[194] Henry Bullock, who studied under Erasmus, had his version of the brief *Dipsades* printed in Cambridge by Siberch in 1521.[195]

The translations of Erasmus and Thomas More did much to stimulate interest in Lucian in Northern Europe. In July 1508, eighteen months after their versions had been printed in Paris, Aleandro chose the Aldine Lucian as his text for his lessons there.[196] That month, he wrote to Aldus to ask for at least twelve copies of Lascaris's grammar, six copies of the Aldine lexicon, and at least six copies of Lucian. Lucian had already made an appearance in France: a manuscript of five dialogues had been made by the industrious George Hermonymus for Guillaume Budé.[197] Selections of Lucian emerged in print, in Greek only, in Paris around 1509, at which time they must have been lectured on by Aleandro.[198] Charles Brachet arranged for a different selection of texts from Lucian to be printed, again in Greek only, before he began his public lectures in Paris in 1512 or 1513.[199] In Louvain, Thierry Martens printed a textbook in 1523 that shows that Lucian's works could play a part in the difficult transition from elementary prayers to the more complex profane authors: after Aleandro's tables, this has short passages from Matthew, from Paul's letter to the Romans, prayers and graces, followed by twelve short dialogues of Lucian.[200] In the same period, Martens printed a series of plain Greek editions of short works of Lucian aimed squarely at the educational market: *Prometheus* in 1519; *Icaromenippus*, *Menippus*, and *Vitarum auctio* in 1519; *Dialogi Deorum*, *Dialogi marini*, and *Dialogi mortuorum* in 1520; *Nigrinus* in 1521; *Charon* in 1522; *Timon* in 1523; *Somnium* in 1524; and *Muscae encomium* in 1525.[201] In Bruges, Jean Strazelius read dialogues of Lucian with his pupils.[202] About 1525, Christopher Rianus used the first book of Gaza's grammar, Aleandro's tables, and an unidentified work of Lucian with students in Etten, near Breda.[203] Lucian was also used with students in Spain. The first time any part of Lucian was printed in that country was in Francisco Vergara's anthology of short texts of 1524. It included two dialogues: *Icaromenippus* and a dialogue between Mercury and Neptune.

In Germany, Lucian was circulating among a handful of students before any works were printed north of the Alps. Between 1479 and 1484, Rudolf Agricola translated Lucian's *Calumnia*, *Gallus*, and *Micyllus*.[204] An autograph manuscript that belonged to Adolf Occo contains several works of Lucian, two of which are followed by a brief Greek–Latin lexicon of words in the text.[205] In a letter dated 1503, Willibald Pirckheimer refers vaguely to some Latin translations of Lucian.[206] His version of Lucian's *De ratione conscribendae historia* was printed in Nuremberg in 1515;[207] *Piscator* emerged in Nuremberg in 1517;[208] and *Rhetor* was printed in Hagenau in 1520.[209] Aleandro's pupil Ottomar Nachtgall saw an edition through the press in Strasbourg in 1515, a parallel Greek–Latin text prepared for those "graecitatis adhuc rudes"[210] (who are still beginners in Greek). In Basle, Johann Cuno seems to have taught the young Amorbach brothers Greek with the help of Lucian.[211] Three works are connected with Melanchthon's teaching in Wittenberg: he was lecturing on *Hercules Gallicus* in 1520; he lectured on *Calumnia* in 1521, and his own translation of this work survives; and the Greek text of *Cupido* was regularly printed with editions of his grammar.[212]

The availability of Latin translations of certain texts made them more likely to receive the attentions of Greek printers. In the same year that Martens published *Icaromenippus*, *Menippus*, and *Vitarum auctio* in Greek, he also printed the versions of Erasmus, More, and Nicolas Bérault.[213] In Basle, Curio's edition of 1522 printed Erasmus's version of *Tyrannicida* and *Abdicatus* opposite the Greek. In a prologue to the dialogues, Curio wrote that they had been chosen because Latin translations were available: "Porro quod eos deligimus quorum bona pars versa est, ideo factum est partim quod elegantissimi, partim etiam ut conferri commode possint ab iis qui praeceptoris destituuntur praesidio praesertim ii qui ab Erasmo versi sunt"[214] (Moreover, we selected the dialogues that have, for the most part, been translated—and especially those that have been translated by Erasmus—because they are very elegant, and so that the texts might be easily compared by those who lack the assistance of a tutor). However, the versions of Erasmus and More also aroused an enthusiasm independent of the Greek text. Erasmus had said that his translations of Lucian should be in the first volume of his complete works, those "quae spectant ad institutionem litterarum" (that pertain to the teaching of literature), but he does not say which literature they should teach. He would not have been unhappy that his Lucian was used to teach Latin as well as Greek. Gourmont glossed Erasmus's difficult Latin words in the margin of his 1535 edition for the benefit of younger readers.[215] While the medieval Latin educational texts attributed to Aesop, Homer, and Cato became Greek, such was the Latinity of Erasmus's versions of Lucian that the Greek author was used in the classroom to teach Latin.

ARISTOPHANES

In 1524, John Froben prefaced his edition of Aristophanes' *Ranae* with an explanation of the relative value of poets and prose authors to students of Greek:

> Qui graecas litteras exacte callent, existimant huius sermonis elegantiam rectius disci ex oratoribus quam ex poetis; quod apud latinos secus est, quibus eadem est utrorumque lingua, nisi quod in poetis maior est verborum delectus ac sententiarum vigor. Apud graecos dicis alia lingua loqui poetas, alia qui soluta scripserunt, sed hoc discrimine: ut qui in oratoribus sit primum exercitatus, facile assequatur phrasim poeticam. Contra secus. Caeterum Aristophanes, si choros excipias, sic in carmine praestat Attici sermonis elegantiam, ut vix Lucianus in prosa felicius.[216]

> [Precise scholars of Greek think that the finer points of this language are more correctly learned from the orators than from the poets; which is not so with Latin, where the same language is used by both, except that the poets have a broader vocabulary and force of expression. Among the Greeks, you might say that the poets speak one language and the prose authors another, but with this proviso: whoever is well practiced in the orators can easily understand the poetic language but not the other way around. But Aristophanes, if you exclude the choruses, demonstrates the finer points of Attic so well in verse that Lucian is hardly better in prose.]

The student of Greek would have encountered Aristophanes before the other dramatists. Of the nine surviving plays, he would have first encountered *Plutus*, the first play on the Byzantine curriculum. It is likely that many students read no further in Aristophanes than this, but those who did persist would next have studied *Nubes* and *Ranae*, the remaining plays of the Byzantine triad. This would seem to have been the experience of Guarino Veronese. Guarino bought his Greek manuscript of these three plays of Aristophanes at Constantinople on March 1, 1406, a manuscript that has already been noticed as the earliest dated copy of Chrysoloras's grammar.[217] Rinuccio Aretino had clearly read *Plutus* by 1417.[218] Leonardo Bruni attempted to put the opening lines of the play into Latin verse, his only attempt at verse translation and not a very successful one.[219] Giovanni Tortelli used *Plutus* and *Nubes* in his Greek studies in Constantinople.[220]

With the exception of Bruni, all these early readers of Aristophanes seem to have first come across these plays during their time in the East. The role of the great Aristotelian scholar Theodore Gaza in bringing Aristophanes into Western classrooms has not received much attention. Gaza taught Greek to the great teacher Vittorino da Feltre in Mantua between 1443 and 1446, and Vittorino's library certainly contained a copy of Aristophanes by 1445.[221] Vittorino valued Aristophanes, as "doctrina linguae, puritate sermonis Attici, ad formandum bonum virum, quod vitia insectaretur, aptum"[222] (with his knowledge of the language, with the Attic purity of his Greek, and because he attacks vices, he is well suited to shape a good man). After Vittorino's death in 1446, Gaza moved to teach Greek in Ferrara, where Aristophanes is known to have been among the texts he taught.²²³ His students appear to have included Giorgio Valagussa, and some years after Gaza's departure, the dramatist was still being studied in the city: Valagussa was unable to send his manuscript of Aristophanes to Bartolomeo Platina in Mantua in 1453 because he and other students were making frequent use of it.²²⁴

In the second half of the fifteenth century, Aristophanes became well established in Italy as a student text. The Chrysoloras–*Plutus* combination of Guarino's manuscript finds an echo in a later manuscript that belonged to Pietro da Montagnana. In this autograph manuscript, Aristophanes follows a Latin translation of Scholarios's Greek grammar.²²⁵ These facts connect the play either with Pietro's own studies or with his teaching of the language in Padua in the 1450s. That Constantine Lascaris made a collection of brief glosses on *Plutus* suggests that he, too, used the play with his students.²²⁶ In Rome, Andrea Brenta lectured on *Plutus* sometime between 1475 and 1484. The prolusion to these lectures survives, and he makes it clear that Aristophanes' pure Attic diction recommends his work to beginners:

> Aristophanem in primis vobis exponere constitui, poetam suavissimum et Actio [*sic*] lepore praestantissimum et praesertim incipientibus convenientissimum, quippe qui non adhuc declinationum, verborum et diversarum linguarum usus calleatis; in quo non multum vobis dubitandum inherendumque erit. Est enim facilis, apertus, planus, suavis et Actica [*sic*] lingua quasi melle conditus.²²⁷
>
> [I have chosen to expound Aristophanes, a poet who is pleasant, preeminent for Attic charm, and particularly appropriate for beginners, to you who have not yet mastered the nouns, the verbs, or the dialects. He will not cause you to hesitate and get stuck, for he is straightforward, clear, direct, pleasant, and founded in the Attic tongue as if in honey.]

We have other evidence that Aristophanes was studied in Rome during this period: Giovanni Francesco Maraschi borrowed manuscripts of Aristophanes from the Vatican Library in 1475, 1476, and 1479, while Demetrio Guazzelli borrowed two manuscripts in the summer and fall of 1477.²²⁸ At Florence, Poliziano was about to teach Aristophanes to the young Piero de' Medici in 1482.²²⁹ *Plutus* was being read in another Florentine classroom in 1493. In that year, Girolamo Amaseo wrote home from the city to his brother Gregorio: "In effingendos graecarum litterarum characteres contuli meme, et Aristophanis *Plutum* (sic illa comoedia, ut graece dicam, Πλοῦτος inscribitur) exscribere coepimus; tot autem versus exaravimus quot per aliquot dies mihi suppeditarentur ad auditionem"²³⁰ (I applied myself to forming the Greek letters, and we began to copy out Aristophanes' *Plutus* (that comedy is titled Πλοῦτος in Greek). We transcribed as many lines as I was given over several days in our lectures). The young Girolamo included with his letter a sample of his transcription of the play so that Gregorio could judge his progress.²³¹ He describes the texts that Guarino of Favera lectured on in Florence and the rate at which they advanced through their texts: "Legit mane *Odysseam* versus autem triginta; post prandium Aristophanem, versus saltem viginti; vicesima secunda hora *Iliadem*, versus quadraginta"²³² (He reads thirty lines of the *Odyssey* in the morning; after lunch, at least twenty lines of Aristophanes; and in the evening, forty lines of the *Iliad*). At this rate, it would have taken Guarino and his students about two months to cover all of *Plutus*.

Aldus Manutius printed nine plays of Aristophanes in 1498 and sold copies of the edition for two-and-a-half Venetian ducats.[233] The comedies were printed directly after the fifth and final volume of the Aldine Aristotle, and the editor of the plays, Marcus Musurus, suggests that they might provide the reader with some light relief after the severities of the philosopher.[234] Aldus's preface includes Gaza's recommendation of the poet:

Quibus graece discere cupientibus nihil aptius, nihil melius legi potest, non meo solum iudicio (quod non magnifacio) sed etiam Theodori Gazae, viri undecunque doctissimi, qui, interrogatus quis ex graecis auctoribus assidue legendus foret graecas literas discere volentibus, respondit: 'Solus Aristophanes,' quod esset sane quam acutus, copiosus, doctus et merus Atticus.[235]

[Nothing more suitable, nothing better can be read by those who want to learn Greek. And this is not only my opinion (which I do not rate highly) but also the opinion of that most learned of men, Theodore Gaza. When he was asked which of the Greek authors should be carefully read by those who want to learn Greek, he replied, "Aristophanes alone," because he is very pointed, abundant, learned, and writes in pure Attic.]

To the modern reader, this praise of Aristophanes seems to miss the point, but humor was not prominent among the qualities required of an educational text. Aldus's words are less surprising when we notice that Vittorino, Gaza, and Brenta found the very same virtues in Aristophanes that Quintilian had found in the Old Comedy in Imperial times.[236] The failure of the fifteenth century to find the humor in Aristophanes may also have been due to the fact that it was *Plutus*, the most allegorical of the plays, that attracted the most attention. In 1501, it was the first Greek play to be printed in Latin, in a verse adaptation by Francesco Passio. Passio had heard Taddeo Ugoleto lecture on the plays of Aristophanes in Parma, perhaps from the Aldine edition. Passio, who could apparently have chosen from a number of plays of Aristophanes, says that he was drawn to *Plutus* partly by its novelty and "partim quod non minus gravitatis in se contineret quam facetiarum"[237] (partly because it has as much serious matter in it as it has humor). It was not only the Byzantine curriculum that gave *Plutus* pride of place among the corpus but also fifteenth-century tastes.

It was only in the sixteenth century that Aristophanes moved north of the Alps. He does not figure prominently in early teaching in France. Aleandro's teaching in Paris is not known to have included Aristophanes, although he did pass a request for a copy of the *editio princeps* to Aldus from Paris in July 1508.[238] In Germany, Aristophanes was more popular. Willibald Pirckheimer used the plays to sharpen his Greek. In 1501, he wrote to a friend in Pavia, "Cuperem etiam ut inquireres si aliquis pauper graeculus Papiae esset, qui convenienti precio transferret mihi de verbo ad verbum aliquas comoedias Aristophanis"[239] (I would also like you to find out whether there is some poor Greekling in Pavia who would, for a suitable fee, make me a literal translation of some comedies of Aristophanes). Perhaps Pirckheimer found his poor *Graeculus*, or perhaps he struggled on alone. He certainly made some progress with Aristophanes. A manuscript now in London contains an anonymous translation of the first part of *Plutus* that is continued in Pirckheimer's hand until the end.[240] This may be the version that Pirckheimer later provided for another friend, apparently to help him advance in his Greek studies. He wrote to him, "Quemadmodum desideras, interpretationem graecarum ad te mitto, quamvis elegantius aliqua verti potuissent; sed volui verbum verbo reddere. Non mirum, cum dictionario careas, si ea minus intellexisti . . . Nam ego illo duce ingredior, absque eo vero claudus sum" (As you requested, I am sending you a translation of those Greek things. Granted, they might have been translated in some more elegant way, but I wanted to translate word for word. It is not surprising you did not understand them, when you have not got a dictionary . . . I myself proceed with its help, and I am quite lame without it).[241] Pirckheimer owned a copy of the Aldine edition and, as an avid collector of Aldine editions, he probably also had at his disposal a copy of the Aldine lexicon of 1497.[242]

In September 1504, Joannes Gregoropoulos was lecturing on Aristophanes' *Nubes* in Venice.[243] We know of these lectures because a talented German student, Johann Cuno, made notes on his teaching. Cuno's notebook has a Latin translation of a portion of *Nubes*.[244] Cuno's manuscript of three plays—*Plutus, Nubes,* and *Ranae*—also survives, and it has a partial interlinear gloss.[245] Cuno seems to have used Aristophanes in his own teaching in Basle between 1510 and 1513, for in 1516, three years after Cuno's death, Bruno Amorbach spoke to his brother Boniface of "tralationes Luciani et Aristophanis, ubi verbum verbo respondet, quas habui a communi praeceptore nostro Conone"[246] (the word-for-word translations of Lucian and Aristophanes that I have from our teacher Cuno).

By this time, Aristophanes had become a staple of northern classrooms. When, in 1517, Petrus Mosellanus took over the Greek chair in Leipzig from Richard Croke, one of his first tasks was to edit the Greek text of *Plutus* for his classes.[247] Mosellanus refers to Quintilian's recommendation of Menander and says that, since the works of Menander have been lost, Aristophanes is the next best thing: "[Comoedia] si qua caeteras vel argumenti commoditate, vel morum correctione, vel festivis sed tamen castis salibus antecellit, ea meo quidem iudicio erit Πλοῦτος"[248] (If any comedy is to surpass the others either in the fitness of its contents, or in the correction of behavior, or in its lively but pure wit, in my opinion it will be *Plutus*). This edition, printed in Hagenau by Anshelm, was dedicated to the respected teacher Joannes Caesarius, to whom Erasmus had dedicated his version of Gaza's first book the previous year. This edition certainly found its way into Reuchlin's classroom, for a surviving copy contains notes taken from his lectures of 1520.[249] It may well have been used by Caesarius in Cologne alongside the translations of Gaza's first and second book dedicated to him by Erasmus in 1516 and 1518. Aleandro's pupil, Rutger Rescius, was appointed first professor of Greek in Louvain in September 1518.[250] Martens, for whom Rescius had worked as a corrector, printed *Plutus* in Greek in Louvain the same year, and it is natural to suppose that the new professor made use of this new edition.[251]

The other plays of the triad attracted much less attention. In Wittenberg, Melanchthon lectured on a freshly printed text of *Nubes* in 1521;[252] in Basle, Froben printed *Ranae* in Greek in 1524; in Hagenau, Secer reprinted Melanchthon's *Nubes* and added a plain Greek text of *Plutus* in 1528. No other play was printed separately before 1530.

XENOPHON

Cyropaedia and *Hiero* were the only works of Xenophon to be printed in Latin in the fifteenth century, and both proved popular with students of Greek. *Cyropaedia* attracted the most interest during the first half of the fifteenth century. It had been brought to the attention of the Latin West by Cicero, who provided subsequent generations of students with a paraphrase of part of Cyrus's dying speech.[253] A manuscript of the complete Greek text of the work has been connected with Manuel Chrysoloras.[254] His student Leonardo Bruni was asking after for a copy in 1407,[255] and while Guarino Veronese was in Florence, from 1410 to 1414, he received a manuscript of the work.[256] Giannozzo Manetti, whose earliest Greek studies appear to have occupied the late 1420s or early 1430s, is said to have read *Cyropaedia* in Florence with Ambrogio Traversari,[257] and Vittorino da Feltre owned two manuscripts of *Cyropaedia*.[258] Francesco Filelfo proved a particularly diligent student of the work. When he left Constantinople for Venice toward the end of August 1427, it seems that he left behind a commission with the scribe George Chrysococces for a copy of *Cyropaedia*. This manuscript was completed in November, but it is not certain that it reached Filelfo.[259] He must, in any case, have had a manuscript of Xenophon by 1429, for in that year he proposed to lecture on "Xenophontis monarchiam" in Florence.[260]

Xenophon's image of the education of the perfect prince struck a chord in Italy, and there was something of a race to translate the work. Lorenzo Valla translated the first four chapters and dedicated them to Alfonso of Aragon in 1438 with a hint that he could translate the rest.[261] Giovanni Aurispa wrote to Alfonso in 1444 with another proposal to translate *Cyropaedia*, one that also came to nothing.[262] It was Poggio Bracciolini who finally turned it into Latin, a translation that was completed between 1445 and 1446 and dedicated to Alfonso around 1447.[263] As Poggio was putting the finishing touches to his version, Theodore Gaza was lecturing on *Cyropaedia* in Ferrara.[264] Poggio's version was very readable and very popular, but his meaning often diverged from his author's, and some years later, Filelfo attempted to replace it. His new version may have been under way as early as 1454; it was certainly in hand in 1466, complete by 1469, and reached print in 1477.[265] Interest in the Greek text of *Cyropaedia*, which had always tended to focus on its content rather than its language, subsided thereafter.

Hiero was the first of Xenophon's works to be translated into Latin in quattrocento Italy: Bruni's version was ready by 1403.[266] Copies of the Greek text can be connected with many of the eminent teachers of the Italian Renaissance: Chrysoloras, Guarino, Vittorino, Aurispa, Filelfo, Gaza, and Callistus all made or owned copies.[267] *Hiero* was the first work of Xenophon to be printed in Greek, in a student anthology of four Greek works in Florence around 1496.[268] When this anthology came to be reprinted in Rome around 1517, *Hiero* was still the only work to have been printed separately from the complete works of Xenophon.[269] The work made another appearance in Spain in Francisco Vergara's student anthology in Alcalá in 1524.

In 1520, however, Johann Reuchlin chose to teach another work of Xenophon to his students. He had been teaching Aristophanes' *Plutus* from Thomas Anshelm's edition of 1517.[270] The decision to change to another text seems to have been dictated by the fact that by 1520 all or most of Anshelm's edition of Aristophanes had been sold. Reuchlin complained to Michael Hummelberg in March 1520,

> Nam cum ne unus quidem habeatur ullus vel graecus vel hebraicus liber impressus qui tot inter auditores numero plusquam trecentos distribui possit, cogor in quatuor tabulas utramque linguam quotidie conscribere et easdem quotidie duabus horis docere publiceque legere, quousque pro fato eiuscemodi ad nos libri ex emporiis ducantur.[271]

[For since not even a single printed copy of any book printed in Greek or Hebrew is to be had, which could be used by an audience of more than three hundred, I am obliged to write both languages every day on four boards, and every day to teach and lecture publicly from them for two hours, until such time as books may be brought to us from the sellers to free us from this fate.]

Reuchlin's own early Greek studies seem to have included Xenophon's *Apologia Socratis*, and he had made a Latin version of the work in Basle between 1474 and 1477.[272] Now he chose the *Apologia*, together with *Hiero* and *Agesilaos*, for his own Greek students. In April 1520, he sent these three works to Thomas Anshelm with a letter:

Auditorium frequens colo exornoque diligenti mea doctrina, audiunt me discipuli prope quadringenti quotidie graece docentem et hebraice, nec opera mea desit, nec illorum attentio. Quare mitto Thomae nostro Xenophontem in tribus opusculis—in *Apologia*, in *Agesilao*, et in *Hierone*—ut tu quamprimum posthabitis rebus omnibus eum graece perquam diligenter concinnes et imprimi facias.[273]

[I cultivate a crowded lecture hall, and I supply it with my careful teaching. About forty students hear me teaching Greek and Hebrew every day; my labors are not lacking, nor is their attention. For this reason, I am sending Xenophon in three short works—the *Apology*, *Agesilaos*, and *Hiero*—to Thomas so that, as soon as possible and neglecting all other tasks, you can carefully prepare him in Greek and have him printed.]

Anshelm duly printed them in Hagenau in July 1520, and Reuchlin was still using this edition in February 1522, when he wrote to Hummelberg, "Ego vero a.d. III Id. Martias, connivente deo, incipiam praelegere utriusque linguae suavissimos oratores: graece Xenophontem in suo *Tyrannico*, et hebraice Salomonem regem Iudaeorum, ambos ad eundem finem et σκόπον tendentes . . . Habemus centum et quinquaginta Xenophontes, omnia volumina quae minimi venalia"[274] (God willing, on March 13, I shall begin lecturing on the great orators of each language: Xenophon's *Tyrant* in Greek, and Solomon, king of the Jews, in Hebrew, both of which have the same end and purpose in view . . . We have one hundred and fifty copies of Xenophon, all of which are very cheap). Reuchlin may have believed that he would soon exhaust his supplies of Anshelm's Xenophon because, as we shall see, he was already looking to his next classroom text.[275] These classes on *Hiero* were ended by Reuchlin's death at the end of June 1522.

One last center of interest in Xenophon is worth noticing here. In Louvain in the late 1520s, several works of Xenophon were printed in Greek for the educational market: *Oeconomicus* and *Cyropaedia* both appeared in 1527, the first in April, the second in June; *Hiero* emerged in August 1528; and *Memorabilia* came off the presses in 1529. In the preface to this last edition, Rutger Rescius notes that he has lectured on all of the works of Xenophon previously printed in Louvain and that he is now going to lecture on *Memorabilia*.[276]

Demosthenes

In 1532, Erasmus wrote in the preface to an edition of Demosthenes his judgment on the educational value of the ancient orator:

> Verum ut puerilibus ingeniis romanae linguae non statim accommodus est M. Tullius, qui, Fabio iudice, nulli valde placet nisi qui egregie profecerit, ita graecarum literarum peritiam ambientibus non arbitror admodum convenire Demosthenem, qui plus artis habet in recessu quam prima fronte prae se ferat.[277]
>
> [But just as Cicero is not appropriate for young students of Latin at the beginning of their studies—according to Quintilian, he is only really appreciated by those who are already proficient—neither do I think Demosthenes quite suitable for those looking to acquire skill in Greek. He has more subtlety about him than is apparent at first reading.]

As one of the greatest of the Greek prose authors, Erasmus did not regard Demosthenes as suitable reading for the tyro.

These reservations about the use of Demosthenes with beginners did not apply to the mature scholars who attended the classes of Chrysoloras in Florence in the late fourteenth century. The Greek text of Demosthenes first returned to the West with Chrysoloras: two manuscripts that associate the orator with a grammar have been connected with him, and he gave a manuscript of Demosthenes to his students Leonardo Bruni and Roberto de' Rossi.[278] Bruni's first translations—of *For Ctesiphon*, *For Diopithes*, and one of the *Philippic* orations—did not appear until 1406, by which time neither scholar was in Florence.[279] It is difficult to link any of these directly with Chrysoloras's teaching, but Chrysoloras's praise of Bruni's translation of Plutarch's life of Demosthenes did somehow reach Bruni in 1412.[280] Bruni was not the only student of Chrysoloras to produce translations of Demosthenes. Among Palla Strozzi's papers were found some Latin translations, "sermoni di Demostene, non choretti" (uncorrected speeches of Demosthenes).[281] These versions have not survived, and the description suggests that they were merely rough drafts not intended for publication. These versions may be connected to another manuscript of Palla's: a list of his books, dated August 1431, includes among the Greek manuscripts a volume described as "grammaticha et sermones Demostenis."[282] Strozzi's lost "translations" may in fact have been his Greek exercises.[283]

It was long believed that Cicero had translated the speeches of Aeschines and Demosthenes prosecuting and defending Ctesiphon and that his versions had been lost.[284] Under the influence of this spurious ancient precedent, Bruni had translated both of these speeches by 1412.[285] To judge from the number of surviving manuscripts, Bruni's translations were enormously popular and were printed five times before 1500.[286] Greek texts of Aeschines can be connected with Giovanni Aurispa, Niccolò Niccoli, Palla Strozzi, and Antonio Corbinelli.[287] When Francesco Filelfo returned from Constantinople in 1427, he brought Greek manuscripts of both orators with him. He chose to lecture on Aeschines in Florence in 1431 and 1432, and it is likely that he spent much of his time on the speech against Demosthenes.[288] In his teaching in Ferrara, between 1446 and 1449, Theodore Gaza lectured on the Aeschines-Demosthenes confrontation and may have done so using Bruni's translations.[289] In the 1440s and 1450s, Latin versions of Demosthenes' speech for Ctesiphon were made by George of Trebizond, Lorenzo Valla, and Nicolaus Secundinus.[290] Gaza's relative Andronicus Callistus lectured on Demosthenes in Florence sometime between 1471 and 1475, and there is some evidence that he, too, lectured on the confrontation between the orators.[291] Ermolao Barbaro taught Demosthenes in Padua in 1484, apparently an informal arrangement,[292] while around 1493, Janus Lascaris proposed to lecture on the orator in Florence.[293]

The first printed text is closely related to another course of lectures. In Venice, in January 1504, Scipione Forteguerri delivered a speech *De laudibus litterarum graecarum*, the prolusion to his lectures on Demosthenes. This lecture course in Venice must have been short, for by the time the prolusion was printed by Aldus in May, its author had left the city.[294] This printed prolusion was no doubt intended as a piece of advance publicity for the projected *editio princeps* of the works of the orator, but the Aldine Edition of the works was published too late to capitalize on Forteguerri's lectures. Aldus may originally have hoped to sell copies to Forteguerri's students: his comments in the preface suggest that the edition of Demosthenes had been delayed, and he seems to have been obliged to print fewer copies than he would have liked.[295] By October, Forteguerri was in Florence, and it was from there, on the eleventh of the month, that he wrote to Aldus to ask for a copy of the new edition. This request could not be met immediately: although Aldus's preface to Daniel Clario is dated October 1504, the volume did not receive its colophon until November. As a result, Forteguerri had to repeat his request for a copy in a letter dated December 2, 1504. It must have been around this time that copies of the edition were finally put up for sale in Venice for three ducats apiece.[296] It is possible that this edition was used by Demetrius Chalcondyles for his lectures on Demosthenes in Milan between 1507 and 1508.[297]

The first works of Demosthenes printed in the Aldine edition were the three Olynthiac orations. In Louvain in 1521, the next time that any part of Demosthenes' work was printed in Greek, it was the *Olynthiacs* that were chosen.[298] These speeches had been used with students before. George Hermonymus made four manuscripts of Demosthenes, at least three of which belonged to Guillaume Budé. One of these contains the speeches of Aeschines and Demosthenes for and against Ctesiphon with many of Budé's notes. Another, one of Hermonymus's two extant copies of the *Olynthiacs*, was also used by Budé.[299] It has been noticed that in 1522 Reuchlin was looking for a new Greek text to have printed for his students in Tübingen.[300] In January of that year, he wrote to Anshelm asking him to print the speeches of Demosthenes and Aeschines for and against Ctesiphon in Greek and send them to him. Anshelm printed the works in April, but since Reuchlin died at the end of June 1522, these classes may have come to nothing.[301] In Paris, Gourmont printed Chéradame's edition of the *Olynthiacs* in Greek in about 1523.[302] In Vergara's student anthology, printed in Alcalá in 1524, Demosthenes is also represented by the three *Olynthiac* orations. The same year, a Greek–Latin text of the first *Olynthiac* emerged in Hagenau, apparently in connection with Melanchthon's Greek course.[303] Melanchthon lectured regularly on Demosthenes in Wittenberg: on the *Olynthiac* orations in 1524; on the speeches for and against Ctesiphon and the Philippic orations in 1525; on *Against Aristogeiton* in 1526; and on *For Ctesiphon* the following year.[304] In 1528, Chéradame was responsible for another Paris edition of the *Olynthiacs*, which he prefaced with an anti-Lutheran dedication to Guillaume Briçonnet.[305]

In practice, the interest of teachers and students tended to gather in two areas of Demosthenes' work: on the three *Olynthiac* orations, and on the great rhetorical struggle between Demosthenes and Aeschines played out in their speeches for and against Ctesiphon. Other speeches were used, but much more rarely. In Louvain, for example, Martens printed a plain Greek text of *Against Midias* in December 1525, and another of *Against Leptines* in June 1526. At Hagenau in 1527, Demosthenes' two speeches *Against Aristogeiton*, the subject of Melanchthon's lectures the previous year, were printed in the Latin versions of Melanchthon and Vitus Vuinshemius, followed by the Greek text of both.[306]

ISOCRATES

Quintilian thought Isocrates "palaestrae quam pugnae magis accommodatus"[307] (better suited for training than for real combat). Renaissance students certainly exercised their command of Greek on the works of Isocrates. Three works of Isocrates were established as canonical student texts in the fifteenth century: *Ad Nicoclem*, *Ad Demonicum*, and *Nicocles*. This status is reflected in the large number of Latin translations of these works made during the period. There are at least five extant Latin translations of his *Nicocles*, sixteen of *Ad Demonicum*, and no fewer than twenty-two of *Ad Nicoclem* before 1530.[308]

The popularity of these three texts is partly due to the fact that they made appropriate gifts for monarchs: versions of *Ad Nicoclem*, for example, were dedicated to a host of Italian princes. However, these dedications often seem to represent revisions of versions first made in the classroom. Their use seems to have been a well-established tradition, one that can be tentatively traced to the beginning of the fifteenth century. Guarino Veronese made a version of *Ad Demonicum* in 1407, and we know that in 1416 he was using this speech to teach Greek to Guiniforte Barzizza.[309] The influential teacher Vittorino da Feltre owned a manuscript of Isocrates' orations.[310] Giorgio Valagussa, who seems to have studied Greek in Ferrara under Guarino and Theodore Gaza, was in possession of a Greek manuscript of Isocrates in the 1450s. He offered to send it to, or commission another copy for, his friend Antonio Palazzolo, and since this offer was made in connection with a collection of Greek fables, we may guess that Palazzolo, too, was learning the language.[311] Angelo Poliziano had the young Piero de' Medici learn passages from Isocrates by heart in his classes in Florence between 1475 and 1479.[312] In 1494 the scribe Joannes Serbopoulos, working in England, made a manuscript that combined Gaza's grammar with Isocrates.[313] It is likely that Giovanni Boerio's translation of *Ad Nicoclem* originated from the period in which he studied Greek under Erasmus.[314] We also know that Marcus Musurus lectured on this triad, either in Padua or Venice, sometime between 1503 and 1516.[315]

We owe the first printed text of Isocrates to Demetrius Chalcondyles. Chalcondyles arrived in Milan in October 1491 and began his lectures in the city in November.[316] At the start of 1493, the Greek press in the city completed the *editio princeps* of the complete works of Isocrates, the first Greek work printed in Milan since Bonaccorso's Psalter of 1481.[317] Chalcondyles may have been about to lecture on this author to his students in Milan. However, we should note that this edition also sold more slowly than any other Greek book of the fifteenth century: over forty years later, copies remained unsold, and in 1535 these were given a new title page and colophon and passed off as a new edition.[318] This does not suggest a popular student text: it appears to have been an expensively produced book, and as such, it may have been beyond the means of students. In the years after its publication, its idiosyncratic font may have deterred readers who had grown used to fonts modeled on those of the Aldine Press.

None of Isocrates' speeches were printed in Greek again until 1509. In that year, the speeches *Ad Demonicum* and *Ad Nicoclem* were both printed in Greek by

Gourmont, in plain, slim pamphlets for Aleandro's students in Paris.[319] These same speeches were printed in a parallel Greek–Latin edition by Aleandro's pupil, Ottomar Nachtgall, for his own Greek classes in Strasbourg in 1515.[320] All three speeches were edited in Greek by Janus Lascaris and printed in Rome in 1517.[321] *Ad Nicoclem* and *De pace* were printed alongside the versions of Erasmus and Petrus Mosellanus in Basle in 1522,[322] and *Ad Demonicum* and *Ad Nicoclem* were printed in Louvain the same year.[323] *Ad Demonicum* appears again in Spain in Vergara's Greek anthology of student texts of 1524.[324] Ercole Girlando's translation of Gaza's grammar, printed in November 1527, has already been noticed.[325] Two months earlier, he had seen to the production of a collection of elementary Greek prose texts: the three canonical essays of Isocrates and Aristides' *Encomium of Rome*. He explained in the preface that poor Greek students needed cheap books: "Vos, quibus a graecis auctoribus bonas disciplinas exhaurire cura est, multas magnis graecorum emendis libris pecunias impendere nunquam patiar. Curavi igitur ut minimus sed maximae frugis libellus excuderetur, quem vobis, qui boni sed pauperes estis, vel minimo aere comparare possitis"[326] (I shall never allow you, who want to draw good learning from the Greek authors, to spend lots of money on the great books of the Greeks. So I have caused a booklet, very small but very profitable, to be printed, which you, who are good but poor, might buy for yourselves for a very small sum). Girlando's solicitude produced a very small, closely printed book with no room for marginalia.

PLUTARCH

At the beginning of the fifteenth century, Manuel Chrysoloras had recommended the study of Plutarch to his Western students because his *Parallel Lives* brought the Greek world into contact with the Latin.[327] Later in the century, Poliziano recommended Plutarch because he combined the traditional—and complementary—virtues of both races: "Plutarchus ipse graeco vir ingenio, romana gravitate"[328] (Plutarch, a man of Greek intellect and Roman restraint). Plutarch's capacity to bridge the gap between the Greek and Roman worlds commended him to many teachers.

The sheer number of the *Lives* kept students and historians busy over translation for much of the first half of the fifteenth century. It has been plausibly suggested that some of Guarino Veronese's versions of Plutarch's *Lives* were made for teaching purposes and that the literal Latin used in the classroom was later revised for publication.[329] It should be noted, however, that few of the lives were translated more than once during the period, and it seems that for most scholars their interest lay in the fact that they could be used to fill holes in the Latin historical record.[330] The year 1470 was a milestone in the history of the *Parallel Lives*: the various translations of the *Lives*, made over the preceding decades by different scholars of varying abilities and for their own purposes, were brought together in a single printed volume.[331] This composite text with all its faults and peculiarities was often reprinted, and it effectively put an end to new translations of the lives until well into the sixteenth century.[332] I know of no Latin translation of any of the *Lives* made between 1462—the date of Alamanno Rinuccini's version of Plutarch's *Agesilaos*—and the end of this survey in 1529.[333] The *Lives* were not printed in Greek until 1517, and no life was printed alone in Greek before 1530.[334] The *Lives* do seem to have had a role in educating Greek students in the first half of the fifteenth century, but they played no part in educating their successors over the following decades.

More use was made by teachers of Plutarch's *Moral Essays*. Three of the *Moralia* attracted an unusual number of translations: *Quomodo ab adulatore discernatur amicus* had accumulated seven Latin translations by 1514;[335] *De utilitate quae habetur ex inimicis* inspired the same number of Latin versions in the same period;[336] and *De cohibenda iracundia* had acquired seven versions by 1525.[337] Part of their popularity derives from the fact that these short essays made fine presents to potential patrons. It is worth noting that two of the translators of *De cohibenda iracundia*, Salutati and Platina, seem to have known little Greek and that Latin interest in the work was probably stimulated by Aulus Gellius's anecdote about it in the *Attic Nights*.[338]

We are on surer ground with another popular essay. The pseudo-Plutarchan *De liberis educandis* had been used as early as 1402 to 1403 by Pier Paolo Vergerio for his own work, *De ingenuis moribus*.[339] The Latin version of Guarino Veronese, published in 1411, survives in many manuscripts and was often reprinted. Later in the century, a version was made by the Padua teacher Giovanni Calfurnio, and another may have been made by Lodovico Odasio.[340] *De liberis educandis* was the first work from among the *Moralia* to be printed in Greek: around 1496 it was issued in Florence with three other popular student texts,[341] a collection thought worth reprinting in Rome about 1517.[342] At least three scholars lectured on the text: Marcus Musurus seems to have done so, either in Padua or Venice, at some time between 1503 and 1516;[343] Philip Melanchthon lectured on the work in Wittenberg in 1519;[344] Johann Metzler published a Latin version of *De liberis educandis* in 1527, and his preface indicates that he lectured on the Greek text in Vratislava.[345]

Some of the *Moralia* attracted the attention of teachers and students in Northern Europe in the first decades of the sixteenth century. George Hermonymus produced a number of manuscripts of interest. He made a Latin–Greek manuscript of the *Praecepta coniugalia*.[346] He made a large manuscript for Guillaume Budé that contained a selection of twenty-one essays from the *Moralia* and from which Budé subsequently made Latin versions of three essays.[347] The first of these, his translation of *De placitis philosophorum*, was made in 1502; Budé's versions of Plutarch's *De fortuna et virtute Alexandri* and *De fortuna Romanorum* were completed the following year; and his version of *De animi tranquillitate* was complete by 1505.[348] Hermonymus made a manuscript of Budé's versions of these last three essays, and all four of Budé's translations were printed in Paris by Josse Bade in 1505. Besides the larger selection he made for Budé, Hermonymus also made at least two more manuscripts of the Greek text of *De animi tranquillitate*, *De fortuna Romanorum*, and *De fortuna et virtute Alexandri*, one of which is found bound with the printed texts of Budé's translations printed by Bade in 1505.[349] It appears that the availability of Budé's Latin translations was a factor in the demand for the Greek texts that Hermonymus copied.

Girolamo Aleandro, who left Venice in 1508, seems to have contributed to the editing of the Aldine *editio princeps* of the Greek text of the *Moralia*, completed in March 1509.[350] In Paris, Aleandro supervised the printing of three essays from this collection for his students, all copied from the Aldine edition and all printed by the end of April 1509: *De virtute et vitio*, *De fortuna*, and *Quomodo adolescens poetas audire debeat*.[351] He notes in the preface that the expense of importing Greek books from Italy is an obstacle to the many eager students of the language in Paris. None of these essays had previously attracted much attention from scholars or translators.[352] About three years later, presumably after the stocks of Gourmont's first edition of

Plutarch had been sold, Gourmont printed another three essays from the Aldine edition of the essays: *De utilitate quae habetur ex inimicis*, *De amicorum multitudine*, and *De superstitione*.[353] The first, as we have seen, had already been translated many times by 1512; the other two had not received the attentions of any translator. He also printed, probably at about the same time, his own revision of the Aldine text of a single essay, *De audiendo*.[354]

Aleandro made more use of Plutarch's *Moralia* than any other teacher of the period. From a passing comment of Joachim Camerarius, we learn that Aleandro's pupil Richard Croke taught some of the moral essays in Leipzig between 1515 and 1517.[355] The fact that Erasmus's translation of the essay Λάθε βιώσας had been printed in 1514 may have inspired Melanchthon, already lecturing on another essay, to edit the Greek text in Leipzig in 1519.[356] In 1525, Erasmus's translations of *De cohibenda iracundia* and *De curiositate* were printed alongside the Greek in Basle, an edition that may indicate some interest in the works for students of Greek but that may as easily reflect contemporary interest in Erasmus's fine Latin.[357] It is as well to close with this observation: the popularity of Plutarch in Latin always far outstripped his popularity as a first Greek text.

PLATO

Petrarch acquired a manuscript of nine of the more important works of Plato around 1353, but he was never able to read them.[358] It was not until Chrysoloras arrived in Florence that Western students were finally able to approach Plato in his own language. With an author of such central importance, the fact that most Greek teachers of the period can be connected in one way or another with a Greek manuscript does not tell us very much.[359] We have seen that Chrysoloras used Lucian in his classroom, and it is very likely that he expounded some of the *Parallel Lives* of Plutarch. The only other text that we can be certain that he introduced to his students is Plato. These pioneering students of the early fifteenth century were rather different from their successors a century later. They were mature scholars who could shape their studies according to their tastes. They studied Plato in Greek because he was an author that they wanted to read, not because his works were particularly appropriate for beginners.

Chrysoloras's students wanted to make Plato available to Latin scholars. After Chrysoloras had left Florence, one of them, Roberto de' Rossi, expressed around 1406 a desire to translate Plato.[360] If we link Palla Strozzi's lost drafts of Demosthenes with his early Greek studies, we may also want to notice that the same source tells us that he also left behind other lost translations, "sermoni di Platone, non choretti," rough drafts or classroom jottings.[361] However, the earliest version actually made by a student of Chrysoloras seems to have been Leonardo Bruni's translation of *Phaedo*, which was under way by September 1400 and complete before September 1408.[362] Bruni's next translation from Plato was of *Gorgias*, a work that had attracted particular attention among Chrsoloras's Florentine students. We know that Jacopo Angeli owned a Greek manuscript of *Gorgias*.[363] We also know that Angeli loaned his fellow student Pier Paolo Vergerio a manuscript of *Gorgias* that Vergerio read carefully in the winter of 1400–1401.[364] Even after Bruni's Latin version was published, the work still attracted students to the original language.[365] In 1425, we find that Poggio Bracciolini is reading *Gorgias* in Greek with Rinucio

Aretino in Rome,³⁶⁶ and in his lectures in Ferrara in 1446, Theodore Gaza translated or paraphrased most of *Gorgias* for his students.³⁶⁷

One Platonic work in which Chrysoloras is known to have taken an interest is the *Republic*. He may have lectured on it in Florence: it seems unlikely that a classroom that included Bruni, Vergerio, and Palla Strozzi would have failed to express an interest in this famous work.³⁶⁸ Coluccio Salutati was able to cite the work, perhaps by consulting a translation, in Florence in 1402.³⁶⁹ Chrysoloras's sustained efforts on the *Republic*, however, seem to belong to the period after he had left Florence. Between 1400 and 1403, while he was in Milan and Pavia, a translation was produced as a result of a collaboration between Chrysoloras and his pupil Uberto Decembrio. It has been suggested that Uberto's role was to make readable Latin prose from his master's literal translation.³⁷⁰

Chrysoloras's Roman pupil Cincio also encouraged the use of some works of Plato. After Chrysoloras's death in Constance in 1415, Bartolomeo Aragazzi da Montepulciano began to take Greek lessons from Cincio. His new master told him to copy out the text of *Protagoras*, *Lysis*, and *Laches*, and this copy, made in Constance sometime between March 1415 and January 1417, still survives.³⁷¹ It is unlikely to be a coincidence that Zomino of Pistoia, who was in Constance from 1417 to 1418, copied a manuscript that has a very similar combination of texts.³⁷² The dialogue *Meno* was used by Joannes Argyropoulos with his students: writing to Donato Acciaiuoli, Pier Filippo Pandolfini describes how he came across the Greek scholar at home reading the work with some of them.³⁷³ It is also worth observing that there are at least six versions of the pseudo-Platonic *Axiochus*, a level of activity that may indicate that some students cut their teeth on it.³⁷⁴

By the 1430s, many important works had been translated, and interest in the Greek text had become less lively. Certainly, in the second half of the fifteenth century, while manuscripts abound, Plato's works do not seem to have been much used with students of Greek. After Marsilio Ficino published his translation of the complete works around 1484, Latin philosophers had access to most of what they wanted from Plato.³⁷⁵ The letters were the first of the works of Plato to reach print in Greek, in the large collection of Greek letters published by Aldus in 1499.³⁷⁶ The Aldine *editio princeps* of the remaining works had to wait until 1513.³⁷⁷ Only one work was printed separately in Greek before 1530: *Cratylus* was printed in 1523 in Louvain by Martens, apparently as a student text.³⁷⁸ By and large, Plato was an author whom students read in Latin, not in Greek.

Hesiod

In 1444, Giannozzo Manetti delivered the funeral oration for Leonardo Bruni.³⁷⁹ He noted that among other poets, Bruni was familiar with Hesiod.³⁸⁰ He goes on to praise the poet: "Hesiodus autem pastor rudis et indoctus, aquula Castalii fontis libata, ita ad summum poeticae evasit ut nobilissima dogmata sua a Platone et Aristotele in mediis eorum utriusque philosophiae naturalis et moralis voluminibus magna cum veneratione velut oracula saepenumero frequententur"³⁸¹ (Having drunk from the spring of the Muses, the ignorant and uncultured shepherd Hesiod became such a great poet that his most noble judgments are often cited with great respect as if they were oracles by Plato and Aristotle in the midst of their works on moral and natural philosophy). This perspective is worth bearing in mind before looking more closely at the diffusion of Hesiod's works. In the first half of the fifteenth century, his verse was first encountered in the works of the two writers in whom contemporary readers were particularly interested: Plato and Aristotle.

In the fourteenth century, Manuel Moschopoulos had included Hesiod's *Works and Days* in his influential classroom anthology of classical poetry.[382] This ensured the work a secure place in the Byzantine curriculum and a ready supply of manuscripts when the work came to the attention of Western students. Among the very earliest manuscripts to reach the West was that of Simon Atumano: he had a Greek manuscript of Hesiod with him in Avignon in 1348, and this manuscript came to Florence.[383] A large number of manuscripts of Hesiod can be located in Italy in the first half of the fifteenth century. In Florence, Antonio Corbinelli owned two Greek manuscripts of Hesiod, both of which remained in the city after his death in 1425.[384] Niccolò Niccoli owned a manuscript of Hesiod and Oppian.[385] A list of the books owned by Palla Strozzi, compiled in 1431, includes two manuscripts of Hesiod.[386] Manetti himself owned a copy of *Works and Days*.[387] Copies of Hesiod can be connected with four teachers of the language: Filelfo brought a manuscript to Italy in 1427 and took it with him to Florence in 1429; Zomino of Pistoia made a copy; Vittorino da Feltre owned two copies; and Guarino Veronese, a further two.[388]

The earliest documented use of Hesiod in a Western classroom seems to date to the 1450s, when Gregorio Tifernas taught the poet to the young Giorgio Merula.[389] This may have been in Milan, and circumstantial evidence indicates that Constantine Lascaris taught Hesiod's *Works and Days* a few years later in the same city. Lascaris owned a manuscript of *Works and Days* with the scholia of Moschopoulos, which he may have acquired in Rhodes around 1455.[390] If this is so, it followed him when he went to Milan in 1458. A number of other manuscripts belong to his time in Milan. Lascaris made a careful copy, possibly for presentation, of a manuscript that included *Works and Days*.[391] Around 1462, he made a copy of Hesiod's works and was able to correct this copy in Milan using Filelfo's valuable thirteenth-century manuscript, a circumstance that suggests that their once-difficult relationship had become civil. Giorgio Valla copied this manuscript of Lascaris before his teacher left the city in 1465. Lascaris's copy of scholia on *Works and Days* survives in a manuscript from his Milan period.[392] Evidence that Lascaris taught Hesiod in Messina is also available. Around 1460, Andronicus Galiziotes made a copy of *Works and Days* for the Sicilian Ludovico Saccano. After Saccano's death around 1480, this manuscript passed to the cathedral library in Messina and was subsequently used by Lascaris for his teaching there: the text of Hesiod has interlinear Greek and Latin glosses in Lascaris' hand.[393] Elsewhere, Hartmann Schedel, a student of Demetrius Chalcondyles, notes that his master expounded Hesiod to his students in Padua after he had taken up the chair of Greek in October 1463.[394] If Andronicus Callistus lectured on Hesiod while he was in Bologna in the 1460s, the fact is not recorded. He did, however, make one manuscript of *Theogony* and *Scutum* and another of scholia to *Works and Days*.[395]

These classes seem to have stimulated translators in the 1460s. A translation of the *Theogony* was made by Marsilio Ficino, apparently in the 1460s.[396] Niccolò della Valle made his popular verse translation of *Works and Days* in 1462 when he was eighteen years old,[397] and Lorenzo Lippi da Colle made a lost version of *Works and Days* in 1469.[398] The first printed translation of *Works and Days* was that by Della

Valle, published in Milan about 1483 and reprinted many times before the end of the century.³⁹⁹ Bonino Mombrizio had signed the petition to have Constantine Lascaris installed in the Greek chair at Milan in 1463, and Lascaris produced some of his grammatical works for his benefit.⁴⁰⁰ A verse translation of the *Theogony* made by Mombrizio was printed in Ferrara in 1474.⁴⁰¹

The Greek text was first printed in Milan alongside Theocritus around 1480 as one of the texts of Bonaccorso's program of Greek studies.⁴⁰² It is possible that it was printed from a manuscript from Callistus's library, acquired by Bonaccorso and his partner in 1475. Callistus's pupil Angelo Poliziano lectured on Hesiod in Florence from 1483 to 1484, and Poliziano's students may thus have used a printed text of the work that was based on his master's manuscript.⁴⁰³ It is likely that when Antonio Codro Urceo lectured on Hesiod, perhaps between 1486 and 1487, his students made use of the same edition.⁴⁰⁴ The next edition, in the Aldine book of Greek poets of 1496, was probably based on a corrected copy of the Milan edition.⁴⁰⁵ Copies of this edition passed through the hands of Codro, Aleandro, and Forteguerri.⁴⁰⁶ Chalcondyles owned a copy of this edition in which he made extensive notes on *Works and Days*.⁴⁰⁷ By the time Vettor Fausto began to lecture on Hesiod and Pindar in Venice in November 1524, the Giunta had produced another Italian edition in Florence.⁴⁰⁸

The third printed edition of Hesiod emerged in Northern Europe: the Greek text of *Works and Days* was reproduced from the Aldine edition as part of François Tissard's program in Paris in 1507.⁴⁰⁹ The Strasbourg edition of *Works and Days* in Greek and Latin, dated to 1515, seems to have been part of Ottomar Nachtgall's course in that city.⁴¹⁰ It contains the first printed prose translation of the work, a very literal one to help the student into the Greek text. This version is likely to go back to Nachtgall's own lessons in Paris with Aleandro. Two other lecture courses are attested in Germany at this period: the grammars of Ceporinus, printed in Basle in 1522 and Zurich in 1526, include a portion of the Greek text of *Works and Days* and his notes on the work, apparently a relic from his classes;⁴¹¹ Philip Melanchthon is also known to have lectured on Hesiod in Wittenberg in 1522.⁴¹²

Most students, Byzantine and Latin, studied *Works and Days* with its sound practical and moral advice. The great majority of the Latin translations printed during this period are of this work, and it was the preferred Greek text in the classroom. The *Theogony* was much less read and may have been thought inappropriate for young Christian readers. The *Shield of Hercules* seems never to have been used in the classroom before 1530.

THEOCRITUS

In addition to Hesiod's *Works and Days*, Manuel Moschopoulos's influential anthology of classical poetry also included the first eight poems of Theocritus.⁴¹³ The popularity of this selection ensured that there were a good number of manuscripts of these poems to be had in the fifteenth century. The great manuscript collectors naturally acquired copies: Francesco Filelfo brought a copy of the poems to Italy in 1427;⁴¹⁴ Palla Strozzi owned two manuscripts in 1431;⁴¹⁵ and Vittorino da Feltre gave Gian Pietro da Lucca a manuscript of Theocritus in 1445.⁴¹⁶ However, in the first half of the fifteenth century, there are few signs that Theocritus had many Italian readers.

Among the earliest-known Western students of Theocritus was Giovanni Antonio Campano. Around 1452, Campano wrote to a friend asking for a manuscript of Theocritus.[417] In another letter, apparently to the same person, he wrote, "Habes libellum quendam graecum, superioribus his diebus a te summa cum diligentia transcriptum, ubi quantum a Martino accepi graeca vocabula latina absoluuntur. Hoc mihi vel maxime est opus . . ."[418] (You have a certain short Greek book, which you have recently copied with great care, in which the Greek words are glossed in Latin as I had them from Martino. I need this urgently . . .). It is likely that this refers to Martino Filetico, who would have been in his early twenties in 1452. Campano's words need not imply that Filetico taught Theocritus to students, but he did produce a translation of the first seven *Idylls* in the 1450s.[419] Thereafter, evidence of interest in Theocritus begins to accumulate. While teaching in Milan in the 1460s, Constantine Lascaris made two copies of Theocritus and copied notes on the text in another manuscript; in Messina, one of his students made a copy of Theocritus.[420] Andronicus Callistus is the first scholar known to have lectured on Theocritus in the West: he taught the poet in Bologna sometime between 1462 and 1466. It is possible that an extant translation of the first seven *Idylls* had its origins in Callistus's classroom.[421] Another translation, made by Pietro da Montagnana sometime before 1478, may be connected with Pietro's teaching.[422]

Theocritus was first printed as part of the Milanese program of Bonaccorso around 1480, perhaps from a manuscript that had been sold by Callistus in Milan.[423] This edition ensured that when Angelo Poliziano decided to lecture on Theocritus at the Florentine Studio in 1482, his students would have easy access to copies of the text.[424] The appearance of Filetico's version in print around 1482 would have provided any student who wanted it with a handy crib for the first poems.[425] Poliziano had himself studied Greek bucolic poetry in his youth, perhaps with Callistus who arrived in Florence when Poliziano was seventeen years old.[426] Poliziano's own annotated manuscript of Theocritus's poems is extant, and he translated Moschus's *Runaway Cupid* into Latin verse, a version that he made "pene puer."[427] This Greek poem occurs separately in a good number of fifteenth-century manuscripts and was first printed as an appendix to Lascaris's grammatical compendium in 1489.[428] In what sounds like an informal arrangement, Ermolao Barbaro expounded Theocritus and the pattern poems in Padua in 1484.[429] From a comment in the Florentine edition of Theocritus, we learn that Marcus Musurus taught the poet in Venice sometime before 1516.[430]

The most influential edition was that which emerged from the Aldine Press in 1496.[431] Girolamo Aleandro, in Padua, requested a copy from Aldus on March 10, 1506, and presumably took it with him to Paris in 1508.[432] At least one copy had preceded him: François Tissard seems to have taken this book with him when he left Italy, and Gourmont printed a number of texts from it in Paris between 1507 and 1508. In France, Aleandro made a remark in a letter to Aldus that suggests that one of these texts was an edition of Theocritus, probably printed by Gourmont in the early months of 1508.[433] Not a trace of it survives today, a reminder that entire editions of printed Greek books could disappear in the sixteenth century. Theocritus seems to have been particularly popular in Paris, with further editions around 1511 and another a few years later.[434] A German student who attended Aleandro's lectures on Theocritus tells us that Aleandro had reached the tenth *Idyll* by November 1511 and regrets that his lecturer did not spend more time on Koine Greek rather than on his author's Doric dialect.[435]

Despite the reservations of this student, Theocritus remained a popular classroom text in Northern Europe. In January 1516, the Juntine edition emerged, defended by a five-year privilege from Leo X; within the week, the more ambitious edition of Callierges appeared in Rome bearing a ten-year privilege from the same pontiff.[436] A plain text of Theocritus was printed by Martens in Louvain in 1520, and classes were taught in Gouda from this edition in about 1521.[437] It is likely that these texts were used for Melanchthon's lectures on Theocritus in Wittenberg the same year and perhaps for his lectures on the poet in 1526.[438] Martens's edition must have sold out by 1528, for in that year he printed another Greek text of the poet.[439]

EURIPIDES

The influence of the Byzantine curriculum on Western students of Aristophanes has been noticed.[440] It also shaped the way these students approached the plays of Euripides. In the East, *Hecuba* was the first play studied; of the others, only *Orestes* and *Phoenissae* were regularly used.[441] The plays reappeared very early in Western Europe: Simon Atumano had a manuscript that included eighteen plays of Euripides with him in Avignon in 1348.[442] Moreover, Euripides is the only Greek author besides Homer who is known to have been taught in the West in the fourteenth century, for Leonzio Pilato used *Hecuba* in his teaching. After Pilato's teaching came to an end, his manuscript of the plays remained in Florence. Euripides, however, seems to have been forgotten in the West for the better part of half a century.[443]

The revival began with Giovanni Aurispa. In 1413, Aurispa bought a manuscript of the Byzantine select plays of Sophocles and Euripides in Chios, and in 1417, he sold it to Niccolò Niccoli in Florence.[444] Antonio Corbinelli owned no fewer than five manuscripts of Euripides at his death in 1425.[445] Copies of Euripides can be connected with the teachers Vittorino da Feltre and Guarino Veronese.[446] Francesco Filelfo took a special interest in the plays, and three of his manuscripts are known. More importantly, we know that he studied the plays: he translated Polydorus's opening speech from *Hecuba* in a consolatory address to the Marcello family, and he translated fifty lines from *Phoenissae*.[447] Other early owners can also be identified. Theodore Gaza and his relative Andronicus Callistus made and owned manuscripts.[448] The Englishman John Free, who traveled to Ferrara in 1456 to study under Guarino, acquired a portion of the dramatist's work in Italy sometime before his death in 1465.[449] Around 1475, Constantine Lascaris was reunited with a manuscript of the triad that he had owned in his youth in Constantinople.[450] Another extant Latin version of *Hecuba*, in prose, is often attributed to Pietro da Montagnana.[451] Whoever made the version, its context suggests that it was prepared in connection with learning or teaching the language. In Northern Europe, George Hermonymus made two manuscripts, apparently while he was teaching in Paris: one of these is of *Hecuba* alone and the other of *Hecuba* and *Orestes*.[452] The text of the Byzantine triad of Euripides was certainly in the hands of most of the prominent teachers of the language.

There was a quickening of interest in the plays of Euripides in Italy in the second half of the fifteenth century. The holdings of the Vatican Library are revealing: in 1455, the library had four manuscripts of Euripides; by 1475, this number had grown to seven; and by 1481, it had a total of thirteen.[453] The library records also show that in the last quarter of the fifteenth century, manuscripts of Euripides were borrowed more often than those of any other Greek author. Indeed, between late 1477 and the middle of 1484, a total of eleven loans are recorded to eleven different individuals. It is plausible that someone in Rome was lecturing on the plays during this period.[454] Lectures on Euripides may be tentatively assigned to Janus Lascaris in Florence some years later. In October 1492, Lascaris was appointed to give two lecture courses at the Florentine *Studio*: one on Greek philosophy and the other on poetry.[455] Girolamo Amaseo writes of Lascaris the following April, "Nec te praetereat complures graecos ex Graecia in Laschari domum confluxisse et latinas litteras discunt ut possint postmodum profiteri. Unus ex ipsis mihi tragoediam, quam mense maio explicaturus est Lascharus, conscribit"[456] (And let it not escape you that many Greeks have gathered together from Greece in the house of Lascaris, and they are learning Latin so that they may find employment afterward. One of these is copying a tragedy for me, which Lascaris is to lecture on in May). This tragedy is very unlikely to be the work of Aeschylus, who was rarely studied in the fifteenth century and never, to my knowledge, used in the classroom.[457] It may refer to a work of Sophocles, on whom Lascaris certainly lectured around this time, but it is possible that he was about to lecture on one of Euripides' plays.[458] Lascaris's interest in Euripides during the 1490s is well attested: sometime after this, and certainly before June 18, 1495, he oversaw the printing of four plays in Florence: *Medea*, *Hippolytus*, *Alcestis*, and *Andromache*.[459] The Aldine edition of the complete plays emerged in February 1503.[460] It is dedicated to Demetrius Chalcondyles, apparently in the hope that the elderly scholar—who was then lecturing on the Aldine edition of Sophocles—would soon lecture on the Aldine Euripides.[461] There is, however, no evidence that he did so.

The appearance of a number of translations of Euripides demonstrates the author's growing popularity in the early years of the sixteenth century. The earliest of these translations was made by Erasmus. He seems to have had an interest in Euripides as early as 1501, and he translated *Hecuba* in 1504.[462] His choice of play is not surprising, since every student began with it. Thus it was *Hecuba* that was translated by Giorgio Anselmi and printed in Parma in 1506,[463] and it was *Hecuba* with which Johann Cuno began his own studies of Euripides.[464] Erasmus himself claimed in the preface to his *Hecuba* that he translated Euripides because he wanted to train his Greek on a profane author before he turned to the New Testament; he later indicated that he had also been dissatisfied with Filelfo's rendering of the opening lines of the play.[465] Erasmus's decision to translate *Iphigenia in Aulis*, which had recently become more easily available in the Aldine edition, is more interesting.[466] Perhaps the author of the *Querela pacis* found Euripides' hostility to war congenial; perhaps the religious reformer in him enjoyed its attacks on superstition. Erasmus's two translations were printed by Badius in Paris in September 1506.[467] By November, Erasmus was in Bologna, where he remained for at least a year.[468] He remained in contact with Paris because he was aware in October 1507 that Badius's first edition of his translation had sold out and that the printer now hoped to print a new edition.[469] However, Erasmus chose to give his new edition to Aldus in Venice, where it was printed in December.[470]

Erasmus's stay in Bologna coincides with the presence of another contemporary translator of Euripides. François Tissard was certainly in Bologna on March 19, 1507, when he received his doctorate in civil and canon law at the university; he was still in Bologna when, on April 1, 1507, he signed the dedication of his translations of Euripides to the future king of France, François Duke of Valois.[471] Tissard apparently carried these versions into France himself, for by August, he was editing Greek texts for Gourmont's new Greek press in Paris. Tissard translated three plays, *Medea*, *Hippolytus*, and *Alcestis*, and we may suppose that he translated these from the Florentine edition that prints these plays in this order. Although he avoided the plays that Erasmus had recently translated, the translators seem to have worked independently. Neither mentions the other, and Tissard's versions seem to have originated in the summer of 1506, before the publication of Badius's edition of Erasmus's version, and before Erasmus himself arrived in Bologna.[472] The success in Paris of Erasmus's translation, however, does seem to have moved François of Valois to express an interest in Tissard's work in December 1506, and Tissard consequently revised his earlier, more literal, rendering for dedication to the prince.[473]

Despite Tissard's later work with Gourmont's press, his versions of Euripides were never printed. Erasmus's translations, however, remained very popular in Northern Europe. Like several of Erasmus's translations, they appealed to many as fine examples of modern Latin literature. They even graced the stage: Erasmus's translation of *Hecuba* was acted in Louvain in September 1506, and one of his translations appears to have been produced again in Louvain in September 1514.[474] Erasmus's versions were also used as an aid to the study of the works in their original language: Martens printed the Greek text of *Hecuba* and *Iphigenia in Aulis* in Louvain in 1520, and Erasmus's versions were printed alongside the Greek texts in Basle in 1524 and in 1530.[475]

Sophocles

Sophocles made an early reappearance in Western Europe in two manuscripts owned by Simon Atumano. Atumano certainly had one of these manuscripts with him in Avignon in 1348.[476] The tutor of Petrarch and Boccaccio, Leonzio Pilato, owned another manuscript of the plays that was in Florence by 1362.[477] Yet despite this early start, Sophocles made little impression in the West for many decades. Some Italian owners can, of course, be identified from the first half of the fifteenth century. Giovanni Aurispa was the first, buying a manuscript that included *Aiax*, *Electra*, and *Oedipus Rex* in Chios in 1413. In 1417, he sold this manuscript to Niccolò Niccoli, and Niccoli subsequently acquired another manuscript of Sophocles from Aurispa.[478] Antonio Corbinelli, who bequeathed his library to the Badia Fiorentina on his death in 1425, owned a number of manuscripts of Sophocles.[479] A list of Palla Strozzi's books, compiled in 1431, includes two manuscripts of Sophocles.[480] Cyriaco of Ancona had a Greek manuscript of Sophocles, and Francesco Filelfo owned one that contains all the plays except *Oedipus Coloneus*.[481]

The first Western student known to have used Sophocles in his early Greek studies was introduced to him in Constantinople: Giovanni Tortelli studied *Aiax* and *Electra* in that city between 1435 and 1437. Later, in his *De orthographia*, he says that it was Isidore of Kiev who taught him to love Sophocles.[482] The first documented use of Sophocles in an Italian classroom was by Theodore Gaza: his students Lodovico Carbone and Basino da Parma tell us that Gaza lectured on Sophocles while he was in Ferrara in the years 1446 to 1449.[483] Andronicus Callistus made a copy of *Antigone* that has interlinear Latin glosses, and he produced a manuscript of scholia on the Byzantine triad.[484] A translation of *Aiax* that has been attributed to Pietro da Montagana survives in one of his manuscripts: it may have been connected with his Greek teaching in Padua, perhaps during the 1460s.[485]

The Vatican Library accumulated many manuscripts during the middle decades of the century. In 1455, at the end of the pontificate of Nicholas V, the library held five manuscripts of Sophocles; twenty years later, in 1475, it had twelve.[486] During the same period, Cardinal Bessarion was gathering his own library of classical Greek literature in Rome. His collection included two manuscripts of Sophocles by 1468, and another soon joined them.[487] After the cardinal's death in 1472, this library was dispatched to Venice. In Venice, the library of Ermolao Barbaro included a manuscript of Sophocles, apparently acquired between 1485 and Barbaro's death in 1493.[488] The prolific scribe Joannes Rhosos completed a manuscript of the Byzantine triad in the city in 1489.[489] The substantial private library of Giorgio Valla included a manuscript of four plays, and some time after August 1483, Valla acquired the two manuscripts of Callistus noted previously.[490] Bartolomeo Zamberti, at the age of about eighteen, made a copy of *Aiax* and *Electra* in Venice in 1491.[491] At about the same time, Giorgio Merula is known to have taught *Aiax* in Milan.[492]

In Florence, Joannes Argyropoulos may have introduced his students to Sophocles: one of these students, Pier Filippo Pandolfini, praises his master's reading of Sophocles in a surviving letter.[493] Two manuscripts, apparently both from the 1490s, are associated with the Florentine monk Pier Candido of Santa Maria degli Angeli.[494] We have seen that Janus Lascaris was about to lecture on an unidentified Greek tragedy in Florence in 1493.[495] He certainly lectured on Sophocles in Florence, probably around 1492. It is unlikely to be a coincidence that, in about 1493, Alessandra di Bartolomeo Scala recited the part of *Electra* in Greek in a Florentine production of the play.[496]

Contact with the works of Sophocles was largely confined to Italy during the fifteenth century. It is, however, curious that Humphrey, Duke of Gloucester, who knew no Greek, chose to name one of his illegitimate children Antigone.[497] John Free's manuscript of Euripides, already noticed, also contained some plays of Sophocles. Free's copy, acquired sometime between 1456 and his death in 1465, was probably the first copy of Sophocles to reach England.[498] The Frisian physician and scholar Adolf Occo, who studied Greek in Italy during the 1470s, made a copy of four plays and made extracts from *Aiax* and *Antigone*. His manuscripts were among the first texts of Sophocles to reach Germany.[499]

The plays of Sophocles were first printed in the Aldine edition of August 1502, and the volume was dedicated to the editor of Euripides, Janus Lascaris.[500] The Aldine edition seems to have been taken up immediately in Milan by Demetrius Chalcondyles, who lectured on the seven plays of Sophocles for nine months, from November 1502 until the end of July the following year.[501] Aldus no doubt anticipated that some students at these lectures would want to acquire copies of the Aldine text, which were available in Venice for three ducats in 1503.[502] Reuchlin ordered a copy from Venice in November 1502;[503] Franciscus Vitalis Bodianus asked Aldus for a copy in 1504;[504] and Scipione Forteguerri owned a copy.[505] Marcus Musurus seems to have lectured on *Oedipus Coloneus* at some point between 1503 and 1516 while he was teaching in Padua and Venice.[506] The notebook of the German scholar Johann Cuno has a Latin translation of much of *Aiax* and part of *Electra*, a version apparently copied during his time in northern Italy in the first decade of the sixteenth century.[507]

Two observations indicate that Sophocles was not often used with beginners in the language: before 1530, there were no editions of single plays, and there was no printed Latin translation of any play. Scholars of some experience were better served: in 1518, Janus Lascaris edited the ancient scholia in Rome.[508] The seven plays of the Aldine edition were reprinted in Florence in 1522 and again in Paris in 1528.[509] By this time, the plays had attracted an enthusiast. In 1527, Alessandro de' Pazzi, Florentine ambassador to Venice, sent his Latin version of Sophocles' *Electra* to Pietro Bembo for his comments, and he tells Bembo that he is working on an *Oedipus*, presumably a version of *Oedipus Rex*. Bembo politely suggests that his *Electra* needs more work.[510]

Pindar

Pindar's *Olympian Odes* were included in the compendium of classical poetry that Manuel Moschopoulos compiled in the fourteenth century.[511] Despite the influence of this handbook, it does not seem that the poet was much read in the West in the fifteenth century. One of our earliest notices comes from George of Trebizond, who wrote that Guarino Veronese was either reading or teaching Pindar between 1417 and 1418.[512] The poet was certainly available in Italy from several sources by the 1420s: Giovanni Aurispa brought a Greek manuscript of Pindar to Italy in 1423; Antonio Corbinelli had two in his library at his death in 1425; Francesco Filelfo brought one back from Constantinople in 1427; and Palla Strozzi is known to have had a copy by 1431.[513] It is harder to be sure that these scholars read the works they owned. Filelfo, at least, seems to have read his Pindar, and he loaned a copy to Giovanni Patrizio sometime before April 10, 1437.[514] In 1444, Giannozzo Manetti stated that Leonardo Bruni knew the poet, a claim for which there is otherwise no evidence.[515]

One scholar certainly taught Pindar to his students. In a letter dated between 1463 and 1466, Andronicus Callistus writes that he is lecturing on Pindar in his Greek classes in Bologna.[516] Callistus's teaching clearly had an impact on one of his pupils, Bartolomeo Fonzio. Fonzio made a manuscript of a Latin version of the *Olympian Odes* that probably represents his reworking of a rough version derived from Callistus.[517] Thereafter, Pindar reappears in a number of contexts that suggest his use with students. Three manuscripts are associated with Constantine Lascaris in Milan: he seems to have had a manuscript of the *Olympian Odes* with him when he arrived in 1458; he made a careful copy of these odes during his time in the city; and he copied scholia on the *Olympians* toward the end of his time in the city.[518] Adolphe Occo wrote out the *Olympian Odes* in the 1480s.[519] We do not know when George Hermonymus made the copy of the *Olympians* and scholia that is extant in his hand, but it would appear to be connected with his teaching in France, that is, after 1475.[520] One Girolamo Scotti of Siena seems to have paid particular attention to Pindar in the 1480s, for between 1484 and 1488, he borrowed the text three times from the Vatican Library.[521] We would like to know what inspired Jacopo Sannazaro to make a translation of the first lines of the first *Olympian Ode* at some point between 1495 and 1501, and why he went no further.[522] Urbano Bolzanio taught Pindar at some point in his long career, as we learn from a passing comment made by his nephew.[523] One thing is clear from this brief survey: students of the poems tended to confine their attention to the *Olympian Odes*.

Pindar reached print in 1513, when the Aldine edition was dedicated to Andrea Navagero.[524] Only two years later, a new scholarly edition of the poems and scholia was printed in Rome by Zacharias Callierges, the first Greek text to be printed in Rome.[525] A single ode, the *Fourteenth Olympian*, was printed in Greek in Leipzig in 1519, apparently under the direction of Philip Melanchthon.[526] Stefano Negri lectured publicly on Pindar in Milan sometime before August 1521, while in Venice, Vettor Fausto began to lecture on Hesiod and Pindar in November 1524.[527] The complete Greek text was reprinted in Basle in 1526, edited by Jacobus Ceporinus, and prepared for publication after Ceporinus's death by Ulrich Zwingli.[528] This edition may have done something to stimulate interest in Germany: early in the following year, Menrad Molther translated the first two *Olympian Odes* in Heidelberg, a modest work that was thought worthy of the press in Hagenau.[529] In 1528, Joannes Lonicer's Latin prose translation of all of Pindar was printed in Basle.[530]

Apollonius of Rhodes

At Constantinople in January 1423, Francesco Filelfo bought a famous thirteenth-century manuscript that included Apollonius from the wife of John Chrysoloras. This manuscript came with him to Venice in 1427 and remained part of his library until his death in 1481.[531] It was not, however, the first manuscript of the *Argonautica* of Apollonius to reach Italy since ancient times. This honor belongs to the oldest extant manuscript of the poem, which was acquired by Niccolò Niccoli in Florence from Giovanni Aurispa in 1424.[532] In Florence, sometime in the following decades, its evident antiquity inspired a faithful imitation that belonged to the Giannozzo Manetti.[533] The text can be connected with a number of prominent teachers. The library of Vittorino da Feltre in Mantua contained a manuscript of the poem, while Vittorino's student Basinio da Parma was preparing a Latin poem on the Argonauts and owned a manuscript of the work at his death in 1457.[534] Guarino Veronese owned at least one Greek manuscript of Apollonius.[535] Constantine Lascaris was able to use Filelfo's manuscript of the work to make a copy for his own use in Milan in 1465.[536] Demetrius Chalcondyles also made a copy of Apollonius.[537]

The late 1460s and early 1470s saw a great deal of interest in Apollonius's poem. It was copied repeatedly among the circle around Bessarion in Rome. The cardinal himself owned two copies, and George Trivizias, a scribe in his pay, made four copies between 1468 and 1472.[538] Domizio Calderini, in Rome, borrowed from Lorenzo de' Medici a Greek manuscript of Apollonius in October 1473.[539] In Venice, Marco Aurelio borrowed a manuscript of the work from Bessarion's collection in 1474.[540] The first certain use of Apollonius with students was by Andronicus Callistus, who lectured on the poet in Florence at some point between 1471 and 1475.[541] The young Angelo Poliziano appears to have made his version of the fifth book of the *Iliad* during Callistus's time in Florence. In the marginalia to this version Poliziano refers to Pherecydes, a learned allusion that can be traced back to the scholia on Apollonius.[542] It is possible that such an able young student came across this passage in his own reading, but it seems more likely that he was directed to it by his master. Callistus's teaching made a particular impression on one student, Bartolomeo Fonzio, who was attempting to acquire a copy of the text in 1472.[543] Fonzio made use of Callistus's lectures in two ways. First, he compiled a complete translation of the poem based on these lectures.⁵⁴⁴ Second, after Callistus had left Florence, Fonzio made use of material on the *Argonautica* of Apollonius for his own lectures in Florence on the *Argonautica* of Valerius Flaccus. Valerius was first printed in 1474, and Fonzio began to annotate his copy of this edition in 1476. We know from this source that, from November 1481 to July 1482, he lectured on Valerius at the Florentine *Studio*. He finished another course on Valerius in 1504.⁵⁴⁵

After Callistus left Italy in 1475, interest in the poem seems to have subsided for a few years. From the mid-1480s, however, copies multiplied rapidly, with Venice and her Cretan scribes playing an important role.⁵⁴⁶ Ermolao Barbaro was reading the poet in Venice in 1484;⁵⁴⁷ Giorgio Valla acquired a copy in the city in the 1490s;⁵⁴⁸ and the Cretan Zacharias Callierges made two copies, probably in Venice in the 1490s.⁵⁴⁹ The same decade saw Demetrius Moschus produce four manuscripts, probably all in Venice.⁵⁵⁰ Meanwhile in Florence, Poliziano was reading Apollonius in the 1480s,⁵⁵¹ and the Florentine scribe Joannes Scutariota made at least two copies.⁵⁵²

A printed edition of the text was meditated in Florence by Janus Lascaris as early as 1493.⁵⁵³ This edition finally emerged from the press in Florence in 1496, a fine piece of printing with the text printed in Greek capitals and the surrounding scholia in lowercase type.⁵⁵⁴ A teacher at the *Studio*, Lorenzo Ciati, copied his manuscript of the poem, completed in 1498, from this edition.⁵⁵⁵ The remainder of the edition was subsequently acquired by Aldus Manutius, who was able to offer a copy to Johann Reuchlin in August 1502 and was advertising copies for sale in his catalog of June 1503.⁵⁵⁶ Of this edition, Willibald Pirckheimer owned a copy that he had decorated by Albrecht Dürer;⁵⁵⁷ Scipione Forteguerri owned one;⁵⁵⁸ Hermann, Count of Neuenahr, seems to have taken delivery of a copy around 1514;⁵⁵⁹ Hernan Nuñez de Guzman owned a copy;⁵⁶⁰ and Cuthbert Tunstall donated his copy of the edition to Cambridge University Library in 1528.⁵⁶¹ Although Agosto Valdo chose to lecture on Apollonius in Rome in 1516, these copies of the text still sold very slowly.⁵⁶² In fact, the Florentine edition satisfied the printers, and presumably the students, of Europe until 1521 when the Aldine Press reprinted the text.⁵⁶³

Pseudo-Orpheus

The *Hymns* and the *Argonautica* attributed to Orpheus were not part of the Byzantine curriculum that did so much to shape the early tradition of Greek studies in the West. Both works were brought to Italy by Giovanni Aurispa in 1423, and Antonio Corbinelli had a copy of the *Orphic Argonautica* in his library in Florence at the time of his death in 1425.⁵⁶⁴ Francesco Filelfo brought another Greek manuscript of these works with him on his return to Italy in 1427.⁵⁶⁵ It is likely that Giannozzo Manetti found the exemplar for his own copy in Florence.⁵⁶⁶ However, the works do not seem to have made much of an impression in Italy in the first half of the fifteenth century. Among the first Western students of Greek to use pseudo-Orpheus was Marsilio Ficino, who translated the *Orphic Argonautica* and *Hymns* in his youth, perhaps in the 1450s. This literal translation seems to have been made as an exercise and never intended for publication.⁵⁶⁷

Constantine Lascaris was an enthusiastic champion of this work. He was lecturing publicly on the *Orphic Argonautica* in Milan in about 1463.⁵⁶⁸ A passage in Lascaris's grammatical work on the Greek noun, published there in that year, informs us,

"[Τὰ Ἀργοναυτικὰ] δὴ πάλαι καταμεληθέντα μόλις ποτὲ αὐτὸς ἐν Μεδιολάνῳ εὑρὼν σεσηπότα, ἐκγράψας τε καὶ τοῖς ἄλλοις μεταδούς, δημοσίως ἀναγινώσκω, πολλῶν καὶ λογίων νέων φοιτώντων. Καὶ νῦν ἐς τὰ ἔσχατα τῶν δυστυχῶν· Ἑλλήνων ἀνεβίω ὁ ἠγνοημένος ἐκεῖνος Ὀρφεύς"[569] (Then some time ago, I myself found it with difficulty moldering away in Milan; and having copied it and shared it with others, I am lecturing on it publicly to many erudite young men. And now that unknown man Orpheus has risen up again among the last of the unhappy Greeks). Lascaris certainly subscribed a manuscript that included the *Orphic Argonautica* and *Hymns* in Milan in 1464 and made another copy that may also belong to this period.[570] His teaching in the city made at least one convert. Some of the signatories of the petition that helped Lascaris to the chair of Greek in Milan have already been noticed. Leodrisio Crivelli signed this petition in December 1462.[571] Crivelli made a translation of the *Orphic Argonautica* in 1463 or 1464, and it is reasonable to suppose that this version owed a great deal to Lascaris's lectures.[572] A copy of Crivelli's version is bound with the Greek text of the work and the epitome of Chrysoloras's grammar.[573] The version of the *Orphic Hymns* made by Filelfo's son, Giovanni Mario, may have been inspired by increased interest in pseudo-Orpheus in Milan in the 1460s.[574]

Lascaris maintained his interest in pseudo-Orpheus after his move to Messina in 1466. There he composed prefatory material for the poetry, Εἰς τὰ προλεγόμενα τοῦ σοφοῦ Ὀρφέως, which he added to the manuscript of the work that he had copied in Milan in 1464.[575] Such material would have made an appropriate prolusion to any lecture on the poetry attributed to Orpheus. Another manuscript made by Lascaris in Messina has a Greek extract relating to Orpheus, and he added interlinear glosses to a manuscript of the *Orphic Argonautica* copied in Messina by his pupil Manuel.[576] Filelfo had already in 1440 sounded a note of skepticism about the identification of the author of this poetry with the legendary Orpheus, but Lascaris's preface shows that he entertained no such doubts.[577] He believed that the ancient poet wrote the work in Phoenician letters, just as Dictys Cretensis did his.[578] Lascaris's belief in the high antiquity of these works accounts for his sustained interest in them.

It is possible that Lascaris was responsible for the text of the *Orphic Argonautica* and *Orphic Hymns* that was printed for the first time in Florence in 1500.[579] The Aldine Press reissued the text in 1517, and this circumstance may have influenced Vettor Fausto's decision to lecture on the *Orphic Argonautica* in his attempt to secure the chair of Greek in Venice the following year.[580] In Florence, the Giunta published another edition in 1519, and in the same year Crivelli's version was first printed with the *Argonautica* of Valerius Flaccus in Bologna.[581] In 1523, this version was printed in Basle alongside the Greek text.[582]

Quintus of Smyrna

The late classical epic poet Quintus, author of the *Posthomerica*, tells the story from the end of the *Iliad* to the fall of Troy in fourteen books. A reference to Smyrna in the poem has been taken to be autobiographical, and the epithet *Smyrnaeus* appears to have been in use by the 1460s.[583] The poet was also known as Quintus Calaber because his work was rediscovered in Calabria. The use of this name by the Aldine *editio princeps* established it among scholars for many decades. Like pseudo-Orpheus,

Quintus was not part of the Byzantine curriculum, and his brief vogue in fifteenth-century Italy is a distinctive episode in the history of Greek studies.

Quintus was rediscovered by Cardinal Bessarion, or by his agents, not long after the fall of Constantinople in a monastery near Otranto in southern Italy. The manuscript that Bessarion brought to light is no longer extant, but the copy that he commissioned from Michael Apostolis gave rise to many descendants, and copies of the work multiplied rapidly during the following decades.[584] Although this rapid diffusion suggests some lively interest in the recovered work, it does not seem to have been often taught. The poem was, however, used in Italy with students of Greek by at least one influential teacher, Constantine Lascaris.

Buried in Lascaris's grammatical work on the Greek noun is an interesting aside on Quintus. He writes, "Ὁ δὲ θεοσεβέστατος Βησσαρίων . . . ταύτην ἐξ Ἀπουλίας ἀνασώσας, τοῖς βουλομένοις μετέδωκεν· ἣν καὶ αὐτὸς πάλαι μὲν ἐπόθουν, νῦν δὲ ἀγαθῇ τύχῃ κτησάμενος, δημοσίως ἀναγνώσομαι μετὰ τὰ Ἀργοναυτικὰ τοῦ σοφοῦ Ὀρφέως"[585] (The devout Bessarion, having recovered this work from Apulia, gave it to those who wanted it. I myself had long wanted it, and now that I have the good fortune to possess it, I shall lecture on it publicly after the *Orphic Argonautica*). The grammatical work was published in 1463.[586] If we assume that Lascaris could only lecture publicly after he had taken up his chair in Milan, on July 24, 1463, this statement (if it is not a later revision) must be placed between that date and the end of the year. Bessarion, it seems, made a transcript of the work available to interested parties. Although Lascaris knew of Quintus and was eager to secure a copy, it still took the text a good eight years to travel from Otranto to his study in Milan.

Only one manuscript can be certainly connected with Lascaris's time in Milan. This manuscript, as we learn from one of his notes written on it, was copied in haste by Lascaris himself and by a number of Italian scribes.[587] This hurried copy was made from Apostolis's apograph of the lost Otranto manuscript, but its precise date remains to be established.[588] Lascaris certainly makes it sound like a recent acquisition in 1463. Later, in Messina, he recalls that he acquired it with difficulty.[589] We may perhaps press Lascaris's words in his grammar and suppose that the manuscript of Quintus was completed after he had begun to lecture on the *Orphic Argonautica*. Lascaris had been teaching privately in Milan since 1458, but the *Orphic Argonautica* was the first text he lectured on publicly, presumably after his appointment to the chair of Greek in July 1463.[590] We know that Apostolis's copy of the work was bought in Ferrara by Giorgio Merula from Nardo Palmieri for four gold pieces in October 1462.[591] It thus seems that Lascaris's copy was made from this manuscript after Merula had acquired it. This would establish an otherwise unattested link between Merula and Lascaris.[592]

The various Italian hands in Lascaris's Milan transcript of Quintus have not yet been identified. These scribes were presumably Lascaris's students, enlisted by their master to make a rapid copy of a text that was passing through Milan.[593] We know the names of many of his students in Milan and may guess that some of these had heard him lecture on Quintus before he left the city two years later. Lascaris took his enthusiasm for Quintus with him when he transferred his school to Messina in 1466. Thirty years later, in 1496, he brought his editorial work on Quintus to completion: in June, he finished a copy of the complete text, heavily revised and corrected, based on the hasty Milan transcript. He has supplied each book with an argument and the whole work with a preface.[594] A copy of the first book alone appears to have been made from this complete manuscript in the same year.[595] The following year, a pupil, Francesco Giovanelli, made another copy from Lascaris's manuscript in Messina.[596] A further manuscript survives today in Naples, perhaps dating to the 1490s, that has a nearly complete interlinear Latin translation of the first five books.[597] Thus we have evidence of Lascaris's interest in the *Posthomerica* at both ends of his long career.

Lascaris's interest in the work is the most sustained of any Greek scholar, but copies of the work belonged to several teachers of the language. Theodore Gaza may have owned one, and Demetrius Chalcondyles made a copy.[598] Andronicus Callistus may also have owned the *Posthomerica*.[599] Callistus was closer to Bessarion than Lascaris and could probably have procured a copy in the 1450s had he wanted. Failing this, Merula, who was in possession of Apostolis's influential transcript of Quintus from late 1462, is known to have attended Callistus's lectures on Theocritus in Bologna sometime between 1462 and 1466.[600] When Callistus left Florence in 1475, he moved to Milan and sold his fine library; he then set out for Northern Europe.[601] By 1476, he was in London with his compatriot George Hermonymus, where another copy of Quintus was made, but it seems that only Hermonymus survived to return to France later the same year. Returning from England, Hermonymus evidently had with him at least one manuscript of Quintus because he completed a copy of it soon after his arrival in Paris. The manuscript—now lost—from which he made this copy was not derived from Apostolis's copy.[602] It is plausible that it had belonged to Callistus. If Hermonymus's exemplar was Callistus's own manuscript, then it is worth noting that from the sale of most of his library he chose to retain this particular work and carry it northward with him.

The Callistus–Hermonymus copy of the text was probably the first to reach Northern Europe, but it seems to have been closely followed by another survival from the classroom of Lascaris. The Frisian physician Adolf Occo owned a Greek manuscript of Quintus that has the text in the hand of Lascaris and marginalia by Occo. This manuscript has interlinear glosses to books one to seven, probably in Lascaris's hand.[603] This is one of three manuscripts owned by Occo that contains Lascaris's hand, but it is not clear that Occo studied under the Greek scholar.[604] The manuscripts were probably acquired by Occo or by Rudolf Agricola during their time in Italy in the 1470s. Agricola was able to quote some memorable lines from Quintus in a letter to Johann Reuchlin of 1484, an unusual piece of erudition for a German scholar of the period. At Agricola's death in October 1485, Occo acted as his literary executor.[605]

The first edition of the Greek text around 1504 was well in advance of poets such as Pindar and Aeschylus and of prose authors such as Plato and Plutarch. However, after half a century of sustained interest in the newly recovered poetry of Quintus, the attentions of scholars and students subsided. The edition of 1504 was the last of the Greek text until 1569.[606]

Epilogue

For much of the fifteenth century, a shortage of Greek texts, and of competent Greek teachers, frustrated would-be students of the language. In the first decades of the fifteenth century, Florentine libraries held more Greek manuscripts than those of any other Italian city, but even in Florence, the scarcity of elementary Greek texts hindered students. In 1425, Ambrogio Traversari asked Francesco Barbaro to give his monastery a Greek Psalter to allow Greek studies to continue there.[1] Traversari himself, having advised Francesco Coppola to learn Greek by collating a Greek Psalter with a Latin translation, was unable to lend him a copy for this purpose: "Psalterium quidem et evangelia et huiusmodi teneo, sed ita ut ea mittere nequeam; sunt enim partim amicorum, et que nostra sunt occuparunt adulescentes nostri quidam graecitatis item studiosi; venale vero prorsus nihil habeo"[2] (I do have a Psalter and the Gospels, and suchlike, but I cannot send them to you. Some of them belong to friends, and those that are mine are being used by some of my young Greek students. I really have none I can sell). Traversari was obliged to cobble together his classroom texts from a number of sources. Students had to use the Greek manuscripts that were at hand, not necessarily those that they or their teachers would have chosen. The Byzantine curriculum shaped Greek studies in the West not only because Byzantine teachers taught the texts they had studied in their youth but also because these texts were the most numerous and widely available.

By the end of the fifteenth century, the early Greek presses had transformed this situation. In December 1507, Aldus Manutius wrote in the preface to his edition of Erasmus's translation of two plays of Euripides his optimistic assessment of the state of contemporary learning: "Deerant olim boni libri, deerant docti praeceptores; eorum enim qui callerent utranque linguam, mira paucitas. Nunc est, Deo gratia, et bonorum librorum copia et doctorum hominum, tam in Italia quam extra"[3] (Once there were few good books, and few learned teachers; there was a terrible shortage of men who knew both languages. Now, by the grace of God, there is an abundance of good books and learned men, both in Italy and abroad). The distribution of large numbers of printed Greek books reduced the need for students of the language to chase them throughout Europe. The ready availability of bilingual grammars, elementary Greek texts, and Greek–Latin lexica made it easier for determined scholars to teach themselves the language. For most of the fifteenth century, the teacher of Greek was valued not only because of his knowledge of the language but also because he had Greek manuscripts and the ability to multiply them. By the beginning of the sixteenth century, students were no longer dependent on their teachers for the elementary texts of the language. One consequence of this development was that self-instruction became an increasingly common alternative to formal lessons.

Some attempt must be made to address the difficult issue of the size of these early editions. Here, examples may be adduced that will allow a plausible conjecture. Thus 1,025 copies of the *editio princeps* of Marsilio Ficino's Latin translation of Plato were printed;[4] 800 copies of the Suda lexicon were printed in 1499;[5] there were 600 seven-volume sets of the Complutensian polyglot Bible printed in Spain from 1514 to 1517;[6] there were 1,200 to 1,300 copies of Erasmus's Greek–Latin New Testament of 1516, and about 2,000 of the second edition of 1519.[7] These are all rather unusual books, and it is difficult to generalize on the basis of such numbers. We are on surer ground with the Aldine Press. In the preface to the Aldine edition of Euripides, completed in 1503, Aldus says that he usually printed one thousand copies of his books.[8] Demetrius Ducas seems to confirm this number in the Greek preface to the Aldine Greek rhetoricians of 1508 to 1509, although there, "one thousand" may simply be a round and rhetorically convenient number.[9] There were perhaps one thousand copies printed of Nachtgall's *Collectanea sacrosancta*, a pamphlet of Greek texts in sixteen leaves printed in Strasbourg in 1515.[10] According to the contract for the first edition of the Latin grammar of Francesco Faraone, dated 1500, one thousand copies of this work were to be printed.[11] Eight hundred copies of another contemporary textbook, a compilation of Latin exercises intended for students at Eton, were printed in 1519.[12] From the end of our period, we know that the first editions of Nicolas Clénard's Greek grammar, all apparently printed in 1530, numbered something more than four thousand copies.[13] By far, the highest figure known comes from Ferrara and the years between 1508 and 1510: a contemporary document tells us that there were to be three thousand copies of Pontico Virunio's edition of Guarino's epitome of Chrysoloras.[14]

These figures for edition sizes permit a tentative estimate of the number of Greek students in Western Europe during the period. From the years between 1471 and 1529, there survive more than one hundred Greek grammars from the presses of Europe.[15] If we assume an average print run of one thousand copies for each edition, this amounts to some one hundred thousand grammars produced over a period of fifty-eight years. We may guess that for each volume there was one student of the language. This figure underestimates the number who had some acquaintance with Greek for two reasons. First, it is likely that there were more than the one hundred known grammars printed between these dates: the survival rate for elementary grammars is low because they were heavily used by a succession of students, and they were more likely to be discarded because they could be cheaply replaced. They are the sort of books that do not, as a matter of course, find their way into the relative safety of institutional libraries. Second, there were certainly more—and probably many more—than one student of Greek for every grammar because the books were shared and reused. This figure of one hundred thousand students of Greek is all the more remarkable when we recollect that from the first decade of the fifteenth century we have the names of just ten students.[16]

If it is difficult to estimate the number of Greek students in Western Europe, it is still harder to assess their competence. Many of these students would not have gone very far with their Greek studies. The Greek alphabets and pamphlets put out by printers and teachers to attract students may actually have satisfied the appetites they were intended to quicken. But if the attainments of most of these students were inevitably modest, this figure still represents an extraordinary transformation of the educational environment in Western Europe. Although there is now a great deal of evidence available to the historian of this phenomenon, a clear picture of it has been obscured by the fact that this evidence is fragmentary and widely dispersed. It is hoped that the detailed chronological and bibliographical framework established in this book will enable a clearer understanding of the origins and development of Renaissance Hellenism.

APPENDIX 1

Printed Texts for Students of Greek, 1471–1529

This appendix contains every student manual known to me. It includes works that have only a page or two of grammatical material, such as the brief introduction in the New Testament volume of the Complutensian Polyglot or the few leaves bound with the Psalter of 1518. It does not include works on the pronunciation of Greek, such as Jacobus Ceratinus's *De sono litterarum*. It is unlikely that the list presented here is complete. Because catalog entries are sometimes misleading or ambiguous, I have attempted to look at as many of these works as possible. Editions that I have not seen are marked with an asterisk. All editions in the Bayerische Staatsbibliothek in Munich recorded here have been consulted in digital facsimiles. One of the purposes of this list is to banish a number of bibliographical ghosts from the record. Consequently, while I have made use of standard bibliographies, I have been reluctant to acknowledge the existence of any edition that does not have a verifiable library shelfmark attached to it. Where I do not give a shelfmark among the references, I have been unable to locate a copy.

A second purpose of this appendix is to define the uncertainties surrounding the dating of many of these editions. In describing the contents, I do not remark on final colophons, but I do notice all colophons that interrupt the sequence of texts in the edition. I have recorded dates attached to prefatory material. Where the dating of an edition is controversial or uncertain, I have attempted to indicate some of the boundaries within which speculation must move. A further problem with dating these books arises from the use by some printers of Greek dates in their colophons. I have dealt more fully with this problem in another place.[1] Here it is sufficient to note that these have usually been dated according to the interpretation of the calendar expounded by Theodore Gaza in his treatise *De mensibus*, published in Rome around 1470.[2] The translations of the Athenian months printed in all early Greek lexica supply a rather different calendar, one that was certainly used on some occasions by Aldus Manutius and John Froben in Venice and Basle, and very probably used by Gilles de Gourmont in Paris.

I have provided details of editions of prefatory or other material, but I cannot have located all the available reprints of these texts. For this reason, I have provided *incipits* for these works so that these references may be expanded. All information supplied in square brackets is inferred. In the transcription of titles I have preserved capitalization and punctuation while silently expanding abbreviations. I have not supplied or corrected the accentuation of Greek titles.

INCUNABLES

1. *SUPER. ερωτηματα. μικρα. πολλυ ωφελιμα.* [Venice: A. von Ambergau, c. 1471.] **Content**: Preface, *inc.* Cum nos libellum . . . (no date, Pertusi " Ἐρωτήματα," 324); Latin explanation of Chrysoloras, not by Guarino Veronese. **Reference**: ISTC ic00492000; Manchester, John Rylands Library, 19651.

2. [Chrysoloras, *Erotemata.*] [Vicenza: printer of Chrysoloras's *Erotemata*, c. 1475–76.] **Content**: Chrysoloras, abbreviated by Guarino, in Greek and Latin; *Ave Maria; Pater noster;* alphabet. **Reference**: ISTC ic00493000; BL, IA.31762.

3. *ΕΠΙΤΟΜΉ ΤΩ͂Ν ΌΚΤΩ͂ ΤΟΥ ΛΌΓΟΥ ΜΕΡΩ͂Ν ΚΑΙ͂ ἌΛΛΩΝ ΤΙΝΩ͂Ν ἈΝΑΓΚΑΊ ὨΝ ΣΥΝΤΕΘΕΙ͂ΣΑ ΠΑΡΑ͂ ΚΩΝΣΤΑΝΤΊΝΟΥ ΛΑΣΚΆΡΕΩΣ ΤΟΥ BYZANTÍ NOY.* Milan: D. Paravisinus, January 30, 1476. **Content**: D. Damilas to young students, *inc.* ʿΟρῶν ὑμᾶς τῶν . . . (Botfield, *Prefaces*, 163–64; Legrand, *Bibliographie hellénique*, 1:4–5); Latin version, *inc.* Cum vos rerum . . . (Botfield, *Prefaces*, 164–65); Lascaris, *Compendium*, in Greek; pseudo-Tryphon; *De anomalis verbis; De spiritibus.* **Reference**: Legrand, *Bibliographie hellénique*, item no. 1; Fraenkel, "Introduction"; ISTC il00065000; Cambridge, University Library, Inc.4.B.7.6 [1894].

4. *Saxoli Pratensis viri doctissimi de accentibus ac diphthongis et formatione praeteritorum graecorum.* [Milan: Bonaccorso, c. 1480.] **Content**: Alphabet and its divisions. Seven printed leaves. **Reference**: ISTC is00300500; BL, IA.26563.

5. [Lascaris, *Compendium.*] Milan: Bonaccorso, September 29, 1480. **Content**: Bonaccorso to J. Pomponius, *inc.* Cum mea opera . . . (Milan, September 29, 1480.); Lascaris, *Compendium*, with G. Crastoni's translation. **Date**: The preface and the colophon have the same date. **Reference**: ISTC il00066000; BL, IB.26559.

6. [Chrysoloras, *Erotemata.*] [Parma: printer of Hieronymus, *Epistolae*, c. 1481.] **Content**: Chrysoloras, abbreviated by Guarino, in Greek and Latin; *Pater noster* and *Ave Maria*, in Greek and Latin; alphabet. **Reference**: ISTC ic00493500; Oxford, Bodleian, Auct.Q.5.48.

7. [Chrysoloras, *Erotemata.*] Venice: P. Bononiensis, February 5, 1484. **Content**: Alphabet; *Pater noster; Ave Maria;* Chrysoloras, abbreviated by Guarino, in Greek and Latin; colophon; alphabet. **Reference**: Cammelli, *Manuele Crisolora*, plates; ISTC ic00494000; BL, IA.22223; BL, 7526.

8. *Coniugationes verborum graecae Davantriae [sic] noviter extremo labore collectae et impressae.* [Deventer: R. Pafraet, before December 12, 1488.] **Content**: The conjugation of τύπτω. Eighteen leaves. **Date**: PBN, Res-X-740 has a manuscript note on the title page with this date. **Reference**: ISTC ic00826850; BL, 7536.

9. * *Erotemata.* [Florence: no printer, c. 1488–94.] **Content**: Chrysoloras's grammar. **Reference**: ISTC ic00489500.

10. [Lascaris, *Compendium.*] Vicenza: L. Achates, June 14, 1489. **Content**: Bonaccorso to J. Pomponius, *inc.* Cum mea opera . . . (no date); Lascaris, *Compendium*, with G. Crastoni's translation; pseudo-Tryphon; *De anomalis verbis; De spiritibus;* Moschus, *Runaway Cupid.* No title page. **Reference**: ISTC 00067000; Cambridge, University Library, Inc.5.B.25.1 [2217].

11. *Κωνσταντίνου λασκάρευς τοῦ βιζαντίου προοίμιον τοῦ περὶ ὀνόματος καὶ ῥήματος τρίτου βιβλίου.* [Vicenza: L. Achates, c. 1489, after June 14, 1489.] **Content**: C. Lascaris,

inc. Ἐν τοῖς προεκδοθεῖσιν . . .; *De verbo*, in Greek, a shorter text than that printed in [1502?] (this appendix, no. 26). The preface is close to the text edited in Martínez-Manzano, *Konstantinos Laskaris*, 207–8. *De nomine* is mentioned in the epilogue, but this edition does not contain the work. For the epilogue, see chapter 1, section "Constantine Lascaris," n. 311. **Date**: Apparently printed after, and probably issued with, Lascaris's *Compendium* of June 14, 1489 (this appendix, no. 10). **Reference**: Legrand, *Bibliographie hellénique*, item no. 6; ISTC 00069000; Cambridge, University Library, Inc.5.B.25.1 [2217].

12. [Chrysoloras, *Erotemata*.] Vicenza: [L. Achates], September 1, 1490. **Content**: Alphabet; *Pater noster* and *Ave Maria*, in Greek and Latin; Chrysoloras, abbreviated by Guarino, in Greek and Latin; alphabet. **Reference**: ISTC ic00495000; BL, IA.31727.

13. *Erotemata*. Vicenza: L. Achates, December 23, 1491. **Content**: Alphabet; *Pater noster* and *Ave Maria*, in Greek and Latin; Chrysoloras, abbreviated by Guarino, in Greek and Latin; alphabet. **Reference**: ISTC ic00496000; Cambridge, University Library, Inc.5.B.25.1 [4276].

14. Δημητρίου χαλκονδύλου ἐρωτήματα συνοπτικὰ τῶν ὀκτώ τοῦ λόγου μερῶν μετά τινων χρησίμων κανόνων. [Milan: U. Scinzenzeler, c. 1493.] **Content**: Errata; Chalcondyles, *Erotemata*; Moschopoulos, *Erotemata*; Gregory Pardus, *De dialectis*. Of the edition of Moschopoulos, Pertusi writes, "Sembra che egli abbia dato due edizioni dei suoi *Erotemata*, di cui la seconda «riveduta e coretta» sarebbe quella a stampa" ("Ἐρωτήματα," 323). **Date**: Apparently not printed by April 28, 1493, when G. Amaseo wrote from Florence, "Impressaeque sunt Mediolani orationes Isocratis auctore Demetrio, nec dubium est quod paulo post complura volumina imprimentur" (Pozzi, "Da Padova a Firenze nel 1493," 194). This edition of Isocrates is dated January 1493 new style. It has been claimed that the grammar is after February 11, 1494 (Motta, "Demetrio Calcondila editore," 157; Cammelli, *Demetrio Calcondila*, 123n2). This is the date of a ten-year privilege (originally edited in *Archivio Storico Lombardo* 1 (1874): 85–86, new edition in Friggi, *Gli studi greci a Milano al tempo di Ludovico il Moro*, 152–53) granted to the grammar and to an edition of Tertullian. This edition of Tertullian is dated December 4, 1493 (ISTC it00116900), and the privilege cannot be used as a *terminus post quem* for the grammar. **Reference**: Legrand, *Bibliographie hellénique*, item no. 8; ISTC ic00419860; BL, IB.26860.

15. *In hoc libro haec Continentur. Constantini Lascaris Erotemata cum interpretatione latina. De literis graecis ac diphthongis et quemadmodum ad nos veniant. Abbreviationes quibus frequentissime graeci utuntur. Oratio Dominica et duplex salutatio Beatae Virginis. Symbolum Apostolorum. Evangelium divi Ioannis Evangelistae. Carmina Aurea Pythagorae. Phocilidis viri sapientissimi moralia. Omnia suprascripta habent e regione interpretationem latinam de verbo ad verbum*. Venice: A. Manutius, March 8, 1495, new style. **Content**: *Aldus . . . studiosis. inc.* Constantini Lascaris, viri . . . (no date, Legrand, *Bibliographie hellénique*, 1:27–28; Renouard, *Annales de l'imprimerie des Alde*, 3; Orlandi, *Aldo Manuzio editore*, 1:3); Lascaris, *Compendium*; pseudo-Tryphon; *De anomalis verbis*; *De spiritibus*; colophon; *Aldus . . . studiosis. inc.* Nihil praetermittere est . . . (no date, Legrand, *Bibliographie hellénique*, 1:28–29; Renouard, *Annales de l'imprimerie des Alde*, 3–4; Orlandi, *Aldo Manuzio editore*, 1:3–4); Aldine Greek appendix; colophon; errata; Moschopulos, extract. Aldus had received BAV, Vat.gr.1401 of Lascaris's grammar from P. Bembo and A. Gabrieli, and he boasts of it in his preface. However, this manuscript was not prepared by Lascaris for the press, it did not serve as printer's copy, and it was only used sometimes to correct a text based on Bonaccorso's text of 1480 (Martínez-Manzano, *Konstantinos*

Laskaris, 228). **Date**: The colophon to the grammar reads "ultimo februarii" 1494. This is according to the *mos venetianus*. Some copies have the last leaf of the grammar reprinted with alterations and the date "ultimo februarii" 1495. The appendix has its own colophon: March 8, 1495. **Reference**: Legrand, *Bibliographie hellénique*, item no. 12; Renouard, *Annales de l'imprimerie des Alde*, 1–4; Christie, "The Chronology of the Early Aldines," 203–4; Orlandi, *Aldo Manuzio editore*, 1:3–5; ISTC il00068000; Cambridge, University Library, Inc.5.B.3.134 [1800].

16. *In hoc volumine haec insunt. Theodori Introductivae grammatices libri quatuor. Eiusdem de mensibus opusculum sane quam pulchtum* [sic]. *Apollonii grammatici de constructione libri quatuor. Herodianus de numeris.* Venice: A. Manutius, December 25, 1495. **Content**: *Aldus... lectori. inc.* Non sum nescius... (no date, Orlandi, *Aldo Manuzio editore*, 1:7–9; Schneider, Uhlig, and Hilgard, *Grammatici Graeci*, 2, ii:xiii–xiv); Gaza, books 1 through 4; Gaza, *De mensibus*; Apollonius Dyscolus, books 1 through 4; all in Greek. The *editio princeps* of both texts. Apollonius has a large *lacuna* in book 2 and a smaller one at the end of book 4: see Schneider, Uhlig, and Hilgard, *Grammatici Graeci*, 2, ii:xv. Copies of this edition were corrected by Aldus's own hand (Quaranta, "Osservazioni intorno," 126, and n2). The second page of the first leaf was reprinted (Christie, "The Chronology of the Early Aldines," 204n1). **Reference**: Legrand, *Bibliographie hellénique*, item no. 17; Renouard, *Annales de l'imprimerie des Alde*, 4–5; ISTC ig00110000; Cambridge, University Library, Inc.3.B.3.134 [1804].

17. [Chrysoloras, *Erotemata*.] [Florence: Lorenzo-Francesco di Alopa, c. 1496.] **Content**: The *editio princeps* of the full text of Chrysoloras, in Greek. No title page. **Reference**: Legrand, *Bibliographie hellénique*, item no. 20; ISTC ic00490000; BL, IA.28031; BL, 7534.

18. ΘΗΣΑΥΡΟΣ Κέρας ἀμαλθείας, καὶ κῆποι Ἀδώνιδος. THESAVRVS Cornu copiae et Horti Adonidis. Τάδε ἔνεστι ἐν τῇδε τῇ βίβλῳ. Αἰλίου Διονυσίου περὶ ἀκλίτων ῥημάτων. Ἐκ τῶν Εὐσταθίου καὶ ἄλλων ἐνδόξων ἐκλογαὶ κατὰ στοιχεῖον. Σχηματισμοὶ τῶν εἰμὶ καὶ εἶμι ῥημάτων. Περὶ τῶν τοῦ καθέζεσθαι σημαντικῶν. Τὰ τοῦ πορεύεσθαι σημαντικά. Ἐκ τῶν Ἡρωδιανοῦ παρεκβολαὶ μεγάλου ῥήματος. Ἐκ τῶν αὐτοῦ παραγωγαὶ δισκλίτων ῥημάτων. Κοιροβοσκοῦ πρὸς τοὺς ἐν πᾶσι ῥήμασι κανόνας ζητοῦντας, καὶ ὁμοιότητας. Τοῦ αὐτοῦ περὶ τοῦ ἐφελκυστικοῦ ν. Περὶ ἀνωμάλων ῥημάτων κατὰ στοιχεῖον. Ἡρωδιανοῦ περὶ ἐγκλινομένων καὶ ἐγκλιτικῶν καὶ συνεγκλιτικῶν μορίων. Ἐκ τῶν Χοιροβοσκοῦ περὶ ἐγκλινομένων. Ἀνώνυμον περὶ ἐγκλινομένων. Ἐκ τῶν Ἰωάννου γραμματικοῦ περὶ διαλέκτων. Εὐσταθίου περὶ τῶν παρ' Ὁμήρῳ διαλέκτων. Καὶ ἄλλως περὶ διαλέκτων τῶν παρὰ κορίνθου παρεκβληθεισῶν. Περὶ τῶν εἰς ω θηλυκῶν ὀνομάτων. Venice: A. Manutius, August 1496. **Content**: Latin version of title page; *Aldus... studiosis, inc.* Dura quidem provincia... (no date, Botfield, *Prefaces*, 205–9; Lemke, *Aldus Manutius*, sigs. *2r–*3v; Orlandi, *Aldo Manuzio editore*, 1:10–13); A. Poliziano to Guarino of Favera, *inc.* Consulis me Varine... (no date, Botfield, *Prefaces*, 209); verses: Poliziano, *inc.* Ἑλλάδι ἰδίοις πεπλανημένη...; A. Apostolides, *inc.* Σπουδαίων ἕνεκεν Γωάρινος...; S. Forteguerri, *inc.* Βίβλον ὁ γραμματικῆς...; Aldus, *inc.* Λῆς γνὼν᾽ Ἡσίοδον... (all in Botfield, *Prefaces*, 209–10; Lemke, *Aldus Manutius*, sig. *4r); Forteguerri to Guarino, *inc.* Τὸ μὲν κατὰ... (no date, Lemke, *Aldus Manutius*, sig. *4v); Guarino to P. de' Medici, *inc.* Πᾶσα γῆ πατρὶς... (no date, Lemke, *Aldus Manutius*, sigs. *5r–*6v). A collection of Greek grammatical works, the *editio princeps* of most of the texts it prints. **Reference**: Renouard, *Annales de l'imprimerie des Alde*, 48; ISTC it00158000; Lemke *Aldus Manutius*; Cambridge, University Library, Inc.3.B.3.134 [1807].

19. * *Brevissima introductio ad literas graecas.* Venice: A. Manutius, [1497.] **Content**: Alphabet and its divisions; abbreviations; *Pater noster*; *Ave Maria*; *Credo*; prologue to John's Gospel; *Salve regina*; *Benedictio mensae*; other prayers. Bühler notes that it seems to be a copy of the Aldine Appendix of 1495; Bateman records some changes from 1495. **Date**: Renouard knew a copy of this Aldine pamphlet had been bound before the Aldine Greek *Horae* of 1497. Aldus seems to have sent Conrad Celtis a copy with a letter of October 13, 1497. See Rupprich, *Die Briefwechsel*, letter no. 175, where it is wrongly identified with Urbano's grammar. **Reference**: Renouard, *Annales de l'imprimerie des Alde*, 15; Bühler, "Notes on Two Incunabula"; Bateman, "Aldus Manutius," 255–56; ISTC im00226400.

20. *INSTITUTIONES GRAECAE GRAMMATICES.* Venice: A. Manutius, January 1497. **Content**: Aldus to G. F. Pico della Mirandola, *inc.* Cogitanti mihi iam . . . (no date, Botfield, *Prefaces*, 210–11; Orlandi, *Aldo Manuzio editore*, 1:21–22); alphabet and its divisions; *Pater noster* and *Ave Maria* in Greek; Urbano's grammar; register; colophon; errata. **Date**: Gualdo Rosa assumes that this is 1498 new style ("Urbano dalle Fosse (Bolzanio)," 89); Christie found no decisive evidence ("The Chronology of the Early Aldines," 208). **Reference**: Renouard, *Annales de l'imprimerie des Alde*, 11–12; Polain, *Catalogue des livres imprimés*, item no. 3887; ISTC iu00066000; BL, G.7583.

21. [Chrysoloras, *Erotemata.*] [Florence: B. di Libri, c. 1498–1500.] **Content**: Chrysoloras, the full text, in Greek. No title page, no preface. **Reference**: ISTC ic0049100; BL, G.7459.

1501

22. *Aldi Manutii Romani rudimenta grammatices latinae linguae. De literis graecis et diphthongis, et quemadmodum ad nos veniant. Abbreviationes, quibus frequenter graeci utuntur. Oratio dominica, et duplex Salutatio ad Virginem gloriosiss. Symbolum Apostolorum. Divi Ioannis Evangelistae Evangelium. Aurea Carmina Pythagorae. Phocylidis Poema ad bene, beateque vivendum. Omnia haec cum interpretatione latina. Introductio perbrevis ad hebraicam linguam.* Venice: A. Manutius, February 1501 new style. **Content**: *Aldus . . . ludi magistris, inc.* Rudimenta grammatices . . . (Venice, June "MCI," i.e., 1501); Aldus's Latin grammar, the *editio princeps*; *Aldus . . . studiosis, inc.* Nihil praetermittere est . . . (no date, Legrand, *Bibliographie hellénique*, 1:28–29; Renouard, *Annales de l'imprimerie des Alde*, 3–4); Greek appendix, in sixteen leaves, with interlinear translation; *Aldus studiosis, inc.* Quoniam hebraicam linguam . . . (no date, Orlandi, *Aldo Manuzio editore*, 1:38); Hebrew appendix, in four leaves. The Greek appendix is signed consecutively with the grammar; the Hebrew appendix is unsigned. Both appendices have their own title pages. I have no evidence that they circulated separately. **Date**: A letter of Aldus to Celtis mentions the book as complete in July 1501, and so the date of the colophon is 1501 new style (Christie, "The Chronology of the Early Aldines," 214). **Reference**: Renouard, *Annales de l'imprimerie des Alde*, 31–32; BL, G.7581.

23. *Erotemata Guarini.* Reggio nell'Emilia: S. Bombasius and others, July 10, 1501. **Content**: *P. Virunius . . . studioso, inc.* Compendiolum a Guarino . . . (no date); Chrysoloras, abbreviated by Guarino, in Greek; pseudo-Libanius, *Epistolici Characteres*, in Greek; the Greek numbers; *Virunius lectori, inc.* Promisi in praefatione . . .; verses: *Ambr. Rhegiensis Scazon, inc.* Quicunque graiarum sititor . . .; colophon. **Reference**: Pertusi, "Ἐρωτήματα," 345–46n3; Cambridge, University Library, F150.d.2.22.

24. * *Εισαγωγη προς των γραμματων ελληνων. Elementale Introductorium in Ideoma Graecanicum. Alphabetum graecum et eius lectura De divisione litterarum graecarum De*

diphthongis graecis propriis et impropriis De potestate litterarum graecarum De potestate diphthongorum propriarum et impropriarum Quemadmodum diphthongi graecae et litterae graecae in latinis litteris transferuntur Quonammodo diphthongi graecae ad latinos venere Abbreviaturae frequentariae graecanicarum litterarum. Erfurt: W. Schenck, September 1501. **Content**: This is not the Hachenborg edition described in Horawitz, "Griechische Studien," 417. It is not clear whether this is a rival or a relative of the next edition listed in this appendix (item no. 25). Eight leaves. **Date**: Colophon: "Expressum Erphordiae per Lupambulum οινοχοον alias Schenken, Anno Christi MCCCCCI ad XXV. Calendas Octobres" (*sic.* Horawitz, "Griechische Studien," 418n1). The catalog of the Bibliothèque nationale de France records the colophon as "MCCCC ad XXV. Calendas Octobres," and the date as 1525, apparently in error. **Reference**: Harlfinger and Barm, *Graecogermania*, 100–101; PBN, Rés. X-1634.

25. *Εισαγωγη προς των γραμματων ελληνων. I.S.* Erfurt: P. Hachenborg, September 18, 1501. **Content**: Alphabet; diphthongs; pronunciation; abbreviations; Greek prayers; colophon. The abbreviations are printed from a woodcut, not from type. Eight leaves. **Date**: Colophon: "Impressum Erphordiae per venerabile virum Paulum hachenborg presbyterum: Anno Christi.M.CCCCC.I. xiiii Kal Octobrias" [*sic*]. **Reference**: Oxford, Bodleian, Vet.D1.e.26.

1502

26. *Constantini Lascaris Byzantini de octo partibus orationis Liber Primus. Eiusdem de Constructione Liber secundus. Eiusdem de nomine et verbo Liber tertius. Eiusdem de pronomine secundum omnem linguam, et poeticum usum opusculum. Haec omnia habent e regione latinam interpretationem ad verbum fere propter rudes, ita tamen ut et amoveri, et addi possit pro cuiuscunque arbitrio. Cebetis tabula et graeca et latina, opus morale, et utile omnibus, et praecipue adulescentibus. De literis graecis ac diphthongis et quemadmodum ad nos veniant. Abbreviationes, quibus frequentissime graeci utuntur. Oratio Dominica et duplex salutatio ad Beatiss. Virginem. Symbolum Apostolorum. Evangelium divi Ioannis Evangelistae. Carmina Aurea Pythagorae. Phocylidis Poema ad bene, beateque vivendum. Omnia haec cum interpretatione latina. Introductio perbrevis ad Hebraicam linguam.* Venice: A. Manutius, [1502?] **Content**: Aldus to A. Gabrieli, *inc.* Cum plurimis in . . . (no date); *Aldus lectori, inc.* Si forte nescieris . . . (no date, Orlandi, *Aldo Manuzio editore*, 1:35–36); Lascaris, book 1: *Compendium*; pseudo-Tryphon; *De anomalis verbis*; *De spiritibus*; Lascaris, book 2: *De constructione*; *Aldus . . . lectori, inc.* Etsi eram typicis . . . (no date, Orlandi, *Aldo Manuzio editore*, 1:38); Lascaris, book 3: *De nomine et verbo*; *De pronominibus*; *De subscriptis vocalibus*; verses: S. Forteguerri, *inc.* Τὴν Κωνσταντίνοιο μαθὼν . . .; *Aldus studiosis, inc.* Nihil praetermittere est . . . (no date, Legrand, *Bibliographie hellénique*, 1:28–29; Renouard, *Annales de l'imprimerie des Alde*, 3–4); Greek appendix; *Aldus studiosis, inc.* Quoniam hebraicam linguam . . . (no date, Orlandi, *Aldo Manuzio editore*, 1:38); Hebrew appendix; errata; two registers: (1) "Ordo quaternionum, si separatum a latino graecum fore placuerit"; and (2) "Ordo quaternionum, si latinum graeco inserere quis voluerit." The *editio princeps* of the full text of Lascaris. The Latin version can be removed. The text and translation of pseudo-Cebes occupy the central pages of each gathering; the central pages of the "H" gathering have *Laudatio in sanctissimam Dei genetricem*. **Reference**: Renouard, *Annales de l'imprimerie des Alde*, 262–63; Cambridge, University Library, Aa*.3.39 (D).

1505

27. Εισαγωγη προς των γραμματων ελληνων. *Elementale Introductorium in Idioma Graecanicum. Alphabetum graecum et eius lectura. De divisione litterarum graecarum. De diphthongis graecis propriis et impropriis. Abbreviationes et colligaturae. De accentibus graecis. Oratio dominica graecae et iuxta latine. Salutatio angelica graecae et iuxta latine. Symbolum apostolorum graecae et iuxta latine. Evangelium Ioannis graecae et iuxta latine. Salutatio angelica alia graecae et iuxta latine. Benedictio mensae graecae et iuxta latine. Gratiae post mensam graecae et iuxta latine. Dicteria id est proverbia septem sapientum metrice.* [Erfurt, 1505.] **Content**: The Latin text is in red, and the Greek in black. The Greek font has no accents or breathings. The abbreviations are printed from woodcuts. Four leaves. **Reference**: Bühler, "Notes on Two Incunabula," 19n4; BL, G.7578.

28. * *Brevissima introductio ad litteras graecas*. Siena: S. Cartolaro, February 15, 1505. **Content**: four leaves. **Reference**: Bühler, "Notes on Two Incunabula," 19n4; Sander, *Le livre à figures italien*, 2:612, item no. 3522.

1507

29. Βίβλος ἡ γνωμαγυρικὴ. *LIBER GNOMAGYRICUS. In hoc volumine contenta. Alphabetum grecum. Regule pronunciandi grecum. Sententie septem sapientum. Opusculum de invidia. Aurea carmina pythagorae. Phocylidae poema admonitorium. Carmina Sibyllae erythraeae de iudicio christi venturo. Differentiae vocum succincta traditio.* [Paris:] G. de Gourmont, August 12, 1507. **Content**: F. Tissard . . . [*studiosis*], *inc.* Nemini dubium est . . . (no date, Omont, "Essai sur les débuts de la typographie grecque à Paris," 39–42); alphabet; pronunciation; sentences of the seven sages; pseudo-Pythagoras; pseudo-Phocylides; acrostich verses; *Tissardi . . . paraclesis, inc.* Praestaturus operam, egregii . . . (no date, ibid., 42–43); verses in Latin and Greek (ibid., 43–45). Some of this was drawn from the Aldine Theocritus of 1495 or 1496 (ibid., 5). Gourmont's first device. Twenty-six leaves. **Reference**: Omont, "Essai sur les débuts de la typographie grecque à Paris," 17–19; Moreau, *Inventaire chronologique*, 1:256; Oxford, Bodleian,. Byw.T.7.22.

30. *ΕΡΩΤΗΜΑΤΑ ΧΡΥΣΟΛΩΡΑ. Grammatica Chrysolorae.* Paris: G. de Gourmont, December 1, 1507. **Content**: F. Tissard to J. d'Orléans, Archbishop of Toulouse, *inc.* Profuturus mea opinione . . . (October 1 *sine anno*; Omont, "Essai sur les débuts de la typographie grecque à Paris," 48–51); Chrysoloras, the full text, in Greek; verses: Tissard to the Archbishop of Toulouse, *inc.* Foelix perpetuos ades . . .; verses: Tissard to Oliverius of Lyons, *inc.* Doctus es et . . .; C. Rousseus to the reader, *inc.* Primus Parrhisia Graiae . . . (all in ibid., 50–51). Gourmont's first device. **Reference**: Omont, "Essai sur les débuts de la typographie grecque à Paris," 20–21; ISTC ic00491500; Moreau, *Inventaire chronologique*, 1:227; BL, G.7529 (1).

1508

31. *ALPHABETUM HEBRAICUM ET GRAECUM.* Paris: G. de Gourmont, [1508?] **Content**: The first of the three undated editions of Gourmont's *Alphabetum*. Eight leaves. **Date**: Omont tentatively dates it to 1510 ("Essai sur les débuts de la typographie grecque à Paris," 25); it is dated [1514?] in BLC. It does not use Gourmont's first or second devices. It has Gourmont's first Greek font, with the accents cast separately from the letters. The last dated use of this font alone was in Gourmont's Plutarch of April 30, 1509 (see chapter 3, section "Plutarch," p. 98 and n. 351), although Gourmont's undated

editions of Isocrates (see chapter 3, section "Isocrates," pp. 96–97), which use the same type, seem to be later. Gourmont was printing Hebrew in Tissard's grammar of January 29, 1508, new style (this appendix, no. 32). **Reference**: Omont, "Essai sur les débuts de la typographie grecque à Paris," 25–26; BL, C.29.h.19.

32. [Hebrew grammar.] Paris: G. de Gourmont, January 29, 1508, new style. **Content**: Tissard to François de Valois, *inc.* Saepenumero cum mecum ... (no date, Omont, "Essai sur les débuts de la typographie grecque à Paris," 51–52); *Dialogus, inc.* Vecordis atque pusillanimis ... (extracts in ibid., 52–53); Tissard to François de Valois, *inc.* Fama tametsi levissima ... (no date, extracts in ibid., 53–54); Hebrew grammar; Greek alphabet; Greek prayers with interlinear translation; the Hippocratic oath; diphthongs; pronunciation; abbreviations; errata; the Greek numbers; verses: P. Corderius to Tissard, *inc.* Gallia te solo ... (January 12, 1508; ibid., 54); verses: [Tissard] to Corderius, *inc.* Non Demosthenes vel ... (January 13, *sine anno.*); contents; colophon. Ninety leaves, seventeen in Greek. **Date**: Omont assumes the date is old style. It seems more plausible that it was printed soon after Tissard's edition of Chrysoloras, after which there was a hiatus of fifteen months before Greek printing resumed in Paris with Aleandro. **Reference**: Omont, "Essai sur les débuts de la typographie grecque à Paris," 21–23; Moreau, *Inventaire chronologique,* 1:299; Oxford, Bodleian, Byw.T.7.23.

33. *ALDI MANUTII ROMANI INSTITUTIONUM GRAMMATICARUM LIBRI QUATTUOR.* Venice: A. Manutius, April 1508. **Content**: *Aldus ... literarii ludi magistris, inc.* Rudimenta grammatices ... (Venice, October 1507); Aldus's Latin grammar; register; colophon; title: *De literis graecis, ac diphthongis, et quemadmodum ad nos veniant. De potestate literarum graecarum, et quomodo quis per se discat legere graeca verba. Item quare Christus. et Iesus. sic scribimus Xps. IHS. Cur in alphabeto y psilon a quibusdam fio dicitur. Abbreviationes, quibus frequentissime graeci utuntur. Oratio Dominica et duplex salutatio ad Beatiss. Virginem. Symbolum Apostolorum. Evangelium Divi Ioannis Evangelistae. Carmina Aurea Pythagorae. Procylidis* [sic] *Poema ad bene, beateque vivendum. Omnia haec cum interpretatione latina. Introductio perbrevis ad hebraicam linguam*; *Aldus ... studiosis, inc.* Nihil praetermittere est ... (no date, Legrand, *Bibliographie hellénique,* 1:28–29; Renouard, *Annales de l'imprimerie des Alde,* 3–4); Greek appendix in sixteen leaves; *Aldus studiosis, inc.* Quoniam hebraicam linguam ... (no date, Orlandi, *Aldo Manuzio editore,* 1:38); Hebrew appendix in four leaves. The appendix is a light revision of that of [1502?] (this appendix, item no. 26): see Bateman, "Aldus Manutius," 232, 257–58. The grammar is signed a through z; the Greek appendix is signed aa through bb. Bateman's statement that the appendix is "separately signed" is thus debatable ("Aldus Manutius," 230). **Date**: The date is from the colophon after the Latin grammar. Neither appendix is dated. **Reference**: BL, 625.c.14.

1509

34. * ἐξεψάλματα, περιέχοντα τὰ κάτω γεγραμμένα. ἤγουν, Τὴν ἀλφάβητον. Τὸ παναγία τριάς. Τὸ πάτερ ἡμῶν. Τὴν εὐλογίαν τῆς τραπέζης, πρὸ τοῦ γεύσασθαι. Τὴν μετὰ τὸ γεύσασθαι εὐχαριστίαν. Τὰ ἐν τῷ ἑσπερινῷ ἀδόμενα, καὶ ἀναγινωσκόμενα. Τὰ ἐν τῇ θείᾳ λειτουργίᾳ. Τὰ ἐν τῶ μικρῶ ἀποδείπνω. Τὸ μεγαλύνει ἡ ψυχή μου. Τὸ ἐλέησόν με ὁ θεὸς κατὰ τὸ μέγα ἔλεός σου. Τὸ ὁ κατοικῶν ἐν βοηθείᾳ τοῦ ὑψίστου. Venice: Z. Callierges, April 14, 1509. **Content**: Alphabet and prayers. Sixteen leaves. **Reference**: Legrand, *Bibliographie hellénique,* item no. 34.

35. *Erotemata Guarini, cum multis additamentis, et cum commentariis latinis.* Ferrara: J. Mazochius, June 23, 1509, to March 13, 1510, new style. **Content:** *J. Maria Tricaelius studiosis,* inc. Quoniam vos nollem . . . (no date); Chrysoloras, abbreviated by Guarino, in Greek; the Greek dialects; Greek numbers; colophon; *Virunius Magnifico A. Vicecomiti Lod. Sfor. Subrorum ducis Consiliario, ac oratori Ferrariae,* inc. Ad doctrinam hominis . . . ; *Vita Chrysolorae; De inventione litterarum; Virunii declamationes quaedam ad magnificum Antonium . . . in erotemata Guarini tumultuarie;* Virunio's Latin commentary; colophon. Virunio's autograph of this commentary is now Rome, Bibl. Angelica, lat.1491. **Date:** The colophon after the Greek numbers is June 23, 1509; the colophon after the commentary is March 13, 1509. Despite the gap between the dates, the letter appears to be 1510 new style. Cambridge University Library has a copy of the first part only, which may indicate that it was issued separately. **Reference:** Pertusi, " Ἐρωτήματα," 345–46n3; Cambridge, University Library, F150.d.2.23; Cambridge, University Library, Norton.e.29 (first part only).

1510

36. *C. Lascaris institutiones universae cum plurimis auctariis nuperrime impressae, tanta diligentia, et rerum copia quanta nunquam alias.* Ferrara: J. Mazochius, July 30, 1510. **Content:** *J. Maciochus bonis ac studiosis,* inc. Quicunque animum ad . . . (Ferrara, no date); Psalm 50 (51), *Miserere mei,* in Greek and Latin; original title page; to L. Bonaciolus, inc. Qui aut suos . . . (July 15, 1510); Lascaris, in three books, in Greek and Latin; *De anomalis verbis; De spiritibus; De constructione; De nomine et verbo; De pronominibus; De subscriptis vocalibus;* verses: S. Forteguerri, inc. Τὴν Κωνσταντίνοιο μαθὼν . . . ; pseudo-Cebes; *B. Piso . . . T. Calcagnino,* inc. Habes tu quidem . . . (Ferrara, January 28, 1509); *Oratio dominica;* Apostolic Creed; prologue to John's Gospel; *Philolai Crotoniatae carmina aurea, quae falso hactenus Pythagorae adscripta sunt* (i.e., the *Aurea verba*); pseudo-Phocylides; C. Calcagninus to Bishop T. Fuscus, inc. Quod tumultuario . . . (no date); Lucian, *Iudicium vocalium,* in Greek and Latin; colophon: July 30, 1510; an apology for misplacing Lucian: *J. Maria Tricaelius Aequina,* inc. Viri studiosi subticui . . . (no place, no date). Psalm 50 (51), advertised in the original title page, was accidentally omitted during printing. A gathering of four leaves was prefaced to the volume, which has the title given earlier, another preface, and the Psalm. **Reference:** BL, 624.c.11.

1511

37. Εισαγωγη προς των γραμματων ελληνων. *Elementale introductorium in idioma Graecanicum. Contenta in Hoc Opello. Alphabetum graecum et eius lectura. Abbreviationes et colligaturae. Oratio Dominica. Salutacio Angelica. Symbolum sanctorum patrum. Bendicite. Gratias. Salutacio Mortalium ad Virginem Mariam. Missa de Diva Virgine. Evangelium Divi Ioannis. Canticum Mariae. Canticum Angelorum. Oratio ad Deum. Dicteria septem sapientum. Aliquot Psalmi penitenciales. Haec omnia Graecae cum interpretatione Latina.* Wittenberg: J. Gronebergius, *sine mense* 1511. **Content:** Verses: H. Trebelius Notianus. The Greek font has no accents or breathings; the "abbreviationes" are woodcuts. Twelve leaves. **Reference:** Oxford, Bodleian, Linc. B.15.21.

38. *THEODORI INTRODUCTIVAE GRAMMATICES LIBRI QUATUOR.* Paris: G. de Gourmont, [before October 16, 1511.] **Content:** Gaza, book 1, in Greek. **Date:** Omont dates it c. 1512 ("Essai sur les débuts de la typographie grecque à Paris," 32); in Moreau,

Inventaire chronologique, 2, item no. 92, it is dated c. 1511. It has Gourmont's first device. The last dated use of this device was in the prefatory gathering of Gourmont's lexicon, printed in the last days of 1512 (appendix 2, no. 14). It has Gourmont's first Greek font, in which the accents and breathings are cast separately from the letters. The last dated use of this font alone was in Gourmont's Plutarch of April 30, 1509 (see chapter 3, section "Plutarch," p. 98 and n. 351), although Gourmont's undated editions of Isocrates (see chapter 3, section "Isocrates"), which use the same type, seem to be later. I believe that this edition was printed before Erasmus decided to change from Chrysoloras's to Gaza's grammar, a decision that he recorded in a letter of October 16, 1511. See Botley, "Learning Greek in Western Europe, 1476–1516," 216n53. **Reference**: Omont, "Essai sur les débuts de la typographie grecque à Paris," 32; Moreau, *Inventaire chronologique*, 2:79; BL, G.7592.

1512

39. *Elementale Introductorium In Nominum et Verborum declinationes Graecas.* Strasbourg: [M. Schurer], *sine mense* 1512. **Content**: No preface. Alphabet; *de divisione literarum*; *de potestate literarum*; *de mutatione literarum graecarum in latinas*; *de accentibus*. Eight leaves. **Reference**: Baillet, "Le premier manuel," 25–26; Benzing and Muller, *Bibliographie strasbourgeoise*, 1:91, 2:183; Chrisman, *Bibliography of Strasbourg Imprints*, 123; Munich, Bayerische Staatsbibliothek, 4 L.lat.258 (1).

40. Ἐρωτήματα τοῦ χρυσολωρᾶ. Περὶ ἀνομάλων ῥημάτων. Περὶ σχηματισμοῦ τῶν χρόνων ἐκ τῶν χαλκονδύλου. Τὸ τέταρτον τοῦ Γαζῆ, περὶ συντάξεως. Περὶ ἐγκλιτικῶν. Γνῶμαι μονόστιχοι ἐκ διαφόρων ποιητῶν. *Erotemata Chrysolorae. De anomalis verbis. De formatione temporum ex libro Chalcondylae. Quartus Gazae de constructione. De Encliticis. Sententiae monostichi ex variis poetis.* Venice: A. Manutius, *sine mense* 1512. **Content**: *Aldus Caesari Aragonio, inc.* Manuel Chrysoloras qui . . . (no date, Legrand, *Bibliographie hellénique*, 1:98–99; Orlandi, *Aldo Manuzio editore*, 1:104); Chrysoloras, the full text; *De anomalis verbis*; Chalcondyles on the verb; Gaza, book 4; Herodian on enclitics; gnomic verses. All in Greek only. Renouard notes some copies on vellum. **Reference**: Legrand, *Bibliographie hellénique*, item no. 37; Renouard, *Annales de l'imprimerie des Alde*, 59; BL G.7460.

41. *Quae hoc libro continentur. Georgii Simler Vuimpinensis observationes de arte grammatica. De literis graecis ac diphthongis et quemadmodum ad nos veniant. Abbreviationes quibus frequentissime graeci utuntur. Erotemata Guarini ex Chrysolorae libello maiusculo cum interpretatione latina. Isagogicum sive introductorium in literas graecas.* Tübingen: T. Anshelm, March 1512. **Content**: Verses: N. Gerbel; verses: *J. Spiegel Selestanus caesaris a secretis, inc.* Si sua cuique . . . (extract in Horawitz, "Griechische Studien," 425); Simler to G. Lamparter, J. Lemp, and J. Luphdich, *inc.* Non me fugit . . . (no date); verses: Simler to J. Haliaenetus, *inc.* Interpres iuris legum . . .; J. Hiltebrant to the reader, *inc.* Adest studiose lector . . . (no date); Simler's *observationes* on Latin grammar in five parts: (1) *Orthographia* (folios 1–7), (2) *Prosodia* (folios 7–16), (3) *Etymologia* (folios 17–83), (4) Simler to G. Forstmaister and T. Berner, *inc.* Legimus viri celebres . . . (no date); *Syntaxis* (folios 84v–99v); (5) *Idiomata* (folios 99v–126); *Peroratio* (folio 126). Another title page lists the remaining four works. Simler to J. Reuchlin, *inc.* Incidimus nuper . . . (no date); *De literis graecis*, the first part of the Aldine Greek appendix; Chrysoloras, abbreviated by Guarino, in Greek and Latin; *Isagogicum in literas graecanicas*; Simler to J. Ofterdingen, B. von Canstatt, A. Lemp, and J. Rheningen, *inc.* Utrum difficilis aut . . . (no date, extract in Horawitz, "Griechische Studien," 429–30 and 429n1); errata;

colophon. **Reference**: Horawitz, "Griechische Studien," 422–30; Baillet, "Le premier manuel," 26–27; BL, 625.d.7; Oxford, Bodleian, Byw.T.1.13.

42. *ΕΡΩΤΗΜΑΤΑ ΤΟΥ ΧΡΥΣΟΛΩΡΑ͂. Grammatica Chrysolorae*. Paris: [G. de Gourmont], [May or July] 13, 1512. **Content**: F. Vatable to B. Doria, *inc.* Quantam prae te ... (May 29, *sine anno*. Rice, *The Prefatory* Epistles, 270–73; Omont, "Essai sur les débuts de la typographie grecque à Paris," 57–59); Chrysoloras, the full text, in Greek; colophon. **Date**: The first dated use of Gourmont's new Greek font, which has breathings and accents cast with the letters. The preface, signed consecutively with the grammar, was not printed last. The colophon reads "Μεταγειτνιῶνος ἐπὶ δέκα τρίτῃ," which Omont renders July 13. Metageitnion is July in *De mensibus*; in the dictionaries it is May. **Reference**: Omont, "Essai sur les débuts de la typographie grecque à Paris," 27; Rice, *The Prefatory Epistles*, 270–73; Moreau, *Inventaire chronologique*, 2:118; BL, 624.c.4.

43. *Institutiones graecae grammatices*. Paris: G. de Gourmont [between May and August 1512?]. **Content**: Alphabet; diphthongs; *Pater noster*; *Ave Maria*; all in Greek; Aldus to G. F. Pico della Mirandola, *inc.* Cogitanti mihi iamdiu ... (no date, Botfield, *Prefaces*, 210–11; Orlandi, *Aldo Manuzio editore*, 1:21–22); Urbano's grammar. **Date**: Omont dates it [1514] ("Essai sur les débuts de la typographie grecque à Paris," 34). Gualdo Rosa repeats Omont's date ("Urbano dalle Fosse (Bolzanio)," 91). It is dated [1510?] in BLC, and it is dated [c. 1513] in Moreau, *Inventaire chronologique*, 2, item no. 739. Three considerations are relevant: (1) It is a copy of the first edition of 1497, not of the expanded Venetian edition of August 20, 1512. (2) It has Gourmont's first device. The last dated use of this device is in the prefatory gathering of the Gourmont's first lexicon (appendix 2, no. 14), printed in the last days of 1512. (3) This edition of Urbano uses Gourmont's second Greek font. The first dated use of this font is in the Chrysoloras of [May or July] 13, 1512 (this appendix, no. 42). **Reference**: Omont, "Essai sur les débuts de la typographie grecque à Paris," 34; Moreau, *Inventaire chronologique*, 2:225; BL, G.7485 (1); PBN, Rés. P-X-485 (2).

44. *De literis graecis ac diphthongis et quemadmodum ad nos veniant. Abbreviationes quibus frequentissime graeci utuntur. Oratio dominica et duplex salutatio ad beatiss. Virginem. Symbolum apostolorum. Evangelium divi Ioannis evangelistae. Carmina aurea Pythagorae. Phocylidis viri sapientissimi moralia, quae omnia habent e regione interpretationem latinam de verbo ad verbum*. Tübingen: T. Anshelm, July 1512. **Content**: *Aldus ... studiosis*, *inc.* Nihil praetermittere est ... (no date, Legrand, *Bibliographie hellénique*, 1:28–29; Renouard, *Annales de l'imprimerie des Alde*, 3–4); Greek appendix; *Aldus studiosis, inc.* Quoniam hebraicam linguam ... (no date, Orlandi, *Aldo Manuzio editore*, 1:38); Hebrew appendix. This is not to be confused with the copy bound with Simler's work (this appendix, no. 41). **Reference**: BL, 12923.b.2.

45. *Vrbani Grammaticae institutiones iterum per quam diligenter elaboratae. Quippe quod alias unum ac satis incompositus fuerat corpus in duo nunc politissima membra defluxit: quorum alterum per compendia ducet adulescentes alterum iam artis arcana consultet indagaturis. De passionibus dictionum ex tryphone. De spiritibus ex theodorito et aliis. De linguarum varietate opus ad enodandos poetas utillimum*. Venice: J. de Tridinus (Tacuinus), August 20, 1512. **Content**: *Urbanus ... studiosis, inc.* Superioribus annis, studiosi ... (no date); verses: V. Fausto, *inc.* Εἴαρος ἀρχομένοιο ...; verses: S. Forteguerri, *inc.* Οὐρβανοῖο λαβὼν ...; Urbano's revised grammar; pseudo-Tryphon; *De spiritibus*; verses: *D. Caietani discipuli, inc.* Foelix pagina ...; Gregory Pardus, *De dialectis*, in Greek; register; colophon; postscript: *Urbanus P. Valeriano, inc.* Grammaticis institutionibus ... (Venice, June 24, 1512); verses: M. Musurus, *inc.* Τοῦ πρὸς θεὸν ...; errata. **Reference**: BL, 1560/1692; Oxford, Bodleian, Byw.U.4.8.

46. *IN HOC LIBRO HAEC HABENTUR. Constantini Lascaris Byzantini de octo partibus orationis Lib.I. Eiusdem de Constructione Liber Secundus. Eiusdem de nomine et verbo Liber Tertius. Eiusdem de pronomine in omni Idiomate loquendi, ac ut poetae utuntur opusculum. Haec omnia habent e regione latinam interpretationem ad verbum fere propter rudiusculos, ita tamen ut et amoveri, et addi possit pro cuiusque arbitrio. Cebetis tabula et graeca et latina, opus morale, et utile omnibus, et praecipue adulescentibus. De literis graecis ac diphthongis et quemadmodum ad nos veniant. Abbreviationes, quibus frequentissime graeci utuntur. Oratio Dominica et duplex salutatio ad Beatiss. Virginem. Symbolum Apostolorum. Evangelium divi Ioannis Evangelistae. Carmina aurea Pythagorae. Phocylidis Poema ad bene beateque vivendum. De Idiomatib. Linguarum tres tractatus Ioannis grammatici. Eustathii Corinthi. Cum interpretatione latina. Introductio perbrevis ad hebraicam linguam.* Venice: A. Manutius, October 1512. **Content:** Aldus to A. Gabrieli, *inc.* Cum plurimis in . . . (no date, Orlandi, *Aldo Manuzio editore,* 1:37; Martínez-Manzano, *Konstantinos Laskaris,* 228–29); *Aldus lectori, inc.* Si forte nescieris . . . (no date, Orlandi, *Aldo Manuzio editore,* 1:35–36); Lascaris, book 1; pseudo-Tryphon; *De anomalis verbis;* Lascaris, *De spiritibus;* Lascaris, book 2; *Aldus lectori, inc.* Etsi eram typicis . . . (no date, Orlandi, *Aldo Manuzio editore,* 1:38); Lascaris, book 3; Lascaris, *De pronominibus;* Lascaris, *De subscriptis vocalibus; Aldus lectori, inc.* Hoc libello et . . . (no date, Orlandi, *Aldo Manuzio editore,* 1:105); J. Grammaticus, *De dialectis;* pseudo-Plutarch, *De dialectis;* Gregory Pardus, *De dialectis.* Interleaved texts: pseudo-Cebes, *Tabula;* errata; *Aldus lectori, inc.* Quoniam hae duae . . . (no date, Orlandi, *Aldo Manuzio editore,* 1:105–6); Aldus on Greek pronunciation (Bateman, "Aldus Manutius," 258–59); Greek appendix, a reprint of the appendix in the Aldine edition of 1508 (Bateman, "Aldus Manutius," 230n19). The Latin version can be removed. **Reference:** Renouard, *Annales de l'imprimerie des Alde,* 58; BL, G.7589.

47. *ΓΝΩΜΟΛΟΓΙΑ. GNOMOLOGIA. Index eorum quae in hoc volumine, quam Gnomologiam. i. Moralium sententiarum collectanea merito appelles, comprehenduntur. Hieronymi Aleandri, qui librum recognovit, Epistola. Theognidis poetae vetustissimi Elegiaco carmine sententiae. Pythagorae Carmina aurea. Epigrammata duo in Phocylidem, cum eiusdem sanctissimis heroico carmine praeceptis. Carmina Sibyllae Erythraeae nomen Iesu dei filii in primis literis pre se ferentia. Diversorum animalium differentia vocis. Catonis, quem pro pueris appellat vulgus, hexametro versu sententiae in graecum e latino conversae. Variorum poetarum sententiae ordine Alphabetico, cum indice rerum fronti nuper apposito. Epigramma in septem sapientes. Eorumdem praeclara dicta. Sententiae in invidiam. Illustrium quorumdam virorum scitu dignissimae sententiae nunquam antea impressae. Addita sunt fini rudimenta quaedam graeca, cum Dominica Angelica et aliis quibusdam piis orationibus. Quae omnia et bonos mores, et una graecas literas desiderantibus non parum conducant.* Paris: impensis M. Bolseci, December 22, 1512. **Content:** Greek verses of Posidippus and Metrodorus (*Greek Anthology* 9:359 and 360); *Aleander Claudio debrillaco discipulo suo, inc.* In omni studiorum . . . (Paris, November 17, 1512); Greek texts as in the title; *Sententiae in invidiam;* register; *Illustrium virorum sententiae; rudimenta;* colophon; register. A reworking of the *Liber Gnomagyricus* of 1507. Twenty-six leaves. **Reference:** Omont, "Essai sur les débuts de la typographie grecque à Paris," 27–28; Moreau, *Inventaire chronologique,* 2:160; BL, 832.h.1.

1513

48. *ALPHABETUM HEBRAICUM ET GRAECUM.* Paris: G. de Gourmont, [1513?] **Content:** Apparently Gourmont's second undated *Alphabetum,* to be identified with that

described in Omont, "Essai sur les débuts de la typographie grecque à Paris," 35. The Greek abbreviations are from woodcuts. Six leaves. **Date**: It uses Gourmont's second Greek font, which has accents and breathings cast with the letters. The first dated use of this font is [May or July] 13, 1512 (this appendix, no. 42). It has Gourmont's first device. The last dated use of this device is in the prefatory gathering of the Paris lexicon, printed in the last days of 1512 (appendix 2, no. 14). **Reference**: Omont, "Essai sur les débuts de la typographie grecque à Paris," 35; BL, 621.g.40 (1).

49. *HIERONYMI ALEANDRI MOTTENSIS TABULAE SANE QUAM UTILES GRAE-CARUM MUSARUM ADYTA COMPENDIO INGREDI CUPIENTIBUS.* Paris: G. de Gourmont, [early 1513?] **Content**: *Aleander . . . studiosis, inc.* Quemadmodum ii qui . . . (no date, Omont, "Essai sur les débuts de la typographie grecque à Paris," 70–71; Horawitz, "Griechische Studien," 430); alphabet and its divisions; pronunciation; accentuation and breathings; notes on parts of speech. Four leaves. **Date**: There are at least three undated Paris editions of Aleandro's *Tabulae* (Omont, "Essai sur les débuts de la typographie grecque à Paris," 12–13), all with the same title. This edition is the third in Omont's list, and apparently the first printed. BL has two of the three undated editions of the *Tabulae*. This one is dated [1515?] in BLC. It appears to be the same as Moreau, *Inventaire chronologique*, 2, item no. 222, where it is dated [c. 1512]. The work was composed during a break in Aleandro's lecturing caused by an illness. The first edition postdates the Paris Gaza of [before October 16, 1511] (this appendix, no. 38) and the Paris lexicon of [after December 25, 1512] (appendix 2, no. 14), both of which are mentioned in the preface. It predates the Strasbourg edition of March 1514 (this appendix, no. 54), which reprints the preface. Gourmont uses his first Greek font without accents or breathings, and his new Greek font that has these cast with the letters. The first dated use of this second font is [May or July] 13, 1512 (this appendix, no. 42). The two other editions identified by Omont have Gourmont's second device, of which the first dated use is [March or June] 22, 1516 (this appendix, no. 72). **Reference**: Omont, "Essai sur les débuts de la typographie grecque à Paris," 12–13; perhaps Moreau, *Inventaire chronologique*, 2:107; BL, 621.b.42.

50. *Aldi manutii romani institutionum Grammaticarum. Libri Quatuor.* Paris: Poncet Le Preux, February 1, 1513, new style. **Content**: [Aldus] *Literarii Ludimagistris, inc.* Rudimenta grammatices . . . (Venice, October 1507); Aldus's Latin grammar; Greek appendix with its own title page: *De literis graecis ac diphthongis et quemadmodum ad nos veniant. De potestate literarum graecarum et quomodo quis per se discat legere graeca verba. Item quare Christus et Iesus sic scribimus Xps. IHS. Cur in Alphabeto y psilon a quibusdam fio dicitur. Oratio dominica et duplex salutatio ad Beatissimam Virginem. Symbolum Apostolorum. Evangelium divi Ioannis Evangelistae. Carmina Aurea Pythagorae. Procylidis [sic] Poema ad bene beateque vivendum. Omnia haec cum interpretatione latina.* The Greek texts detailed on the title page have an interlinear Latin translation. *Aldus . . . Studiosis adolescentibus, inc.* Nihil praetermittere est . . . (no date, Legrand, *Bibliographie hellénique*, 1:28–29; Renouard, *Annales de l'imprimerie des Alde*, 3–4). The error "Procylidis" on the title page shows that this edition was set from a copy of the Aldine edition of April 1508 (this appendix, no. 33)—no other edition has this error. No *abbreviationes*. No Hebrew appendix. The Greek font has no accents or breathings. **Date**: The colophon to the grammar is "Anno Domini M.D. Decimo tertio kalendas Februarias." This is not 13 Kal. Feb. 1500, nor 3 Kal. Feb. 1510, but Kal. Feb. 1513. **Reference**: BL, C.142.c.19 (grammar only); BL, G.7579 (appendix only).

51. * *Tabulae in graecas literas.* Deventer: A. Pafraet, February 27, 1513. **Content**: The work of J. Aedicollius. **Reference**: Nijhoff, *L'art typographique*, 1:8, plates VI:26–29.

52. *Elementale Introductorium in Nominum et Verborum declinationes Graecas. Graecas dictiones cum eorum characteribus, accentibus, ac vocum moderamentis, hic insertas offendes. LECTOR EME, LEGE, ET GAUDEBIS.* Strasbourg: M. Schurer, May 1513. **Content**: Alphabet and its divisions; pronunciation; transliteration; accentuation; the article; Greek numbers; colophon. Ten leaves. **Reference**: Baillet, "Le premier manuel," 27; Chrisman, *Bibliography of Strasbourg Imprints,* 123; Oxford, Bodleian, Antiq.e.G.1513.3.

1514

53. *Novum testamentum grece et latine in academia complutensi noster noviter impressum.* Alcalá: A. Brocar, January 10, 1514, new style. **Content**: The fifth volume of the Complutensian Polyglot Bible, the New Testament, contains a brief introduction to Greek and a Greek–Latin lexicon. To the reader, *inc.* Ne mireris aut . . . (no date); letters of Eusebius and Jerome; Gospels, in Greek and Latin; St. Paul's journeys, *inc.* Ἀπὸ Δαμασκοῦ . . .; Romans 1 and 2, Corinthians 1 and 2, Galatians, Ephesians, Philippians, Colossians, Thessalonians 1 and 2, Timothy 1 and 2, Titus, Philemon, Hebrews, Acts, James, Peter 1 and 2, John 1–3, Jude, Revelation; colophon; Greek and Latin poems; *Interpretationes hebreorum chaldeorum grecorumque nominum noui testamenti; Introductio quam brevissima ad grecas litteras;* Greek–Latin lexicon. **Date**: The New Testament volume has a colophon: January 10, 1514. The sixth volume, the Hebrew lexicon and grammar, has colophons of March 17, 1515, and May 31, 1515. The most plausible interpretation of these colophons is that Brocar dated his volumes new style. **Reference**: Norton, *A Descriptive Catalogue,* 11–15; Abad, *La Imprenta,* 222–33; Cambridge, University Library, Sel.2.73; Cambridge, University Library, Young 5; Cambridge, University Library, Ta.56.1.

54. *Elementale introductorium in Nominum et Verborum declinationes Graecas. Graecas dictiones cum eorum characteribus, accentibus ac vocum moderamentis hic insertas offendes. ITEM Hieronymi Aleandri Mottensis tabulae, sane quam utiles Graecarum Musarum adyta compendio ingredi cupientibus. LECTOR EME, LEGE, ET GAUDEBIS.* Strasbourg: M. Schurer, March 1514. **Content**: No preface. Alphabet; its divisions; pronunciation; transliteration; accentuation; gender; the article; numbers; *Aleander . . . studiosis, inc.* Quemadmodum ii qui . . . (no date, Horawitz, "Griechische Studien," 430; Omont, "Essai sur les débuts de la typographie grecque à Paris," 70–71); alphabet; its divisions; pronunciation; accentuation and breathings; notes on parts of speech; abbreviations; colophon. Fifteen printed leaves. Schurer added a copy of Aleandro's *Tabulae,* first printed at Paris [early 1513?] (this appendix, no. 49), to a reprint of his pamphlet of May 1513 (this appendix, no. 52). This duplicated much of the substance of the pamphlet. **Reference**: Horawitz, "Griechische Studien," 430; Baillet, "Le premier manuel," 27–28; Benzing and Muller, *Bibliographie strasbourgeoise,* 2:189; Chrisman, *Bibliography of Strasbourg Imprints,* 123; Manchester, John Rylands Library, 20033; Munich, Bayerische Staatsbibliothek, Res/4 L.gr.80 (1).

55. Ἐρωτήματα τοῦ χρυσολωρᾶ. Περὶ σχηματισμοῦ τῶν χρόνων ἐκ τῶν χαλκονδύλου. Τὸ τέταρτον τοῦ Γαζῆ περὶ συντάξεως. Περὶ ἀνωμάλων ῥημάτων. Περὶ ἐγκλιτικῶν. Γνῶμαι μονόστιχοι ἐκ διαφόρων ποιητῶν. *Erotemata chrysolorae. De formatione temporum ex libro chalcondylae. Quartus gazae de constructione. De anomalis verbis. De encliticis. Sententiae monostichi ex variis poetis.* Alcalá: A. Brocar, April 10, 1514. **Content**: Alphabet; *Per signum sanctae crucis; Gloria; Sanctus; Pater noster; Ave Maria; Salve regina; Credo;* prologue to John's Gospel; Chrysoloras, the full text; Chalcondyles on the verb; Gaza,

book 4; *De anomalis verbis*; Herodian on enclitics; *Sententiae*; Δημήτριος Δουκᾶς ὀρκῆς τοῖς ἐν κομπλούτου ἀκαδημία σπουαίοις, *inc.* Ἐγὼ ἐλθὼν ... (no date, Legrand, *Bibliographie hellénique*, 1:119); verses: L. M. Bradyglossus to the readers, *inc.* Intumuit pharia cithara ... (Legrand, *Bibliographie hellénique*, 1:119-20). All texts up to the end of Chalcondyles have an interlinear translation; thereafter the text is in Greek. This edition was based on the Aldine of 1512, probably on a copy brought to Spain by Ducas. The *Sententiae* reproduce those in the Aldine Theocritus of 1495 or 1496. **Date**: For a possible date of c. 1513, see Abad, *Post-Incunables Ibéricos*, 195-96. **Reference**: Legrand, *Bibliographie hellénique*, item no. 41; Norton, *A Descriptive Catalogue*, 16; Abad, *La Imprenta*, 234-35; Cambridge, University Library, F151.c.8.2; Oxford, Bodleian, Byw.L.6.21.

56. *Aldi Pii Manutii institutionum grammaticarum libri quatuor*. Venice: A. Manutius, December 1514. **Content**: *Aldus ... literarii ludi magistris. inc.* Rudimenta grammatices ... (Venice, October 1507); Latin grammar, with the first gathering only in red and black; register; colophon; *Aldus ... studiosis, inc.* Nihil praetermittere est ... (no date, Legrand, *Bibliographie hellénique*, 1:28-29; Renouard, *Annales de l'imprimerie des Alde*, 3-4); Greek appendix, in sixteen leaves; *Aldus studiosis, inc.* Quoniam hebraicam linguam ... (no date, Orlandi, *Aldo Manuzio editore*, 1:38); Hebrew appendix in four leaves. The Greek appendix printed here is a revision of that printed with Lascaris's grammar in 1512 (Bateman, "Aldus Manutius," 230n19). **Date**: The colophon follows the Latin grammar. Neither appendix is dated. **Reference**: BL, 625.c.15.

1515

57. *Collectanea sacrosancta, graece discere cupientibus non aspernanda. CONTENTA. Introductiones elementares Hellenismi: cum quibusdam aliis pronunciationi legitime subservientibus.* Πάτερ ἡμῶν. *Pater noster.* Χαῖρε Μαρία. *Ave Maria.* Σύμβολον τῶν Ἀποστόλων. *Symbolum Apostolorum.* Σύμβολον τῶν Πατέρων. *Symbolum Patrum.* Μεγαλύνει. *Magnificat.* Νῦν ἀπολύσεις. *Nunc dimittis.* Χαῖρε βασίλεια. *Salve regina.* Εὐλογεῖτε. *Benedicite.* Εὐχαριστία. *Gratiarum actio.* Ὠδὴ [sic] τῶν ἀγγέλων. *Cantus angelicus.* Σύμβολον τοῦ Ἀθανασίου. *Symbolum Athanasii.* Η μακαρίσμοι. *8 beatitudines.* Η στίχοι τοῦ μακαρίου βερνάρδου. *8 Versus b. Bernardi.* Εὐαγγέλιον τοῦ Ἰωάννου. *Evangelium Ioannis.* Ἐξομολόγησις. *Confessio. Supradictis adnexae sunt, sententiae illustres, septem Sapientum Graeciae. Et de invidia, scitu quaedam dignissima.* Strasbourg: J. Schottus, *sine mense* 1515. **Content**: Nachtgall to J. Schottus, *inc.* Duae res sunt ... (Strasbourg, no date); alphabet and its divisions; Greek texts as detailed in the title. Sixteen leaves. According to the preface, one thousand copies were printed. **Reference**: BL, 1560/1738.

58. ΕΓΧΕΙΡΙΔΙΟΝ ΓΡΑΜΜΑΤΙΚΗΣ ΕΙΣΑΓΩΓΗΣ ΕΚ ΔΙΑΦΟΡΩΝ ΣΥΓΓΡΑΦΕΩΝ ΣΥΛΛΗΦΘΕΝ. ΕΝ ΤΩιΔΕ ΤΩι ΒΙΒΛΙΩι ΤΑΔΕ ΠΕΡΙΕΧΕΤΑΙ. Ερωτήματα τοῦ χρυσολωρᾶ. Περὶ ἀνομάλων ῥημάτων. Περὶ σχηματισμοῦ τῶν χρόνων ἐκ τοῦ χαλκονδύλου. Θεοδώρου γραμματικῆς εἰσαγωγῆς τῶν εἰς τέσσαρα τὸ τέταρτον, περὶ συντάξεως. Ηρωδιανοῦ περὶ ἐγκλιτικῶν. Γνῶμαι μονόστιχοι ἐκ διαφόρων ποιητῶν. Κάτωνος ῥωμαίου γνῶμαι παραινετικαὶ δίστιχοι ἃς μετήνεγκεν ἐκ τῆς λατίνων φονῆς εἰς τὴν ἑλληνίδα διάλεκτον μάξιμος μοναχὸς ὁ πλανούδιος. Florence: P. Junta, February 1, 1514. [1515 new style]. **Content**: *E. Boninus Aloysio Alamanno. inc.* Cum graiae te ... (no date); Chrysoloras, the full text; Chalcondyles on the verb; Gaza, book 4; Herodian on enclitics; *sententiae*; Planudes' translation of the *Disticha Catonis*; errata; colophon; device. All in Greek only. **Reference**: Renouard, *Annales de l'imprimerie des Alde*, xxxviii; BL, C.66.d.9.

59. ΕΝ ΤΩιΔΕ ΤΩι ΒΙΒΛΙΩι ΤΑΔΕ ΠΕΡΙΕΧΕΤΑΙ. Ἀπολλωνίου ἀλεξανδρέως περὶ συντάξεως. Μεγάλου βασιλίου περὶ γραμματικῆς γυμνασίας. *IN HOC LIBRO HAEC CONTINENTUR. Apollonii alexandrei de constructione. Magni Basilii de grammatica exercitatione.* Florence: P. Junta, *sine mense* 1515, after March 10. **Content**: E. Boninus... C. Sernisio, *inc.* Dum tibi mnemosines... (no date, Schneider, Uhlig, and Hilgard, *Grammatici Graeci recognit*, 2, ii:xv); life of Apollonius; Apollonius, *De constructione*, books 1–4; "Basil"; all in Greek. The work attributed to Basil is the first part of Manuel Moschopoulos's Περὶ σχεδῶν (ibid.). Apollonius's books 2 and 4 have the same *lacunae* as the Aldine *editio princeps*. **Date**: Printed in the third year of the pontificate of Leo X, that is, March 11, 1515, to March 10, 1516. **Reference**: Schneider, Uhlig, and Hilgard, *Grammatici Graeci recognit*, 2, ii:xv; BL, 58.B.28.

60. Θεοδώρου γραμματικῆς εἰσαγωγῆς βιβλία Δ΄. Τοῦ αὐτοῦ περὶ μηνῶν. Γεωργίου τοῦ Λεκαπηνοῦ περὶ συντάξεως τῶν ῥημάτων. *Theodori Grammatices Introductionis libri quatuor. Eiusdem de mensibus. Georgii lagapeni [sic] de constructione verborum.* Florence: P. Junta, March 28, 1515. **Content**: E. Boninus Ludovico Martello Laurentii filio, *inc.* Cum novis Theodori...; Gaza, books 1 through 4, in Greek. The work attributed to Lecapenus is by Michael Syncellus. The *editio princeps* of Syncellus's work, based for this text on Venice, Bibl. Marciana, gr.314 (Donnet, "La tradition imprimée," 473). **Reference**: Renouard, *Annales de l'imprimerie des Alde*, xxxviii–xxxix; Cambridge, University Library, F151.e.2.21; BL, 622.c.16.

61. *Elementale introductorium in Nominum, et Verborum declinationes Graecas. Graecas dictiones cum earum characteribus, accentibus, ac vocum moderamentis, hic insertas offendes. ITEM. Hieronymi Aleandri Mottensis tabulae, sane utiles Graecarum Musarum adyta compendio ingredi cupientibus. LECTOR EME, LEGE, ET GAUDEBIS.* Strasbourg: M. Schurer, October 1515. **Content**: Alphabet and its divisions; pronunciation; transliteration; accents; the article; Greek numbers; *Aleander... studiosis, inc.* Quemadmodum ii qui... (no date, Horawitz, "Griechische Studien," 430; Omont, "Essai sur les débuts de la typographie grecque à Paris," 70–71); *tabulae*; noun declensions 1 through 5: "de contractis per crasin, sive synaeresis, apud alios reperies" (sig. e1r); *De verbo*; abbreviations. Twenty leaves. **Reference**: Baillet, "Le premier manuel," 28–29; Benzing and Muller, *Bibliographie strasbourgeoise*, 2:192; Chrisman, *Bibliography of Strasbourg Imprints*, 123; BL, 1560/1737.

62. *IN HOC LIBRO HAEC CONTINENTUR. Constantini Lascaris Byzantini de octo partibus orationis Lib.I. Eiusdem de Constructione Liber Secundus. Eiusdem de nomine et verbo Liber Tertius. Eiusdem de pronomine in omni idiomate loquendi, ac ut poetae utuntur opusculum. Cebetis Thebani Tabula. Plutarchi de his quae apud Homerum linguis. De literis graecis ac diphthongis et quemadmodum ad nos veniant. De potestate literarum graecarum, et quo modo quis per se discat legere graeca verba. Item quare Christus et Iesus sic scribimus Xps IHS. Cur in alphabeto ypsilon a quibusdam fio dicitur. Oratio Dominica et duplex salutatio ad Beatiss. Virginem. Symbolum Apostolorum. Evangelium divi Ioannis Evangelistae. Carmina aurea Pythagorae. Phocylidis Poema ad bene, beateque vivendum. Introductio perbrevis ad hebraicam linguam. Omnia haec cum interpretatione latina.* Florence: P. Junta, November 1515. **Content**: B. Junta P. Victorio Pauli filio, *inc.* Dum sopitos ne... (no date); Lascaris, book 1; pseudo-Tryphon; *De anomalis verbis*; *De spiritibus*; Lascaris, book 2: *De constructione*; *Aldus... lectori, inc.* Etsi eram typicis... (no date, Orlandi, *Aldo Manuzio editore*, 1:38); Lascaris, book 3: *De nomine et verbo*; *De pronominibus*; *De subscriptis vocalibus*; pseudo-Cebes; *Laudatio in sanctissimam dei genetricem*; pseudo-Plutarch on the Homeric dialects; Greek appendix; colophon; register.

The Hebrew appendix, lacking in BL, 624.c.12, may not have been printed. **Reference**: Renouard, *Annales de l'imprimerie des Alde*, xl; BL, 624.c.12.

63. *ALDI MANUTII ROMANI GRAMMATICAE INSTITUTIONES GRAECAE.* Venice: Manutius, November 1515. **Content**: *M. Musurus J. Grolierio . . . inc.* Multum equidem ac . . . (Venice, November 13, 1515. Legrand, *Bibliographie hellénique*, 1:131–33; Renouard, *Annales de l'imprimerie des Alde*, 73–74); Aldus's Greek grammar, in Greek. **Reference**: Legrand, *Bibliographie hellénique*, item no. 48; Renouard, *Annales de l'imprimerie des Alde*, 73–74; Cambridge, University Library, Aa*.11.70 (E).

1516

64. *Alphabetum hebraicum et Graecum.* Paris: G. de Gourmont, [1516?] **Content**: Gourmont's third undated *Alphabetum*. Six leaves. This edition is not in Omont. **Date**: BLC records it as [1516?]; the Bodleian catalog dates it [c. 1520]. It may be Moreau, *Inventaire chronologique*, 2, item no. 749, where it is dated [c. 1514] and where four copies are recorded; or it may be ibid., 2, item no. 1508, where a single Oxford copy is recorded. It has Gourmont's second device, of which the first dated use is [March or June] 22, 1516 (this appendix, no. 72). **Reference**: BL, 624.c.7 (1); BL, G.7532 (3); Oxford, Bodleian, Byw.N.6.8 (1).

65. * *Hieronymi Aleandri Mottensis tabulae sane quam utiles Graecarum musarum adyta compendio ingredi cupientibus.* Paris: G. de Gourmont, [1516?] **Content**: *Aleander . . . studiosis, inc.* Quemadmodum ii qui . . . (no date, Horawitz, "Griechische Studien," 430; Omont, "Essai sur les débuts de la typographie grecque à Paris," 70–71); alphabet and its divisions; pronunciation; accentuation and breathings; notes on parts of speech. Four leaves. There are at least three undated Paris editions of Aleandro's *Tabulae* (Omont, "Essai sur les débuts de la typographie grecque à Paris," 12–13). This is the second in Omont's list. It is not in BLC. **Date**: It has Gourmont's second device, of which the first dated use is [March or June] 22, 1516 (this appendix, no. 72). It is unclear which of the two undated editions with Gourmont's second device was printed first. **Reference**: Perhaps Moreau, *Inventaire chronologique*, 2:289; Paris, Bibl. Mazarine, 10487 (6).

66. *Constantini Lascaris Byzantini de octo partibus orationis liber primus. Eiusdem de constructione Liber secundus. Eiusdem de nomine et verbo Liber tertius. Eiusdem de pronomine secundum omnem linguam et poeticum usum Opusculum. Haec omnia habent e regione latinam interpretationem ad verbum fere propter rudes.* Louvain: T. Martens, [1516.] **Content**: *Aldus . . . A. Gabrieli, inc.* Cum plurimis in . . . (no date, Orlandi, *Aldo Manuzio editore*, 1:37; Martínez-Manzano, *Konstantinos Laskaris*, 228–29); verses: S. Forteguerri, in Greek and Latin; Lascaris, the full text, in Greek and Latin. This has *Laudatio in sanctissimam dei genetricem*, found interleaved in the Aldine edition. **Date**: BLC dates it [1519?]. It is dated 1516 or 1517 in Hoven, "Enseignement du grec," 79. It appears to be the edition dated [1516?] in the John Rylands Catalogue, 2:1011. Van Iseghem dates it [1516], citing the device and the condition of the type. **Reference**: Van Iseghem, *Biographie de Thierry Martens d'Alost*, 266–67; BL, 624.c.9.

67. * *ALPHABETUM GRAECUM, Oratio dominica, Angelica Salutatio, Symbolum Apostolorum Christi Servatoris apud Matthäum evangeliographum decreta, cum hoc genus aliis, Graece et latine, In usum iuventutis Graecarum adyta literarum subingressurae.* Basle: J. Froben, 1516. **Content**: Froben *studiosis, inc.* Quoniam dilectissimum filiolum . . . (no date, Horawitz, "Griechische Studien," 440). Eight leaves. The earliest extant Basle *Alphabetum*. **Reference**: Horawitz, "Griechische Studien," 439–40.

68. *Theodori viri undecunque doctissimi Liber quartus et ultimus de constructione, R. Croco Britanno interprete.* Leipzig: V. Schumann, *sine mense* 1516. **Content**: Croke to Albertus, bishop of Magdeburg, *inc.* Plutarchus ille Cheroneus ... (Leipzig, December 31, *sine anno*. See Geiger, *Johann Reuchlins Briefwechsel*, 362); verses: Croke and G. C. Aubanus; Gaza, book 4, trans. Croke. **Date**: Croke's preface is dated December 31, *sine anno*. Croke sent this edition to J. Reuchlin with an undated letter (edited by Dall'Asta and Dörner, *Johannes* Reuchlin 3:99–402). **Reference**: Cambridge, University Library, Syn.6.51.13; Oxford, Bodleian, Byw.T.6.2.

69. THEODORI INTRODUCTIVAE GRAMMATICES LIBRI QUATUOR. Paris: G. de Gourmont, [early 1516?] **Content**: Gaza, book 1, in Greek. **Date**: This edition of the first book is different from the Paris Gaza of [March or June] 22, 1516 (this appendix, no. 72), although the copy in the British library is bound with books 2 through 4 of that edition. It has Gourmont's second device, of which the first dated use is in that edition (this appendix, no. 72). Omont dates it [1515?] ("Essai sur les débuts de la typographie grecque à Paris," 36). **Reference**: Omont, "Essai sur les débuts de la typographie grecque à Paris," 36; BL, 1568/3159 (miscataloged as 1568/3157).

70. *ΕΡΩΤΗΜΑΤΑ ΤΟΥ ΧΡΥΣΟΛΩΡΑ. Grammatica Chrysolorae.* Paris: G. de Gourmont, [February or December] 5, 1516. **Content**: F. Vatable to B. Doria, *inc.* Quantam prae te ... (Paris, May 29, *sine anno*; Rice, *The Prefatory Epistles*, 270–73; Omont, "Essai sur les débuts de la typographie grecque à Paris," 57–59); Chrysoloras, the full text, in Greek; colophon. **Date**: The colophon reads, "Ἐλαφηβολιῶνος ἱσταμένου πέμπτῃ." This is February in *De mensibus*; in the lexica it is December. It has Gourmont's second device of which the first dated use is [March or June] 22, 1516 (this appendix, no. 72). The date of Vatable's preface is copied from the edition printed by Gourmont in [May or July] 1512 (this appendix, no. 42). **Reference**: Omont, "Essai sur les débuts de la typographie grecque à Paris," 38; Rice, *The Prefatory Epistles*, 270–73; Moreau, *Inventaire chronologique*, 2:358; BL, G.7531 (3).

71. *Theodori introductivae grammatices libri quatuor.* Louvain: T. Martens, March 1516. **Content**: Verses: G. Aleandro; Gaza, book 1, in Greek. **Date**: The books of the grammar sometimes found bound together under this title page were not printed at the same time. The block used on the title page was used to print the title page of the second book three months later (this appendix, no. 76), by which time it had lost some of its border. It appears that book 1 was issued with the title page for 1 through 4 in anticipation of the remaining books. **Reference**: Van Iseghem, *Biographie de Thierry Martens d'Alost*, 260–61; Cambridge, University Library, Rel.c.51.10 (3), book 1 only; BL, 624.c.6 (1 and 3), books 1 and 2 only.

72. THEODORI INTRODUCTIVAE GRAMMATICES LIBRI QUATUOR. Paris: G. de Gourmont, [March or June] 22, 1516. **Content**: Gaza, books 1 through 4, in Greek. Each book has its own title page. **Date**: Books 1 through 3 are undated. The colophon at the end of the fourth book reads, "Σκιροφοριῶνος ἐννάτῃ ἀπιόντος" 1516. This month is June in *De mensibus*; it is March in the lexica. Omont makes this June 9 ("Essai sur les débuts de la typographie grecque à Paris," 36). Each book has its own title page with Gourmont's second device, the first dated use of this device. Another edition from Gourmont's press of book 1 only, here dated [early 1516?] (this appendix, no. 69), is found bound with books 2 through 4 of this edition (BL, 1568/3159). Gourmont may have sold the remainder of this earlier edition with his new copies of the later books. **Reference**: Omont, "Essai sur les débuts de la typographie grecque à Paris," 36–37; Moreau, *Inventaire chronologique*, 2:370; BL, 624.c.7 with Erasmus's translations (Louvain 1516 and 1518) interleaved; BL, 1568/3159; Oxford, Bodleian, Byw.N.6.8.

73. *Hieronymi Aleandri Mottensis tabulae sane quam utiles Graecarum musarum adyta compendio ingredi cupientibus. Rutgeri Rescii Dryopolitani in nominum, et verborum declinationes. Tabulae ad normam Theodori grammatices redactae. Urbani tabulae in nominum declinationes. Oratio dominica cum angelica salutatione, et aliis quibusdam piis orationibus. Symbolum Apostolorum. Symbolum sanctorum patrum. Symbolum divi Athanasii. Στίχοι Σιββύλλας τῆς Ἐρυθραίας περὶ τοῦ κυρίου ἡμῶν ἔχοντες ἀκροστιχίδα τήνδε, ιησους χριστὸς θεοῦ υἱὸς σωτὴρ σταυρός. Hoc est, Carmina Sibyllae Erythraeae de domino nostro haec imprimis versuum literis pre se ferentia, Iesus Christus dei filius salvator crux. Epigramma in septem sapientes. Eorundem praeclara dicta. Sententiae in invidiam, in amicos, et in tempus.* Louvain: T. Martens, March 1516. **Content**: Alphabet; *Aleander... studiosis, inc.* Quemadmodum ii qui... (Horawitz, "Griechische Studien," 430; Omont, "Essai sur les débuts de la typographie grecque à Paris," 70–71); Rescius to J. Paludanus, *inc.* Cum omnis eloquentiae... (March 9, 1516); *tabulae*; *Urbani tabulae*; prayers and texts, in Greek. **Reference**: Cambridge, University Library, Rel.c.51.10 (1).

74. *Aldi Manutii Romani Institutionum grammaticarum. Libri Quattuor. Ad Exemplar Aldinum: cum graeco suis locis inserto. Quae autem in singulis libris contineantur in tergo huius videbis.* Paris: N. de Pratis, April 1, 1516. **Content**: *Aldus... literarii ludimagistris, inc.* Rudimenta grammatices... (Venice, October 1507). Aldus's Latin grammar; Greek appendix, no preface; colophon. **Reference**: BL, 1568/3281.

75. *M. R. Croci, londoniensis, Tabulae, Grecas literas compendio discere cupientibus, sane quam utiles, in quibus haec habentur contenta. De pronunciatione literarum grecarum ex Aleandro. De formatione comparativorum et superlativorum. De temporum et modorum deductione. Ver. in ω. baryto. De verbis circumflexis. De verbis in Mi. Ex Theodori quarto de constructione adverbiorum. Ex Urbano de verbis defectivis.* Leipzig: V. Schumann, [1516, after April 1]. **Content**: Verses: G. C. Aubanus, *inc.* Si cui nec...; verses: [*isdem*] *inc.* Vidit ut has...; verses: [*isdem*] *inc.* Ταῦτα ὁρῶσα Κρόκου... (all in Horawitz, "Griechische Studien," 432–33); *Crocus Academie senatui et philosophorum in urbe Lipsiensi coronae, inc.* Utcunque de me... (February 25, *sine anno*); privilege of four years (April 1, 1516); verses: *Ad librum...*; verses: *In beatam tranquillitatem Muttiani.* **Reference**: Horawitz, "Griechische Studien," 432–34; Cambridge, University Library, Syn.7.51.29; BL, 826.c.26 (2).

76. *THEODORI GRAMMATICES INTRODUCTIONIS LIBER SECUNDUS.* Louvain: T. Martens, June 1516. **Content**: Gaza, book 2, in Greek; colophon. No preface. See this appendix, no. 71. **Reference**: Van Iseghem, *Biographie de Thierry Martens d'Alost*, 262–63; Cambridge, University Library, Rel.c.51.10 (3); Oxford, Bodleian, Byw.T.6.5 (2).

77. *Primus liber grammaticae institutionis Theodori Gazae sic translatus per Erasmum Roterodamum, ac titulis et annotatiunculis explanatus, ut citra negocium et percipi queat et teneri.* Louvain: T. Martens, July 1516. **Content**: *Erasmus... J. Caesario, inc.* Habent in omni... (June 23, 1516; EE 2:264–66); Gaza, book 1, trans. Erasmus. **Reference**: BL, 624.c.7 (3).

78. *ΕΓΧΕΙΡΙΔΙΟΝ ΓΡΑΜΜΑΤΙΚΗΣ. ΕΝ ΤΗιΔΕ ΤΗι ΒΙΒΛΩι ΤΑΔΕ ΕΙΣΙ. Ἐρωτήματα τοῦ χρυσολωρᾶ. Περὶ ἀνομάλων ῥημάτων. Περὶ σχηματισμοῦ τῶν χρόνων ἐκ τῶν χαλκονδύλου. Θεοδώρου περὶ συντάξεως. Ἡρωδιανοῦ περὶ ἐγκλιτικῶν. Γνῶμαι μονόστιχοι ἐκ διαφόρων ποιητῶν. Κάτωνος ῥωμαίου γνῶμαι ἃς μετήνεγκεν ἐκ τῆς λατίνων φωνῆς εἰς τὴν ἑλληνίδα διάλεκτον μάξιμος μοναχὸς ὁ πλανούδης. ENCHIRIDIUM GRAMMATICES. IN HOC LIBRO HAEC SUNT. Erotemata chrisolorae. De anomalis verbis. De formatione temporum chalcondilae. Theodori de constructione. Herodiani de encleticis [sic] Sententiae unius carminis ex diversis poetis. Catonis Romani*

sententiae quas transtulit ex latina voce in graecam linguam maximus monachus planudes. Florence: P. Junta, September 22, 1516. **Content**: *Euphrosynus Boninus Aloysio Alamanno, inc.* Cum Graiae te . . . (no date); Chrysoloras, the full text; *De anomalis verbis*; Chalcondyles on the verb; Gaza, book 4; Herodian on enclitics; gnomic verses; *Disticha Catonis*, trans. Planudes. All texts in Greek only. **Date**: This edition, and its preface, is a reprint of the Juntine edition of February 1, 1515, new style (this appendix, no. 58). **Reference**: Renouard, *Annales de l'imprimerie des Alde*, xli; BL, 236.g.29.

79. *THEODORI GAZAE Thessalonicensis, Grammaticae institutionis liber primus, sic translatus per ERASMUM ROTERODAMUM, ac titulis et annotatiunculis explanatus ut citra negocium et percipi queat et teneri. IDEM Graece, pro iis qui iam aliquantulum profecerunt. COLLOQUIORUM FAMIliarium incerto autore libellus Graece et Latine, non pueris modo, sed quibusvis, in cottidiano colloquio, graecum affectantibus sermonem, impendio futurus utilis, nunquam antehac typis excusus.* Basle: J. Froben, November 1516. **Content**: *Erasmus . . . J. Caesario, inc.* Habent in omni . . . (Antwerp, June 23, 1516; EE 2:264–66). Gaza, book 1, trans. Erasmus; B. Rhenanus to J. Froben, *inc.* Rogas ut quamprimum . . . (Basle, October 27, 1516; Horawitz and Hartfelder, *Briefwechsel des Beatus Rhenanus*, 583); Gaza, book 1, in Greek; Rhenanus to L. Edenberg, *inc.* Proximis superioribus diebus . . . (Basle, November 5, 1516; Horawitz and Hartfelder, *Briefwechsel des Beatus Rhenanus*, 89–90); *colloquia*, in Greek and Latin. A reprint of Erasmus's translation printed at Louvain in July (this appendix, no. 77). Allen says that this edition did not sell well and that the remainder of the edition was bound with Erasmus's version of book 2, printed by Froben in March 1518 (this appendix, no. 93; EE 3:214). However, different ornamental capitals show that at least some copies of the first book were reprinted in 1518. **Reference**: Horawitz and Hartfelder, *Briefwechsel des Beatus Rhenanus*, 603; Harlfinger and Barm, *Graecogermania*, 99–100; *Griechischer Geist*, 36, item no. 18; BL, 624.c.5 (1).

80. *ΕΡΩΤΗΜΑΤΑ ΤΟΥ ΧΡΥΣΟΛΩΡΑ. EROTEMATA CHRYSOLORAE.* Strasbourg: J. Knoblouch, December 3, 1516. **Content**: Chrysoloras, the full text, in Greek. **Reference**: Benzing and Muller, *Bibliographie strasbourgeoise*, 1:75, 2:131; Chrisman, *Bibliography of Strasbourg Imprints*, 124; BL, 624.c.3.

1517

81. *ALDI PII MANUTII INSTITUTIONUM GRAMMATICARUM LIBRI QUATUOR. Quae quoque libro continentur hanc volventi chartam statim se offerunt.* Florence: P. Junta, [July 1516–January 1517 new style] **Content**: *Aldus . . . literarii ludi magistris, inc.* Rudimenta grammatices . . . (no date); Aldus's Latin grammar; register; colophon; Greek appendix, with its own title page; colophon; register; Aldus, *inc.* Quoniam hebraicam linguam . . . (no date, Orlandi, *Aldo Manuzio editore*, 1:38); Hebrew appendix. The first gathering only of the grammar is in red and black. Apparently a copy of the Aldine of 1514. **Date**: The grammar colophon is July 1516; its register includes the gatherings of the Greek appendix. The colophon of the Greek appendix is January 1516 *stylo florentino*; its register includes the gatherings of the grammar. **Reference**: BL, 1568/3746.

82. * *ELEMENTALE INTROductorium in Nominum, et Verborum declinationes Graecas, praeterea et alia quaedam iam addita, quae legendo, studiosiss. Quisque Lector facile deprehendet. ITEM Hieronymi Aleandri Mottensis tabulae, sane utiles Graecarum musarum adyta compendio ingredi cupientibus.* Strasbourg: M. Schurer, March 1517. **Reference**: Baillet, "Le premier manuel," 29; Benzing and Muller, *Bibliographie strasbourgeoise*, 2:199; Chrisman, *Bibliography of Strasbourg Imprints*, 123; PBN, Rés. P-X-361.

83. *PROGYMNASMATA GRAECAnicae literaturae ab Ottomaro Luscinio pro studiosis iampridem concinnata, In quibus sequentia insunt. Quae ad elementorum Nomen pertinent. Figuram et potestatem. Quae ad literarum divisionem. Quae ad literarum nexus sive abbreviationem. Quae ad pronunciationem. Quae ad Accentum. Quae ad facilem nominum inflexionem per casus et comparationem, et ibi de Heteroclitis. Quae ad temporum in verbo cognationem et confinitatem quam ex voce deprehendas licebit, qua via non est alia facilior ad percipienda coniugationem. De alii orationis partibus.* Strasbourg: J. Knoblouch, March 29, 1517. **Content:** Nachtgall to H. Gebuilerus, *inc.* Rogatus iampridem a . . . (no date); alphabet and its divisions; abbreviations; pronunciation; accentuation; nouns; verbs; pronouns; prepositions; adverbs; conjunctions; *Ad lectorem, inc.* Haec sunt amice . . . (no date). Fourteen leaves. **Reference:** Benzing and Muller, *Bibliographie strasbourgeoise*, 1:188, 2:135; Chrisman, *Bibliography of Strasbourg Imprints*, 124; BL, 1560/1740.

84. *Ex Aldo Manutio de literis Graecis et diphthongis, ac earum proprietatibus, una cum abbreviaturis, quibus frequentius utuntur, ex quorum cognitione, tyrunculus facillime literas Graecas lectitabit, et ne desit ei, quod lecturiat, addita sunt ex ordine haec quae sequuntur. Oratio Dominica, Salutatio angelica, Symbolum apostolorum, Benedictio mensae, Gratiarum actio post mensam dicenda, Addidimus praeterea breviusculam institutionem in literas Hebraeas, ab ipso Volphango [sic] Fabro mutuatam, qua profecto facillimus ad Hebraeorum scripta perlegenda datur aditus.* Cologne: E. Cervicornus, August 7, 1517. **Content:** Alphabet and its divisions; pronunciation; abbreviations; Greek prayers; Hebrew appendix. Eight leaves. **Reference:** BL, T.2236 (2).

85. Ἐρωτήματα τοῦ Χρυσολωρᾶ. Περὶ ἀνομάλων ῥημάτων. Περὶ σχηματισμοῦ τῶν χρόνων ἐκ τοῦ χαλκονδύλου. Τὸ τέταρτον τοῦ γαζῆ, περὶ συντάξεως. Περὶ ἐγκλητικῶν. Γνῶμαι μονόστιχοι ἐκ διαφόρων ποιητῶν. Κάτων. Ἐρωτήματα τοῦ Γουαρίνου. *Erotemata Chrysolorae. De anomalis verbis. De formatione temporum ex libro Chalcondylae. Quartus Gazae De constructione. De encleticis [sic]. Sententiae monostichi ex variis poetis. Cato. Erotemata Guarini.* Venice: in aedibus Aldi et Andreae Soceri, November 1517. **Content:** *Aldus Caesari Aragonio, inc.* Manuel Chrysoloras qui . . . (no date); Chrysoloras, the full text; Chalcondyles on the verb; Gaza, book 4; Herodian on enclitics; *sententiae*; Planudes' Greek version of the *Disticha Catonis*, printed on its own gathering in different font; Chrysoloras, abbreviated by Guarino; notes on the dialects; Greek numbers. This is the first edition to print both texts of Chrysoloras together. **Reference:** Renouard, *Annales de l'imprimerie des Alde*, 80; BL, 1067.c.26.

1518

86. *Hieronymi Aleandri Mottensis tabulae sanequam utiles Graecarum Musarum adyta compendio ingredi cupientibus.* Paris: G. de Gourmont, [c. 1518?]. **Content:** *Aleander . . . studiosis, inc.* Quemadmodum ii qui . . . (no date, Horawitz, "Griechische Studien," 430; Omont, "Essai sur les débuts de la typographie grecque à Paris," 70–71); alphabet and its divisions; pronunciation; accentuation and breathings; notes on parts of speech. Four leaves. **Date:** There are at least three undated Paris editions of Aleandro's *Tabulae*. This is the first in Omont's list ("Essai sur les débuts de la typographie grecque à Paris," 12–13). BLC dates this edition [1516?]. Apparently to be identified with the third of the undated Paris tables in Moreau, *Inventaire chronologique*, 2, item no. 1734, where it is dated [c. 1518]. It has Gourmont's second device, of which the first dated use is [March or June] 22, 1516 (this appendix, no. 72). Gourmont uses two Greek fonts and two Latin for his main text. His smaller Greek font has no accents or breathings. With this font he

uses his smaller Latin font. The second Greek font has all accents and breathings cast with the letter. With this larger font he uses a larger Latin font on the same line. This makes the page look peculiar. It is unclear which of the two undated editions with Gourmont's second device was printed first. **Reference**: Moreau, *Inventaire chronologique*, 2: 457; BL. G.7485 (2).

87. * *Alphabetum graecum. Oratio dominica. Angelica salutatio. Symbolum apostolorum. Christi Salvatoris apud Matthaeum Evangeliographum Decreta. Cum quibusdam aliis.* [Louvain: T. Martens, c. 1518.] **Date**: Dated 1518 by Van Iseghem (*Biographie de Thierry Martens d'Alost*, 294). **Reference**: Van Iseghem, *Biographie de Thierry Martens d'Alost*, 294; *Index Aureliensis* 1:388; PBN, Rés. X-1305.

88. * *Contenta. De literis Graecis ac diphthongis et quemadmodum ad nos veniant. Abbreviationes quibus frequentissime Graeci utuntur. Oratio Dominica et duplex Salutatio ad Beatiss. Virginem. Symbolum Apostolorum. Evangelium Divi Ioannis Evangelistae. Carmina aurea Pythagorae. Phocylidis poema ad bene beateque vivendum. Omnia haec cum tralatione Latina. Introductio perbrevis ad Hebraicam linguam.* Hagenau: T. Anshelm, [1518.] **Date**: This undated edition appears to be noticed in Melanchthon's grammar, complete by May 1518 (this appendix, no. 94, sig. a3r). The John Rylands catalog dates it 1520. **Reference**: Horawitz, "Griechische Studien," 440n3; Manchester, John Rylands Library, 17662.2.

89. *PRIMUS LIBER grammaticae institutionis Theodori Gazae, sic translatus per Erasmum Roterodamum ac titulis et annotatiunculis explanatus, ut citra negotium et percipi queat et teneri. Cum gratia et privilegio.* Louvain: T. Martens, March 1, 1518. **Content**: *Erasmus . . . J. Caesario, inc.* Habent in omni . . . (Antwerp, June 23, 1516; EE 2:264–66); Gaza, book 1, trans. Erasmus; colophon; device. This was probably intended for issue with Marten's contemporary edition of book 2. **Date**: The date is from the title page; the colophon reads "Anno. M.D.XVIII. Mense Martio." **Reference**: Van Iseghem, *Biographie de Thierry Martens d'Alost*, 281–82; EE 2:214; Oxford, Bodleian, Byw.T.6.4.

90. *THEODORI GAZAE de linguae graecae institutione liber secundus, Erasmo Roterodamo interprete. Cum gratia et privilegio.* Louvain: T. Martens, [perhaps March 1–5, 1518.] **Content**: *Erasmus . . . J. Caesario, inc.* Queso te, Caesari . . . (Louvain, February 20, 1518; EE 3:214–15); abbreviations; Gaza, book 2, trans. Erasmus; device. **Date**: The *terminus post quem* is provided by the date of Erasmus's letter to Caesarius. The *terminus ante quem* is supplied by the fact that Erasmus sent a copy of this edition of the second book alone to John Fisher with a letter c. March 5 (EE 3:236–38). It is likely that it was printed with or shortly after Martens's edition of book 1 (this appendix, no. 89), with which it was probably issued. **Reference**: Van Iseghem, *Biographie de Thierry Martens d'Alost*, 282; EE 3:214; BL, 624.c.26; Oxford, Bodleian, Byw.N.6.8 (2).

91. *THEODORI GRAMMATICAE INTRODUCTIVAE LIBER QUARTUS.* Louvain: T. Martens, [c. 1518, after March 1, 1518.] **Content**: Gaza, book 4, in Greek; device. **Date**: Martens's device is more worn than in his edition of Erasmus's translation of book 1, March 1, 1518 (this appendix, no. 89); it is less worn than in his edition of the Greek text of book 3, November 1521 (this appendix, no. 123); it is in a similar state to that in Aleandro's *Tabulae*, December 1518 (no. 97). **Reference**: Cambridge, University Library, Rel.c.51.10 (3); Oxford, Bodleian, Byw.T.6.5 (4).

92. *ALPHABETUM GRAECUM, Oratio dominica, Angelica Salutatio, Symbolum Apostolorum, CHRISTI Servatoris apud Matthaeum Evangeliographum Decreta. Cum hoc genus aliis. Graece et Latine. IN USUM IUVENTUTIS GRAECARUM ADYTA LITERARUM SUBINGRESSURAE.* Basle: J. Froben, March 15, 1518. **Content**: *Frobenius*

studiosis, inc. Quoniam dilectissimum filiolum . . . (no date, Horawitz, "Griechische Studien," 440); prayers, in Greek and Latin. The second Basle *Alphabetum*. **Date**: The British Library copy has a colophon of March 1518 (sig. a8r). It is followed by a single unsigned leaf with the same device and a second colophon: March 15, 1518. **Reference**: BL, 827.d.43.

93. *THEODORI Gazae Thessalonicensis, Grammaticae institutionis libri duo, nempe Primus et Secundus, sic translati per ERASMUM ROTERODAMUM ac titulis et annotatiunculis explanati, ut citra negotium et percipi queant et teneri. IIDEM Graece, pro iis qui iam aliquantulum profecerunt. COLLOQUIORUM FAMILIArium incerto autore libellus Graece et Latine, non pueris modo, sed quibusvis, in cottidiano colloquio, graecum affectantibus sermonem, impendio futurus utilis, nunquam antehac typis excusus.* Basle: J. Froben, March 1518. **Content**: Erasmus . . . *J. Caesario, inc.* Habent in omni . . . (Antwerp, June 23, 1516. EE 2:264–66); Gaza, book 1, trans. Erasmus; Gaza, book 2, trans. Erasmus; B. Rhenanus to J. Froben, *inc.* Rogas ut quamprimum . . . (Basle, October 27, 1516; Horawitz and Hartfelder, *Briefwechsel des Beatus Rhenanus*, 583); Gaza, book 1, in Greek; Gaza, book 2, in Greek; errata; register; Rhenanus to L. Edenberg, *inc.* Proximis superioribus diebus . . . (Basle, November 5, 1516; Horawitz and Hartfelder, *Briefwechsel des Beatus Rhenanus*, 89–90); colloquia, in Greek and Latin. **Date**: Each of the five parts of this volume begins on a new gathering. Erasmus suggested that his version of book 2 be bound with unsold copies of his version of book 1, printed by Froben in November 1516 (this appendix, no. 79): "Mitto primum librum Theodori castigatum, et secundum versum. Si multos adhuc habes primae editionis, adde chartulam in qua notes errata et adiunge secundum" (August 1517, EE 3:53). In a letter of November 18, 1517, Rhenanus claims that this is being printed at Basle (Horawitz and Hartfelder, *Briefwechsel des Beatus Rhenanus*, 98). The claim in the title that the colloquies had not been printed before, reproduced from the title page of the edition of 1516, is strictly true: Froben bound unsold copies of his 1516 edition into this new edition. The colophon after the Greek text of book 2 gives the date as Σκιροφοριών 1518. This is May in *De mensibus*, and March in the lexica. Froben writes toward the end of March 1518 that the volume has been printed (EE 3:256). **Reference**: *Griechischer Geist*, 39, item no. 20; BL, 12924.f.15; BL, 1560/1745 (incomplete).

94. *INSTITUTIONES GRAECAE GRAMMATICAE Accentuum exquisita ratio. Etymologia. Ex Homero, Thersita et Chelys cum scholiis. PHILIP. MELANCHT. Proderunt haec non solum graeca discentibus sed iis etiam qui non turpissime latina tractare conantur. Tubingae.* Hagenau: T. Anshelm, May 1518. **Content**: On the dialects, *inc.* Ampla fuit regio . . .; verses: Johannes Secerius, *inc.* Hac iter ad Musas . . .; Philip Melanchthon to Bernhard Maurus, *inc.* Sive hoc nostro . . . (Hagenau, *sine mense* 1518; Wetzel and others, *Melanchthons Briefwechsel* 1:62–64); Melanchthon's grammar, the *editio princeps*. Before *De verbo*, Hesiod, *Theogony*, 36–79, with commentary. After the grammar, *Thersites* (*Iliad* 2:212–20), with commentary; *Chelys* (*Homeric Hymn* 4:29–55), in Greek and Latin, with scholion; postscript, *inc.* Pauca haec de . . . (Tübingen, no date; Wetzel and others, *Melanchthons Briefwechsel*, 1:64–64). **Reference**: Harlfinger and Barm, *Graecogermania*, 106–7; Wetzel and others, *Melanchthons Briefwechsel*, 1:62–65; Munich, Bayerische Staatsbibliothek, Res/4 L.gr.80.

95. *Psalterium in Quattuor linguis Hebraea Graeca Chaldaea Latina*. Cologne, June 1518. **Content**: A brief pamphlet precedes the title page: "Introductiunculae in tres linguas externas. Hebraeam Graecam Chaldaeam." Postscript: *Io. Potken Praepositus Ecclesiae Sancti Georgii Colonien. Peregrinarum literarum studiosis, inc.* Dumdum Romae in . . . (June 10, *sine anno*). **Reference**: Cambridge, University Library, Bury.22.3.

96. * *DRAGMATA GRAECAE LITERATURAE, A IO. OECOLAMPADIO CONGESTA. Cum privilegio.* Basle: A. Cratander, September 1518. **Content**: *Andreas Cratander studiosis* (Basle, August 30, 1518); *Io. Oecolampadius Hartmanno Hallwilero, inc.* Equidem, mi Hartmanne . . . (Basle, August 31, 1518); Oecolampadius's grammar, the *editio princeps*. **Reference**: Staehelin, "Oekolampad-Bibliographie," 11–12, item no. 7; Hoven, *Bibliographie*, 5; *Griechischer Geist*, 40, item no. 21.

97. *HIERONYMI Aleandri Mottensis tabulae sane quam utiles graecarum musarum adyta compendio ingredi cupientibus. Oratio dominica cum angelica salutatione, et aliis quibusdam piis orationibus. Symbolum Apostolorum. Symbolum sanctorum patrum. Symbolum divi Athanasii.* Στίχοι Σιβύλλας τῆς Ερυθραίας περὶ τοῦ κυρίου ἡμῶν, ἔχοντες ἀκροστιχίδα, τήνδε, Ιησοῦς χριστὸς θεοῦ υἱὸς σωτὴρ σταυρός. *Hoc est. Carmina Sibyllae Erythraeae de domino nostro, haec in primis versum literis prae se ferentia, Iesus Christus dei filius salvator crux. Epigramma in septem sapientes. Eorundem praeclare dicta. Sententiae in invidiam.* Louvain: T. Martens, December 1518. **Content**: Alphabet; *Aleander . . . studiosis, inc.* Quemadmodum ii qui . . . (no date, Omont, "Essai sur les débuts de la typographie grecque à Paris," 70–71; Horawitz, "Griechische Studien," 430); alphabet and its divisions; pronunciation; accentuation; Greek texts; abbreviations; colophon; device. **Reference**: Van Iseghem, *Biographie de Thierry Martens d'Alost*, 290; Oxford, Bodleian, Byw.J.2.28 (miscataloged as Byw.F.2.28).

1519

98. * *Elementale in graecas literas introductorium. Hieronymi Aleandri Mottensis de eisdem tabulae. Quaedam non inutilis in graecorum nominum et verborum declinationes introductio. Ad calcem praeterea est adjecta explanatio abbreviationum quae Graecis admodum sunt familiares.* Cologne: E. Cervicornus, 1519. **Reference**: PBN, Rés. P-Y2-259.

99. * *De literis Graecis: abbreviationes: oratio dominica: symbolum apostolorum: evangelium Ioannis: carmina Pythagorae: Phocylidis poema: Introductio in literas Hebraeas.* Hagenau: T. Anshelm, 1519. **Content**: This edition is in octavo. The undated edition previously noted, Hagenau, [1518] (this appendix, no. 88), is in quarto. **Reference**: Manchester, John Rylands Library, 17811.

100. *ALDI PII MANUTII INSTITUTIONUM GRAMMATICARUM LIBRI QUATUOR. Quae quoque libro continentur hanc volventi chartam statim se offerunt.* Toscolano: Alexander de paganinis, 24 December 1519. **Content**: *Aldus . . . literarii ludi magistris, inc.* Rudimenta grammatices . . . (no date); Aldus's Latin grammar; register; colophon; Greek appendix, with its own title page; Aldus, *inc.* Quoniam hebraicam linguam . . . (no date, Orlandi, *Aldo Manuzio editore*, 1:38); Hebrew appendix. **Reference**: Cambridge, University Library, Norton.e.44.

1520

101. * *Brevissima introductio ad literas Graecas.* [Rome?: Z. Callierges? c. 1520.] **Content**: Eight leaves. **Reference**: Manchester, John Rylands Library, 19963.

102. *THEODORI GAZAE LIBER PRIMUS de Rudimentis Graecarum Literarum.* Tübingen: ex Charisio Thomae Anshelmi, [c. 1520]. **Content**: *Philippus Mela Paulo Geraeandro, inc.* Qui Graeca iuventuti . . . (Tübingen, no date); Gaza's grammar, book 1, in Greek; *ex Callistrato in Orphei statuam*, in Greek. **Reference**: Munich, Bayerische Staatsbibliothek, Res/A.gr.b.1572.

103. *ELEMENTALE INTRODUCTORIUM IN Nominum, et Verborum declinationes Graecas, praeterea et alia quaedam iam addita, quae legendo, studiosiss. Quisque Lector facile deprehendet. Item. Hieronymi Aleandri Mottensis tabulae, sane utiles Graecarum musarum adyta compendio ingredi cupientibus.* Selestadt: L. Schurer, *sine mense* 1520. **Content**: Alphabet; pronunciation; the article; Greek numbers; *Aleander . . . studiosis, inc.* Quemadmodum ii qui . . . (no date, Horawitz, "Griechische Studien," 430; Omont, "Essai sur les débuts de la typographie grecque à Paris," 70–71); *tabulae*; five declensions: "De contractis per crasin sive synaeresin apud alios reperies" (sig. d4v); *De verbo*: τύπτω, full conjugation; ποιέω, full conjugation; εἶναι, abbreviated conjugation; *De formatione temporum*; abbreviations. **Reference**: BL, 1568/3129.

104. *ALDI PII MANUTII INSTITUTIONUM GRAMMATICARUM LIBRI QUATUOR. Addito in fine de octo partium orationis libello. Erasmo Roterodamo auctore. Quae quoque libro continentur hanc volventi chartam statim se offerunt.* Florence: Heredes P. Junta, January 1519 [1520 new style]. **Content**: Aldus's Latin grammar, with the first gathering printed in red and black; register; colophon; Greek appendix, with its own title page; no preface, abbreviations, or colophon; Manutius, *inc.* Quoniam hebraicam linguam . . . (no date, Orlandi, *Aldo Manuzio editore*, 1:38); Hebrew appendix; no colophon; J. Colet to W. Lily, *inc.* Haud aliter . . . (1513); Erasmus *lectori, inc.* Ipsa re comperio . . . (Basle, July 30, 1515; EE 2:118–20); Erasmus, *De octo partium orationis libello*; colophon. **Date**: Both colophons are January 1519 *stylo florentino*. **Reference**: BL, 66.a.6.

105. *ALPHABETUM GRAECUM, Oratio dominica, Angelica Salutatio, Symbolum Apostolorum, CHRISTI servatoris apud Matthaeum evangeliographum decreta, cum hoc genus aliis, Graece et Latine, in usum iuventutis Graecarum adyta literarum subingressurae.* Basle: J. Froben, February 1520. **Content**: *Ioannes Frobenius studiosis, inc.* Quoniam dilectissimum filiolum . . . (no date, Horawitz, "Griechische Studien," 440); alphabet; prayers, in Greek and Latin. Eight leaves. Apparently the third Basle *Alphabetum*, after the second of 1518. **Reference**: Munich, Bayerisches Staatsbibliothek, Res/L.gr.6.

106. * *GRAECAE LITERATURAE DRAGMATA, IO. OECOLAMPADIO AUTORE.* Basle: A. Cratander, March 1520. **Content**: *And. Cratander studiosis* (Basle, 22 Kal. Apr. 1520); *Io. Oecolampadius Hartmanno Hallwilero, inc.* Equidem, mi Hartmanne . . . (Basle, August 31, 1518); grammar. **Date**: The date of Cratander's preface is impossible. It is not clear whether the error belongs to Staehelin or to his source. **Reference**: Staehelin, "Oekolampad-Bibliographie," 19, item no. 23.

107. *ΘΕΟΔΩΡΟΥ ΓΡΑΜΜΑΤΙΚΗΣ ΕΙΣΑΓΩΓΗΣ ΒΙΒΛΙΑ Δ΄. Τοῦ αὐτοῦ περὶ μηνῶν. Γεωργίου τοῦ λεκαπηνοῦ περὶ συντάξεως τῶν ῥημάτων. Theodori grammatices introductionis libri quatuor. Eiusdem de mensibus. Georgii legapeni [sic] de constructione verborum.* Florence: Heredes P. Juntae, March 28, 1520. **Content**: Gaza, books 1 through 4, in Greek; Gaza, *De mensibus*, in Greek; Syncellus, *De constructione*, in Greek; colophon; register. The second edition of "Lecapenus," that is, Syncellus. For Syncellus, at least, the text is based on the *editio princeps* of 1515 (Donnet, "La tradition imprimée," 473). **Reference**: Renouard, *Annales de l'imprimerie des Alde*, xliv–xlv; BL, G.16800.

108. *RICHARDI CROCI BRITANni introductiones in Rudimenta Graeca.* Cologne: E. Cervicornus, May 1520. **Content**: Croke to William Warham, Archbishop of Canterbury, *inc.* Exigua profecto res . . . (London, January 1, *sine anno*); Croke's grammar. **Reference**: Manchester, John Rylands Library, 7844.

109. *INTEGRAE GRAECAE GRAMMATICES INSTItutiones, a Philippo Melanchthone conscriptae, atque pluribus in locis auctae.* Hagenau: T. Anshelm, August 1520. **Content**: On the dialects, *inc.* Lata fuit regio . . . ; Melanchthon to the reader, *inc.* Semper optavi

libellos... (Wittenberg, no date; Wetzel and others, *Melanchthons Briefwechsel*, 1:240–42); grammar; *Chelys* (*Homeric Hymn* 4:29–55), in Greek and Latin, with scholion; postscript, *inc.* Pauca haec de... (Tübingen, no date; Wetzel and others, *Melanchthons Briefwechsel*, 1:64–64); Lucian, *Cupido*, in Greek. **Reference**: BL, C.190.a.28.

110. *HADRIANI AMEROTII Suessionensis Compendium Graecae Grammatices, perspicua brevitate complectens, quicquid est octo partium orationis. Cum gratia et privilegio.* Louvain: T. Martens, October 15, 1520. **Content**: Amerot to Antoine de la Marck, *inc.* Abhinc annos complusculos... (Louvain, 18 Kal. Nov. 1520); alphabet and its divisions; article; accentuation; nouns; verbs; other parts of speech; dialectal variants; abbreviations. **Date**: The impossible date of the preface may be an error for 17 Kal. Nov., the date of the colophon. **Reference**: Van Iseghem, *Biographie de Thierry Martens d'Alost*, 310–11; Hummel, "Un opuscule-relais"; Hoven, *Bibliographie*, 8; Cambridge, Corpus Christi College, EP.S.4/4 (Ben Jonson's copy).

1521

111. * *Alphabetum graecum*. Paris: N. de la Barre, [1521.] **Content**: *Pater noster; Salutatio ad beatissimam virginem; Benedictio mensae; Gratiarum actio mensae; Symbolum apostolorum; Confessio; Supplicatio filiorum Evae.* Four leaves. **Reference**: Moreau, *Inventaire chronologique*, 3:50; PBN, Rés. P-X-386 (1).

112. * *Liber quartus et ultimus de constructione, R. Croco Britanno interprete.* [Cologne: H. Novesiensis, 1521.] **Content**: Gaza, book 4, trans. Croke. **Reference**: Cathedral Libraries Catalogue, *Books Printed Before 1701*, vol. 2, part 1, 615; York Minster Library, VII.M.11 (3).

113. *ELEMENTALE INTRODUctorium in Nominum, et Verborum declinationes Graecas, praeterea et alia quaedam iam addita, quae legendo, studiosiss. quisque Lector facile deprehendet. ITEM Hieronymi Aleandri Mottensis tabulae, sane utiles Graecarum musarum adyta compendio ingredi cupientibus.* Strasbourg, January 10, 1521. **Content**: Alphabet and its divisions; pronunciation; article; Greek numbers; *Aleander... studiosis, inc.* Quemadmodum ii qui... (no date, Horawitz, "Griechische Studien," 430; Omont, "Essai sur les débuts de la typographie grecque à Paris," 70–71); *tabulae*; declensions; *De verbo*. **Reference**: Cambridge, St. John's College, 12.F.29 (2).

114. *THEODORI GAZAE THESSAlonicensis, Grammaticae institutionis libri duo priores, sic translati per ERASMUM ROTERODAMUM, ac titulis et annotatiunculis explanati, ut citra negotium et percipi queant et teneri. IIDEM Graece pro iis qui iam aliquantulum profecerunt ut conferri commode possint.* Basle: J. Froben, February 1521. **Content**: *Erasmus... J. Caesario, inc.* Habent in omni... (Antwerp, June 23, 1516; EE 2:264–66); Gaza, books 1 and 2, trans. Erasmus; Gaza, books 1 and 2, in Greek. **Date**: Colophon in Greek and Latin: Θαργηλιών 1521 and February 1521. Θαργηλιών is April in *De mensibus*, February in the lexica. **Reference**: Oxford, Bodleian, Vet.D1 e.23 (2).

115. * *THEODORI GAZAE GRAMmaticae institutionis Liber Secundus, ERASMO interprete.* [Cologne: H. Novesiensis, March 1, 1521.] **Content**: Gaza, book 2, trans. Erasmus. **Reference**: PBN, Rés. X-1916 (2); York Minster Library, VII.M.11 (1); Reuck, *Bibliotheca Erasmiana Bruxellensis*, 187, item no. 432.

116. *PROGYMNASMATA Graecae literaturae ab Ottomaro Luscinio Argentino iureconsul. Cum accessione auctarii quo docetur, qua ratione citra praeceptoris operam graecae discere possis, plurimis in locis iam recentiore foetura locupletata. Nuncupatoria epistola de utilitate graecarum literarum et praefracta cervice quorundam Mataeologorum qui iis*

contemptis, ac in publicis concionibus theonino dente laceratis, falso sibi scientiae opinionem induerunt. Strasbourg: J. Knoblouch, 1521, [after March 1.] **Content**: *Nuncupatoria epistola*: Nachtgall to J. Botzheim, *inc.* Meminisse potes, vir . . . (Strasbourg, March 1, 1521); verb tables; *De anomalis verbis; De constructione* (verb case constructions); *Auctarium quo docetur qua ratione citra praeceptoris operam graece discere possis, inc.* Quandoquidem ubere ingeniorum . . .; *Epigramma* in Greek with Latin translations; notes on the epigrams. **Reference**: Benzing and Muller, *Bibliographie strasbourgeoise*, 2:148; Chrisman, *Bibliography of Strasbourg Imprints*, 124; BL, 622.d.2.

117. *GRAECAE LITERATURAE DRAGMATA, IO. OECOLAMPADIO AUTORE.* Basle: A. Cratander, March 1521. **Content**: *A. Cratander studiosis, inc.* Queruntur aliqui de . . . (Basle, February 1, 1521); *Oecolampadius Hartmanno Hallwilero, inc.* Equidem, mi Hartmanne . . . (Basle, August 31, 1518); grammar. The text was revised for publication in some particulars: "Est ergo nunc annus ab incarnatione salvatoris αφκα," that is, 1521 (sig. B1v). **Reference**: Staehelin, "Oekolampad-Bibliographie," 24, item no. 37; Harlfinger and Barm, *Graecogermania*, 107–8; Munich, Bayerische Staatsbibliothek, Res/L.gr.241.

118. * *Grammaticae Graecae institutiones.* Hagenau: T. Anshelm, August 1521. **Content**: P. Melanchthon to the reader, *inc.* Semper optavi libellos . . . (Wittenberg, no date; Wetzel and others, *Melanchthons Briefwechsel*, 1:240–42); Melanchthon's grammar. **Reference**: Wetzel and others, *Melanchthons Briefwechsel*, 1:241.

119. *GRAMMATICA ISAGOGICA IOANNIS CHERADAMI SAGIENSIS ex diversis autoribus ad studiosorum utilitatem multo labore selecta.* Paris: G. de Gourmont, 21 August 1521. **Content**: Chéradame to L. Guilliardus, *inc.* Cogitavi saepenumero . . . (Paris, August 13, 1521); verses: Chéradame and G. Hopylius; Chéradame's grammar; Chéradame to the reader, *inc.* Errata si forsitan . . . (no date); verses from M. Caradasius, J. Ligarius, and A. Ligarius. **Date**: It is dated "sole leonis 29 gradum occupante." **Reference**: Moreau, *Inventaire chronologique*, 3:63; BL, 65.a.19.

120. *THEODORI GAZAE GRAMMATICAE INstitutionis libri quatuor, latine e regione ad verbum fere expositi, Ioanne Vatello concinnatore.* Paris: J. Bade, October 1521. **Content**: *Vatellus . . . F. Deloino, inc.* Comparatum aut fato . . . (Paris, October 1521); Gaza, books 1 through 4, in Greek and Latin; two-year privilege, dated October 8, 1521. See chapter 1, section "Theodore Gaza," p. 23. **Reference**: Delaruelle, "L'étude du grec à Paris de 1514 à 1530," 60–62; Moreau, *Inventaire chronologique*, 3:77; BL, 1560/1742; Oxford, Bodleian, Byw.L.6.9 (2).

121. *IN HOC LIBRO HAEC CONTINENTUR. Constantini Lascaris Byzantini de octo partibus orationis Lib.I. Eiusdem de Constructione Liber Secundus. Eiusdem de nomine et verbo Liber Tertius. Eiusdem de pronomine in omni Idiomate loquendi, ac ut poetae utuntur opusculum. De Graecarum proprietate linguarum ex scriptis de arte Ioannis Grammatici. De Graecarum proprietate linguarum ex his quae a corintho decerpta. Plutarchi de his quae apud Homerum linguis. Cebetis Thebani tabula. De literis graecis ac diphthongis et quemadmodum ad nos veniant. De potestate literarum Graecarum, et quo modo quis per se discat legere graeca verba. Item quare Christus et Iesus sic scribimus Xps IHS. Cur in alphabeto ypsilon a quibusdam fio dicitur. Oratio Dominica et duplex salutatio ad Beatiss. Virginem. Symbolum Apostolorum. Evangelium divi Ioannis Evangelistae, Carmina Aurea Pythagorae. Phocylidis poema ad bene, beateque vivendum. Introductio perbrevis ad hebraicam linguam. Omnia haec cum interpretatione latina.* Venice: M. Sessa and P. de Ravanis, October 17, 1521. **Content**: *M. Sessa and P. de Ravanis studiosis, inc.* Cum nuper studiosi . . . (no date); Lascaris, book 1; pseudo-Tryphon; *De anomalis verbis; De spiritibus;*

Lascaris, book 2: *De constructione*; Lascaris, book 3: *De nomine et verbo*; *De pronominibus*; *De subscriptis vocalibus*; J. Grammaticus, pseudo-Plutarch, and Gregory Pardus on the dialects, in Greek and Latin; pseudo-Cebes, in Greek and Latin; *Laudatio in sanctissimam dei genetricem*, in Greek and Latin; *Aldus studiosis, inc.* Nihil praetermittere est . . . (no date, Legrand, *Bibliographie hellénique*, 1:28–29; Renouard, *Annales de l'imprimerie des Alde*, 3–4); Greek appendix; colophon; *Aldus studiosis, inc.* Quoniam hebraicam linguam . . . (no date, Orlandi, *Aldo Manuzio editore*, 1:38); Hebrew appendix. **Reference:** BL, 624.c.13; Oxford, Bodleian, Byw.G.1.1.

122. *M. R. CROCI, LONDONIENSIS, TABULAE, GRAECAS LITEras compendio discere cupientibus, sane quam utiles, in quibus haec habentur contenta. De graecarum literarum pronunciatione. De formatione comparativorum et superlativorum. De temporum et modorum deductione. Ver. in ω. baryto. De verbis circumflexis. De verbis in Mi. Ex Theodori quarto, de constructione adverbiorum. Ex urbano de verbis defectivis.* Leipzig: V. Schumann, [after October 23, 1521.] **Content:** P. Novenianus to J. Kuchel, *inc.* Inolevit iam consuetudo . . . (Leipzig, October 23, 1521); *Crocus Academie senatui et philosophorum in urbe Lipsiensi coronae, inc.* Utcunque de me . . . (March 25, *sine anno*). **Date:** Croke's preface is reprinted from 1516. The volume is dated by the first preface. **Reference:** Harlfinger and Barm, *Graecogermania*, 109; Oxford, Bodleian, Vet.D1.e.38.

123. *THEODORI GRAMMATICAE INTRODUCTIVAE LIBER TERTIUS.* Louvain: T. Martens, November 1521. **Content:** Gaza, book 3, in Greek; device. No preface. **Date:** Dated on the title page. **Reference:** Cambridge, University Library, Rel.c.51.10 (3).

1522

124. *GRAECAE LITERATURAE DRAGMATA, IO. OECOLAMPADIO AUTORE.* Paris: C. Reschius and P. Vidovaeus, *sine mense* 1522. **Content:** Vidovaeus to Reschius, *inc.* Videbar mihi apud . . . (Paris, 1522); Oecolampadius to H. Hallwilerus, *inc.* Equidem mi Hartmanne . . . (no date); grammar. In the *editio princeps*, this letter of Oecolampadius is dated Basle, August 31, 1518. Apparently a reprint of the Basle edition of 1521, not the *editio princeps* of 1518, for in the discussion of the Greek numbers we find "Est ergo nunc annus ab incarnatione salvatoris αφκα," that is, 1521 (sig. B1v). **Reference:** Moreau, *Inventaire chronologique*, 3:146; Oxford, Bodleian, Byw.Q.7.5.

125. *ALPHABETUM GRAECUM, ORatio dominica, Angelica Salutatio, Symbolum apostolorum, Christi servatoris apud Matthaeum evangeliographum decreta, cum duobus epigrammat. Graecis humanae vitae commoda et incommoda complectentibus ab Eras. Rot. versis, nonnullisque hoc genus aliis, Graece et Latine, in usum iuventutis Graecarum adyta literarum ingressurae.* Basle: J. Froben, [1522–27?] **Content:** *Ioannes Frobenius studiosis, inc.* Quoniam dilectissimum filiolum . . . (no date, Horawitz, "Griechische Studien," 440); prayers, in Greek and Latin. Eight leaves. **Date:** Perhaps the fourth Basle *Alphabetum*, after the third of 1520 and before Froben's death in 1527. **Reference:** BL, C.24.e.21.

126. *ΕΡΩΤΗΜΑΤΑ ΤΟΥ ΧΡΥΣΟΛΩΡΑ. ΠΕΡΙ ΣΧΗΜΑΤΙΣΜΟΥ ΤΩΝ ΧΡΟΝΩΝ ΕΚ ΤΩΝ ΧΑΛΚΟΝΔΥΛΟΥ. EROTEMATA CHRYSOLORAE. DE FORMATIONE TEMPORUM EX LIBRO CHALCONDYLAE.* Rome: [Z. Callierges], June 1522. **Content:** Alphabet and diphthongs; Chrysoloras, the full text, with interlinear translation; Chalcondyles on the verb, with interlinear translation. **Reference:** Legrand, *Bibliographie hellénique*, item no. 67; BL, 1568/3048.

127. *COMPENDIUM GRAECAE GRAMMATICAE IACOBI CEPORINI IAM RECENS EDITUM.* Basle: V. Curio, June 1522. **Content:** *V. Curio lectori, inc.* Nunquam mihi

probatum . . . (no date); Ceporinus's grammar, the *editio princeps, Domus Alcinoi*, in Greek (*Odyssey*, 7:80–133). **Reference**: *Griechischer Geist*, 53, item no. 26; Munich, Bayerische Staatsbibliothek, A.gr.a.665 (1).

128. * *Grammaticae Graecae institutiones.* Cologne: J. Soter, June 1522. **Content**: P. Melanchthon to the reader, *inc.* Semper optavi libellos . . . (Wittenberg, no date; Wetzel and others, *Melanchthons Briefwechsel*, 1:240–42); Melanchthon's grammar. **Reference**: Wetzel and others, *Melanchthons Briefwechsel*, 1:241.

129. *INTEGRAE GRAECAE GRAMMATICES INSTITUTIOnes, a Philippo Melanchthone conscriptae, atque pluribus in locis auctae.* Hagenau: T. Anshelm, August 1522. **Content**: On the dialects, *inc.* Lata fuit regio . . .; grammar. Before *De verbo*: Hesiod, *Theogony*, 36–79, with commentary. After grammar: *Thersites* (*Iliad* 2:12–20), with commentary; *Chelys* (*Homeric Hymn* 4:29–55), in Greek and Latin, with scholion; postscript, *inc.* Pauca haec de . . . (no date; Wetzel and others, *Melanchthons Briefwechsel*, 1:64–64); Lucian, *Cupido*, in Greek. **Reference**: Wetzel and others, *Melanchthons Briefwechsel*, 1:241; Munich, Bayerische Staatsbibliothek, A.gr.a.665 (2).

130. * *COMPENDIUM GRAMMAticae graecae Iacobi Ceporini, iam de integro ab ipso authore et castigatum et locupletatum. Hesiodi georgicon, ab eodem Ceporino brevi scholio adornatum, ubi dictiones et sententiae quaedam obscuriores, atque obiter graecorum carminum ratio declarantur. Epigrammata quaedam lepidiora vice coronidis adiecta.* Basle: V. Curio, December 1522. **Content**: V. Curio to U. Zwingli, *inc.* Diu sane multumque . . . (no date, Egli and others, *Huldreich Zwinglis sämtliche Werke*, 7:651–52); the second edition of the grammar of Ceporinus; Hesiod, *Opera et dies*, in Greek; *Brevis declaratio grammatica in Hesiodi γεωργικὸν Ceporini*; nine Greek epigrams. **Reference**: Egli, "Ceporins Leben und Schriften," 148n3; Harlfinger and Barm, *Graecogermania*, 110–11; Manchester, John Rylands Library, 17804.

1523

131. * *Theodori Gazae Grammaticae institutionis liber tertius. Graeca e regione exposita sunt latinis, ita ut versus versui, immo verbo pene verbum . . . respondeat, autore Iohanne Vatello.* Cologne, 1523. **Content**: Gaza, book 3, trans. Vatel. **Reference**: PBN, Rés. X-1916 (3); York Minster Library, VII.M.11 (2).

132. *PROGYMNASMATA GRAEcae literaturae ab Ottomaro Luscinio Argentino iureconsul. Cum accessione auctarii, quo docetur, qua ratione citra praeceptoris operam, graecae discere possis, plurimis in locis iam recentiore foetura locupletata.* Strasbourg: J. Knoblouch, *sine mense* 1523. **Content**: Alphabet and its divisions; abbreviations; pronunciation; accents; noun declensions; verb conjugations; article; pronouns; prepositions; adverbs; conjunctions; verb tables; *De anomalis verbis*; *De constructione* (verb-case constructions); *Auctarium quo docetur qua ratione citra praeceptoris operam graece discere possis, inc.* Quandoquidem ubere ingeniorum . . .; *Epigramma* in Greek with Latin translations; notes on the epigrams; device. This lacks the *Nuncupatoria epistola* of 1521. **Reference**: Benzing and Muller, *Bibliographie strasbourgeoise*, 1:188, 2:156; Cambridge, University Library, XV.6.45.

133. *D. Hieronymi Aleandri Mottensis tabulae sane quam utiles Graecarum musarum adyta compendio ingredi cupientibus. Selecti aliquot Luciani dialogi, cum aliis nonnullis.* Louvain: T. Martens, *sine mense* 1523. **Content**: *Aleander . . . studiosis, inc.* Quemadmodum ii qui . . . (no date, Horawitz, "Griechische Studien," 430; Omont, "Essai sur les débuts de la typographie grecque à Paris," 70–71); *tabulae*; passages from Matthew's

Gospel and Paul, *Ad Romanos; Pater noster; Ave Maria; Credo;* graces; twelve short dialogues of Lucian. **Reference:** Van Iseghem, *Biographie de Thierry Martens d'Alost,* 332; BL, 1067.m.23.

134. *THEODORI INSTITUTIONIS GRAMMATICES LIBRI QUATUOR.* Louvain: T. Martens, *sine mense* 1523. **Content:** Verses: Aleandro, *inc.* Τίπτε διδασκαλίας μετιθηνήτειραν . . .; Gaza, book 1, in Greek. These verses were first printed in Aleandro's lexicon in 1512 (appendix 2, no. 14). **Reference:** Oxford, Bodleian, Byw.T.6.5 (1).

135. * *THEODORI GAZAE THESSAlonicensis, grammaticae institutionis liber primus, sic translatus ab Erasmo Roterodamo, ac titulis et annotatiunculis explanatus, ut citra negotium et percipi queat et teneri.* Cologne: E. Cervicornus, *sine mense* 1523. **Content:** *Erasmus . . . J. Caesario, inc.* Habent in omni . . . (June 23, 1516; EE 2:264–66); Gaza, book 1, trans. Erasmus. **Reference:** Reuck, *Bibliotheca Erasmiana Bruxellensis,* 186, item no. 29.

136. * *ELEMENTALE INTRODUCTORIUM In Nominum, et Verborum declinationes Graecas . . . ITEM HIERONYMI ALEANDRI Mottensis tabulae . . .* Strasbourg: J. Knoblouch, March 1523. **Reference:** Benzing and Muller, *Bibliographie strasbourgeoise,* 2:154.

137. *GRAECAE LITERATURAE DRAGMATA, IO. OECOLAMPADIO AUTORE. Tandem accuratius recognita.* Basle: A. Cratander, April 1523. **Content:** *Cratander studiosis, inc.* Queruntur aliqui de . . . (Basle, March 1, 1523); *Oecolampadius Hartmanno Hallwilero, inc.* Equidem, mi Hartmanne . . . (Basle, August 31, 1518); grammar. **Date:** Oecolampadius's preface is reprinted from the *editio princeps.* **Reference:** Staehelin, "Oekolampad-Bibliographie," 38–39, item no. 76; BL, 622.d.3; Oxford, Bodleian, Med. Seld. 8o W.28 (1).

138. *IOANNIS CHERADAMI SAGIENSIS INTRODUCTIO SANE QUAM UTILIS GRAECARUM MUSARUM ADYTA COMPENDIO INGREDI CUPIENTIBUS.* Paris: G. de Gourmont, [c. 1523, after April 1523.] **Content:** *Cheradamus . . . Pastori Adamo Pluyette, inc.* Cogitanti mihi iamdiu . . . (no date); alphabet and its divisions; pronunciation; accentuation; the article; abbreviations; verses; *A. Galli ad librum, inc.* Nunc vises latias . . .; Gourmont's second device. Six leaves. **Date:** BLC supplies a date of [1520?]. Moreau, *Inventaire chronologique,* dates it [c. 1523]. From the preface it appears that the lexicon of April 1523 (appendix 2, no. 28) has been printed, as has a Paris edition of Demosthenes. This undated edition of Demosthenes was printed c. 1523: see chapter 3, section "Demosthenes." **Reference:** Moreau, *Inventaire chronologique,* 3:163; BL, G.7564; Oxford, Bodleian, Byw.L.6.9 (1).

139. *ALDI PII MANUTII INSTITUTIONUM GRAMMATICARUM LIBRI QUATUOR. Erasmi Roterodami opusculum de octo orationis partium constructione. Quae quoque libro continentur hanc volventi chartam statim se offerunt.* Venice: in aedibus Aldi et Andreae soceri, July 1523. **Content:** *Aldus . . . ludimagistris, inc.* Rudimenta grammatices . . . (Venice, October 1507); Latin grammar of Aldus. The first gathering only is printed in red and black; register; colophon; *Aldus . . . studiosis, inc.* Nihil praetermittere est . . . (no date, Legrand, *Bibliographie hellénique,* 1:28–9; Renouard, *Annales de l'imprimerie des Alde,* 3–4); Greek appendix with its own title page, interlinear Latin translation; no colophon or register. **Reference:** BL, 625.c.16.

140. *THEODORI GAZAE INTRODUCTIOnis grammaticae libri quattuor, una cum interpretatione Latina, eorum usui dicati, qui vel citra praeceptoris operam Graecari cupiunt. Ubi quid expectes, sequentis paginae indicat epistolium.* Basle: V. Curio, August 1523. **Content:** *Curio . . . tyronibus, inc.* Theodorus Gaza vir . . . (Basle, August 28, 1523); verses: *Studiosis J. Denglius,* Gaza, books 1 through 4, in Greek and Latin. **Reference:** *Griechischer Geist* 57, item no. 31; BL, 624.d.37; BL, 624.c.8 (lacks title page).

141. * *THEODORI GAZAE GRAMMATICAE INSTITUTIONIS LIber Tertius interprete Ioanne Vatello*. Louvain: T. Martens, September 1523. **Reference**: Nijhoff and Kronenberg, *Nederlandsche Bibliographie*, 2:411–12; Nijhoff, *L'art typographique*, 2, plates, VII no. 23.

142. *EROTEMATA PER GEORGIUM RITHAYMER PRO REI NECESSITATE NONNIHIL AUCTA. ANOMALA VERBA. FORMATIONES TEMPORUM GEORGII RITHAYMER. SENTENTIAE MONOSTICHI EX VARIIS POETIS*. Vienna: J. Singrenius, November 14, 1523. **Content**: *G. Rithaymer Stirus lectori, inc.* Cum in animo ... (November 14, 1523); Greek verses of Rithaimer; Greek verses of Andreas Nountallius Stirus; Greek verses of J. Prousinouscus; Chrysoloras, abbreviated by Guarino, in Greek; *anomala verba*; Rithaimer's *formationes*, in Latin; *sententiae*, in Greek; errata; colophon: November 14, 1523. **Reference**: Cambridge, University Library, F152.e.7.1.

1524

143. * *Compendium in octo partes orationis et temporum formationes: Gregorii Theologi sententiae: Carmina aurea Pythagorae*. Vienna: J. Singrenius, 1524. **Content**: The work of Georg Rithaimer. **Reference**: Manchester, John Rylands Library, 13641.

144. *ELEMENTALE INTRODUCTORIUM IN NOMInum et Verborum declinationes Graecas, praeterea et alia quaedam iam addita, quae legendo, studiosiss. quisque Lector facile deprehendet. ITEM. HIERONYMI ALEANDRI MOTtensis tabulae, sane utiles Graecarum musarum adyta compendio ingredi cupientibus, quibus annexa sunt. Dominica Oratio. Angelica Salutatio. Apostolicum Symbolon. Benedictio mensae, una cum gratiarum actione.* [Cologne]: P. Quentell, February 1524. **Content**: Alphabet; its divisions; pronunciation; transliteration; accentuation; the article; Greek numbers; *Aleander ... studiosis, inc.* Quemadmodum ii qui ... (no date, Horawitz, "Griechische Studien," 430; Omont, "Essai sur les débuts de la typographie grecque à Paris," 70–71); alphabet; pronunciation; accentuation; noun declensions: "De contractis per crasin sive synaeresin apud alios reperies" (sig. D4v); *De verbo*: τύπτω, full conjugation; εἶναι, abbreviated conjugation; *De formatione temporum*; abbreviations; *Ioannes Knoblouchius iuventuti, inc.* Quoniam apertissimum est ... (no date); prayers, in Greek and Latin. **Reference**: Munich, Bayerische Staatsbibliothek, 4.L.gr.81 (1).

145. *URBANI GRAMMATICAE INSTItutiones, iam tanta adhuc iterum cura excussae, ut maiore vix potuerint, in quibus quid operae ultra priorem aeditionem expectes, versa pagella, et deinde in mox sequente epistola reperies*. Basle: V. Curio, March 7, 1524. **Content**: *Glareanus ... lectori, inc.* Cum nuper Homeri ... (Basle, 1524); *Urbanus ... studiosis, inc.* Superioribus annis ... (no date); verses: V. Fausto, *inc.* Εἴαρος ἀρχομένοιο ...; verses: S. Forteguerri, *inc.* Οὐρβανοῖο λαβὼν ...; Urbano's revised grammar; *Collectio ΤΩΝ HN. HΣ. H. Ex diversis autoribus per eundem Urbanum*; pseudo-Tryphon, in Greek with Latin notes; *De spiritibus ex Theodorito et aliis*, in Latin; *De dialectis ex Corintho*, in Greek; errata. **Reference**: *Griechischer Geist*, 57–58, item no. 32; Oxford, Bodleian, D.8.13, 14 Linc. (bound out of order); Cambridge, University Library, Aa*.3.8 (D).

146. * *PRIMUS LIBER GRAMMATICAE INSTITUTIonis. Theodori Gazae, sic translatus per Erasmum Roterodamum, ac titulis et annotatiunculis explanatus, ut citra negotium et percipi queat, et teneri.* Louvain: T. Martens, May 1524. **Reference**: Nijhoff and Kronenberg, *Nederlandsche Bibliographie*, 2:412; Reuck, *Bibliotheca Erasmiana Bruxellensis*, 187, item no. 430.

147. *Habes candide lector grammaticen doctissimi Ghrysolorae* [sic] *a I. Chaeradamo Hypocrate, longe quam antea emendatiorem.* Paris: G. de Gourmont, [c. 1524, after May 1524.] **Content**: Chéradame to Guilelmus, abbot of Sainte Geneviève, *inc.* Vetus ille amor . . . (no date); Chrysoloras, the full text, in Greek; Chéradame to C. Boucher, abbot of Saint Magloire, *inc.* Gravissima est temporis . . . (no date). **Date**: Dated [c. 1524] in Moreau, *Inventaire chronologique*, 3:206, where it is noted that Boucher was named abbot of Saint Magloire in May 1524. **Reference**: Moreau, *Inventaire chronologique*, 3:206; Cambridge, University Library, Aa*.5.31 (1) (G); BL, 622.c.2.

148. *Aldi Manutii Romani Institutionum Grammaticarum, libri quatuor, Ad exemplar Aldinum, ab Ascensio cum accentibus Graecis restituti. Quae autem in singulis libris contineantur, sequens pagella enucleabit.* Paris: P. Vidovaeus, September 3, 1524. **Content**: Aldus . . . ludi magistris, *inc.* Rudimenta grammatices . . . (Venice, October 1507); Latin grammar; Greek appendix, with interlinear Latin translation. No preface to the appendix. **Reference**: BL, C.66.c.1.

1525

149. *Alphabetum Graecum, Oratio Dominica, Angelica salutatio, Symbolorum Apostolorum, Christi servatoris apud Matthaeum Evangeliographum Decreta. Cum hoc genus aliis. Graece et Latine. In usum iuventutis Graecarum adyta literarum subingressurae.* Basle: J. Bebel, [1525?] **Content**: Brief religious texts, in Greek and Latin. Eight leaves. **Date**: The date is from the Cambridge University Library guard book catalog. The Cambridge copy is bound with Wechel's Paris editions of Lucian, Clenardus, and Gaza of 1530. **Reference**: Cambridge, University Library, U*.7.204 (1).

150. * *D. H. Aleandri . . . tabulae sane quam utiles Graecarum musarum adyta compendio ingredi cupientibus: Selecti aliquot Luciani dialogi, cum aliis nonnullis.* Louvain: T. Martens, 1525. **Reference**: Manchester, John Rylands Library, Christie Coll. 27 a 12.

151. *GRAMMATICAE GRAECAE INSTITUTIONES integrae, a Phil. Melancht. conscriptae, atque pluribus in locis auctae.* Hagenau: J. Secerius, *sine mense* 1525. **Content**: On the dialects: *inc.* Lata fuit regio . . .; Melanchthon . . . lectori, *inc.* Semper optavi libellos . . . (Wittenberg, no date; Wetzel and others, *Melanchthons Briefwechsel*, 1:240–42); grammar; *Thersites* (*Iliad* 2:212–20), with commentary; *Chelys* (*Homeric Hymn* 4:29–55), in Greek and Latin. **Reference**: Oxford, Bodleian, Med.Seld. 8o W28 (2).

152. *Theodori Gazae introductionis Grammaticae libri quatuor, una cum interpretatione Latina sane quam doctissima.* Cologne: J. Soter, *sine mense* 1525. **Content**: Gaza, books 1 through 4, in Greek and Latin; device. No preface. **Reference**: BL, 1568/3263.

153. *Habes candide lector duos tomos isagogae ad linguam graecam capessendam septem continentes libros: quibus et lexicon annexum est ordine alphabetico secundum declinationes: et coniugationes (ut index tibi ostendet) quo lucidius: copiosiusve nullum extitit antehac. Hos edidit Reverendus pater sacrae theologiae professor: et concionator apostolicus frater Sanctes pagninus Lucensis praedicatorii ordinis. Cum privilegio.* Avignon: J. de Channey, February 1, 1525. **Content**: Device; Pagninus to F. G. de Castelnau, cardinal and papal legate, *inc.* Ea literarum dignitas . . . (no date); verses: C. Lucius to Pagninus, *inc.* Graeca prius fuerant . . .; verses: Lucius to the reader, *inc.* Affinis latiae graeca . . .; index; errata; register; privilege of Hadrian VI, *inc.* Cum nobis exponi . . . (Rome, March 11, 1523); part one: grammar, books 1 through 3; device; part 2: device; grammar, books 4 through 7; colophon; register; device. **Reference**: Baudrier, *Bibliographie lyonnaise*, 300–301; BL, G.7593; Oxford, Bodleian, Byw.Q.8.4.

154. *Enchiridion ad capessendam linguam graecam editum a Reverendo patre magistro Sancte pagnino Lucensi concionatore apostolico, graecas literas Avenioni profitente ordinis praedicatorum.* Avignon: [J. de Channey, after February 1, 1525.] **Content**: Pagninus to J. Nicolaus, *inc.* Quamquam nostris in . . . (no date); alphabet and its divisions; *Ave Maria; Pater noster; Salve domina; Credo; Beatus vir,* all in Greek, with transliteration and translation; grammar in fifty-four chapters; verses: B. Ruffus; verses: J. Perreonus; seven penitential psalms, in Greek and Latin; pseudo-Phocylides (forty-nine lines); *Aurea verba* (twelve lines); one hundred *Adagia,* in Greek and Latin with notes; J. Nicolaus to Pagninus, *inc.* Cum nuper expenderem . . . (no date); Perreonus's panegyric of Pagninus. **Date**: From the preface, it appears that this followed the publication of his *Isagoga.* **Reference**: BL, G.7468.

155. *DEMETRII CHALCONDYLAE GRAMMATICAE INSTITUTIONES GRAECAE, GRAECE INITIANDIS MIRE UTILES.* Paris: G. de Gourmont, February 18, 1525. **Content**: *M. Volmarius . . . Petro xylotecto . . . discipulo suo, inc.* Si nihil aliud . . . (ex aedibus Beraldi, prima primae septimanae mensis Januarii, 1525); Chalcondyles, in Greek. Volmar used an exemplar provided by Pierre Danès (sig. a3r). **Date**: Moreau, *Inventaire chronologique,* mistakenly says that the date is February 28. **Reference**: Moreau, *Inventaire chronologique,* 3:244; Oxford, Bodleian, Byw.D 1.5.

156. *ALPHABETUM GRAECUM CUM ABbreviationibus perpulchre scitu, quibus frequentissime Graeci utuntur indifferenter et in principio, et in medio, et in fine dictionis. Oratio dominica, Angelica Salutatio, Symbolum Apostolorum, CHRISTI servatoris apud Matthaeum evangeliographum decreta, cum hoc genus aliis, Graece et Latine, In usum iuventutis Graecarum adyta literarum subingressurae.* [Basle or Zurich], June 1525. **Content**: No preface. Alphabet; abbreviations; *Pater noster, Ave Maria; Credo; Magnificat; Cantus Symeonis; Christi decreta; Salve regina;* four Graces; *Gloria;* eight beatitudes (Matthew 5:3–12); each Greek prayer is followed by its Latin version. For the place of printing, see chapter 1, section "Jacobus Ceporinus," and n. 535. **Reference**: Leeds, Brotherton, Ripon Cathedral XVIII.E.35 (3) (consulted in facsimile).

157. ΘΕΟΔΩΡΟΥ ΓΡΑΜΜΑΤΙΚΗΣ ΒΙΒΛΙΑ Δ΄. Περὶ μηνῶν ἐκ τῶν τοῦ αὐτοῦ. Γεωγίου τοῦ Λεκαπηνοῦ επὶ συντάξεως ῥημάτων. Εμανουὴλ Μοσχοπούλου περὶ τῆς τῶν ὀνομάτων, καὶ ῥημάτων συντάξεως. Τοῦ αὐτοῦ περὶ προσῳδιῶν. *Theodori grammatices libri IIII. De mensibus liber eiusdem. Georgii Lecapeni de constructione verborum. Emmanuelis moschopuli de constructione nominum, et verborum. Eiusdem de accentibus.* Venice: In aedibus Aldi et Andreae Asulani soceri, June 1525. **Content**: *F. Asulanus lectori, inc.* Non minoris tibi . . . (no date); Gaza, books 1 through 4, in Greek. The third edition of "Lecapenus," that is, of Syncellus. For this text, at least, it is based on the *editio princeps* of 1515 (Donnet, "La tradition imprimée," 473). **Reference**: Renouard, *Annales de l'imprimerie des Alde,* 100–101; BL, 687.d.11.

158. *GRAMMATICAE GRAECAE INSTITUtiones integrae, a Philippo Melancht. conscriptae, atque pluribus in locis auctae.* Cologne: E. Cervicornus, June 23, 1525. **Content**: On the dialects: *inc.* Lata fuit regio . . .; *Melanchthon . . . lectori, inc.* Semper optavi libellos . . . (Wittenberg, no date; Wetzel and others, *Melanchthons Briefwechsel,* 1:240–42); grammar; *Thersites (Iliad* 2:12–20), with commentary; *Chelys (Homeric Hymn* 4:29–55), in Greek and Latin. **Reference**: Manchester, John Rylands Library, R28474.

1526

159. * *Brevissima Introductio ad literas graecas.* Venice: Manutius, 1526. **Content**: Alphabet and its divisions; abbreviations; *Pater noster, Ave Maria; Credo;* prologue to John's

Gospel; *Salve regina; Magnificat; Nunc dimisit; Christi decreta* (Matthew 5:39–48); *Benedictio mensae; Dicteria septem sapientium.* In Greek with interlinear Latin translation. Sixteen leaves. **Reference**: Renouard, *Annales de l'imprimerie des Alde*, 103; Bühler, "Notes on Two Incunabula," 20–21.

160. * *Elementale introductorium in nominum et verborum declinationes graecas, praeterea et alia quaedam iam addita. Item H.A. Mottensis Tabulae utilissimae.* Cologne: Apud Hieronem Alopeau, 1526. **Reference**: Besançon, Doubs, Bibl. Municipale, 210410.

161. * *Introductivae grammatices libri quatuor.* Paris: G. de Gourmont, *sine mense* 1526. **Content**: Gaza, book 1, in Greek, edited by J. Chéradame. **Reference**: Moreau, *Inventaire chronologique*, 3:294.

162. *COMPENDIUM GRAMMATICAE Graecae Iacobi Ceporini, iam tertium de integro ab ipso authore et castigatum et locupletatum. HESIODI Georgicon, ab eodem Ceporino brevi Scholio adornatum, ubi dictiones et sententiae quaedam obscuriores, atque obiter Graecorum carminum ratio declarantur. EPIGRAMMATA quaedam lepidiora vice coronidis adiecta.* Zurich: C. Froschauer, *sine mense* 1526. **Content**: *Froschover graecae linguae candidatis, inc.* En vobis adolescentes . . . (Zurich, 1526); third edition of the grammar of Ceporinus; Hesiod, *Opera et dies,* in Greek; *Brevis declaratio grammatica in Hesiodi γεωργικὸν Ceporini; Obvia de ratione carminum Graecorum;* twenty Greek epigrams. **Date**: The preface assumes that Ceporinus (d. December 1525) is still alive, which suggests that it was printed late in 1525 or early in 1526. **Reference**: BL, 1568/3043.

163. Θεοδώρου γραμματικῆς βιβλία Δ΄. Περὶ μηνῶν ἐκ τοῦ αὐτοῦ. Γεωργίου Λεκαπηνοῦ περὶ συντάξεως ῥημάτων. Ἐμμανουὴλ Μοσχοπούλου περὶ τῆς τῶν ὀνομάτων καὶ ῥημάτων συντάξεως. Τοῦ αὐτοῦ περὶ προσῳδιῶν. Ἡφαιστίωνος ἐγχειρίδιον. *Theodori grammatices libri IIII. De mensibus liber eiusdem. Georgii lecapeni de constructione verborum. Emmanuelis Moscopuli de constructione nominum et verborum. Eiusdem de accentibus. Hephaestionis Enchiridion.* Florence: Heredes P. Juntae, April 1526. **Content**: *A. Francinus . . . lectori, inc.* Cauta est quadam . . . (no date); Gaza, books 1 through 4; Gaza, *De mensibus;* Syncellus and Moschopoulos on syntax; Hephaestion with the B scholia, the *editio princeps;* all in Greek. The fourth edition of "Lecapenus," that is, of Syncellus. For this text, at least, it is based on the edition of 1520 (Donnet, "La tradition imprimée," 473). Hephaestion has its own title page and colophon and is sometimes found alone. **Reference**: Renouard, *Annales de l'imprimerie des Alde*, xlix; BL, G.7535 (Hephaestion only); BL, 622.c.18.

1527

164. * *Introductio sane quam utilis Graecarum musarum adyta compendio ingredi cupientibus.* Paris: G. de Gourmont, *sine mense* 1527. **Content**: Apparently a reprint of the introductory pamphlet of J. Chéradame, first printed [after April 1523] (this appendix, no. 138). **Reference**: Moreau, *Inventaire chronologique*, 3:333.

165. *Grammatica Graeca Phil. Mel. Iam denuo recognita, atque multis in locis locupletata.* Hagenau: J. Secerius, January 1527. **Content**: On the dialects: *inc.* Lata fuit regio . . . *Melanchthon studioso lectori, inc.* Semper optavi libellos . . . (Wittenberg, no date; Wetzel and others, *Melanchthons Briefwechsel*, 1:240–42); grammar. Before *De verbo,* Hesiod, *Theogony,* 36–79, with commentary. After grammar, *Homeric Hymn* 4:29–55, in Greek and Latin; pseudo-Herodotus, *Vita Homeri,* in Greek and Latin; Lucian, *Cupido,* in Greek. **Reference**: A facsimile of this volume has been published: Menston: Scolar Press, 1969.

166. *SYNTAXIS GRAECA NUNC RECENS, ET NATA, ET AEDITA, AUTORE GUINTERIO IOANNE ANDERNACO.* Paris: G. de Gourmont, April 1527. **Content**:

Johann Winther of Andernach to Antoine de la Marck: *inc.* Cum superiore anno . . . (Paris, no date); *Andernacus lectori, inc.* En habes libellum . . .; errata; *Syntaxis graeca*; *In Mercurium* (*Homeric Hymn* 18), in Greek. **Reference**: Moreau, *Inventaire chronologique*, 3:347; BL, 12923 (3).

167. *THEODORI GAZAE INTRODUCTIONIS GRAMmaticae libri quattuor, una cum interpretatione latina, nuper ab Hercule Girlando Mantuano, et recognita, et ab omni vitio expurgata, ubi quae passim obscura, caeca, recondita, multis perplexa nodis, hactenus lectoris animum latuere, ea nunc omnia omnibus aperta, candida manifesta, ac intellectu facilia leguntur. quare lector, si bonus es, nos quoque bonos, boni aliquid tibi quotidie ferentes, bene ama: et sis felix.* Venice: F. Garonus, November 1527. **Content**: *Federico Malatestae . . . Hercules Girlandus, inc.* Ἀχάριστος ὅστις εὖ . . . (no date); Gaza, books 1 through 4, in Greek and Latin. **Date**: Title page: November 1521. Colophon: October 21, 1527. An undated privilege from the Venetian Senate is on the title page. **Reference**: BL, G.7591; BL, 1211.k.18.

1528

168. *ELEMENTALE INTRODUCTOrium in nominum et verborum declinationes Graecas, praeterea et alia quaedam iam addita. ITEM, Hieronymus Aleandri Mottensis Tabulae utilissimae.* Paris: G. de Gourmont, *sine mense* 1528. **Content**: Alphabet and its divisions; pronunciation; transliteration; accentuation; Greek numbers; *Aleander . . . studiosis, inc.* Quemadmodum ii qui . . . (Horawitz, "Griechische Studien," 430; Omont, "Essai sur les débuts de la typographie grecque à Paris," 70–71); notes on the alphabet, accents, and pronunciation; noun declensions; verb conjugations; abbreviations; prayers, in Greek and Latin. **Reference**: Moreau, *Inventaire chronologique*, 3:379; Cambridge, University Library, Peterborough H.1.17 (2).

169. *Alphabetum Graecum: Modus orandi, graece et latine, abbreviationes aliquot graecae: Alphabetum hebraicum: Decalogus, hebraice et latine.* Paris: R. Stephanus, *sine mense* 1528. **Content**: Alphabet and its divisions; Matthew 6:5–13; 21:22; Luke 18:1; in Greek and Latin; abbreviations; Hebrew alphabet; Hebrew vowel points; *Decalogue*, in Hebrew and Latin; Deuteronomy 27; Galatians 3; *titulus crucis Christi*. **Reference**: Renouard, *Annales de l'imprimerie des Estienne*, 28, item no. 5; Moreau, *Inventaire chronologique*, 3:380, which records two states of the title page; PBN, Rés. X-1706.

170. *EMANUELIS CHRYSOLORAE, BYzantini, Oratoris eximii, integrae Grammatices, epitoma quidem, sed undecunque absolutissima, institutio. ALBANO Torino Vitudurensi interprete.* Basle: J. Bebel, March 1528. **Content**: *J. Bebelius pio lectori, inc.* Exhibuere nobis bonarum . . . (no date); Chrysoloras's grammar, trans. Torinus; *Torinus pusionibus suis, inc.* Ecce quanta simplicitate . . . (no date); *de nomine comparativo*, trans. Torinus; *de spiritibus*, trans. Torinus; Lucian, *Dialogues of the Courtesans*, no. 1, in Greek and Latin. **Reference**: National Library of Scotland, *A Short-Title Catalogue*, 89; Edinburgh, National Library, K 84.f.1 (2); Munich, Bayerische Staatsbibliothek, A.gr.b.1091.

171. *GRAECAE LITERATURAE DRAGMATA. IO. OECOLAMPADIO AUTORE. Tandem accuratius recognita.* Paris: P. Vidovaeus, impensis G. de Gourmont and C. Wechel, June 1528. **Content**: *A. Cratander studiosis, inc.* Quaeruntur aliqui de . . . (Basle, March 1, 1523); Oecolampadius to Hartmann Hallwilerus, *inc.* Equidem, mi Martmanne . . . (*sic.* Basle, August 31, 1518); grammar. **Reference**: Moreau, *Inventaire chronologique*, 3:431; Cambridge, University Library, Peterborough H.1.17 (1).

172. * *Grammaticae Graecae institutiones.* Cologne: E. Cervicornus, April 3, 1528. **Content**: P. Melanchthon to the reader, *inc.* Semper optavi libellos . . . (Wittenberg, no date;

Wetzel and others, *Melanchthons Briefwechsel*, 1:240–42); Melanchthon's grammar. **Reference**: Wetzel and others, *Melanchthons Briefwechsel*, 1:241.

173. * *Grammatica Graeca*. Paris: Gourmont, Vidovaeus and Wechel, August 1528. **Content**: P. Melanchthon to the reader, *inc.* Semper optavi libellos . . . (Wittenberg, no date; Wetzel and others, *Melanchthons Briefwechsel*, 1:240–42); Melanchthon's grammar; pseudo-Herodotus, *Vita Homeri*, in Greek followed by Conrad Heresbach's version; Lucian, *Cupido*, in Greek. **Reference**: Moreau, *Inventaire chronologique*, 3:428; Wetzel and others, *Melanchthons Briefwechsel*, 1:241.

1529

174. * *Integrae graecae grammatices institutiones a Philippo Melanchthone conscriptae, auctae a Nic. Gerbellio*. Cologne, 1529. **Reference**: Clermont-Ferrand, Bibl. Municipale et Universitaire, Fonds Vincent I 641.

175. *Compendium Grammaticae Graecae Iacobi Ceporini, iam tertium de integro ab authore castigatum*. Paris: S. Colinaeus, *sine mense* 1529. **Content**: Grammar of J. Ceporinus, in nine chapters. No preface. **Reference**: Renouard, *Bibliographie des éditions de Simon de Colines*, 132–33; Moreau, *Inventaire chronologique*, 3:460; Oxford, Bodleian, 8o St Amand 42 (2).

176. *Theodori grammaticae introductionis libri IIII*. Paris: P. Gaudoul and P. Gromors, *sine mense* 1529. **Content**: *Candido lectori, inc.* Scripsere in hanc . . . (Paris, January 30, *sine anno*); life of Gaza, *inc.* Theodorus cognomento Gaza . . .; Gaza, books 1 through 4, in Greek. **Reference**: Moreau, *Inventaire chronologique*, 3:479; BL, G.7463.

177. * *Theodori Gazae Institutionis Grammaticae libri quatuor, addita versione latina: ad omnium hactenus impressorum exemplarium collationem, et graece studiosorum castigationem tam emendate excusi, quam et res ipsa indicabit, et loca quaedam nunc tandem suae integritati restituta testabuntur*. Paris: C. Wechel, *sine mense* 1529. **Content**: Gaza, books 1 through 4, in Greek with Jean Vatel's version. Each book save the first has its own title page. **Reference**: Delaruelle, "L'étude du grec à Paris de 1514 à 1530," 147–48; Moreau, *Inventaire chronologique*, 3:480; PBN, Rés. X-1914.

178. *PRIMAE GRAMMATICES GRAECAE PARTIS Rudimenta, Iohanne Metzler authore*. Hagenau: J. Secerius, July 1529. **Content**: Greek verses: J. Camerarius; *J. Rullo et A. Winckler, ludimagistris Vratislaviensibus, J. Metzler, inc.* Bonae literae studiaque . . . (Vratislava, January 1, 1529); *Pater noster, Ave Maria, Credo,* all in Greek; grammar. **Reference**: BL, 622.c.36.

179. *Theodori Gaza introductionis grammaticae libri quattuor, Graece, simul cum interpretatione latina iam de integro recogniti atque aucti, cum argumentis, et indicibus librorum singulorum, ac aliis luculentis castigationibus, quae in aliis exemplaribus desyderabantur. Quid autem in universum hic expectes, sequentis paginae indicat epistolion*. Basle: V. Curio, September 1529. **Content**: *Curio . . . tyronibus, inc.* Theodorus Gaza, vir . . .; Gaza, book 1 through 4, in Greek and Latin. Curio says that books 1 and 2 are Erasmus's version, while for books 3 and 4, he used the versions of C. Heresbach, J. Toussain, and R. Croke. **Reference**: Cambridge, University Library, M*.10.25.

180. * *Alphabetum Graecum una cum Prosodia, Oratione Dominica, Angelica Salutatione, Symbolo Apostolico, Decem praeceptis, Christi Servatoris apud Matthaeum evangeliographum decretis atque abbreviationibus quibus passim Graeci utuntur*. Paris: C. Wechel, December 1529. **Reference**: Moreau, *Inventaire chronologique*, 3:446.

Appendix 2

Printed Greek Lexica, 1478–1529

The conventions and caveats described at the beginning of Appendix 1 apply to this appendix. I have inspected a copy of every edition detailed below.

1. [*Lexicon graeco–latinum.*] [Milan:] Bonaccorso, [by March 28, 1478.] **Content**: G. Crastoni to F. Ferrarius, *inc.* Non difficulter adductus ... (no date, Botfield, *Prefaces*, 167–68); Bonaccorso to J. F. Turrianus, *inc.* Nemo potest mea ... (no date, Botfield, *Prefaces*, 168–70); Greek–Latin lexicon, edited by G. Crastoni. **Date**: A copy in the Vatican Library (Inc.II.454) has a note of acquisition, March 28, 1478 (Sheehan, *Incunabula*, 1:421). A copy in the British Library (C.5.c.4) records its donation by Pietro da Montagnana in 1478. **Reference**: ISTC ic00958000; BL, C.5.c.4.

2. [*Lexicon latino–graecum.*] [Milan:] Bonaccorso, [c. 1480.] **Content**: Bonaccorso to A. Bracellus, *inc.* Quo pacto fieri ... (no date, ISTC image); Latin–Greek lexicon, edited by G. Crastoni. This is not a reversal of the Greek–Latin lexicon (this appendix, no. 1). **Reference**: ISTC ic00962000; BL, G.7538.

3. [*Lexicon latino–graecum.*] [Vicenza: D. Bertochus, c. 1483.] **Content**: Bonaccorso to A. Bracellus, *inc.* Quo pacto fieri ... (no date, ISTC image); Latin–Greek lexicon, edited by G. Crastoni. **Date**: Gualdo Rosa discusses the date of this, the second *Vocabulista*, but the letter cited probably refers to the third edition of 1497 (Gualdo Rosa, "Crastone, Giovanni," 579). **Reference**: ISTC 00963000; BL, IA.31877.

4. *Lexicon graeco–latinum.* Vicenza: D. Bertochus, November 10, 1483. **Content**: Bonaccorso to J. F. Turrianus, *inc.* Nemo potest mea ... (no date, *Botfield*, Prefaces, 168–70); Greek–Latin lexicon, edited by G. Crastoni. **Reference**: ISTC ic00959000; Cambridge, University Library, Inc.3.B.25.11 [2227].

5. [*Lexicon latino–graecum.*] Reggio Emilia: D. Bertochus and M. A. de Bacileriis, *sine mense* 1497. **Content**: Bonaccorso to A. Bracellus, *inc.* Quo pacto fieri ... (no date, ISTC image); Latin–Greek lexicon, edited by G. Crastoni. **Date**: Gualdo Rosa discusses the date of the second *Vocabulista* (1483), but the letter she cites probably refers to this, the third *vocabulista* (Gualdo Rosa, "Crastone, Giovanni," 579). **Reference**: ISTC ic00964000; BL, IA.34068.

6. *Dictionarium graecum copiosissimum secundum ordinem alphabeti cum interpretatione latina. Cyrilli opusculum de dictionibus, quae variato accentu mutant significatum secundum ordinem alphabeti cum interpretatione latina. Ammonius de differentia dictionum per literarum ordinem. Vetus instructio et denominationes praefectorum militum. Significata τοῦ ἦ. Significata τοῦ ὡς. Index oppido quam copiosus, docens latinas dictiones fere omneis graece dicere et multas etiam multis modis.* Venice: A. Manutius, December 1497.

Content: *Aldus . . . studiosis, inc.* Constitueram τὰ τῶν ἑλλήνων . . . (no date, Botfield, *Prefaces*, 211-12; Orlandi, *Aldo Manuzio editore*, 1:19-20); verses: S. Forteguerri, *inc.* Μαιομένοις ξείνοις, ἑλληνίδος . . . (Botfield, *Prefaces*, 212); verses: M. Musurus, *inc.* Τῆσδε πέρι μαίνεσκε . . . (Botfield, *Prefaces*, 213); Greek–Latin lexicon; pseudo-Cyril; Ammonius; Τάξις παλαιά; meanings of η and ως; *Ad lectorem, inc.* Cum indicem istum . . . (no date, Orlandi, *Aldo Manuzio editore*, 1:20-21); Latin–Greek index. **Reference**: Renouard, *Annales de l'imprimerie des Alde*, 13-14; ISTC ic00960000; Cambridge, University Library, Inc.3.13.3.134 [1819]; BL, IB.24450.

7. *ΕΤΥΜΟΛΟΓΙΚΟΝ ΜΕΓΑ ΚΑΤΑ ΑΛΦΑΒΗΤΟΝ, ΠΑΝΥ ΩΦΕΛΙΜΟΝ*. Venice: Z. Callierges, [May or July] 8, 1499. **Content**: Verses: M. Musurus, *inc.* Ἔκποθεν ἀφράστοιο φανεὶς . . . (Botfield, *Prefaces*, 225; Firmin-Didot, *Alde Manuce et l'Hellénisme à Venise*, 549-52; Legrand, *Bibliographie hellénique*, 1:58-59); verses: J. Gregoropoulos, *inc.* Ἄνθεα γραμματικῆς δρέψαι . . . (Botfield, *Prefaces*, 226; Firmin-Didot, *Alde Manuce et l'Hellénisme à Venise*, 547; Legrand, *Bibliographie hellénique*, 1:59); Musurus to Paduan students, *inc*: Οἱ μὲν ἑλληνικῶς . . . (no date; Botfield, *Prefaces*, 226-28; Firmin-Didot, *Alde Manuce et l'Hellénisme à Venise*, 553-54; Legrand, *Bibliographie hellénique*, 1:59-62); *Etymologicum magnum*, the *editio princeps*. **Date**: "Μεταγειτνιῶνος, ὀγδόη ἱσταμένου." This is July according to *De mensibus*; in the lexica it is May. **Reference**: Firmin-Didot, *Alde Manuce et l'Hellénisme à Venise*, 546-61; Legrand, *Bibliographie hellénique*, item no. 23; ISTC ie00112000; Cambridge, University Library, Inc.1.B.3.146 [1849].

8. [*Lexicon graeco–latinum. Lexicon Latino–Graecum.*] Modena: D. Bertochus, October 20, 1499, to after July 5, 1500. **Content**: Bonaccorso to J. F. Turrianus, *inc.* Nemo potest mea . . . (no date, Botfield, *Prefaces*, 168-70); Greek–Latin lexicon; *Ambrosius Regiensis studiosis, inc.* Sententia illa celebratissima . . . (Reggio, July 5, 1500); Latin–Greek lexicon; errata for Greek–Latin lexicon; *L. Manii Regiensis Scazon*. **Date**: Colophon to part 1 is October 20, 1499. Part 2 has no colophon and is dated by its preface. **Reference**: ISTC ic00961000; BL, IB.32333.

9. *ΤΟ ΜΕΝ ΠΑΡΟΝ ΒΙΒΛΙΟΝ ΣΟΥΙΔΑ. ΟΙ ΔΕ ΣΥΝΤΑΞΑΜΕΝΟΙ ΤΟΥΤΟ, ΑΝΔΡΕΣ ΣΟΦΟΙ. ΕΥΔΗΜΟΣ ΡΗΤΩΡ. ΠΕΡΙ ΛΕΞΕΩΝ ΚΑΤΑ ΣΤΟΙΧΕΙΟΝ. ΕΛΛΑΔΙΟΣ ΕΠΙ ΘΕΟΔΟΣΙΟΥ ΤΟΥ ΝΕΟΥ ΟΜΟΙΩΣ. ΕΥΓΕΝΙΟΣ ΑΥΓΥΣΤΟΠΟΛΕΩΣ ΤΗΣ ΕΝ ΦΡΥΓΙΑ ΟΜΟΙΩΣ. ΖΩΣΙΜΟΣ ΓΑΖΑΙΟΣ ΛΕΞΕΙΣ ΡΗΤΟΡΙΚΑΣ, ΚΑΤΑ ΣΤΟΙΧΕΙΟΝ. ΚΕΚΙΛΙΟΣ ΣΙΚΕΛΙΩΤΗΣ ΕΚΛΟΓΗΝ ΛΕΞΕΩΝ ΚΑΤΑ ΣΤΟΙΧΕΙΟΝ. ΛΟΓΓΙΝΟΣ Ο ΚΑΣΙΜΟΣ, ΟΜΟΙΩΣ. ΛΟΥΠΕΡΚΟΣ ΒΕΡΥΤΤΙΟΣ, ΑΤΤΙΚΑΣ ΛΕΞΕΙΣ. ΙΟΥΣΤΙΝΟΣ ΙΟΥΛΙΟΣ ΣΟΦΙΣΤΗΣ, ΕΠΙΤΟΜΗΝ ΤΩΝ ΠΑΜΦΙΛΟΥ ΓΛΩΣΣΩΝ. ΠΑΚΑΤΟΣ ΠΕΡΙ ΣΥΝΗΘΕΙΑΣ ΑΤΤΙΚΗΣ. ΠΑΜΦΙΛΟΣ, ΛΕΙΜΩΝΑ ΛΕΞΕΩΝ. ΕΣΤΙ ΔΕ ΑΠΟ ΤΟΥ Ε ΣΤΟΙΧΕΙΟΥ ΕΩΣ ΤΟΥ Ω. ΤΑ ΓΑΡ ΑΠΟ ΤΟΥ Α, ΜΕΧΡΙ ΤΟΥ Δ, ΖΩΠΥΡΙΩΝ ΠΕΠΟΙΗΚΕ. ΠΩΛΙΩΝ ΑΛΕΞΑΝΔΡΕΥΣ, ΑΤΤΙΚΩΝ ΛΕΞΕΩΝ ΣΥΝΑΓΩΓΗΝ ΚΑΤΑ ΣΤΟΙΧΕΙΟΝ.* Milan: J. Bissolus and B. Mangius, November 15, 1499. **Content**: Dialogue: *inc.* Βι. Δεῦρ' ἴθι φιλομαθὲς . . . (Botfield, *Prefaces*, 230; Legrand, *Bibliographie hellénique*, 1:64); verses: A. Motta, *inc.* Demetri, aeternos debet . . . (Botfield, *Prefaces*, 230; Legrand, *Bibliographie hellénique*, 1:64); verses: Motta, *inc.* Olim Phocis erat . . . (Botfield, *Prefaces*, 231; Legrand, *Bibliographie hellénique*, 1:64-65); J. M. Cataneus to Alberto Pio, *inc.* In omni re . . . (Botfield, *Prefaces*, 231-32); D. Chalcondyles, *inc.* Τὸ παρὸν βιβλίον . . . (no date, Botfield, *Prefaces*, 232-33; Legrand, *Bibliographie hellénique*, 1:65-66); Suda lexicon; register; colophon; verses: J. Salandus to Chalcondyles, *inc.* Maiestas decus et . . . (ISTC image); verses: Salandus to the reader, *inc.* Qui plenis monumenta . . . (ISTC image). **Reference**: Legrand, *Bibliographie hellénique*, item no. 25; ISTC is00829000; Cambridge, University Library, Inc.2.B.7.28 [1499].

10. *ΣΤΕΦΑΝΟΣ ΠΕΡΙ ΠΟΛΕΩΝ. STEPHANUS DE URBIBUS*. Venice: A. Manutius, January 1502, new style. **Content**: Aldus to J. Taberius Brixiensis, *inc.* Quantum voluptatis

ceperim... (Venice, March 18, 1502. Botfield, *Prefaces*, 262–63; Orlandi, *Aldo Manuzio editore*, 1:55–56); Stephanus, in Greek. **Date**: For the date, see Christie, "The Chronology of the Early Aldines," 200–203. The colophon is January 1502. The prefatory letter, printed last, is dated April 18, 1502. It was printed by August 1502, when Aldus sent Reuchlin a copy. See Geiger, *Johann Reuchlins Briefwechsel*, 77–78, letter no. 83. **Reference**: Renouard, *Annales de l'imprimerie des Alde*, 38–39; Diller, "The Tradition of Stephanus Byzantinus," 337; BL, 679.h.2 (2).

11. *ΙΟΥΛΙΟΥ ΠΟΛΥΔΕΥΚΟΥΣ ΟΝΟΜΑΣΤΙΚΟΝ. IULII POLLUCIS VOCABULARIUM.* Venice: A. Manutius, April 1502. **Content**: Aldus to Helias Capreolus, *inc.* Julius Pollux Naucratita... (Venice, April 11, 1502. Botfield, *Prefaces*, 259–60; Orlandi, *Aldo Manuzio editore*, 1:57–58); Julius Pollux, in Greek; S. Forteguerri τοῖς φιλολόγοις, *inc.* Τὰ ὄντα καθ᾽ ἑαυτὰ... (no date); register; colophon; index, in Greek; index, in Latin. **Date**: The indices, sometimes bound before the main work, are signed separately and correct Forteguerri's concluding letter. They were printed after the colophon. **Reference**: Renouard, *Annales de l'imprimerie des Alde*, 32–33; Cambridge, University Library, Aa*.2.12 (1) (C); BL, 679.h.2 (1).

12. *Οὐλπιανοῦ ῥήτορος, προλεγόμενα εἴς τε τοὺς ὀλυνθιακούς, καὶ φιλιππικοὺς δημοσθένους λόγοις. Ἐξήγησις ἀναγκαιοτάτη, εἰς δεκατρεῖς δημοσθένους λόγοις. Vlpiani commentarioli in olynthiacas philippicasque Demosthenis orationes. Enarrationes sanequam necessariae in tredecim orationes Demosthenis.* Venice: A. Manutius, October 1503. **Content**: Ulpian's preface and commentaries on Demosthenes; Harpocration. The lexicon is not mentioned on the title page. Harpocration begins on the first page of a new gathering and is often found separated from Ulpian. **Reference**: Renouard, *Annales de l'imprimerie des Alde*, 41; BL, 674.k.6.

13. *DICTIONUM GRAECARUM THESAURUS COPIOsus quantum nunquam antea. Annotationesque innumerae, tum ad rem graecam, tum latinam pertinentes, ceu flosculi toto opere interspersi. Quantum dictiones quaedam mutato accentu differant autore Cyrillo. De differentia plurimarum dictionum Autore Ammonio. Vocabula militaria ex institutione veterum. Super .ῆ. καὶ .ὡς, annotata quaedam oppido quam diligenter. Dictionum latinarum thesaurus nunquam alias impressus cum graeca interpretatione, laboriosum sane opus, quo neque utilius, neque optatius bene studiosis aliud afferri poterat.* Ferrara: J. Maciochus, [after September 27, 1510.] **Content**: *J. Maciochus... N. signorello Priori Carmelitarum, inc.* Nihil est pater... (Ferrara, April 3, 1510); *Annotationum, quae toto opere inveniuntur, elenchus*; Greek–Latin lexicon; pseudo-Cyril; Ammonius; Τάξις παλαιά; meanings of η and ως; J. M. Tricaelius, *inc.* Non potui diu... (no date); Latin–Greek lexicon; *Maciochus lectori, inc.* Cum huic dictionario... (Ferrara, September 27, 1510); colophon: September 27, 1510; register; Tricaelius, *inc.* Habetis expositionem qualemcumque... (no date); A. Fanuccio to Tricaelius, *inc.* Compulsus amore amplissimae... (no date); Greek verses: Tricaelius to Fanuccio; Latin verses: *incertum*; D. Finus to the reader; B. Piso. **Reference**: Cambridge, University Library, Sel.3.99; Oxford, Bodleian, Byw.B.5.18.

14. *Lexicon graecolatinum multis et preclaris additionibus locupletatum: quod vel ex indice eorum: quae in toto volumine comprehenduntur: in sequenti pagina cognoscas.* Paris: G. de Gourmont, [after December 25, 1512.] **Content**: G. Aleandro to Prince Wolfgang of Bavaria, *inc.* Si quamlibet parvam... (Paris, December 23, 1512); *Aleander lectoribus, inc.* Scio plaerosque expectaturus... (December 25, 1512; Omont, "Essai sur les débuts de la typographie grecque à Paris," 59–60); verses: Aleandro, *inc.* Τίπτε διδασκαλίας μετιθηνήτειραν...; Greek–Latin lexicon; pseudo-Cyril; Latin–Greek lexicon of words from Gaza's versions of Aristotle, *De animalibus*, and Theophrastus, *De plantis*; Ammonius; Τάξις παλαιά; meanings of η and ως; Latin–Greek lexicon. **Date**: The Greek–Latin

lexicon is in Gourmont's first Greek font. The last dated use of this font alone was in Gourmont's Plutarch of April 30, 1509 (see chapter 3, section "Plutarch," p. 98), although Gourmont's undated editions of Isocrates (see chapter 3, section "Isocrates"), which use the same type, seem to be later. From Ammonius, Gourmont's second font is used. The first dated use of this font is in the Chrysoloras of [May or July] 13, 1512 (appendix 1, no. 42). This part of the lexicon was completed December 13, 1512. The prefatory gathering was printed in this font after December 25, 1512. There are two title pages and two colophons for this edition. The different title pages are described in Omont, "Essai sur les débuts de la typographie grecque à Paris," 28–29; Omont does not notice the colophon change. **Reference**: Omont, "Essai sur les débuts de la typographie grecque à Paris," 28–31; Harlfinger and Barm, *Graecogermania*, 118–20; Moreau, *Inventaire chronologique*, 2:146, item no. 396; Oxford, Bodleian, Byw.G 1.3.

15. *ΗΣΥΧΙΟΥ ΛΕΞΙΚΟΝ. HESYCHII DICTIONARIUM.* Venice: A. Manutius, August 1514. **Content**: Aldus to J. J. Bardellonus, *inc.* Si caeteri studiosi . . . (Venice, August 1514. Botfield, *Prefaces*, 304–5; Legrand, *Bibliographie hellénique*, 1:123–24; Orlandi, *Aldo Manuzio editore*, 1:143–44) Hesychius, the *editio princeps*, edited by M. Musurus. **Reference**: Renouard, *Annales de l'imprimerie des Alde*, 66–67; Legrand, *Bibliographie hellénique*, item no. 44; Cambridge, University Library, Aa*.2.13 (C); Cambridge, University Library, Adams.3.51.3.

16. *Novum testamentum grece et latine in academia complutensi noster noviter impressum.* Alcalá: A. Brocar, January 10, 1514, new style. See appendix 1, no. 53. This Greek–Latin lexicon claims to contain all the words from the New Testament, Wisdom, and Ecclesiasticus.

17. *ΣΥΙΔΑ. ΣΟΥΙΔΑ. ΤΟ ΜΕΝ ΠΑΡΟΝ ΒΙΒΛΙΟΝ, ΣΟΥΙΔΑ. ΟΙ ΔΕ ΣΥΝΤΑΞΑΜΕΝΟΙ ΤΟΥΤΟ ΑΝΔΡΕΣ ΣΟΦΟΙ.* Εὔδημος ῥήτωρ, περὶ λέξεων κατὰ στοιχεῖον. Ἑλλάδιος ὑθὶ θεοδοσίου τοῦ νέου, ὁμοίως. Εὐγένιος αὐγουστοπόλεως τῆς ἐν φρυγίᾳ παμμιγῆ λέξιν κατὰ στοιχεῖον. Ζώσιμος γαζαῖος λέξεις ῥητορικὰς, κατὰ στοιχεῖον. Καικίλιος σικελιώτης ἐκλογὴν λέξεων κατὰ στοιχεῖον. Λογγῖνος ὁ κάσσιος, λέξεις κατὰ στοιχεῖον. Λούπερκος βηρύτιος, ἀττικὰς λέξεις. Ἰουστῖνος Ἰούλιος σοφιστής, ἐπιτομὴν τῶν παμφίλου γλωσσῶν, βιβλίων ἐννενήκοντα ἑνός. Πάκατος περὶ συνηθείας ἀττικῆς κατὰ στοιχεῖον. Πάμφιλος, λειμῶνα λέξεων ποικίλων περιοχὴν βιβλίων ἐννενήκοντα πέντε. ἔστι δὲ ἀπὸ τοῦ ε στοιχείου, ἕως τοῦ ω. τὰ γὰρ ἀπὸ τοῦ α, μέχρι τοῦ δ, Ζωπυρίων ἐπεποιήκει. Πωλίων ἀλεξανδρεὺς, ἀττικῶν λέξεων συναγωγὴν κατὰ στοιχεῖον. Venice: A. Manutius, February 1514, new style. **Content**: Aldus to the readers, *inc.* ἐπειδὴ ἐπὶ τουτουΐ . . . (Orlandi, *Aldo Manuzio editore*, 1:128); Suda lexicon; register; colophon. **Date**: Aldus advertised this in his third catalogue of November 1513 (Orlandi, *Aldo Manuzio editore*, 2: plate XVII), so the date in the colophon appears to be new style. **Reference**: Renouard, *Annales de l'imprimerie des Alde*, 70; Cambridge, University Library, Aa*.2.15 (C).

18. Θωμᾶ τοῦ μαγίστρου κατὰ ἀλφάβητον, ἀτθίδος διαλέκτου ἐκλογαί. αἷς οἱ δοκιμώτατοι χρῶνται τῶν παλαιῶν. καὶ τινες αὐτῆς, παρασημειώσεις. *Thome Magistri per alphabetum, hoc est elementorum ordinem attici eloquii, elegantie quibus approbatissimi priscorum usi sunt. Atque nonnulle, circa eandem annotationes et differentie.* Rome: Z. Callierges, March 4, 1517. **Content**: Callierges to M. Silva, Portuguese ambassador, *inc.* Οὔ μοι δοκεῖ . . . (no date, Firmin-Didot, *Alde Manuce et l'Hellénisme à Venise*, 566–69; Legrand, *Bibliographie hellénique*, 1:151–52); verses: L. Ptolemaeus, *inc.* Λυσιτανῆς γαίης . . . and *inc.* Ζαχαρίας ὁ Κρὴς . . . (Firmin-Didot, *Alde Manuce et l'Hellénisme à Venise*, 567–68; Legrand, *Bibliographie hellénique*, 1:152); ten-year privilege from Leo X (Legrand, *Bibliographie hellénique*, 1:153); Magister's *Eclogues*. This is in the same small format as Callierges'

edition of Phrynichus (this appendix, no. 19) with which it is often bound. **Reference**: Firmin-Didot, *Alde Manuce et l'Hellénisme à Venise*, 565–69; Legrand, *Bibliographie hellénique*, item no. 52; BL, 236.g.35; BL, G.7457; Oxford, Bodleian, Byw.T.7.12 (1).

19. *ΦΡΥΝΙΧΟΥ, ΕΚΛΟΓΗ ΑΤΤΙΚΩΝ ΡΗΜΑΤΩΝ, ΚΑΙ ΟΝΟΜΑΤΩΝ.* "Ητις οὐκ εὐνομίου χωρὶς, ἀλλὰ κατὰ τὸν ὅρον ἐτυπώθη καὶ αὕτη, τοῦ δοθέντος ἡμῖν ἀρχιερατικοῦ ἐπιτάγματος. Rome: Z. Callierges, July 1, 1517. **Content**: Phrynichus, *Eclogues*, the *editio princeps*. No prefatory matter. This is in the same small format as Callierges' edition of Thomas Magister (this appendix, no. 18) with which it is often bound. **Reference**: Legrand, *Bibliographie hellénique*, item no. 53; Oxford, Bodleian, Byw.T.7.12 (2).

20. *DICTIONARIUM GRAECUM, ULTRA FERRARENSEM aeditionem locupletatum locis infinitis, idque ex optimis autoribus, quod iam nunc sufficere potest legendae linguae communi, atque Atticae propemodum. Cyrilli opusculum, de dictionibus, quae accentu variant significatum. Ammonius de similitudine ac differentia dictionum. De re militari veterum, et nominibus praefectorum, libellus graecus, incerto autore. Orbicii, de ordinibus exercitus. Significata τοῦ ἤ. Significata τοῦ ὡς. DICTIONARIUM, quo latina graecis exponuntur.* Basle: A. Cratander, March 1519. **Content**: V. Curio to the reader, *inc.* Lexicon hoc ex . . . (Basle, April 4, 1519); Greek–Latin lexicon; pseudo-Cyril; Ammonius; Τάξις παλαιά; Orbicius; meanings of η and ως; Latin–Greek lexicon; *Cartander* [sic] *lectori, inc.* Nova mihi officina . . . (Basle, March 24, 1519); colophon: March 1519. **Reference**: *Griechischer Geist*, 40–43, item no. 22; Oxford, Bodleian, Antiq.d.GS.1519.1.

21. *Hesychii Dictionarium*. Florence: Heredes P. Juntae, August 9, 1520. **Content**: A. Francino to P. F. Portinari, *inc.* Non te latet . . . (no date); Hesychius. **Reference**: Renouard, *Annales de l'imprimerie des Alde*, xlv; Cambridge, University Library, Aa*.2.23 (1) (C).

22. *ΙΟΥΛΙΟΥ ΠΟΛΥΔΕΥΚΟΥΣ ΟΝΟΜΑΣΤΙΚΟΝ. IULII POLLUCIS VOCABULARIUM.* Florence: B. Junta, November 1520. **Content**: A. Francino to T. Linacre, *inc.* Lege quadam naturae . . . (no date); index, in Greek and Latin; extract from the Suda on Pollux; Julius Pollux, in Greek; S. Forteguerri τοῖς φιλολόγοις, *inc.* Τὰ ὄντα καθ' ἑαυτὰ . . . (no date); register; colophon. **Reference**: Renouard, *Annales de l'imprimerie des Alde*, xlv; Cambridge, University Library, M*.9.21 (C).

23. *ΣΤΕΦΑΝΟΣ ΠΕΡΙ ΠΟΛΕΩΝ. STEPHANUS DE URBIBUS.* Florence: Heredes P. Juntae, April 30, 1521. **Content**: Stephanus, in Greek; register; colophon; device. **Reference**: Renouard, *Annales de l'imprimerie des Alde*, xlvi; BL, 70.f.8 (2).

24. *Dictionarium Graecum innumeris locis auctum, ac locupletatum, Impressum nunc primum in Gallia his elegantissimis typis, Cui vel assurgere, vel cedere iure debeant Dictionaria alia omnia alicubi antehac excusa. In gratiam studiosae Iuventutis, abs qua non vulgarem quoque gratiam vicissim expectamus ipsi. Cyrilli opusculum de dictionibus, quae accentu atque apice variant significatum. Ammonius de similitudine ac differentia quarundam dictionum. De Re Militari veterum, ac praefectorum nominibus libellus Graecus, Authore incerto. Orbicii de Ordinibus exercitus. Significata τοῦ ἤ. τοῦ ὡς. Dictionarium quo Latina Graecis exponuntur. Ioannis Grammatici libellus de differentiis linguarum, adulescentibus Graecae linguae candidatis non utilis modo, sed etiam necessarius, cum nullo alio Lexico Impressus.* Paris: P. Vidovaeus, July 1521. **Content**: *N. Beraldus . . . Guielmo Marsiboio, inc.* Quicunque ingeniis favent . . . (Paris, June 27, 1521); Greek–Latin lexicon; pseudo-Cyril; Ammonius; Τάξις παλαιά; Orbicius; meanings of η and ως; Latin–Greek lexicon; register; colophon; Vidovaeus to the reader, *inc.* Habes lector . . . (no date); J. Grammaticus, Eustathius (pseudo-Plutarch), and Gregory Pardus on the dialects. **Date**: The works on the dialects, only one of which appears in the title, may have been printed after the colophon. They are separately signed and not foliated. **Reference**: Moreau, *Inventaire chronologique*, 3:68, item no. 73; BL, 1505/232.

25. *Hesychii Dictionarium locupletiss, ea fide ac diligentia excusum, ut hoc uno, ad veterum autorum fere omnium, ac poetarum in primis lectionem, iusti Commentarii vice, uti quivis possit, et plane nihil sit, quod ad rectam interpretationem desyderari hic queat.* Hagenau: T. Anshelm, December 1521. **Content**: Aldus to J. J. Bardellonus, *inc.* Si caeteri studiosi . . . (Botfield, *Prefaces*, 304–5; Legrand, *Bibliographie hellénique*, 1:123–24; Orlandi, *Aldo Manuzio editore*, 1:143–44); Hesychius. Some copies have a brief title page: *ΗΣΥΧΙΟΥ ΛΕΞΙΚΟΝ. HESYCHII DICTIONARIUM.* **Reference**: BL, C.79.d.8 (2) (brief title); Cambridge, University Library, U*.3.31 (B).

26. *QUAE HOCCE LIBRO CONTENTA. LEXICON GRAECUM IAM SECUNDUM, PLUS trium millium dictionum auctario locupletatum, ad hoc multis ante parum latine redditis, elegantius ac magis apposite interpretatis. Ammonii de similibus et differentibus dictionibus ordine alphabetico. Vetus instructio militarium praefectorum, et eorundem denominationes. Orbicii de nominibus ordinum militarium. Cyrilli dictiones, quae pro literae vel accentus immutatione diversa significant. Quam multiplici sint significato τὸ ὡς καὶ τὸ η. Corinthii libellus de linguarum proprietatibus iam noviter adpressus. De anomalis et inaequabilis verbis ordine alphabetico. Herodiani et Choerobosci de encliticis et enclinomenis. Omnia iam recens adiecta.* Basle: V. Curio, March 1522. **Content**: *Curio lectoribus philograecis, inc.* Vulgavimus abhinc opinor . . . (Basle, March 1522); Greek–Latin lexicon; pseudo-Cyril; Ammonius; Τάξις παλαιά; Orbicius; the meanings of ως and η; J. Grammaticus, Eustathius (pseudo-Plutarch), and Gregory Pardus on the dialects; *De anomalis verbis*; Herodian, J. Grammaticus, and Choeroboscus on enclitics; Latin–Greek lexicon; colophon; verses: H. Buschius; *errata*. **Reference**: *Griechischer Geist*, 50–52, item no. 25; BL, C.79.d.8 (1).

27. *ΜΕΓΑ, ΚΑΙ ΠΑΝΥ ΩΦΕΛΙΜΟΝ ΛΕΞΙΚΟΝ ΟΠΕΡ ΓΑΡΙΝΟΣ, ΦΑΒΩΡΙΝΟΣ, ΚΑΜΗΡΣ, Ο ΝΟΥΚΑΙΡΙΑΣ ΕΠΙΣΚΟΠΟΣ, ΕΚ ΠΟΛΛΩΝ ΚΑΙ ΔΙΑΦΟΡΩΝ ΒΙΒΛΙΩΝ, ΚΑΤΑ ΣΤΟΙΧΕΙΟΝ ΣΥΝΕΛΕΞΑΤΟ. MAGNUM AC PER UTILE DICTIONARIUM. QUODQUIDEM VARINUS PHAVORINUS CAMERS NUCERINUS EPISCOPUS EX MULTIS VARIISQUE AUCTORIBUS IN ORDINEM ALPHABETI COLLEGIT.* Rome: Z. Callierges, [March or May] 28, 1523. **Content**: Verses: J. Lascaris, *inc.* ʽΗ βίβλος μεγάλη . . . (Legrand, *Bibliographie hellénique*, 1:175); verses: A. Poliziano, *inc.* ʽΕλλάδι τοῖς ἰδίοις . . . (Legrand, *Bibliographie hellénique*, 1:176); verses: S. Forteguerri, *inc.* Βίβλον ὁ γραμματικῆς . . . (Legrand, *Bibliographie hellénique*, 1:176); ten-year privilege from Leo X; Guarino of Favera to Giulio de' Medici, *inc.* Ἐάν τινες πάνυ . . . (no date, Legrand, *Bibliographie hellénique*, 1:176–78); lexicon of Guarino, in Greek only. **Date**: Colophon: "σκιρο[φο]ριῶνος τετάρτῃ φθίνοντος." This is May in *De mensibus*; it is March in the lexica. **Reference**: Legrand, *Bibliographie hellénique*, item no. 68; Cambridge, University Library, Aa*.2.17 (B); BL, G.7646.

28. *HABES TANDEM GRAECARUM LITERARUM ADMIRATOR, LEXIcon Graecum, caeteris omnibus aut in Italia, aut Gallia Germaniave antehac excusis multo locupletius, utpote supra ter mille additiones Basiliensi Lexico An. M.D.XXII. apud Curionem impresso adiectas, amplius quinque recentiorum additionum milibus auctum. Quibus ex receptissimo quoque scriptore seligendis, plurimum tibi desudarunt, Partim Gulielmus Mainus liberorum D. Budaei praeceptor ut doctissimus ita diligentissimus, Partim Iohannes Chaeradamus Hypocrates Matheseos et Graecae linguae professor non Poenitendus. Quae vero, quamque multa hoc Lexico contineantur, sequens Pagina Elencho te docebit luculentissimo.* Paris: G. de Gourmont, April 1523. **Content**: G. de Maine to F. Poncher, *inc.* Nisi de ingenii . . . (no date); J. Chéradame to F. de Valois, *inc.* Sum equidem nescius . . . (no date); Chéradame to G. Petit, *inc.* Cum plaeraque in . . . (no date); Greek–Latin lexicon; *Additiones quae passim omissae fuerunt*; pseudo-Cyril; Ammonius; Τάξις παλαιά; Orbicius; meanings of η and ως; Chéradame to H. Savevsius, *inc.* Non te latet . . . (no

date); J. Grammaticus, pseudo-Plutarch, and Gregory Pardus on the dialects; Chéradame to J. Odoardus, *inc.* Pithagoras numerorum perscrutator . . . (1523); Chéradame, *De numeris; De anomalis verbis;* Herodian on enclitics; *Additiones quae iam in Germania editae fuerunt;* Latin–Greek lexicon; Gourmont to the Provost of Paris, *inc.* Supplie humblement Gilles . . .; privilege of three years, April 13, 1523; Chéradame to J. Nervet, *inc.* Non modo utiles . . . (1523). **Reference**: Moreau, *Inventaire chronologique,* 3:170, item no. 475; Cambridge, University Library, Aa*.3.1 (D); Oxford, Bodleian, Byw.G.1.4.

29. *DICTIONARIUS GRAECUS, PRAEter omnes superiores accessiones, quarum nihil est omissum, ingenti vocabulorum numero locupletatus per utriusque literaturae non vulgariter peritum, IACOBUM CERATINUM. Ac ne libellorum quidem ac fragmentorum, quae superiores adiecerant, hic quicquam desiderabis.* Basle: J. Froben, July 1524. **Content**: *Erasmus graecae literaturae candidatis, inc.* Crescentem, inquit Oratius . . . (Basle, July 1, 1524; EE 5:483–85); Greek–Latin lexicon; pseudo-Cyril; Ammonius; Τάξις παλαιά; Orbicius; J. Grammaticus, pseudo-Plutarch, and Gregory Pardus on the dialects; *De anomalis verbis;* J. Chéradame, *De Graecorum numeris methodus;* Herodian and Choeroboscus on enclitics; colophon; **errata. Reference**: Dufrane and Isaac, "Jacques Ceratinus et son dictionnaire"; Harlfinger and Barm, *Graecogermania,* 120–21; Cambridge, University Library, Aa*.2.24 (C).

30. *DICTIONARIUM GRAECUM cum interpretatione latina, omnium, quae hactenus impressa sunt, copiosissimum. Collectio dictionum, quae differunt significatu, per ordinem literarum. Dictiones latinae graece redditae. Ammonius de similibus et differentibus dictionibus. Vetus instructio et denominationes praefectorum militum. Orbicius de nominibus ordinum militarium. Significata τοῦ ἦ καὶ ὥς. Io. Grammatici quaedam de proprietatibus linguarum. Eustathii quaedam de proprietatibus linguarum apud Homerum. Corinthus de proprietatibus linguarum. Verborum anomalorum declinationes secundum ordinem literarum. Herodiani quaedam de encliticis. Io. Grammatici Characis quaedam de encliticis. Choerobosci quaedam de encliticis. Thomae Magistri eclogae atticorum nominum, et verborum. Phrynichi ecloge [sic] atticorum nominum, et verborum. Emanuelis Moschopuli eclogae [sic] atticarum dictionum, nunc primum impressae.* Venice: in aedibus Aldi et Andreae Asulani soceri, December 1524. **Content**: *F. Asulanus lectori, inc.* Cum sororius noster . . . (no date); Greek–Latin lexicon; pseudo-Cyril; Latin–Greek lexicon; Ammonius; Τάξις παλαιά; Orbicius; meanings of η and ως; J. Grammaticus, Eustathius (pseudo-Plutarch), and Gregory Pardus on the dialects; *De anomalis verbis;* Herodian and J. Grammaticus on enclitics; *Eclogae* of Magister, Phrynichus, and Moschopoulos, in Greek; register; colophon. The title page claims a ten-year privilege. **Reference**: Renouard, *Annales de l'imprimerie des Alde,* 99; BL, 623.l.8.

31. *Habes candide lector duos tomos isagogae ad linguam graecam capessendam septem continentes libros: quibus et lexicon annexum est ordine alphabetico secundum declinationes: et coniugationes (ut index tibi ostendet) quo lucidius: copiosiusve nullum extitit antehac. Hos edidit Reverendus pater sacrae theologiae professor: et concionator apostolicus frater Sanctes pagninus Lucensis praedicatorii ordinis.* Avignon: J. de Channey, February 1, 1525. **Content**: For a description, see appendix 1, no. 153. For its vocabularies, see chapter 1, section "Sanctes Pagninus."

32. *LEXICON GRAECUM IAM DENUO SUPRA OMNEIS OMNIUM auctiones longe auctissimum, et locupletissimum, cui praeter superiores aeditiones magna vis dictionum accessit, ex optimis quibusque autoribus deprompta, non sine locorum citatione, et accuratissima restitutione eorum, quae aut depravata erant, aut tumultuarie assuta. Accessit et libellorum aliquot ex non pessimis non poenitenda farrago, eaque in numeros, et indices suos tam apte digesta, ut nihil supervacuum resecari, nihil diminutum desiderari possit.*

Basle: V. Curio, March 1525. **Content**: Curio to the reader, *inc.* Erat animus, candide lector . . . (March 1525); Greek–Latin lexicon; pseudo-Cyril; index; Ammonius; Τάξις παλαιά; Orbicius; meanings of η and ως; index; J. Grammaticus, Eustathius (pseudo-Plutarch), and Gregory Pardus on the dialects; index; pseudo-Tryphon; *De anomalis verbis;* C. Lascaris, *De constructione;* *De spiritibus;* C. Lascaris, *De subscriptis vocalibus;* Herodian, J. Grammaticus, and Choeroboscus on enclitics; On paragogic nu; verbs of being, going, and sitting; J. Chéradame, *De Graecorum numeris methodus;* Herodian, *De numeris,* register. This edition has no Latin–Greek lexicon. **Reference**: Cambridge, University Library, Aa*.2.19 (C); Oxford, Bodleian, 304.x.16 (lacks first and last leaves).

33. *DICTIONARIUM GRAECUM. Cyrilli collectio dictionum quae different significato, Dictiones latinae graecis expositae. Ammonii de similibus et differentibus dictionibus. Vetus instructio, et denominationes praefectorum militum. Orbicii de nominibus ordinum militarium. Choerobosci de his in quibus attrahatur v. Significata η et ως. Io. Grammatici de dialectis cum interp. lat. De faemininis nominibus quae desinunt in ω. Eustathii de dialectis cum interp. lat. Corinthi de dialectis cum interp. lat. De figures soloecis quae cuius sint dialecti. De anomalis verbis cum interp. lat. Tryphonis de passionibus dictionum. Herodiani de numeris. Herodiani de encliticis. Io. Grammatici de encliticis. Choerobosci de encliticis. Theodori Gazae de mensibus. Thomae magistri eclogae acticorum [sic] nominum, et verborum. Phrynichi eclogae atticorum nominum, et verborum. Epistolares styli.* Venice: M. Sessa and P. de Ravanis, December 24, 1525. **Content**: Sessa and de Ravanis . . . *studiosis, inc.* Homo homini deus . . . (no date); Greek–Latin lexicon; pseudo-Cyril; Latin–Greek lexicon; Ammonius; Τάξις παλαιά; Orbicius; Choeroboscus; meanings of η and ως; J. Grammaticus on the dialects; *De foemininis nominibus quae desinunt in ω* (printed on a page left blank by mistake); Eustathius (pseudo-Plutarch) and Gregory Pardus on the dialects; *De figuris soloecis; De anomalis verbis;* pseudo-Tryphon; Herodian, *De numeris;* Herodian, J. Grammaticus, and Choeroboscus on enclitics; Gaza, *De mensibus;* colophon. Magister, Phrynichus, and the *epistolares styli* are not in BL, 623.1.9. **Reference**: BL, 623.1.9.

34. Οὐλπιανοῦ ῥήτορος προλεγόμενα εἴς τε τοὺς Ὀλυνθιακοὺς καὶ Φιλιππικοὺς Δημοσθένους λόγους. Ἐξέγησις . . . εἰς δεκατρεῖς τοῦ Δημοσθένους λόγους. Ἁρποκρατίωνος λεξικὸν τῶν δέκα ῥητόρων. *Vlpiani Commentarioli in olynthiacas, philippicasque Demosthenis orationes. Enarrationes sane quam necessariae in tredecim orationes Demosthenis, Arpocrationis dictionarium decem Rhetorum.* Venice: in aedibus Aldi et A. Asulani, June 1527. **Reference**: Renouard, *Annales de l'imprimerie des Alde,* 104; Cambridge, University Library, Aa*.2.23 (2) (C) (Harpocration only); BL, G.8514.

35. *INTRODUTTORIO NUOVO INTItolato Corona Preciosa, per imparare, legere, scrivere, parlare, & intendere la Lingua greca volgare & literale, & la lingua latina, & il volgare italico con molto facilita e prestezza sanza precettore (cosa molto utile ad ogni conditione di persone o literate, o non literate) compilato per lo ingenioso huomo Stephano da Sabio stampatore da libri greci & latini nelle inclita Citta di Vinegia.* Venice: J. A. et fratres de Sabio, August 1527. **Content**: S. da Sabio to A. Gritti, *inc.* Tutti gl'huomini . . . (Venice, May 1527); verses: J. Eterno Senese, *inc.* Ecco che adempirai . . . (Legrand, *Bibliographie hellénique,* 1:201); Greek alphabet and its divisions; abbreviations; *Pater noster* and *Ave Maria* in Greek, transliterated into Latin letters; *Pater noster* and *Ave Maria* in Latin, transliterated into Greek letters; vocabulary in four columns: Italian, vulgar Greek, Latin, and classical Greek. All forms are transliterated. The title is printed in Italian, Greek, and Latin. **Date**: August 1527 in the colophon. A privilege is dated August 17, 1527. Legrand mistakenly records the date of the preface as May 1529. **Reference**: Legrand, *Bibliographie hellénique,* item no. 79; Cambridge, University Library, F152.d.2.28.

Notes

Preface

1. Botley, *Latin Translation in the Renaissance*.
2. See, for example, Proctor, *The Printing of Greek*; Scholderer, *Greek Printing Types 1465–1927*.
3. Renouard, *Annales de l'imprimerie des Alde*; Legrand, *Bibliographie hellénique*.
4. Hirsch, "Early Printed Greek Grammars, 1471–1550," is of limited use. Pertusi, " Ἐρωτήματα," is valuable.
5. Bakelants and Hoven, *Bibliographie des oeuvres de Nicholas Clénard*.
6. It has been studied in a recent monograph: Sanchi, *Les Commentaires de la langue grecque de Guillaume Budé*.

Chapter 1

1. See chapter 3, section "Quintus of Smyrna."
2. Lake, "The Greek Monasteries of South Italy. IV," 196. The discovery is recorded in a note on BAV, Vat.gr.1351, folio 11r, dated 1498. See De Nolhac, "Inventaire des manuscrits grecs," 153; Rabe, "Konstantin Laskaris," 5; Martínez-Manzano, *Konstantinos Laskaris*, 324–25.
3. Quoted in Wilson, "The Libraries of the Byzantine World," 73.
4. Forteguerri's *Oratio de laudibus literarum graecarum* was first printed at Venice in 1504, here cited from *Thesaurus graecae linguae*, 1:xiii.
5. Cammelli, *Demetrio Calcondila*, 121n2.
6. "Quod si quis pronunciationis tantum graecae studio . . . graecum sibi cupit praeceptorem, Quintilianum audiat praecipientem non esse dandam operam literis graecis superstitiose . . ." (*Oratio* [as in n. 4], 1:xiii). The reference is to Quintilian, *Institutio oratoria*, 1.1.13.
7. See Hesseling and Pernot, "Érasme et les origines," 296–301.
8. 15 May 1511, De Nolhac, *Les correspondants d'Alde Manuce*, 52–53, letter no. 43. For Colocci, see Gaisser, *Pierio Valeriano*, 53–57. In March 1510, Colocci borrowed from the Vatican Library a Greek manuscript of Aristotle's logical works with the commentary of Alexander of Aphrodisias (Bertola, *I due primi registri*, 47). This suggests some competence with the language.
9. Appendix 1, no. 8.
10. Pozzi, "Da Padova a Firenze nel 1493," 193.
11. Girolamo, whose home was in Padua, is most likely to have owned the latest edition of Lascaris's *compendium*, printed at nearby Vicenza in 1489. Lascaris's full grammar was not printed until around 1502. See chapter 1, section "Constantine Lascaris," and appendix 1, nos. 10 and 26.
12. See his letter to Ambrogio Traversari, August 27, 1424, Sabbadini, *Carteggio di Giovanni Aurispa*, 10–15.

13. On April 13, 1441, Filelfo wrote to Pietro Perleone at Constantinople: "Cum istic essem, diu multumque studui quaesiviique diligenter comparare aliquid mihi ex Apollonii Erodianique iis operibus quae ab illis de arte grammatica copiose fuerant et accurate scripta. Nihil usquam potui odorari. Nam a magistris ludi quae publicae docent[ur] plena sunt nugarum omnia. Itaque neque de constructione grammaticae orationis, de syllabarum quantitate, neque de accentu quicquam aut perfecti aut certi ex istorum praeceptis haberi potest" (Filelfo, *Epistolare Francisci Philelfi*, sig. i4v). This digression on Apollonius is a non sequitur in the letter and seems to be an answer to a lost question of Perleone. It is clear that at this date Filelfo does not have either author.
14. For Filelfo's copy of the Suda lexicon, see chapter 2, section "The Suda Lexicon."
15. Letter of April 13, 1441, cited previously, n. 13. For details of Filelfo's search, see Calderini, "Ricerche intorno alla biblioteca."
16. Letter of May 1456. Legrand, *Cent-dix lettres greques de F. Filelfo*, 83–84.
17. PBN, suppl.gr.541. To the first half of this manuscript, written by Georgios Gregoropoulos, Callistus added other works: see Centanni, "La biblioteca di Andronico Callisto," 217. For its contents, see Omont, *Inventaire-sommaire*, 3:274–75.
18. Diller, "Greek Codices of Palla Strozzi and Guarino Veronese," 316. See Filelfo's letter of January 28, 1461, to Palla Strozzi (Milan, Bibl. Trivulziana, ms. 873, folio 205v). He returned it in April 1461 (ibid., folio 212v).
19. Lascaris copied Madrid, Bibl. Nacional, 4650 at Milan c. 1460 (Andrés, *Catálogo de los códices griegos*, 196–97). Vienna, Österreichische Nationalbibl., Phil.gr.138 was largely copied by Lascaris at Milan by 1464 (Martínez-Manzano, *Konstantinos Laskaris*, 236). He may have corrected PBN, gr.2547, made in 1496. See Omont, "Les manuscrits grecs," 30; Schneider, Uhlig, and Hilgard, *Grammatici Graeci recogniti*, II, ii: xxxvi–xxxvii; Martínez-Manzano, *Konstantinos Laskaris*, 236n15. Venice, Bibl. Marciana, gr.8.2 (1388) (which has Apollonius, folios 126–211) was seen by Bartolomeo Bardella (folio 297v), apparently at Milan, and has some notes in Lascaris's hand (folios 126r and 199v; Martínez-Manzano, *Konstantinos Laskaris*, 284, 288).
20. A manuscript described simply as "Apolonius" [*sic*] is in a list of books sent by Vittorino da Feltre to Gian Pietro da Lucca in 1445. See Cortesi, "Libri e vicende di Vittorino da Feltre," 92. See chapter 3, section "Apollonius of Rhodes."
21. Perhaps Florence, Bibl. Laurenziana, 60.26, fourteenth century (Martinelli, "Grammatiche greche," 267 and n26).
22. Appendix 1, no. 16.
23. *De fructu qui ex doctrina percipitur*, Manley and Sylvester, *De fructu qui ex doctrina percipitur*, 94. For Pace, see Curtis, "Pace, Richard (1483?–1536)."
24. See chapter 1, section "Theodore Gaza."
25. Dyck, "Aelius Herodian," 777.
26. Ibid., 776–77; OCD, 140, *s. v.* Arcadius (1). For an edition, see Schmidt, Ἐπιτομή.
27. Lascaris's autograph of the epitome is now Madrid, Bibl. Nacional, 4575. It is detailed in Andrés, *Catálogo de los códices griegos*, 55–56, where it is dated c. 1480. See also Fernández Pomar, "La colección de Uceda," 237; Martínez-Manzano, *Konstantinos Laskaris*, 233. The discovery of the παλαιὰ βίβλος is referred to in the colophons to Lascaris's epitomes in Madrid 4689, folios 117v (1482) and 199r (November 25, 1488). Both epitomes suppose access to the Theodosian epitome of the *Catholica Prosodia*.
28. This epitome has been edited: Lenz, "Constantini Lascaris epitome," 162–75. The preface, with a Latin translation, is in PG 161:939–42. A modern edition of this preface is in Martínez-Manzano, *Konstantinos Laskaris*, 231–32.
29. This treatise is in Madrid, Bibl. Nacional, 4689, folios 137r–199r. Lascaris's epilogue is in PG 161:941. For the treatise and the epilogue, see Martínez-Manzano, *Konstantinos Laskaris*, 232–33.
30. For this grammar, see Pertusi "Ἐρωτήματα," 323, 331–32, 337–38. For the *editio princeps*, see appendix 1, no. 14. For a tendency to attribute anonymous *schedographia* to Moschopoulos, see Keaney, "Moschopulea," 304.

31. Baiophoros is studied in Gamillscheg, "Zur handschriftlichen Überlieferung."
32. See Cortesi, "Il «Vocabularium» greco di Giovanni Tortelli."
33. See Pertusi, " Ἐρωτήματα," 329.
34. Florence, Bibl. Laurenziana, S.Marco.317 (Ullman and Stadter, *The Public Library of Renaissance Florence*, 266).
35. Formerly S. Mich. 122 (Mioni, "I manoscritti greci di S. Michele di Murano," 335). Now Leningrad, Inst. of History of the Akad. Nauk. I.666 (Mioni, "Altri due manoscritti greci di S. Michele di Murano"; Diller, "The Library of Francesco and Ermolao Barbaro," 260).
36. BAV, Vat.gr.21, for which see Mercati and Cavalieri, *Codices vaticani graeci*, 20–21. It was certainly in the Vatican by 1475 (Devreesse, *Le fonds grec*, 9n5, 48; Mercati and De' Cavalieri, *Codices vaticani graeci*, 20–21). For Garatone, see Moro, "Garatone."
37. Oxford, Bodleian, Canon.gr.14. See RGK 1, no. 352; Wilson, *From Byzantium to Italy*, 38.
38. Strozzi's manuscript is now Cambridge, St. John's College, manuscript 265 (note on folio 1). Poliziano's may be Florence, Bibl. Laurenziana, 28.24 or Bibl. Laurenziana, 59.45: see Martinelli, "Grammatiche greche, 269, 282.
39. Baiophoros's Vienna, Österreichische Nationalbibl., Phil.gr.286 has a note on folio 42v that appears to be in Lascaris's hand (Gamillscheg, "Zur handschriftlichen Überlieferung," 229n116). Lascaris owned Madrid, Bibl. Nacional, 4646 and Bibl. Nacional, I/1988 (Andrés, *Catálogo de los códices griegos*, 190–91, 545–46). For the *editio princeps*, see appendix 1, no. 14.
40. Tübingen, Universitätsbibliothek, Mb.8, which has a note: "Liber grammaticalis Moschopuli emptus per Joannem Reuchlin Phorcensem. Esse perpetuo debet τῇ χρήσει familiae Capnionum." This manuscript is possibly that manuscript of Moschopoulos listed among the books of Cardinal Giovanni of Ragusa (d. 1443). See Vernet, "Les manuscrits grecs," 100–101.
41. Vienna, Österreichische Nationalbibl., Phil.gr.92: see Kalatzi, "Georgios Hermonymos," 145–46.
42. Novati, *Epistolario di Coluccio Salutati*, 3:109; 18 February, to Cydones; 3:125, 8 March, to Chrysoloras; 3:131, 25 March, to Angeli.
43. PBN, gr.425, folios 80–87, for which see Bernardinello, "La grammatica di Manuele Caleca," 207–10. For the manuscript, see Omont, *Inventaire-sommaire*, 1:45–46. It is a composite manuscript: folios 1–10, 11–18v, 19, and 27–28 were copied by Cyriaco of Ancona (d. c. 1453; RGK 2, no. 307).
44. For the date, see Bernardinello, "La grammatica di Manuele Caleca," 203–5.
45. Novati, *Epistolario di Coluccio Salutati*, 3:129–32.
46. Weiss, "Iacopo Angeli da Scarperia," 255–77.
47. Bernardinello, "La grammatica di Manuele Caleca," 208.
48. Folios 80–87 (Bernardinello, "La grammatica di Manuele Caleca," 208n3).
49. Bernardinello, "La grammatica di Manuele Caleca," 214. For the declensions, see Pertusi " Ἐρωτήματα," 339.
50. Bernardinello, "La grammatica di Manuele Caleca," 216. For Dionysius on the conjugations, see Lallot, *La grammaire de Denys le Thrace*, 58.
51. For surviving copies, see Bernardinello, "La grammatica di Manuele Caleca," 206–11.
52. Pietro: Venice, Bibl. Marciana, gr.10.7, perhaps the exemplar for Salutati's PBN, gr.425 (Bernardinello, "La grammatica di Manuele Caleca," 206, 208). Calfurnio: Venice, Bibl. Marciana, gr.10.8, for which see ibid., 207. For Calfurnio's ownership, see Marcotte, "La bibliothèque de Jean Calphurnius," 197.
53. Weiss, "Iacopo Angeli da Scarperia," 258.
54. See Pertusi " Ἐρωτήματα," 324n2.
55. Ibid., 324–25.
56. BAV, Pal.gr.116, for which see Stevenson, *Codices manuscripti palatini graeci*, 55. Theodore Gaza copied folios 23–24v of this manuscript (RGK 3, no. 211), possibly a repair. Guarino studied at Constantinople from 1403 to 1408. Guarino had a manuscript at his death in 1460: "Volumen antiquissimum in quo ars grammatica copiosissime traditur, cuius auctor

fortasse fuit Chrisoloras, Guarini praeceptor; et in eodem Aratus cum scholiis, et Ammonius in quinque voces." I know no manuscript that fits this description.

57. For Salutati's request, see Novati, *Epistolario di Coluccio Salutati*, 4:269–71. Of Chrysoloras's reply, which accompanied the treatise, only a part survives. Omitted by Novati, it was edited by Mercati, "Una lettera negletta," 232–34. For this letter, see Mercati, "Una lettera negletta," 227–32, and Ullman, "Chrysoloras' Two Letters to Coluccio Salutati."

58. Salutati writes, "Omissa responsione graecis litteris scripta a Manuele, tractatum eius illico subieci et ex eius manu exaratum transcripsi" (Bernardinello, "La grammatica di Manuele Caleca," 209n6). The *responsio* is the fragmentary letter mentioned above. The *tractatus* is the treatise on the breathings.

59. Fiocco, "La biblioteca di Palla Strozzi," 309–10. Diller's proposed identification of the former is, as he acknowledges, unlikely ("Greek Codices of Palla Strozzi and Guarino Veronese," 316). PBN, gr.2489, a composite manuscript, has a descriptive note on folio 88r: "gramatica et sermones demosthenis," while PBN, gr.2508, has a description on folio 1r: "gramatica et demosthenis sermones." Both have been connected with Chrysoloras (Zorzi, "I Crisolora," 109), but neither has the *Erotemata*.

60. Sabbadini quotes the letter, "Alvisius Mainerius tibi defert Erotimata graeca, seu mavis latine interrogationes grammaticas ordinatas per virum ill. Emanuelem Chrysoloram et transcriptas manu genitoris nostri. Scio Guarinum eiusque sequaces amplioribus uti regulis" (Florence, Bibl. Riccardiana, 827, folio 48v; Sabbadini, *Epistolario di Guarino Veronese*, 3:77).

61. Cammelli, *Manuele Crisolora*, 123.

62. For which tradition, see Pertusi, "Ἐρωτήματα," 330–33.

63. Edited in ibid,. 324.

64. A description and sample of Chrysoloras's grammar is in Robins, *The Byzantine Grammarians*, 237–44.

65. Pertusi summarizes the ancient and Byzantine tradition for the categorization of the nouns and verbs from Dionysios Thrax to Georgios Choeroboscos ("Ἐρωτήματα," 329).

66. Nolan and Hirsch, *The Greek Grammar of Roger Bacon*, 146–47.

67. These ten declension are detailed in Pertusi, "Ἐρωτήματα," 44, and n2.

68. Ibid., 345.

69. See chapter 1, section "Manuel Calecas," p. 7.

70. Chrysoloras probably used the treatise of Gregorius Pardus of Corinth *On the Dialects* when he composed the *Erotemata*. See Berti, "Alla scuola di M. Crisolora," 25–26; Donnet, "La place de la syntaxe."

71. Sabbadini, *Epistolario di Guarino Veronese*, 1:180; Percival, "The Place of the *Rudimenta Grammatices*," 235.

72. See Guarino's letter of January 12, [1418] to Nicola Pirondolo in Sabbadini, *Epistolario di Guarino Veronese*, 1:176; 3:76–77. He may have done this for Francesco Barbaro. See Sabbadini, *Epistolario di Guarino Veronese*, 1:310–11.

73. The omissions made by Guarino in his compendium are discussed in Bernardinello, "Gli studi propedeutici di greco," 123–25.

74. *De ordine docendi et studendi* (edited by Kallendorf, *Humanist Educational Treatises*, 280–82).

75. The epitome and the full text are not always distinguished by the catalogs. Full text *incipit*: Εἰς πόσα διαιροῦνται τὰ εἰκοσιτέσσαρα γράμματα ἃ καὶ στοιχεῖα λέγονται; εἰς δύο ... Epitome *incipit*: Εἰς πόσα διαιροῦνται τὰ εἰκοσιτέσσαρα γράμματα; εἰς δύο.

76. BL, Harl. 6506. Zamponi dates it by its hand ("Un ignoto compendio sozomeniano," 258). This manuscript includes the treatise on the breathings (folios 28–31v). For Zomino's time in Constance from 1417 to 1418, see chapter 3, section "Plato," n. 372.

77. Pistoia, Archivio Capitolare, ms c 74; Zamponi, "Un ignoto compendio sozomeniano," 260–61. For Zamponi's detailed analysis of the differences between the two manuscripts of Zomino, see ibid., 256–57, 263–70.

78. Vespasiano, edited by Greco, *Vespasiano da Bisticci*, 1:560–61.

79. For his copy of Calecas, see chapter 1, section "Manuel Calecas."

80. Venice, Bibl. Marciana, lat.13.15, folios 1r–42v, for which, see Bernardinello, "Gli studi propedeutici di greco," 125–26.
81. Venice, Bibl. Marciana, gr.10.13 (Bernardinello, "Gli studi propedeutici di greco," 125).
82. Padua, Anton.lat.123. The interlinear translation may be Guarino's (Mancini, "Codices graeci patavini," 163–64; Pertusi " Ἐρωτήματα," 325n4).
83. Hartmann Schedel wrote, "Iste Grecus fuit Demetrius Atheniensis, qui publice Padue primo Erothimata deinde Hesiodum nobis exposuit." This is prefaced to a document dated 1463 (Geanakoplos, "Translation of Chalcondyles' Discourses," 296). Chalcondyles made two manuscripts of Chrysoloras: he copied PBN, suppl.gr.170, folios 1–47v (RGK 2, no. 138); in the 1460s, he made Jena, Prov.o.25, which was in the hands of Johann Löffelholtz of Nuremberg by 1467 (Stockhausen, "Katalog der griechischen Handschriften," 698–700).
84. Lascaris copied Modena, Bibl. Estense, γ.K.7.19. He copied folios 33v–34v of Florence, Bibl. Riccardiana 96, a manuscript partially copied by Joannes Scutariota (Martínez-Manzano, *Konstantinos Laskaris*, 236–37, 291). Riccardiana 96 has notes of ownership: "Georgii Antonii Vespucci liber, ad usum D. Io. eius nepotis" (folio 1); and "Hic liber est Georgii Antonii et Amerigii Vespucci καὶ τῶν φίλων et amicorum. Nunc vero Laurentii Petri Francisci de Medicis" (folio 34v). BAV, Vat.gr.2388 is described in Martínez-Manzano, *Konstantinos Laskaris*, 331, and dated there between 1462 and 1465: Lascaris copied the grammar on folios 1–57. Giorgio Valla added prayers on folios 57v–58v.
85. PBN, gr.2611, and PBN, gr.2613, folios 2–60 (RGK 2, no. 242). Dated manuscripts in his hand are from the years 1442 to 1494 (Omont, "Catalogue des manuscripts grecs des bibliothèques de Suisse," 3:13).
86. BAV, Reg.gr.134. Rhosos subscribed only one other manuscript at Bologna: BAV, Vat.gr.27 of Homer, dated May 28, 1465 (RGK 3, no. 298).
87. See chapter 2, section "Greek Lexica in Western Europe 1396–1529," n. 132. Here we may notice a Greek grammar, in Latin, that survives in a single manuscript, Wolfenbüttel, Guelf.17 21 4 August 4o. It is discussed and edited by Cortesi, "Aspetti linguistici della cultura greca di Francesco Filelfo." Cortesi concludes that it shows affinities with Chrysoloras's grammar. It has a brief Greek autograph letter of Filelfo to Zenone Amidani, and the manuscript once belonged to Giovanni Andrea Amidani. The grammar itself is not in Filelfo's hand, and his connection with its contents remains a matter for speculation.
88. Appendix 1, no. 23.
89. For Urbano's grammar, see chapter 1, section "Urbano Bolzanio."
90. Appendix 1, no. 35.
91. Appendix 1, no. 1.
92. Appendix 1, no. 9.
93. Appendix 1, no. 30; Girot, *Pindare avant Ronsard*, 20–21n42.
94. This information derives from Tissard's Hebrew grammar (ed.) Omont, "Essai sur les débuts de la typographie grecque à Paris," 53. Tissard claims to have been taught by Guarino Veronese (d. 1460). In the preface to his unpublished versions of Euripides, he says his teacher was Battista Guarino (ibid., 66). Calfurnio died at Padua in 1503. Beroaldo taught at Bologna between 1472 and 1476 and from 1479 until his death in 1505. Tissard graduated doctor of canon and civil law at Bologna in March 1507 (ibid., 2). A search among the Spartan Demetrii active in northern Italy in the late quattrocento suggests that this teacher may have been Demetrius Moschus. Moschus copied Rome, Bibl. Vallicelliana, E.37 (71), folios 92–127v of Lascaris and Michael Syncellus (RGK 1, no. 97).
95. Appendix 1, nos. 17 and 21.
96. Omont, "Essai sur les débuts de la typographie grecque à Paris," 69. For the Aldine Lascaris, see appendix 1, nos. 15 and 26.
97. Appendix 1, no. 42.
98. Appendix 1, nos. 38 (Gaza, 1511), 43 (Urbano, 1512), 69 (Gaza, 1516), 70 (Chrysoloras, 1516), 72 (Gaza, 1516).

168   Notes to Chapter 1

99. Appendix 1, no. 147. *Emanuelis Chrysolorae . . . Graecae grammaticae institutiones. Latina e regione opposita sunt graecis . . . Dominico Sylvio interprete.* Paris: Wechel, 1534.
100. This preface is edited in Legrand, *Bibliographie hellénique*, 1:98–99 and Orlandi, *Aldo Manuzio editore*, 1:104.
101. See Renouard, *Annales de l'imprimerie des Alde*, 59, for surviving copies on vellum.
102. As appears from Ducas's postscript to the Alcalá grammar, sig. X3v.
103. See appendix 1, no. 55. For the date of the Complutensian Polyglot Bible, see appendix 1, no. 53.
104. BL, Arundel 526, folios 1–54, with *ex libris* on folio 55. Sgouropoulos (fl. 1443–73) made at least one other copy of Chrysoloras: Modena, Bibl. Estense, α.F.9.21 (RGK 1, no. 101).
105. BL, Arundel 526, note on folio 1.
106. A copy of appendix 1, no. 21, has on the flyleaf "Ἑνρίκος Ἀγρίκολα" (Rhodes, *Incunabula in Greece*, 37). For Hendrik, see Van der Laan and Akkerman, *Rudolf Agricola*, 310.
107. Reuchlin to Hummelberg, February 20, 1522: "Edocui nunc artem grammaticam in utraque lingua graecam Chrysolorae, hebraicam Mose Kimhi" (edited by Horawitz, "Zur Biographie und Correspondenz Johannes Reuchlins," 187).
108. For Nachtgall, see chapter 1, section "Ottomar Nachtgall."
109. Prefaced to his edition of Chalcondyles' grammar, appendix 1, no. 155, sigs. a2v–a3r.
110. Vossius repeated this judgment: "Emanuel Chrysoloras idoneus est unde discantur principia linguae graecae, nisi quod verborum formationes omittit. Plenior Demetrius Chalcondyles'" (*De arte grammatica*, 1:4, cited in Huntingford, *An Introduction to the Writing of Greek*, vii).
111. For Winther, see chapter 1, section "Johann Winther." For Thorer, see Milham, "Apicius," 325–27; Rice, "Paulus Aegineta," 161–65.
112. *Erotemata Chrysolorae. De anomalis verbis. De formatione temporum ex libro Chalcondylae. Quartus Gazae De constructione* (Venice, 1564). A copy is recorded at Gubbio (*Censimento nazionale* vol. 4, item no. 4143).
113. Grammar: Petit, Sidéridès, and Jugie, *Oeuvres complètes de Georges Scholarios*, 8:351–424. Lexicon: ibid., 425–98.
114. Padua, Bibl. Commun. C.M.938 (Bernardinello, "Gli studi propedeutici di greco," 111–14).
115. Raudnizianus X (olim VI.F.e.6), now Prague, Bibl. Univ. A watermark supplies a date of c. 1446 (Bernardinello, "Gli studi propedeutici di greco," 114n47, 120–21).
116. The two versions of this can be compared in Petit, Sidéridès, and Jugie, *Oeuvres complètes de Georges Scholarios*, 8:417–19.
117. Thirteen manuscripts are listed in Bernardinello, "Gli studi propedeutici di greco," 111–16.
118. For the nouns, see Petit, Sidéridès, and Jugie, *Oeuvres complètes de Georges Scholarios*), 8:355–76; for the verbs, see ibid., 383–411.
119. See chapter 1, section "Manuel Chrysoloras," p. 8.
120. Milan, Bibl. Ambrosiana, E.65 sup. (gr. 291), which has the lexicon and was revised and corrected by Scholarios (Petit, Sidéridès, and Jugie, *Oeuvres complètes de Georges Scholarios*, 8:ix and n2, xi; Cortesi, "Il «Vocabularium» greco di Giovanni Tortelli," 459n4 and 466). Theodore died in 1456.
121. See Cortesi, "Il «Vocabularium» greco di Giovanni Tortelli," 458–73
122. Padua, Bibl. Commun. C.M.938.
123. Some Greek marginalia seem to be in Palla's hand (Bernardinello, "Gli studi propedeutici di greco," 120–22).
124. BAV, Vat.gr.1314, dated March 12, 1449. The grammar is in folios 32v–66v. See Petit, Sidéridès, and Jugie, *Oeuvres complètes de Georges Scholarios*, 8:x–xi; Bernardinello, "Gli studi propedeutici di greco," 115; Diller, "Three Greek Scribes Working for Bessarion," 408; Mioni, "Bessarione scriba ed alcuni suoi collaboratori," 299; Centanni, "La biblioteca di Andronico Callisto," 218.
125. Venice, Bibl. Marciana, lat.14.10 (4659). See Kristeller, *Iter Italicum*, 2:262–63.
126. Madrid, Bibl. Nacional, 4854 (Andrés, *Catálogo de los códices griegos*, 471).
127. Raudnizianus X (olim VI.F.e.6): see in this section n. 115.

128. Raudnizianus X (olim VI.F.e.6), now in Prague, Bibl. Univ., is one of the few manuscripts to retain Scholarios's early name, Κουρτέζης (Petit, Sidéridès, and Jugie, *Oeuvres complètes de Georges Scholarios*, 8:x n6). Reuchlin's copy was descibed as *Georgii Cortesii grammatica scripta* (Förstel, "Jean Cuno et la grammaire grecque," 304). The Prague manuscript seems to be the only such copy surviving outside Italy.
129. For Cuno's use of the grammars of Lascaris, Gaza, and Scholarios, see Förstel, "Jean Cuno et la grammaire grecque."
130. Camariotes received the dedication of Scholarios's *De ente et essentia*, translated from Aquinas between 1444 and 1450 (Jugie in Vacant, Mangenot and Amann, eds. *Dictionnaire de théologie catholique*, XIV, part 2, cols 1551–52). His lament on the city of Constantinople has been printed, with a Latin translation, in PG 160:1060–69.
131. Modena, Bibl. Estense, α.U.2.10 (gr.10, olim ii.A.10) was copied by Camariotes (RGK 1, no. 269). It has Arrian's *Dissertationes* and Timaeus Locrus's *De natura mundi*. A note on the flyleaf reads, "Liber hic scriptus est manu clarissimi viri domini Matthaei camarioti constantinopolitani: quem mihi dono dedit Anno domini M cccc Lxxxiiii praeceptor ille optimus." Below this, deleted, is Giorgio Valla's note of ownership.
132. For Ficino's Proclus, see Saffrey, "Notes platoniciennes de Marsile Ficin." For a summary of Camariotes' career and works, see Biedl, "Matthaeus Camariotes," and see also Saffrey, "Nouveaux manuscrits."
133. A *Synopsis rhetorica* has also been ascribed to him, edited in Walz, *Rhetores Graeci ex codicibus*, 6:546–98 and PG 160:1019–60. The ascription is very uncertain: see Walz, *Rhetores Graeci ex codicibus*, 6:544–45. The compendium from Hermogenes is edited in ibid. 6:601–4; the work from the *Progymnasmata* is in ibid. 1:121–26.
134. I have not seen Athos, ms. 4216, described in Lampros, *Catalogue of the Greek Manuscripts*, 2:18–19. The possibility that the other manuscript, Oxford, Bodleian, Auct.F.6.26 (misc. 120), is an autograph is raised in Wilson, "Greek Grammars," 78. An image from the grammar, showing the declension of Αἴας, is in ibid. 78, figure 53. Camariotes' hand is well documented: facsimiles are in Astruc, "La fin inédite," plates 30 and 31; Astruc, "Manuscrits autographes," plate 12; Harlfinger, *Specimena Griechischen Kopisten*, plates 39–41; RGK 1, no. 269; RGK 1, part c, plate 269.
135. Oxford, Bodleian, Auct.F.6.26, folios 28v, 29r.
136. Ibid., folios 10r–26r.
137. Monfasani states that he was born c. 1415 ("L'insegnamento di Teodoro Gaza a Ferrara," 5). Bianca believes he was born c. 1408 to 1410 ("Gaza, Teodoro," 737). A letter of October 1440, written by Filelfo to Gaza, implies that Gaza had not long before arrived from Constantinople (Legrand, *Cent-dix lettres greques de F. Filelfo*, 40–41).
138. Monfasani, "L'insegnamento di Teodoro Gaza a Ferrara," 5.
139. As appears from Filelfo, letter of October 1440 (Legrand, *Cent-dix lettres greques de F. Filelfo*, 40–41).
140. Bianca, "Gaza, Teodoro," 738.
141. For the texts that he taught at Ferrara, see chapter 3, sections "Homer," "Aristophanes," "Xenophon," "Demosthenes," "Plato," and "Sophocles."
142. Edited by Mohler, *Kardinal Bessarion*, 253–59.
143. Bianca, "Gaza, Teodoro," 739.
144. Monfasani, "L'insegnamento di Teodoro Gaza a Ferrara,"12; Bianca, "Gaza, Teodoro," 739.
145. "... ea nos ad duorum ipsius authoris exemplorum constantiam et fidem emendasse, quorum alterum Baptistae Guarini fuit, Ferrariae Gaza docente descriptum, alterum vero Codri Urcei Bononiensis" (Moschopoulos, *Grammaticae artis graecae methodus*, sig. a3r).
146. See chapter 1, section "Manuel Chrysoloras," p. 9.
147. See in this section, n. 151.
148. "ἐν ‘Ρώμῃ ... ὅπου κάλλιστα τὴν γραμματικὴν συνέστειλεν εἰς τέσσαρα διελών" (PG 161: 933). For the date of this preface, see chapter 1, section "Constantine Lascaris," p. 28 and n. 307.

149. Bianca, "Gaza, Teodoro," 739.
150. Leone, "Le lettere di Teodoro Gaza," 206.
151. C. Lascaris wrote a letter to Gaza at Policastro, undated, but in the spring of 1462 (PG 161: 960–61; Laurent and Guillou, Le «Liber Visitationis» d'Athanase Chalkéopoulos (1457–1458), 199–200; Martínez-Manzano, Konstantinos Laskaris, 167–68). Gaza wrote to Alexios from Policastro on September 8, probably 1462 (edited by Mohler, Kardinal Bessarion, 3:585–86; Leone, "Le lettere di Teodoro Gaza," 206).
152. His movements in 1463 are based on two letters, both *sine anno*: see Legrand, Cent-dix lettres greques de F. Filelfo, 334–40; Leone, "Le lettere di Teodoro Gaza," 207; Bianca, "Gaza, Teodoro," 741–42. Bessarion became patriarch on March 15, 1463 (Monfasani, "Bessarion Latinus," 171).
153. Bianca, "Gaza, Teodoro," 741.
154. Legrand, Bibliographie hellénique, 1:xxxvi n1; Legrand, Cent-dix lettres greques de F. Filelfo, 331–32; Leone, "Le lettere di Teodoro Gaza," 209; Bianca, "Gaza, Teodoro," 741–42.
155. Gaza wrote to Alexios of his intention to leave Rome in a letter dated March 29, [1474] (Leone, "Le lettere di Teodoro Gaza," 217; edited in Mohler, Kardinal Bessarion, 3:582–83). Soon after April 27, 1474, Gaza wrote to Alexios, confirming that he was to leave Rome (Leone, "Le lettere di Teodoro Gaza," 217–18; edited in Mohler, Kardinal Bessarion, 583–85). On May 19, 1475, Gaza's version of pseudo-Aristotle, Problemata, was printed in Rome. The editor, Gupalatinus, says Gaza revised it. See Bianca, "Gaza, Teodoro," 740; Legrand, Bibliographie hellénique, 1:xlii.
156. Apostolis: Mohler, Kardinal Bessarion, 3:169, lines 18–21; Callistus: ibid., 3:201, lines 28–31. These references were first noticed in Monfasani, "Theodore Gaza as a Philosopher," 272n18.
157. Cammelli, "Andronico Callisto," 115.
158. The letter is edited in Powell, "Two Letters." It was written after Chalcondyles' election to the chair at Padua (Cammelli, Demetrio Calcondila, 27–28) and before Filelfo's letter to Callistus at Rome (Legrand, Cent-dix lettres greques de F. Filelfo, 123–25).
159. For Callistus's copy of Scholarios's grammar, see chapter 1, section "George Scholarios." For his copy of Apollonius, see chapter 1, section "Ancient and Byzantine Greek Grammatical Works." For his correspondence with Filelfo, see ibid., and in the present section, p. 17.
160. For Greek grammatical works in the Vatican Library in 1455, see Devreesse, Le fonds grec, 33–35.
161. The letter of June 13, *sine anno* is in Legrand, Cent-dix lettres greques de F. Filelfo, 339–40; for the year, see Bianca, "Gaza, Teodoro," 741.
162. None of the grammatical works listed in the inventories of 1455 or 1475 appear to be Gaza's work. Callistus seems to have owned BAV, Vat.gr.13, copied by George Hermonymus (Mercati and Cavalieri, Codices vaticani graeci, 10; RGK 3, no. 102). He added marginalia to this copy (Centanni, "La biblioteca di Andronico Callisto," 217; RGK 1, no. 18). It has some Latin verses on the Greek declensions appended. Demetrius Trivolis copied a single leaf of this manuscript (Vat.gr.13, folios 22r-v, RGK 1, no. 103), perhaps a repair after it had left Callistus's possession. Trivolis was in Corfu in 1462, apparently in Rome from at least 1469 to 1472, and in Corfu again in 1481. His hand appears in a manuscript of several *opuscula* of Gaza (Florence, Bibl. Laurenziana, 55.9, folios 82–86v), of which the first item, De mensibus, was copied by Joannes Rhosos at Rome in 1471: see Speranzi, "L'Anonymus Δ-Καί." Trivolis also copied Florence, Bibl. Laurenziana, 55.16 of Gaza (RGK 1, no. 103).
163. Hody, De graecis illustribus linguae graecae, 72. For a manuscript that might have misled Hody, see this section, n. 165.
164. Madrid, Bibl. Nacional, 4635. For a description, see Andrés, Catálogo de los códices griegos, 165–68, who dates this portion of the manuscript c. 1463. It was seen at Milan by Bartolomeo Bardella, for whom see Martínez-Manzano, Konstantinos Laskaris, 291–93.
165. Nürnberg, Stadtbibliothek, Norimb. Cent.V, App. 49a. See Harlfinger and others, Graecogermania, 98. Kalatzi dates the manuscript c. 1470–73 on palaeographical grounds (Kalatzi,

"Georgios Hermonymos," 244–45). Regiomontanus went to Italy and Rome with Bessarion in 1461 and on to Venice in 1465; by 1467, he was in Hungary (Bietenholz and Deutscher, *Contemporaries of Erasmus*, 3:134–35).

166. Padua, Bibl. Seminarii, 40, dated by Rhosos February 1, 1467, probably 1468 new style (Mioni, *Catalogo*, 1:241; Mancini, "Codices graeci patavini," 158–59).
167. Venice, Bibl. Marciana, gr.625, which has a watermark dated 1468 to 1470 by Bricquet. For Vitali, see RGK 1, no. 375; 3, no. 603.
168. Rhusotas made BL, Harl.5641, Modena, Bibl. Estense, α.P.5.16 and Perugia, Perus.d.3 of Gaza (RGK 1, no. 154). The first of these was not owned by Pier Candido Decembrio (*pace* British Library, *Summary Catalogue*, 150), but by the monk Pietro Candido, and may belong to the 1490s. I am grateful to David Speranzi for this information. Rhusotas made two copies of Chrysoloras: Wolfenbüttel, Guelf.38.3 August 4o and Oxford, Bodleian, D'Orv. 114.
169. Shirwood's copy is Cambridge, UL, Ii.4.16, bought by Thomas Gale from the estate of Meric Casaubon (Weiss, *Humanism in England*, 152; Oates, *Cambridge University Library*, 412–13). Madrid, Bibl. Nacional, 4590, subscribed in Rome on March 22, 1481 (Andrés, *Catálogo de los códices griegos*, 77–78). Cambridge, King's College, ms. 10, part 2, folios 1–5, and Oxford, Bodleian, Bywater 35 (RGK 1, no. 178). BAV, Ottob.gr.52, for which see Feron and Battaglini, *Codices manuscripti graeci ottoboniani*, 36; complete by 1475 because it has a marginal note in Callistus's hand (folio 37v; RGK 3, nos. 31 and 298). PBN, gr.2585 (Omont, *Inventaire-sommaire*, 3:8; RGK 2, no. 237).
170. BL, Add.18492, copied c. 1470–73. The title was copied by George Trivizias and the volume may have come from the same scriptorium as another copy of the work made by Trivizias, BL, Harl. 6290: see this section, n. 181, and Kalatzi, "Georgios Hermonymos," 162–64.
171. For a discussion and sample of Gaza's grammar, see Robins, *The Byzantine Grammarians*, 253–61.
172. In the fifteenth century, Aldus, Chalcondyles, and Urbano did so: see chapter 1, sections "Aldus Manutius," "Demetrius Chalcondyles," and "Urbano Bolzanio."
173. These debts are traced in Donnet, "Théodore de Gaza," 133–55; Donnet, "Théodore de Gaza et Apollonius Dyscolus," 619–29.
174. Callistus's letter is implied by Filelfo's letters, which are in Legrand, *Cent-dix lettres greques de F. Filelfo*, 80–82, 83–84. Filelfo calls Syncellus "Lecapenus" a common confusion, for the origins of which see Donnet, "La tradition imprimée," 476–77. I have not found the words in Syncellus.
175. See Cammelli, "Andronico Callisto," 111–12.
176. Donnet showed that, for his grammar, Gaza used a copy of Syncellus that belonged to the family headed by Florence, Bibl. Laurenziana, S.Marco.314 (Donnet, "Théodore de Gaza," 147). This was Gaza's manuscript, according to Ullman and Stadter, *The Public Library of Renaissance Florence*, 266; after Rostagno and Festa, "Indice dei codici greci," 33*. Donnet is more circumspect about Gaza's ownership (*Le traité de la construction de la phrase de Michel le Syncelle*, 74). It was later used for the *editio princeps* of Syncellus in 1515 (Donnet, "La tradition imprimée," 473).
177. For Merula, see Wilson, *From Byzantium to Italy*, 117; for Argino, see Filelfo's letter of March 21, 1465 (Filelfo, *Francisci Philelfi . . . epistolarum familiarum libri xxxvii*, folios 167r–v) and Cosenza, *Biographical and Bibliographical Dictionary*, 1:293.
178. Harris, *Greek Emigres in the West, 1400–1520*, 134.
179. He was in Canterbury by March 1469, where he subsequently taught Greek, perhaps before he became prior, September 10, 1472 (Weiss, *Humanism in England*, 154–57 and n6; Clough, "Selling [Celling, Tyll], William," 723).
180. Dursos copied Florence, Bibl. Laurenziana, 55.14, 1–42v (RGK 1, no. 9). Demetrius Damilas wrote folios 43–196 of this manuscript (RGK 1, no. 93).
181. Trivizias copied Gaza's work in BAV, Ottob.gr.55 (RGK 3, no. 123), and made BL, Harl.6290, folios 1–146 (see this section, n. 170). To this manuscript Bravus added folios 146v–151r, a short work on the dialects attributed to Moschopulos, which he subscribed at Padua, June

3, *sine anno*. (RGK 1, no. 345; British Library, *Summary Catalogue*, 196). Bravus directed an undated invective against one Andronicus, probably Andronicus Contoblacas, for whom see Monfasani, "In Praise of Ognibene and Blame of Guarino." The invective is edited in Hankins, "Renaissance Crusaders," 203–4, where its target is said to be Callistus. Girolamo Avanzi of Verona notes Bravus's contribution to the text of Catullus in the preface to his commentary on the poet, first published in Venice in 1495 (Hausmann, "Carmina Priapea," 436). For Bravus, see also Cengarle, "Ps. Moschopuli compendium," 234 and n27.

182. Trivizias copied BAV, Ottob.gr.198 of Gaza's grammar (RGK 1, no. 123). For Bonamico's notes in this manuscript, see Feron and Battaglini, *Codices manuscripti graeci ottoboniani*, 116; for his biography, see Avesani, "Bonamico."
183. Cammelli, "Andronico Callisto," 190–91; Reeve, "Classical Scholarship," 35.
184. See Avezzù, "ΑΝΔΡΟΝΙΚΙΑ ΓΡΑΜΜΑΤΑ," 87 and n34. For Valla's connection to a copy of Chrysoloras in Milan, ca. 1462–65, see chapter 1, section "Manuel Chrysoloras."
185. See chapter 1, section "Demetrius Chalcondyles."
186. Phill.2356. RGK 1, no. 105.
187. Reuchlin studied under Chalcondyles at Florence and Milan: "Basileae primum . . . deinde Parisiis . . . post Romae . . . ad extremum Florentiae Mediolanique a Demetrio Chalcondyle, graecorum linguam frustillatim et quasi micas de mensa domini cadentes, accepi" (*De rudimentis hebraicis*, edited in Geiger, *Johann Reuchlins Briefwechsel*, 96). Linacre was at Florence from 1487 to 1491 and perhaps until 1494. In 1488, Grocyn resigned as reader in divinity at Magdalen College, Oxford, and went to Italy. Both men studied in Florence for at least two years under Chalcondyles and Poliziano (EE 2:441–42; DNB; Tilley, "Greek Studies in England," 221–22).
188. For Chalcondyles' reluctance to teach beginners, see chapter 1, section "Demetrius Chalcondyles." The edition of Chrysoloras is appendix 1, no. 9.
189. Perosa, "Due lettere inedite del Poliziano," 352–55. Piero was born February 15, 1472.
190. Woodward, *Vittorino da Feltre and Other Humanist Educators*, 225n2. For Poliziano's use of Gaza in his commentary on the *Odyssey*, see Martinelli, "Grammatiche greche," 281–83.
191. Legrand, *Bibliographie hellénique*, 1:xcix.
192. Milan, Bibl. Ambrosiana, G.26 sup. (gr. 388). This has the following note inside the cover: "MCCCCLXXXIIII ~ Iste liber est Bernardi Nerli Tanais, die xv Februarii ~ Quem emi σ.46 β.10" (Martini and Bassi, *Catalogus codicum graecorum*). The date February 15, 1484, *stylo florentino*, is February 15, 1485, new style. Chalcondyles' verses are in Legrand, *Bibliographie hellénique*, 1:xli. Gaza died in Calabria in 1475 or 1476 and left most of his books to Chalcondyles. In May 1477, Chalcondyles began legal proceedings to acquire these books: see Dorez, "Un document."
193. For the fortunes of Callistus's library, see Motta, "Demetrio Calcondila editore," 154; Legrand, *Bibliographie hellénique*, 1:liv–lv; Cammelli, "Andronico Callisto," 202–11. On September 1, 1483, Ermolao Barbaro wrote to Giorgio Merula from Venice: "Libros Andronici non haberi amplius istic [i.e., Mediolano] doleo, quanquam si verum est pervenisse illos in manus Pici nostri minus moleste fero" (edited in Branca, *Ermolao Barbaro, 1454–1493*, 1:44).
194. See this section, p. 16 and n. 162.
195. It accompanied a letter of February 1478 old style, edited by Omont, "Georges Hermonyme de Sparte," 88–89; Rhein, dall'Asta, and Dörner, *Johannes Reuchlin*, 1:26–27.
196. Hermonymus copied Albi ms.71, BL, Burn.76, PBN, gr.2586, PBN, gr.2587 (Toussain's copy), Aix-en-Provence, Bibl. Méjanes, Aquensis 1385 (1229), and BAV, Reg.gr.148, all of book 1. He copied PBN, suppl.558 of book 2 (Omont, "Georges Hermonyme de Sparte," 87–89; Kalatzi, "Georgios Hermonymos," 180–81, 261–62).
197. Sandys, *From the Revival of Learning*, 62.
198. Besides Lascaris's manuscript noted previously, ca. 1485, Lascaris made excerpts from the third book of Gaza's grammar in Madrid, Bibl. Nacional, 4615 (Andrés, *Catálogo de los códices griegos*, 123–24). In the late fifteenth century, someone, possibly a pupil of Lascaris,

made Madrid, Bibl. Nacional, 4576, which contains *inter alia* the fourth book of Gaza's grammar in Greek (ibid., 57).
199. For an account of Vitelli's movements, see Trapp, "Vitelli, Cornelio." Serbopoulos made Dublin, Trinity College, 925 (RGK 1, no. 180).
200. Cambridge, Trinity College, R.9.22 (823) (RGK 1, no. 180).
201. Oxford, New College, 254, which also contains Isocrates. See RGK 1, no. 180. Serbopoulos also made two undated manuscripts of Gaza in England: Oxford, Bodleian, gr.class.e.96 (RGK 1, no. 180; Wilson, "Greek Grammars," 78) and Oxford, Bodleian, 36205 (Madan and Craster, *Summary Catalogue*, 428).
202. Musurus taught at Padua from 1503 to 1509, at Venice from 1512 to 1516, and at Rome from 1516 to 1517 (Bietenholz and Deutscher, *Contemporaries of Erasmus*, 2:472–73). BAV, Vat.gr.1377 has Gaza's grammar, Gregory of Corinth's *De dialectis*, and Phrynichus. A note on folio 153 (Gaza's fourth book) reads, "Gaza a nostro Musuro reprehenditur hoc in loco" (De Nolhac, *La bibliothèque de Fulvio Orsini*, 348n140; Fischer, *Die Ekloge des Phrynichos*, 3). Lazzaro Bonamico's manuscript of Gaza, BAV, Ottob.gr.198, may have been connected with his studies under Musurus: see Feron and Battaglini, *Codices manuscripti graeci ottoboniani*, 116. BAV, Vat.gr.1405 is two manuscripts bound as one: the second is Gaza's grammar, annotated by Forteguerri (De Nolhac, *La bibliothèque de Fulvio Orsini*, 179). Bartolomeo Comparini copied much of this manuscript (RGK 3, no. 58). For Musurus's annotated copy of the *editio princeps* of Gaza's grammar, see this section, n. 210.
203. Appendix 1, no. 16.
204. *De fructu qui ex doctrina percipitur*, edited in Manley and Sylvester, *De fructu qui ex doctrina percipitur*, 94. Only the 1495 Aldine edition combined these texts before 1518. For Pace, see Curtis, "Pace, Richard (1483?–1536)."
205. The catalogs are reproduced in Orlandi, *Aldo Manuzio editore*, 2: plates IX and X–XIII.
206. For Urbano's grammar, see chapter 1, section "Urbano Bolzanio."
207. Urbano's grammar appears in the Aldine catalog of 1503 but not in the catalog of 1513.
208. ISTC ig00110000.
209. A note reads, "1496 die ultimo februarii haec opera accepi ego Antonius Vicens dono ab Aldo Romano Mo. quem diu nobis immortalis deus servet" (sig. MM4r). It is at the Harry Ransom Humanities Research Center in Texas (Kallendorf and Wells, *Aldine Press Books*, 54).
210. BAV, Inc.II.128 and BAV, Inc.II.152 (Sheehan, *Incunabula*, 2:540). Sheehan and his predecessors attribute the marginalia in BAV, Inc.II.128 to Janus Lascaris, but they are by Musurus: see Pagliaroli, "Nuovi autografi di Marco Musuro," 356–62. I am grateful to David Speranzi for bringing this to my attention.
211. Venice, Bibl. Marciana, gr.10.10 (1230). See Marcotte, "La bibliothèque de Jean Calphurnius," 192, 195.
212. De Nolhac, *Les correspondants d'Alde Manuce*, 22, letter no. 17. For Clario, see Orlandi, *Aldo Manuzio editore*, 2:327n1.
213. Salamanca, Inc.128, which has the following note: "Ego Fernandus Nugnius Pincianus Comendatarius ordinis divi Iacobi emi hunc codicem Bononiae praecio unius nummi aurei cum dimidio" (Codoñer, Merino, and Malvadi, *Biblioteca y epistolario de Hernán Núñez de Guzmán*, 4). For the date of purchase, see ibid., 11–12.
214. Oates, *A Catalogue of the Fifteenth-Century Printed Books*, item no. 2166, and see ibid., p. 5. Bullock was a fellow of Queens' College in 1506; his version of a work of Lucian was printed at Cambridge in 1521; he was vice-chancellor of the university from 1524 to 1525, and died in 1526 (Firmin-Didot, *Alde Manuce et l'Hellénisme à Venise*, 602–3; Bietenholz and Deutscher, *Contemporaries of Erasmus*, 1:220).
215. It is now at Shrewsbury school: see Oates, *A Catalogue of the Fifteenth-Century Printed Books*, 49.
216. BL, Arundel 550, folios 17r–24v.
217. Utrecht, University Library, no. 1532 (Tiele, *Catalogus codicum manu scriptorum*, 1:354). For the Amorbachs, see EE 2:66–67, 237.

218. See this section, p. 22.
219. Lefèvre graduated with a master's degree in Paris in 1504 at the age of sixteen and seems to have begun teaching there immediately: "Robertus du Gast, Cocqueretici primarius, eum [*sc.* Fabrum] post annum revocavit; et ille, praeter publicam grammatices explanationem, Theodorus Gazam interpretatus est; quae prima fere fuit Atticae linguae in Academiam Parisiensem introductio" (Égasse du Boulay, *Historia Universitatis Parisiensis*, 928–29).
220. See chapter 1, section "Manuel Chrysoloras," p. 10.
221. Appendix 1, no. 38.
222. To Ammonius, October 16, 1511. EE 1:472–73, letter no. 233. See Tilley, "Greek Studies in England," 227.
223. For Fox's program of Greek studies, set out in the statutes, see Ward, *The Foundation Statutes*, 101. His donation of books to Corpus Christi in 1519 included a copy of Gaza's grammar (Sotheby's, *Early Printed Books*, 76).
224. *De ratione studii* seems to have been extant in some form by 1498. It was first printed, without Erasmus's consent, in Paris on October 20, 1511: see Margolin, *De ratione studi*, 89–96, 113–46 (expanded text), 147–51 (shorter text). This quotation is ibid., 148, and see 114.
225. For the date of this work, see appendix 1, no. 49.
226. Edited in Omont, "Essai sur les débuts de la typographie grecque à Paris," 70.
227. See EE 2:497. For Rescius, see Roersch, "Un bon ouvrier."
228. Appendix 1, nos. 71 (Gaza) and 73 (*Tabulae*).
229. Hoven, "Enseignement du grec," 81.
230. Appendix 1, no. 77. It was revised and issued by Froben a few months later: see appendix 1, no. 79.
231. For Caesarius, see De Vocht, *History of the Foundation*, 281n2; Nauert, "Caius Plinius Secundus," 363–67. He travelled to Italy in December 1508 with the Count of Neuenahr and studied Greek at Bologna (EE 2:172).
232. Glareanus matriculated at Cologne in 1506 (EE 2:279).
233. Ibid., 282.
234. Mosellanus matriculated at Cologne on January 2, 1512 (ibid., 517). In 1517, he dedicated to Caesarius an edition of Aristophanes' *Plutus* (Hagenau: Anshelm). For Aristophanes in Germany, see chapter 3, section "Aristophanes."
235. March 20, 1515 (Woolfson, "Croke, Richard (1489–1558)," 266).
236. EE 2:264. Erasmus later echoed these words, writing that he made his version of Gaza "ut plures alliceremus ad studium graecanici sermonis vel ipsa facilitate velut esca quadam" (EE 1:9, January 30, 1523). See also Erasmus's second preface to Caesarius, EE 3:215.
237. "Ad haec titulis distinximus et annotatiunculis additis nonnihil lucis addidimus . . ." (EE 2:265).
238. This story is told in Rhenanus's preface to the *Colloquia*, which are printed with Erasmus's version and the Greek text (appendix 1, no. 79, sig. Q1r). Erasmus seems to have complained that Martens's interests had been damaged by Froben's reprint of November 1516: see Rhenanus's letter to Erasmus of 24 April 1517 (EE 2:549–50).
239. I know of five such combinations before 1530: appendix 1, nos. 40 (Venice, 1512), 55 (Alcalá, 1514), 58 (Florence, 1515), 78 (Florence, 1516) and 85 (Venice, 1517).
240. He began teaching on June 19. Delaruelle, "L'étude du grec à Paris de 1514 à 1530," 52n2; Paquier, *Jérôme Aléandre*, 49.
241. Sheppard, "Richard Croke," 14.
242. See Bietenholz and Deutscher, *Contemporaries of Erasmus*, 1:359; EE 1:19; ibid., letter nos. 221, 222, 256.
243. Woolfson, "Croke, Richard (1489–1558)," 266.
244. On April 16, 1515, Croke was voted ten florins if he would give two lectures in Leipzig (Boehme, *De litteratura lipsiensi opuscula academica*, 187). In October, he wrote the preface to his edition of Ausonius at Leipzig.
245. See appendix 1, no. 75.

246. In a speech of 1518 or 1519, Croke announced to his students at Cambridge that the bishop had given him sixty gold pieces for this dedication (Croke, *Orationes Richardi Croci duae*, sig. b3r).
247. For Amoenus, see Bietenholz and Deutscher, *Contemporaries of Erasmus*, 1:51. I know of no such edition.
248. For Croke's return to England, see EE 2:517–19; 3:142, note to line 29. For his *Introductiones*, see appendix 1, no. 108.
249. Appendix 1, no. 90.
250. He owned a copy of book one of Gaza's grammar in Hermonymus's hand: see this section, p. 19, n. 196.
251. Appendix 1, no. 120.
252. "Studium in hoc nostrum fuit Aldum ipsum ut possemus imitari, qui latinam in grammaticam Constantini Lascaris interpretationem αὐτολεξεὶ e regione edidit" (appendix 1, no. 120, sig. a1v).
253. Appendix 1, no. 140, sig. A1v.
254. This is the text from PG 161:938–39; the text of the postscript in the printed edition of c. 1489 is identical; a similar statement is found in the preface to *De nomine et verbo* in the first Aldine edition. Lascaris took the Delian diver from the Suda (edited by Adler, *Suidae Lexicon*, 2:37) or from the Suda's source, Diogenes Laertius, *Lives of the Philosophers*, 2.22 and 9.12.
255. Orlandi, *Aldo Manuzio editore*, 1:8.
256. Ibid., 1:7.
257. Appendix 1, no. 68, preface.
258. Appendix 1, no. 120, sig. a2r. Croke's orations on the value of Greek learning had just been printed in Paris in 1520.
259. Appendix 1, no. 120, sig. a2r. For Giustiniani, see Cevolotto, "Giustiniani, Agostino."
260. Appendix 1, no. 140, sig. A1v. For the "proverb," see Plautus, *Poenulus*, lines 435–36: "Oedipo opust coniectore."
261. Appendix 1, no. 140, sigs. A1v–A2r.
262. Appendix 1, no. 145, sig. aa2r.
263. Appendix 1, no. 155, sig. a2v. Stephanus quotes this judgment in his *Dialogus de bene instituendis graecae linguae studiis* of 1587, p. 41. For the quotation, see Stevens, "How the French Humanists of the Renaissance Learned Greek," 245n17.
264. Appendix 1, no. 155, sig. a2v.
265. This is from Stevens, "How the French Humanists of the Renaissance Learned Greek," 244, where he cites Chauvain and Roersch, *Étude sur la vie et les travaux de Nicolas Clénard*, 76–77.
266. "Gaza in quarto libro difficillime praecipit atque obscurissime, secutus Apollonium, et ipsum in primis tenebricosum" (cited in Hody, *De graecis illustribus linguae graecae*, 75).
267. Appendix 1, no. 167, sigs. A1v–A2r.
268. The grammar was printed with a commentary by Gerasinus of Byzantium at Venice by A. Bortoli in 1757. The nineteenth-century edition is of the grammar alone: Θεωδώρου τοῦ Γαζῆ γραμματικῆς εἰσαγωγῆς βιβλία τέσσαρα, Venice, 1807.
269. For Lascaris's biography, see De Rosalia, "La vita di Costantino Lascaris"; Fernández Pomar, "La colección de Uceda"; Martínez-Manzano, *Konstantinos Laskaris*, 6–32.
270. June 13, 1451 (Filelfo, *Epistolare Francisci Philelfi*, sig. t3r). Donato studied Greek at Florence under Francesco da Castiglione and later under Joannes Argyropoulos (Vespasiano, edited in Greco, *Vespasiano da Bisticci*, 2:25).
271. Fernández Pomar, "La colección de Uceda," 218–19.
272. This was not printed until c. 1502 in the second Aldine edition of Lascaris's grammar (appendix 1, no. 26). For the treatise, see Martínez-Manzano, *Konstantinos Laskaris*, 233.
273. The work, apparently a summary of pseudo-Plutarch on the Homeric dialects, has never been printed. The preface is in PG 161:953–54, reprinted in Martínez-Manzano, *Konstantinos Laskaris*, 235.
274. As he states in the postscript to his grammatical works, for which see Legrand, *Bibliographie hellénique*, 1:lxxxv.

275. Filelfo first wrote to Castreno on January 21, 1458, encouraging him to come to Milan. He reinforced the invitation on March 1, 1458 (letters in Legrand, *Cent-dix lettres greques de F. Filelfo*, 99–102). Castreno arrived shortly afterward, and his private teaching at Milan appears from the document of October 9, 1462, edited in Motta, "Demetrio Calcondila editore," 161–62.
276. Cammelli, *Demetrio Calcondila*, 101. The document is in Motta, "Demetrio Calcondila editore," 161–62.
277. Ibid., 103. The documents are in Motta, "Demetrio Calcondila editore," 145–49, 162–63.
278. The list of signatories was published by Motta, "Demetrio Calcondila editore," 147–49. It has been edited again in Friggi, *Gli studi greci a Milano al tempo di Ludovico il Moro*, 33–37. Friggi prints for the first time a shorter, undated petition to the same end: ibid., 38–39. The relationship between the two petitions is unclear.
279. For Decembrio, see Viti, "Decembrio, Pier Candido."
280. For Birago, see Miglio, "Birago, Lampugnino."
281. For Crivelli, see Petrucci, "Crivelli, Lodrisio," 149–50; for the translation, see chapter 3, section "Pseudo-Orpheus."
282. Percival, "The Place of the *Rudimenta Grammatices*," 236. Bartolomeo, who studied under Lorenzo Valla in Rome, wrote his grammar between Valla's death in August 1457 and his consecration as bishop of Sulmona in October 1463 (Percival, "The *Artis Grammaticae Opusculum* of Bartolomeo Sulmonese," 43).
283. Percival, "The *Artis Grammaticae Opusculum* of Bartolomeo Sulmonese," 41 and n13.
284. This letter is in Milan, Bibl. Ambrosiana, gr.87, folios 23r–24v, edited in Martínez-Manzano, *Konstantinos Laskaris*, 109–11. Relations between Lascaris and Filelfo may have improved a few years later: see chapter 3, section "Hesiod," p. 101 and n. 392, and chapter 3, section "Apollonius of Rhodes," p. 109 and n. 536.
285. For Calco, see Stumpo, "Calco, Bartolomeo," and chapter 3, section "Aesop," p. 80. For Gregorio's movements, see Pagliaroli, "Gregorio da Città di Castello." The presence of both Lascaris and Castreno in Milan from 1458 did not prevent an attempt to bring Gregorio back to Milan in 1459.
286. Filelfo's letter encourages Filippo to return to Milan now that the plague has passed: "ἡ γὰρ ἀκαδημία ἡμῶν λυπεῖται τῇ σῇ ἀπουσίᾳ. ἐλθὲ γοῦν σὺν θεῷ μὴ βραδέως, τὰ ἡμῶν καὶ Συμπόσια συγκομίσας" (edited in Legrand, *Cent-dix lettres greques de F. Filelfo*, 59–60). This refers to Filelfo's *Convivia*, in which Domenico Feruffini appears as an interlocutor. Filelfo wrote to Filippo's father, Giovanni, in 1439 and 1447 (Legrand, *Cent-dix lettres greques de F. Filelfo*, 60n1). A manuscript with a variant of Lascaris's grammar, Milan, Bibl. Ambrosiana, C.16 sup. (gr. 170), has a note on folio IIv: ιωνις ἰακώβοὶ φερούφηνοῖ ἀρκιγραμαθεοῖ [corr. ἀρκιγραμαθεαῖ] τοῦ λοῦδουικοῦ. Beneath is written, "Ferre feruffino propera mea musa salutem: / Namque mei proprio nomine saluus erit . . ." (Martini and Bassi, *Catalogus codicum graecorum*, 1:182–83). For Domenico, Filippo, and Giovanni Feruffini, see Spinelli, "Feruffini, Domenico," "Feruffini, Filippo," and "Feruffini, Giovanni."
287. Their request is recorded in Lascaris's postscript to Περὶ ὀνόματος καὶ ῥήματος, for which see Legrand, *Bibliographie hellénique*, 1:lxxxv.
288. Martínez-Manzano, *Konstantinos Laskaris*, 15. Valla owned two manuscripts of Lascaris's grammar, both now at Modena: Bibl. Estense, α.W.2.8, which has *De nomine*, and Bibl. Estense, α.R.7.22, which has *De verbo* (Martínez-Manzano, *Konstantinos Laskaris*, 226). Valla seems to have used copies of the grammars of Chrysoloras and Scholarios: see chapter 1, section "Manuel Chrysoloras," and chapter 1, section "George Scholarios."
289. Legrand prints the dedicatory letter to the manuscript of Lascaris's *Compendium*, now PBN, gr.2590 (*Bibliographie hellénique*, I:lxxii). Lascaris may have written only the Greek part of the manuscript (Martínez-Manzano, *Konstantinos Laskaris*, 184–85). Legrand's belief that he tutored Ippolyta is repeated in Fraenkel, "Introduction," 14–15; Manoussakas and Staikos, *The Publishing Activity of the Greeks*, 56; and Martínez-Manzano, *Konstantinos Laskaris*, 13, 184. Motta disputed it ("Demetrio Calcondila editore," 151–52). A fine copy of Lascaris's

grammatical works, Milan, Bibl. Trivulziana, ms. 2147, belonged to Gian Galeazzo Sforza. It was made between 1475 and 1476, after Lascaris had left Milan (Motta, "Demetrio Calcondila editore," 153; Pellegrin, *La bibliothèque*, 380).

290. See Legrand, *Bibliographie hellénique*, 1:lxxiii–lxxv. For Mombrizio, see chapter 3, section "Hesiod," p. 102.
291. Motta, "Demetrio Calcondila editore," 152. Fernando's letter is in Legrand, *Bibliographie hellénique*, 1:lxxvi–lxxviii.
292. This appears from an overlooked variant of the postscript to Περὶ ὀνόματος καὶ ῥήματος, printed at Vicenza, c. 1489, and apparently composed not long after leaving Naples. See appendix 1, no. 11, and in this section, n. 311.
293. De Rosalia, "La vita di Costantino Lascaris," 36–37; but see also Martínez-Manzano, *Konstantinos Laskaris*, 21.
294. Lascaris made his will August 15, 1501, and probably died shortly afterward.
295. This development is described in Martínez-Manzano, *Konstantinos Laskaris*, 192–93.
296. For a description and a sample of Lascaris's grammar, see Robins, *The Byzantine Grammarians*, 247–53. For the nouns, see appendix 1, no. 26, sigs. α3r–α6r, and Martínez-Manzano, *Konstantinos Laskaris*, 188–89.
297. For the verbs, see appendix 1, no. 26, sigs. α7v–β8v, and Martínez-Manzano, *Konstantinos Laskaris*, 189–90. His scheme is that of Dionysius Thrax, Chrysoloras, and Scholarios.
298. Madrid, Bibl. Nacional, 4689 (Martínez-Manzano, *Konstantinos Laskaris*, 191; Andrés, *Catálogo de los códices griegos*, 247–49).
299. Martínez-Manzano, *Konstantinos Laskaris*, 191.
300. Ibid., 191, 232–33. For this work, see chapter 1, section "Ancient and Byzantine Greek Grammatical Works," pp. 4–5.
301. Martínez-Manzano, *Konstantinos Laskaris*, 192.
302. Περὶ σοφῶν ἀνδρῶν βραχυτάτη συνόψις ἐκ τοῦ Σουδᾶ ἐκγραφεῖσα, now Madrid, Bibl. Nacional, 4621, folios 37r–99v, perhaps made at Milan, c. 1463 (Andrés, *Catálogo de los códices griegos*, 138–40).
303. Madrid, Bibl. Nacional, 4621, folios 12–21, 24–34, 101–12 (Andrés, *Catálogo de los códices griegos*, 138–42). The extracts from Plutarch were translated into Greek from a Latin text.
304. Sicilian writers, edited in PG 161:915–24: "Nos quotquot potuimus ex Laertio, Philostrato, Suida aliisque veterum monumentis carptim collectos in hoc notavimus compendio . . ." (916–17). Calabrian writers, edited in PG 161:923–28: "Ego in compendium viros litteris ac virtute insignes . . . congeram" (923).
305. See chapter 1, section "Ancient and Byzantine Greek Grammatical Works."
306. He abbreviated it at Messina according to the epilogue edited in PG 161: 937–38, also edited in Martínez-Manzano, *Konstantinos Laskaris*, 224. In the epilogue printed at Vicenza c. 1489, Lascaris says that he did this at Naples. For the edition of c. 1489, see appendix 1, no. 11.
307. No printed edition of Lascaris's grammar includes this preface, which is printed in PG 161:931–36. It talks of Chalcondyles' teaching at Padua and Florence but not of his teaching at Milan, so it would appear to have been composed while Chalcondyles was at Florence, between September 1475 and October 1491. The manuscript in which it appears is detailed in Andrés, *Catálogo de los códices griegos*, 247–49, who dates it c. 1480.
308. PG 161:932–33.
309. Ibid., 933.
310. Ibid., 936.
311. This postscript is extant in at least three forms. The first is in the *editio princeps* of *De verbo*, printed c. 1489 (appendix 1, no. 11). The second is in Madrid, Bibl. Nacional, 4689, printed in PG 161:937–40, and Martínez-Manzano, *Konstantinos Laskaris*, 223–25. The third was printed in the first edition of the complete grammar, c. 1502 (appendix 1, no. 26). The first two forms are closely related; the third is quite different.
312. Appendix 1, no. 26, sig. Z7r.
313. For Guarino's summary, see chapter 1, section "Manuel Chrysoloras," p. 9.

314. PG 161:935.
315. Martínez-Manzano, *Konstantinos Laskaris*, 223 (the same text is in PG 161:937). The text of the edition of c. 1489 and that of the Aldine edition c. 1502 are close but not identical at this point. Lascaris's pupil Urbano also uses the idea of grammar as an ocean: see chapter 1, section "Urbano Bolzanio."
316. PG 161:935.
317. Madrid, Bibl. Nacional, 4854, for which see chapter 1, section "George Scholarios"; for the postscript, see PG 161: 937.
318. Appendix 1, no. 3.
319. For the grammar, see appendix 1, no. 5; for Crastoni's dictionary, see chapter 2, "Greek Lexica in Western Europe, 1396–1529," pp. 64–65.
320. Appendix 1, no. 10.
321. Poliziano copied extracts into PBN, gr.3069, folios 215r–223r, June 9, 1484 (Martinelli, "Grammatiche greche," 268, 270). For his use of Lascaris in the commentary, see ibid., 277, 284–85, 289.
322. See the introduction to the present chapter, p. 3.
323. Legrand, *Bibliographie hellénique*, 1:27.
324. Piccolomini, "Una lettera greca di Pietro Bembo," 307.
325. BAV, Vat.gr.1401. This manuscript, described in Martínez-Manzano, *Konstantinos Laskaris*, 327–29, carries three dates: May 30, 1494, Messina (folio 50v inf.); July 18, 1494, Messina (folio 129r); and November 25, 1494, no place, presumably at Venice (folio 164 inf.). Printing of the grammar was completed in February 1495 new style. See appendix 1, no. 15.
326. Appendix 1, no. 15. The price is from the catalog of October 1, 1498, reproduced in Orlandi, *Aldo Manuzio editore*, 2: plate IX.
327. "rudibus et ignaris penitus litterarum graecarum Lascaris institutiones imprimendas curavimus" (Legrand, *Bibliographie hellénique*, 1:28).
328. For the Aldine Appendix, see chapter 3, section "Elementary Pamphlets."
329. Appendix 1, no. 26. The price was added in manuscript, apparently by Aldus, to a catalog dated June 22, 1503, reproduced in Orlandi, *Aldo Manuzio editore*, 2: plate X.
330. De Nolhac, *Les correspondants d'Alde Manuce*, 70–71, letter no. 59.
331. He says, "Ex hiis qui scripsere grammaticam, Lascarem habent tantum, Theodorum enim non advexi mecum..." (edited in Surtz and Hexter, *The Complete Works of St Thomas More*, 180).
332. See chapter 1, section "Manuel Chrysoloras."
333. See chapter 1, section "Theodore Gaza," p. 20.
334. For Chalcondyles' grammar, see chapter 1, section "Demetrius Chalcondyles."
335. Prefaced to his edition of Chalcondyles' grammar, sigs. a2v–a3r.
336. For its influence on the grammar of Sophianos (d. after 1551), see Elioudes, "Η γραμματική του Κωνσταντίνου Λασκάρεως."
337. Editions of 1802, 1808, and 1819 are in the British Library.
338. This account appears in Geiger, *Johann Reuchlins Briefwechsel*, 90–91, letter no. 95.
339. "... Graeca elementa quae ipse ego quondam in vestra Gallia ex discipulis Gregorii Tiphernatis adulescens Parisius acceperam anno Domini 1473" (cited in Girot, *Pindare avant Ronsard*, 8n6). Gregorio was in France from late 1456 until perhaps early 1459 (Pagliaroli, "Gregorio da Città di Castello," 263).
340. For Contoblacas, see Monfasani, "In Praise of Ognibene and Blame of Guarino." His grammar, written in Greek, is BAV, Vat.gr.1822, folios 146r–192r. Some leaves have watermarks associated by Briquet with Vicenza 1460 and Verona 1462 (ibid., 309n3). This copy was made by one Lazarus (RGK 3, no. 378), perhaps an Italian student of Contoblacas.
341. For Hermonymus, see chapter 1, section "Johann Reuchlin," and chapter 3, section "Quintus of Smyrna."
342. Reuchlin, *De Rudimentis Hebraicis*, Pforzheim: Anshelm, March 27, 1506, pp. 2–3.
343. Edited in Omont, "Georges Hermonyme de Sparte," 88–89. The letter is dated February 8, 1478, old style.

Notes to Chapter 1   179

344. For Bacon's work, see Nolan and Hirsch, *The Greek Grammar of Roger Bacon*.
345. The account is from Veit Dietrich in 1533 (Kusukawa, *Philip Melanchthon*, 35–36). Reuchlin alludes to this episode in another account of his Greek studies: "Basileae primum ab Andronico Contoblaca; deinde Parisiis a Georgio Hieronymo Spartiata; post Romae ab Argyropulo Byzantio publice in Vaticano Thucydidem legente Xisto IV pontefice, ad extremum Florentiae Mediolanique a Demetrio Chalcondyle, graecorum linguam frustillatim et quasi micas de mensa domini cadentes, accepi" (*De rudimentis hebraicis*, preface to book 3, edited in Geiger, *Johann Reuchlins Briefwechsel*, 96).
346. He wrote to Jacob Louber in July 1488, "Verti e graeco Proclum de laudibus beatissimae virginis Christique nativitate eamque omiliam tibi latinam feci tuoque nomini propriamque dicavi . . ." (edited in Geiger, *Johann Reuchlins Briefwechsel*, 14, letter no. 14). He gave a copy of this version to Gregory Lamparter in 1521 (edited in Geiger, *Johann Reuchlins Briefwechsel*, 332–33, letter no. 302).
347. Saffrey, "Un humaniste dominicain," 20.
348. The work is edited in Horawitz, "Griechische Studien," 445–50, who does not date it. A copy was made by a German monk, Nicolaus Basellius, on September 1, 1508.
349. Munich, Bayerische Staatsbibl., gr.582a, folios 117–c.187v. For the contents of this manuscript, see Knauer, "*Iter per miscellanea*," 33–35.
350. Appendix 1, no. 5. Reuchlin's inscription is reproduced in Rhein, "Johannes Reuchlin (1455–1522)," 65.
351. See chapter 1, section "George Scholarios."
352. With a letter dated September 13, 1516. De Vocht, *History of the Foundation*, 276n3.
353. Orlandi, *Aldo Manuzio editore*, 1:160–64; Bateman, "Aldus Manutius," 226n4.
354. For the Aldine Appendix, see chapter 3, section "Elementary Pamphlets."
355. Orlandi, *Aldo Manuzio editore*, 1:165; Bateman, "Aldus Manutius," 228n11.
356. Milan, Bibl. Ambrosiana, p. 35 sup. has been identified as Aldus's autograph by Quaranta, "Osservazioni intorno," 123–27.
357. Appendix 1, no. 63, folios 6r, 8v.
358. Appendix 1, no. 63, folio 7v. For this reversal, see chapter 1, section "Theodore Gaza," p. 17.
359. Appendix 1, no. 63, folio 6r.
360. Appendix 1, no. 63, folio 37v.
361. Appendix 1, no. 63, folio 42r.
362. See chapter 1, section "Manuel Chrysoloras," pp. 11–12.
363. Celtis's travels in Italy are recorded in Spitz, *Conrad Celtis*, 10–15.
364. It occupies folios 1v–11v in Vienna, Österreichische Nationalbibl., sup.gr.43.
365. For Bacon's work, see Nolan and Hirsch, *The Greek Grammar of Roger Bacon*; for Urbano's, see chapter 1, section "Urbano Bolzanio."
366. See Rupprich, *Die Briefwechsel*, 25–26, 162–63.
367. Spitz, *Conrad Celtis*, 43.
368. Ibid., 8.
369. Wuttke, "Zur griechischen Grammatik des Konrad Celtis," 303.
370. Vienna, Österreichische Nationalbibl., lat.3748, folios 23r–247v. See Wuttke, "Zur griechischen Grammatik des Konrad Celtis," 303.
371. Ibid., sup.gr.43, has Celtis's grammar, colloquies, and a Greek–Latin vocabulary. Folios 1v–11v (the grammar) were written by Rosenperger. See Wuttke, "Zur griechischen Grammatik des Konrad Celtis," 296, 298–99.
372. Edited in Rupprich, *Die Briefwechsel*, 568–69, who revised the date from 1501 to 1504 on the basis of internal evidence.
373. For the Aldine Appendix, see chapter 3, section "Elementary Pamphlets," and appendix 1, no. 15.
374. This plausible supposition is often presented as fact. Cammelli concluded that the Demetrius who taught Campano was Chalcondyles (*Demetrio Calcondila*, 8–13). His conclusion was repeated by Hausmann, "Giovanni Antonio Campano (1429–1477): Erläuterungen,"

51–53; Hausmann, "Giovanni Antonio Campano (1429–1477): Ein Beitrag," 133; Petrucci, "Calcondila," 543; Hausmann, "Campano, Giovanni Antonio (Giannantonio)," 424; Monfasani, "L'insegnamento universitario," 48. See also chapter 3, section "Theocritus."
375. Cammelli, *Demetrio Calcondila*, 27–28.
376. Schedel writes, "Iste Grecus fuit Demetrius Atheniensis qui publice padue primo Erothimata deinde Hesiodum nobis exposuit" (Geanakoplos, "Translation of Chalcondyles' Discourses," 296). For two manuscripts of Chrysoloras's work copied by Chalcondyles, one of which belongs to the 1460s, see chapter 1, section "Manuel Chrysoloras," n. 83.
377. See chapter 1, section "Theodore Gaza."
378. For which, see chapter 2, section "The Suda Lexicon."
379. Appendix 1, no. 14, where the date is discussed. A vellum copy survives: BAV, urb.gr.153 (Sheehan, *Incunabula*, 1: 361).
380. For this reversal, see chapter 1, section "Theodore Gaza," p. 17.
381. Pozzi, "Da Padova a Firenze nel 1493," 196. For Tomeo, see De Bellis, "La vita e l'ambiente."
382. A copy of Chalcondyles' grammar appears in an inventory of his father's property, compiled in March 1499 (Rebecchini, "The Book Collection," 18, 27).
383. Salamanca, Inc.157, which has the following note: "Ego Comendatarius Fernandus Nugnius Pincianus emi hunc codicem Mediolani praecio unius nummi aurei." The deletion appears to be later. It was probably bought in Italy between 1500 and 1505 (Codoñer, Merino, and Malvadi, *Biblioteca y epistolario de Hernán Núñez de Guzmán*, 4, 11–12).
384. PBN, Rés.X.490; Maillard and others, *La France des Humanistes*, 96.
385. Andrés, *Catálogo de los códices griegos*, 545–46.
386. See chapter 1, sections "Manuel Chrysoloras" and "Aldus Manutius."
387. Appendix 1, no. 40.
388. Appendix 1, no. 55.
389. "Atque hoc erroris Demetrio imputant Chalcondylo, viro tum probo tum erudito, sed cuius mediocritas exactum illud ac sublime Theodori iudicium haudquaquam assequi potuerit" (EE 2:265).
390. Appendix 1, no. 155, sig. a3r. For Danès, see Delaruelle, "L'étude du grec à Paris de 1514 à 1530," 140–41; De Morembert, "Danès, Pierre"; RGK 2, no. 473.
391. Bietenholz and Deutscher, *Contemporaries of Erasmus*, 3:370; Gualdo Rosa, "Urbano dalle Fosse (Bolzanio)," 88–89. In his funeral oration, Castrifrancanus says that Urbano, returning from Constantinople with Andrea Gritti, studied under Lascaris in Messina (Castrifrancanus, *Alberti Castrifrancani oratio*, sigs. b2r–v). Urbano's only known trip to the east with Gritti was in 1503 or 1504 (Gualdo Rosa, "Urbano dalle Fosse (Bolzanio)," 89). By this date Lascaris was dead, and Castrifrancanus may be conflating two separate incidents.
392. Gualdo Rosa, "Urbano dalle Fosse (Bolzanio)," 89.
393. Bietenholz and Deutscher, *Contemporaries of Erasmus*, 2:323–24.
394. Orlandi, *Aldo Manuzio editore*, 2:342.
395. Castrifrancanus, *Alberti Castrifrancani oratio*, sig. a2r.
396. Pellegrini, "Χεὶρ χεῖρα νίπτει," 224–25.
397. Gaisser, *Pierio Valeriano*, 270; Gualdo Rosa, "Urbano dalle Fosse (Bolzanio)," 89.
398. "Multa enim addidi, plurima immutavi, adiuvante interdum Urbano … a quo brevi habebitis quas summa cura ac doctissime composuit in graecam linguam introductiones" (Orlandi, *Aldo Manuzio editore*, 1:12).
399. "meo rogatu ac impulsu" (Orlandi, *Aldo Manuzio editore*, 1:22).
400. Gualdo Rosa, "Urbano dalle Fosse (Bolzanio)," 90; Bustico, "Due umanisti veneti," 100. For an image of this medal, see Doglioni, *Memorie di Urbano Bolzanio*, frontispiece.
401. Appendix 1, no. 45, sig. A1v.
402. "editionem celerius quam instituteram maturavi" (postscript to appendix 1, no. 45, sig. Cc10v).
403. Appendix 1, no. 20, sig. m5v.
404. Urbano included nouns declined like νόος and ἁπλόος in this fifth contracted declension (Martínez-Manzano, *Konstantinos Laskaris*, 188–89).

405. "Quoniam communem ordinem declinationum mutavimus Theodorum Gazam imitati, sciri velim hoc non temere factum esse . . ." (appendix 1, no. 20, sig. b8v). For this innovation, see chapter 1, section "Theodore Gaza," p. 17.
406. Appendix 1, no. 20, sig. c1v. The printed text reads "cognitione"; the [et] is my addition.
407. Appendix 1, no. 20, sig. e6v.
408. Appendix 1, no. 23.
409. See chapter 1, section "Philip Melanchthon."
410. EE 1:367, letter no. 159. Pizzi is wrong to say that Erasmus does not mention the grammar of Constantine Lascaris ("La grammatica greca," 187).
411. Appendix 1, no. 26.
412. The three catalogs produced in Aldus's lifetime are reproduced in Orlandi, *Aldo Manuzio editore*, 2: plates IX–XVIII. Urbano's grammar must have sold out before November 1513, since it does not appear in the third catalog that carries that date. Willibald Pirckheimer, nearer to Venice and better connected, managed to acquire a copy at an unknown date (Offenbacher, "La bibliothèque de Willibald Pirckheimer," 255).
413. Appendix 1, nos. 43 and 45.
414. Appendix 1, no. 45, sigs. A1v–A2r, which reads *excutere* for *excudere*.
415. Appendix 1, no. 45, sig. A2r. Urbano made Oxford, Bodleian, Auct.T.4.7 (misc. 245), a grammatical collection containing Choeroboscos, Moschopoulos, and Lascaris, which has some marginal notes in Lascaris's hand (RGK 1, nos. 223 and 337). This manuscript has Lascaris's *De nomine*, the preface to which was copied from a manuscript written before Lascaris's *De constructione* became book 2 of his grammar. See folio 88r: Ἐν τῷ προεκδωθέντα ἡμῖν πρώτῳ βιβλίῳ. . . . For its arrival in the Bodleian Library, see Wilson, "Greek Grammars," 78. Urbano copied and owned an important grammatical manuscript, Copenhagen, GKS 1965, 40, described in Schartau, *Codices Graeci Haunienses*, 168–77.
416. "In priori tractatu de octo partibus orationis locuti sumus, sed secundum linguam communem. Nunc, quia magna inter hanc et alias diversitas est, de eisdem secundum eas dicemus, additis quibusdam regulis generalibus, quas inutiles fore non puto . . ." (appendix 1, no. 45, sig. H3r).
417. Urbano's preface is undated (appendix 1, no. 45, sigs. A1v–A2r); the postscript is dated June 24 (sig. Cc10v); the colophon is August 20 (sig. Ee10v).
418. See Gaisser, *Pierio Valeriano*, 242–47.
419. "non qui eruditissimus eo in negotio fuerit, mihi tum quaerebatur, sed qui maxime accommodus et auditoribus adhuc rudibus, et negotio pro rudibus suscepto" (appendix 1, no. 145, preface, sig. aa2r).
420. Appendix 1, no. 145, preface, sig. aa2r.
421. Appendix 1, no. 145, preface, sig. aa2v.
422. See the edition of 1545: *Urbano, Urbani Bolzanii Bellunensis grammaticae institutiones*, sig. *5v.
423. Ibid., sig. *6r. I have emended "orationi[s]." The *recta semita* may be an echo of Mark's Gospel, 1:3. Urbano may have picked up the idea of grammar as an ocean from his teacher Lascaris: see chapter 1, section "Constantine Lascaris," p. 29.
424. I know of eight editions between 1530 and 1566. The edition of 1585, noticed in Doglioni, *Memorie di Urbano Bolzanio*, 41, was printed by Joannes Variscus and Paganinus de Paganinis.
425. To whom he addressed the postscript of the edition, appendix 1, no. 41, sigs. EE3v–EE4r.
426. For Simler's career, see Scheible, "Melanchthons Pforzheimer Schulzeit," 15–21.
427. He notices Gaza at sigs. AA2v (book 3), BB1r (book 3), and GG7r; he notices Apollonius at sigs. BB3r and BB3v. The passage from sig. AA2v is quoted in Horawitz, "Griechische Studien," 428.
428. Sigs. AA2v (on the subscript), ΓΓ5v, ΓΓ7r.
429. Sig. BB1r.
430. He corrects a trivial error of Urbano's grammar at sig. DD4r. Two editions of this grammar were printed immediately after Simler's work (appendix 1, nos. 43 and 45).

182   Notes to Chapter 1

431. Sig. BB2v.
432. The former is appendix 1, no. 18; the latter is appendix 2, no. 7. For the latter, see chapter 2, section "The *Etymologicum magnum.*"
433. Reuchlin completed *Sergius* in 1504 (Bietenholz and Deutscher, *Contemporaries of Erasmus*, 3:146). Simler's commentary on it emerged in 1507. For the *Rudimenta*, see Simler's letter in Reuchlin, *De Rudimentis Hebraicis*, Pforzheim: Anshelm, 27 March 1506, p. 622. The belief that Simler wrote a commentary on Reuchlin's *Scaenica progymnasmata* of 1498 is unfounded: see Scheible, "Melanchthons Pforzheimer Schulzeit," 18–19.
434. For which, see chapter 2, section "The Suda Lexicon."
435. Sig. ΓΤ4r.
436. Sig. ΓΤ1v.
437. Sig. ΓΤ5r.
438. Peutinger wrote to Reuchlin on December 12, 1512: "Simler ipsum, hactenus mihi incognitum, virum in Germanis nostris nunquam satis laudatum et qui nos post te graecissare curat, grammaticam cuius graecam et in septem psalmos interpretationes tuas Thomas Anshelmus, elegans ille chalcographus, ad me misit, salvum optato" (edited in König, *Konrad Peutingers Briefwechsel*, 177). Beatus Rhenanus owned a copy: Sélestat, Bibl. Municipale, K998a, Incunables: "Sum Beati Rhenani Nec muto dominum Basileae An. MDXIII." The same library holds Rhenanus's copy of Chrysoloras (Basle, 1528, appendix 1, no. 170).
439. For his biography, see Niemöller, "Othmar Luscinius"; Bietenholz and Deutscher, *Contemporaries of Erasmus*, 3:3–4.
440. Preface to his *Musicae institutiones* (Strasbourg, [1515]) sig. a2r); Niemöller, "Othmar Luscinius," 46.
441. This appears from his preface to his edition of Lucian, edited in Omont, "Essai sur les débuts de la typographie grecque à Paris," 63. Niemöller assigns his studies in Paris to the years 1511 to 1514 ("Othmar Luscinius," 48). Aleandro was absent from Paris from December 10, 1510, to June 14, 1511; in December 1513, he became secretary to the bishop of Paris, a role that seems to have ended his teaching (Alberigo, "Aleandro, Girolamo," 129).
442. Niemöller, "Othmar Luscinius," 49–50.
443. As appears from the preface to Nachtgall's edition of Lucian (Omont, "Essai sur les débuts de la typographie grecque à Paris," 63).
444. For Lucian, see chapter 3, section "Lucian"; for Isocrates, see chapter 3, section "Isocrates"; for the prayers, see appendix 1, no. 57. The gnomic verse is in *Senarii graecanici* (Strasbourg: Knoblouch, 1515). It postdates Nachtgall's preface to Nicolaus Wurmser, August 5, 1515.
445. Appendix 1, nos. 61 and 80.
446. Appendix 1, no. 83. Nachtgall first used the name *Luscinius* in two Strasbourg imprints of 1517: in the *Progymnasmata* and in his versions from Lucian. Both editions are dated March 29, 1517.
447. Appendix 1, no. 83, sig. A1v. For Gebweiler, see *Allgemeine Deutsche Biographie*, 8:486–87. Guida and Dieler are mentioned by Beatus Rhenanus as members of the Strasbourg *Sodalitas Literaria* in a letter to Nachtgall of 1515 (Horawitz and Hartfelder, *Briefwechsel des Beatus Rhenanus*, 80–81).
448. Appendix 1, no. 83, sig. A1v. Ergersheim seems to be the Ergerinus to whom Beatus Rhenanus dedicates his edition of Synesius, *Laus Calvitii* (Basle: Froben, 1515). See Horawitz and Hartfelder, *Briefwechsel des Beatus Rhenanus*, 72.
449. "Haec sunt, amice lector, in eum quem vides ordinem paucissimis sane diebus a nobis congesta, quo memoriam saltem studiosorum iuvaremus, cui nihil tam tenaciter infigitur quam quod nativa quadam serie in unum corpus est compactum" (appendix 1, no. 83, sig. C6r).
450. "Huic loco conveniunt typi maioris chartae" (appendix 1, no. 83, sig. B4r). "Verborum coniugationem nemo unquam citra sudorem aggressus sit, ob tam immensum rei copiam et varietatem" (ibid., sig. B4v).
451. Appendix 1, no. 83, sig. B4v.
452. Appendix 1, no. 83, sig. A1v. For *transenna*, see Cicero, *De Oratore*, 1.35.162.

453. See Niemöller, "Othmar Luscinius," 51–52. One preface in his *Moralia quaedam*, dated June 13, 1518, begins, "Reducem me nuper ex Italia . . ." (Nachtgall, *Moralia quaedam*, sig. O5v).
454. The letter is dated March 1, 1521. Leo "collegium graecanicum in monte Caballino loco amoenissimo et plurimum tranquillo urbis, pube e media Graecia lecta magno aere instituit. Id nos abhinc annum exporrecta fonte duntaxat in urbe vidimus, caetera enim quae agebamus ibi male nobis erant ominata" (appendix 1, no. 116, sig. b4v).
455. Niemöller, "Othmar Luscinius," 51–53.
456. Appendix 1, no. 113.
457. For editions of the *Tabulae* before 1521, see appendix 1, nos. 49, 54, 61, 65, 73, 82, 86, 97, 98, 103.
458. For example, in 1521, "Huic loco convenit typus Declinationis, quem censeo separatim habendum" (appendix 1, no. 116, p. 15); "Huic loco convenit typus Coniugationis" (appendix 1, no. 116, p. 25). See also in 1517, appendix 1, no. 83, sig. B4r, and in 1523, appendix 1, no. 132, pp. 15 and 26.
459. For this innovation by Gaza, see chapter 1, section "Philip Melanchthon," p. 47. In Nachtgall's book, see appendix 1, no. 116, sig. c7r for the Attic declension, and sig. d2r for Gaza's influence on the verbs.
460. See appendix 1, no. 116, pp. 39–40, 82, and sig. i1v.
461. The prefatory epistle is edited by Omont, "Essai sur les débuts de la typographie grecque à Paris," 63.
462. Appendix 1, no. 116, sig. h2r.
463. Appendix 1, no. 116, sig. [a1r]. For "theonino dente," see Horace, *Epistulae*, 1.18.82.
464. Appendix 1, no. 116, sigs. a2r–b6v.
465. Niemöller, "Othmar Luscinius," 52–53.
466. Hartmann's *patruus* was Johann Rudolf Hallwiler, "Basiliensis templi custos" (appendix 1, no. 123, sig. A3v).
467. For Melanchthon's grammar, see chapter 1, section "Philip Melanchthon."
468. "Agentem etenim me in Heydelbergensi gymnasio, Petrus Scybenardus, primae autoritatis theologus adeoque solidioris theologiae antistes, ὥσπερ ἐργοδιώκτης ad id muneris perurgebat" (appendix 1, no. 124, sig. A2r). Oecolampadius may have picked up the word ἐργοδιώκτης from the Septuagint translation of Exodus, where it is applied to the Egyptian masters of the Jews (3:7, 5:6, 10:13). The word is also used by Gregory Nazianzenus (Lampe, *A Patristic Greek Lexicon*, 546). Oecolampadius translated some works of Gregory.
469. The dedication reads, "D. Billibaldo Pyrckaymer, patritio et senatori Norimbergensi, domino suo Oecolampadius dono mittit" (Offenbacher, "La bibliothèque de Willibald Pirckheimer," 245–46, 255).
470. Appendix 1, no. 124, sig. A3r.
471. For Lascaris's work, see chapter 1, section "Constantine Lascaris," p. 27.
472. "De vocativo singulari tradit Chrysoloras quinque regulas. Prima . . ." (appendix 1, no. 124, sig. E7r).
473. "Duplices sunt declinationes: simplices et contractae, quae alias *synaeresiatae* dicuntur. Et sub unaquaque inveniuntur quinque formulae declinandi: simplicium enim declinatio habet quatuor formas declinandi parisyllaba et unam imparisyllaborum, ex qua etiam fluunt quinque formulae declinandi contracta" (appendix 1, no. 124, sig. C7r).
474. For this innovation, see chapter 1, section "Theodore Gaza," p. 17.
475. "Tredecim sunt coniugationes apud graecos: sex sunt barytonorum in ω; a quibus descendunt etiam aliae septem: tres circumflexorum, et quatuor verborum in μι" (appendix 1, no. 124, sigs. G3r–v).
476. The work was revised in at least one particular in 1521: see appendix 1, nos. 117 and 124.
477. See appendix 1, no. 137.
478. The Paris edition is appendix 1, no. 171. For the Basle editions, see Staehelin, "Oekolampad-Bibliographie," 87 (no. 180) and 97 (no. 199).
479. For this gift, see chapter 1, section "Johann Reuchlin."

480. Horawitz, "Griechische Studien," 422–23. For Simler, see chapter 1, section "George Simler."
481. Appendix 1, no. 94.
482. Melanchthon dedicated his *De Rhetorica* to Maurus in January 1519: see Wetzel and others, *Melanchthons Briefwechsel*, 1:99–103.
483. Appendix 1, no. 165, sig. A2r.
484. For Urbano, see chapter 1, section "Urbano Bolzanio"; for Oecolampadius, see chapter 1, section "Joannes Oecolampadius."
485. *Allgemeine Deutsche Biographie*, 21:269.
486. See appendix 1, nos. 94, 109, 118, 128, 129, 151, 158, 165, 172, 173, 174.
487. "Germanicus sermo habet articulum, nec graeci articuli vim exacte cognoveris, nisi ex Germanico idiomate" (appendix 1, no. 165, sig. b5r).
488. Wetzel and others, *Melanchthons Briefwechsel*, 1:63.
489. Appendix 1, no. 165, sig. A4v.
490. Appendix 1, no. 165, sig. A8r.
491. "Constat enim res observatione, observationem vero adiuvant regulae. Haec est prosodia summa" (Wetzel and others, *Melanchthons Briefwechsel*, 1:63).
492. Appendix 1, no. 165, sig. C2r.
493. Appendix 1, no. 165, sig. B5v.
494. "Quinque sunt ordines graecae declinationis quos simplices vocamus; et ex quinta nascuntur quidam ordines flectendi nomina quae contracta vocant" (appendix 1, no. 165, sig. C3r).
495. Appendix 1, no. 165, sig. C4v.
496. Appendix 1, no. 165, sig. C8v.
497. Appendix 1, no. 165, sig. D2r.
498. Appendix 1, no. 165, sig. D1v; *Aeneid* 2:371, 382, 392; 6:20. For Gaza's innovation, see chapter 1, section "Theodore Gaza," p. 17.
499. Appendix 1, no. 165, sig. H1r.
500. Appendix 1, no. 165, sig. L5r.
501. Appendix 1, no. 165, sig. L5v.
502. See appendix 1, no. 165, sigs. G6r, I4r, N3r–v, N6v.
503. For Amerot's biography, see Hoven, *Bibliographie*, 1–6; Hummel, "Un opuscule-relais," 483–84.
504. Appendix 1, no. 110. "Nicolaus Buscoducensis . . . qui ante biennium me ad aeditionem exhortatus est . . . Paschasius Berselius . . . qui ad eandem me plane perpulit . . ." (sig. A3v). For Berselius, see chapter 1, section "Johann Winther of Andernach," n. 545; De Vocht, *History of the Foundation*, 1:493–500.
505. Appendix 1, no. 110, sigs. k3v, n3r.
506. Cited in Hummel, "Un opuscule-relais," 487.
507. Appendix 1, no. 110, sig. a3r.
508. Ibid. I have added "id est." It is possible that a marginal gloss on the Greek has crept into the text here.
509. "Ausim persancte deierare quicquid est in octo partibus orationis id totum studio trimestri ab ingenio mediocri perdisci posse" (sig. a3r).
510. The woodcut is interleaved between sig. 7e4v ("Sequitur arbor") and sig. f1r ("Declaratio arboris"). It is reproduced in Hummel, "Un opuscule-relais," 486.
511. Hoven, *Bibliographie*, 8–9. Sigs. 7e1v–7e3v in the edition of 1530.
512. See Hummel, "Un opuscule-relais." The extract, *De declinationibus et coniugationibus graecis secundum varia idiomata*, is from appendix 1, no. 110, sigs. q1v–r3r.
513. According to Theodore Beza's *Histoire ecclésiastique* (Veissière, "Une dédicace de Jean Chéradame," 397). For a brief notice of Chéradame, see Prevost, "Chéradame, Jean." For the epithet *Sagiensis*, or of Séez, see Delaruelle, "L'étude du grec à Paris de 1514 à 1530," 132n2.
514. Appendix 1, no. 119.
515. For Toussain, see *Biographie Universelle*, 42:68–69.
516. Appendix 1, no. 119, sigs. b2r–b4v.

Notes to Chapter 1   185

517. Appendix 1, no. 119, sigs. c1r–v.
518. "Sunt omnia defectiva et anomala. Deducunturque a verbis circumflexis per synaeresin ..." (appendix 1, no. 119, sig. c3r).
519. "E tertia coniugatione nascuntur circumflexa verba ... Formae tres sunt ..." (appendix 1, no. 119, sig. d4r).
520. Appendix 1, nos. 138 and 164.
521. Appendix 1, no. 147.
522. Appendix 1, no. 161.
523. Appendix 2, no. 28.
524. Appendix 1, nos. 29 and 32.
525. For Ceporinus's early career, see Egli, "Ceporins Leben und Schriften," 145–48.
526. Appendix 1, no. 127. Egli did not know this, the *editio princeps*, and postulated another edition of the grammar between 1522 and 1526 (Egli, "Ceporins Leben und Schriften," 152 and n2). This edition is a ghost.
527. Appendix 1, no. 130.
528. Appendix 1, no. 127, sig. A1v.
529. Appendix 1, no. 162, p. 8.
530. Appendix 1, no. 162, pp. 26, 44–49.
531. In 1526, in a postscript to Ceporinus's posthumous edition of Pindar, he wrote, "grammaticas praeceptiones adeo probe tradidit ut qui diligenter legerunt palmam ei offerant, praesertim quod ad διαλέκτους attinet" (Egli, Finsler, Köhler, and others, *Huldreich Zwinglis sämtliche Werke*, 4:874). Conrad Gesner repeated this judgment (Egli, "Ceporins Leben und Schriften," 159).
532. For the date of his death, see Egli, "Ceporins Leben und Schriften," 155 and n3.
533. Egli, "Ceporins Leben und Schriften," 150; Parks and Cranz, "Dionysius Periegetes," 39–41.
534. Basle: Bebel, August 1524, sig. 1v.
535. See appendix 1, no. 162. A pamphlet, dated June 1525, contains the Greek alphabet and a collection of Greek–Latin prayers: appendix 1, no. 156. The only copy known to me is bound with Froschauer's 1526 edition of Ceporinus's grammar. The typography of this pamphlet is consistent with Basle or Zurich. If it was printed at Zurich, it was the first Greek work printed in that city.
536. The Paris edition is appendix 1, no. 175. Egli notices an edition of the grammar (Basle: Bebel, 1528), which I have been unable to locate (Egli, "Ceporins Leben und Schriften," 157). For later editions, see ibid., 157–58.
537. Appendix 1, no. 153.
538. Appendix 1, no. 153, folio 65r.
539. Appendix 1, no. 154.
540. The cardinal subsidized Pagninus's *Hebraicae institutiones*, printed at Lyons in October 1526.
541. Leo X granted a privilege to Callierges' edition of Thomas Magister in 1517. See appendix 2, no. 18. The date of Hadrian's privilege may indicate an earlier grammatical work. Fabricius records an edition at Paris in 1523 that I have been unable to find: *Santis Pagnini ad linguam graecum capessendam*.
542. Kelly, *The Oxford Dictionary of Popes*, 258–59. In January 1516, Ximenes became regent of Castile and Aragon (EE 2:488, note to line 37); Hadrian was made a cardinal in Spain on July 1, 1517 (EE 3:21 and note to line 12); the last volume of the Polyglot received its colophon July 10, 1517 (volume 4, sig. G4r); Ximenes died November 8, 1517 (EE 2:488, note to line 37).
543. EE 4:69, 94, 103.
544. Appendix 1, no. 166. For his biography, see Turner, "Jean Guinther d'Andernach (1505–1574)"; Bernays, "Zur Biographie Johann Winthers von Andernach"; Rice, "Paulus Aegineta," 171–72.
545. "Cum superiore anno utramque linguam apud Leodium profiterer, clarissime princeps, hortabatur me Paschasius ille Perselius [*sic*] ... ut nonnihil de constructione graecanici

sermonis . . . conscriberem" (appendix 1, no. 166, sig. a2r). For Paschasius Berselius, see chapter 1, section "Adrien Amerot."

546. In late 1528, Chéradame published his edition of Aristophanes. He dedicated *Nubes* to one Thomas Winther, possibly a relative of the grammarian. His preface to *Aves* is addressed to Bérault, while *Pax* is dedicated to another translator of Greek medical works, Joannes Ruellius. For the edition of Aristophanes, see Botley, "Renaissance Scholarship and the Athenian Calendar," 428–29. For Chéradame, see chapter 1, section "Jean Chéradame."
547. Rice, "Paulus Aegineta," 171.
548. Appendix 1, no. 166, sig. a2v.
549. See chapter 1, section "Theodore Gaza" and chapter 1, section "Ancient and Byzantine Greek Grammatical Works."
550. Appendix 1, no. 166, sigs. c1v–c2r.
551. Appendix 1, no. 166, sig. i5v.
552. As appears from the preface to his grammar, appendix 1, no. 178, sig. A2r.
553. For which teaching, see chapter 3, section "Plutarch."
554. Appendix 1, no. 178.
555. Appendix 1, no. 178, sigs. A2v–A3r.
556. Appendix 1, no. 178, sig. B1r.
557. "Eas si voles adpellare declinationes contractas per me licet, modo memineris eas oriri ex quinta et veluti partem eius esse" (appendix 1, no. 178, sig. B1v).
558. For Ceporinus, see chapter 1, section "Jacobus Ceporinus."
559. See Schimmelpfennig, "Metzler."

Chapter 2

1. Novati, *Epistolario di Coluccio Salutati*, 3:131; Oliver, "Plato and Salutati," 318n17.
2. See chapter 3, section "Homer," p. 81.
3. Grosseteste owned Leiden, Univ. Bibl., Voss.gr.F.2. From this was copied BAV, Vat.gr.1296, dated 1204. BL, Harl.3100 was also made from Grosseteste's manuscript. Grocyn's copy is now Oxford, Corpus Christi College, ms. 76 and 77 (Adler, *Suidae Lexicon*, 5:230–38; Dionisotti, "On the Greek Studies of Robert Grosseteste," 37–38). The Oxford manuscripts were made by Emmanuel of Constantinople and John Serbopoulos (James, "Two More Manuscripts"; RGK 1, nos. 115 and 180).
4. "Suidas Rhodi a Guarino emptum, sed ita vetustate confectum ut multis in locis legi non possit" (Adler, *Suidae Lexicon* 5:262–63; Diller, "Greek Codices of Palla Strozzi and Guarino Veronese," 319).
5. Florence, Bibl. Laurenziana, 55.1 (Adler, *Suidae Lexicon*, 5:228–29; Diller, "Greek Codices of Palla Strozzi and Guarino Veronese," 319; RGK 1, no. 352). For the date, see Wilson, *From Byzantium to Italy*, 169n21.
6. For Filelfo's Suda, see Mehus, *Ambrosii Traversarii epistolae*, vol. 2, columns 1010–11, book 24, letter no. 32. PBN, gr.2623 of the Suda belonged to Filelfo and appears to have been the manuscript he brought to Italy in 1427: see Calderini, "Intorno ad un passo di Suida," 15–16; Adler, *Suidae Lexicon*, 5:238–40; Eleuteri, "Francesco Filelfo," 176; Speranzi, "Codici greci appartenuti a Francesco Filelfo," 476–82. Adler's attribution of the hand to Caesar Strategos is incorrect (RGK 2, no. 292). For a list of articles used by Filelfo, see Calderini, "Ricerche intorno alla biblioteca," 398n1. Filelfo's version, made between 1445 and 1446 for Fra Alberto da Sarteano, was dedicated to Pope Sixtus IV in 1476 and printed at Milan around 1480 (ISTC ip00612800). "Narratio hagiographica quam sub verbo Ἰησοῦς legimus, multis in codicibus exstat, ubi e Suida descripta non est" (Adler, *Suidae Lexicon*, 5:257). On Filelfo's death in 1481, his manuscripts were acquired for the Medici library, and his Suda subsequently passed to Janus Lascaris (Adler, *Suidae Lexicon*, 5:261–62).
7. BAV, Vat.gr.3 and 4, largely copied by Leo Atrapes (RGK 3, no. 383). These were certainly in the Vatican by 1475 (Devreesse, *Le fonds grec*, 9n5, 48). They were copied from PBN,

gr.2625 and PBN, gr.2626 (Adler, *Suidae Lexicon*, 5:223). For Garatone, see chapter 1, section "Ancient and Byzantine Greek Grammatical Works," p. 5, n. 36.
8. Oxford, Bodleian, Holkh.gr.111 (RGK 1, no. 98).
9. Calderini, "Ricerche intorno alla biblioteca," 397n3.
10. In 1455, Apostolis wrote to Ang. Vadius, who seems to have been in Cyprus, promising to bring him a manuscript of the Suda. Adler knew of no manuscript in Apostolis's hand (*Suidae Lexicon*, 5:262), but he copied BAV, Urb.gr.160, folios 1r–224v and 363r–396r; Calophrenas copied folios 225r–362v. Apostolis copied BAV, Pal.gr.244, folios 7r–359v, 395v–403r; Lygizos copied folios 360r–95r (RGK 1, no. 278; 3, no. 103; 3, no. 454; 3, no. 465).
11. Perugia, Perus.E.43. RGK 1, no. 58. Gregoropoulos is recorded between 1450 and 1501.
12. He had "partem unam Suide," presumably a single volume of a two-volume copy. Adler was unable to identify this with any extant manuscript and believed it lost (Adler, *Suidae Lexicon*, 5:262).
13. BAV, Vat.gr.2317, December 27, 1463, apparently copied from BL, Add.11892 and Add.11893 (Adler, *Suidae Lexicon*, 5:227–28; RGK 3, no. 392).
14. Venice, Bibl. Marciana, gr.448 (1047) (Adler, *Suidae Lexicon*, 5:255–56; Labowsky, *Bessarion's Library and the Biblioteca Marciana*, 177, item no. 469) and Venice, Bibl. Marciana, gr.449 (588) (Labowsky, *Bessarion's Library and the Biblioteca Marciana*, 229, item no. 680).
15. For his commentary on the *Odyssey* (Martinelli, "Grammatiche greche," 278–81, 284, 287–90). He refers to the Suda in an undated letter to Bernardo Riccio (Poliziano, *Angeli Politiani Opera*, 359).
16. Lascaris's manuscript is now BAV, Vat.gr.1296, made in 1204 (Adler, *Suidae Lexicon*, 5:233–35; Martínez-Manzano, *Konstantinos Laskaris*, 287, 336): see this chapter, n. 3. His extracts are in Madrid, Bibl. Nacional, 4621, folios 37r–99v (Andrés, *Catálogo de los códices griegos*, 138–40).
17. Faraone's preface, from the edition of Venice, 1499, can be consulted in ISTC id0018700. For Faraone, see Ceresa, "Faraone (Faragonio), Francesco."
18. Travi, *Pietro Bembo*, 1:15. Adler was unable to identify the manuscript (*Suidae Lexicon*, 5:263).
19. See De Rosalia, "La vita di Costantino Lascaris," 48–49. For Lascaris's manuscript of the Suda, see this chapter, nn. 3 and 16.
20. ISTC is00829000. See Motta, "Demetrio Calcondila editore," 163. The scribe Joannes copied Brussels 11281 of the Suda at Koroni in the Peloponnese in 1475 (RGK 1, no. 203). Adler suggests that this was the basis for the *editio princeps* (*Suidae Lexicon*, 5:251–52).
21. In the preface he describes himself as "πλείοσιν ἀντιγράφοις χρησάμενος" (Botfield, *Prefaces*, 232; Legrand, *Bibliographie hellénique*, 1:65; Adler, *Suidae Lexicon*, 1:xi; 5:277).
22. The contract is in Motta, "Demetrio Calcondila editore," 163–65. For Taddeo, see Lasagni, *Dizionario biografico dei parmigiani*, 4:658–63.
23. Ludovico Sforza left Milan on September 2, 1499. French troops entered the city on September 11, and Louis XII formally took possession of it on October 6 (Williams, *Chronology*, 16). The colophon of the lexicon is November 15.
24. The prefatory Greek matter, verses of Antonius Motta, and Latin and Greek prefaces are edited in Botfield, *Prefaces*, 230–33. The prefatory Greek dialogue is translated in Greswell, *A View of the Early Parisian Greek Press*, 1:5n.
25. Williams, *Chronology*, 18.
26. See the document edited in Motta, "Demetrio Calcondila editore," 166. It is dated March 23, 1500, certainly new style, for Ludovico was in France in 1501.
27. Cammelli, *Demetrio Calcondila*, 126–27.
28. Williams, *Chronology*, 18.
29. Petrucci, "Calcondila," 546.
30. Geiger, *Johann Reuchlins Briefwechsel*, 77, letter no. 83.
31. De Nolhac, *Les correspondants d'Alde Manuce*, letter no. 15.

32. Giovanni Calfurnio owned a copy of the Milan edition: see Marcotte, "La bibliothèque de Jean Calphurnius," 196. Calfurnio's close links with Aldus make it plausible that Calfurnio acquired this volume from him before his death in January 1503.
33. "Libros omneis quos volebas cui iussisti dedimus praeter Nonnum et Gregorium" (Geiger, *Johann Reuchlins Briefwechsel*, 79, letter no. 85).
34. The catalog of June 22, 1503, is reproduced in Orlandi, *Aldo Manuzio editore*, 2: plates X–XIII. The price is added in manuscript, apparently by Aldus himself.
35. On August 18, Aldus wrote to Reuchlin: "Imprimuntur et quasi absolutae sunt Sophoclis tragoediae septem cum commentariis" (Geiger, *Johann Reuchlins Briefwechsel*, 78, letter no. 83). The Latin colophon dates it as August 1502. The Greek colophon dates it as 14 Μαιμακτηριών (Legrand, *Bibliographie hellénique*, 1:77). See chapter 3, section "Sophocles."
36. See Lucchesi, "Una prolusione," 54, and n1. This undated letter was written after Piero Egineta took up his chair in 1510 and before Virunio's death in 1520.
37. Appendix 2, no. 17. Adler states that the second Aldine edition used the *editio princeps* supplemented by an unidentified manuscript (*Suidae Lexicon*, 1:xi).
38. Reeve, *Erasmus' Annotations on the New Testament*, 40, 80, 94, 105, 108, 111, 119, 116. In 1516, he wrote of a passage, "Suidas aut quisquis is fuit alius hominumve deumve, corrigit hunc locum . . ." (ibid., 228). In 1515, a commentary on Erasmus's *Moriae Encomium* was printed, much of which came from Erasmus's pen. It cites the Suda a number of times, all in the second half of the commentary: Erasmus, *Moriae encomium*, 145, 150, 190, 191, 199, 200.
39. Forteguerri's copy is BAV, Inc.I:20; Lascaris' is BAV, Inc.I:51 (Sheehan, *Incunabula*, 3:1216).
40. Offenbacher, "La bibliothèque de Willibald Pirckheimer," 255.
41. Madrid, Univ. Complutense, Nov. I/283, which has the following note: "Ego Ferdinandus Pincianus . . . emi hunc codicem Bononiae a D. Ioviano de Sancta Maura praeceptore meo praecio ducatorum 3" (Codoñer, Merino, and Malvadi, *Biblioteca y epistolario de Hernán Núñez de Guzmán*, 5). This was probably between 1500 and 1505 (ibid., 11–12). The fact that he paid the cover price, not Aldus's price, may indicate a date between 1500 and 1502.
42. Pollux is on his list of 1421 (Sabbadini, *Le scoperte dei codici*, 46). See also Omont, "Catalogue des manuscrits grecs," 186.
43. Aurispa to Traversari, February 11, 1424, Sabbadini, *Carteggio di Giovanni Aurispa*, 7–8; Traversari to Niccoli, February 26 and July 26 [1424], Mehus, *Ambrosii Traversarii epistolae*, vol. 2, columns 376, 386, book 8, letter nos. 12 and 28; Ullman and Stadter, *The Public Library of Renaissance Florence*, 95n4; Stinger, *Humanism and the Church Fathers*, 51 and 246n92.
44. Calderini, "Ricerche intorno alla biblioteca," 379–80. Filelfo to Aurispa, April 4, 1428: "Pollucem quem petis dabo ad te propediem" (Filelfo, *Epistolare Francisci Philelfi*, sig. a8v). Filelfo owned Florence, Bibl. Laurenziana, 28.32, a fifteenth-century manuscript made by three scribes. It has Filelfo's note of possession: see Calderini, "Ricerche intorno alla biblioteca," 379–81; Eleuteri, "Francesco Filelfo," 169. Filelfo did not copy Florence, Bibl. Laurenziana, 58.1, folios 1r–12v, of Pollux, *pace* Eleuteri, "Francesco Filelfo," 171: see Speranzi, "Codici greci appartenuti a Francesco Filelfo," 475.
45. Omont, "Les manuscrits grecs," 79.
46. Trivizias (d. 1485) made Oxford, Bodleian, D'Orv. 60, folios 1–112v (RGK 1, no. 73); Rhosos made folios 113–50 (RGK 1, no. 178). Trivizias also made BAV, Urb.gr.159 and Florence, Bibl. Laurenziana, 58.3 (RGK 1, no. 73).
47. Madrid, Bibl. Nacional, 4625. Andrés, *Catálogo de los códices griegos*, 147–48.
48. He wrote on it, "emptus fuit per me Georgium Ferrariae a Nardo Aurispae die XXVI februarii 1462" (Milan, Bibl. Ambrosiana, M 94 sup., folio 1r; Friggi, "Libri greci alla corte di Ludovico il Moro," 122).
49. Venice, Bibl. Marciana, gr.493 was part of the donation of 1468; Venice, Bibl. Marciana, gr.490, which has excerpts from Pollux, was listed in the inventory of 1474 (Nickau, *Ammonii*

qui dicitur liber, xv; Labowsky, *Bessarion's Library and the Biblioteca Marciana*, 178, item no. 481; 200, item no. 169).
50. For the citations, see PG 19:1168, 1209; for the date, see PG 19:1216.
51. For this version, see chapter 3, section "Homer." In his *Rusticus*, published in 1483, Poliziano knows the fable of the discovery of purple from Pollux (Fantazzi, *Angelo Poliziano*, 50).
52. See Diller, "The Library of Francesco and Ermolao Barbaro," 257; and see Barbaro's letters in Branca, *Ermolao Barbaro, 1454–1493*, 2:20, 54, 56, 78, 83. Barbaro died in 1493.
53. Bartolomeo of Capo d'Istria, Gabriele Braccio, Giovanni Bissoli, and Benedetto Mangio were licensed to print the Letters of Phalaris and Brutus, Aesop, Pollux, and Philostratus. Only the first two works were printed (Brown, *The Venetian Printing Press*, 43).
54. Aldus's preface is in Botfield, *Prefaces*, 259–60; Orlandi, *Aldo Manuzio editore*, 1:57–58. For Capriolo, see Giansante, "Capriolo (Caprioli, Cavriolo), Elia," 218–19. Capriolo had published a number of minor works by 1502, but his most famous work, *Chronica de rebus Brixianorum*, did not appear until 1505.
55. Geiger, *Johann Reuchlins Briefwechsel*, 77–78, letter no. 83.
56. Offenbacher, "La bibliothèque de Willibald Pirckheimer," 255.
57. Firmin-Didot, *Alde Manuce et l'Hellénisme à Venise*, 290–92.
58. For the New Testament citation of κόφινος, see Reeve, *Erasmus' Annotations on the New Testament*, 64. Pollux is mentioned in the commentary on the *Moriae encomium*, first printed in 1515, at least some of which came from Erasmus's pen.
59. Florence, Bibl. Laurenziana, S. Marco 304, which also has the lexicon known as the *Etymologicum parvum*. See Rostagno and Festa, "Indice dei codici greci," 32*; Pintaudi, *Etymologicum parvum*, xvi.
60. For Traversari's copy, see Ullman and Stadter, *The Public Library of Renaissance Florence*, 62.
61. For the use of the work in his version of the *Iliad*, book 3, see Levine Rubinstein, "The Notes to Poliziano's «Iliad»," 205, 223; for its use in his commentary on the *Odyssey*, see Martinelli, "Grammatiche greche," 276–79, 281, 283–90.
62. Florence, Bibl. Laurenziana, S. Marco 303: see Rostagno and Festa, "Indice dei codici greci," 32*; Ullman and Stadter, *The Public Library of Renaissance Florence*, 265. For Guarino's dictionary, printed in 1523, see chapter 2, section "Greek Lexica in Western Europe, 1396–1529," p. 70.
63. Legrand, *Cent-dix lettres greques de F. Filelfo*, 125–26.
64. Calofrenas made Florence, Bibl. Laurenziana, 57.11 (Eleuteri, "Francesco Filelfo," 171). Florence, Bibl. Laurenziana, 57.15 was made at Milan (Calderini, "Ricerche intorno alla biblioteca," 306–8). Both manuscripts were mistakenly said by Bandini to have been written by Filelfo: see Eleuteri, "Francesco Filelfo," 168.
65. Venice, Bibl. Marciana, gr.530 (Labowsky, *Bessarion's Library and the Biblioteca Marciana*, 177, item no. 470).
66. Lake, "The Greek Monasteries of South Italy," 196.
67. Müller, "Neue Mittheilungen," 389.
68. For the manuscript, see ibid., 385. For Benedetti, see Crespi, "Benedetti, Alessandro," 244.
69. Appendix 2, no. 7. Caesar Strategos (floruit 1475–1500) wrote Venice, app. cl.XI.3, of the *Etymologicum magnum*. This manuscript and Copenhagen, Haun.gr.44, are closely related to the printer's copy for the *editio princeps* (Wilson, "The Book Trade in Venice ca. 1400–1515," 394). For Callierges, see Mioni, "Calliergi (Callergi), Zaccaria," 750–53.
70. The price is written beside the edition in the catalog of June 22, 1503, reproduced in Orlandi, *Aldo Manuzio editore*, 2: plates X–XIII.
71. For the catalog, see Orlandi, *Aldo Manuzio editore*, 2: plates XIV–XVIII. The reprint was written in Venice by F. Tarrisanus, 1549. For the sale of the first edition of the Suda, see chapter 2, section "The Suda Lexicon," p. 57.
72. Geiger, *Johann Reuchlins Briefwechsel*, 77, letter no. 83.
73. Marcotte, "La bibliothèque de Jean Calphurnius," 196.
74. Firmin-Didot, *Alde Manuce et l'Hellénisme à Venise*, 290–92.

190   Notes to Chapter 2

75. Ibid., 552n1.
76. Offenbacher, "La bibliothèque de Willibald Pirckheimer," 255.
77. Madrid, RBI/3, which has the following note: "Ego Fernandus Pincianus . . . emi hunc codicem Bononiae a domino Ioviano de Sancta Maura praeceptore meo praeci [sic] ducatorum duorum cum dimidio" (Codoñer, Merino, and Malvadi, *Biblioteca y epistolario de Hernán Núñez de Guzmán*, 4). For the date, see ibid., 11–12.
78. It is cited in the 1519 edition of his *Annotations* on the New Testament (Reeve, *Erasmus' Annotations on the New Testament*, 238).
79. Cambridge, University Library, Inc.1.B.3.146 [1849]. Sturge, *Cuthbert Tunstall*, 392–94.
80. PBN, Rés.X.63; Grafton, *Commerce with the Classics*, 168.
81. For Filelfo's Harpocration, see Calderini, "Intorno ad un passo di Suida," 15–16; Calderini, "Ricerche intorno alla biblioteca," 320. When Filelfo cites Hyperides in letters to Sassuolo da Prato of 1444 and 1451, his citations are taken from Harpocration.
82. BAV, Vat.gr.871 (Devreesse, *Le fonds grec*, 35).
83. Madrid, Bibl. Nacional, 7211, folios 205–45v (Andrés, *Catálogo de los códices griegos*, 497–500). For the subscription (folio 245v), see ibid., 499. For the turn of phrase, compare Plato, *Phaedrus*, 276d.
84. Florence, Bibl. Laurenziana, 55.14, folios 1–42v, has Gaza's grammar (1461–62), written by Alfonsos Dursos (recorded 1473; RGK 1, no. 9). Demetrius copied folios 43–262v (RGK 1, no. 93).
85. PBN, gr.2552, folios 24–88. See RGK 2, no. 202; Keaney, *Harpocration*, xxii. This scribe may be the monk Hilarion of Verona, for whom see Fuiano, "Ilarione da Verona." His location in 1496 is not known.
86. Florence, Bibl. Laurenziana, 58.4, folios 1–71. For the history of this manuscript, see Ullman and Stadter, *The Public Library of Renaissance Florence*, 259–60. Its annotations are by Quirini (d. 1475–79), not Marsilio Ficino: see D. Speranzi's forthcoming article in *Segno e testo* 8 (2009). For Apostolis's other manuscripts, see RGK 1, no. 278; 2, no. 379; 3, no. 454.
87. The manuscript brought to Florence by Lascaris seems to have been BL, Royal 16 C.17: see Speranzi, "Per la storia della libreria medicea privata," 201–3. Folios 1 though 78 of this manuscript were probably written by Demetrius Trivolis (Keaney, *Harpocration*, xiv–xv). For Trivolis (recorded 1456–92), see Oleroff, "Démétrius Trivolis," and RGK 1, no. 103.
88. Genavensis m g 43, folios 1–53 (Procopius), folios 54–158 (Harpocration). See Haury, *Procopius caesariensis omnia opera*, 4:vii.
89. Venice, Bibl. Marciana, gr.443 (Mioni, *Bibliothecae Divi Marci Venetiarum*, 2:214–15; Labowsky, *Bessarion's Library and the Biblioteca Marciana*, 177). Venice, Bibl. Marciana, gr.490 also has Harpocration and is listed in the 1474 inventory of Bessarion's books (Labowsky, *Bessarion's Library and the Biblioteca Marciana*, 200).
90. BL, Burn.96. For Musurus's movements, see RGK 1, no. 265.
91. Rome, Bibl. Angelica, gr.3 (RGK 1, no. 67).
92. Appendix 2, no. 12.
93. Appendix 2, no. 34.
94. Henry, *Photius*, 2:115–19.
95. De Borries, *Phrynichi Sophistae Praeparatio Sophistica*, edited from PBN, Coislin.gr.345, for which see Devreesse, *Catalogue des manuscrits grecs*, 329–30.
96. For the manuscripts, see Fischer, *Die Ekloge des Phrynichos*, 3–24.
97. Venice, Bibl. Marciana, gr.486, fifteenth century, has Moschopulus, Thomas Magister, and Phrynichus, *inter alia* (Fischer, *Die Ekloge des Phrynichos*, 18; Labowsky, *Bessarion's Library and the Biblioteca Marciana*, 177, item no. 480).
98. BAV, Vat.gr.1377 has Gaza's grammar (folios 1–160), Gregory of Corinth's *De dialectis*, and Phrynichus (folios 161–205). Folios 161 through 205 were copied by Trivizias (RGK 3, no. 123). This portion seems to have been copied between the publication of Gaza's grammar, 1461–62, and Trivizias's death in 1485. The first part found itself in Musurus's classroom: a

note on folio 153 reads, "Gaza a nostro Musuro reprehenditur hoc in loco" (De Nolhac, *La bibliothèque de Fulvio Orsini*, 348n140; Fischer, *Die Ekloge des Phrynichos*, 3–24).

99. Florence, Bibl. Laurenziana, 6.22. The colophon is in Rutherford, *The New Phrynichus*, 505.
100. PBN, gr.1045. Bartolomeo Comparini da Prato copied folios 1 through 280v of this manuscript at Padua (RGK 2, no. 46; Fischer, *Die Ekloge des Phrynichos*, 5; Wilson, "The Book Trade in Venice ca. 1400–1515," 391).
101. Legrand, *Bibliographie hellénique*, item no. 53.
102. Appendix 2, no. 27. Guarino used a manuscript of Fischer's "c" family, perhaps Rhosos's Florence, Bibl. Laurenziana, 6.22. He did not use Callierges's edition (Fischer, *Die Ekloge des Phrynichos*, 33). For Guarino's dictionary, see chapter 2, section "Greek Lexica in Western Europe, 1396–1529," p. 70
103. Appendix 2, no. 30.
104. Trivizias made BAV, Pal.gr.253 (Diller, "Three Greek Scribes Working for Bessarion," 405; RGK 3, no. 123). He spent the years 1474 to 1485 in Venice (RGK 3, no. 123), so this copy was probably made in that city.
105. Souliardos made PBN, gr.1413 (RGK 2, no. 392), PBN, gr.1412 (January 1486; Omont, "Les manuscrits grecs," 26), and Toledo, Chapter Library 45–30 (1496; Diller, "The Tradition of Stephanus Byzantinus," 340). Diller suspected the date of PBN, gr.1412, because he believed that Stephanus was rediscovered by Janus Lascaris in 1491 and because he believed that in 1486 Souliardos was in Greece. However, Trivizias's copy shows that the work was available by 1485, while another manuscript, PBN, gr.3048, was subscribed by Souliardos in Florence in January 1486 (RGK 2, no. 392). The dates of both manuscripts of 1486 are probably *stylo florentino*, that is, 1487 new style.
106. Rhosos copied Florence, Bibl. Laurenziana, 4.3, folios 23 through 308. It was probably made at Rome: he dated PBN, gr.1857 (Aristotle) at Rome, February 22, 1492, and Florence, Bibl. Laurenziana, 58.11 (Stobaeus) at Rome, July 10, 1493 (RGK 1, no. 178). Calfurnio's manuscript, unidentified, was still in his library at his death in 1503 (Müller, "Neue Mittheilungen," 389; Diller, "The Tradition of Stephanus Byzantinus," 336, 339; Marcotte, "La bibliothèque de Jean Calphurnius," 193).
107. Otherwise known as Didymus Zenoteles. This is now Venice, Bibl. Marciana, gr.7.52. See Diller, "The Library of Francesco and Ermolao Barbaro," 260.
108. Moschus made Breslau, Rehdig. 47 (Wiesner and Victor, "Griechische Schreiber der Renaissance," 60; RGK 1, no. 97) and Escorial Σ.III.7 (Diller, "The Tradition of Stephanus Byzantinus," 340; Fernández Pomar, "Copistas en los códices griegos escurialenses," 9).
109. For the date, see appendix 2, no. 10. Aldus omitted one quire marking. In the colophon he wrote, "Nota, lector, deesse in libro quaternionem ZF, quia non extat reliquum cappae literae. Relictus est igitur locus ut si forte quispiam quod deest aliquando invenerit, illud commode huic libro queat adiungere" (folio 58r, sig. ΛL8r). In the catalog of June 22, 1503, this volume has the price of three lire added in manuscript, apparently by Aldus himself (Orlandi, *Aldo Manuzio editore*, 2: plate XI). Taberio produced a commentary on Persius, and in 1486, he revised Omnibonus Leonicenus's commentary on Lucan (Robathan, Kristeller, and Bischoff, "Persius," 271–72).
110. Orlandi, *Aldo Manuzio editore*, 1:56.
111. Venice, Bibl. Marciana, gr.622, copied by the scribe of Oxford, Bodleian, Holkh.gr.88 of Aristophanes. The date is derived from its watermarks (Wilson, "On the Transmission of the Greek Lexica," 372–73). Wilson does not notice Diller's claim that Caesar Strategos copied the manuscript (Diller, "Pausanias in the Middle Ages," 494n60).
112. Calderini, "Ricerche intorno alla biblioteca," 325. In the letter, Filelfo conflates articles from Hesychius and the *Etymologicum magnum*.
113. For Musurus's editorial work on this manuscript, see Wilson, *From Byzantium to Italy*, 152–53.
114. Irigoin, "L'édition princeps d'Athénée et ses sources," 418.
115. See Allen, "Speculations on St. Thomas More's Use of Hesychius."

116. Reeve, *Erasmus' Annotations on the New Testament*, 33.
117. Offenbacher, "La bibliothèque de Willibald Pirckheimer," 255.
118. Bertalot, "Zwölf Briefe des Ambrogio Traversari," 262–63; Sabbadini, *Il metodo degli umanisti*, 18–20.
119. *De ordine docendi et studendi*, edited by Kallendorf, *Humanist Educational Treatises*, 282.
120. Appendix 1, no. 137, preface.
121. Florence, Bibl. Laurenziana, Ashb.1439 (Pintaudi, *Marsilio Ficino*).
122. Basle, Universitätsbibliothek, F.VIII.3, folios 141r–167v. For this vocabulary, see Cortesi, "Il «Vocabularium» greco di Giovanni Tortelli," 478–81.
123. In the preface he writes, "ho voluto formare et compilare uno breve introduttorio onde ciascuno latino per se stesso et sanza precettore possi introdursi a sapere, legere, scrivere, intendere, et parlare greco volgare et litterale, et che essi greci possino acquistare la lingua latina et la volgare italiana." See appendix 2, no. 35.
124. "vocabularium graecum... cuius significata latine interpretata sunt" (cited in Thiermann, "I dizionari greco-latini fra medioevo e umanesimo," 674).
125. S. Mich.182, now Venice, Bibl. Marciana, gr.10.30. For a description and the note of ownership, see Mioni, "I manoscritti greci di S. Michele di Murano," 336. See also Diller, "The Library of Francesco and Ermolao Barbaro," 261.
126. BL, Harl.5792. The lexicon seems to have reemerged in the West in this manuscript (Goetz, *Corpus Glossariorum Latinorum*, 2:20; Berti, "Alla scuola di M. Crisolora," 70n163; Thiermann, "I dizionari greco-latini fra medioevo e umanesimo," 659).
127. BAV, Pal.gr.195 has a Latin–Greek lexicon of adverbs, the Greek letters, the verb εἰμί, *Credo, Ave Maria*, the prologue of John's Gospel, and pseudo-Cyril's lexicon, with Michael's subscription. Over two hundred fables of Aesop follow (RGK 3, no. 474).
128. Basle, Universitätsbibliothek, A.III.17. Giovanni's manuscript was used for the *editio princeps* of the lexicon by Stephanus in 1573. See Thiermann, "I dizionari greco-latini fra medioevo e umanesimo," 661. For a description, see Omont, "Catalogue des manuscripts grecs des bibliothèques de Suisse," 406. One manuscript must be eliminated from the inquiry. Gerardo of Patras (recorded 1420–43), a scribe known to have worked for Vittorino da Feltre at Mantua, made Oxford, Bodleian, Barocc.gr.95. This has a lexicon identified in the manuscript as (pseudo-) Cyril, an identification repeated in RGK 1, no. 80. It is, in fact, the shorter version of the lexicon attributed to Zonaras (Naoumides, "The Shorter Version of Pseudo-Zonaras' Lexicon," 441).
129. Vienna, Österreichische Nationalbibl., suppl.gr.45, described in Hunger and Hannick, *Katalog der griechischen Handschriften der Österreichischen Nationalbibliothek*, 85–87. See Thiermann, "I dizionari greco-latini fra medioevo e umanesimo," 660 and n. 15. It once had a note, since lost: "Ἴανος ὁ παννόνιος ἰδίᾳ χειρὶ ἔγραψεν ὅταν τα ἑλληνικα γράμματα μάθεν ἐμελεν" [*sic*]. See Csapodi, *The Corvinian Library*, 456.
130. Milan, Bibl. Ambrosiana, B.46 sup. *olim* T.211 (gr. 90) has pseudo-Cyril and a note: "1472 die 11 septb" (Martini and Bassi, *Catalogus codicum graecorum*, 1:105–6). Merula died in 1494.
131. Florence, Bibl. Laurenziana, Acq.92 (Kristeller, *Supplementum ficinianum*, 340–41; Thiermann, "I dizionari greco-latini fra medioevo e umanesimo," 658, and n6). Francesco died in 1484.
132. Vienna, Österreichische Nationalbibl., suppl.gr.47, described in Hunger and Hannick, *Katalog der griechischen Handschriften der Österreichischen Nationalbibliothek*, 4:89–90. The scribe of the lexicon has not been identified, but Persona (d. 1485) added Guarino's epitome of Chrysoloras to the manuscript (folios 94r–101r). See also Thiermann, "I dizionari greco-latini fra medioevo e umanesimo," 660, and n16.
133. Yale, University Library, Beinecke 291, has pseudo-Cyril, folios 1r–151v (Shailor, *Catalogue of Medieval and Renaissance Manuscripts*, 2:67–68).
134. BL, Harl.6313, described in Thiermann, *Das Wörterbuch der Humanisten*, 22–24. On the fortunes of this manuscript, see Zamponi, "Un ignoto compendio sozomeniano," 252–53. The verso of the first leaf, of vellum and apparently a guard leaf, has the following note in

Zomino's hand: "Greci habent usque in presentem annum—viz Mccccxx—annos mundi 6927, et incip[iunt] annum [de] mense Septembris, et discrepant a nobis q[uonia]m usque in presentem diem ha[be]mus annos mundi 6621." Thiermann suspected the date (*Das Wörterbuch der Humanisten*, 148–49, 174; "I dizionari greco-latini fra medioevo e umanesimo," 670).

135. Basle, Universitätsbibliothek, F.VIII.3, folios 168r–211v (Cortesi, "Il «Vocabularium» greco di Giovanni Tortelli"). Ferrara 84 and BAV, Vat.gr.5, folios 1r–61r, have a similar dictionary in a more complete form (Thiermann, "I dizionari greco-latini fra medioevo e umanesimo," 658n3). BAV, Vat.gr.5 was copied by Nicolaus Rhaxes (RGK 3, no. 514).

136. Greco, *Vespasiano da Bisticci*, 2:371. Vespasiano seems to be referring to a manuscript with columns in Greek and Latin. This, at least, appears to be his meaning when he commented that the library of Federigo Duke of Urbino contained "tutti e' vocabolisti de' Greci, et greco con la expositione latina . . ." (Greco, *Vespasiano da Bisticci*, 1:396).

137. Filelfo wrote to Niccolò in January 1431, January 1432, and April 1433 (Milan, Bibl. Trivulziana, ms. 873, folios 18v–20r, 22r, 25v). From the first of these, it appeared that the young man had an interest in Latin vocabulary. Niccolò wrote to Giannozzo Manetti, in about 1444, a letter in which he displayed his Greek learning, now Florence, Bibl. Riccardiana, 1166, folios 13v–14r. He entered a monastery around 1450 and may have died soon afterward (Field, *The Origins of the Platonic Academy of Florence*, 64).

138. Thiermann assigned this compilation to Guarino Veronese on slender circumstantial evidence (Thiermann, *Das Wörterbuch der Humanisten*, 149–55). He later repeated this identification without caveats (Thiermann, "I dizionari greco-latini fra medioevo e umanesimo," 662). The compiler used BAV, Vat.gr.877, a Greek–Latin lexicon that has notes by Poggio Bracciolini (Thiermann, *Das Wörterbuch der Humanisten*, 44–45; Thiermann, "I dizionari greco-latini fra medioevo e umanesimo," 661–62, and n20). For copies of the lexicon, see the list in Thiermann, "I dizionari greco-latini fra medioevo e umanesimo," 661–63.

139. BL, Add.14083 (RGK 1, no. 382; Thiermann, *Das Wörterbuch der Humanisten*, 21–22; Thiermann, "I dizionari greco-latini fra medioevo e umanesimo," 662–63).

140. BAV, Pal.gr.194 (Cagni, "I codici vaticani," 6–7; Thiermann, *Das Wörterbuch der Humanisten*, 51–52; Thiermann, "I dizionari greco-latini fra medioevo e umanesimo," 662–63; RGK 3, no. 302).

141. For the possibility that a Greek–Latin lexicon, Florence, Bibl. Laurenziana, Conv. soppr. 580, is in Traversari's hand, see Thiermann, *Das Wörterbuch der Humanisten*, 17–18.

142. Rome, Bibl. Angelica, lat.1094 and BAV, Barb.gr.585 (RGK 1, no. 183; 3, no. 302; Thiermann, *Das Wörterbuch der Humanisten*, 40–41, 48–49; Thiermann, "I dizionari greco-latini fra medioevo e umanesimo," 663).

143. BAV, Vat.gr.2355 (Thiermann, *Das Wörterbuch der Humanisten*, 47). Lascaris copied the Greek columns, and an unidentified Italian copied the Latin. It has Crivelli's signature (folio 245v), and is dated around 1464 in Martínez-Manzano, *Konstantinos Laskaris*, 331. For Crivelli, see chapter 1, section "Constantine Lascaris."

144. Madrid, Bibl. Nacional, Res.224 (Andrés, *Catálogo de los códices griegos*, 540–41; Thiermann, "I dizionari greco-latini fra medioevo e umanesimo," 662–63).

145. Lygizos: PBN, Coislin.179, folios 3r–317v (RGK 2, no. 386; Thiermann, *Das Wörterbuch der Humanisten*, 38–39; Thiermann, "I dizionari greco-latini fra medioevo e umanesimo," 663). Apostolis: Oxford, Bodleian, D'Orv. 117 (RGK 1, no. 278; Thiermann, *Das Wörterbuch der Humanisten*, 35–36; Thiermann, "I dizionari greco-latini fra medioevo e umanesimo," 663). Rhusotas: Bologna, Bibl. Univ., ms. 2498, and PBN, suppl.gr.1318, which lacks the Latin column (RGK 1, no. 154; 2, no. 203; Thiermann, *Das Wörterbuch der Humanisten*, 11–12, 39–40; Thiermann, "I dizionari greco-latini fra medioevo e umanesimo," 658–59, 662).

146. Legrand, *Cent-dix lettres greques de F. Filelfo*, 174.

147. Appendix 2, no. 1.

148. Appendix 2, no. 2.

149. The grammar is appendix 1, no. 5. His preface to the Psalter, addressed to Lodovico Donato, is in Botfield, *Prefaces*, 13–16.

150. Translated by Angelo Cospo, first printed in 1516 (Cosenza, *Biographical and Bibliographical Dictionary*, 2:1138–40; Gualdo Rosa, "Crastone, Giovanni," 580–81).
151. Terentianus Maurus. Milan, February 4, 1497 (ISTC it00063000). The earliest extant edition of Cruceius's Callimachus is undated, but after 1500 (ISTC ic00061500). An earlier edition may have been lost.
152. The exploration of Crastoni's debts was begun by Delaruelle, "Le dictionnaire grec-latin de Crastone." For additions, see Thiermann, *Das Wörterbuch der Humanisten*, 132–44, although only one bears Crastoni's name (ibid., 134).
153. See chapter 1, section "Theodore Gaza," pp. 18–19. Crastoni's lexicon refers twice to Gaza's grammar for clarification (Thiermann, *Das Wörterbuch der Humanisten*, 137).
154. He seems to have owned BAV, Vat.gr.1314, which has *Etymologica varia* (folios 66–99), and Modena, Bibl. Estense, α.W.5.5, of which folios 26v through 66v and 75r through 90v were made by Emmanuel Zacharides and most of the rest by Callistus (RGK 1, nos. 18 and 114). Modena, Bibl. Estense, α.W.5.5, contains the longer version of the lexicon of pseudo-Zonaras (Naoumides, "The Shorter Version of Pseudo-Zonaras' Lexicon," 487). Both manuscripts were subsequently owned by Giorgio Valla. For details, see Centanni, "La biblioteca di Andronico Callisto 215," 218.
155. Thiermann, "I dizionari greco-latini fra medioevo e umanesimo," 674, and n50.
156. BAV, Vat.gr.2355 (Thiermann, "I dizionari greco-latini fra medioevo e umanesimo." 674–75; Martínez-Manzano, *Konstantinos Laskaris*, 331).
157. PBN, gr.2628 (Omont, "Georges Hermonyme de Sparte," 89–90; Thiermann, *Das Wörterbuch der Humanisten*, 37–38). Hermonymus also made Montpellier, École de médicine, ms. 415, a Latin–Greek lexicon examined in Decharme, "Extraits d'un lexique." For the categorization of the text of this lexicon, see Thiermann, "I dizionari greco-latini fra medioevo e umanesimo," 674. Reuchlin saw a Greek lexicon among Hermonymus's books at Paris, between 1477 and 1478. In January 1479, now at Orléans, he asked the Greek for it. Hermonymus replied that it was not his, but that Reuchlin could have it for six scudi (Rhein, Dall'Asta, and Dörner, *Johannes Reuchlin*, 1:26–27).
158. ISTC ic00958000 has an image of this preface.
159. Breen, "Francesco Zambeccari," 51n18.
160. This is the price in the catalog of October 1, 1498, and the same figure is written beside the volume in the catalog of June 22, 1503 (Orlandi, *Aldo Manuzio editore*, 2: plates IX–X). For the lexicon, see appendix 2, no. 6.
161. Orlandi, *Aldo Manuzio editore*, 1:20–21.
162. *Georgics*, 2:103–8. The vines are listed in lines 89–102.
163. Dorez, "Études aldines III," 325.
164. Appendix 2, no. 13.
165. "Hae [*sc.* annotationes] statim quidem inveniuntur quibusdam signis vel lunulis quae extant in margine animadversis quibus declaratur ibi adnotatum vel reformatum aliquid esse" (sig. N1r).
166. Appendix 2, no. 29, sig. a1v.
167. Appendix 2, no. 29, sig. a1v.
168. Appendix 2, no. 8.
169. The work is now attributed to Joannes Philoponus (Daly, *Ioannis Philoponi*, xxvii–xxviii, 141–95).
170. Lucchesi, "Una prolusione," 58. These *vocabularia* are not known to me.
171. *De adfinium vocabulorum differentia*, Nickau, *Ammonii qui dicitur liber de adfinium vocabulorum differentia*. Urceo noticed it; see this chapter, pp. 65–66.
172. Omont, "Essai sur les débuts de la typographie grecque à Paris," 59–60.
173. For other evidence for the shortage of Greek type in Gourmont's shop, see Shaw, "Setting by Formes."
174. In the preface to his edition of three of Plutarch's *Moralia*: "Quare . . . facturus precium curae mihi visus sum si ex optimo quoque graecae primum linguae auctore . . . aliquod quasi

specimen imprimendum curarem quibusdam characteribus qui prius in hac urbe habebantur; non multis illis quidem elimatis, sed quos tamen pro tempore speremus fore non inutiles" (Omont, "Essai sur les débuts de la typographie grecque à Paris," 55).
175. Ibid., 60. The "furtivae notae" may be the ligatures and abbreviations. Since at least some of the type is already in use, "exscalpuntur" seems to describe the process of removing freshly cast type from its mold. It may, however, refer to the process of cutting new punches.
176. For the edition, and this date, see appendix 1, no. 42.
177. EE 3:421–22. Erasmus, writing from Louvain, also took this opportunity to ask Froben to send him a copy of the Ferrara dictionary of 1510.
178. For Curio's preface, see appendix 2, no. 20.
179. Ibid.
180. Appendix 1, nos. 18 and 46. For the work, see Hoffman, *Die griechischen Dialekte*, 2:204–22.
181. Appendix 2, no. 24, sig. Q5v.
182. EE 5:484–85.
183. For the genesis of the dictionary, see Guida, "Il *Dictionarium* di Favorino e il *Lexicon Vindobonense*," 269–73.
184. Ceresa, "Favorino, Guarino (Varino, Guerino)," 477. These reprints are Basle: R. Winter, 1538–41; Venice: A. Bortolis, 1712; Venice: N. Glykeos, 1801.

Chapter 3

1. Battista Guarino, *De ordine docendi et studendi*, edited by Kallendorf, *Humanist Educational Treatises*, 282.
2. Pozzi, "Da Padova a Firenze nel 1493," 193.
3. *Contra Aristogitonem, orationes duae doctissimae, a Philippo Melanchthone iam primum latinitate donatae* (Hagenau: Secer, 1527) sig. aa2r.
4. Edited by Rupprich, *Die Briefwechsel*, 288. I believe that the text referred to in this letter, variously identified as Urbano's or Lascaris's grammar, was actually this pamphlet.
5. A pupil of Vittorino da Feltre. Vittorino gave him a Greek manuscript of Xenophon: see Woodward, *Vittorino da Feltre and Other Humanist Educators*, 49 and n3.
6. Appendix 1, nos. 24 and 25.
7. For these instructions, see Wuttke, "Zur griechischen Grammatik des Konrad Celtis," 296, and chapter 1, section "Conrad Celtis."
8. See chapter 2, section "Greek Lexica in Western Europe, 1396–1529," pp. 67–68.
9. Appendix 1, no. 37.
10. Croke's Ausonius is dated 1515 and the preface is dated October 23 *sine anno*. His *Achademie Lipsensis encomium congratulatorium* is undated, but the prefatory letter is December 28 *sine anno*. The *encomium*, apparently Croke's prolusion to his lectures on Ausonius, is edited in Boehme, *De litteratura lipsiensi opuscula academica*, 191–205. For the date of Croke's *Tabulae*, see appendix 1, no. 75.
11. Appendix 1, no. 8.
12. Agricola was staying at Paffraet's house in Deventer in April 1484 (EE 1:581).
13. That is, I know of no copy of the appendix in a fifteenth-century binding.
14. Appendix 1, nos. 22, 26, 33, 46, 56, 139.
15. Appendix 1, nos. 19 and 159.
16. Appendix 1, nos. 24, 25, 27.
17. Appendix 1, no. 28.
18. Appendix 1, no. 36.
19. Appendix 1, no. 50.
20. Appendix 1, no. 49, apparently the *editio princeps*.
21. Appendix 1, no. 44. Melanchthon arrived in September 1512, and graduated January 1514, after which he worked for the printer Thomas Anshelm (EE 2:319n).
22. The pamphlet is appendix 1, no. 88. Melanchthon refers to it in appendix 1, no. 94, sig. a3r.

23. Appendix 1, no. 129, sig. A3r.
24. *De liberorum educatione*, edited by Kallendorf, *Humanist Educational Treatises*, 162–63.
25. Nolan and Hirsch, *The Greek Grammar of Roger Bacon*, 17–24.
26. Omont, "Georges Hermonyme de Sparte," 78–79.
27. The *editio princeps* of *Homerocentra*, 1502, included the translation of Petrus Candidus Monachus. See Botfield, *Prefaces*, 254–56. For the technique of interleaving, see Botley, "Learning Greek in Western Europe, 1476–1516," 207–11.
28. Cited in chapter 2, section "Greek Lexica in Western Europe, 1396–1529," p. 61–62.
29. *De ordine docendi et studendi*, edited in Kallendorf, *Humanist Educational Treatises*, 296.
30. Edited in Sabbadini, "Andrea Contrario," 418.
31. Now Cambridge, Corpus Christi College, ms. 480. Farley died young in 1464. See Weiss, *Humanism in England*, 136–38.
32. To Celtis, April 1495 (edited in Rupprich *Die Briefwechsel*, 145–47, letter no. 88).
33. Milan: Bonaccorso, September 20, 1481 (ISTC ip01035000).
34. The preface, addressed to Lodovico Donato, is in Botfield, *Prefaces*, 13–16.
35. Psalter: [Milan], September 20, 1481 (ISTC ip0103500); Venice, November 15, 1486 (ISTC ip01034000); Venice, [c. 1496–98] (ISTC ip01033000). New Testament: appendix 1, no. 53.
36. Fiocco, "La biblioteca di Palla Strozzi," 297.
37. See Cortesi, "Il «Vocabularium» greco di Giovanni Tortelli," 476–77.
38. Woodward, *Vittorino da Feltre and Other Humanist Educators*, 70.
39. Mondrain, "L'étude du grec en Italie," 316.
40. PBN, gr.45 and PBN, gr.98, were copied in 1478 and 1479 for David Chambellan; PBN, gr.99, of Luke's Gospel belonged to Germain de Brie and Jacques Toussain; PBN, gr.59 (Acts, Epistles, Apocalypse), and PBN, gr.108–11 (Epistles), have marginalia by Budé; Cambridge, University Library, Kk.v.35; Cambridge, University Library, Ll.ii.13, has marginalia by Budé (Omont, "Georges Hermonyme de Sparte," 74–77).
41. All at Oxford: see RGK 1, no. 180.
42. "Si quid est novae graecanitatis, vestem citius oppigneraverimus quam non potiamur; maxime si qua Christiana, ut Ψαλμοί, ut Evangelia" (EE 1:368, ep. 160).
43. Stinger, *Humanism and the Church Fathers*, 188; to Michael, 4 October [1435], edited in Mehus, *Ambrosii Traversarii epistolae*, 2: column 617, book 13, letter no. 5. Planudes translated *De consolatione philosophiae*, *De differentiis topicis*, and *De hypotheticis syllogismis* (edited in Papathomopoulos, *Anicii Manlii Severini Boethii*). Planudes was also responsible for a version of Augustine's *De Trinitate* (edited in Papathomopoulos, Tsabare, and Rigotti, *Αὐγουστίνου Περὶ Τριάδος*). A manuscript of the Greek text of *De Trinitate* was given to Traversari by Vittorino da Feltre in July 1433 (Ullman and Stadter, *The Public Library of Renaissance Florence*, 97, 253, item no. 1102). Palla Strozzi's manuscript of this work is BAV, Urb.gr.26. It was sold to Palla in 1459 (Diller, "Greek Codices of Palla Strozzi and Guarino Veronese," 316).
44. Saffrey, "Une exercise de latin philosophique," 374–79.
45. Gaza's version of *De senectute* has been edited by Salanitro, *Theodorus Gaza*. Gaza may have made a version of the *Somnium Scipionis* (Geanakoplos, "Theodore Gaza, a Byzantine Scholar," 71) and of Pliny, *Historia Naturalis*, 2:12–13 (Bianca, "Gaza, Teodoro," 743). A lost Florentine manuscript seems to have contained a Greek version made by Gaza of the first letter of the first volume of Cicero's correspondence (Diller, "The Manuscript Tradition of Aeschines' Orations," 61–62). Gaza has been proposed as the author of a Greek translation of Caesar's *De bello gallico* 1 through 7 (i.e., excluding book 8), but this version is more probably by Piero degli Strozzi (1500?–1558). See Brown, "Caesar," 97.
46. For Occo's manuscript, see Mondrain, "La collection de manuscrits grecs d'Adolphe Occo," 173; for Hermonymus's, see Omont, "Georges Hermonyme de Sparte," 81, 93; for Lascaris's, see Salanitro, *Theodorus Gaza*, x.
47. Bianca, "Gaza, Teodoro," 740.
48. *Cato Maior* 79 renders *Cyropaedia* 8:7, 17. See Jones, "Cicero as a Translator," 25. For the use of the *Cyropaedia* in the classroom, see chapter 3, section "Xenophon."

49. This manuscript contains homilies of Saint Basil, extracts from the Greek Fathers, and Planudes' translation of the *Disticha Catonis*. It is a copy of one loaned to Occo by Johann Reuchlin and returned in July 1494 (Mondrain, "La collection de manuscrits grecs d'Adolphe Occo," 166–67 and n39).
50. Mondrain, "L'étude du grec en Italie," 315. Planudes translated the *Distichs* in the late thirteenth or early fourteenth century.
51. Florence, Bibl. Laurenziana, gr.314. After Poliziano's death, it entered the library of San Marco in 1497 (Ullman and Stadter, *The Public Library of Renaissance Florence*, 266; Ortoleva, "La traduzione di Massimo Planude dei *Disticha Catonis*," 98n17).
52. Aix-en-Provence, Bibl. Méjanes, 1385, and Vienna, Österreichische Nationalbibl., suppl. gr.83 (Ortoleva, "La traduzione di Massimo Planude dei *Disticha Catonis*," 98n17); Berne 629, once owned by Budé (Omont, "Georges Hermonyme de Sparte," 84; Omont, "Catalogue des manuscrits grecs des bibliothèques de Suisse," 426).
53. See chapter 3, section "Hesiod," p. 102 and n. 405.
54. Appendix 1, no. 47 (1512). Appendix 1, no. 57 (1515). The work was printed with Hesiod, *Works and Days*; *Aurea verba*; pseudo-Phocylides; pseudo-Cebes, *Tabula* (Strasbourg: Knoblouch, [1515]). This volume may have been edited by Nachtgall, for whom see chapter 1, section "Ottomar Nachtgall."
55. See EE 2:1–3, letter no. 298 to John de Neve.
56. After printing, a gathering of four leaves was printed to correct an omission and prefaced to the main text. The original title page announced, "Philolai Crotoniatae carmina aurea, quae falso hactenus Pythagorae adscripta sunt." In the volume itself they are, however, titled "Aurea Carmina Pythagorae" (sig. m2r). See appendix 1, no. 36.
57. PG 161:924–25. In his grammar, Melanchthon cites lines 9 through 11 (κρατεῖν ... θυμοῦ) of which he says, "Philolai sunt in Pythagoricis institutis" (appendix 1, no. 165, sig. K6r).
58. "Phocylides ... synchronus Theognidis ... Exstat eius *admonitorium poema* heroico metro utilissimum" (*De scriptoribus graecis, patria siculis*, PG 161:923–24).
59. Derron, "Inventaire des manuscrits du Pseudo-Phocylide," item no. 112.
60. Chrysococces: BAV, Urb.gr.132, Pythag.; PBN, gr.3047, Phoc., Pythag. (Derron, "Inventaire des manuscrits du Pseudo-Phocylide," item no. 110; Derron, "Inventaire des manuscrits des *Vers d'Or* pythagoriciens," item nos. 140 and 174; RGK 2, no. 95 and 3, no. 127). Scutariota: Escorial T.III.15, Pythag.; BL, Burn.70, Pythag. (Fernández Pomar, "Copistas en los códices griegos escurialenses," 9; Derron, "Inventaire des manuscrits des *Vers d'Or* pythagoriciens," item nos. 48 and 82; RGK 1, no. 183). Lygizos: PBN, gr.2008, Phoc., Pythag. (Derron, "Inventaire des manuscrits du Pseudo-Phocylide," item no. 100; Derron, "Inventaire des manuscrits des *Vers d'Or* pythagoriciens," item no. 131; RGK 2, no. 386). Rhosos: Salamanca, Bibl. Univ. 243 (I.2.10), Phoc., Pythag.; Venice, Bibl. Marciana, gr.192, Pythag. (Derron, "Inventaire des manuscrits des *Vers d'Or* pythagoriciens," item no. 175; Centanni, "La biblioteca di Andronico Callisto," 219). Apostolis: BAV, Vat.gr.72, Pythag.; PBN, gr.1804, Pythag. (Wiesner and Victor, "Griechische Schreiber der Renaissance," 53; Derron, "Inventaire des manuscrits des *Vers d'Or* pythagoriciens," item nos. 125 and 154). Damilas: Florence, Bibl. Laurenziana, 58.33, Pythag. (Derron, "Inventaire des manuscrits des *Vers d'Or* pythagoriciens," item no. 57). Souliardos: probably Milan, Bibl. Ambrosiana, D.15 sup. (gr. 218), Phoc., Pythag.; certainly PBN, gr.2600, Phoc., Pythag. (Derron, "Inventaire des manuscrits du Pseudo-Phocylide," item nos. 75 and 105; Derron, "Inventaire des manuscrits des *Vers d'Or* pythagoriciens," item nos. 95 and 136; RGK 2, no. 392). Hypselas: BL, Burn.85, Phoc., Pythag. (Derron, "Inventaire des manuscrits du Pseudo-Phocylide," item no. 69; Derron, "Inventaire des manuscrits des *Vers d'Or* pythagoriciens," item no. 83; RGK 1, no. 349). Donos: Oxford, Bodleian, Barocc.gr.64, Phoc., Pythag.; BL, Harl.5664, Phoc. (Derron, "Inventaire des manuscrits du Pseudo-Phocylide," item nos. 71 and 91; Derron, "Inventaire des manuscrits des *Vers d'Or* pythagoriciens," item no. 114; RGK 1, no. 14).
61. Argyropoulos: PBN, gr.1806, Pythag. (Derron, "Inventaire des manuscrits des *Vers d'Or* pythagoriciens," item no. 127; RGK 2, no. 212). Callistus: BAV, Vat.gr.1314, Pythag.;

Venice, Bibl. Marciana, gr.522, Phoc., Pythag. (Derron, "Inventaire des manuscrits du Pseudo-Phocylide," item no. 143; Eleuteri *Storia della tradizione manoscritta* 26–27; Centanni, "La biblioteca di Andronico Callisto," 218, 220). Hermonymus: Leiden, Univ. Library, Voss.gr.Q.65, Phoc.; PBN, lat.16707, Phoc. (Derron, "Inventaire des manuscrits du Pseudo-Phocylide," item nos. 65 and 118; Omont, "Georges Hermonyme de Sparte," 90–91). Lascaris: Naples, II.A.19, Phoc., Pythag. (Derron, "Inventaire des manuscrits du Pseudo-Phocylide," item no. 85; Derron, "Inventaire des manuscrits des *Vers d'Or* pythagoriciens," item no. 110; Cyrillus, *Codices graeci MSS regiae bibliothecae borbonicae*, 1:49–50). Chalcondyles: PBN, suppl.gr.170, Pythag. (Derron, "Inventaire des manuscrits des *Vers d'Or* pythagoriciens," item no. 143; RGK 2, no. 138). Moschus: Vienna, Österreichische Nationalbibl., Phil.gr.331, Phoc., Pythag.; PBN, gr.2568, Moschop., Phoc. (Derron, "Inventaire des manuscrits du Pseudo-Phocylide," item nos. 103 and 157; Derron, "Inventaire des manuscrits des *Vers d'Or* pythagoriciens," item no. 195; RGK 1, no. 97, and 2, no. 131).

62. Hankins, *Plato in the Italian Renaissance*, 2:410–11 and n11.
63. Poliziano: BAV, Vat.gr.1373, verses 1–34 only (Derron, "Inventaire des manuscrits du Pseudo-Phocylide," item no. 132). Zamberti: Vienna, Österreichische Nationalbibl., Phil.gr.270, Phoc. (Derron, "Inventaire des manuscrits du Pseudo-Phocylide," item no. 154). Urceo: BAV, Ottob. gr.166, Phoc., Pythag.; Florence, Bibl. Laurenziana, .31.20, Phoc., Pythag. (Derron, "Inventaire des manuscrits du Pseudo-Phocylide," item no. 42; Derron, "Inventaire des manuscrits des *Vers d'Or* pythagoriciens," item nos. 52 and 169). Valla: Modena, Bibl. Estense, α.P.5.7, Phoc. (Derron, "Inventaire des manuscrits du Pseudo-Phocylide," item no. 79). Vitali: Vienna, Österreichische Nationalbibl., Phil.gr.167, Phoc. (Derron, "Inventaire des manuscrits du Pseudo-Phocylide," item no. 149; RGK 1, no. 375). Occo: Munich, Staatsbibliothek, gr.313, Pythag. (Mondrain, "La collection de manuscrits grecs d'Adolphe Occo," 172; Derron, "Inventaire des manuscrits des *Vers d'Or* pythagoriciens," item no. 105).
64. Appendix 1, no. 47, sig. a2v.
65. Escorial R.III.5, Phoc., Pythag. (Derron, "Inventaire des manuscrits du Pseudo-Phocylide," item no. 38; Derron, "Inventaire des manuscrits des *Vers d'Or* pythagoriciens," item no. 47).
66. A description of the edition, which I have not seen, is in Girot, *Pindare avant Ronsard*, 410–11.
67. The Aldine text of pseudo-Phocylides, frequently reprinted, has 217 lines. Many of the copies made in the fifteenth century have 230 lines.
68. Twenty-three are in appendix 1: nos. 15, 22, 26, 29, 33, 36, 44, 46, 47, 50, 56, 62, 74, 81, 88, 99, 100, 104, 121, 139, 143 (Pythag. only), 148, 154 (part only). To these may be added six more: Theocritus (Venice, February 1496 new style; ISTC it00144000); Hesiod (Strasbourg: Knoblouch, [1515]: see chapter 3, section "Greek Translations of Latin Texts," n. 54); Hesiod (Florence: Junta, January 1515, *stylo florentino*, Pythag. only); *Sententiae*, edited by J. Musurus (Paris: Gourmont, [by 1517]; Omont, "Essai sur les débuts de la typographie grecque à Paris," 37); *Scriptores aliquot gnomici* (Basle: Froben, February 1521); *Moralia quaedam* (Augsburg: Ruff, December 1523).
69. For Hierocles' work, see Köhler, *Hieroclis in aureum Pythagoreorum carmen commentarius*. For the version, see Aurispa's letter to Panormita (Sabbadini, *Carteggio di Giovanni Aurispa*, letter no. 96). This version was first printed in 1474 (ISTC ih00151000). The Greek text of the commentary was first printed in Paris in 1583.
70. Perhaps 1440 to 1443 (Lockwood, "De Rinucio Aretino," 54, 108–9).
71. On August 12, 1485, Fonzio wrote to Pier Filippo Pandolfini, "Ego quidem ut filio tuo valde consulerem, ei dicavi Phocylidem, aequissimum et continentissimum hominem, ut eius admonitionibus perfecte vivere consuescit" (edited in Juhász, *Bartholomaeus Fontius*, 33). For this Latin version, not located, see Resta, *Apollonio Rodio*, 1096–97n41.
72. Lucca, Bibl. governativa, ms. 3002 (Derron, "Inventaire des manuscrits des *Vers d'Or* pythagoriciens," item no. 91). For this manuscript, see Lavagnini, "Un codicetto lucchese."
73. Augsburg: Froschauer, after April 5, 1500 (ISTC ip00629000). The author's prefatory verses show his use of the Aldine Appendix (sigs. b3v–b4r).

74. Celtis matriculated at Ingolstadt on May 7, 1494. He left for Vienna in October 1497 (Spitz, *Conrad Celtis*, 42, 55). For Locher, see Reicke, *Willibald Pirckheimers Briefwechsel*, 2:52–54.
75. Quintilian, *Institutio oratoria*, 1.ix.
76. For Guarino, see Berrigan, "The Aesopic Fables of Guarino da Verona," 4. Esopo was born September 1422. A translation of twenty-eight fables is in Milan, Bibl. Ambrosiana, R.21 sup., fols. 162v–170r. The manuscript identifies this version as Guarino's, but Cocco believes that it may have been made by a pupil (Cocco, *Ermolao Barbaro il vecchio*, 20, and n38, and 21n42).
77. Milan, Bibl. Ambrosiana, A.69 sup. (gr. 7) (RGK 1, no. 352).
78. BAV, Pal.gr.195 (RGK 3, no. 474). The lexicon is dated 1431 by Michael the Notary. For pseudo-Cyril, see chapter 2, section "Greek Lexica in Western Europe, 1396–1529," p. 63.
79. Valla: edited by Ruelle, "Les 'Apologues' de Guillaume Tardif," 38–49; and see Berrigan, "The Latin Aesop of Ermolao Barbaro," 146–47. For his Greek exemplar, see Finch, "The Greek Source," 118–20. The dedication to Arnau Fenolleda is in Achelis, "Die Aesopübersetzungen des Lorenzo Valla," 243–44. Barbaro: edited in Cocco, *Ermolao Barbaro il vecchio*; and see Berrigan, "The Latin Aesop of Ermolao Barbaro," 143–45. The dedication is in Mehus, *Ambrosii Traversarii epistolae*, 2, cols. 997–98, book 24, letter no. 19.
80. Ognibene: dedicated to Gian Francesco Gonzaga, Marchese of Mantua; probably made before Correr's (Cocco, *Ermolao Barbaro il vecchio*, 23). For the family of the Greek exemplar, see Berrigan, "The Latin Aesop of Ermolao Barbaro," 143 and n15. Correr: dedicated to "fratello Filippo" (Cocco, *Ermolao Barbaro il vecchio*, 23). He claims in the preface to have translated sixty fables, but there are only fifty-nine. He may not have made it directly from the Greek (Berrigan, "The Latin Aesop of Ermolao Barbaro," 143).
81. Rinuccio's dedication to Cardinal Antonio Cerdano is in Lockwood, "De Rinucio Aretino," 69–70. The version is in Österley, *Steinhöwels Äsop*. Rinuccio also translated a life of Aesop, not that of Planudes. For Rinuccio's versions, see Lockwood, "De Rinucio Aretino," 55–56, 61–72.
82. Bonaccorso writes in the preface, "Nunc vero, quo maior liberis tuis ac facilior aditus sit ad utramque linguam et graecam et latinam, quasdam electiores fabulas quae in communi sunt nostrorum hominum usu . . . informari curavimus" (ISTC ia00104000; Botfield, *Prefaces*, 171–72). Ognibene's version was first printed in [Venice, c. 1470–71] (ISTC ia00108500); Valla's was printed in [Valencia, c. 1473–74] (ISTC ia00104500) and [the Netherlands, c. 1465–80] (ISTC ia00104200).
83. ISTC ia00098000, part III, fol. 38r.
84. For Poliziano's instruction, see Perosa, "Due lettere inedite del Poliziano," 353.
85. See chapter 1, section "Constantine Lascaris," p. 27.
86. "Perchè Marco Antonio comincia a intendere qualche cosa, priegho la V. M. si degni di fare vedere un pocho tra li mei libri che li è uno volume che ha la vita e le Fabule di Esopo grece et latine, perchè mi pare al proposito al principio di farli legere le Fabule di Esopo grece, per essere breve e assai chiare . . ." (cited in Calderini, "Ricerche intorno alla biblioteca," 248n5).
87. Reggio: ISTC ia00104000. Venice: ISTC ia00097000. For the Aldine edition, see Botley, "Learning Greek in Western Europe, 1476–1516," 210.
88. See chapter 1, section "Theodore Gaza," p. 19.
89. Edited in Omont, "Georges Hermonyme de Sparte," 88–89; Rhein, Dall'Asta, and Dörner, *Johannes Reuchlin*, 1:26–27. See also Irigoin, "Georges Hermonyme de Sparte," 23.
90. Copenhagen, Bibl. Royale, 212b. See Adler, *Catalogue supplémentaire*, 313–14.
91. Zurich, Zentralbibliothek, C.136, fols. 27r–52r, described in Mondrain, "La collection de manuscrits grecs d'Adolphe Occo," 173.
92. Einsidl.19, described in Omont, "Catalogue des manuscrits grecs des bibliothèques de Suisse," 428. Here, Matthias copied a collection of Greek-Latin vocabularies (September 30, 1503), edited in Goetz, *Corpus Glossariorum Latinorum*, 3:221–79. Matthias copied it from Reuchlin's

autograph (Sicherl, "Pseudodositheana," 189). Einsidl.19 has *inter alia* a work on the Greek verb (January 16, 1504), Aesop (January 27, 1504), and a Greek Psalter (March 1, 1504).
93. Quintilian, *Institutio oratoria*, 1.6.5; 10.1.85. Augustine, *Confessiones*, 1:xiv.
94. For Livius Andronicus (third century BC), see OCD, "Livius Andronicus, Lucius." For Matius (first century BC), see OCD, "Matius, Gnaeus." For Labeo, see Persius, *Satire* no. 1 and the ancient scholia. For Polybius (d. 46 or 47 AD), see OCD, "Polybius (2)." For the *Ilias latina*, see OCD, "*Ilias latina*." It seems to have been made before 68 AD, perhaps by Baebius Italicus.
95. Scaffai, "Pindarus seu Homerus," 932–39.
96. Diller, "Petrarch's Greek Codex of Plato," 270.
97. Pfeiffer, *History of Classical Scholarship*, 14; Pertusi, *Leonzio Pilato fra Petrarca e Boccaccio*, 522. See Petrarch's letter to Boccaccio, 18 August 1360 (*Epistolae Variae*, letter no. 25) and his *Epistola ad Homerum* (*Epistolae Familiares*, book XXIV, letter no. 12).
98. PBN, lat.7880, 1 and 2.
99. Boccaccio, *Genealogiae*, 15:7. See Diller, "Petrarch's Greek Codex of Plato," "Boccaccio's Acquaintance with Homer," 45.
100. Diller, "Petrarch's Greek Codex of Plato," 272n10.
101. Novati, *Epistolario di Coluccio Salutati*, 2:354–58; Stinger, *Humanism and the Church Fathers*, 102; Gualdo Rosa, "Le traduzioni dal greco nella prima metà del '400," 185.
102. For Atumano's version of 1373, see Weiss, "Lo studio di Plutarco nel trecento," 207–10; Lockwood, "De Rinucio Aretino"; Resta, "Antonio Cassarino," 238. Salutati revised this version circa 1396 and 1397. See Novati, *Epistolario di Coluccio Salutati*, 2:480–83; Weiss, "Lo studio di Plutarco nel trecento," 216–19; Gualdo Rosa, "Le traduzioni dal greco nella prima metà del '400," 185.
103. Vienna, Österreichische Nationalbibl., Phil.gr.56, c. 1300, *Odyssey*, which had been annotated by Atumano; BL, Harl.5674, thirteenth century, *Odyssey*; BAV, Vat.gr.30, fourteenth century, *Iliad* (Zorzi, "I Crisolora," 103, 107, 109).
104. Smith, *Epistolario di Pier Paolo Vergerio*, 240–42, letter no. 95.
105. Pertusi, *Leonzio Pilato fra Petrarca e Boccaccio*, 522.
106. Venice, Bibl. Marciana, lat.12.23, which has a note: "Franciscus de Zabarellis feci scribi 1398" (fol. 108v). It was later owned and annotated by Giovanni Calfurnio (Marcotte, "La bibliothèque de Jean Calphurnius," 199).
107. Florence, Bibl. Laurenziana, St. Croce, lat.XXI sin. 8, fols. 158v–160v. An anonymous translation of the *Letter of Aristeas*, dated May 26, 1403, is dedicated to one Frater Thedaldus. For Tedaldo, see Mattesini, "La biblioteca francescana."
108. *Iliad* 9.222–603. After ca. 1422–24, according to Baron, *Leonardo Bruni Aretino*, 172. For the revised date, see Thiermann, *Die Orationes Homeri*, 118–29.
109. He translated passages from, perhaps all of, *Iliad* 10 and *Odyssey* 23: see Sabbadini, *La scuola e gli studi di Guarino Guarini Veronese*, 124, 195–97; Sabbadini, *Epistolario di Guarino Veronese*, 1:581–83.
110. *De ordine docendi et studendi*, edited in Kallendorf, *Humanist Educational Treatises*, 282.
111. The evidence is circumstantial. Gerardo of Patras, who worked for Vittorino in the 1430s, copied PBN, gr.2687 of Homer (RGK 2, no. 107). Traversari saw the pseudo-Herodotean *Vita Homeri*, a work usually associated with the poems, in Vittorino's library in 1433 (Ullman and Stadter, *The Public Library of Renaissance Florence*, 97). In 1440, Guarino wrote to Carlo Brugnolo, "Commenda me viro doctissimo magistro Victorino [da Feltre] et mihi respondeat ora ad ea quae de Homeri commento nuper ad eum scripsi" (*Epistolario* 2:402, cited in Cortesi, "Libri e vicende di Vittorino da Feltre," 89). An "Etymologicon super Homerum" and a "Commentarium super Homerum" are in a list of books, dated June 12, 1445, sent to Gian Pietro da Lucca by Vittorino (Cortesi, "Libri e vicende di Vittorino da Feltre," 88–89).
112. Bianca, "Gaza, Teodoro," 739. Gaza acquired Cambridge, Corpus Christi College, ms. 81 of *Iliad, Posthomerica*, and *Odyssey* (Easterling, "From Britain to Byzantium," 110–11). It cannot be connected with his teaching at Ferrara, since the *Posthomerica* were not rediscovered

until around 1454: see chapter 3, section "Quintus of Smyrna." Demetrius Xanthopoulos, who dated manuscripts in 1450–1451 and 1454, was the scribe (RGK 1, no. 98). Bessarion's Venice, Bibl. Marciana, gr.456, which he donated to Venice in 1468, was made from Xanthopoulos's transcript (Labowsky, *Bessarion's Library and the Biblioteca Marciana*, 176). It has been suggested that Gaza's manuscript came to England with William Selling (d. 1494; Weiss, *Humanism in England*, 158 and n5).

113. Gaza made Florence, Bibl. Laurenziana, 32.1 for Filelfo (Woodward, *Vittorino da Feltre and Other Humanist Educators*, 72). On January 23, 1448, Filelfo declined to sell this manuscript to Bessarion (Calderini, "Ricerche intorno alla biblioteca," 330). Filelfo's letter to Bessarion is in PG 161:iii–iv, and Legrand, *Bibliographie hellénique*, 1:xlvii–xlviii. The *Iliad* paraphrase is edited by Theseus, ʽΟμήρου Ἰλιάς.

114. Lascaris copied Madrid, Bibl. Nacional, 4462, fols. 56–83v, of the *Homeric Hymns* at Milan in 1464 (Andrés, *Catálogo de los códices griegos*, 35–37). He used Madrid, Bibl. Nacional, 4560, commissioned by Ludovico Saccano, which had the *Iliad* with Greek and and Latin glosses and some scholia. Half was copied by Andronicus Galiziotes, and the rest by Cosmas Trapezuntius. A note by Lascaris (fol. 363) says that Cosmas finished it after the death of Andronicus (c. 1460?). After Saccano's death (c. 1480), it passed to the cathedral library at Messina and it was used by Lascaris in his lessons: . . . ἐδίδαξε δὲ ταύτην πολλάκις ἐν Μεσσήνῃ Κωνσταντῖνος ὁ Λάσκαρις (Andrés, *Catálogo de los códices griegos*, 31–33). He finished Madrid, Bibl. Nacional, 4841, of the *Iliad* in Messina on June 2, 1488 (Andrés, *Catálogo de los códices griegos*, 451–53). He owned and glossed Madrid, Bibl. Nacional, 4565 (Andrés, *Catálogo de los códices griegos*, 42–43; Martínez-Manzano, *Konstantinos Laskaris*, 298). He made Perugia, Perus.D.56, fols. 4r–208v, 210r–303v, 304r–348v (RGK 1, no. 223). He bought Madrid, Bibl. Nacional, 4626, *scholia in Iliadem*, in Messina (Andrés, *Catálogo de los códices griegos*, 148–50).

115. Prague, BU PSK, VIII.H.36, has *inter alia* Aristophanes, Proclus, Homer, Oppian, and Theocritus. It was copied by Petrus in 1485, apparently while he studied under Lascaris in Messina (Martínez-Manzano, *Konstantinos Laskaris*, 293). In 1503 Adolf Occo owned three manuscripts in Lascaris's hand, but it remains to be shown that he studied under him. Munich gr.519a has *Iliad* 13–24: folios 1 through 73 are in Occo's hand, as are interlinear glosses and marginalia; folios 74 through 198 are in Lascaris's hand, and there are numerous Greek interlinear glosses in Occo's hand. Martínez-Manzano dates Lascaris's portion around 1460 to 1470. For the Lascaris–Occo manuscripts, see Mondrain, "La collection de manuscrits grecs d'Adolphe Occo," 168–69, 174; Martínez-Manzano, *Konstantinos Laskaris*, 244, 339–40, 341.

116. Oxford, Bodleian, Holkham.gr.84 (Wilson, "The Book Trade in Venice ca. 1400–1515," 389).

117. Gualdo Rosa, "Cortesi Urceo, Antonio, detto Codro," 776.

118. Castrifrancanus, *Alberti Castrifrancani oratio*, sigs. b2v, c1r; Bustico, "Due umanisti veneti," 347.

119. Sabbadini, *Le scoperte dei codici*, 48; Wilson, *From Byzantium to Italy*, 49.

120. For extant fragments, see Calderini, "Ricerche intorno alla biblioteca," 330–39. One edition has the versions of Bruni and Niccolò della Valle, Marsuppini's versions of *Iliad* 1 and *Batrachomyomachia*, and a translation of the *Odyssey* attributed to Filelfo (Venice: B. de Vitalibus, 1516). See Bertalot, "Zur Bibliographie der Übersetzungen," 280–81; Thiermann, "Redécouverte et influence," 55n2.

121. Manetti mentions his copy of Pilato in his treatise *Contra Iudaeos et Gentes* (Baldassari and Bagemihl, *Giannozzo Manetti: Biographical Writings*, 146). His *Iliad* is BAV, Pal.gr.180 (Stevenson, *Codices manuscripti palatini graeci*, 94; RGK 3, no. 302). Scutariota was working in Manetti's house in 1442 (Cagni, "Agnolo Manetti e Vespasiano da Bisticci," 296n1). Manetti also owned BAV, Pal.gr.179, of the *Homeric Hymns* (Stevenson, *Codices manuscripti palatini graeci*, 93–94).

122. Bietenholz and Deutscher, *Contemporaries of Erasmus*, 2:27. "Argonautica et hymnos Orphei et Homeri . . . quae adolescens nescio quomodo ad verbum mihi soli transtuli, quemadmodum tu nuper hospes ad me vidisti, edere nunquam placuit" (Cytowska, "Érasme de Rotterdam," 342).

123. Rhosos made BAV, Vat.gr.27, at Bologna, subscribed on May 28, 1465. For an undated manuscript made by Rhosos at Bologna, see chapter 1, section "Manuel Chrysoloras," p. 10 and n. 86.
124. Resta, *Apollonio Rodio*, 1058. Florence, Bibl. Laurenziana, 66.31, has a version of the *Iliad* (fols. 7r–256v), disordered and with gaps, which may have originated with Callistus (Resta, *Apollonio Rodio*, 1092–95n31). He copied Modena, Bibl. Estense, α.U.5.1 of the *Iliad*, and Modena, Bibl. Estense, α.P.5.19, fols. 2r–43r, of the *Odyssey*; Demetrius Xanthopoulos copied fols. 43r–199v. Both manuscripts were made perhaps between 1455 and 1460 (Centanni, "La biblioteca di Andronico Callisto," 210, 212–13, 218). Callistus copied some *Homeric Hymns* in Modena, Bibl. Estense, α.T.9.14; he wrote scholia on Homer in Modena, Bibl. Estense, α.U.9.22; and he copied Venice, Bibl. Marciana, gr.611, fols. 46–243v, of the *Odyssey* (Günther, "Andronikos Kallistos," 316 and n4, 323, 334).
125. Only lines 1 through 525 remain. Parts of the two versions are compared by Ferri in "Per una supposta traduzione." Ferri calls this a revision of Pilato's translation. For Fonzio's version of the *Posthomerica*, see chapter 3, section "Quintus of Smyrna."
126. BAV, Vat.lat.3298, which has books 2 and 3, was presented to Lorenzo de' Medici in 1472; BAV, Vat.lat.3617, which has books 4 and 5, was complete by 1475 (Levine Rubinstein, "The Notes to Poliziano's «Iliad»," 205).
127. Perosa, "Due lettere inedite del Poliziano," 353.
128. September 1475 (Cammelli, *Demetrio Calcondila*, 56).
129. The preface to his verse prolusion, *Ambra*, addressed to Lorenzo Tornabuoni, is dated November 4, 1485 (edited in Fantazzi, *Angelo Poliziano*, 68–109). Martinelli, "Grammatiche greche," 258–59, 261.
130. On April 2, 1507, Cipriano Senile wrote to Giangiorgio Trissino that he had tried unsuccessfully to persuade Chalcondyles to lecture on Apollonius or pseudo-Orpheus rather than the *Homeric Hymns* (Morsolin, *Giangiorgio Trissino*, 29–30, n1; Friggi, *Gli studi greci a Milano al tempo di Ludovico il Moro*, 206). On April 7, 1508, Chalcondyes wrote to Trissino, "Io sono al quinto libro de la *Iliade*. Lego etiam privatim Basilio nonum librum τῆς Ὀδυσσείας" (Pontani, "Omero, Appiano e l'ombra di un padre," 263–84; Friggi, *Gli studi greci a Milano al tempo di Ludovico il Moro*, 210).
131. ISTC ih00300000. ISTC dates it March 18, 1487, to 1488. The colophon is December 9, 1488; the preface, apparently printed last, is January 13, 1488, *stylo florentino*.
132. He also owned the two-volume Aldine edition of 1504 (Offenbacher, "La bibliothèque de Willibald Pirckheimer," 253). On March 10, 1503, Pirckheimer asked Celtis to send him a ἑρμενεία of Homer (edited in Reicke, *Willibald Pirckheimers Briefwechsel*, 1:195). It is not clear whether this is a translation or a commentary.
133. Marcotte, "La bibliothèque de Jean Calphurnius," 197.
134. Venice, Bibl. Marciana, gr.454, annotated with notes from the A scholia (Grafton, *Commerce with the Classics*, 174–75).
135. Cambridge, University Library, Inc.2.B.8.8 [1943]. He also donated his edition of the *Iliad* scholia (Rome, 1517). See Sturge, *Cuthbert Tunstall*, 392–94.
136. It was not advertised in the Aldine catalog of October 1, 1498 (Orlandi, *Aldo Manuzio editore*, 2: plate IX), but it was in that of June 22, 1503. However, it has been deleted from this catalog, probably when the following Aldine editions were added to the catalog in manuscript: Demosthenes (November 1504); Homer (November 1504); Quintus (c. 1504); Aesop (October 1505; Orlandi, *Aldo Manuzio editore*, 2: plates X–XIII).
137. Edited in Müllner. "Eine Rede des Ioannes Lascaris," 137.
138. Antinori (1470–1503) copied Madrid, Bibl. Nacional, 64, extracts from Eustathius's commentary on Homer, on which he wrote, "Καρῖλος ὁ Ἀντίνωρος, νεανίας πάνυ πεπαιδευμένος τὴν Ἑλλάδα φωνήν, ταύτην τὴν βίβλον ἔγραψε, ἐκ τοῦ Εὐσταθίου ταύτας τὰς ἐκλογὰς Βαρίνου τοῦ Φαβωρίνου ἐκλέγοντος καὶ ἀναγινώσκοντος. αὐτὸς δὲ ὁ Καρῖλος, οὐ προσβλέπων μεταξὺ γράφων, ὅλην τὴν βίβλον ἔγραψε, Βαρίνου αὐτοῦ διδασκάλου

ἀναγινώσκοντος καὶ ἐκλέγοντος ἐκ τοῦ Εὐσταθίου ἅπερ αὐτῷ ἤρεσκεν . . ." (Guida, "Il *Dictionarium* di Favorino e il *Lexicon Vindobonense*," 267n10).

139. Appendix 1, no. 18, "Eustathii de idiomatibus quae apud Homerum," probably 1493, according to Guida, "Il *Dictionarium* di Favorino e il *Lexicon Vindobonense*," 268n15.
140. Appendix 1, no. 18, sig. *6r.
141. Pozzi, "Da Padova a Firenze nel 1493," 193.
142. Forteguerri, at Florence, asked for a copy of the Aldine Homer on October 11, 1504, and again on December 2. See De Nolhac, *Les correspondants d'Alde Manuce*, 39–41, letter nos. 32 and 33.
143. June 3, 1510 (De Nolhac, *Les correspondants d'Alde Manuce*, 49, letter no. 40).
144. Browning, "Homer in Byzantium," 16.
145. Munich, gr.519a, *Iliad* 13–24, copied by Occo and Lascaris; Munich, gr.519b, *Odyssey* and *Batrachomyomachia*, thirteenth or fourteenth century (Mondrain, "La collection de manuscrits grecs d'Adolphe Occo," 168–70). See in this chapter, n. 115. For Occo and Lascaris, see chapter 3, section "Quintus of Smyrna."
146. Agricola wrote to Occo from Dillingen, August 24, 1479: "Causa propter quam manere volui fuit ut Homerum exscriberem. Scis ut sine eo Greca studia mihi prorsus sint manca. Scriberemque si non utrumque volumen, saltem tamen Ἰλιάδα" (edited in Van der Laan and Akkerman, *Rudolf Agricola*, 116).
147. For the timing of Lascaris's departure, see Knös, *Un ambassadeur de l'hellénisme*, 80. Lascaris owned PBN, Rés.Yb 3–4 (Grafton, *Commerce with the Classics*, 180 and n126). The marginalia in BAV, Inc.I.50 have long been attributed to Janus Lascaris (e.g., in De Nolhac, *La bibliothèque de Fulvio Orsini*, 158; Sheehan, *Incunabula*, 2:631), but they are by Marcus Musurus: see Pontani, *Sguardi su Ulisse*, 481–83. I am grateful to David Speranzi for this notice. For Aemilius, see Grafton, *Commerce with the Classics*, 161.
148. Ibid., 135. For this book, now at Princeton University, see Hanford, "An Old Master Restored."
149. Budé used the B scholia preserved in Venice, Bibl. Marciana, gr.453, and the A scholia preserved in Venice, Bibl. Marciana, gr.454 (Grafton, *Commerce with the Classics*, 174). The first of these appears in the inventory of 1468, the second in that of 1474 (Labowsky, *Bessarion's Library and the Biblioteca Marciana*, 176, item no. 442, and 226, item no. 633). A likely opportunity for studying these manuscripts would have been during Lascaris's time as ambassador to Venice, 1504 to 1509.
150. EE 1:305–6. Perhaps an echo of Petrarch: "Homerus tuus apud me mutus, imo vero ego apud illum surdus sum. Gaudeo tamen vel aspectu solo . . ." (to Nicolas Sigeros, Milan, 10 January [1354]; Rossi, *Francesco Petrarca*, 3:277, book 18, letter no. 2).
151. Pierre d'Angleberme, who studied Greek under Erasmus at Paris (apparently 1504–5), refers to "Odyssea quam praeceptor meus Desiderius feliciter traduxit" (EE 1:306n, 329n). Allen says "Pyrrhus" (his son), possibly an error.
152. In the eighteenth century, this copy was owned by J. A. Ernestus. See Ernestus, *Homeri Opera Omnia*, viii.
153. Cambridge, University Library, Adv.d.13.4, has annotations, some by Melanchthon.
154. Spitz, *Conrad Celtis*, 58. In 1503, Celtis was in possession of a copy of Homer that belonged to Willibald Pirckheimer. Pirckheimer had some difficulty retrieving this copy, and in 1504, he declined Celtis's suggestion that he translate the *Odyssey*. See Reicke, *Willibald Pirckheimers Briefwechsel*, 1:195, 198, 206.
155. Lectures are recorded in 1518, 1519, 1522, 1523, and 1524. See Rhein, "Melanchthon and Greek Literature," 164–65.
156. Appendix 1, no. 94; *Iliad* 2:211–20; *Homeric Hymn* 4:29–55.
157. He says that the Paris lectures were given by a Cretan. Delaruelle suggests that he might have meant Jacques Musurus of Rhodes ("L'étude du grec à Paris de 1514 à 1530," 58). In November 1520, Gleareanus writes, "Vide quam *Iliada* nunc tibi recito. Fortasse quod nunc *Iliada* lego et Livium" (ibid., 59).

158. *Homeri Ulysseae lib. I et II. Angeli Politiani in Homerum Praefatio.* Basle: A. Cratander, July 1520. Oecolampadius's grammar had been printed by Cratander at Basle in September 1518 and March 1520 (appendix 1, nos. 96 and 106). The lexicon was printed in March 1519 (appendix 2, no. 20). Cratander's preface to the *Odyssey* records that he was encouraged by two enthusiastic students of Greek, Caspar Hedius (1494–1552) and Jacobus Nepos (d. 1527), for whom see Bietenholz and Deutscher, *Contemporaries of Erasmus*, 2:11–12, 169–70.
159. *Homeri Ulysseae lib. I et II. Angeli Politiani in Homerum Praefatio.* Basle: A. Cratander, July 1520, sig. A1v.
160. Appendix 1, no. 166.
161. In two parts: *Iliad*, March 1523; *Odyssey, Batrachomyomachia, Hymni*, 1523 *sine mense* (Van Iseghem, *Biographie de Thierry Martens d'Alost*, 327–28).
162. See Delaruelle, "L'étude du grec à Paris de 1514 à 1530," 136. *Homeri Iliados libri duo una cum annotatiunculis Volmarii.* [Paris]: Gourmont, October 1523. An edition of *Iliad* books 1 and 2 by Martens, tentatively ascribed to 1521 (Van Iseghem, *Biographie de Thierry Martens d'Alost*, 317–18), may have followed Gourmont's edition.
163. Dedicated to Giovanni Marrasio (Zippel, "Carlo Marsuppini da Arezzo," 203n20). The preface is in Sabbadini, *Biografia documentata di Giovanni Aurispa*, 179. See also Bertalot, "Zwölf Briefe des Ambrogio Traversari," 259–60, and Stinger, *Humanism and the Church Fathers*, 34.
164. See Salanitro, "Teodoro Gaza traduttore di testi classici," 224.
165. A revised version was printed in 1503. For Calenzio, see Foà, "Gallucci, Luigi (Elisio Calenzio)." In the preface, written many years later, he says that he wrote the work at the age of eighteen, from which it is calculated that he was born in 1430.
166. BAV, Vat.gr.1314. See Diller, "Three Greek Scribes Working for Bessarion," 408; Mioni, "Bessarione scriba ed alcuni suoi collaboratori," 299; Centanni, "La biblioteca di Andronico Callisto," 218.
167. For this manuscript, see chapter 1, section "Manuel Chrysoloras," n. 83, and in the present chapter, n. 174.
168. ISTC ih00300800, the *editio princeps* of Marsuppini's verse translation and the first printed interlinear Greek–Latin text. For the date, see Balsamo, "Revisiting Early Printed Books at Brescia," 22. A single copy survives at the John Rylands Library in Manchester.
169. Edited by Leonicus of Crete. Legrand, *Bibliographie hellénique*, item no. 3; ISTC ih000301000.
170. Gourmont, September 18, 1507 (Omont, "Essai sur les débuts de la typographie grecque à Paris," 19).
171. Venice, circa 1475 (ISTC ih00302000); Parma, 1492 (ISTC ih00303000); Modena, 1498 (ISTC ih00304000); Pesaro: Soncinus, 1509 [Vienna: Winterburg, c. 1509] (see in the present chapter, n. 172); Florence: Zuchetta, 1512; Venice: De Vitalibus, 1516.
172. The edition published at Vienna by Winterburg, around 1509, prints Marsuppini's version but ascribes it to Reuchlin: see Knauer, "*Iter per miscellanea.*"
173. Paris: Bade, [1511?]; Wittenberg: Gronenberg, 1513.
174. A manuscript of the work in the hand of Demetrius Chalcondyles, dated 1460 to 1467, attributes the work either to Homer or to Τίγρης τοῦ Καρός (Jena, Prov.o.25, fol. 84). In 1467, this manuscript belonged to Johann Löffelholtz of Nuremberg: see Stockhausen, "Katalog der griechischen Handschriften," 698–700. The Greek edition of the text in 1486 attributes it to the same author (sig. i1r). Reuchlin's version in Munich 582a, dated 1486 to 1495, is titled "Homeri Batrachomyomachia: In quibusdam autem Tigretis Caris" (Knauer, "*Iter per miscellanea*," 29). Froben records that in a manuscript belonging to Beatus Rhenanus it is attributed to "Tigres Cares" (*Batrachomyomachia*, Basle: Froben, January 1518, p. 3). For this attribution, a corruption of *Pigres*, see Bliquez, "Frogs and Mice and Athens," 13–16. In the commentary on the *Moriae encomium*, published 1515, partly written by Erasmus, it is said of *Batrachomyomachia*, "extat autem titulo Homeri, quanquam docti magis putant esse compositum alicuius faceta quaedam Homeri imitatione" (Erasmus, *Moriae encomium*, 8). For Erasmus's role in this commentary, see Gavin and Miller, "Erasmus' Additions to Listrius' Commentary."

175. Kusukawa, *Philip Melanchthon*, 56.
176. Robinson, *Luciani Dialogi*, 369.
177. Chrysoloras owned BAV, Vat.gr.87, of Lucian and Philostratus's *Heroicus*. This was in the Vatican Library by 1455. It was borrowed by Cardinal Isidore of Kiev in May 1455 and returned on his death in 1463 (Devreesse, *Catalogue des manuscrits grecs*, 38). For the manuscript and its subscriptions, see Berti, "Uno scriba greco-latino," 441–42 and figure 8. Another manuscript of Lucian, BAV, Vat.gr.1324, tenth century, has also been connected with Chrysoloras (Zorzi, "I Crisolora," 108, 110).
178. The glossed manuscript is BAV, Urb.gr.121, which has *Charon, Calumnia, Piscator, Icaromenippus, Timon,* and *Iuppiter tragoedus* (incomplete). Since this manuscript seems to have been used to make the version of *Timon*, it is likely that it was made between 1397 and 1400 (Berti, "Uno scriba greco-latino," 427, 440–41). For the use of *Calumnia* in this classroom, and for an edition of the Greek text of this work, with its Latin glosses and scholia, see Deligiannis, *Fifteenth-Century Latin Translations*, 31–61, 267–95. For Bertoldo's version, see Weiss, "Gli inizi dello studio del greco a Firenze," 245 and n119. The evidence for Bertoldo's dedication of this work to Zambeccari is in Sabbadini, "Ancora Pietro Marcello," 260–61. For the date of Zambeccari's death, see Frati, *Epistolario di Pellegrino Zambeccari*.
179. Florence, Bibl. Laurenziana, 25.9, copied at Florence by Tedaldo della Casa, dated May 26, 1403 (Berti, "Uno scriba greco-latino," 416–17); BAV, Vat.lat.989, which belonged to Salutati (Ullman, *The Humanism of Coluccio Salutati*, 184–85). In a letter of January 26, 1403, to Pietro Marcello, Antonio di Romagno acknowledges a loan of "tuum Timonem" (Goldschmidt, "The First Edition of Lucian of Samosata," 12–13).
180. Complete no later than May 26, 1403, when it was copied by Tedaldo della Casa in Florence (Weiss, "Gli inizi dello studio del greco a Firenze," 245; Berti, "Uno scriba greco-latino," 416–17). Salutati owned BAV, Vat.lat.989, fols. 90v–96v (Ullman, *The Humanism of Coluccio Salutati*, 184–85). This version, possibly also made by Bertoldo, is in Heymeryck, "Les traductions latines du 'Charon,'" 168–95. It was not (*pace* Sabbadini, "Ancora Pietro Marcello," 260–62) printed at Venice in 1494 (Berti, "Uno scriba greco-latino," 418n3).
181. He probably owned Wolfenbüttel, ms. 2907 (Diller, "Greek Codices of Palla Strozzi and Guarino Veronese," 318), for which, see Sidwell, "Manoscritti umanistici di Luciano," 242.
182. *Calumnia*: For the sources and diffusion of this version, see Deligiannis, *Fifteenth-Century Latin Translations*, 65–110; for an edition, see ibid., 111–37. *Muscae encomium*: dedicated to Scipione Mainente: "Nuper inter versandum scedas nonnullas amoenum quoddam occurit opusculum, quod dum linguae graecae rudimenta pridem exercere coepi, iuvenilis quondam lusit aetas: inscribitur autem *Muscae laudes*" ([October 1440?], Sabbadini, *Epistolario di Guarino Veronese* 2:406; Marsh, *Lucian and the Latins*, 28). *Parasitus*: completed after Guarino's return to Venice in 1408 and dedicated to Pietro Donà (then archbishop of Crete) between 1408 and 1418. The version survives in two manuscripts and is edited in Marsh, "Guarino of Verona's Translation of Lucian's *Parasite*."
183. Lapo da Castiglionchio, perhaps 1436 (Deligiannis, *Fifteenth-Century Latin Translations*, 141–205); Francesco Griffolini, circa 1460 (ibid., 209–54); Lorenzo Lippi da Colle (De Marinis and Perosa, *Nuovi documenti*, 49–50); anonymous version (Venice: Bevilaqua, 1494; Sidwell, "Manoscritti umanistici di Luciano," 245); Rudolf Agricola, circa 1479, printed Louvain: Rescius and Sturm, 1530 (Allen, "The Letters of Rudolf Agricola," 312); Giovanni Boerio, circa 1506 (BL, Add.19553; EE 8:324); Philip Melanchthon (Venice, Bibl. Marciana, lat.12.98 [4726], fols. 1–4; Kristeller, *Iter Italicum*, 2:258).
184. Anonymous version in Venice: Bevilaqua, 1494 (Sidwell, "Manoscritti umanistici di Luciano," 245). Bérault's version was published at Paris in 1517 (Delaruelle, "L'étude du grec à Paris de 1514 à 1530," 52).
185. Bologna, B.3471 (Kristeller, *Iter Italicum*, 1:17).
186. See appendix 1, no. 36. For Calcagnini, see Marchetti, De Ferrari, and Mutini, "Calcagnini, Celio," 492–98; Bietenholz and Deutscher, *Contemporaries of Erasmus*, 1:242–43. I know of

no other version before 1530. In a letter to Aldus dated December 19, 1505, Forteguerri talks of translating this work (De Nolhac, *Les correspondants d'Alde Manuce*, 43–45, letter no. 36).
187. Lorenzo de Alopa. ISTC il00320000. The edition excludes *Nero* and the *Epigrammata*, and the editor marks *Philopatris* and *Charidemus* as spurious. It was probably edited by Janus Lascaris, but see Sidwell, "Manoscritti umanistici di Luciano," 253n77.
188. Marcotte, "La bibliothèque de Jean Calphurnius," 192.
189. BAV, Inc.I.19, is annotated by Tomeo; BAV, Inc.I.18, by Forteguerri (Sheehan, *Incunabula*, 2:788).
190. Offenbacher, "La bibliothèque de Willibald Pirckheimer," 254. For Pirckheimer's attempts to acquire leaves missing from a printed edition of Lucian, see Reicke, *Willibald Pirckheimers Briefwechsel*, 2:236, 328, 330.
191. *Luciani opera. Icones Philostrati. Eiusdem Heroica. Eiusdem vitae Sophistarum. Icones Iunioris Philostrati. Descriptiones Callistrati.* The colophon to the text of Lucian is February 1503, apparently new style; the colophon to Philostratus's *Vitae sophistarum* is June.
192. The price is written next to the book in the catalog of June 22, 1503, reproduced in Orlandi, *Aldo Manuzio editore*, 2: plates X–XIII.
193. Erasmus's versions are edited by Robinson, *Luciani Dialogi*, 362–603. In 1506, *Toxaris* (EE 1:416–17), *Tyrannicida* (EE 1:422–23), *Timon* (EE 1:423–24), *Gallus* (EE 1:424–26), *De mercede conductis* (EE 1:429–30), *Alexander* (EE 1:430–31), *Eunuchus*, and *De sacrificiis* (EE 1:434–35). In 1512, *Abdicatus*, *Icaromenippus* (EE 1:512–13), and *De astrologia* (EE 1:519–20). In 1514, *Cronosolon* and *Saturnalia* (EE 1:561–62). In 1517, *Convivium* (EE 2:502–3).
194. BL, Add.19553 has this Latin translation of *Calumnia* and of Isocrates' *Ad Nicoclem*: see EE 8:324. In 1512, Erasmus dedicated his version of *De astrologia* to Boerio's father, the king's physician (EE 1:519–20).
195. Firmin-Didot, *Alde Manuce et l'Hellénisme à Venise*, 602–3. For Bullock, see chapter 1, section "Theodore Gaza," p. 20, n. 214.
196. Aleandro's letter to Aldus is printed in the original Italian in Omont, "Essai sur les débuts de la typographie grecque à Paris," 68–70. It is translated by De Nolhac, "Le grec à Paris sous Louis XII," 63–67.
197. PBN, gr.1638, which also has Thucydides, Planudes, and Demosthenes (Omont, "Georges Hermonyme de Sparte," 94).
198. This has *Somnium, Ad Prometheum, Ad Nigrinum, Nigrinus, Iudicium vocalium, Timon, Alcyon*, and *Prometheus*. Omont dates it [c. 1510] (Omont, "Essai sur les débuts de la typographie grecque à Paris," 26). It has Gourmont's first Greek font, with the accents cast separately from the letters. The last dated use of this font is in the Paris Plutarch of April 30, 1509, although Gourmont's undated Isocrates uses the font and seems to postdate the Plutarch. The first dated use of Gourmont's new Greek font, which has breathings and accents cast with the letters, is in the Chrysoloras of [May or July] 13, 1512, appendix 1, no. 42.
199. The edition, described in Omont, "Essai sur les débuts de la typographie grecque à Paris," 26, 33–34, 61–62, *Dialogi deorum, Dialogi marini*, and *Dialogi mortuorum*. Omont dates it [c. 1513]. It has Gourmont's first device. The last dated use of this device was in the prefatory gathering of Gourmont's dictionary (appendix 2, no. 14), printed in the last days of 1512. This edition uses Gourmont's second Greek font, of which the first dated use is in the Chrysoloras of [May or July] 1512. The title page of this edition advertises Brachet's lectures (Omont, "Essai sur les débuts de la typographie grecque à Paris," 33). The preface is reprinted in Omont, "Essai sur les débuts de la typographie grecque à Paris," 61–62.
200. Appendix 1, no. 133; reprinted in 1525, appendix 1, no. 150.
201. For details of these editions, see Van Iseghem, *Biographie de Thierry Martens d'Alost*, 304–5, 309, 320, 323, 332, 334–35, 336.
202. Hoven, "Enseignement du grec," 81. For Strazelius, see *Biographie Nationale de Belgique* 24: cols. 168–69.
203. Hoven, "Enseignement du grec," 81.

204. *Calumnia*, 1479; *Gallus*, 1479, revised 1484; *Micyllus*, 1484 (Vander Laan and Akkerman, *Rudolf Agricola*, 106–9; 232, 236, 366, 369; 224).
205. It has *Calumnia, Icaromenippus, Somnium, Menippus,* and *Cynicus.* The last two works have lexica attached (Mondrain, "La collection de manuscrits grecs d'Adolphe Occo," 171).
206. Reicke, *Willibald Pirckheimers Briefwechsel*, 1:195.
207. See EE 2:151, letter no. 362, note to line 3.
208. *Luciani Piscator . . . Bilibaldo Pirckheymero . . . interprete, eiusdem epistola apologetica.* Nuremberg: F. Peypus, October 2, 1517. The long preface to Laurentius Beheym defends Reuchlin.
209. Hagenau: T. Anshelm, January 1520. Dedicated to Hieronymus Emser.
210. The edition, printed by Johann Schott, is dated 1515 *sine mense*. It is presumably before November 26, 1515, the date of a letter of P. Aperbach, at Leipzig, to M. Hummelberg: "Estne cognitus tibi Othmarus Nachtgall? Transtulit e graeco Luciani dialogos deorum" (Horawitz, "Zur Biographie und Correspondenz Johannes Reuchlins," 141–42). For this translator, see chapter 1, section "Ottomar Nachtgall."
211. In 1516 Bruno Amorbach spoke to his brother Boniface of "tralationes Luciani et Aristophanis, ubi verbum verbo respondet, quas habui a communi praeceptore nostro Conone" (Saffrey, "Un humaniste dominicain," 36).
212. *Hercules Gallicus* was printed at Wittenberg, [1520]: see Wetzel and others, *Melanchthons Briefwechsel*, 1:181–82. The Greek text of *Calumnia* was printed there [c. March 1521]: see ibid., 1:272–73. For his version, see the present chapter, n. 183. For his lectures, see Rhein, "Melanchthon and Greek Literature," 164–65. *Cupido* was printed in Greek with the grammar in 1520, 1522, 1527, and 1528: see appendix 1, nos. 109, 129, 165, 173. I have not seen every edition of Melanchthon's grammar and this list is incomplete.
213. Martens's edition of *Prometheus*, and his edition of *Icaromenippus, Menippus,* and *Vitarum auctio*, are undated. Van Iseghem dates the first to 1519 from the state of the device, and he is certain that the second was printed the same year as the first (Van Iseghem, *Biographie de Thierry Martens d'Alost*, 304–5). A third edition, a translation of the second, is also undated. It has been printed to allow binding with the Greek text and is very likely contemporary with it.
214. Basle: Curio, 1522, sig. [A1v]; Robinson, *Luciani Dialogi*, 369.
215. Robinson, *Luciani Dialogi*, 369.
216. *Aristophanis inter comicos summi Ranae* (Basle: Froben, 1524), sig. a1v.
217. BAV, Pal.gr.116, for which see Stevenson, *Codices manuscripti palatini graeci*, 55. See also Sabbadini, *La scuola e gli studi di Guarino Guarini Veronese*, 11–12; Sabbadini, *Le scoperte dei codici*, 45; Diller, "Greek Codices of Palla Strozzi and Guarino Veronese," 319. Guarino may have owned Oxford, Bodleian, Holkh.gr.88, of eight plays: see Giannini, "Holkham Hall 88." For Chrysoloras's grammar, see chapter 1, section "Manuel Chrysoloras."
218. Lockwood, "De Rinucio Aretino," 51–52, 72–76.
219. Lines 1 through 269. This version is edited, as prose, by Lockwood, "De Rinucio Aretino," 163–72, and see Cecchini and Cassio, "Due contributi sulla traduzione," 472–82. Bruni's preface indicates that he knew, or knew of, *Nubes*. Wilson evaluates the version and suggests a date circa 1439 (Wilson, *From Byzantium to Italy*, 30–31). Piccolomini commented on Bruni's poetry, "in carmine quoque nihil potuit; nam etsi artem habuit, venam tamen naturae non habuit" (Van Heck, *Enee Silvii Piccolominei postea Pii PP. II De viris illustribus*, 36).
220. See Cortesi, "Il «Vocabularium» greco di Giovanni Tortelli," 481–82. The scholia preserved in Modena, Bibl. Estense, α.U.5.101, or a related manuscript, seem to have been used by Tortelli at Constantinople (ibid., 476).
221. Bianca, "Gaza, Teodoro," 738. A list of books to be sent to Gian Pietro da Lucca by Vittorino, dated 1445, includes one titled "Aristophanes" (Cortesi, "Libri e vicende di Vittorino da Feltre," 92).
222. Woodward, *Vittorino da Feltre and Other Humanist Educators*, 50.
223. Bianca, "Gaza, Teodoro," 739.

224. He wrote to Platina, "Aristophanis particulam illam impraesentiarum ad te minime mitto, cum mihi ipse sit opus: quibusdam lectito; cum illum explevero, ilico accipies, eo tamen foedere ut, cum illum acceperis, non insolenter eum tractes, non asperneris propterea quod tam male vestitus, tam obsitus, tam turpis decrepitusque accedat. Si eum olim in tuas manus aliquando perventurum putassem, diligentius in illo ordinando ac scribendo elaborassem" (Resta, *Giorgio Valagussa*, 179). For Valagussa's Greek studies at Ferrara, see ibid., 162–64, 183–84.
225. Venice, Bibl. Marciana, lat.14.10 (4659), fols. 41r–65v. Pietro donated this manuscript to the monastery of San Giovanni in Verdara at Padua in 1478. For Scholarios's grammar, see chapter 1, section "George Scholarios." Copenhagen, GKS 418, 20, of *Plutus* also belonged to Pietro (Bernardinello, "Gli studi propedeutici di greco," 127 and n109).
226. Madrid, Bibl. Nacional, 4629, fols. 21ff. Lascaris added *Plutus* to Madrid, Bibl. Nacional, 4677. This manuscript was owned by Lascaris in Constantinople, lost in the fall of the city, rediscovered, and bought by him in Fera circa 1457, and then given to a friend there along with other manuscripts. He later recovered and restored it at Messina circa 1475 (Martínez-Manzano, *Konstantinos Laskaris*, 10 and n19). In 1490 at Messina, Lascaris completed Madrid, Bibl. Nacional, 4683, a thirteenth-century manuscript of *Plutus, Nubes, Ranae*, and *Equites* (Andrés, *Catálogo de los códices griegos*, 224–26, 236–38). Prague, BU PSK, VIII.H.36, which has Aristophanes *inter alia*, was copied by Petrus Castellus of Paris in 1485, apparently while he studied under Lascaris at Messina. See Martínez-Manzano, *Konstantinos Laskaris*, 293.
227. Pincelli, *Andrea Brenta*, 30, which reads, "declinationes verborum." The prolusion survives in BAV, Vat.lat.2713, fols. 45r–46v, edited in Pincelli, *Andrea Brenta*, 30–38. Brenta is recorded as lecturer in Latin and Greek at the *Studium urbis* from 1481 to 1483 (Dorati, "I lettori dello Studio," 125), but the records are incomplete and he probably lectured there earlier. He died February 11, 1484 (Pincelli, *Andrea Brenta*, 40).
228. Bertola, *I due primi registri*, 3, 7, 9, 18. For Guazzelli, see Russo, "Guazzelli, Demetrio."
229. Piero, at Fiesole, to Niccolò Michelozzi, at Florence, 29 July 1482: "Cum Angelus comicum illum Graecum atque elegantissimum, et in quo est id quod proprie dicitur ἀττικισμός, Aristophanem mihi exponere cupiat, et mihi eius non sit copia, peto a te mihi ut tuum commodes" (De Marinis and Perosa, *Nuovi documenti*, 74).
230. Pozzi, "Da Padova a Firenze nel 1493," 193.
231. "Inserui autem huic epistolae dimidium folii mei libelli ubi ipsam comoediam conscribo, ut videres si placerent illi litterularum lineares tractus" (ibid., 193).
232. Ibid.
233. See the Aldine catalogs of October 1, 1498, and June 22, 1503, reproduced in Orlandi, *Aldo Manuzio editore*, 2: plates IX–XIII. In a letter dated April 15, 1498, Antonio Codro Urceo declined an opportunity to buy two copies of the edition for one gold piece (Dorez, "Études aldines III," 325). This date is three months before the colophon of the Aldine Aristophanes. *Thesmophoriazousai.* and *Lysistrata* were first printed at Florence in the Juntine edition of 1515 and 1516.
234. The fifth volume of Aristotle is dated June 1498; the Aldine Aristophanes (ISTC ia00958000) is dated July 15, 1498. Aldus's Latin preface is in Botfield, *Prefaces*, 218–19; Orlandi, *Aldo Manuzio editore*, 1:23–24; and Legrand, *Bibliographie hellénique*, 1:46–47. Musurus's Greek preface is in Botfield, *Prefaces*, 219–21; Legrand, *Bibliographie hellénique*, 1:47–49.
235. Orlandi, *Aldo Manuzio editore*, 1:24. Aldus's source for this remark is unknown. Gaza died circa 1475.
236. "Antiqua comoedia cum sinceram illam sermonis Attici gratiam prope sola retinet, tum facundissimae libertatis est et in insectandis vitiis praecipua . . ." (Quintilian, *Institutio oratoria*, 10.1).
237. *Plutus antiqua comoedia* (Parma: A. Ugoletus, 1501) preface. Passio writes, [*Plutus*, comoedia] "quam olim cum caeteris Aristophanis fabulis mihi et condiscipulo Balthasari Alioto (non vulgaris doctrinae iuveni) interpretatus est Thadaeus Ugoletus Parmensis . . ." It appears from the preface that the version had been made not long before.
238. De Nolhac, *Les correspondants d'Alde Manuce*, 65–69, letter no. 57.

239. To Anton Kress, December 19, 1501, edited in Reicke, *Willibald Pirckheimers Briefwechsel*, 1:141.
240. Lines 1 through 269 and Pirckheimer's continuation are in BL, Arundel 338 (Kristeller, *Iter Italicum*, 4:131).
241. To an unidentified friend, [1502?], edited in Reicke, *Willibald Pirckheimers Briefwechsel*, 1:177–78; Mondrain, "L'étude du grec en Italie," 314. The translation is not stated in the letter to be of Aristophanes. Pirckheimer wrote in 1502 (after June 19), "Iam pridem secum [Adolph Occo] egi, Iohane [*sic*] Peutinger intercessore, ut aliquid praecipue Aristo[phanis] extorquere possem, sed in cassum omnis noster fuit labor; quamvis ego amplius opera sua non indigeam, comentaria [*sic*] nactus Aristophanis quae mihi sensum poetae aperiunt" (Rupprich, *Die Briefwechsel*, no. 359; Reicke, *Willibald Pirckheimers Briefwechsel*, 1:192).
242. Pirckheimer's copy of the *editio princeps* of Aristophanes was decorated by Albrecht Dürer (Offenbacher, "La bibliothèque de Willibald Pirckheimer," 253).
243. Saffrey, "Un humaniste dominicain," 28.
244. Lines 1340ff (Meyer, "Ein Kollegheft des humanisten Cono," 281).
245. Cuno died in Basle in 1513. His manuscript, Cambridge, Trinity College, R.1.42 (459), copied by Michael Lygizos (RGK 1, no. 282), passed to Beatus Rhenanus the same year (Saffrey, "Un humaniste dominicain," 36n51).
246. Ibid., 36.
247. As appears from Mosellanus's preface, dated August 25, 1517 (*Aristophanis comici facetissimi Plutus, graeci sermonis studiosis mire utilis*. Hagenau: T. Anshelm, November 1517), sig. α2v.
248. Ibid., sig. α2v.
249. As appears from the inscription on the title page (Oxford, Bodleian, Auct.S.8.12). Carlotta Dionisotti brought this volume to my attention.
250. EE 2:497. For Rescius, see Roersch, "Un bon ouvrier."
251. Detailed in Van Iseghem, *Biographie de Thierry Martens d'Alost*, 280–82.
252. Wittenberg: M. Lotter, [after April] 1521. Wetzel and others, *Melanchthons Briefwechsel*, 203–5; Rhein, "Melanchthon and Greek Literature," 164.
253. Cicero, *De senectute*, 79 renders Xenophon, *Cyropaedia*, 8:7.17. See Jones, "Cicero as a Translator," 25. Cicero wrote, "at Cyri vitam et disciplinam legant, praeclaram illam quidem, sed neque tam nostris rebus aptam nec tamen Scauri laudibus anteponendam" (*Brutus*, 29).
254. BAV, Vat.gr.1335, tenth century, *Cyrop., Anab., Apol., Ages., Hiero, Lac. Resp., Ath. Resp., Poroi* (Zorzi, "I Crisolora," 101, 108). It was subsequently owned by Aurispa (Haltinner and Schmoll, "The Older Manuscripts of Xenophon's *Hiero*," 231–32).
255. Bruni wrote to Pietro Miani in October or November 1407, "Librum Xenophontis de Cyri infantia, quem tu fore apud Demetrium [Cydones] arbitrabare, cupio scire an habere possimus" (Luiso, *Studi su l'epistolario*, 2:16).
256. Guarino received a manuscript of *Anab., Oecon., Hiero* from a Greek monk named Isidore (Diller, "Greek Codices of Palla Strozzi and Guarino Veronese," 320). This is probably Florence, Bibl. Laurenziana, Conv. soppr. gr.112 (*Oecon., Cyrop., Anab., Hiero*), copied by Isidore, subsequently Latin patriarch of Constantinople (RGK 1, no. 155). Since it belonged to Antonio Corbinelli (d. 1425), Guarino may have left it in Florence. Guarino owned a manuscript of *Oecon., Anab., Cyrop., Ages., Mem.* (Sabbadini, *La scuola e gli studi di Guarino Guarini Veronese*, 105) and seems to have owned Erlangensis 89 of *Cyrop*. (Diller, "Greek Codices of Palla Strozzi and Guarino Veronese," 320).
257. Vespasiano, edited in Greco, *Vespasiano da Bisticci*, 522. Manetti owned BAV, Pal.gr.174 (*Oecon., Hiero* and *Cyrop.*) Traversari died in 1439.
258. Petrus Creticus wrote most of Florence, Bibl. Laurenziana, 55.21 (*Mem., Oecon., De ven., Cyrop., Anab., Hipparch., Hiero, Hippias, Lac. Resp.*, and *Ath. Resp.*) for Vittorino, who later gave it to his pupil Sassuolo da Prato (note on fol. 1v). It passed to Guarino and Filelfo (Diller, "Greek Codices of Palla Strozzi and Guarino Veronese," 320; Gamillscheg, "Beobachtungen zur Kopistentätigkeit des Petros Kretikos," 142n35; Haltinner and Schmoll, "The Older Manuscripts of Xenophon's *Hiero*," 234–35; RGK 1, no. 352; Eleuteri, "Francesco Filelfo," 178;

Speranzi, "Codici greci appartenuti a Francesco Filelfo," 475–76). Gerardo da Patrasso, who worked for Vittorino, wrote Perugia, Perus.B.34 (*Mem.*, *Oecon.* [imperfect.], *Symp.* [imperfect.], *Cyneg.*, *Cyrop.*, *Anab.*, *Hipparch.*, *Hiero, De re equestri*, *Lac. Resp.*, *Ath. Resp.* [imperfect.], *Poroi* [imperfect.]; Cirignano, "The Manuscripts of Xenophon's Symposium," 193).

259. Filelfo left Constantinople August 27, 1427, and was in Venice by October 10 (Filelfo, *Epistolare Francisci Philelfi*, sigs. a2r–v). Florence, Bibl. Laurenziana, 55.19 (*Symp.*, *Oecon.*, and *Cyrop.*) was copied for him at Constantinople by Chrysococces November 23, 1427 (Cirignano, "The Manuscripts of Xenophon's Symposium," 204; Calderini, "Ricerche intorno alla biblioteca," 406; Eleuteri, "Francesco Filelfo," 170).

260. Filelfo to Traversari, 31 January 1429, edited in Mehus, *Ambrosii Traversarii epistolae*, 2, col. 1016, book 24, letter no. 40. Filelfo's subsequent interest in the work suggests that this refers to *Cyrop.* It may, however, refer to *Hiero*. Filelfo copied BAV, Vat.gr.1337, fols. 1–83, *Lac. Resp.* and *Cyrop.* (Eleuteri, "Francesco Filelfo," 178; Calderini, "Ricerche intorno alla biblioteca," 406). He acquired Florence, Bibl. Laurenziana, 55.21: see in the present chapter, n. 258.

261. See Marsh, "Xenophon."

262. Sabbadini, *Carteggio di Giovanni Aurispa*, letter no. 88.

263. Loomis, "The Greek Studies of Poggio Bracciolini," 494–500; Marsh, "Xenophon," 118. Poggio's preface is in Fubini, *Poggio Bracciolini*, 4:671–77. Vespasiano gives an account of this version (edited in Greco, *Vespasiano da Bisticci*, 1:546–47).

264. 1446 to 1449 (Bianca, "Gaza, Teodoro," 739). Gaza and Chrysococces copied BAV, Vat. gr.1334 (*Hipparch.*, *De re equestri, Hiero, Lac. Resp.*, *inter alia*) for Filelfo at Constantinople (Calderini, "Ricerche intorno alla biblioteca," 406; RGK 3, nos. 127 and 211). For Florence, Bibl. Laurenziana, 32.1, see chapter 3, section "Homer," n. 113.

265. Filelfo's wrote in a letter of November 5, 1454, to Malatesta Novello, "Non diu post ad te dabo historiam Cyri iunioris quam Xenophon Socraticus libris quinque complexus est" (Filelfo, *Epistolare Francisci Philelfi*, sig. B6r). This may refer to Xenophon's *Anab.* (7 books) or to *Cyrop.* (8 books). On December 1, 1466, Filelfo wrote to Bessarion about dedicating his version of *Cyrop.* to Pope Paul II, and included a sample of the translation. A version was complete by September 1467, and in September 1469, he received four hundred ducats for the work. He had a copy of his version dedicated to Nicholas Canale, with a preface dated April 1, 1470. The *editio princeps* was printed by April 1477 (Legrand, *Cent-dix lettres greques de F. Filelfo*, 128–29, 131, and n1; Sheppard, "A Fifteenth-Century Humanist"; De Keyser, "Francesco Filelfo traduttore di Senofonte," xlix–lv). Filelfo's version is edited in De Keyser, "Francesco Filelfo traduttore di Senofonte," 45–269.

266. For Bruni and Xenophon, see Botley, *Latin Translation in the Renaissance*, 9–10.

267. For Chrysoloras and Aurispa, see the present chapter, p. 92, n. 254; for Guarino, see the present chapter, p. 92, n. 256; for Vittorino, see the present chapter, p. 92, n. 258; for Gaza and Filelfo, see the present chapter, p. 92, n. 264. Callistus copied most of Modena, Bibl. Estense, gr.145 (*Hiero, Lac. Resp., Ath. Resp., Poroi, Apol., inter alia*), later owned by Giorgio Valla (Schmoll, *Plato in the Italian Renaissance*, 315; Centanni, "La biblioteca di Andronico Callisto," 214).

268. With pseudo-Cebes, *Tablet*; Plutarch, *De liberis educandis*; Basil's letter *Ad iuvenes*. ISTC ic00356000.

269. The Aldine *editio princeps* of the works in Greek appeared in 1503. For the edition of 1517, see Legrand, *Bibliographie hellénique*, item no. 58.

270. See chapter 3, section "Aristophanes," p. 91.

271. Edited in Horawitz, "Zur Biographie und Correspondenz Johannes Reuchlins," 182.

272. Reuchlin's version is noticed in a letter dated [1477] (Rhein, Dall'Asta, and Dörner, *Johannes Reuchlin*, 15–18).

273. Reuchlin to Johann Secer, 12 April 1520 (Geiger, *Johann Reuchlins Briefwechsel*, 323, letter no. 292).

274. Edited in Horawitz, "Zur Biographie und Correspondenz Johannes Reuchlins," 187–88.

275. See chapter 3, section "Demosthenes," p. 95.

276. Van Iseghem, *Biographie de Thierry Martens d'Alost*, 336–40. In the preface to his 1529 edition of *Mem.*, Rescius says that he taught *Oecon.*, *Cyrop.*, and *Hiero* the previous year and that he has taught Greek at the Trilingual College in Louvain for about eleven years (ibid., 339–40). For Rescius, see Roersch, "Un bon ouvrier."
277. Demosthenes, edited in Herwagen (Basle, 1532). EE 10:74. For the turn of phrase, compare Quintilian, *Institutio oratoria*, 1.4.2. Quintilian states that Cicero is very good for beginners, *Institutio oratoria*, 2.5.20.
278. PBN, gr.2489, and PBN, gr.2508, for which see Omont, *Inventaire-sommaire*, 2:268–69, 274. For the link with Chrysoloras, see Zorzi, "I Crisolora," 109, 115. For Chrysoloras's gift, see Bruni's letter to Niccolò Niccoli, 12 October 1405: "Orationes Demosthenis, quas Manuel mihi et Roberto nostro donavit, certior fieri cupio an Florentiae sint" (Luiso, *Studi su l'epistolario*, 1:10).
279. *Pro Ctesiphonte* was largely finished by 1406 and published in 1407: see Botley, *Latin Translation in the Renaissance*, 18n73. *Pro Diopithe* was completed between November 6 and 30, 1406 (Hankins, *Plato in the Italian Renaissance*, 2:376–77). One of the *Philippics* was complete by December 1406: Bruni to Niccoli, December 23, 1406: "Mitto unam ex Demosthenis Philippicis, quam proximis diebus interpretatus sum . . ." (Mehus, *Leonardi Bruni Aretini epistolarum libri VIII*, 1:36, book II, letter no. 4; Luiso, *Studi su l'epistolario*, book II, letter no. 3).
280. "Chrysoloras, qui nuper eam [*sc.* Demosthenis vitam] legit, miris laudibus elegantiam et conversionis fidelitatem extollit" (December 26, 1412; Mehus, *Leonardi Bruni Aretini epistolarum libri VIII*, 1:101, book IV, letter no. 1; Luiso, *Studi su l'epistolario*, book IV, letter no. 1). This letter provides a *terminus ante quem* for the version of the life of Demosthenes. For Plutarch in the classroom, see chapter 3, section "Plutarch."
281. Perosa, *Giovanni Rucellai ed il suo Zibaldone I*, 64.
282. Fiocco, "La biblioteca di Palla Strozzi," 310.
283. Chrysoloras did not copy BAV, Vat.gr.1368 (*De corona*, *Philippics I* and *II*, and *De pace*), made at Milan before 1414. The inventory of Fulvio Orsini's library claimed that it was in Chrysoloras's hand, a judgment accepted by several later writers: see De Nolhac, *La bibliothèque de Fulvio Orsini*, 144–45, 348; Pertusi, "La scoperta di Euripide nel primo Umanesimo," 121n2. Another copy of Demosthenes, Cesena, Bibl. Malatestiana, D XXVII 1, which has been connected with Chrysoloras, seems to have come to Italy later: it was bought at Constantinople in 1431 by Niccolò Martinozzi (Zorzi, "I Crisolora," 124).
284. For the debate over the authenticity of the work, see Dihle, "Ein Spurium."
285. See Botley, *Latin Translation in the Renaissance*, 19–21.
286. For the number of manuscripts, see Hankins, *Repertorium Brunianum*, 253, *s. v.* "Aeschines," and 257, *s. v.* "Demosthenes." Bruni's versions were printed at Venice: B. Alexandrinus and A. Asulanus, March 5, 1485; Venice: De Blavis, May 16, 1488; Venice: P. Pincius, July 15, 1495; [Nuremberg]: A. Koberger, March 26, 1497; and Milan, November 23, 1498.
287. Aeschines: BAV, Barb.gr.159 was probably in Florence early in the fifteenth century and Florence, Bibl. Laurenziana, 60.4, belonged to Niccoli (Diller, "The Manuscript Tradition of Aeschines' Orations," 51, 56). He certainly had a Greek manuscript of Aeschines by March 1416 (Ullman and Stadter, *The Public Library of Renaissance Florence*, 94). Milan, Bibl. Ambrosiana, J.22 sup., may have been the manuscript from which Bruni made his version. It belonged to Strozzi at his death in 1462 (Diller, "The Manuscript Tradition of Aeschines' Orations," 50–51). Florence, Bibl. Laurenziana, Conv. soppr. gr.84, belonged to Corbinelli (Diller, "The Manuscript Tradition of Aeschines' Orations," 49). Wolfenbüttel, 902, was made for Aurispa by George Chrysococces, probably in the 1420s, and later owned by Guarino Veronese (Diller, "Greek Codices of Palla Strozzi and Guarino Veronese," 318; Diller, "The Manuscript Tradition of Aeschines' Orations," 56).
288. Sabbadini, *Le scoperte dei codici*, 48; Wilson, *From Byzantium to Italy*, 49. Filelfo was very familiar with Demosthenes: in a letter of February 15, 1451, he correctly observes that the

words ἄτομος and ἐντελέχεια do not appear in his works (Calderini, "Ricerche intorno alla biblioteca," 286).

289. See Bianca, "Gaza, Teodoro," 739. Monfasani discusses his method and suggests that he used Bruni's version (Monfasani, "L'insegnamento di Teodoro Gaza a Ferrara," 10).

290. George: 1444 to 1446, dedicated to Alfonso of Aragon, 1452 to 1453. An earlier anonymous translation by George was perhaps dedicated to Vittorino da Feltre (Monfasani, *Collectanea Trapezuntiana*, 720–21; Accame Lanzillotta, *Leonardo Bruni traduttore di Demostene*, 23). Valla: 1455 to 1457 (Lo Monaco, "Per la traduzione valliana della 'Pro Ctesiphonte' di Demostene," 162–64). Secundinus: 1458 to 1460 (Mastrodemetres, Νικόλαος Σεκουνδινός, 214–16). An anonymous version in Venice, Bibl. Marciana, lat.11.129 (4198), fols. 29r–59v, was made between 1444 and 1453 (Monfasani, *George of Trebizond*, 66 and n163).

291. Resta, *Apollonio Rodio*, 1058. In August 1471, Bessarion commended Callistus, newly arrived in Florence, to Lorenzo de' Medici. He left Florence in March 1475 (Cammelli, "Andronico Callisto," 178–81, 185). Florence, Bibl. Laurenziana, 66.31, includes a version of the *Iliad* (fols. 7r–256v) that may have originated with Callistus, and the speeches of Aeschines and Demosthenes for and against Ctesiphon (fols. 257r–400v). See Resta, *Apollonio Rodio*, 1092–95n31.

292. He wrote to Pontico Faccino, June 25, 1484, "Cupierunt hic boni quidam iuvenes ut poetas eis graecos temporibus succisivis meis praelegerem: satisfecimus. Nunc in Demosthene delectamur, nunc in Theocrito conquiescimus, quoius *Bipennis* et *Fidicula* (sive malis *Pinnula*) vice bellariorum a prandio nobis hodie lecta sunt admirabili voluptate" (edited in Branca, *Ermolao Barbaro, 1454–1493*, 1:56).

293. Müllner, "Eine Rede des Ioannes Lascaris," 143.

294. Piovan, "Forteguerri (Carteromaco), Scipione," 164. For Forteguerri's *oratio*, see chapter 1, note 4.

295. For the edition, see Renouard, *Annales de l'imprimerie des Alde*, 47–48. The preface is in Botfield, *Prefaces*, 269–74; Orlandi, *Aldo Manuzio editore*, 1:84–89. There, Aldus wrote: ". . . admodum quam pauca earum orationum exempla imprimenda curaverim; idque coactus, quod in nullo ante accidit volumine excuso in thermis nostris" (Orlandi, *Aldo Manuzio editore*, 1:88).

296. De Nolhac, *Les correspondants d'Alde Manuce*, 39–41, letter nos. 32 and 33. F. V. Bodiano asked Aldus for a copy of the edition in a letter dated 6 Kalend. Brumae 1504, "si iam absolutae sint." He says that he cannot pay until Christmas (De Nolhac, *Les correspondants d'Alde Manuce*, 38–39, letter no. 31). This edition, and its price, were added in manuscript to a copy of the Aldine catalog of June 1503 (Orlandi, *Aldo Manuzio editore*, 2: plate XIII).

297. Chalcondyles wrote to Giangiorgio Trissino, April 7, 1508, "Io da poi la partita vostra ho letto qualche tre orazione de Demostene brevi" (Friggi, *Gli studi greci a Milano al tempo di Ludovico il Moro*, 209–12, 210).

298. Louvain: Martens, February 1521.

299. Hermonymus made Leiden, Univ. Library, Voss.gr.65 (*Olynthiacs* I–III, *De pace*, *Philippic* I, *inter alia*); PBN, gr.1638, used by Budé (*Olynthiacs* I–II, *inter alia*; Omont, "Georges Hermonyme de Sparte," 90, 94); Cambridge, University Library, Nn.4.2 (pseudo-Demosthenes, funeral oration) owned by Budé (Grafton, *Commerce with the Classics*, 159); PBN, gr.3004 (For and Against Ctesiphon; Omont, "Georges Hermonyme de Sparte," 90; Diller, "The Manuscript Tradition of Aeschines' Orations," 45).

300. See chapter 3, section "Xenophon."

301. *Graeciae excellentium oratorum Aeschinis et Demosthenis, orationes adversariae* (Hagenau: Anshelm, April 1522). The text was drawn from the Aldine (Dilts, *Aeschinis orationes*, xxi, xxiv). Reuchlin's letter of January 13, 1522 (edited in Geiger, *Johann Reuchlins Briefwechsel*, 333–35, letter no. 303), supplies the preface.

302. The edition is undated. The preface to Chéradame's pamphlet of circa 1523 (appendix 1, no. 138) says that the dictionary of April 1523 (appendix 2, no. 28) and Demosthenes have both been printed. This must refer to this edition of Demosthenes. Since the preface of the

second Paris edition of the *Olynthiacs* (1528) seems to respond to Melanchthon's edition of *Olynthiac* I (1524: see this chapter, n. 303), it is likely that the first Paris edition preceded Melanchthon's. For Chéradame, see chapter 1, section "Jean Chéradame."

303. *Demosthenis Olynthiaca prima in latinam versa a Phil. Mel.* (Hagenau, 1524). This edition includes another Latin version by Joachim Camerarius.
304. Rhein, "Melanchthon and Greek Literature," 165–66. One student complained that a lack of textbooks limited the size of classes for Melanchthon's lectures on the *Philipics*. "Auditores illi eramus', inquit Vitus Vuinsemius, 'numero tantum quattuor, propter exemplorum inopiam. Describere enim cogebamur, et unicum tantum erat exemplum praeceptoris unde describeremus" (Boehme, *De litteratura lipsiensi opuscula academica*, 178).
305. For this edition and its dedication, see Veissière, "Une dédicace de Jean Chéradame."
306. See chapter 3, introduction, p. 72 and n. 3.
307. Quintilian, *Institutio oratoria*, 10.1.79.
308. *Nicocles*: For four fifteenth-century versions, see Gualdo Rosa, "Le traduzioni latine dell' «A Nicocle» di Isocrate," 278–79, 288, 290n28, 302n25. J. L. Vives's version was printed in 1526. *Ad Demonicum*: For twelve fifteenth-century versions, see Sabbadini, "Una traduzione medievale del Πρὸς Δημόνικον"; Allen, "The Letters of Rudolf Agricola," 312; Gualdo Rosa, "Le traduzioni latine dell' «A Nicocle» di Isocrate"; Gualdo Rosa, "Niccolò Loschi; Gualdo Rosa, *La fede nella "Paideia,"* 64n27, 67–68, 185–89. W. Pirckheimer mentions his Latin version in November 1503 (Rupprich, *Die Briefwechsel*, letter no. 302; Reicke, *Willibald Pirckheimers Briefwechsel*, 1:198, 200); B. Zamberti (Gualdo Rosa, *La fede nella "Paideia,"* 68, 59n4); O. Nachtgall (Strasbourg, 1515); Erasmus (Louvain, 1517). *Ad Nicoclem*: for fifteen fifteenth-century versions, see Gualdo Rosa, "Le traduzioni latine dell' «A Nicocle» di Isocrate"; and Gualdo Rosa, *La fede nella "Paideia,"* 190–97. Five more were printed by 1516: D. Bonominus (Brescia, 1503); M. Filetico (Strasbourg, 1514); O. Nachtgall (Strasbourg, 1515); J. Marinus ('s-Hertogenbosch, 1516); Erasmus (Louvain, 1516). BL, Add.19553 has a version made circa 1506 by Erasmus's pupil, J. Boerio (FE 8:324). M. Chesserius made a version between 1506 and 1524 (Gualdo Rosa, *La fede nella "Paideia,"* 88n16).
309. See Gualdo Rosa, "Le traduzioni latine dell' «A Nicocle» di Isocrate," 288n13. Guarino's preface and poem are in Sabbadini, "Una traduzione medievale del Πρὸς Δημόνικον," 684–86. For Barzizza, see Gualdo Rosa, *La fede nella "Paideia,"* 24. Wolfenbüttel, 902 (Isocrates *inter alia*), was made for Aurispa by George Chrysococces, probably in the 1420s, and later owned by Guarino (Diller, "Greek Codices of Palla Strozzi and Guarino Veronese," 318; Diller, "The Manuscript Tradition of Aeschines' Orations," 56).
310. In 1445 he gave "Orationes Isocratis" to Gian Pietro da Lucca (Cortesi, "Libri e vicende di Vittorino da Feltre," 93). Gerardo da Patrasso, who worked for Vittorino in the 1430s, copied Oxford, Bodleian, Canon.gr.87 of Isocrates (RGK 2, no. 107).
311. Valagussa to Palazzolo: "orationes Isocratis, si a Demetrio transcribi vis, aureum unum cum dimidio mittas: hoc pretio ipsum, non minore sane, transcripturum puto; si tamen eis magnopere in praesentia indigeres, meas accipe: postmodum alias ego curabo" (Resta, *Giorgio Valagussa*, 154–55). Resta suggests that this scribe was Demetrius Castrenus and dates the letter to 1454. For Valagussa's Greek studies, see ibid., 183–84.
312. Perosa, "Due lettere inedite del Poliziano," 353.
313. Oxford, New College, 254, dated October 5, 1494. For Serbopoulos's manuscripts and Greek studies in England, see chapter 1, section "Theodore Gaza," p. 19.
314. See this chapter, n. 308.
315. A commentary from his classroom survives in BAV, Vat.lat.11483, for which see Gualdo Rosa, *La fede nella "Paideia,"* 73–75. A commentary on *Nicocles*, anticipated in the manuscript, is absent: either it was not delivered or the student did not record it.
316. Chalcondyles, at Florence, accepted a place in Milan in July 1491. On October 3, 1491, he returned borrowed books to the Medici Library at Florence. By October 8, 1491, he was in Milan. On November 6, 1491, he gave the prolusion to his first lecture: "El principio suo è

stata una oratione in laude de lettere . . ." wrote a listener (Cammelli, *Demetrio Calcondila*, 94, 108, 109n2, 111). This prolusion seems not to have survived.
317. The Milan Isocrates, ISTC ii00210000, is dated January 24, 1493. The date is new style because Amaseo talks of the work as printed in a letter of April 1493: "impressaeque sunt Mediolani orationes Isocratis auctore Demetrio" (Pozzi, "Da Padova a Firenze nel 1493," 194). For the manuscripts from which it was drawn, see Menchelli, "Isocrate commentato," and Martinelli Tempesta, "Per l'identificazione delle fonti manoscritte."
318. See Legrand, *Bibliographie hellénique*, 1:17.
319. Described and dated in Omont, "Essai sur les débuts de la typographie grecque à Paris," 24–25. The two works are printed, and may have been sold, separately.
320. Strasbourg: Knoblouch, September 1, 1515. For Nachtgall, see chapter 1, section "Ottomar Nachtgall."
321. Legrand, *Bibliographie hellénique*, item no. 57. This edition has been misdated to 1495 (ISTC ii00210200).
322. Basle: Froben, May 1, 1522.
323. Hoven, "Enseignement du grec," 80.
324. Alcalá: Eguia, June 1524.
325. See chapter 1, section "Theodore Gaza," p. 25.
326. Venice: Garonus, August 20, 1527, sig. α1v.
327. See Chrysoloras's letter to Salutati, in Greek, in Novati, *Epistolario di Coluccio Salutati*, 4:333–44. BAV, Barb.gr.182, tenth to eleventh centuries (*Moralia*), and BAV, Vat.gr.138, eleventh century (*Lives*), have been connected with Chrysoloras (Zorzi, "I Crisolora," 108).
328. *Miscellanea* I (Poliziano, *Angeli Politiani Opera*, 510).
329. Pade, "The Dedicatory Letter as a Genre," 561.
330. For this use of Plutarch and other Greek historians, see Botley, *Latin Translation in the Renaissance*, 13–41.
331. ISTC ip00830000, undated but on sale in Milan by April 27, 1470. The paired lives are arranged chronologically according to the Roman lives. It also has Nepos, *Atticus*; Isocrates, *Evagoras*, trans. Guarino; Guarino, *Plato*; Bruni, *Aristotle*; pseudo-Herodotus and pseudo-Plutarch, *Homer*, trans. Pellegrino degli Agli; Donatus, *Vergil*; Donato Acciaiuoli, *Charlemagne*, *Hannibal*, and *Scipio*. Xenophon, *Agesilaos*, trans. Battista Guarini, was printed instead of Plutarch, *Agesilaos*.
332. In his Greek grammar, Melanchthon cites the life of Solon in Greek and comments, "Id, si non falso interpreteris, aliter leges in iis Plutarchi vitis, quae nescio a quibus versae passim mendosissimae manibus volvuntur studiosorum" (appendix 1, no. 165, sig. M6v).
333. For the Latin versions of the *Lives*, the essential work is Giustiniani, "Sulle traduzioni latine delle 'Vite' di Plutarco nel quattrocento," but see also Pade, "The Latin Translations of Plutarch's *Lives*."
334. The *editio princeps* is Florence: Junta, August 27, 1517. Filippo Giunta's preface to Marcello Virgilio is in Botfield, *Prefaces*, 331–32. Plutarch's *Demosthenes* was printed as a preface to the Aldine edition of Demosthenes' *Opera* in 1504, for which see chapter 3, section "Demosthenes."
335. (1) Guarino Veronese, trans. 1–25 (Sabbadini, *La scuola e gli studi di Guarino Guarini Veronese*, 135–36); (2) A. Cassarino (Resta, "Antonio Cassarino," 230–31); (3) Lapo Biraghi (Resta, "Antonio Cassarino," 231n3); (4) L. Odasio (Resta, "Antonio Cassarino," 231–32 and 232n1; Bevegni, "Appunti sulle traduzioni latine dei «Moralia»," n33); (5) G. Boninsegna (Resta, "Antonio Cassarino," 232, n2); (6) G. Lorenzi, made before 1501, printed in Rome, 1514 (Paschini, "Un ellenista veneziano del Quattrocento," 140); (7) Erasmus, printed in Basle, 1514 (EE 1:529–30). Chrysoloras refers to this work in an undated Greek letter to Traversari on friendship (edited in Cyrillus, *Codices graeci MSS regiae bibliothecae borbonicae*, 2:259–78, 265).
336. (1) A. Cassarino (Resta, "Antonio Cassarino," 234–35); (2) Janus Pannonius, 1456 (Resta, "Antonio Cassarino," 235n1; Bevegni, "Appunti sulle traduzioni latine dei «Moralia»," 73);

(3) L. Odasio (Resta, "Antonio Cassarino," 235, n2); (4) G. Lorenzi (Resta, "Antonio Cassarino," 236; Paschini "Un ellenista veneziano del Quattrocento 140"); (5) G. Corsi (Resta, "Antonio Cassarino," 236); (6) Erasmus (Resta, "Antonio Cassarino," 236; EE 1:548–49). (7). R. Pace (Resta, "Antonio Cassarino," 236). The anonymous translation in Florence, Bibl. Riccardiana, 906, may bring the total to eight (Bevegni, "Appunti sulle traduzioni latine dei «Moralia»," 84).

337. (1) Simon Atumano, 1373 (Weiss, "Lo studio di Plutarco nel trecento," 207–10; Lockwood, "Plutarch in the Fourteenth Century"; Resta, "Antonio Cassarino," 238); (2) Salutati revised Atumano's Latin, ca. 1396–97 (Weiss, "Lo studio di Plutarco nel trecento," 216–19; Gualdo Rosa, "Le traduzioni dal greco nella prima metà del '400," 185; Novati, *Epistolario di Coluccio Salutati*, 2:480–83); (3) A. Cassarino, perhaps 1443 (Resta, "Antonio Cassarino," 237); (4) Lapo Biraghi (Resta, "Antonio Cassarino," 241); (5) G. Lorenzi (Resta, "Antonio Cassarino," 241; Paschini, "Un ellenista veneziano del Quattrocento," 140); (6) Platina, 1472 to 1473 (Resta, "Antonio Cassarino," 239); (7) Erasmus, printed in Basle, 1525 (EE 6:70–72; Resta, "Antonio Cassarino," 241–43).
338. *Attic Nights* 1:26.
339. Edited in Kallendorf, *Humanist Educational Treatises*, 321n4, 322n21, 322n30, 324n60, 324n78, 326n112.
340. Calfurnio's version is noticed by Marcotte, "La bibliothèque de Jean Calphurnius," 186. For a possible version by Odasio, see Bevegni, "Appunti sulle traduzioni latine dei «Moralia»," 74, 81n18.
341. See chapter 3, section "Xenophon," p. 92 and n. 268.
342. Legrand, *Bibliographie hellénique*, item no. 58.
343. See Gualdo Rosa, *La fede nella "Paideia,"* 74.
344. Rhein, "Melanchthon and Greek Literature," 164.
345. "non est commodius in praesentia quicquam visum quam si publice Plutarchi philosophi et oratoris gravissimi *De liberorum educatione* libellum graece praelegerem. Ita enim futurum ut iuventus nostra graecam disceret linguam et simul cum animi eorum optimis monitis ac praeceptis imbuerentur?" (Hagenau: Secer, 1527, sigs. L1v–L2r). For Metzler, see chapter 1, section "Johann Metzler."
346. PBN, suppl.gr.167. The Greek text follows the Latin (Omont, "Georges Hermonyme de Sparte," 83). It is not clear that the version was made by Hermonymus. A version of this essay was made by Giovanni Volta (Bevegni, "Appunti sulle traduzioni latine dei «Moralia»," 79) and Pierio Valeriano mentions one by Piero de' Medici (Gaisser, *Pierio Valeriano*, 2:27).
347. Leiden, Univ. Library, Voss.gr.2. The three essays translated by Budé appear first in this manuscript. It has notes in Budé's hand. The first two essays are not in Hermonymus's hand (Omont, "Georges Hermonyme de Sparte," 81).
348. A manuscript of the version of *De placitis*, dedicated to Germain de Ganay, January 1, 1503, new style, is now PBN, lat.6633. It has autograph corrections by Budé (Omont, "Georges Hermonyme de Sparte," 83n1). It was published by Faber d'Étaples, who addressed it to Hermonymus (Paris: Bade, March 18, 1505; Rice, *The Prefatory Epistles*, 148–49). *De fortuna et virtute Alexandri* and *De fortuna Romanorum* were dedicated to Pierre de Courthardy, August 18, 1503 (Rice, *The Prefatory Epistles*, 139n3), and both were printed with *De animi tranquillitate* (Paris: Bade, October 15, 1505).
349. See Omont, "Georges Hermonyme de Sparte," 81–83.
350. Aleandro's prefatory Greek poem is in Legrand, *Bibliographie hellénique*, 1:92. For his involvement in the Aldine edition, see Hillyard, "Girolamo Aleandro," 527–28.
351. April 30, 1509. Description and preface in Omont, "Essai sur les débuts de la typographie grecque à Paris," 23–24, 54–57.
352. Cincio Romano translated *De virtute et vitio*, now Oxford, Balliol College, ms. 315 (Weiss, *Humanism in England*, 93).
353. Description in Omont, "Essai sur les débuts de la typographie grecque à Paris," 32. For the date, see Hillyard, "Girolamo Aleandro," 518–19.

354. The edition of *De audiendo*, not known to Omont, "Essai sur les débuts de la typographie grecque à Paris," is not a reprint of the Aldine text. It may have been based on collations made by Aleandro in Italy. See Hillyard, "Girolamo Aleandro," 519–21.
355. Aleandro appears to have said that the editor of the Aldine *Moralia*, Demetrius Ducas, did the job badly. Croke repeated the gossip to Camerarius, who passed it on to posterity: "Recordor me audisse ex magistro meo, Ricardo Croco Britanno, qui quosdam libellos Plutarchi explicare nobis pueris solebat . . ." (cited in Boehme, *De litteratura lipsiensi opuscula academica*, 188). The context makes it clear that these *libelli* are from the *moralia*, not the *vitae*. Camerarius studied in Leipzig from 1512 to 1518 (Bietenholz and Deutscher, *Contemporaries of Erasmus*, 1:247).
356. Basle: Froben, 1514; Leipzig: Schumann, 1519. The latter is described in Girot, *Pindare avant Ronsard*, 410.
357. Basle: Froben, May 1525. See EE 6:70–72.
358. Petrarch's manuscript was probably PBN, gr.1807. It was in Padua from 1374 to 1388, and in Pavia from 1388 to circa 1499. Giorgio Valla and George Hermonymus made copies of it. Janus Lascaris later owned it, perhaps from 1499. See Diller, "Petrarch's Greek Codex of Plato."
359. Chrysoloras has been connected with PBN, gr.1811, and BAV, Vat.gr.226, both fourteenth century (Zorzi, "I Crisolora," 109).
360. In his preface circa 1406 to his version of Aristotle's *Posterior Analytics*, edited in Manetti, "Roberto de' Rossi," 54.
361. See chapter 3, section "Demosthenes"; Perosa, *Giovanni Rucellai*, 64. No extant version of any work of Plato has been connected with Palla. He added marginalia to a manuscript of Plato (BAV, Vat.gr.226, fols. 235r–422v), and he copied BAV, Urb.gr.31 of Plato (RGK 3, no. 534). A list of his books, dated August 24, 1431, includes a Greek manuscript, "Sermones Platonis" (Fiocco, "La biblioteca di Palla Strozzi," 310).
362. Mehus, *Leonardi Bruni Aretini epistolarum libri VIII*, 1:15–17, book 1, letter no. 8; Luiso, *Studi su l'epistolario*, book 1, letter no. 1, and book 3, letter no. 3. Chrysoloras left Florence March 10, 1400 (Weiss, "Gli inizi dello studio del greco a Firenze," 238).
363. Sabbadini, *Le scoperte dei codici*, 44n5.
364. Vergerio says, "Gorgiam bis ex integro evolvi" (Smith, *Epistolario di Pier Paolo Vergerio*, 240–42, letter no. 95). He quoted *Gorgias* in Latin in *De ingenuis moribus*, circa 1402 and 1403 (Kallendorf, *Humanist Educational Treatises*, 26).
365. On November 1, [1409], Bruni sent the version to Niccolò Niccoli for copying (Mehus, *Leonardi Bruni Aretini epistolarum libri VIII*, 1:88–89, book 3, letter no. 13; Luiso, *Studi su l'epistolario*, book 3, letter no. 19). It was dedicated to Pope John XXIII after May 17, 1410. Bruni's preface is in Bertalot, "Zur Bibliographie der Übersetzungen," 268–70.
366. Harth, *Poggio Bracciolini*, 1:139–40, letter no. 48.
367. Monfasani, "L'insegnamento di Teodoro Gaza a Ferrara," 10; Bianca, "Gaza, Teodoro," 739.
368. Bruni did not find the work congenial. When Niccolò Ceva encouraged him to make a translation, he replied in a letter of 1441, "libros illos iampridem latinos facere aggressus essem, si michi placerent. Sed multa sunt in iis libris abhorrentia a moribus nostris, quae pro honore Platonis tacere satius est quam proferre" (Mehus, *Leonardi Bruni Aretini epistolarum libri VIII*, 2:148, book 9, letter no. 4; Luiso, *Studi su l'epistolario*, book 9, letter no. 5).
369. See Novati, *Epistolario di Coluccio Salutati*, 4:84; Ullman, *The Humanism of Coluccio Salutati*, 245–46.
370. Wilson, *From Byzantium to Italy*, 20–21.
371. "Quo mortuo, ad C[incium] Romanum probatissimum quidem virum saepenumero me contuli . . . Ab hoc multa quae ab illo audierat didici; quae sciebam non perdidi; plurima Platonis opuscula—*Protagoram, De amicitia, De fortitudine*, eius viri *De laudibus utriusque Romae*—ipso hortante et suadente conscripsi" (to A. Traversari, January 21, 1417, cited in Förstel, "Bartolomeo Aragazzi et Manuel Chrysoloras," 111). Bartolomeo's transcript, Wroclaw, BU Akc.1949.kn.60, has Chrysoloras's *Comparatio* of Rome and Constantinople, *Lysis, Laches*, two letters of Chrysoloras and Aristides' *Oratio in Bacchum* (ibid., 112–13).

372. BL, Harl.5547, has Plato, *Protagoras, Lysis*, and *Laches*; Aristides, *Dionysus* and *Hercules* (RGK 1, no. 371; British Library, *Summary Catalogue*, 106). Zomino went to Constance in response to a letter dated April 1417; he was certainly there by July 23, 1417, and he was back in Florence by February 1418: see De la Mare, "Sozomeno (Zomino) of Pistoia 1387–1458," 92–93.
373. Cited in Cammelli, *Giovanni Argiropulo*, 106. Acciaiuoli (d. 1478) may have observed this in Rome in the 1470s.
374. (1) Rinuccio Aretino, 1423 to 1431 (Lockwood, "De Rinucio Aretino," 103–4; Belli, "Le versioni umanistiche dell'Assioco pseudo-platonico," 442; Resta, "Antonio Cassarino," 252n2; Hankins, *Plato in the Italian Renaissance*, 1:87); (2) Cincio Romano, 1436 to 1437 (Garin, "Ricerche sulle traduzioni di Platone nella prima meta del secolo XV," 368–69; Hankins, *Plato in the Italian Renaissance*, 1:82, 87); (3) A. Cassarino, before 1447 (Belli, "Le versioni umanistiche dell'Assioco pseudo-platonico," 442; Resta, "Antonio Cassarino," 252); (4) R. Agricola, perhaps 1477 (Van der Laan and Akkerman, *Rudolf Agricola*, 98–99, 294–95); (5) W. Pirckheimer, 1523 (Belli, "Le versioni umanistiche dell'Assioco pseudo-platonico," 443); (6) J. Cornarius (Belli, "Le versioni umanistiche dell'Assioco pseudo-platonico," 443).
375. Florence: De Alopa, [1484–85]. ISTC ip00771000.
376. Legrand, *Bibliographie hellénique*, item no. 22; Botfield, *Prefaces*, 243–44; Orlandi, *Aldo Manuzio editore*, 1:26; ISTC ie00064000.
377. Legrand, *Bibliographie hellénique*, item no. 39; Botfield, *Prefaces*, 286–96; Renouard, *Annales de l'imprimerie des Alde*, 62; Orlandi, *Aldo Manuzio editore*, 1:120–23.
378. Van Iseghem, *Biographie de Thierry Martens d'Alost*, 331.
379. Edited in Mehus, *Leonardi Bruni Aretini epistolarum libri VIII*, 1:lxxxix–cxiv. For its delivery, see Vespasiano, edited in Greco, *Vespasiano da Bisticci*, 1:498.
380. "Admirabilis in eo erat memoria poetraum Pindari, Aristophanis, Euripidis, Hesiodi, Homeri . . ." (Mehus, *Leonardi Bruni Aretini epistolarum libri VIII*, 1:c).
381. Mehus, *Leonardi Bruni Aretini epistolarum libri VIII*, 1:cx–cxi.
382. Browning, "Homer in Byzantium," 16.
383. Florence, Bibl. Laurenziana, 32.2, fourteenth century, has Sophocles (six plays), Euripides (eighteen plays), Aeschylus (three plays), and Hesiod (Ullman and Stadter, *The Public Library of Renaissance Florence*, 264; Weiss, "Lo studio di Plutarco nel trecento," 208).
384. Florence, Bibl. Laurenziana, Conv. soppr. 15 and Bibl. Laurenziana, Conv. soppr. 8 (Blum, *La biblioteca della Badia Fiorentina*, 74; Fera, "La prima traduzione umanistica delle *Olimpiche* di Pindaro," 698n12).
385. Ullman and Stadter, *The Public Library of Renaissance Florence*, 64.
386. Fiocco, "La biblioteca di Palla Strozzi," 310.
387. BAV, Pal.gr.190, written by Joannes Scutariota, who worked in Manetti's house in the 1440s.
388. Filelfo owned Florence, Bibl. Laurenziana, 32.16, which preserved Nonnus's *Dionysiaca*, and has Theocritus, Apollonius Rhodius, Triphiodorus, and Hesiod. He bought it in January 1423 from the wife of John Chrysoloras (Calderini, "Ricerche intorno alla biblioteca," 347–48; Diller, "A Lost Manuscript of Nonnus' *Dionysiaca*"). It is mentioned in Filelfo's letter to Traversari of June 13, 1428 (Mehus, *Ambrosii Traversarii epistolae*, 2, cols. 1010–11, book 24, letter no. 32). Zomino made Pistoia, Bibl. Forteguerriana A.24 of Hesiod and Theocritus (Festa, "Indice de' codici greci di Lucca e di Pistoia," 225; De la Mare, "Sozomeno (Zomino) of Pistoia 1387–1458," 100, plate XXIIe). A list of books sent to Gian Pietro da Lucca by Vittorino, dated June 12, 1445, includes "Hesiodi Theogonia" and "Hesiodus" (Cortesi, "Libri e vicende di Vittorino da Feltre," 92). Petrus Creticus, who worked for Vittorino, copied Florence, Bibl. Laurenziana, Acq.60, *Works and Days* with Tzetzes' commentary (RGK 1, no. 352). Guarino owned BAV, Vat.gr.1507 and PBN, gr.2772, both of which contain Hesiod (Diller, "Greek Codices of Palla Strozzi and Guarino Veronese," 319).
389. Around 1491, Merula (1430–94) wrote a work critical of Poliziano's *Miscellanea* in which he stated, "Audivi iuvenis haec dicentem Gregorium Tifernatem, cum Hesiodi libros interpretaretur, ubi Pandoram fictam tradit . . ." (Perotto Sali, "L'opuscolo inedito di Giorgio Merula

contro i *Miscellanea* di Angelo Poliziano," 182). The reference is to Hesiod, *Works and Days*, 73. Gregorio (1414–64) seems to have been at Naples from 1440 to 1453, and at Rome from 1453 to 1455. He taught briefly at Milan from around May 1456 until the autumn of the same year, when he left for France. Returning to Italy in 1460, he taught privately at Venice until his death: see Pagliaroli, "Gregorio da Città di Castello."

390. Madrid, Bibl. Nacional, 4617: Sophocles, *Aiax, Electra, Oedipus Rex*; Hesiod, *Works and Days* with Moschopoulos's scholia; Pindar, *Olympians*, 114. It was owned by Lascaris at Messina (1466–1501; Andrés, *Catálogo de los códices griegos*, 130–32). Folios 122 and 123 were copied by an unidentified scribe who worked with Lascaris and copied BAV, Vat.gr.1121, fols. 69–84 (Martínez-Manzano, *Konstantinos Laskaris*, 304).
391. Munich, gr.470: Theocritus, 8 *Idylls*; Hesiod, *Works and Days*; Pindar, *Olympians*, 114. It is described in Martínez-Manzano, *Konstantinos Laskaris*, 343–44.
392. Lascaris copied Madrid, Bibl. Nacional, 4607, of Hesiod and Theocritus. Filelfo's manuscript was Florence, Bibl. Laurenziana, 32.16. Lascaris copied Apollonius Rhodius from Filelfo's manuscript in the first half of 1465, and we may guess that these corrections were made at the same time: see chapter 3, section "Apollonius of Rhodes," n. 536, and for Lascaris's relations with Filelfo, see chapter 1, section "Constantine Lascaris," pp. 26–27. Valla copied Modena, Bibl. Estense, α.N.5.9 (West, "The Medieval and Renaissance Manuscripts of Hesiod's *Theogony*," 166–68; Andrés, *Catálogo de los códices griegos*, 108–11). Lascaris copied Madrid, Bibl. Nacional, 4629, which includes scholia on *Works and Days* (Andrés, *Catálogo de los códices griegos*, 153–57).
393. Madrid, Bibl. Nacional, 4642, fols. 1r–53v (Fernández Pomar, "La colección de Uceda," 261–62; Andrés, *Catálogo de los códices griegos*, 183–85).
394. "Iste Grecus fuit Demetrius Atheniensis qui publice padue primo *Erothimata* deinde Hesiodum nobis exposuit" (Geanakoplos, "Translation of Chalcondyles' Discourses," 296). For the date, see Cammelli, *Demetrio Calcondila*, 27–28.
395. Modena, Bibl. Estense, α.T.9.14 and Bibl. Estense, α.Q.9.20: see Günther, "Andronikos Kallistos," 315, 315n3.
396. Vian, "Leodrisio Crivelli," 63–64.
397. The dedication to Pius II can be consulted in ISTC ih00136000, image of sig. a1v. Niccolò says that he translated it at the age of "7 + 7 + 4," that is, eighteen. Since he was born in 1444, the translation was made around 1462. It was first printed with Calpurnius Siculus [Rome: Sweynheym and Pannartz, c. 1471]. For Niccolò, see De Nichilo, "Niccolò della Valle."
398. Hankins, *Plato in the Italian Renaissance*, 2:486n2. For a sample of this version, see Lippi's speech in Giustiniani, "L'orazione di Lorenzo Lippi," 282. This speech was delivered in November 1473.
399. ISTC ih00136500. His version was printed nine times before 1500 (ISTC).
400. See chapter 1, section "Constantine Lascaris," p. 27.
401. ISTC ih00141000, dedicated to Borso d'Este. Mombrizio cited Hesiod in his edition of Papias in 1476: see Daly, "Hesiod and Theocritus in the Text of Papias."
402. ISTC it00143000. For Bonaccorso's program, see Botley, "Learning Greek in Western Europe, 1476–1516," 201–6.
403. Poliziano's prolusion to his lectures on Hesiod and Vergil's *Georgics* was published not long after its delivery, October 26, 1483 (Fantazzi, *Angelo Poliziano*, xii, 30–67). On Filelfo's death in Florence in 1481, his manuscript, Florence, Bibl. Laurenziana, 32.16, entered the Medici library (Resta, *Apollonio Rodio*, 1081). Poliziano consulted Nonnus's *Dionysiaca* in this manuscript (*Miscellanea*, article nos. 11, 12, 28, 80). Material from Nonnus appeared in his poetic prolusion *Ambra*, dated November 4, 1485 (Fantazzi, *Angelo Poliziano*, 76, 84, 175n33, 177n63).
404. For Codro's lectures, see Gualdo Rosa, "Cortesi Urceo, Antonio, detto Codro," 776. He copied Florence, Bibl. Laurenziana, 31.20. For *Theogony*, at least, this was copied from Florence, Bibl. Laurenziana, Conv. soppr. gr.158 (West, "The Medieval and Renaissance Manuscripts of Hesiod's *Theogony*," 172–74).

405. The Aldine edition of the Greek poets has Theocritus, Planudes' Greek Cato, Theognis, *Aurea verba*, pseudo-Phocylides, Hesiod, and gnomic verse. The Milan edition of circa 1480, corrected against BAV, Vat.gr.1311, was certainly used for the Aldine text of Theocritus (Lowry, "Two Great Venetian Libraries," 142). The colophon of the edition, February 1495, is probably February 1496 new style (Christie, "The Chronology of the Early Aldines," 204). It is for sale at eight *marcelli* in the catalog of October 1, 1498; the price of four lire has been added to the catalog of June 22, 1503 (Orlandi, *Aldo Manuzio editore*, 2: plates IX–XIII).
406. Urceo sold two copies (letter of April 15, 1498; Dorez, "Études aldines III," 324). Aleandro, at Padua, requested a copy from Aldus on March 10, 1506 (De Nolhac, *Les correspondants d'Alde Manuce*, 63, letter no. 53). Forteguerri annotated a copy now bound with BAV, Vat.gr.1948 (De Nolhac, *La bibliothèque de Fulvio Orsini*, 176, 351).
407. BL, IB.24403. The other works in this volume do not have marginalia.
408. For Fausto's lectures, see Wilson, "Vettor Fausto," 91–92. For the Juntine Hesiod, dated January 20, 1515, *stylo florentino*, and edited by Euphrosynus Boninus, see Renouard, *Annales de l'imprimerie des Alde*, xl.
409. Described in Omont, "Essai sur les débuts de la typographie grecque à Paris," 19–20. Tissard's preface is in ibid., 47.
410. Strasbourg: Knoblouch, no date. Hesiod is followed by Planudes' Greek Cato, the *Aurea Verba*, and pseudo-Phocylides. The edition has no prefatory matter: its connection with Nachtgall is inferred from his certain connection with other Greek works printed by Knoblouch in 1515. For Nachtgall, see chapter 1, section "Ottomar Nachtgall."
411. Appendix 1, nos. 130 and 162. For Ceporinus, see chapter 1, section "Jacobus Ceporinus."
412. Rhein, "Melanchthon and Greek Literature," 165.
413. Browning, "Homer in Byzantium," 16.
414. Filelfo bought Florence, Bibl. Laurenziana, 32.16, in 1423: see chapter 3, section "Hesiod," n. 388. In a letter of October 5, 1450, to Pietro Perleone, Filelfo cites and translates Theocritus 4:41–43 (Filelfo, *Epistolare Francisci Philelfi*, sig. o3r). After 1460, Filelfo owned Florence, Bibl. Laurenziana, 58.19, of scholia on Theocritus (Calderini, "Ricerche intorno alla biblioteca," 399–400; Cortesi, "Aspetti linguistici della cultura greca di Francesco Filelfo," 183n73). This manuscript stayed in Florence after Filelfo's death in 1481 and seems to have been used by Poliziano (Martinelli, "Grammatiche greche," 268).
415. Fiocco, "La biblioteca di Palla Strozzi," 310.
416. Cortesi, "Libri e vicende di Vittorino da Feltre," 94.
417. "Vellem Tehocritum [*sic*] illum Roberti Siculi, optimi atque humanissimi viri, quamprimum nacta occasione remitteres" (Campano to "P," no date, Campano, *Ioannis Anthonii Campani opera omnia*, book 2, sig. b2r; Hausmann, "Giovanni Antonio Campano (1429–1477)," 48–49). Other letters in this book were written by Campano at Perugia. The date derives from a letter (see this chapter, n. 418) apparently addressed to the same person in the same book, in which he still has not sent this manuscript, and Constantinople has not yet fallen.
418. Campano to "P," no date (Campano, *Ioannis Anthonii Campani opera omnia*, book 2, sig. b4r; Hausmann, "Giovanni Antonio Campano (1429–1477)," 51–52). Campano says here that he is twenty-three years old. For the possibility that Campano was taught by Chalcondyles, see chapter 1, section "Demetrius Chalcondyles."
419. Filetico studied at Ferrara under Guarino sometime between 1447 and 1454, and his version was made at Urbino between 1454 and 1458. A dedication to Alfonso of Aragon (d. June 27, 1458) is extant (Bianca, "Filetico (Filettico), Martino," 636).
420. Lascaris copied Munich, gr.470, which includes Theocritus: see chapter 3, section "Hesiod," n. 391. In Messina, he added *Syrinx*, Theocritus (eighteen *Idylls*), and Moschus's *Epitaphium Bionis, Europa*, and *Amor fugitivus* to Madrid, Bibl. Nacional, 4607 (fols. 133–53v; Andrés, *Catálogo de los códices griegos*, 108–11). He copied Madrid, Bibl. Nacional, 4629, which includes notes on Theocritus (ibid., 153–57). In 1485 Petrus Castellus of Paris copied Prague, BU PSK, VIII.H.36, which has Theocritus *inter alia*. It was apparently copied while he studied under Lascaris in Messina. See Martínez-Manzano, *Konstantinos Laskaris*, 8n10, 293.

421. His lectures appear from a comment by one of his pupils, Merula (Centanni, "La biblioteca di Andronico Callisto," 202; Wilson, *From Byzantium to Italy*, 117). Callistus owned BL, Burn.109 of Theocritus; he copied Modena, Bibl. Estense, α.Q.5.20, which has scholia on Theocritus (Centanni, "La biblioteca di Andronico Callisto," 209, 211; RGK 1, no. 18). For his treatment of the *scholia vetera*, see Günther, "Andronikos Kallistos," 326. Florence, Bibl. Laurenziana.66.31, has *inter alia*, a version of the *Iliad* (fols. 7r–256v), which may have originated with Callistus. It also has a version of Theocritus, *Idylls* 1–7 (fols. 404r–411v). For this manuscript and its possible connection with Callistus, see Resta, *Apollonio Rodio*, 1092–95n31.
422. Venice, Bibl. Marciana, lat.14.10 (4659), fols. 66r–83v (Kristeller, *Iter Italicum*, 2:262; Bernardinello, "Gli studi propedeutici di greco," 127).
423. ISTC it00143000. For the sale of Callistus's manuscripts, see chapter 1, section "Theodore Gaza," p. 18. For Bonaccorso's program, see Botley, "Learning Greek in Western Europe, 1476–1516," 201–6.
424. Garin, "La 'Expositio Theocriti' di Angelo Poliziano."
425. [Rome]: Silber, [circa 1482]. ISTC it00146000. Printed under the author's supervision. At this date, Filetico is recorded as a lecturer on Latin and Greek at the *Studium urbis* (Dorati, "I lettori dello Studio," 125).
426. Poliziano was born in July 1454 (Bietenholz and Deutscher, *Contemporaries of Erasmus*, 3:106); Callistus arrived in Florence in August 1471 (Cammelli, "Andronico Callisto," 178–81).
427. He owned Florence, Bibl. Laurenziana, 32.46, of eighteen *Idylls* (Wilson, *From Byzantium to Italy*, 107). His version is addressed to Antonio Zeno (Poliziano, *Angeli Politiani Opera*, 207–10).
428. For example, in Giannozzo Manetti's BAV, Pal.gr.179; in the manuscript made by Joannes Rhosos, Florence, Bibl. Riccardiana, 53 Kii 13; and in Milan, Bibl. Ambrosiana, S.31.sup., copied by Demetrius Damilas. Lascaris's *compendium* is appendix 1, no. 10.
429. See chapter 3, section "Demosthenes," n. 292.
430. The preface of Filippo di Alessandro Pandolfino to the Juntine Theocritus: "Διατρίβων Ἐνετίῃσι καὶ τῶν Μουσουρείων εἷς ὢν ἀκροατῶν, ἐνέτυχον ἀντιγράφῳ τινὶ . . ." (edited in Legrand, *Bibliographie hellénique*, 1:125). For the date, see this chapter, n. 436.
431. For this edition, see chapter 3, section "Hesiod," n. 405.
432. De Nolhac, *Les correspondants d'Alde Manuce*, 63, letter no. 53.
433. "L'e vero che in questa terra hanno stampito l'*Erotemati* di Chrysolora dal typo di Regio et Theocrito; le letre in men sono facte qui et ancora che io non le habia viste, tamen credo che non siano ne belle ne bone" (Omont, "Essai sur les débuts de la typographie grecque à Paris," 6, 68–69).
434. The first of these, which I have not seen, was printed by Gourmont and has a dedication dated 1511 (Moreau, *Inventaire chronologique*, 2, item no. 465). The second may be a reprint of the first, removing the date from the dedication to Aleandro. See Omont, "Essai sur les débuts de la typographie grecque à Paris," 33, 61; Moreau, *Inventaire chronologique*, 2, item no. 209.
435. Kierher, at Paris, to M. Hummelberg, November 1511: [Aleander] "exposuit, ut opinor, iam decem Theocriti eclogas non sine summa sua laude. Sed ut tibi verum fatear—non tam ego quam ceteri—mallem potius linguam communem ut doceret quam Doricam illam scabram certe et subrusticam, tametsi rei rusticae alioqui accomodatissimam" (cited in Girot, *Pindare avant Ronsard*, 33).
436. For the Juntine edition, see Legrand, *Bibliographie hellénique*, item no. 45. Legrand does not notice the privilege. The edition is dated January 10, 1515, in the third year of Leo's pontificate. This third year began March 11, 1515, so the date is *stylo florentino*. For Callierges' edition, see Legrand, *Bibliographie hellénique*, item no. 49. The privilege is edited at Legrand, *Bibliographie hellénique*, 1:134–35. This edition is dated in the colophon January 15, 1516. Since this privilege refers to Callierges' edition of Pindar, August 13, 1515, as *nuper editus*, the Theocritus colophon is new style. Neither privilege specifies territorial limitations.
437. January 1520 (title page), February 1520 (colophon; Van Iseghem, *Biographie de Thierry Martens d'Alost*, 307; Hoven, "Enseignement du grec," 80).

438. The lectures of 1521 are derived from Albert Burer's letter to Basil Amorbach, 31 August 1521, from Wittenberg: "Lutherum nondum vidi ... Audimus a ministro eius in coenobio Augustinensium Theocriti εἰδύλλια" (Allen, "Some Letters of Masters and Scholars," 746). For the lectures of 1526, see Rhein, "Melanchthon and Greek Literature," 166.
439. Van Iseghem, *Biographie de Thierry Martens d'Alost*, 340.
440. For Aristophanes, see chapter 3, section "Aristophanes."
441. Wilson, "Erasmus as a Translator of Euripides," 87.
442. Florence, Bibl. Laurenziana, 32.2, which also has Sophocles, Aeschylus, and Hesiod (Ullman and Stadter, *The Public Library of Renaissance Florence*, 264).
443. Pilato's version of *Hecuba*, lines 1–466, is in Florence, Bibl. Laurenziana, 31.10, a manuscript that was in Florence in 1362. It also has seven plays of Sophocles (Wilson, *Scholars of Byzantium*, 163–64). Pilato's version of *Hecuba*, lines 1–396, is in Florence, Bibl. Laurenziana, S. Marco.226 (Wilson, *From Byzantium to Italy*, 4–5).
444. Now Florence, Bibl. Laurenziana, Conv. soppr. 71 (Sophocles, *Aiax, Electra, Oedipus Rex*; Euripides, *Hecuba, Orestes, Phoenissae*; Sabbadini, *Carteggio di Giovanni Aurispa*, 3–4; Ullman and Stadter, *The Public Library of Renaissance Florence*, 62; Browning, "Greek Manuscripts in Medieval Chios," 46).
445. Three of the triad: Florence, Bibl. Laurenziana, Conv. soppr. gr.11, gr.71, gr.98; Bibl. Laurenziana, Conv. soppr. gr.66 (*Hecuba, Orestes*.); and Bibl. Laurenziana, Conv. soppr. gr.172 (*Heraclidae* (part), *Hercules, Helena, Electra, Hecuba, Orestes, Phoenissae*). See Blum, *La biblioteca della Badia Fiorentina*, 74.
446. A list of books to be sent to Gian Pietro da Lucca by Vittorino, dated June 12, 1445, includes "Tragedie Euripidis" (Cortesi, "Libri e vicende di Vittorino da Feltre," 94). Guarino owned a manuscript "Euripidis tragediae nonnullae" (Diller, "Greek Codices of Palla Strozzi and Guarino Veronese," 318).
447. Filelfo brought PBN, gr.2713 to Italy in 1427, and it has marginalia in his hand (Speranzi, "Codici greci appartenuti a Francesco Filelfo," 482–88). Vittorino gave a manuscript of Euripides to Jacopo Cassiano for delivery to Filelfo in 1440 (Filelfo, *Epistolare Francisci Philelfi*, sigs. h3r–v, h8v, o4v). Filelfo lent a copy to Cato Sacco, which he attempted to retrieve in 1440 (ibid., sig. h8r). He owned Florence, Bibl. Laurenziana, 31.1 of eleven plays, copied for Filelfo at Rome from Atumano's Florence, Bibl. Laurenziana, 32.2 by Angelo Thytes (Calderini, "Ricerche intorno alla biblioteca," 309; Turyn, *Studies in the Manuscript Tradition*, 41, 66–67; Eleuteri, "Francesco Filelfo," 169). He owned Florence, Bibl. Laurenziana, 31.34 (Eleuteri, "Francesco Filelfo," 169; Günther, "Andronikos Kallistos," 326). His version from *Hecuba* is edited in Calderini, "Ricerche intorno alla biblioteca," 310–11, and evaluated in Wilson, *From Byzantium to Italy*, 5. His version of *Phoenissae*, lines 360–410, is edited in Calderini, "Ricerche intorno alla biblioteca," 312–13.
448. PBN, gr.2713, fols. 9r–16v, are by Gaza (Eleuteri, "Francesco Filelfo," 168; RGK 2, no. 165). Gaza copied or restored BAV, Vat.gr.52 (Günther, "Andronikos Kallistos," 326). Callistus made Modena, Bibl. Estense, α.U.9.22, which has scholia on *Electra, Hecuba, Orestes*, and *Phoenissae* (Centanni, "La biblioteca di Andronico Callisto," 213). He restored Cremona 130, which has *Hecuba, Orestes*, and *Phoenissae* (Günther, "Andronikos Kallistos," 327, 333). Florence, Bibl. Laurenziana, 31.21, scholia on Euripides, is in a hand rather like Callistus's (Günther, "Andronikos Kallistos," 321).
449. Oxford, Bodleian, Auct.F.3.25. Free arrived at Ferrara to study under Guarino in the autumn of 1456. In 1458, he wrote to his patron for money to buy Greek books. He moved to Padua in 1458, where he was until at least 1461. He died in Rome (Weiss, *Humanism in England*, 106–11). For the fate of his books after his death, see ibid., 111, 123.
450. Madrid, Bibl. Nacional, 4677 (Andrés, *Catálogo de los códices griegos*, 224–26). He also copied *Hecuba* in Madrid, Bibl. Nacional, 4555 (Andrés, *Catálogo de los códices griegos*, 22–24).
451. Venice, Bibl. Marciana, lat.14.54 (4328), an autograph. See Bernardinello, "Gli studi propedeutici di greco," 127; Porro, "La versione latina dell' Écuba euripidea," 343–63.

452. Leiden, Univ. Library, Voss.gr.61 (*Hecuba* and *Orestes*, with scholia); PBN, gr.2813 (*Hecuba*). The Paris manuscript is signed by Jacques Toussain (Irigoin, "Georges Hermonyme de Sparte," 26; Omont, "Georges Hermonyme de Sparte," 92).
453. Devreesse, *Catalogue des manuscrits grecs*, 34–35, 46–47, 98, 101–2.
454. Bertola, *I due primi registri*, 9, 12, 13, 15, 20, 21, 25, 29, 30. For lectures on Aristophanes in Rome at this period, see chapter 3, section "Aristophanes."
455. Perosa, Review of Knös, *Un ambassadeur de l'hellénisme*, 362.
456. Pozzi, "Da Padova a Firenze nel 1493," 194.
457. No translation of Aeschylus was made in the fifteenth century. The Greek text was not printed until 1518. There was no new edition until 1552 and no translation until 1555. Amid the general neglect, George Hermonymus made Leiden, Bibl. Publ., gr.51 (*Prometheus* and *Septem* with scholia) and PBN, Coislin.gr.353 (*Prometheus* and *Septem*) (Omont, "Georges Hermonyme de Sparte," 91–92).
458. For Lascaris and Sophocles, see chapter 3, section "Sophocles."
459. ISTC ie00115000; Legrand, *Bibliographie hellénique*, item no. 15.
460. Legrand, *Bibliographie hellénique*, item no. 31. The colophon is February 1503: "The book itself affords no evidence whether the date is 1503 or 1504 n.s." (Christie, "The Chronology of the Early Aldines," 216). However, see Fletcher "Three New-Style Dates," 107, which makes it certainly new style. The book appears in the Aldine catalog of June 22, 1503, where the price of one ducat and three lire is added in manuscript. This has eighteen plays, although only seventeen are advertised on the title page. *Electra* was first printed at Rome in 1545.
461. For Chalcondyles, see chapter 1, section "Demetrius Chalcondyles"; for his lectures on Sophocles, see chapter 3, section "Sophocles."
462. In July 1501, he wrote to his sometime pupil, Nicholas Bensrott, "Euripidem et Isocratem ad te mittimus" (EE 1:365 and note on line 6.). It is unclear whether this refers to a Greek or Latin text. His version of *Hecuba* was made in Louvain between February 1504 and the end of the year (Waszink, *Euripidis Hecuba*, 195; EE 1:4).
463. Parma: Franciscus Ugoletus, June 5, 1506. For Anselmi, see Quattrucci, "Anselmi, Giorgio."
464. His notebook has a Latin version of *Hecuba* (minus lines 438–637 and 1280ff) and of *Orestes*, lines 1–280 (Meyer, "Ein Kollegheft des humanisten Cono," 281).
465. EE 1:4; 1:418.
466. "Simulatque me Lutetiam recepissem, inde petiturus Italiam, libro Badio tradidi formulis excudendum, adiecta *Iphigenia Aulidensi*, quam fusius ac liberius veteram agens in Anglia" (EE 1:5). Erasmus went to England toward the end of 1505; he left for France in June 1506 (EE 1:414, headnote to letter no. 185).
467. See EE 1:417–20, 430; Waszink, *Euripidis Hecuba*.
468. Erasmus was in Paris in early August 1506 (EE 1:430 and headnote to letter no. 199). For his journey to Italy, see EE 1:426, headnote to letter no. 194. He was in Bologna in November 1507 (EE 1:439–42).
469. EE 1:438–39.
470. Renouard, *Annales de l'imprimerie des Alde*, 51–52; EE 1:439–40; Orlandi, *Aldo Manuzio editore*, 1:93.
471. Omont, "Essai sur les débuts de la typographie grecque à Paris," 2. The versions survive in the dedication manuscript, PBN, lat.7884. See Omont, "Essai sur les débuts de la typographie grecque à Paris," 4. For a partial transcript of Tissard's dedication, see ibid., 64–68.
472. "primam tragoediam et secundae dimidiam aestate superiori . . . traduxeram" (Omont, "Essai sur les débuts de la typographie grecque à Paris," 67).
473. "ubi primum litteris quibusdam patriis tertio Nonas Decembres te desyderare accepissem, mihi visum fuit longe congruentius illos graecanicos loquendi modos, qui saltem vix latiali sermone tolerari potuissent vel qui duriusculi forent, aliquatenus variare permutareque . . ." (Omont, "Essai sur les débuts de la typographie grecque à Paris," 67).
474. For the first performance, see EE 1:417, headnote to letter no. 188; for a second, see EE 2:388 and note to line 62.

475. Louvain: Martens, August 1520. This is a single volume, not two separately printed texts issued together. Basle: Froben, February 1524 and April 1530.
476. Florence, Bibl. Laurenziana, 31.8 (Aeschylus, Sophocles, Lycophron, and Dionysius Periegetes) belonged to Atumano. It was in the library of San Marco in Florence in 1457 (Pertusi, "La scoperta di Euripide nel primo Umanesimo," 115–16; Ullman and Stadter, *The Public Library of Renaissance Florence*, 263). Atumano had Florence, Bibl. Laurenziana, 32.2 in Avignon in 1348. It has Sophocles (six plays), Euripides (eighteen plays), Aeschylus (three plays), and Hesiod (Weiss, "Lo studio di Plutarco nel trecento," 208; Ullman and Stadter, *The Public Library of Renaissance Florence*, 264).
477. Florence, Bibl. Laurenziana, 31.10, which has Sophocles (seven plays) and Euripides (eight plays; Turyn, *Studies in the Manuscript Tradition*, 166–68; Wilson, *Scholars of Byzantium*, 163–64).
478. The first is Florence, Bibl. Laurenziana, Conv. soppr. 71 (Sabbadini, *Carteggio di Giovanni Aurispa*, 3–4; Browning, "Greek Manuscripts in Medieval Chios," 46). The second is Florence, Bibl. Laurenziana, 32.9, of seven plays. This, the oldest surviving manuscript of Sophocles, is mentioned in Traversari's letter of May 25, [1425] (edited in Mehus, *Ambrosii Traversarii epistolae*, 2, col. 372, book 8, letter no. 8; Stinger, *Humanism and the Church Fathers*, 37).
479. Blum, *La biblioteca della Badia Fiorentina*, 74–75. This list includes the manuscript Aurispa sold to Niccoli, Florence, Bibl. Laurenziana, Conv. soppr. 71, presumably acquired between 1417 and 1425. See chapter 3, section "Euripides," n. 444.
480. Fiocco, "La biblioteca di Palla Strozzi," 310.
481. For Cyriaco's manuscript, see Omont, "Catalogue des manuscrits grecs," 187. Florence, Bibl. Laurenziana, 31.1, was copied for Filelfo in Rome by Angelo Thytes (Eleuteri, "Francesco Filelfo," 169; Calderini, "Ricerche intorno alla biblioteca," 309, 390–93). The copy was made from Atumano's manuscript, Florence, Bibl. Laurenziana, 32.2 (Turyn, *Studies in the Manuscript Tradition*, 41, 66–67).
482. Under the entry "Sophocles" (Cortesi, "Il «Vocabularium» greco di Giovanni Tortelli," 451, 471).
483. Monfasani, "L'insegnamento di Teodoro Gaza a Ferrara," 8; Bianca, "Gaza, Teodoro," 739.
484. He added *Antigone* to Modena, Bibl. Estense, α.T.9.2, and made Modena, Bibl. Estense, α.Q.5.20, which has scholia on the triad. Both were later owned by Giorgio Valla and Alberto Pio (Allen, "Notes upon Greek Manuscripts," 14–15; Turyn, *Studies in the Manuscript Tradition*, 79, 81–83; Centanni, "La biblioteca di Andronico Callisto," 209, 211–12; Günther, "Andronikos Kallistos," 317n18, 319, 323, 325–26, 333). Both were apparently made before Callistus left Italy in 1475.
485. Bernardinello, "Gli studi propedeutici di greco," 127.
486. Devreesse, *Catalogue des manuscrits grecs*, 34–35, 45–47.
487. Venice, Bibl. Marciana, gr.467 (seven plays) and Venice, Bibl. Marciana, gr.468 (six plays) were in the inventory of 1468 (Labowsky, *Bessarion's Library and the Biblioteca Marciana*, 176, item nos. 457 and 450). Georgius Trivizias copied Venice, Bibl. Marciana, gr.470 (seven plays), which first appears in the inventory of 1474 (Labowsky, *Bessarion's Library and the Biblioteca Marciana*, 226, item no. 635).
488. This manuscript, Venice, Bibl. Marciana, gr.617 (Dionysius Periegetes; Sophocles, seven plays), was once owned by Lorenzo Lippi (d. 1485). See Diller, "Greek Codices of Palla Strozzi and Guarino Veronese," 259. Turyn suggests that Venice, Bibl. Marciana, gr.616, fifteenth century, was copied from Barbaro's manuscript (*Studies in the Manuscript Tradition*, 67).
489. Vienna, Österreichische Nationalbibl., Philos.philol.gr.147 (*Aiax, Electra, Oedipus Rex*); subscribed after *Electra*, Venice, December 15, 1488 (fol. 98v); subscribed at the end, Venice, January 23, 1488 (fol. 151r). This last date is January 23, 1489, new style. See Turyn, *Studies in the Manuscript Tradition*, 79, 79n82. For Rhosos, see RGK 1, no. 178; 2, no. 237; 3, no. 298.

490. *Aiax, Electra, Antigone, Oedipus Rex*, and scholia (Müller, "Neue Mittheilungen," 382). For Callistus's Sophocles manuscripts, see this chapter, n. 484. For the fortunes of Callistus's library, see chapter 1, section "Theodore Gaza," p. 18 and n. 193.
491. Vienna, Österreichische Nationalbibl., Phil.gr.270, dated Venice, August 9, 1491 (Turyn, *Studies in the Manuscript Tradition*, 91). He added the text of pseudo-Phocylides at the end (Derron, "Inventaire des manuscrits du Pseudo-Phocylide," no. 154).
492. In his work against Poliziano's *Miscellanea*, Merula wrote, "Nuper cum Sophoclis tragoediam Αἴας μαστιγόφορος discipulis interpretarer, quid coronis esset ex Hephaestionis sententia enarravi . . ." (edited in Perotto Sali, "L'opuscolo inedito di Giorgio Merula contro i *Miscellanea* di Angelo Poliziano," 183). For the date of this work, see ibid., 151–52. Merula owned Milan, Bibl. Ambrosiana, A105 sup. of Sophocles (Friggi, "Libri greci alla corte di Ludovico il Moro," 135).
493. Cammelli, *Giovanni Argiropulo*, 101n3. Argyropoulos began his lectures at Florence, February 4, 1457, new style (Müllner, "Eine Rede des Ioannes Lascaris," 3); he left Florence for Rome after October 3, 1471, and was in Rome by October 26 (Cammelli, *Giovanni Argiropulo*, 135–36).
494. Arsenius (Aristoboulos) Apostolis copied Florence, Bibl. Riccardiana 77, Sophocles, *Aiax, Electra* (part), *Electra* (complete), *Antigone* (part); Euripides, *Electra*; Sophocles, *Philoctetes, Oedipus Coloneus*. One portion of the manuscript is subscribed at Crete, January 22, 1496, Πέτρῳ φλωρεντίνῳ τῷ μοναχῷ (fol. 94v). The later leaves seem to have been made in Florence in the 1490s. For its sources and fortunes, see Turyn, *Studies in the Manuscript Tradition*, 65, 188–89; Günther, "Andronikos Kallistos," 328; Speranzi, "Tra Creta e Firenze." Florence, Bibl. Laurenziana, Conv. soppr. gr.142 has scholia on several plays, *Trachiniae*, and a note: "Monasterii Angelorum Petrus Candidus" (fol. 1r). Part was copied from Bibl. Laurenziana, 32.9, and part from PBN, gr.2799 (Turyn, *Studies in the Manuscript Tradition*, 186–88).
495. Possibly of Euripides: see chapter 3, section "Euripides."
496. In a speech delivered circa 1493, Lascaris said, "interpretati sumus anno superiori duos gravissimos et praestantissimos auctores, Sophoclem et Thucydidem" (Müllner, "Eine Rede des Ioannes Lascaris," 143). For the production of *Electra*, see Cammelli, *Demetrio Calcondila*, 79.
497. Weiss, *Humanism in England*, 68. Antigone was born before 1428.
498. For this manuscript, see chapter 3, section "Euripides," and n. 449.
499. Occo made Munich, gr.500, of *Aiax, Antigone, Oedipus Rex*, and *Electra*. His extracts are in Munich, gr.313 (Turyn, *Studies in the Manuscript Tradition*, 41, 68; Mondrain, "La collection de manuscrits grecs d'Adolphe Occo," 165).
500. Renouard, *Annales de l'imprimerie des Alde*, 34–35; Legrand, *Bibliographie hellénique*, item no. 30; Orlandi, *Aldo Manuzio editore*, 1:61–62; Botfield, *Prefaces*, 261.
501. This appears from a lexicon made during these lectures, BAV, Vat.gr.1880 (Canart, *Codices Vaticani Graeci*, 1:468–69).
502. The price is added in manuscript to a copy of the Aldine catalog of June 22, 1503, reproduced in Orlandi, *Aldo Manuzio editore*, 2: plates X–XIII. For the possibility that Aldus exchanged copies of Sophocles for Chalcondyles' copies of the Suda lexicon, see chapter 2, section "The Suda Lexicon."
503. Aldus offered the edition to Reuchlin in August 1502 (Geiger, *Johann Reuchlins Briefwechsel*, 78, letter no. 83). In November, Reuchlin requested a copy (De Nolhac, *Les correspondants d'Alde Manuce*, 21, letter no. 15).
504. The request was made in a letter dated "6 Kal. Brumae 1504," although he says that he cannot pay until Christmas (De Nolhac, *Les correspondants d'Alde Manuce*, 38–39, letter no. 31). For Bodianus (Fracantius), see Pagano, "Fracanzio da Montalboddo."
505. Now in the Vatican Library (De Nolhac, *La bibliothèque de Fulvio Orsini*, 181).
506. BAV, Vat.lat.11483 has a commentary on *Oedipus Coloneus* from his lectures: see Gualdo Rosa, *La fede nella "Paideia,"* 74. In July 1511, Musurus owned BAV, Pal.gr.287, which has *Antigone, Oedipus Coloneus, Trachiniae*, and *Philoctetes*. He copied PBN, gr.2799, fols. 1–19, 23–164, and scholia on Sophocles (RGK 2, no. 359).

507. *Aiax*, lines 1–787, and the conclusion; *Electra*, lines 1–130, and the conclusion. A note after the translation of *Electra* reads "1508 Agathe" (Meyer, "Ein Kollegheft des humanisten Cono," 281, 283).
508. Legrand, *Bibliographie hellénique*, item no. 60.
509. Florence: heredes P. Juntae, October 27, 1522; Paris: Colinaeus, December 16, 1528.
510. Travi, *Pietro Bembo*, 2:407, 411–12; and see Solerti, *Le tragedie metriche*, 22–26.
511. Browning, "Homer in Byzantium," 16.
512. Monfasani, *Collectanea Trapezuntiana*, 398; Wilson, *From Byzantium to Italy*, 45–46; Fera, "La prima traduzione umanistica delle *Olimpiche* di Pindaro," 695n6.
513. For Aurispa, see Sabbadini, *Carteggio di Giovanni Aurispa*, 10–15; Fera, "La prima traduzione umanistica delle *Olimpiche* di Pindaro," 693n1. For Corbinelli, see Blum, *La biblioteca della Badia Fiorentina*, 74–75; Wilson, *From Byzantium to Italy*, 46; Fera, "La prima traduzione umanistica delle *Olimpiche* di Pindaro," 698n12. For Filelfo, see Fera, "La prima traduzione umanistica delle *Olimpiche* di Pindaro," 693n1. A list of Strozzi's books, dated 1431, includes Pindar (Fiocco, "La biblioteca di Palla Strozzi," 310).
514. See Calderini, "Ricerche intorno alla biblioteca," 355–56.
515. "Admirabilis in eo erat memoria poetarum Pindari, Aristophanis, Euripidis, Hesiodi, Homeri . . ." (Mehus, *Leonardi Bruni Aretini epistolarum libri VIII*, 1:c). Manetti owned Pindar in BAV, Pal.gr.190, copied by Joannes Scutariota.
516. The letter is in Powell, "Two Letters." Florence, Bibl. Laurenziana, Ashburn.1144, which has most of Pindar, was written by Callistus but has no annotations to connect it with his teaching (Todd, "Baltasar Meliavacca," 70–71, 71n15; Wilson, *From Byzantium to Italy*, 116; Fera, "La prima traduzione umanistica delle *Olimpiche* di Pindaro"). Callistus made Modena, Bibl. Estense, α.Q.5.20 (*De metris Pindari* and scholia on Pindar, *Olympians*, no. 1) and Modena, Bibl. Estense, α.T.9.14 (*Pythia*, *Nemea*, 1–4 and 6). See Centanni, "La biblioteca di Andronico Callisto," 211, 212; Günther, "Andronikos Kallistos," 323, 325. The latter manuscript has been dated by its watermarks to the 1460s (West, "The Medieval and Renaissance Manuscripts of Hesiod's *Theogony*," 179).
517. Florence, Bibl. Nazionale Centrale, Magliab.VII.1025, for which see Fera, "La prima traduzione umanistica delle *Olimpiche* di Pindaro," 700–710.
518. Madrid, Bibl. Nacional, 4617, has *Olympians* 1–14 (fols. 195–239v). It was owned and partly copied by Lascaris at Messina (1466–1501), but probably acquired by him at Rhodes in the 1450s (Andrés, *Catálogo de los códices griegos*, 130–32). Lascaris copied Munich, gr.470, at Milan, which includes *Olympians* 1–14. This, perhaps a presentation copy, is described in Martínez-Manzano, *Konstantinos Laskaris*, 343–44. Madrid, Bibl. Nacional, 4633, has scholia on *Olympians* 1–7, copied at Milan circa 1465; he added scholia on *Olympians* 8–10 at Messina circa 1480 (Andrés, *Catálogo de los códices griegos*, 162–64).
519. Munich, gr.550, fols. 1r–31v. See Mondrain, "La collection de manuscrits grecs d'Adolphe Occo," 167–68.
520. Leiden, Univ. Library, Voss.gr.39 (Omont, "Georges Hermonyme de Sparte," 90).
521. August 2, [1484]; November 20, 1485; and July 18, 1488 (Bertola, *I due primi registri*, 31, 35).
522. Fera, "La prima traduzione umanistica delle *Olimpiche* di Pindaro," 694n5.
523. Grafton, *Textual Criticism and Exegesis*, 247n33. Copenhagen, GKS 1979, 4o, was used by Urbano. It has *Olympians*, 1–14, with interlinear glosses; *Vita Pindari*; scholia to *Olympians*, 1–10. See Schartau, *Codices Graeci Haunienses*, 192–93.
524. With Callimachus, Dionysius Periegetes, and Lycophron (Venice: Manutius, January 1513). The date is new style (Christie, "The Chronology of the Early Aldines," 218–19). For this edition, see Botfield, *Prefaces*, 284–85; Renouard, *Annales de l'imprimerie des Alde*, 64–65; Orlandi, *Aldo Manuzio editore*, 1:106–8; Girot, *Pindare avant Ronsard*, 102–5, 408. For manuscripts used, see Irigoin, *Histoire du texte de Pindare*, 399–408. For Navagero, see Orlandi, *Aldo Manuzio editore*, 2:363.

525. Rome: Callierges, August 13, 1515. See Legrand, *Bibliographie hellénique*, item no. 47; Girot, *Pindare avant Ronsard*, 409–10. Cornelio Benigno collaborated with Callierges on this edition, and in doing so alienated his patron, Agostino Chigi: in 1518 Chigi successfully sued him for four hundred ducats that he had advanced for the edition (Gigante, "Benigni, Cornelio," 513).
526. Leipzig: Schumann, 1519. The ode is appended to a Greek text of Plutarch, *An recte dictum sit latenter esse vivendum*. For the edition, see Girot, *Pindare avant Ronsard*, 410.
527. For Negri, see Girot, *Pindare avant Ronsard*, 49–50, 105–8. For Fausto, see Wilson, "Vettor Fausto," 91–92.
528. Basle: Cratander, 1526. See Girot, *Pindare avant Ronsard*, 108–17, 411–12. Probably printed by 1525, since a copy bears the note, "Iacobus Ceporinus Albano Torino dono dedit MDXXV" (Egli, "Ceporins Leben und Schriften," 154, 155n1). For Ceporinus, see chapter 1, section "Jacobus Ceporinus."
529. Hagenau: Gran, September 1527. The version of the first ode is dedicated to Conrad Peutinger; the second, to Joannes Pincianus. Both dedications are dated Heidelberg, March 1527. For Molther, see König, *Konrad Peutingers Briefwechsel*, 380–81, 429–34. For his versions, see Girot, *Pindare avant Ronsard*, 117–19. In a letter preface to Peutinger of November 30, 1528, Molther quotes *Olympians* 13I, lines 6–11 (König, *Konrad Peutingers Briefwechsel*, 434).
530. Basle: Cratander, March 1528. See Girot, *Pindare avant Ronsard*, 119–22, 412–13. Dedicated to M. Adamus from Frankfurt, 1527 *sine mense*.
531. Florence, Bibl. Laurenziana, 32.16, which preserved Nonnus's *Dionysiaca*: see chapter 3, section "Hesiod," nn. 388, 392, and 403.
532. Florence, Bibl. Laurenziana, 32.9, mid-tenth century (Resta, *Apollonio Rodio*, 1080, 1117–18n94; Schade and Eleuteri, "The Textual Tradition of the *Argonautica*," 41).
533. Manetti's BAV, Pal.gr.186, for many years wrongly believed to be of the eleventh century, imitates its exemplar, Florence, Bibl. Laurenziana, 32.9. See Resta, *Apollonio Rodio*, 1080, 1117–18n94; Schade and Eleuteri, "The Textual Tradition of the *Argonautica*," 41.
534. Petrus Creticus made Wolfenbüttel, Guelf.10.2, August 4o (2296) of Apollonius from a lost exemplar. This, probably made in Mantua, was owned by Vittorino (RGK 1, no. 352; Schade and Eleuteri, "The Textual Tradition of the *Argonautica*," 43–44). A manuscript described simply as "Apolonius" [*sic*] is in a list of books sent to Gian Pietro da Lucca (d. 1457) by Vittorino, dated June 12, 1445 (Cortesi, "Libri e vicende di Vittorino da Feltre," 92). Aurispa sold Petrus's copy in Rome on June 10, 1456 (Resta, *Apollonio Rodio*, 1091–92n28, 1119–20n96). It was also owned by Gian Lucido Gonzaga (d. 1448) and Guarino Veronese (d. 1460): see Cortesi, "Libri e vicende di Vittorino da Feltre," 107; Eleuteri, "Francesco Filelfo," 179. For Basinio's poem and manuscript, see Campana, "Basinio da Parma," 93–94.
535. See Diller, "Greek Codices of Palla Strozzi and Guarino Veronese," 319. Probably not the manuscript made by Petrus Creticus: see Resta, *Apollonio Rodio*, 1091–92n28. Guarino did ultimately acquire Petrus's copy, apparently between 1456 and his death in 1460: see this chapter, n. 534.
536. Madrid, Bibl. Nacional, 4691, of Aratus, Apollonius Rhodius, and Triphiodorus (Andrés, *Catálogo de los códices griegos*, 251–53). Presumably made before June 1465, when he was summoned to Naples. It was copied from Filelfo's Florence, Bibl. Laurenziana, 32.16 (Schade and Eleuteri, "The Textual Tradition of the *Argonautica*," 43). Relations between the two scholars were poor in the early 1460s, but this copy suggests that they had improved by 1465: see chapter 1, section "Constantine Lascaris," pp. 26–27; chapter 3, section "Hesiod," n. 392.
537. Parma 355 (Hh.VIII.62). RGK 1, no. 105; Schade and Eleuteri, "The Textual Tradition of the *Argonautica*," 49.
538. Bessarion's inventory of 1468 lists one copy of Apollonius; the inventory of 1474 has two (Labowsky, *Bessarion's Library and the Biblioteca Marciana*, 176, no. 453; 226, no. 639 and no. 641). One of these, Venice, Bibl. Marciana, gr.480, was copied by Trivizias for Bessarion, apparently at Rome, between 1468 and 1472. It was copied from BAV, Pal.gr.280, which must also be placed in Rome at this time. In the same period, Trivizias copied two manuscripts from Bibl. Marciana, gr.480: BAV, Vat.gr.36, fols. 1–225, and BAV, Urb.gr.146.

He also copied Oxford, Bodleian, Auct.T.3.10 (misc. 227), apparently at the same time and place. Bessarion's second copy is BAV, Vat.gr.1619 (RGK 1, no. 73; Schade and Eleuteri, "The Textual Tradition of the *Argonautica*," 42–43).

539. Resta says that this was Niccoli's ancient copy, Florence, Bibl. Laurenziana, 32.9 (Resta, *Apollonio Rodio*, 1106).
540. BAV, Vat.gr.1619, which Aurelio returned to the collection in October 1474 (Labowsky, *Bessarion's Library and the Biblioteca Marciana*, 53–57, 490).
541. Resta, *Apollonio Rodio*, 1059. Callistus made Modena, Bibl. Estense, α.T.8.13, of Apollonius, and Modena, Bibl. Estense, α.P.6.13, which has the scholia: see Centanni, "La biblioteca di Andronico Callisto," 210–11; Günther, "Andronikos Kallistos," 323–24, 333.
542. *Argonautica*, book 4, line 1515. See Levine Rubinstein, "The Notes to Poliziano's «Iliad.»," 205, 238, and chapter 3, section "Homer."
543. Fonzio wrote to Baptista Guarino from Florence, April 19, 1472, that he could not borrow a manuscript from Bessarion: "Apollonium autem, quem deferre mecum sperabam, idcirco habere non potui, quod Bessarion ad obeundam legationem intentus non exhibuit" (Juhász, *Bartholomaeus Fontius*, 10). Bessarion left on his legation on April 20, 1472 (Mohler, *Kardinal Bessarion*, 3:577, note to letter, no. 5); he died in November.
544. Florence, Bibl. Riccardiana, ms. 153, has an interlinear translation of *Argonautica*, book 1, lines 1–247, derived from the lectures of Callistus in Fonzio's hand; Florence, Bibl. Riccardiana, ms. 539 has a complete translation by Fonzio, based on Callistus's interpretation (Resta, *Apollonio Rodio*, 1059–64, 1090–91n25). Resta seems not to have noticed Padua, Bibl. Univ. 1487: "Ex primo libro Argonauticorum Apollonii secundum Andronici interpretationem" (Kristeller, *Iter Italicum*, 2:19).
545. His notes seem to have started July 12, 1476. In November 1481, he began to lecture on Valerius at the *Studio*. This course finished July 24, 1482. He finished another course on Valerius in Florence on July 24, 1504 (Resta, *Apollonio Rodio*, 1071–72).
546. This phase in the transmission of the text is traced in Schade and Eleuteri, "The Textual Tradition of the *Argonautica*," 45–47.
547. Barbaro wrote to Pontico Faccino, July 8, 1484, "Decima [hora] sum in litteris: rogas quibus? Aristotelicis; undecima cum Demosthene vel Hermogene; duodecima cum poetis, nunc Arato, nunc Apollonio" (edited in Branca, *Ermolao Barbaro, 1454–1493*, 1:61). His manuscript entered the library of Alberto Pio of Carpi (Resta, *Apollonio Rodio*, 1125).
548. Valla owned Modena, Bibl. Estense, gr.112. George Alexandrou copied folios 1 through 100 at Crete between 1485 and 1489. It was probably brought to Venice by Arsenius (Aristoboulos) Apostolis, who had it in 1492 (Schade and Eleuteri, "The Textual Tradition of the *Argonautica*," 45, 47).
549. Escorial, Σ.III.20, and Florence, Bibl. Riccardiana, ms. 35 (Schade and Eleuteri, "The Textual Tradition of the *Argonautica*," 47). According to Mioni, Callieges made the latter at Padua in the first decade of the sixteenth century (Mioni, "Calliergi (Callergi), Zaccaria," 751).
550. Demetrius made BAV, Vat.gr.37, PBN, gr.2729, BAV, Vat.gr.1358, fols. 1–120, and Rome, Bibl. Casanatense, gr.408. These were all probably made at Venice (RGK 1, no. 97; 3, no. 165; Schade and Eleuteri, "The Textual Tradition of the *Argonautica*," 47–48).
551. PBN, gr.3069, an autograph of Poliziano, has extracts from Apollonius and scholia (fols. 224r–239v). It is dated October 2, 1485 (Resta, *Apollonio Rodio*, 1122). Pomponio Leto wrote to Poliziano to ask for help with a reading in Valerius's *Argonautica*, March 17, 1488. Poliziano's response used Apollonius, the *Orphic Argonautica*, and Strabo to correct Valerius (Butler, *Angelo Poliziano*, 46–54, 308n7). Florence, Bibl. Laurenziana, 32.45, made in the 1470s or 1480s, was used by Poliziano for his *Miscellanea* of 1489 and was in the Medici Library in 1494 (Schade and Eleuteri, "The Textual Tradition of the *Argonautica*," 48).
552. Scutariota copied BAV, Barb.gr.142, and Barb.gr.143. He probably copied Naples, II.F.13 (Cyrillus, *Codices graeci MSS regiae bibliothecae borbonicae*, 2:160; Schade and Eleuteri, "The Textual Tradition of the *Argonautica*," 49). None of his many manuscripts can be shown to have been made outside Florence. His latest dated manuscript is from 1494.

553. Girolamo Amaseo writes of Lascaris in April 1493, "Is autem paulo post constituit curare ut Apollonius qui *Argonauticam* scripsit imprimatur . . ." (Pozzi, "Da Padova a Firenze nel 1493," 194).
554. Legrand, *Bibliographie hellénique*, item no. 18; Resta, *Apollonio Rodio*, 1125–26n102; ISTC ia00924000.
555. PBN, gr.2844, fols. 140v–78 (Apollonius, Demosthenes, and Libanius) were copied by Ciati (RGK 2, no. 323; Schade and Eleuteri, "The Textual Tradition of the *Argonautica*," 48–49).
556. Aldus to Reuchlin, 18 August 1502 (edited in Geiger, *Johann Reuchlins Briefwechsel*, 77–78, letter no. 83). For the catalog, see Orlandi, *Aldo Manuzio editore*, 2: plate X–XIII. The price is added in manuscript: one ducat, three lire.
557. Offenbacher, "La bibliothèque de Willibald Pirckheimer," 253. In a letter to Anton Kress at Pavia, 14 April 1502, Pirckheimer complains that his copy of Apollonius is incomplete: "Deest . . . integer quaternio, scilicet 19 signatus litera τ" (edited in Reicke, *Willibald Pirckheimers Briefwechsel*, 1:164).
558. Forteguerri made glossaries of Euripides, Apollonius, and Nicander, now BAV, Vat.gr.1389, fols. 1–77v. On his death in 1515, the edition and the glossaries passed to Angelo Colocci (De Nolhac, *La bibliothèque de Fulvio Orsini*, 178, 180). For Colocci, see chapter 1, introduction, p. 2, and n. 8.
559. In a letter to the count, dated 1513 to 1514, Pirckheimer writes, "Spero tamen, libros emptos infra triduum hic affuturos, quos inde proximis suscipies vecturis. Sunt vero isti Luciani opera, Xenophon et Apollonii *Argonautica*" (edited in Reicke, *Willibald Pirckheimers Briefwechsel*, 2:326). These books appear to have arrived, since a later letter complains only of the imperfections of the Lucian, not of the absence of the others (ibid., 328).
560. Madrid, Bibl. Nacional, BN I/322; Codoñer, Merino, and Malvadi, *Biblioteca y epistolario de Hernán Núñez de Guzmán*, 464.
561. Cambridge, University Library, Inc.4.B.8.19 [2028]; Sturge, *Cuthbert Tunstall*, 392–94.
562. Michael Hummelberg wrote from Rome to Nicholas Gerbel in March 1516: "Est professoribus haec: Baptista Pius Plautum, Ianus Parrhasius Ciceronem et Vergilium, Pimpinellus Ovidium, Augustinus τὰ τοῦ Ἀπολλωνίου τοῦ Ἀλεξανδρέως, alii alia profitentur" (Horawitz, "Zur Biographie und Correspondenz Johannes Reuchlins," 157–58). For Valdo (Baldus), see Gaisser, *Pierio Valeriano*, 327–28. He studied under Chalcondyles at Padua in the 1460s (Petrucci, "Calcondila," 543).
563. Copies of the *editio princeps* were still for sale in the Aldine catalog of November 1513 (Orlandi, *Aldo Manuzio editore*, 2: plate XVII). F. Asulanus edited the replacement: Venice, April 1521. Renouard, *Annales de l'imprimerie des Alde*, 90.
564. For Aurispa's manuscript, see his letter to Traversari, August 27, 1424 (edited in Sabbadini, *Carteggio di Giovanni Aurispa*, 10–15). Quandt believed it lost (*Orphei Hymni*, 10*). Corbinelli owned Florence, Bibl. Laurenziana, Conv. soppr. 4, made circa 1388 (Blum, *La biblioteca della Badia Fiorentina*, 74; Vian, "La tradition manuscrite," 4, 46).
565. Filelfo did not have his manuscript of pseudo-Orpheus with him in Florence in 1430 (to Traversari, 13 June 1428; edited in Mehus, *Ambrosii Traversarii epistolae*, 2, col. 1024, book 24, letter no. 32; to Scholarios, March 1, 1430; edited in Legrand, *Cent-dix lettres greques de F. Filelfo*, 9–12; Calderini, "Ricerche intorno alla biblioteca," 348). Quandt believed it lost (*Orphei Hymni*, 10*). He had a copy by July 1440 (Filelfo *Epistolare Francisci Philelfi*, sig. g1v).
566. BAV, Pal.gr.179, has the *Orphic Argonautica* and the *Orphic Hymns* (fols. 21r–82v). It was made by a single unidentified scribe of the fifteenth century (Quandt, *Orphei Hymni*, 9*; Vian, "La tradition manuscrite," 7; Eleuteri, *Storia della tradizione manoscritta*, 32). Manetti died in 1459.
567. See chapter 3, section "Homer," p. 82, n. 122. Vian dates his version to 1462 (Vian "Leodrisio Crivelli," 63). Ficino was born in 1433. Ficino's supposed Greek tutor, Francesco da Castiglione (d. 1484) copied BAV, Barb.gr.43, which includes the *Orphic Argonautica* (Vian, "La tradition manuscrite," 7; RGK 3, no. 601).

568. See chapter 3, section "Quintus of Smyrna," p. 112.
569. Appendix 1, no. 26, sig. D5r. The passage is reprinted in Legrand, *Bibliographie hellénique*, 1:lxxxvi–lxxxvii. Compare Lascaris's words at the end of his preface to pseudo-Orpheus (Rivautella and Ricolvi, *Marmora taurinensia*, 1:104).
570. Madrid, Bibl. Nacional, 4562, has pseudo-Orpheus at fols. 12r–52v, subscribed on fol. 100v (Eleuteri, *Storia della tradizione manoscritta*, 16–17; Andrés, *Catálogo de los códices griegos*, 35–37). Bologna, BU 2612, fols. 1–37 (RGK 1, no. 223). Allen wrongly claimed that these leaves were in the hand of Giorgio Valla (Allen, "Notes upon Greek Manuscripts," 254). See Martínez-Manzano, *Konstantinos Laskaris*, 288.
571. See chapter 1, section "Constantine Lascaris," p. 27.
572. Vian's study of this version, "Leodrisio Crivelli," does not mention this possibility. For Crivelli's Greek–Latin lexicon, copied in part by Lascaris, see chapter 2, section "Greek Lexica in Western Europe, 1396–1529," p. 64.
573. BAV, Vat.gr.35. Vian says that the Greek text is certainly after 1466, perhaps circa 1470, and that it was copied from Milan, Bibl. Ambrosiana, M.52 sup. (gr. 517) (Vian, "La tradition manuscrite," 5–6 and stemma). It was copied by George Hermonymus (RGK 3, no. 102), apparently before he left Italy in 1475.
574. The version is noticed in Pignatti, "Filelfo, Giovanni Mario," 629.
575. Madrid, Bibl. Nacional, 4562, fols. 8v–10r. For this work, see Wilson, *From Byzantium to Italy*, 121. It has been edited with a Latin translation: Rivautella and Ricolvi, *Marmora taurinensia*, 1:93–104. It is followed by a brief digression on the history and function of poetry (fols. 10v–11r; edited in PG 161:951–54). Both works also appear in BAV, Vat.gr.1406, for which see Martínez-Manzano, *Konstantinos Laskaris*, 329–30.
576. The extract is in Madrid, Bibl. Nacional, 4621, fols. 134r–135r, and has been edited by C.-E. Ruelle, "Deux textes concernant le canon musical heptacorde," 156–62. Manuel (for whom, see Martínez-Manzano, *Konstantinos Laskaris*, 295–98) copied Madrid, Bibl. Nacional, 4565 (Andrés, *Catálogo de los códices griegos*, 42–43).
577. Filelfo wrote in July 1440, "Itaque non absurde Orpheus ille in Argonauticis, quicumque tandem is fuerit, quem tamen vetustissimum poetarum fuisse constat, cum loqueretur de summo deo . . ." (Filelfo, *Epistolare Francisci Philelfi*, sig. g1v). At the end of his biography, Lascaris writes, "καὶ ταῦτα μὲν ἐκ πολλοῦ περὶ τοῦ σοφοῦ Ὀρφέως, ὃν ἔνιοι ἀλόγως οὐδὲ γεγονέναι φασίν" (Rivautella and Ricolvi, *Marmora taurinensia*, 1:100). For Lascaris and Dictys, see chapter 2, section "The Suda Lexicon," p. 56.
578. γράμμασι φοινίκων, ὥς δοξάσομεν (Rivautella and Ricolvi, *Marmora taurinensia*, 1:98). Lascaris drew on the entry in the Suda for his biography and rationalizes the story of Eurydice.
579. Florence: F. Giunta, September 19, 1500 (Legrand, *Bibliographie hellénique*, item no. 28; ISTC io00103000). The edition does not mention Lascaris. Legrand wrote that Janus Lascaris probably edited the volume (*Bibliographie hellénique*, 1:73); he later corrected this to Constantine Lascaris (ibid., 1:lxxxvi). In 1500, Janus was in France and Constantine was in Sicily.
580. Venice: in aedibus Aldi et Andrea Soceri, November 1517. This is the *editio princeps* of pseudo-Orpheus, *De lapidibus* (Botfield, *Prefaces*, 182–84; Renouard, *Annales de l'imprimerie des Alde*, 81; Legrand, *Bibliographie hellénique*, item no. 55; Orlandi, *Aldo Manuzio editore*, 1:5). For Fausto's lecture, see Wilson, "Vettor Fausto," 90–91.
581. Florence: heredes P. Juntae, 1519 *sine mense* (Renouard, *Annales de l'imprimerie des Alde*, xliii; Vian, "Leodrisio Crivelli," 65).
582. Basle: Cratander, June 1523.
583. *Posthomerica*, 12:308–13. The argument was first set out by Constantine Lascaris no later than 1496 (PG 161:944), but for its validity, see OCD, 1291. Quintus is called *Smyrnaeus* in Vienna, Österreichische Nationalbibl., Phil.gr.5, copied by Demetrius Trivolis (recorded 1461–92). The watermarks of this manuscript are consistent with a date of circa 1460 to 1465 (Irigoin, "Review of Vian (1959)," 486–87; RGK 1, no. 103).
584. Bessarion wrote to Apostolis, "Κύιντον δὲ καὶ τὰ Πυρρώνεια ὅπως γεγράψονται, σοὶ μελέτω" (edited in Mohler, *Kardinal Bessarion*, 3:483). This letter is undated and *sine loco*,

but is from Bologna between July 1453 and March 23, 1455. Apostolis made Milan, Bibl. Ambrosiana, gr.D.528 inf, which gave rise to Florence, Bibl. Laurenziana, 56.29, Madrid, bibl. Nacional, 4566, Naples, gr.II.E.24, and Cambridge, Corpus Christi College, 81 (Irigoin, Review of Vian, *Histoire de la tradition manuscrite de Quinte de Smyrne*, 486; Vian, *Quintus de Smyrne*, 1:xlvi–xlvii). Lascaris later notes that the discovery was made after the fall of Constantinople, May 29, 1453 (PG 161:945).

585. From the *editio princeps* of *De nomine*, appendix 1, no. 26, sig. Δ5v. The aside is also in Legrand, *Bibliographie hellénique*, 1:lxxxvi–lxxxvii.

586. See chapter 1, section "Constantine Lascaris," pp. 26–27.

587. Madrid, Bibl. Nacional, 4566, has a note: "Κωνσταντίνου Λασκάρεως. τὸ παρὸν βιβλίον ἀναγκαῖον καὶ δυσεύρετον τυγχάνει, ὅθεν μόλις εὑρόντος ἐν ὀλίγαις ἡμέραις ἐποίησα ἐκγραφῆναι ὑπὸ διαφόρων Λατίνων οὕτως ἀνάρμοστον" (fol. III). For the manuscript, see Vian, *Quintus de Smyrne*, 1:xlvi. Vian dates it between 1464 and 1465. Andrés dates it circa 1463, apparently on the basis of its watermarks (*Catálogo de los códices griego*, 43–44). It was seen in Milan by Bartolomeo Bardella, for whom see Martínez-Manzano, *Konstantinos Laskaris*, 291–92.

588. Vian, *Quintus de Smyrne*, 1:xlvi.

589. "Ταύτην μετὰ δυσκολίας κτησάμενος ἐξέγραψα" (preface to Quintus, PG 161:945).

590. For the appointment, see chapter 1, section "Constantine Lascaris," p. 26. For Lascaris's lectures, see chapter 3, section "Pseudo-Orpheus."

591. See Labowsky, *Bessarion's Library and the Biblioteca Marciana*, 9n19, 11; Friggi, "Libri greci alla corte di Ludovico il Moro, 123.

592. It is plausible to place Merula (1430–94) in Milan, circa 1463; the hasty transcription suggests a brief stay. He was in Venice from 1465 to 1482 (Bietenholz and Deutscher, *Contemporaries of Erasmus*, 2:437). Merula studied under Gregorio Tifernas at Mantua, where Gregorio taught from April 1460 to probably 1462. In that year Gregorio moved to Ferrara, where he was still to be found in late 1462. He was in Venice by April 1463 (Pagliaroli, "Gregorio da Città di Castello," 3–64). That is, Gregorio was also in Ferrara when Merula acquired the manuscript from Palmieri.

593. See this chapter, n. 587.

594. Madrid, Bibl. Nacional, 4686, bears the date June 13, 1496, and a note: "Τέλος τῆς δυσευρέτου ποιήσεως τοῦ Κοίντου ἣν Κωνσταντῖνος ὁ Λάσκαρις ἐξέγραψεν ἔτη δύο καὶ ἑξήκοντα γεγονὼς ἐν Μεσσήνῃ τῆς Σικελίας ἐξ ἀντιγράφων σφαλερωτάτων" (Andrés, *Catálogo de los códices griegos*, 242–43). The preface and arguments are in PG 161:941–50.

595. BAV, Ottob.gr.103. For the colophon to this manuscript, see Rabe, "Konstantin Laskaris," 6; Irigoin, Review of Vian, *Histoire de la tradition manuscrite de Quinte de Smyrne*, 486.

596. BAV, Vat.gr.1420, dated January 11, 1496, that is, 1497 new style (Irigoin, Review of Vian, *Histoire de la tradition manuscrite de Quinte de Smyrne*, 486; Martínez-Manzano, *Konstantinos Laskaris*, 337).

597. Vian says that Naples, gr.II.F.11, was made ca. 1460–65 (Vian, *Quintus de Smyrne*, 1:xlvi, lv). It is described in Cyrillus, *Codices graeci MSS regiae bibliothecae borbonicae*, 158–59. The first five books have a nearly complete interlinear Latin translation. A space is left before each book, apparently to accommodate the argument for each book. The date of the composition of these *argumenta* is uncertain, but they seem to belong to Lascaris's Messina period (1466–1501). They may not long predate their appearance in Madrid, Bibl. Nacional, 4686, completed June 1496.

598. Cambridge, Corpus Christi College, ms. 81, was written by Demetrius Xanthopoulos for Gaza between 1454 and 1468. See chapter 3, section "Homer," n. 112. Chalcondyles copied most of Florence, Bibl. Laurenziana, 69.29 (RGK 1, no. 105).

599. It is possible that he taught the *Posthomerica* in Florence between 1471 and 1475. Poliziano writes of Callistus's teaching at Florence, "Smyrnaeique docet iocunda poemata vatis" (Cammelli, "Andronico Callisto," 190; Resta, *Apollonio Rodio*, 1058). This probably refers to his teaching of Homer (see chapter 3, section "Homer"), but may refer to Quintus. Quintus

was certainly called *Smyrnaeus* by the 1460s: see this section, n. 583. In 1482, in his *Manto*, Poliziano does not believe that Homer was from Smyrna; rather, he emphasizes the uncertainty surrounding his birthplace (edited in Fantazzi, *Angelo Poliziano*, 18, lines 199–200). In 1484, in his prose prolusion to his lectures on Homer, he is of the same opinion (Poliziano, *Omnia opera Angeli Politiani*, sigs. &1v–&2r). In 1485, in his verse prolusion *Ambra*, Poliziano makes use of Quintus (edited in Fantazzi, *Angelo Poliziano*, xvi, 74–76), but in the same work, he selects Smyrna as Homer's birthplace (ibid., 82–84, lines 202–32).

600. See chapter 3, section "Theocritus."
601. See chapter 1, section "Theodore Gaza," pp. 18–19.
602. Hermonymus made BAV, Urb.gr.147, from the lost exemplar (Irigoin, Review of Vian, *Histoire de la tradition manuscrite de Quinte de Smyrne*, 488; RGK 3, no. 102). This manuscript, or its exemplar, was made in London (Vian, *Quintus de Smyrne*, 1:xlvii). He made BAV, Barb. gr.166, at Paris from the lost exemplar, dated June 28, 1476 (Omont, "Georges Hermonyme de Sparte," 91; Irigoin, Review of Vian, *Histoire de la tradition manuscrite de Quinte de Smyrne*, 488).
603. Tübingen, Bibl. Univ., Mb.26, described in Martínez-Manzano, *Konstantinos Laskaris*, 339–40. Occo made Munich, gr.313, a miscellany that has an extract from Quintus: see Mondrain, "La collection de manuscrits grecs d'Adolphe Occo," 172–74.
604. Occo also owned Munich, gr.453 (Plato's *Euthyphro, Apologia, Crito*, and *Phaedo*), described by Martínez-Manzano, *Konstantinos Laskaris*, 341, who suggested it was copied by Lascaris at Messina ca. 1466–72. Occo owned Munich, gr.519a of *Iliad*, books 13–24. Folios 1 through 73 are in Occo's hand, as are interlinear glosses and marginalia. There is no trace of Lascaris in this portion of the manuscript; folios 74 through 198 are in Lascaris's hand and Occo has added Greek interlinear glosses. Martínez-Manzano dates Lascaris's portion to the 1460s (Mondrain, "La collection de manuscrits grecs d'Adolphe Occo," 168–69; Martínez-Manzano, *Konstantinos Laskaris*, 244).
605. Occo seems to have studied at Ferrara from at least April 1474 until at least June 1478; a letter of Agricola to Occo (October 1480) indicates that Occo had also studied in Bologna (Mondrain, "La collection de manuscrits grecs d'Adolphe Occo," 158, 158n8). Agricola was at Pavia from 1468 to 1474, and at Ferrara from 1474 to 1479. For Agricola, see Allen, "The Letters of Rudolf Agricola"; Bietenholz and Deutscher, *Contemporaries of Erasmus*, 1:15–17. Agricola quotes *Posthomerica*, 7:70–77 (Van der Laan and Akkerman, *Rudolf Agricola*, 226–31). It may not be a coincidence that the glosses in Occo's manuscript extend as far as the seventh book of Quintus.
606. Venice: Manutius, circa 1504; Basle: Hendricpetrus, 1569. The first printed Latin translation, that of Jodocus Velareus, was printed at Antwerp in 1539.

Epilogue

1. Stinger, *Humanism and the Church Fathers*, 67.
2. Bertalot, "Zwölf Briefe des Ambrogio Traversari," 263. The letter is undated. Traversari died in 1439.
3. Orlandi, *Aldo Manuzio editore*, 1:93.
4. Grafton, "The Availability of Ancient Works," 769n17.
5. See chapter 2, section "The Suda Lexicon."
6. See Botley, *Latin Translation in the Renaissance*, 125n21.
7. See EE 3:387, headnote to letter no. 864.
8. Botfield, *Prefaces*, 265–66; Legrand, *Bibliographie hellénique*, item no. 31; Orlandi, *Aldo Manuzio editore*, 1:73–74.
9. Ἄλδος . . . ἀνθ' ἑνὸς ἀντιγράφου . . . χίλια τοῖς φιλολόγοις ἐπιδιδούς . . . (edited in Legrand, *Bibliographie hellénique*, 1:85–86).

10. Appendix 1, no. 57. In the preface Nachtgall writes, "Tui autem fuerit muneris, amicissime Schotte, id qualecunque laboris nostri mille exemplaribus excussum ταῖς φιλομαθαῖς ἑλληνιστὶ publicitus exponere . . ."
11. No copies of this edition survive, and it may never have been printed: see Ceresa, "Faraone (Faragonio), Francesco," 766.
12. William Horman's *Vulgaria*: see Nugent, *The Thought and Culture of the English Renaissance*, 123.
13. Clénard claimed in July 1531 that previous editions of his grammar amounted to over four thousand copies (Bakelants and Hoven, *Bibliographie des oeuvres de Nicholas Clénard*, 16). Two editions of 1530 are noticed in ibid., 25–26. A third may have been printed by this date: Paris: [C. Wechel, after March 16, 1530], consulted in Cambridge, University Library, U*.7.2043.
14. Appendix 1, no. 35. The contract is dated December 19, 1508: ". . . promiserunt stampire *arotimata* [*sic*] quondam Guirini [*sic*] numero tria milia cum celerarita [*sic*]" (Ferrari, *Documento dell'Archivio di Stato*, 22).
15. This figure is derived from appendix 1, counting only fully-fledged grammars.
16. Jacopo Angeli, Leonardo Bruni, Pier Paolo Vergerio, Coluccio Salutati, Roberto de' Rossi, Antonio Corbinelli, Palla Strozzi, Guarino of Verona, Uberto Decembrio, and Poggio Bracciolini.

Appendix 1

1. Botley, "Renaissance Scholarship and the Athenian Calendar."
2. Edited in PG 19:1167–1218.

Bibliography

Abad, J. M. *La Imprenta en Alcalá de Henares (1502–1600)*. 3 vols. Madrid: Arco/Libros, 1991.

———. *Post-Incunables Ibéricos*. Madrid: Ollero y Ramos, 2001.

Accame Lanzillotta, M., ed. *Leonardo Bruni traduttore di Demostene: la "Pro Ctesiphonte."* Genoa: Università di Genova, Facoltà di lettere, Istituto di filologia classica e medievale, 1986.

Achelis, T. O. "Die Aesopübersetzungen des Lorenzo Valla." *Münchener Museum* 2 (1914): 239–78.

Adler, A. *Catalogue supplémentaire des manuscrits grecs de la Bibliothèque Royale de Copenhague*. Copenhagen: Bianco Luno, 1916.

———, ed. *Suidae Lexicon*. 5 vols. Leipzig: B. G. Teubner, 1928–38.

Alberigo, G. "Aleandro, Girolamo." *Dizionario biografico degli Italiani* 2 (1960): 128–35.

Allen, P. S. "Some letters of Masters and Scholars, 1500–1530." *English Historical Review* 22 (1907): 740–54.

———. "The Letters of Rudolf Agricola." *English Historical Review* 21(1906): 302–17.

Allen, P. S., H. M. Allen, and H. W. Garrod, eds. *Opus Epistolarum Des. Erasmi Roterodami*. 12 vols. Oxford: Clarendon Press, 1906–58.

Allen, T. W. "Notes upon Greek Manuscripts in Italian Libraries." *Classical Review* 3 (1889): 12–22; 252–56; 345–52.

Allen, W. "Speculations on St. Thomas More's Use of Hesychius." *Philological Quarterly* 46 (1967): 156–66.

Allgemeine Deutsche Biographie. 56 vols. Leipzig: Duncker and Humblot, 1875–1912.

Andrés, G. de. *Catálogo de los códices griegos de la Biblioteca Nacional*. Madrid: Ministero de Cultura, 1987.

Astruc, C. "La fin inédite du *Contra Plethonem* de Matthieu Camariotès." *Scriptorium* 9 (1955): 246–62.

———. "Manuscrits autographes de Matthieu Camariotès." *Scriptorium* 10 (1956): 100–102.

Avesani, R. "Bonamico (Bonamici, Buonamici, Buonamico), Lazzaro (Lazzaro da Bassano)." *Dizionario biografico degli Italiani* 11 (1969): 533–40.

Avezzù, G. "ΑΝΔΡΟΝΙΚΙΑ ΓΡΑΜΜΑΤΑ: Per l'identificazione di Andronico Callisto copista. Con alcune notizie su Giano Lascaris e la biblioteca di Giorgio Valla." *Atti e memorie dell'Accademia Patavina di Scienze, Lettere ed Arti* 102, 3, *memorie della classe di scienze morali, lettere ed arti* (1989): 75–93.

Baillet, L. "Le premier manuel du grec paru à Strabourg." In *Festschrift für Josef Benzing zum sechzigsten geburtstag 4. Februar 1964*, edited by E. Geck and G. Pressler, 25–36. Wiesbaden: n. p., 1964.

Bakelants, L., and R. Hoven. *Bibliographie des oeuvres de Nicholas Clénard: 1529–1700*. 2 vols. Verniers: Gason, 1981.

Baldassari, S. U., and R. Bagemihil, eds. *Giannozzo Manetti: Biographical Writings*. Cambridge, MA: Harvard University Press, 2003.

Balsamo, L. "Revisiting Early Printed Books at Brescia: "Thoma Ferrando auctore" (1471–74)." In *Incunabula: Studies in Fifteenth-Century Printed Books Presented to Lotte Hellinga*, edited by M. Davies, 7–26. London: British Library, 1999.

Baron, H. *Leonardo Bruni Aretino: Humanistisch-philosophische Schriften, mit einer Chronologie seiner Werke und Briefe*. Leipzig: Teubner, 1928.

Bateman, J. I. "Aldus Manutius' *Fragmenta Grammatica*." *Illinois Classical Studies* 1 (1976): 226–61.

Baudrier, J. *Bibliographie lyonnaise: Recherches sur les imprimeurs, libraires, relieurs et fondeurs de lettres de Lyon au XVIe siècle*. Lyons: Libraire Ancienne d'Auguste Brun, 1895–1921.

Belli, A. "Le versioni umanistiche dell'Assioco pseudo-platonico." *La parola del passato* 9 (1954): 442–67.

Benzing, J., and J. Muller. *Bibliographie strasbourgeoise: bibliographie des ouvrages imprimés à Strasbourg (Bas-Rhin) au XVIe siècle*. 3 vols. Baden-Baden: Valentin Koerner, 1981–86.

Bernardinello, S. "Gli studi propedeutici di greco del grammatico padovano Pietro da Montagnana." *Quaderni per la storia dell'Università di Padova* 9–10 (1976–77): 103–29.

———. "La grammatica di Manuele Caleca." *Rivista di studi bizantini e neoellenici* 8–9 (1971–72): 203–18.

Bernays, J. "Zur Biographie Johann Winthers von Andernach." *Zeitschrift für die Geschichte des Oberrheins*, n.s. 16 (1901): 28–58.

Berrigan, J. R. "The Aesopic Fables of Guarino da Verona (Milano, Biblioteca Ambrosiana, cod.R.21)." *Manuscripta* 32 (1988): 4.

———. "The Latin Aesop of Ermolao Barbaro." *Manuscripta* 22 (1978): 141–48.

Bertalot, L. "Zur Bibliographie der Übersetzungen des Leonardus Brunus Aretinus." *Quellen und Forschungen aus italienischen Archiven und Bibliotheken* 27 (1936–37): 178–95. Cited from *Studien zum italienischen und deutschen Humanismus*, vol. 2, edited by P. O. Kristeller, 265–83. Rome: Edizioni di storia e letteratura, 1975.

———. "Zwölf Briefe des Ambrogio Traversari." *Römische Quartalschrift* 29 (1915): 91*–106*. Cited from *Studien zum italienischen und deutschen Humanismus*, vol. 1, edited by P. O. Kristeller, 251–67. Rome: Edizioni di storia e letteratura, 1975.

Berti, E. "Alla scuola di M. Crisolora. Lettura e commento di Luciano." *Rinascimento*, ser. 2, 27 (1987): 3–73.

———. "Uno scriba greco-latino: il codice Vaticano Urbinate gr.121 e la prima versione del «Caronte» di Luciano." *Rivista di filologia e di istruzione classica* 118 (1985): 416–43.

Bertola, M. *I due primi registri di prestito della Biblioteca Apostolica Vaticana: codici vaticani latini 3964, 3966*. Vatican City: Biblioteca apostolica vaticana, 1942.

Bevegni, C. "Appunti sulle traduzioni latine dei «Moralia» di Plutarco nel Quattrocento." *Studi umanistici piceni* 14 (1994): 71–84.

Bianca, C. "Filetico (Filettico), Martino." *Dizionario biografico degli Italiani* 47 (1997): 636–40.

———. "Gaza, Teodoro." *Dizionario biografico degli Italiani* 52 (1999): 737–46.

Biedl, A. "Matthaeus Camariotes: Specimen Prosopographiae Byzantinae." *Byzantinische Zeitschrift* 35 (1935): 337–39.
Bietenholz, P. G., and T. B. Deutscher, eds. *Contemporaries of Erasmus: A Biographical Register of the Renaissance and Reformation*. 3 vols. Toronto: University of Toronto Press, 1985–87.
Biographie universelle (Michaud) ancienne et moderne. 45 vols. Paris: Madame C. Desplaces *et alii,* 1854–65.
Bliquez, L. J. "Frogs and Mice and Athens." *Transactions of the American Philological Association* 107 (1977): 11–25.
Blum, R. *La biblioteca della Badia Fiorentina e i codici di Antonio Corbinelli*. Vatican City: Biblioteca apostolica vaticana, 1951.
Boehme, J. G. *De litteratura lipsiensi opuscula academica. Accedunt Rich. Croci britanni Encomium Academiae Lipsiensis et H. Stromeri Auerbachii sermo panegyricus Petro Mosellano dictus cum Mosellani responsione*. Leipzig: Sumptu Guil. Gottlob Sommeri, 1779.
Botfield, B. *Prefaces to the First Editions of the Greek and Roman Classics*. London: H. G. Bohn, 1861.
Botley, P. *Latin Translation in the Renaissance: The Theory and Practice of Leonardo Bruni, Giannozzo Manetti and Desiderius Erasmus*. Cambridge: Cambridge University Press, 2004.
———. "Learning Greek in Western Europe, 1476–1516." In *Literacy, Education and Manuscript Transmission in Byzantium and Beyond,* edited by C. Holmes and J. Waring, 199–223. Leiden: Brill, 2002.
———. "Renaissance Scholarship and the Athenian Calendar." *Greek, Roman, and Byzantine Studies* 46 (2006): 395–431.
Branca, V., ed. *Ermolao Barbaro, 1454–1493: Epistolae, Orationes et Carmina.* 2 vols. Florence: Bibliopolis, 1943.
Breen, Q. "Francesco Zambeccari: His Translations and Fabricated Translations of Libanian Letters." *Studies in the Renaissance* 11 (1964): 46–75.
British Library. *The British Library: Summary Catalogue of Greek Manuscripts.* Vol. 1. London: British Library, 1999.
Brown, H. F. *The Venetian Printing Press: An Historical Study Based upon Documents for the Most Part Hitherto Unpublished*. London: J. C. Nimmo, 1891.
Brown, V. "Caesar." *Catalogus Translationum et Commentariorum* 3 (1976): 87–140.
Browning, R. "Greek Manuscripts in Medieval Chios." In *Chios,* edited by J. Boardman and C. E. Vaphopoulou-Richardson, 43–53. Oxford: Clarendon Press, 1986.
———. "Homer in Byzantium." *Viator* 6 (1975): 15–33.
Bühler, C. F. "Notes on Two Incunabula Printed by Aldus Manutius." *Papers of the Bibliographical Society of America* 36 (1942): 18–26.
Bustico, G. "Due umanisti veneti—Urbano Bolzanio e Pietro Valeriani." *Civiltà moderna* 4 (1932): 86–103, 344–79.
Butler, S., ed. *Angelo Poliziano: Letters.* Vol. 1. Cambridge MA: Harvard University Press, 2006.
Cagni, G. M. "Agnolo Manetti e Vespasiano da Bisticci." *Italia medioevale e umanistica* 14 (1971): 293–312.
———. "I codici vaticani palatino-latini appartenuti alla biblioteca di Giannozzo Manetti (1396–1459)." *Bibliofilía* 62 (1960): 1–43.

Calderini, A. "Intorno ad un passo di Suida e di Arpocrazione riportato da Francesco Filelfo." *Studi italiani di filologia classica* 19 (1912): 11–18.

———. "Ricerche intorno alla biblioteca e cultura greca di Francesco Filelfo." *Studi italiani di filologia classica* 20 (1913): 204–424.

Cammelli, G. "Andronico Callisto." *Rinascita* 5 (1942): 104–21, 174–214.

———. *Demetrio Calcondila*. Vol. 3 of *I dotti bizantini e le origini dell'umanesimo*. Florence: Vallecchi, 1954.

———. *Giovanni Argiropulo*. Vol. 2 of *I dotti bizantini e le origini dell'umanesimo*. Florence: Vallecchi, 1951.

———. *Manuele Crisolora*. Vol. 1 of *I dotti bizantini e le origini dell'umanesimo*. Florence: Vallecchi, 1941.

Campana, A. "Basinio da Parma." *Dizionario biografico degli Italiani* 7 (1965): 89–98.

Campano, G. A. *Ioannis Anthonii Campani opera omnia*. Rome: Eucharius Silber, 1495. Consulted in facsimile, Farnborough: Gregg International, 1969.

Canart, P., ed. *Codices Vaticani Graeci: Codices 1745–1962*. Vatican City: Biblioteca apostolica vaticana, 1970.

Castrifrancanus, A. *Alberti Castrifrancani oratio habita in funere Urbani Bellunensis e minoritana familia unius*. Venice: Per B. de Vitalibus, 1524.

Cathedral Libraries Catalogue. *Books Printed Before 1701 in the Libraries of the Anglican Cathedrals of England and Wales*. 2 vols. London: British Library, 1984–98.

Cecchini, E., and A. C. Cassio. "Due contributi sulla traduzione di Leonardo Bruni del 'Pluto' di Aristofane." *Giornale italiano di filologia*, new series, 3 (1972): 472–82.

Cengarle, S. A. "Ps. Moschopuli compendium de dialectis linguae graecae." *ACME* 24 (1971): 213–92.

Censimento Nazionale: Le edizioni italiane del XVI secolo, edited by Istituto centrale per il catalogo unico delle biblioteche italiane e per le informazioni bibliografiche. 4 vols to date. Rome, 1985–96.

Centanni, M. "La biblioteca di Andronico Callisto: primo inventario di manoscritti greci." *Atti e memorie dell' Accademia Patavina* 97 (1984–85): 201–23.

Cevolotto, A. "Giustiniani, Agostino." *Dizionario biografico degli italiani* 57 (2001): 301–6.

Ceresa, M. "Faraone (Faragonio), Francesco." *Dizionario biografico degli Italiani* 44 (1994): 765–66.

———. "Favorino, Guarino (Varino, Guerino)." *Dizionario biografico degli Italiani* 45 (1995): 474–77.

Chauvain, V., and A. Roersch. *Étude sur la vie et les travaux de Nicolas Clénard*. Brussels: Academie Royale des Sciences, des Lettres et des Beaux-Arts de Belgique, 1901.

Chrisman, M. U. *Bibliography of Strasbourg Imprints, 1480–1599*. New Haven, CT: Yale University Press, 1982.

Christie, R. C. "The Chronology of the Early Aldines." *Bibliographica* 1 (1895): 193–222.

Cirignano, J. "The Manuscripts of Xenophon's Symposium." *Greek, Roman and Byzantine Studies* 34 (1993): 187–210.

Clough, C. H. "Flemming, Robert (1416–1483)." *Oxford Dictionary of National Biography*, vol. 20, edited by H. C. G. Matthew and B. Harrison, 80–82. Oxford: Oxford University Press, 2004.

———. "Selling [Celling, Tyll], William (c. 1430–1494)." *Oxford Dictionary of National Biography*, vol. 49, edited by H. C. G. Matthew and B. Harrison, 722–24. Oxford: Oxford University Press, 2004.

Cocco, C., ed. *Ermolao Barbaro il vecchio: Aesopi Fabulae*. Favolisti latini medievali e umanistici 6. Genoa: Pubblicazioni del D. AR. FI. CL. ET, 1994.

Codoñer, J. S., C. C. Merino, and A. D. Malvadi. *Biblioteca y epistolario de Hernán Núñez de Guzmán (El Pinciano). Una aproximación al humanismo español del siglo XVI*. Madrid: CSIC, 2001.

Cortesi, M. "Aspetti linguistici della cultura greca di Francesco Filelfo." In *Francesco Filelfo nel quinto centenario della morte. Atti del XVII convegno di studi maceratesi (Tolentino 27–30 settembre 1981)*, 163–206. Padua: Antenore, 1986.

———. "Il «Vocabularium» greco di Giovanni Tortelli." *Italia medioevale e umanistica* 22 (1979): 449–83.

———. "Libri e vicende di Vittorino da Feltre." *Italia medioevale e umanistica* 23 (1980): 77–115.

Cosenza, M. E. *Biographical and Bibliographical Dictionary of the Italian Humanists and of the World of Classical Scholarship in Italy 1300–1800*. 6 vols. Boston: Hall, 1962–67.

Coulter, G. G. "Boccaccio's Acquaintance with Homer." *Philological Quarterly* 5 (1926): 44–53.

Crespi, M. "Benedetti, Alessandro." *Dizionario biografico degli Italiani* 8 (1966): 244–47.

Croke, R. *Orationes Richardi Croci duae, altera a cura, qua utilitatem laudemque graecae linguae tractat, altera a tempore, qua hortatus est Cantabrigienses ne desertores essent eiusdem*. Paris: Cura Simonis Colinaei, sumptibus Damiani Ichman, 1520.

Csapodi, C. *The Corvinian Library: History and Stock*. Budapest: Akademiai Kiado, 1973.

Curtis, C. "Pace, Richard (1483?–1536)." In *Oxford Dictionary of National Biography*, vol. 42, edited by H. C. G. Matthew and B. Harrison, 298–302. Oxford: Oxford University Press, 2004.

Cyrillus, S. *Codices graeci MSS regiae bibliothecae borbonicae descripti atque illustrati a Salvatore Cyrillo regio bibliothecario*. Naples: ex Regia Typographia, 1826–32. Consulted in facsimile: Hildesheim: Georg Olms, 1992.

Cytowska, M., ed. *De recta latini graecique sermonis pronuntiatione*. In *Opera omnia Desiderii Erasmi Roterodami recognita et adnotatione critica instructa notisque illustrata*, ord. 1, vol. 4, 1–103. Amsterdam: North-Holland, 1973.

———. "Érasme de Rotterdam, traducteur de Homère." *Eos* 63 (1975): 341–53.

Daly, L. W. "Hesiod and Theocritus in the Text of Papias." *Greek, Roman and Byzantine Studies* 9 (1968): 457–60.

———, ed. *Ioannis Philoponi De vocabulis quae diversum significatum exhibent secundum differentiam accentus*. Philadelphia: American Philosophical Society, 1983.

De Bellis, D. "La vita e l'ambiente di Niccolò Leonico Tomeo." *Quaderni per la storia dell' Università di Padova* 13 (1980): 37–75.

De Borries, J. *Phrynichi Sophistae Praeparatio Sophistica*. Leipzig: Teubner, 1911.

Decharme, M. P. "Extraits d'un lexique manuscrit latin-grec ancien et grec moderne." *Annuaire de l'Association pour l'encouragement des études grecques en France* 7 (1873): 100–113.

De Keyser, J. "Francesco Filelfo traduttore di Senofonte." PhD diss., Università degli studi di Torino, 2008.

De la Mare, A. C. "Sozomeno (Zomino) of Pistoia 1387–1458." In *The Handwriting of Italian Humanists*, vol. 1, fasc I. ed. A. C. De la Mare, 91–105. Oxford: Printed at the University Press for the Association internationale de bibliophilie, 1973.

Delaruelle, L. "L'étude du grec à Paris de 1514 à 1530." *Revue du XVIe siècle* 9 (1922): 51–62, 132–49.

———. "Le dictionnaire grec-latin de Crastone: Contribution à l'histoire de la lexicographie grecque." *Studi italiani di filologia classica* 8 (1930): 221–46.

Deligiannis, J. *Fifteenth-Century Latin Translations of Lucian's Essay on Salnder.* Pisa: Gruppo Editoriale Internazionale, 2006.

De Marinis, T., and A. Perosa. *Nuovi documenti per la storia del rinascimento.* Florence: L. S. Olschki, 1970.

De Morembert, T. "Danès, Pierre." *Dictionnaire de biographie française* 10 (1965): 90–91.

De Nichilo, M. "Niccolò della Valle." *Dizionario biografico degli Italiani* 37 (1989): 759–62.

De Rosalia, A. "La vita di Costantino Lascaris." *Archivio storico siciliano* 9 (1957–58): 21–70.

Derron, P. "Inventaire des manuscrits des *Vers d'Or* pythagoriciens." *Revue d'histoire des textes* 22 (1992): 49–71.

———. "Inventaire des manuscrits du Pseudo-Phocylide." *Revue d'histoire des textes* 10 (1981): 237–47.

De Vocht, H. *History of the Foundation and the Rise of the Collegium Trilingue Lovaniense, 1517–1550.* Louvain: Bibliothèque de l'Université, Bureaux du Recueil, 1951.

Devreesse, R. *Catalogue des manuscrits grecs: fonds Coislin.* Paris: n. p., 1945.

———. *Le fonds grec de la Bibliothèque Vaticane des origines à Paul V.* Vatican City: Biblioteca apostolica vaticana, 1965.

Dihle, A. "Ein Spurium unter den rhetorischen Werken Ciceros." *Hermes* 83 (1955): 303–14.

Diller, A. "Greek Codices of Palla Strozzi and Guarino Veronese." *Journal of the Warburg and Courtauld Institutes* 24 (1961): 313–21.

———. "The Library of Francesco and Ermolao Barbaro." *Italia medioevale e umanistica* 6 (1963): 253–62.

———. "A Lost Manuscript of Nonnus' *Dionysiaca.*" *Classical Philology* 48 (1953): 177.

———. "The Manuscript Tradition of Aeschines' Orations." *Illinois Classical Studies* 4 (1979): 34–64.

———. "Pausanias in the Middle Ages." *Transactions and Proceedings of the American Philological Association* 87 (1956): 84–97. Cited from *Griechische Kodikologie und Textüberlieferung*, edited by D. Harlfinger, 484–500. Darmstadt: Wissenschaftliche Buchgesellschaft, 1980.

———. "Petrarch's Greek Codex of Plato." *Classical Philology* 59 (1964): 270–72.

———. *Studies in Greek Manuscript Tradition.* Amsterdam: Hakkert, 1983.

———. "Three Greek Scribes Working for Bessarion: Trivizias, Callistus, Hermonimus." *Italia medioevale e umanistica* 10 (1967): 403–10.

———. "The Tradition of Stephanus Byzantinus." *Transactions of the American Philological Association* 69 (1938): 333–48.

Dilts, M. R., ed. *Aeschinis orationes.* Stuttgart: Teubner, 1997.

Dionisotti, A. C. "On the Greek Studies of Robert Grosseteste." In *The Uses of Greek and Latin: Historical Essays*, edited by A. C. Dionisotti, A. Grafton, and J. Kraye, 19–40. London: Warburg Institute, 1988.

Doglioni, L. *Memorie di Urbano Bolzanio Bellunese dell'ordine de'minori conventuali.* Belluno: n.p., 1784.

Donnet, D. "La place de la syntaxe dans les traités de grammaire grecque des origines aux xiie siècle." *Antiquité classique* 36 (1967): 22–46.

———. "La tradition imprimée du traité de grammaire de Michel le Syncelle de Jérusalem." *Byzantion* 42 (1972): 441–508.

———. *Le traité de la construction de la phrase de Michel le Syncelle de Jérusalem. Histoire du texte, édition, traduction et commentaire par Daniel Donnet.* Brussels: Institut Historique Belge de Rome, 1982.

———. "Théodore de Gaza, *Introduction à la grammaire*, livre IV: à la recherche des sources byzantines." *Byzantion* 49 (1979): 133–55.

———. "Théodore de Gaza et Apollonius Dyscolus: sur un problème de sources." *Antiquité classique* 48 (1979): 619–29. Dorati, M. C. "I lettori dello Studio e i maestri di grammatica a Roma da Sisto IV ad Alessandro VI." *Rassegna degli Archivi di Stato* 40 (1980): 98–147.

Dorez, L. "Études aldines III: Alde Manuce et Ange Politien." *Revue des bibliothèques* 6 (1896): 311–26.

———. "Un document sur la bibliothèque de Théodore Gaza." *Revue des bibliothèques* 3 (1893): 385–90.

Dufrane, C., and M.-T. Isaac, "Un helléniste hollandais á Tournai: Jacques Ceratinus et son dictionnaire (1524)." In *Écoles et livres d'école en Hainaut du XVIe au XIXe siècle*, 119–55. Mons: Université de Mons, 1971.

Dyck, A. R. "Aelius Herodian: Recent Studies and Prospects for Future Research." In *Aufstieg und Niedergang der römischen Welt/Rise and Decline of the Roman World*, edited by W. Haase and H. Temporini, 772–94. Part 2: *Principate*, vol. 34, part 1, Berlin: W. de Gruyter, 1993.

Easterling, P. "From Britain to Byzantium: The Study of Greek Manuscripts." In *Through the Looking Glass: Byzantium through British Eyes*, edited by R. Cormack and E. Jeffreys, 107–20. Aldershot: Ashgate, 2000.

Égasse du Boulay, C. *Historia Universitatis Parisiensis, ipsius fundationem, nationes, facultates, magistratus, decreta, censuras et iudicia in negotiis fidei, privilegia . . . aliaque id genus cum instrumentis publicis et authenticis a Carolo M. ad nostra tempora ordine chronologico complectens.* 6 vols. Paris: n.p., 1665–73.

Egli, E. "Ceporins Leben und Schriften." In *Analecta Reformatoria*, vol. 2, edited by E. Egli, 145–60. Zurich: n.p., 1899–1901.

Egli, E., G. Finsler, W. Kohler, and O. Farner. *Huldreich Zwinglis sämtliche Werke*. 14 vols. Berlin: Heinsius, 1905–59.

Eleuteri, P. "Francesco Filelfo copista e possessore di codici greci." In *Paleografia e codicologia greca*, vol. 1, edited by D. Harlfinger and G. Prato, 163–79. Alexandria: Edizioni dell'Orso, 1991.

———. *Storia della tradizione manoscritta di Museo*. Pisa: Giardini, 1981.

Elioudes, G. N. "Η γραμματική του Κωνσταντίνου Λασκάρεως πρότυπο της γραμματικής του Νικολάου Σοφιανού." *Ελληνικά* 40 (1989): 413–17.

Erasmus, D. *Moriae Encomium, cum Gerardi Listrii Commentariis. Epistolae aliquot in fine additae. Una cum Erasmi responsione adversus Martini Lutheri Epistolae.* Oxford, Typis W. Hall, impensis F. Oxlad sen. et F. Oxlad jun., 1663.

Ernestus, J. A., ed. *Homeri Opera Omnia ex recensione et cum notis Samuelis Clarkii, accessit varietas lectionum MS. Lips. et Vratislav. et edd. veterum cura Io. Augusti Ernesti qui et suas notas adspersit.* 2nd ed., 2 vols. Leipzig: G. Rimmer, 1824.

Fantazzi, C., ed. and trans. *Angelo Poliziano: Silvae*. Cambridge, MA: Harvard University Press, 2004.

Fera, V. "La prima traduzione umanistica delle *Olimpiche* di Pindaro." In *Filologia umanistica per Gianvito Resta*, vol. 1, edited by V. Fera and G. Ferraú, 693–765. Padua: Antenore, 1997.
Fernández Pomar, J. M. *Copistas en los códices griegos escurialenses: complemento al catálogo de Revilla-Andrés*. Madrid: published by the author, 1986.
———. "La colección de Uceda y los manuscritos griegos de Constantino Lascaris." *Emerita* 34 (1966): 211–88.
Feron, E., and F. Battaglini, eds. *Codices manuscripti graeci ottoboniani bibliothecae vaticanae descripti*. Rome: Ex typographeo vaticano, 1893.
Ferrari, V. *Documento dell'Archivio di Stato in Reggio Emilia interessante la storia della tipografia reggiana e ferrarese*. Reggio Emilia: Rodolfo, 1924.
Ferri, F. "Per una supposta traduzione di Omero del Fonzio." *Athenaeum* 4 (1916): 312–20.
Festa, N. "Indice de' codici greci di Lucca e di Pistoia." *Studi italiani di filologia classica* 5 (1897): 221–30.
Field, A. M. *The Origins of the Platonic Academy of Florence*. Princeton: Princeton University Press, 1988.
Filelfo, F. *Epistolare Francisci Philelfi*. [Basle: n. p., 1492–94].
———. *Francisci Philelfi viri graece et latine eruditissimi epistolarum familiarum libri xxxvii*. Venice: Ex aedibus Ioannis et Gregorii de Gregoriis fratres, 1502.
Finch, C. E. "The Greek Source of Lorenzo Valla's Translation of Aesop Fables." *Classical Philology* 55 (1960): 118–20.
Fiocco, G. "La biblioteca di Palla Strozzi." In *Studi di bibliografia e storia in onore di Tammaro de Marinis*, vol. 2, edited by G. Mardersteig, 289–310. Verona: Stemperia Valdonega, 1964.
Firmin-Didot, A. *Alde Manuce et l'Hellénisme à Venise*. Paris: A. F. Didot, 1875.
Fischer, E., ed. *Die Ekloge des Phrynichos*. Berlin: De Gruyter, 1974.
Fletcher, H. G. "Three New-Style Dates." In *New Aldine Studies: Documentary Essays on the Life and Works of Aldus Manutius*, edited by H. G. Fletcher, 106–7. San Francisco: Bernard M. Rosenthal, Inc., 1988.
Foà, S. "Gallucci, Luigi (Elisio Calenzio)." *Dizionario biografico degli Italiani* 51 (1998): 743–45.
Förstel, C. "Bartolomeo Aragazzi et Manuel Chrysoloras: le codex Vratislav. AKC. 1949 KN. 60." *Scriptorium* 48 (1994): 111–19.
———. "Jean Cuno et la grammaire grecque." *Bibliothèque de l'école de Chartes* 151 (1993): 289–305.
Fraenkel, J. J. "Introduction." In *Constantine Lascaris: Greek Grammar. Milan, Dionysius Paravsinus for Demetrius of Crete, 30 January 1476. Facsimile edition*, 3–16. Amsterdam: A. M. Hakkert, 1966.
Frati, L., ed. *Epistolario di Pellegrino Zambeccari*. Rome: Istituto storico italiano, 1929.
Friggi, A. "Gli studi greci a Milano al tempo di Ludovico il Moro." PhD diss., Università degli studi di Torino, 2006.
———. "Libri greci alla corte di Ludovico il Moro: Giorgio Merula e la sua biblioteca." *Archivio Storico Lombardo* 130 (2004): 109–35.
Fubini, R., ed. *Poggio Bracciolini: Opera Omnia*. 4 vols. Turin: Bottega d'Erasmo, 1964–69.
Fuiano, M. "Ilarione da Verona." In *Studi di storiografia medioevale ed umanistica*, edited by M. Fuiano, 281–328. Naples: Giannini, 1975.
Gaisser, J. H., ed. *Pierio Valeriano on the Ill Fortune of Learned Men: A Renaissance Humanist and His World*. Ann Arbor: University of Michigan Press, 2002.

Gamillscheg, E. "Beobachtungen zur Kopistentätigkeit des Petros Kretikos." *Jahrbuch der Österreichischen Byzantinistik* 24 (1975): 137–45.

———. "Zur handschriftlichen Überlieferung byzantinischer Schulbücher." *Jahrbuch der Österreichischen Byzantinistik* 26 (1977): 211–30.

Gamillscheg, E., and D. Harlfinger. *Repertorium der griechischen Kopisten 800–1600.* 3 vols. Vienna: Verlag der Österreichischen Akademie der Wissenschaften, 1981-97.

Garin, E. "Ricerche sulle traduzioni di Platone nella prima meta del secolo XV." In *Medioevo e Rinascimento: studi in onore di Bruno Nardi,* vol. 1, 341–74. Florence: G. C. Sansoni, 1955.

Garin, F. "La 'Expositio Theocriti' di Angelo Poliziano nello Studio Fiorentino (1482–3?)" *Rivista di filologia classica* 42 (1914): 275–82.

Gavin, J. A., and C. H. Miller. "Erasmus' Additions to Listrius' Commentary on the 'Praise of Folly.'" *Erasmus in English* 11 (1981–82): 19–26.

Geanakoplos, D. J. "The Career of the Byzantine Humanist Professor John Argyropoulos in Florence and Rome (1410–87): The Turn to Metaphysics." In *Constantinople and the West: Essays on the Late Byzantine (Palaeologan) and Italian Renaissances and the Byzantine and Roman Churches,* edited by D. J. Geanakoplos, 92–113. Wisconsin: University of Wisconsin Press, 1989.

———. "The Discourse of Demetrius Chalcondyles on the Inauguration of Greek Studies at the University of Padua in 1463." *Studies in the Renaissance* 21 (1974): 118–44.

———. "Theodore Gaza, a Byzantine Scholar of the Palaeologan 'Renaissance' in the Early Italian Renaissance (c.1400–1475)." In *Constantinople and the West: Essays on the Late Byzantine (Palaeologan) and Italian Renaissances and the Byzantine and Roman Churches,* edited by D. J. Geanakoplos, 68–90. Wisconsin: University of Wisconsin Press, 1989.

———. "Translation of Chalcondyles' Discourses on the Inauguration of Greek Studies at Padua University." In *Interaction of the "Sibling" Byzantine and Western Cultures in the Middle Ages and Italian Renaissance (330–1600)* by D. J. Geanakoplos, 254–64 (English tr.); 296–304 (Latin text), New Haven: Yale University Press, 1976.

Geiger, L., ed. *Johann Reuchlins Briefwechsel.* Tübingen: Fues, 1875.

Giannini, M. A. "Holkham Hall 88: Guarino's Aristophanes." *Greek, Roman and Byzantine Studies* 12 (1971): 287–89.

Giansante, M. "Capriolo (Caprioli, Cavriolo), Elia." *Dizionario biografico degli Italiani* 19 (1976): 218–19.

Gigante, M. "Benigni, Cornelio." *Dizionario biografico degli italiani* 8 (1966): 513–14.

Giles, J. A., ed. *Publii Terentii Carthaginensis Afri Comoediae Sex.* London: Bohn, 1837.

Girot, J.-E. *Pindare avant Ronsard: De l'émergence du grec à la publication des Quatre Premiers livres des Odes de Ronsard.* Geneva: Droz, 2002.

Giustiniani, V. R. "L'orazione di Lorenzo Lippi per l'apertura dell' università di Pisa." *Rinascimento,* ser. 2, 4 (1964): 265–83.

———. "Sulle traduzioni latine delle 'Vite' di Plutarco nel quattrocento." *Rinascimento* ser. 2, 1 (1961): 3–62.

Goetz, G., ed. *Corpus Glossariorum Latinorum.* 7 vols. Leipzig: Teubner, 1855–80. Facsimile reprint Amsterdam: Hakkert, 1965.

Goldschmidt, E. P. "The First Edition of Lucian of Samosata." *Journal of the Warburg and Courtauld Institute* 14 (1951): 7–20.

Grafton, A. "The Availability of Ancient Works." In *The Cambridge History of Renaissance Philosophy*, edited by C. B. Schmidt, with Q. Skinner, E. Kessler, and J. Kraye, 767–91. Cambridge: Cambridge University Press, 1988.

———. *Commerce with the Classics: Ancient Books and Renaissance Readers.* Ann Arbor: University of Michigan Press, 1997.

———. *Joseph Scaliger: A Study in the History of Classical Scholarship.* Vol.1: *Textual Criticism and Exegesis.* Oxford: Clarendon Press, 1983.

Greco, A., ed. *Vespasiano da Bisticci: Le vite.* 2 vols. Florence: Istituto Palazzo Strozzi, 1970–76.

Greswell, E. *A View of the Early Parisian Greek Press.* 2 vols. Oxford: Printed by S. Collingwood, printer to the University, for D. A. Talboys, 1833.

Griechischer Geist aus Basler Pressen: Universitätsbibliothek Basel 4. Juli bis 22. August 1992, Staatsbibliothek zu Berlin, Preussischer Kulturbesitz, 28. Januar bis 6. März 1993, Gutenberg-Museum, Mainz 8. Juni bis 29. August 1993. Basle: Universitätsbibliothek Basel, c. 1993.

Gualdo Rosa, L. "Cortesi Urceo, Antonio, detto Codro." *Dizionario biografico degli Italiani* 29 (1983): 773–78.

———. "Crastone, Giovanni." *Dizionario biografico degli Italiani* 30 (1984): 578–80.

———. *La fede nella "Paideia": Aspetti della fortuna europea di Isocrate nei secoli XV e XVI.* Rome: Istituto storico italiano per il medio evo, 1984.

———. "Le traduzioni dal greco nella prima metà del '400: alle radici del classicismo europeo." *Collection Latomus* 187 (1985): 177–93.

———. "Le traduzioni latine dell' «A Nicocle» di Isocrate nel secolo XV." In *Acta Conventus Neo-Latini Lovaniensis*, edited by J. IJsewijn and E. Kessler, 275–303. Leuven: Leuven University Press, 1973.

———. "Niccolò Loschi e Pietro Perleone e le traduzioni dell'orazione pseudo-isocratea «A Demonico»." *Atti dell' Istituto Veneto di scienze, lettere, ed arti* 131 (1973): 825–56.

———. "Urbano dalle Fosse (Bolzanio)." *Dizionario biografico degli Italiani* 32 (1986): 88–92.

Guida, A. "Il *Dictionarium* di Favorino e il *Lexicon Vindobonense*." *Prometheus* 8 (1982): 264–86.

Günther, H.-C. "Andronikos Kallistos und das Studium griechischer Dichtertexte." *Eikasmos: Quaderni bolognesi di filologia classica* 10 (1999): 315–34.

Haltinner, D. O., and E. A. Schmoll. "The Older Manuscripts of Xenophon's *Hiero*." *Revue d'histoire des textes* 10 (1981): 231–36.

Hanford, J. H. "An Old Master Restored: The Homeric Commentary of Guillaume Budé at Princeton." *Princeton University Library Chronicle* 18 (1956–57): 1–10.

Hankins, J. *Plato in the Italian Renaissance.* 2 vols. Leiden: Brill, 1990.

———. "Renaissance Crusaders: Humanist Crusade Literature in the Age of Mehmed II." *Dumbarton Oaks Papers* 49 (1995): 111–207.

———. *Repertorium Brunianum: A Critical Guide to the Writings of Leonardo Bruni. Volume I: Handlist of MSS.* Rome: Istituto storico Italiano, 1997.

Harlfinger, D. *Specimena griechischen Kopisten der Renaissance.* Berlin: Mielke, 1974.

Harlfinger, D., and R. Barm, eds. *Graecogermania: Griechischstudien deutscher Humanisten. Die Editionstätigkeit der Griechen in der italienischen Renaissance (1469–1523). Austellungskataloge der Herzog August Bibliothek 59.* Weinheim: VCH, acta humaniora, 1989.

Harris, J. *Greek Emigres in the West, 1400–1520.* Camberley: Porphyrogenitus, 1995.

Harth, H., ed. *Poggio Bracciolini: Lettere.* 3 vols. Florence: Olschki, 1984–87.

Haury, J., ed. *Procopius caesariensis omnia opera.* 3 vols in 4. Leipzig: in aedibus B. G. Teubneri, 1905–13. Facsimile reprint in 4 vols, Leipzig: in aedibus B. G. Teubneri, 1963–64.

Hausmann, F. R. "Campano, Giovanni Antonio (Giannantonio)." *Dizionario biografico degli italiani* 17 (1974): 424–29.

———. "Carmina Priapea." *Catalogus Translationum et Commentariorum* 4 (1980): 423–50.

———. "Giovanni Antonio Campano (1429–1477): Ein Beitrag zur Geschichte des italienischen Humanismus im Quattrocento." *Römische Historische Mitteilungen* 12 (1970): 125–78.

———. "Giovanni Antonio Campano (1429–1477): Erläuterungen und Ergänzungen zu seinen Briefen." PhD diss., Freiburg im Breisgau, 1968.

Hegius, A. *Alexandri Hegii gymnasiarchae iampridem Daventriensis diligentissimi artium professoris clarissimi philosophi presbyteri poetae utriusque linguae docti carmina et gravia et elegantia.* Deventer: R. Paffraet, 1503.

Henry, R., ed. *Photius: Bibliothèque.* 9 vols. Paris: Les Belle Lettres, 1959–91.

Hesseling, D.-C., and H. Pernot. "Érasme et les origines de la pronunciation érasmienne." *Revue des études grecques* 32 (1919): 278–301.

Heymeryck, P. "Les traductions latines du 'Charon' de Lucien au quinzième siècle." *Mélanges de l'école française de Rome* 84 (1972): 129–200.

Hillyard, B. "Girolamo Aleandro, Editor of Plutarch's *Moralia.*" *Bibliothèque d'humanisme et renaissance* 36 (1974): 517–31.

Hirsch, R. "Early Printed Greek Grammars, 1471–1550." In *The Printed Word: Its Impact and Diffusion* by R. Hirsch, London, item no. VII, 1978.

———. "Printing in France and Humanism, 1470–80." In *French Humanism 1470–1600,* edited by W. L. Gundersheimer, 113–30. London: Macmillan, 1969.

Hody, H. *De graecis illustribus linguae graecae literarumque humaniorum instauratoribus.* London: C. Davis, 1742.

Hoffmann, O., ed. *Die griechischen Dialekte in ihrem historischen Zusammenhange mit den wichtigsten ihrer Quellen.* 3 vols. Göttingen: Vandenhoeck und Ruprecht, 1891–98.

Horawitz, A. "Griechische Studien: Beiträge zur Geschichte des Griechischen in Deutschland." *Berliner Studien für classische Philologie und Archaeologie* 1 (1883): 409–50.

———. "Zur Biographie und Correspondenz Johannes Reuchlins." *Sitzungsberichte der kaiserlichen Akademie der Wissenschaften* 85 (1877): 117–90.

Horawitz, A., and K. Hartfelder, eds. *Briefwechsel des Beatus Rhenanus.* Leipzig: B. G. Teubner, 1886.

Hornblower, S., and A. Spawforth, eds. *The Oxford Classical Dictionary.* 3rd ed., rev. Oxford: Oxford University Press, 2003.

Hoven, R. *Bibliographie de trois auteurs de grammaires grecques contemporains de Nicolas Clénard: Adrien Amerot, Arnold Oridryus, Jean Varennius.* Aubel: Gason, 1985.

———. "Enseignement du grec et livres scolaires dans les anciens Pays-Bas et la Principauté de Liège de 1483 à 1600. Première partie: 1483–1550." *Gutenberg-Jahrbuch* (1979): 78–86.

Hummel, P. "Un opuscule-relais: le *De dialectis* (1520/1530) d'Adrien Amerot." *Bibliothèque d'humanisme et renaissance* 61 (1999): 479–94.

Hunger, H., and C. Hannick. *Katalog der griechischen Handschriften der Österreichischen Nationalbibliothek.* Vol. 4: *Supplementum Graecum.* Vienna: In Kommission bei Verlag Brüder Hollinek, 1994.

Huntingford, G. I. *An Introduction to the Writing of Greek, in Two Parts for the Use of Winchester College*. 8th ed. Oxford: Oxford University Press, 1811.

Index Aureliensis: Catalogus librorum sedecimo saeculo impressorum. 13 vols. Baden-Baden: n. p., 1965.

Irigoin, J. "Georges Hermonyme de Sparte: ses manuscrits et son enseignement à Paris." In *Bulletin de l'Association Guillaume Budé* (1977): 22–27.

———. *Histoire du texte de Pindare*. Paris: Klincksieck, 1952.

———. "L'édition princeps d'Athénée et ses sources." *Revue des études grecques* 80 (1967): 418–24.

———. Review of Vian, *Histoire de la tradition manuscrite de Quinte de Smyrne*. *Revue des études anciennes* 62 (1960): 484–89.

James, M. R. "Two More Manuscripts Written by the Scribe of the Leicester Codex." *Journal of Theological Studies* 11 (1910): 291–92.

John Rylands Catalogue. *Catalogue of the Printed Books and Manuscripts in the John Rylands Library Manchester*. 3 vols. Manchester, 1899.

Jones, D. M. "Cicero as a Translator." *Institute of Classical Studies Bulletin* 6 (1959): 22–33.

Juhász, L., ed. *Bartholomaeus Fontius: Epistolarum libri III*. Budapest: Királyi magyar egyetemi nyomda, 1931.

Kalatzi, M. "Georgios Hermonymos, a Fifteenth-Century Scribe and Scholar: An Examination of His Life, Activities and Manuscripts." PhD diss., University of London, 1997.

Kallendorf, C. W., ed. and trans. *Humanist Educational Treatises*. Cambridge, MA: Harvard University Press, 2002.

Kallendorf, C. W., and M. X. Wells. *Aldine Press Books at the Harry Ransom Humanities Research Center. The University of Texas at Austin. A Descriptive Catalogue*. Austin: Harry Ransom Humanities Research Center, 1998.

Keaney, J. J. "Moschopulea." *Byzantinische Zeitschrift* 64 (1971): 303–21.

———, ed. *Lexeis of the Ten Orators: Harpocration*. Amsterdam: Hakkert, 1991.

Kelly, J. N. D. *The Oxford Dictionary of Popes*. Oxford: Oxford University Press, 1986.

Knauer, G. N. "*Iter per miscellanea*: Homer's *Batrachomyomachia* and Johannes Reuchlin." In *The Whole Book: Cultural Perspectives on the Medieval Miscellany*, edited by S. G. Nichols and S. Wenzel, 23–36. Ann Arbor: University of Michigan Press, 1996.

Knös, B. *Un ambassadeur de l'hellénisme: Janus Lascaris et la tradition greco-byzantine dans l'humanisme français*. Uppsala, 1945.

Knott, B. I., ed. *De copia verborum ac rerum*, in *Opera omnia Desiderii Erasmi Roterodami recognita et adnotatione critica instructa notisque illustrata*, ord. 1, vol. 6. Amsterdam: North-Holland, 1983.

König, E., ed. *Konrad Peutingers Briefwechsel*. Munich: Beck, 1923.

Köhler, F. G., ed. *Hieroclis in aureum Pythagoreorum carmen commentarius*. Stuttgart: Teubner, 1974.

Kristeller, P. O. *Iter Italicum: A Finding List of Uncatalogued or Incompletely Catalogued Humanistic Manuscripts of the Renaissance in Italian and Other Libraries*. London: Warburg Institute, 1963–97.

———, ed. *Supplementum ficinianum: Marsilii Ficini florentini philosophi platonici opuscula inedita et dispersa*. 6 vols. Florence: L. S. Olschki, 1999.

Kusukawa, S., ed. *Philip Melanchthon: Orations on Philosophy and Education*. Translated by C. F. Salazar. Cambridge: Cambridge University Press, 1999.

Labowsky, L. *Bessarion's Library and the Biblioteca Marciana: Six Early Inventories.* Rome: Edizioni di storia e letteratura, 1979.
Lake, K. "The Greek Monasteries of South Italy. IV: The Libraries of the Basilian Monasteries." *Journal of Theological Studies* 5 (1904): 189–202.
Lallot, J., ed. and trans. *La grammaire de Denys le Thrace.* Paris: CNRS Editions, 1998.
Lampe, G. W. H. *A Patristic Greek Lexicon.* Oxford: Clarendon Press, 1961.
Lampros, S. P., ed. *Catalogue of the Greek Manuscripts on Mount Athos.* 2 vols. Cambridge: Cambridge University Press, 1895–1900.
Lasagni, R. *Dizionario biografico dei Parmigiani.* 4 vols. Parma: PPS, 1999.
Laurent, M. H., and A. Guillou. *Le «Liber Visitationis» d'Athanase Chalkéopoulos (1457–1458). Contribution à l'histoire du monachisme en Italie méridionale.* Vatican City: Biblioteca apostolica vaticana, 1960.
Lavagnini, B. "Un codicetto lucchese delle Χρυσᾶ ἔπη." *Bollettino di filologia classica* 24 (1918): 169–71.
Legrand, E. *Bibliographie hellénique ou description raisonnée des ouvrages publiés en grec par des grecs au XVe et XVIe siècles.* 4 vols. Paris: E. Leroux, 1885–1906.
———, ed. and trans. *Cent-dix lettres grecques de F. Filelfo.* Paris: Ernest Leroux, 1892.
Lemke, A. *Aldus Manutius and His Thesaurus Cornucopiae of 1496.* Syracuse: Syracuse University Press, 1958.
Lenz, A. "Constantini Lascaris epitome libri XVI Herodiani Prosodiae Catholicae e MS. Hamburgensi ope I. Classeni emendatior edita." *Philologus* 23 (1866): 162–75.
Leone, P. L. M. "Le lettere di Teodoro Gaza." In *Dotti bizantini e libri greci nell'Italia del secolo XV: Atti del Convegno internazionale trento, 22–23 ottobre 1990,* edited by M. Cortesi and E. V. Maltese, 201–18. Naples: D'Auria, 1992.
Levine Rubinstein, A. "The Notes to Poliziano's «Iliad.»" *Italia medioevale e umanistica* 25 (1982): 205–39.
Lockwood, D. P. "De Rinucio Aretino graecarum litterarum interprete." *Harvard Studies in Classical Philology* 24 (1913): 51–109.
———. "Leonardo Bruni's Translation of Act I of the *Plutus* of Aristophanes." In *Classical Studies in Honor of J. C. Rolfe,* edited by G. Depue Hadzsits, 163–72. Philadelphia: University of Pennsylvania Press, 1931.
———. "Plutarch in the Fourteenth Century: New Evidence Concerning the Transition from the Middle Ages to the Renaissance." *Transactions and Proceedings of the American Philological Association* 64 (1933): lxvi–lxvii.
Lo Monaco, F. "Per la traduzione valliana della 'Pro Ctesiphonte' di Demostene." In *Lorenzo Valla e l'umanesimo italiano: Atti del convegno internazionale di studi umanistici,* edited by O. Besomi and M. Regoliosi, 141–64. Padua: Antenore, 1986.
Loomis, L. R. "The Greek Studies of Poggio Bracciolini." In *Medieval Studies in Memory of Gertrude Schoepperle Loomis,* 489–512. Paris: Honoré Champion, 1927.
Lowry, M. J. C. "Two Great Venetian Libraries in the Age of Aldus Manutius." *Bulletin of the John Rylands University Library of Manchester* 57 (1974): 128–66.
Lucchesi, C. "Una prolusione di Pontico Virunio a Marziale nel cod. A 1415 della biblioteca dell' Archiginnasio." *L'Archiginnasio* 14 (1919): 53–62.
Luiso, F. P. *Studi su l'epistolario di Leonardo Bruni,* edited by L. Gualdo Rosa. Rome: Nella sede dell'Istituto Palazzo Borromini, 1980.
Madan, F., and H. H. E. Craster. *Summary Catalogue of Western Manuscripts in the Bodleian Library at Oxford.* Vol. 6. Oxford: Clarendon Press, 1924.

Maillard, J.-F., J. Kecskeméti, C. Magnien, and M. Portalier. *La France des Humanistes: Hellenistes I*. Turnhout: Brepols, 1999.

Mancini, A. "Codices graeci patavini." *Studi Italiani di filologia classica* 5 (1927): 157–64.

Manetti, A. "Roberto de' Rossi." *Rinascimento* 2 (1951): 33–55.

Manley, F., and R. S. Sylvester, eds. and trans. *De fructu qui ex doctrina percipitur (The Benefit of a Liberal Education)*. New York: Published for the Renaissance Society of America by Ungar, 1967.

Manoussacas, M., and K. Staikos. *The Publishing Activity of the Greeks during the Italian Renaissance (1469–1523)*. Athens: Greek Ministry of Culture, 1987.

Marchetti, V., A. de Ferrari, and C. Mutini. "Calcagnini, Celio." *Dizionario biografico degli Italiani* 16 (1973): 492–98.

Marcotte, D. "La bibliothèque de Jean Calphurnius." *Humanistica lovaniensia* 36 (1987): 184–211.

Margolin, J.-C., ed. *De ratione studii*, in *Opera omnia Desiderii Erasmi Roterodami recognita et adnotatione critica instructa notisque illustrata*, ord. 1, vol. 2, 79–151. Amsterdam: North-Holland, 1971.

Marsh, D. "Guarino of Verona's Translation of Lucian's *Parasite*." *Bibliothèque d'humanisme et renaissance* 56 (1994): 419–44.

———. *Lucian and the Latins: Humour and Humanism in the Early Renaissance*. Ann Arbor: University of Michigan Press, 1998.

———. "Xenophon." *Catalogus Translationum et Commentariorum* 7 (1992): 75–196.

Martinelli, L. C. "Grammatiche greche e bizantine nello scrittoio del Poliziano." In *Dotti bizantini e libri greci nell'Italia del secolo XV: Atti del convegno internazionale trento, 22–23 ottobre 1990*, edited by M. Cortesi and E. V. Maltese, 257–90. Naples: D'Auria, 1992.

Martinelli Tempesta, S. "Per l'identificazione delle fonti manoscritte dell' *Editio princeps* delle *Orazioni* di Isocrate: il caso de *Panegirico*." *Cuadernos de filologia classica* 16 (2006): 237–67.

Martínez-Manzano, T. *Konstantinos Laskaris. Humanist, Philologe, Lehrer, Kopist*. Hamburg: Universität Hamburg, Institut für Griechische und Lateinische Philologie, 1994.

Martini, A., and D. Bassi, eds. *Catalogus codicum graecorum bibliothecae ambrosianae*. 2 vols. Milan: U. Hoepli, 1906.

Mastrodemetres, P. D. Νικόλαος Σεκουνδινός, 1402–1464. Βίος καὶ ἔργον. Συμβολὴ εἰς τὴν μελέτην τῶν Ἑλλήνων λογίων τῆς Διασπορᾶς. Διατριβὴ ἐπὶ διδακτορίᾳ. Athens: n.p., 1970.

Mattesini, F. "La biblioteca francescana di S. Croce e Fra Tedaldo della Casa." *Studi francescani* 57 (1960): 282–83.

Mehus, L., ed. *Ambrosii Traversarii epistolae a domno Petro Canneto in libros XXV tributae variorum opera distinctae, et observationibus illustratae . . . ex monumentis potissimum nondum editis deducta est a Laurentio Mehus*. 2 vols. Florence: Ex Typographio Caesareo, 1759.

———, ed. *Leonardi Bruni Aretini epistolarum libri VIII . . . recensente Laurentio Mehus . . . qui Leonardi vitam scripsit, Manetti et Poggii orationes praemisit, indices, animadversiones, praefationemque adjecit, librumque nonum ac decimum in lucem protulit*. 2 vols. Florence: Ex Typographia Bernardi Paperinii, 1741.

Menchelli, M. "Isocrate commentato tra manoscritti e stampa. Il laur. 58, 5 e l'incunabolo di Demetrio Calcondila e Sebastiano da Pontremoli. Il Vat. Pal. gr. 135 e l'Aldina di Marco Musuro." *Res publica litterarum* 28 (2005): 5–34.

Mercati, G. "Una lettera negletta di Manuele Crisolora al Salutati e un'altra datata male." *Rendiconti dell' Istituto Lombardo di Scienze e Lettere* 51 (1918): 227–34.

Mercati, G., and P. F. de' Cavalieri, eds. *Codices vaticani graeci: Codices 1–329.* Rome: Typis polyglottis vaticanis, 1923.

Meyer, H. "Ein Kollegheft des humanisten Cono." *Zentralblatt für Bibliothekswesen* 53 (1936): 281–84.

Miglio, M. "Birago, Lampugnino." *Dizionario biografico degli Italiani* 10 (1968): 595–97.

Migne, J.-P., ed. *Patrologiae cursus completus: Series graeca.* 161 vols. Paris: Migne, 1857–66.

———, ed. *Patrologiae cursus completus: Series latina.* 221 vols. Paris: Migne, 1844–90.

Milham, M. E. "Apicius." *Catalogus Translationum et Commentariorum* 2 (1971): 323–29.

Mioni, E. "Altri due manoscritti greci di S. Michele di Murano." *Italia medioevale e umanistica* 3 (1960): 389–90.

———. "Bessarione scriba ed alcuni suoi collaboratori." *Miscellanea marciana di studi bessarionei*, 263–318. Padua: Antenore, 1976.

———, ed. *Bibliothecae Divi Marci Venetiarum: Codices Graeci Manuscripti.* 5 vols. Rome: Ministero della pubblica istruzione, 1972–1985.

———. "Calliergi (Callergi), Zaccaria." *Dizionario biografico degli Italiani* 16 (1973): 750–53.

———, ed. *Catalogo di manoscritti greci esistenti nelle biblioteche italiane.* Rome, Istituto poligrafo dello stato, n.d.

———. "I manoscritti greci di S. Michele di Murano." *Italia medioevale e umanistica* 1 (1958): 317–43.

Mohler, L. *Kardinal Bessarion als Theologe, Humanist und Staatsmann.* 3 vols. Paderborn: Schöningh, 1923–42.

Mondrain, B. "L'étude du grec en Italie à la fin du XVe siècle, vue à travers l'experience d'humanistes allemands." In *Dotti bizantini e libri greci nell'Italia del secolo XV: Atti del Convegno internazionale trento, 22–23 ottobre 1990*, edited by M. Cortesi and E. V. Maltese, 309–19. Naples: D'Auria, 1992.

———. "La collection de manuscrits grecs d'Adolphe Occo." *Scriptorium* 42 (1988): 156–75.

Monfasani, J. "Bessarion Latinus." *Rinascimento* 21 (1981): 165–209.

———, ed. *Collectanea Trapezuntiana: Texts, Documents, and Bibliographies of George of Trebizond.* Binghamton, New York: Medieval and Renaissance Texts and Studies in conjunction with the Renaissance Society of America, 1984.

———. *George of Trebizond: A Biography and Study of His Rhetoric and Logic.* Leiden: Brill, 1976.

———. "In Praise of Ognibene and Blame of Guarino: Andronicus Contoblacas' Invective against Niccolò Botano and the Citizens of Brescia." *Bibliothèque d'humanisme et renaissance* 52 (1990): 309–21.

———. "L'insegnamento di Teodoro Gaza a Ferrara." *Alla corte degli Estensi: Filosofia, arte e cultura a Ferrara nei secoli XV e XVI. Atti del convegno internazionale di studi, Ferrara, 5–7 marzo 1992*, edited by M. Bertozzi, 5–17. Ferrara: Università degli studi, 1994.

———. "L'insegnamento universitario e la cultura bizantina in Italia nel Quattrocento." *Sapere e/è potere: Discipline, dispute e professioni nell'università medievale e moderna: Il caso bolognese a confronto. Atti del 4o Convegno, Bologna, 13–15 aprile 1989*, edited by L. Avellini, 43–65. Bologna: Istituto per la storia di Bologna, 1990.

———. "Theodore Gaza as a Philosopher: A Preliminary Survey." In *Manuele Crisolora e il ritorno del greco in occidente: Atti del convegno internazionale (Napoli, 26–29 giugno 1997)*, edited by R. Maisano and A. Rollo, 269–81. Naples: Istituto universitario orientale, 2002.

Moreau, B. *Inventaire chronologique des éditions parisiennes du XVIe siècle*. 5 vols. Paris: Service des travaux historiques de la ville de Paris, 1972–2004.

Moro, G. "Garatone (Garaton, Garatoni, Garatono, Garatonus, Garathonius), Cristoforo." *Dizionario biografico degli italiani* 52 (1999): 234–38.

Morsolin, B. *Giangiorgio Trissino o monografia di un letterato nel secolo XVI*. Vicenza: G. Burato, 1878.

Moschopoulos, M. *Grammaticae artis graecae methodus Manuele Moscopulo authore. Eiusdem artis Theodori Gazae lib. II*. Basle: Walder, 1540.

Motta, E. "Demetrio Calcondila editore." *Archivio storico lombardo* 20 (1893): 143–66.

Müller, K. K. "Neue Mittheilungen über Janos Laskaris und die Mediceische Bibliothek." *Centralblatt für Bibliothekswesen* 1 (1884): 331–412.

Müllner, K. "Eine Rede des Ioannes Lascaris." *Wiener Studien* 21 (1899): 128–43.

———. *Reden und Briefe italienischer Humanisten*. Vienna: Hölder, 1899.

Nachtgall, O. *Graece et latine Moralia quaedam instituta, ex variis authoribus. Cato noster, Maximo planude graeco interprete. Aurea Carmina Pythagorae. Phocylidis poema exhortatorium. Senarii morales, diversorum poetarum. Cebetis Tabula. Sententiae morales, multorum virorum illustrium*. Augsburg: Simpertus Ruff, expensis S. Grim, 1523.

Naoumides, M. "The Shorter Version of Pseudo-Zonaras' Lexicon." In *Serta Turyniana: Studies in Greek Literature and Palaeography in Honor of Alexander Turyn*, edited by J. H. Heller, 436–88. Urbana: Illinois University Press, 1974.

National Library of Scotland. *A Short-Title Catalogue of Books Printed up to 1600*. Edinburgh: Her Majesty's Stationery Office, 1970.

Nauert, C. G. "Caius Plinius Secundus." *Catalogus Translationum et Commentariorum* 4 (1980): 297–422.

Nickau, K., ed. *Ammonii qui dicitur liber de adfinium vocabulorum differentia*. Leipzig: Teubner, 1966.

Niemöller, K. W. "Othmar Luscinius, Musiker und Humanist." *Archiv für Musikwissenschaft* 15 (1958): 41–59.

Nijhoff, W., and M. E. Kronenberg. *Nederlandsche Bibliographie van 1500 tot 1540*. 's-Gravenhage: M. Nijhoff, 1923–40.

Nijhoff, W. *L'art typographique dans les Pays-Bas pendant les années 1500 à 1540. Reproduction en fac-simile des charactères typographiques, marques d'imprimeurs, gravures sur bois et autres ornements employés pendant cette période*. 2 vols. The Hague: M. Nijhoff, 1926.

Nolan, E., and S. A. Hirsch, eds. *The Greek Grammar of Roger Bacon and a Fragment of His Hebrew Grammar*. Cambridge: Cambridge University Press, 1902.

De Nolhac, P. "Inventaire des manuscrits grecs de Jean Lascaris." *Mélanges d'archéologie et d'histoire* 6 (1886): 251–74.

———. *La bibliothèque de Fulvio Orsini*. Paris: E. Bouillon and E. Vieweg, 1887.

———. "Le grec à Paris sous Louis XII: récit d'un témoin." *Revue des études grecques* 1 (1888): 61–67.

———. *Les correspondants d'Alde Manuce. Matériaux nouveau d'histoire littéraire, 1483–1514*. Rome: Imprimerie vaticane, 1888.

Norton, F. J. *A Descriptive Catalogue of Printing in Spain and Portugal 1501–1520*. Cambridge: Cambridge University Press, 1978.

Novati, F., ed. *Epistolario di Coluccio Salutati*. 4 vols. Rome: Istituto storico italiano, 1891–1911.

Nugent, E. M., ed. *The Thought and Culture of the English Renaissance: An Anthology of Tudor Prose, 1481–1555*. Cambridge: Cambridge University Press, 1956.

Oates, J. C. T. *Cambridge University Library: A History. From the Beginnings to the Copyright Act of Queen Anne*. Cambridge: Cambridge University Press, 1986.

———. *A Catalogue of the Fifteenth-Century Printed Books in the University Library Cambridge*. Cambridge: Cambridge University Press, 1954.

Offenbacher, E. "La bibliothèque de Willibald Pirckheimer." *La Bibliofilía* 40 (1938): 241–63.

Oleroff, A. "Démétrius Trivolis, copiste et bibliophile." *Scriptorium* 4 (1950): 260–63.

Oliver, R. P. "Plato and Salutati." *Transactions and Proceedings of the American Philological Association* 71 (1940): 315–34.

Omont, H. "Catalogue des manuscripts grecs des bibliothèques de Suisse: Bâle, Berne, Einsiedeln, Genève, St. Gall, Schaffhouse et Zürich." *Zentralblatt für Bibliothekswesen* 3 (1886): 385–452.

———. "Catalogue des manuscrits grecs des bibliothèques publiques des Pays-Bas." *Zentralblatt für Bibliothekswesen* 4 (1887): 185–214.

———. "Essai sur les débuts de la typographie grecque à Paris." *Mémoires de la société de l'histoire de Paris et de l'Ile de France* 18 (1891): 1–72.

———. "Georges Hermonyme de Sparte, maître de grec à Paris, et copiste de manuscrits (1476)." *Mémoires de société de l'histoire de Paris et de l'Ile de France* 12 (1885): 65–98.

———. *Inventaire sommaire des manuscrits grecs de la Bibliothèque nationale*. 4 vols. Paris: A. Picard, 1886–98.

———. "Les manuscrits grecs datés des XVe et XVIe siècles de la Bibliothèque nationale et des autres bibliothèques de France." *Revue des bibliothèques* 2 (1892): 1–32, 145–76, 194–215.

Orlandi, G., ed. *Aldo Manuzio editore: Dediche, prefazioni, note ai testi*. 2 vols. Milan: Il polifilo, 1975.

Ortoleva, V. "La traduzione di Massimo Planude dei *Disticha Catonis*: dalla divulgazione del latino a Bisanzio alla didassi del greco in occidente." *Aufidus* 15 (1991): 93–101.

Österley, H., ed. *Steinhöwels Äsop*. Tübingen: Fues, 1873.

Pade, M. "The Dedicatory Letter as a Genre: The Prefaces of Guarino Veronese's Translations of Plutarch." In *Acta Conventus Neo-Latini Torontonensis. Proceedings of the Seventh International Congress of Neo-Latin Studies*, edited by A. Dalzell, C. Fantazzi, and R. J. Schoeck, 559–68. Binghamton, New York: Medieval and Renaissance Texts and Studies, 1991.

———. "The Latin Translations of Plutarch's *Lives* in Fifteenth-Century Italy and Their Manuscript Diffusion." In *The Classical Tradition in the Middle Ages and the Renaissance*, edited by C. Leonardi and B. M. Olsen, 170–83. Spoleto: Centro italiano di studi sull'alto medioevo, 1995.

Pagano, A. "Fracanzio da Montalboddo." *Dizionario biografico degli Italiani* 49 (1997): 531–33.

Pagliaroli, S. "Gregorio da Città di Castello." *Dizionario biografico degli Italiani* 59 (2002): 260–65.

———. "Nuovi autografi di Marco Musuro." *Studi medievali e umanistici* 2 (2004): 356–63.

Papathomopoulos, M., I. Tsabare, and G. Rigotti, eds. Αὐγουστίνου Περὶ Τριάδος βιβλία πεντεκαίδεκα ἅπερ ἐκ τῆς Λατίνων διαλέκτου εἰς τὴν Ἑλλάδα μετήνεγκε Μάξιμος ὁ Πλανούδης. 2 vols. Athens: Κέντρον ἐκδόσεως ἔργων συγγράφεων, 1995.

Papathomopoulos, M., ed. *Anicii Manlii Severini Boethii, de Consolatione Philosophiae: traduction grecque de Maxime Planude*. Athens: Ἀκαδημία Ἀθηνῶν, 1999.

Paquier, J. *Jérôme Aléandre: de sa naissance à la fin de son séjour à Brindes, 1480–1529*. Paris: Leroux, 1900.

Parks, G. B., and F. E. Cranz. "Dionysius Periegetes." *Catalogus Translationum et Commentariorum* 3 (1976): 21–61.

Paschini, P. "Un ellenista veneziano del Quattrocento: Giovanni Lorenzi." *Archivio Veneto* 32–33 (1943): 114–46.

Pellegrin, E. *La bibliothèque des Visconti et des Sforza Ducs de Milan au XVe siècle*. Paris: Vente au Service des publications du C.N.R.S., 1955.

Pellegrini, P. "Χεὶρ χεῖρα νίπτει. Per gli incunaboli di Giovanni Calfurnio, umanista editore." *Italia medioevale e umanistica* 42 (2001): 181–283.

Percival, W. K. "The *Artis Grammaticae Opusculum* of Bartolomeo Sulmonese: A Newly Discovered Latin Grammar of the Quattrocento." *Renaissance Quarterly* 31 (1978): 39–47.

———. "The Place of the *Rudimenta Grammatices* in the History of Latin Grammar." *Res publica litterarum* 4 (1981): 233–64.

Perosa, A. "Due lettere inedite del Poliziano." *Italia medioevale e umanistica* 10 (1967): 345–74.

———, ed. *Giovanni Rucellai ed il suo Zibaldone I: «Il zibaldone quaresimale»*. London: Warburg Institute, 1960.

———. Review of Knös, *Un ambassadeur de l'hellénisme*. *Leonardo* 16 (1947): 359–63.

Perotto Sali, L. "L'opuscolo inedito di Giorgio Merula contro i *Miscellanea* di Angelo Poliziano." *Interpres* 1 (1978): 146–83.

Pertusi, A. "La scoperta di Euripide nel primo Umanesimo." *Italia medioevale e umanistica* 3 (1960): 101–52.

———. "Ἐρωτήματα: Per la storia e le fonti delle prime grammatiche greche a stampa." *Italia medioevale e umanistica* 5 (1962): 321–51.

———. *Leonzio Pilato fra Petrarca e Boccaccio: le sue versioni omeriche negli autografi di Venezia e la cultura greca del primo umanesimo*, Venice: Istituto per la collaborazione culturale, 1964.

Petit, L., X. A. Sidéridès, and M. Jugie. *Oeuvres complètes de Georges Scholarios*. 8 vols. Paris: Maison de la bonne presse, 1928–36.

Petrucci, A. "Calcondila (Calcocondila, Χαλκονδύλης, Χαλκοκανδύλης), Demetrio." *Dizionario biografico degli Italiani* 16 (1973): 542–47.

Petrucci, F. "Crivelli, Lodrisio." *Dizionario biografico degli Italiani* 31 (1985): 146–52.

Pfeiffer, R. *History of Classical Scholarship from 1300 to 1850*. Oxford: Clarendon Press, 1976.

Piccolomini, E. "Una lettera greca di Pietro Bembo a Demetrio Mosco." *Archivio storico italiano*, series 5, 6 (1890): 307–9.

Pignatti, F. "Filelfo, Giovanni Mario." *Dizionario biografico degli Italiani* 47 (1997): 626–31.

Pincelli, M. A. *Andrea Brenta: In principio lectionis Aristophanis praeludia. La prolusione al corso su Aristofane*. Rome: Roma nel Rinscimento, 1993.

Pintaudi, R., ed. *Etymologicum Parvum quod vocatur*. Milan: Cisalpino-Goliardica, 1973.
———, ed. *Marsilio Ficino: lessico greco-latino, Laur.Ashb.1439*. Rome: Ateneo e Bizzarri, 1977.
Piovan, F. "Forteguerri (Carteromaco), Scipione." *Dizionario biografico degli Italiani* 49 (1997): 163–67.
Pizzi, C. "La grammatica greca di T. di Gaza ed Erasmo." *Studi bizantini e neoellenici* 7 (1953): 183–88.
Polain, M.-L. *Catalogue des livres imprimés au quinzième siècle des bibliothèques de Belgique*. 4 vols. Brussels: Pour la Société des Bibliophiles et Iconophiles de Belgique, 1932.
Poliziano, A. *Angeli Politiani Opera. Quorum primus hic tomus complectitur epistolarum libros XII. Miscellaneorum Centuriam I. Omnia iam recens a mendis repurgata*. Lyons: Apud S. Gryphium, 1536.
———. *Omnia opera Angeli Politiani, et alia quaedam lectu digna*. Venice: In aedibus Aldi Romani, 1498.
Pontani, F. "Omero, Appiano e l'ombra di un padre. Giovanni Basilio Romolo Calcondila." *Bollettino della Badia di Grottaferrata* 56–57 (2002–3): 263–84.
———. *Sguardi su Ulisse: la tradizione esegetica greca all'Odissea*. Rome: Edizioni di storia e letteratura, 2005.
Porro, A. "La versione latina dell' Écuba euripidea attribuita a Pietro da Montagnana." In *Dotti bizantini e libri greci nell'Italia del secolo XV: Atti del convegno internazionale trento, 22–23 ottobre 1990*, edited by M. Cortesi and E. V. Maltese, 343–63. Naples: D'Auria, 1992.
Powell, J. E. "Two Letters of Andronicus Callistus to Demetrius Chalcocondyles." *Byzantinische-Neugriechische Jahrbücher* 15 (1939): 14–20.
Pozzi, G. "Da Padova a Firenze nel 1493." *Italia medioevale e umanistica* 9 (1966): 191–227.
Prevost, M. "Chéradame, Jean." *Dictionnaire de biographie française* 8 (1959): 1000.
Proctor, R. *The Printing of Greek in the Fifteenth Century*. London: Bibliographical Society, 1900.
Quandt, W., ed. *Orphei Hymni*. Berlin: Apud Weidmannos, 1955.
Quaranta, E. "Osservazioni intorno ai caratteri greci di Aldo Manuzio." *Bibliofilía* 55 (1953): 123–30.
Quattrucci, M. "Anselmi, Giorgio." *Dizionario biografico degli Italiani* 3 (1961): 378–79.
Rabe, H. "Konstantin Laskaris." *Zentralblatt für Bibliothekswesen* 45 (1928): 1–7.
Rebecchini, G. "The Book Collection and Other Possessions of Baldassarre Castiglione." *Journal of the Warburg and Courtauld Institutes* 61 (1998): 17–52.
Reeve, A., ed. *Erasmus' Annotations on the New Testament: The Gospels. Facsimile of the Final Latin Text (1535) with All Earlier Variants (1516, 1519, 1522 and 1527)*. London: Duckworth, 1986.
Reeve, M. D. "Classical Scholarship." In *The Cambridge Companion to Renaissance Humanism*, edited by J. Kraye, 20–46. Cambridge: Cambridge University Press, 1996.
Reicke, E., ed. *Willibald Pirckheimers Briefwechsel*. 2 vols. Munich: C. Beck, 1940–56.
Renouard, A. A. *Annales de l'imprimerie des Alde, ou Histoire des trois Manuce et de leurs éditions*. 2nd ed. Paris: J. Renouard, 1834.
———. *Annales de l'imprimerie des Estienne ou histoire de la famille des Estienne et de ses éditions*. 2nd ed. Paris: J. Renouard, 1843.

Renouard, P. *Bibliographie des éditions de Simon de Colines, 1520–1546*. Paris: Paul, Huard, and Guillemin, 1894.

———. *Bibliographie des impressions et des oeuvres de Josse Badius Ascensius imprimeur et humaniste 1462–1535*. Paris: E. Paul et fils et Guillemin, 1908.

Resta, G. "Antonio Cassarino e le sue traduzioni da Plutarco e Platone." *Italia medioevale e umanistica* 2 (1959): 207–83.

———. *Apollonio Rodio e gli umanisti*. Rome: Edizioni dell'Ateneo e Bizzarri, 1980.

———. *Giorgio Valagussa umanista del Quattrocento*. Padua: Antenore, 1964.

Reuck, J. de. *Bibliotheca Erasmiana Bruxellensis: Catalogus der werken uitgegeven in de 16de eeuw aanwezig in de Koninklijke Bibliotheek Albert I*. Edited by G. Colin and R. Hoven. Brussels: Koninklijke Bibliotheek Albert I, 1993.

Rhein, S. "Johannes Reuchlin (1455–1522): Ein deutscher «uomo universale»." In *Humanismus im deutschen Südwesten: Biographische Profile*, edited by P. G. Schmidt, 59–76. Stuttgart: Jan Thorbecke, 2000.

———. "Melanchthon and Greek Literature." In *Philip Melanchthon (1497–1560) and the Commentary*, edited by T. J. Wengert and M. P. Graham, 149–70. Sheffield: Sheffield Academic Press, 1997.

Rhein, S., M. dall'Asta, and G. Dörner, eds. *Johannes Reuchlin: Briefwechsel*. 3 vols. Stuttgart: Frommann-Holzboog, 1999–2007.

Rhodes, D. E. *Incunabula in Greece: A First Census*. Munich: Kraus International Publications, 1980.

Rice, E. F. "Paulus Aegineta." *Catalogus Translationum et Commentariorum* 3 (1980): 145–91.

———. *The Prefatory Epistles of Jacques Lefèvre d'Étaples and Related Texts*. New York: Columbia University Press, 1972.

Rivautella, A., and J. P. Ricolvi, eds. *Marmora taurinensia dissertationibus et notis illustrata*. 2 vols. Tours: Ex Typographia Regia, 1743–47.

Robathan, D., with P. O. Kristeller and B. Bischoff. "Persius." *Catalogus Translationum et Commentariorum* 3 (1976): 201–312.

Robins, R. H. *The Byzantine Grammarians: Their Place in History*. Berlin and New York: De Gruyter, 1993.

Robinson, C., ed. *Luciani Dialogi*, in *Opera omnia Desiderii Erasmi Roterodami recognita et adnotatione critica instructa notisque illustrata*, ord. 1, vol. 1, 362–603. Amsterdam: North-Holland, 1969.

Roersch, A. "Un bon ouvrier de la renaissance: Rescius." In *L'humanisme belge à l'époque de la renaissance: études et portraits*, edited by A. Roersch, 37–55. Brussels: Van Oest and Cie, 1910.

Rossi, V., ed. *Francesco Petrarca: Le Familiari*. 4 vols. Florence: G. C. Sansoni, 1933–42.

Rostagno, E., and N. Festa. "Indice dei codici greci laurenziani non compresi nel catalogo del Bandini." *Studi italiani di filologia classica* 1 (1893): 129–232; consulted in *Catalogus codicum Manuscriptorum Bibliothecae Mediceae Laurentianae*, vol. 2, edited by A. M. Bandini, 3*–62*. Leipzig: Zentral-Antiquariat, 1961.

Ruelle, C.-E. "Deux textes concernant le canon musical heptacorde, puis octacorde, publiés d'après le ms. N-72 de la Biblioteca nacional de Madrid, avec une traduction française et des notes." *Annuaire de l'association pour l'encouragement des études grecs en France* 11 (1877): 147–69.

Ruelle, P. "Les 'Apologues' de Guillaume Tardif et les 'Facetiae morales' de Laurent Valla." *Centre d'études franco-italien* 10 (1986): 38–49.

Rupprich, H., ed. *Die Briefwechsel des Konrad Celtis.* Munich: Beck'sche, 1934.

Russo, E. "Guazzelli, Demetrio (Pietro Demetrio)." *Dizionario biografico degli Italiani* 60 (2003): 520–23.

Rutherford, W. G., ed. *The New Phrynichus, Being a Revised Text of the Ecloga of the Grammarian Phrynichus.* London: Macmillan and Co., 1881.

Sabbadini, R. "Ancora Pietro Marcello." *Nuovo archivio veneto* 31 (1916): 260–61.

———. "Andrea Contrario." *Nuovo archivio veneto* 16 (1916): 378–433.

———. *Biografia documentata di Giovanni Aurispa.* Noto: F. Zammit, 1890.

———, ed. *Carteggio di Giovanni Aurispa.* Rome: Tipografia del Senato, 1931.

———, ed. *Epistolario di Guarino Veronese.* 3 vols. Venice: A spese della Società, 1915–19.

———. *Il metodo degli umanisti.* Florence: Le Monner, 1922.

———. *La scuola e gli studi di Guarino Guarini Veronese.* Catania: Galati, 1896. Facsimile reprint in *Guariniana*, edited by M. Sancipriano. Turin: Bottega d'Erasmo, 1964.

———. *Le scoperte dei codici latini e greci nei secoli XIV e XV.* Florence: G. C. Sansoni, 1905.

———. "Una traduzione medievale del Πρός Δημόνικον di Isocrate e una umanistica." *Rendiconti dell'Istituto lombardo di scienze e lettere* 38 (1905): 674–87.

Saffrey, H. D. "Notes platoniciennes de Marsile Ficin dans un manuscrit de Proclus (Cod. Riccardianus 70)." *Bibliothèque d'humanisme et renaissance* 21 (1959): 161–84.

———. "Nouveaux manuscrits copiés par Matthieu Camariotès." *Scriptorium* 14 (1960): 340–44.

———. "Une exercise de Latin philosophique autographe du cardinal Bessarion." In *Miscellanea marciana di studi bessarionei*, 371–79. Padua: Antenore, 1976.

———. "Un humaniste dominicain, Jean Cuno de Nuremberg, précurseur d'Érasme à Bâle." *Bibliothèque d'humanisme et renaissance* 33 (1971): 19–62.

Salanitro, G., ed. "Teodoro Gaza traduttore di testi classici." In *Dotti bizantini e libri greci nell'Italia del secolo XV: Atti del convegno internazionale trento, 22–23 ottobre 1990*, edited by M. Cortesi and E. V. Maltese, 219–25. Naples: D'Auria, 1992.

———. *Theodorus Gaza: M. Tullii Ciceronis liber de senectute in graecum translatus.* Leipzig: B. G. Teubner, 1987.

Sanchi, L.-A. *Les Commentaires de la langue grecque de Guillaume Budé: l'oeuvre, ses sources, sa préparation.* Geneva: Droz, 2006.

Sander, M. *Le livre à figures italien depuis 1467 jusqu'à 1530.* 6 vols. Milan: Hoepli, 1942.

Sandys, J. E. *From the Revival of Learning to the End of the 18th Century in Italy, France, England and the Netherlands.* Vol. 2 of *A History of Classical Scholarship*. Cambridge: Cambridge University Press, 1908.

Scaffai, M. "Pindarus seu Homerus. Un' ipotesi sul titolo dell' *Ilias Latina*." *Latomus* 38 (1979): 932–39.

Schade, G., and P. Eleuteri. "The Textual Tradition of the *Argonautica*." In *A Companion to Apollonius Rhodius*, edited by T. D. Papanghelis and A. Rengakos, 27–49. Leiden: Brill, 2001.

Schartau, B. *Codices Graeci Haunienses: Ein descriptiver Katalog des griechischen Handschriftenbestandes der Königlichen Bibliothek Kopenhagen.* Copenhagen: Museum Tusculanum Press, 1994.

Scheible, H. "Melanchthons Pforzheimer Schulzeit: Studien zur humanistischen Bildungselite." In *Pforzheim in der frühen Neuzeit: Beiträge zur Stadtgeschichte des 16. bis 18. Jahrhunderts*, edited by H.-P. Becht, 9–50. Sigmaringen: Thorbecke, 1989.

Schimmelpfennig, A. "Metzler. Dr Johannes." *Allgemeine Deutsche Biographie* 21 (1885): 531–32.

Schmidt, M., ed. Ἐπιτομὴ τῆς καθολικῆς προσῳδίας Ἡρωδιανοῦ. Jena: Sumptibus et typis F. Maukie, 1860. Facsimile reprint Hildesheim: G. Olms, 1983.

Schmoll, E. A. "The Manuscript Tradition of Xenophon's *Apologia Socratis*." *Greek, Roman and Byzantine Studies* 31 (1990): 313–21.

Schneider, R., G. Uhlig, and A. Hilgard, eds. *Grammatici Graeci recogniti et apparatu critico instructi*. 9 vols. Leipzig: B. G. Teubner, 1867–1910. Facsimile reprint Hildesheim: G. Olms, 1965–1979.

Scholderer, V. *Greek Printing Types 1465–1927: Facsimiles from an Exhibition of Books Illustrating the Development of Greek Printing Shown in the British Museum 1927*. London: British Museum, 1927.

Shailor, B. A., ed. *Catalogue of Medieval and Renaissance Manuscripts in the Beinecke Rare Book and Manuscript Library, Yale University*. 3 vols. Binghamton, NY: Medieval and Renaissance Texts and Studies, 1984–92.

Shaw, D. J. "Setting by Formes in some Early Parisian Greek Books." In *Book Production and Letters in the Western European Renaissance: Essays in Honour of Conor Fahy*, edited by A. L. Lepschy, J. Took, and D. E. Rhodes, 284–90. London: Modern Humanities Research Association, 1986.

Sheehan, W. J., ed. *Bibliothecae Apostolicae Vaticanae Incunabula*. 4 vols. Vatican City: Biblioteca apostolica vaticana, 1997.

Sheppard, J. T. "Richard Croke: A Sixteenth Century Don, Being the Croke Lecture for the May Term, 1919." Cambridge: Heffer and Sons, 1919.

Sheppard, L. A. "A Fifteenth-Century Humanist, Francesco Filelfo." *Library* 16 (1935): 1–26.

Sicherl, M. "Pseudodositheana." In *Catalepton: Festschrift für Bernhard Wyss zum 80. Geburtstag*, edited by C. Schäublin, 183–202. Basle: Seminar für Klassische Philologie der Universität Basel, 1985.

Sidwell, K. "Manoscritti umanistici di Luciano in Italia nel Quattrocento." *Res publica litterarum* 9 (1986): 241–53.

Smith, L., ed. *Epistolario di Pier Paolo Vergerio*. Rome: Tipografia del Senato, 1934.

Solerti, A., ed. *Le tragedie metriche di Alessandro Pazzi de' Medici*. Bologna: Romagnoli-Dall'Acqua, 1887. Facsimile reprint Bologna: Commissione per i testi di lingua, 1969.

Sotheby's, *Early Printed Books from Stonyhurst College Sold in Aid of Bursaries*. London: Sotheby's, 2003.

Speranzi, D. "Codici greci appartenuti a Francesco Filelfo nella biblioteca di Ianos Laskaris." *Segno et testo* 3 (2005): 467–96.

———. "L'*Anonymus Δ-Καί*, copista del *Corpus Aristotelicum*. Un'ipotesi di identificazione." *Quaderni di storia* 69 (2009): 105–23.

———. "Per la storia della libreria medicea privata. Il Laur. 58.2, Giano Lascaris et Giovanni Mosco." *Medioevo e rinascimento* 21 (2007): 181–215.

———. "Tra Creta e Firenze. Aristobulo Apostolis, Marco Musuro e il Riccardiano 77." *Segno e testo* 4 (2006): 191–208.

Spinelli, M. "Feruffini, Domenico." *Dizionario biografico degli Italiani* 47 (1997): 266–67.

———. "Feruffini, Filippo." *Dizionario biografico degli Italiani* 47 (1997): 267–69.
———. "Feruffini, Giovanni." *Dizionario biografico degli Italiani* 47 (1997): 269–71.
Spitz, L. W. *Conrad Celtis: The German Arch-Humanist*. Cambridge, MA: Harvard University Press, 1957.
Staehelin, E. "Oekolampad-Bibliographie." *Basler Zeitschrift für Geschichte und Altertumskunde* 17 (1918): 1–119.
Stevens, L. P. "How the French Humanists of the Renaissance Learned Greek." *Proceedings of the Modern Language Association* 65 (1950): 240–48.
Stevenson, H., senior ed. *Codices manuscripti palatini graeci Bibliothecae Vaticanae descripti praeside I. B. Cardinali Pitra episcopo portuensi S. R. E. bibliothecario*. Rome: Ex typographeo vaticano, 1885.
Stinger, C. L. *Humanism and the Church Fathers: Ambrogio Traversari and Christian Antiquity in the Italian Renaissance*. New York: State University of New York Press, 1977.
Stockhausen, A. von, "Katalog der griechischen Handschriften im Besitz der Thüringer Universitäts- und Landesbibliothek Jena." *Byzantinische Zeitschrift* 94 (2001): 684–701.
Stumpo, E. "Calco, Bartolomeo." *Dizionario biografico degli Italiani* 16 (1973): 526–31.
Sturge, C. *Cuthbert Tunstall: Churchman, Scholar, Statesman, Administrator*. London: Longmans and Co., 1938.
Surtz, E., and J. H. Hexter, eds. *The Complete Works of St Thomas More*, vol. 4: *Utopia*. New Haven: Yale University Press, 1965.
Thesaurus Graecae Linguae. Post editionem Anglicam novis additamentis auctum, ordineque alphabetico digestum tertio, edited by C. B. Hase, G. R. L. von Sinner, T. Fix, G. Dindorf, and L. Dindorf. 8 vols. Paris: A. F. Didot, 1831–65.
Theseus, N., ed. ʿΟμήρου Ἰλιὰς μετὰ παλαιᾶς παραφράσεως ἐξ ἰδιοχείρου τοῦ Θεοδώρου Γαζῆ. 4 vols. Florence: n.p., 1811–12.
Thiermann, P. "Das Wörterbuch der Humanisten: Die griechisch-lateinische Lexikographie des fünfzehnten Jahrhunderts und das 'Dictionarium Crastoni.'" PhD diss., University of Hamburg, 1994.
———. *Die Orationes Homeri des Leonardo Bruni Aretino*. Leiden: Brill, 1993.
———. "I dizionari greco-latini fra medioevo e umanesimo." *Les manuscrits des lexiques et glossaires de l'antiquité tardive à la fin du moyen âge: Actes du colloque international organisé par le "Ettore Majorana Centre for Scientific Culture" (Erice, 23–30 septembre 1994)*, edited by J. Hamesse, 657–76. Louvain-la-neuve: Federation internationale des instituts d'etudes medievales, 1996.
———. "Redécouverte et influence de manuscrits d'auteurs latins classiques au debut du quinzième siècle." *Revue d'histoire des textes* 17 (1987): 55–71.
Tiele, P. A. *Catalogus codicum manu scriptorum bibliothecae universitatis Rheno-Trajectinae*. 2 vols. Utrecht: Typis Kemink et fil., 1887–1909.
Tilley, A. "Greek Studies in England in the Early Sixteenth Century." *English Historical Review* 53 (1938): 221–39, 438–56.
Todd, R. B. "Baltasar Meliavacca, Andronicus Callistus, and the Greek Aristotelian Commentators in Fifteenth-Century Italy." *Italia medioevale e umanistica* 37 (1994): 62–75.
Trapp, J. B. "Vitelli, Cornelio (d. in or before 1554)." In *Oxford Dictionary of National Biography*, vol. 56, edited by H. C. G. Matthew and B. Harrison, 564–65. Oxford: Oxford University Press, 2004.
Travi, E. *Pietro Bembo: Lettere*. 4 vols. Bologna: Commissione per i testi di lingua, 1987–93.

Turner, E. "Jean Guinther d'Andernach (1505–1574): Son nom, son âge, le temps de ses études à Paris, ses titres, ses ouvrages." *Gazette hebdomadaire de médecine et de chirurgie* 18 (1881): 425–34, 441–48, 505–16.

Turyn, A. *Studies in the Manuscript Tradition of the Tragedies of Sophocles*. Urbana: University of Illinois Press, 1952.

Ullman, B. L. "Chrysoloras' Two Letters to Coluccio Salutati." In *Studies in the Italian Renaissance*, 2nd ed., edited by B. L. Ullman, 279–83. Rome: Edizioni di storia e letteratura, 1973.

———. *The Humanism of Coluccio Salutati*. Padua: Antenore, 1963.

Ullman, B. L., and P. A. Stadter. *The Public Library of Renaissance Florence: Niccolò Niccoli, Cosimo de' Medici and the Library of San Marco*. Padua: Antenore, 1972.

Urbano Bolzanio. *Urbani Bolzanii Bellunensis grammaticae institutiones in graecam linguam ultima ipsius censura editioneque probatae. Ac post longam suppressionem tandem in lucem emissae. Addito indice rerum necessariarum locupletissimo*. Venice: Apud haeredes P. Rabani et socios, 1545.

Vacant, A., E. Mangenot, and E. Amann, eds. *Dictionnaire de théologie catholique: contenant l'exposé des doctrines de la théologie catholique, leurs preuves et leur histoire*. 17 vols. Paris: Letouzey et Ane, 1923–72.

Van der Laan, A., and F. Akkerman, eds. *Rudolf Agricola: Letters*. Assen: Royal Van Gorcum, 2002.

Van Heck, A., ed. *Enee Silvii Piccolominei postea Pii PP. II De viris illustribus*. Vatican City: Bibliotheca apostolica vaticana, 1991.

Van Iseghem, A. F. *Biographie de Thierry Martens d'Alost, premier imprimeur de la Belgique, suivie de la bibliographie de ses éditions*. Malines: P. J. Hanicq, 1852.

Veissière, M. "Une dédicace de Jean Chéradame à Guillaume Briçonnet (1528)." *Bibliothèque d'humanisme et renaissance* 53 (1991): 397–403.

Vernet, M. "Les manuscrits grecs de Jean de Raguse (†1443)." *Basler Zeitschrift für Geschichte und Altertumskunde* 61 (1961): 75–108.

Vian, F. *Histoire de la tradition manuscrite de Quinte de Smyrne*. Paris: Presses universitaires de France, 1959.

———. "Leodrisio Crivelli traducteur des *Argonautiques orphiques*." *Revue d'histoire des textes* 16 (1986): 63–82.

———. *Quintus de Smyrne, La suite d'Homère*. 3 vols. Paris: Les Belles Lettres, 1963–69.

———. "La tradition manuscrite des 'Argonautiques orphiques.'" *Revue d'histoire des textes* 9 (1979): 1–46.

Viti, P. "Decembrio, Pier Candido." *Dizionario biografico degli italiani* 33 (1987): 488–98.

Walz, C., ed. *Rhetores Graeci ex codicibus Florentinis, Mediolanensibus, Monacensibus, Neapolitanis, Parisiensibus, Romanis, Venetis, Taurinensibus et Vindobonensibus*. 9 vols. Stuttgart: Sumptibus J. G. Cottae, 1832–36.

Ward, G. R. M. *The Foundation Statutes of Bishop Fox for Corpus Christi College in the University of Oxford A.D. 1517*. London: Longman, Brown and Green, 1843.

Waszink, J. H., ed. *Euripidis Hecuba et Iphigenia latinae factae Erasmo interprete*, in *Opera omnia Desiderii Erasmi Roterodami recognita et adnotatione critica instructa notisque illustrata*, ord. 1, vol. 1, 193–359. Amsterdam: North-Holland, 1969.

Weiss, R. "Gli inizi dello studio del greco a Firenze." In *Medieval and Humanist Greek: Collected Essays*, edited by R. Weiss, 227–54. Padua: Antenore, 1977.

———. *Humanism in England during the Fifteenth Century*. 3rd ed. Oxford: Blackwell, 1967.

———. "Iacopo Angeli da Scarperia (c. 1360–1410–11)." In *Medieval and Humanist Greek: Collected Essays*, edited by R. Weiss, 255–77. Padua: Antenore, 1977. First published in *Medioevo e rinascimento: studi in onore di Bruno Nardi*. 2 vols. Florence: G. C. Sansoni, 1955, 2: 803–17.

———. "Lo studio di Plutarco nel trecento." In *Medieval and Humanist Greek: Collected Essays*, edited by R. Weiss, 204–26. Padua: Antenore, 1977. First published in *La Parola del Passato* 32 (1953) 321–42.

West, M. L. "The Medieval and Renaissance Manuscripts of Hesiod's *Theogony*." *Classical Quarterly* 14 (1964): 165–89.

Wetzel, R., H. Scheible, W. Thüringer, C. Mundhenk, and R. Wartenberg, eds. *Melanchthons Briefwechsel*. 10 vols. Stuttgart: Frommann-Holzboog, 1991–2009.

Wiesner, J., and U. Victor. "Griechische Schreiber der Renaissance." *Rivista di studi bizantini e neoellenici* 8–9 (1971–72): 51–66.

Williams, N. *Chronology of the Expanding World, 1492–1762*. London: Barrie and Rockliff, 1969.

Wilson, N. G. "The Book Trade in Venice ca. 1400–1515." In *Venezia, centro di mediazione tra Oriente e Occidente (secoli XV-XVI): aspetti e problemi*, vol. 2, edited by H. G. Beck, M. Manoussacas, and A. Pertusi, 381–97. Florence: L. S. Olschki, 1977.

———. "Erasmus as a Translator of Euripides: Supplementary Notes." *Antike und Abendland* 18 (1973): 87–8.

———. *From Byzantium to Italy: Greek Studies in the Italian Renaissance*. London: Duckworth, 1992.

———. "Greek Grammars." In *Manuscripts at Oxford: An Exhibition in Memory of Richard William Hunt (1908–1979)*, edited by A. C. de la Mare and B. C. Barker-Benfield, 77–78. Oxford: Bodleian Library, 1980.

———. "The Libraries of the Byzantine World." *Greek, Roman and Byzantine Studies* 8 (1967): 53–80.

———. "On the Transmission of the Greek Lexica." *Greek, Roman and Byzantine Studies* 23 (1982): 369–75.

———. *Scholars of Byzantium*. London: Duckworth, 1983.

———. "Vettor Fausto, Professor of Greek and Naval Architect." In *The Uses of Greek and Latin: Historical Essays*, edited by A. C. Dionisotti, A. Grafton, and J. Kraye, 89–96. London: Warburg Institute, 1988.

Woodward, W. H. *Vittorino da Feltre and Other Humanist Educators: Essays and Versions*. Cambridge: Cambridge University Press, 1905.

Woolfson, J. "Croke, Richard (1489–1558)." In *Oxford Dictionary of National Biography*, vol. 14, edited by H. C. G. Matthew and B. Harrison, 265–67. Oxford: Oxford University Press, 2004.

Wuttke, D. "Zur griechischen Grammatik des Konrad Celtis." In *Silvae: Festschrift für Ernst Zinn*, edited by M. von Albrecht and E. Heck, 289–303. Tübingen: M. Niemayer, 1970.

Zamponi, S. "Un ignoto compendio sozomeniano degli «Erotemata» di Manuele Crisolora (Il ms. c 74 dell'Archivio Capitolare di Pistoia)." *Rinascimento* 18 (1978): 251–70.

Zippel, G. "Carlo Marsuppini da Arezzo: notizie bibliografiche." In *Storia e cultura del rinascimento italiano*, G. Zippel, 198–214. Padua: Antenore, 1979.

Zorzi, N. "I Crisolora: personaggi e libri." In *Manuele Crisolora e il ritorno del greco in occidente: Atti del convegno internazionale (Napoli, 26–29 giugno 1997)*, edited by R. Maisano and A. Rollo, 87–131. Naples: Istituto universitario orientale, 2002.

Index

Asterisks mark pages in which the figure in question is discussed at length.

A

Acciaiuoli, Donato, 26, 100, 175, 214
Accolti, Benedetto, 39
Adamus, M., 226
Aedicollius, Joannes, 131
Aedicollius, Servatius, 85
Aelius Dionysius, 122
Aemilius, Paulus, 84
Aeschines, 94, 95, 211, 212
Aeschylus, 105, 113, 217, 221, 222, 223
Aesop, 52, *79–80, 81, 85, 88, 189, 192, 199, 200, 202
Agricola, Hendrik, 11, 168
Agricola, Rudolf, 11, 74, 84, 87, 113, 195, 203, 205, 217, 231
Albert, bishop of Magdeburg, 22, 136
Alberto da Sarteano, 186
Alcalá, 11, 35, 78, 92, 95
Aldine Appendix, 74, 78, 121, 122, 123, 124, 126, 131, 133, 134, 138, 142, 143, 148, 150
Aldus. *See* Manutius
Aleandro, Girolamo (Aleander), 6, 10, 11, 20, 21, 22, 31, 42, 43, 47, 67, 74, 77, 78, 86, 87, 90, 91, 97, 98, 99, 102, 103, 130, 131, 132, 134, 135, 136, 137, 138, 139, 140, 142, 143, 144, 147, 148, 149, 150, 152, 153, 157, 182, 206, 215, 216, 219, 220
Alexander VI (pope), 79
Alexander of Aphrodisias, 163
Alexios, 170
Alfonso of Aragon, 92, 212, 219
Aliotus, Baltasar (Alioto), 208
Aloysius Alamannus, 133, 138
Amaseo, Girolamo, 3, 30, 35, 71, 83, 89, 105, 121, 163, 214, 228
Amaseo, Gregorio, 89
Ambrogio of Reggio, 123, 156
Amerot, Adrien, 11, *47–48, 144

Amidani, Giovanni Andrea, 167
Amidani, Zenone, 167
Ammonius grammaticus, 41, 67, 155, 156, 157, 158, 159, 160, 161, 162, 166
Amoenus, Gervasius, 23
Amorbach, Basil, 221
Amorbach, Boniface, 91, 207
Amorbach, Bruno, 68, 87, 91, 207
Amorbach, Johann, 20
Andelou, Joannes de, 42
Andronicus, Livius, 80
Anellus, Georgius, 42
Angeli, Jacopo, 6, 8, 55, 99, 165, 232
Anselmi, Giorgio, 105
Anshelm, Thomas, 40, 42, 45, 74, 91, 92, 93, 95, 182, 195
Antigone, daughter of Humphrey Duke of Gloucester, 107, 224
Antinori, Carlo, 83, 202
Antonio de Lebrixa, 17
Antonio di Romagno, 205
Antwerp, 85
Aperbach, Peter, 207
Aphthonius, 14
Apollonius Dyscolus, 3, 4, 15, 17, 19, 20, 25, 41, 52, 122, 134, 164, 181
Apollonius of Rhodes, *109–10, 202, 217, 218, 226, 227, 228
Apostolides. *See* Apostolis, Arsenius
Apostolis, Arsenius (Aristoboulos), 122, 224, 227
Apostolis, Michael, 15, 16, 56, 59, 64, 78, 112, 113, 187, 190, 193, 197, 229, 230
Appian of Alexandria, 27
Aquinas, Thomas, 169
Aragazzi, Bartolomeo, 100, 216
Aratus of Soloi, 50, 166, 226, 227
Arcadius of Antiocheia, 5

Argino da Basseto, 17, 171
Argyropoulos, Joannes, 26, 32, 59, 78, 100, 107, 175, 179, 197, 224
Aristeas, Letter of, 200
Aristides, 97, 216, 217
Aristophanes, 83, *88–91, 92, 104, 186, 191, 201, 207, 208, 209, 217, 222, 225
Aristotle, 14, 33, 36, 67, 68, 90, 100, 101, 157, 163, 191, 208
Arrian of Nicomedia, 169
Asulanus, Franciscus, 151, 161
Athens, 34
Athos, 14
Atrapes, Leo, 186
Atumano, Simon, 81, 101, 104, 106, 215, 221, 223
Aubanus, Gregorius Coelius, 136, 137
Augsburg, 44
Augustinus, Aurelius (saint), 80, 196
Aurea verba, 74, *77–79, 85, 94, 121, 123, 124, 125, 126, 127, 129, 130, 131, 134, 140, 142, 145, 149, 151, 197, 198, 219
Aurelio, Marco, 109, 227
Aurispa, Giovanni, 4, 14, 56, 58, 79, 92, 104, 106, 108, 109, 110, 188, 198, 209, 211, 213, 223, 225, 226, 228
Ausonius, 22, 73, 195
Avanzi, Girolamo, 172
Avignon, 51, 101, 104

B

Bacon, Roger, 8, 32, 34, 75
Bade (Badius), Josse, 98, 105, 106, 222
Baiophoros, George, 5, 165
Barbaro, Ermolao, 58, 60, 79, 94, 103, 107, 110, 172, 199, 223, 227
Barbaro, Francesco, 5, 63, 115, 166
Bardella, Bartolomeo, 164, 170, 230
Bardellone, Jacopo, 61, 158, 160
Bartolomeo of Capo d'Istria, 189
Bartolomeo of Sulmona, 27, 176
Barzizza, Guiniforte, 96
Basellius, Nicolaus, 179
Basil of Caesarea, 197, 210
Basinio da Parma, 106, 109, 226
Basle, 12, 23, 31, 39, 44, 45, 49, 50, 63, 66, 67, 68, 69, 70, 84, 87, 91, 92, 97, 99, 102, 109, 111, 119, 172, 179, 182, 185, 204
Bebel, Johann, 153
Beheym, Laurentius, 207
Bembo, Pietro, 30, 56, 108, 121
Benedetti, Alessandro, 59
Benigno, Cornelio, 226
Benna, Cristoforo, 64

Bensrott, Nicholas, 222
Bentivolus, Antonius, 76
Bérault, Nicholas, 51, 86, 87, 159, 186, 205
Berner, Thomas, 128
Beroaldo, Filippo, 10, 34, 167
Berselius, Paschasius, 47, 184, 185
Bertoldo, 86, 205
Bessarion (Cardinal), 1, 15, 56, 58, 59, 60, 77, 84, 107, 109, 112, 113, 170, 171, 201, 210, 211, 226, 227, 229
Birago, Lampugnino, 26, 214, 215
Bisner, Baltasar, 42
Bissoli, Giovanni, 189
Boccaccio, Giovanni, 81, 106
Bodianus (Fracantius), Franciscus Vitalis, 107, 212, 224
Boerio, Giovanni, 86, 96, 205, 206, 213
Boethius, Anicius Manlius Severinus, 76
Bologna, 10, 15, 17, 18, 19, 20, 34, 59, 76, 82, 84, 101, 103, 105, 106, 111, 113, 167, 188, 190, 202, 222, 230, 231
Bolzanio, Urbano, 1, 10, 11, 20, 22, 24, 31, 34, *36–40, 41, 46, 47, 49, 52, 53, 82, 108, 123, 129, 137, 146, 149, 178, 180, 181, 195, 225
Bombasio, Paulo, 83
Bonaccorso Pisano, 18, 32, 64, 65, 79, 80, 96, 102, 103, 120, 121, 155, 156, 199
Bonaciolus, Ludovicus, 127
Bonamico, Lazzaro, 18, 171, 173
Boninsegna, G., 214
Boninus, Euphrosinus, 133, 134, 138, 219
Bonominus, Domenico, 213
Borso d'Este, 218
Botzheim, Johann, 44, 145
Boucher, Charles, 49, 150
Braccio, Gabriele, 189
Bracellus, Antonius, 155
Brachet, Charles, 86, 206
Bradyglossus, Laurentius Martinus, 133
Bravus, Petrus, 18, 171, 172
Brenta, Andrea, 89, 90, 208
Brescia, 61, 85
Briçonnet, Guillaume, 95
Brie, Germain de, 196
Brocar, Arnao, 132
Bruges, 87
Brugnolo, Carlo, 200
Bruni, Leonardo, 8, 82, 88, 92, 94, 99, 100, 108, 201, 207, 209, 211, 212, 214, 216, 232
Brutus, Marcus Junius, 189
Budé, Guillaume, xiii, 5, 19, 25, 35, 59, 70, 77, 78, 84, 86, 95, 98, 163, 196, 197, 203, 212

Bullock, Henry, 20, 86, 173
Bünau, Heinrich von, 34
Burer, Albert, 221
Buschius, Hermannus, 160
Byzantium. *See* Constantinople

C

Caesar, Gaius Julius, 196
Caesar Aragonius, 128, 139
Caesarius, Joannes, 22, 23, 91, 137, 138, 140, 141, 144, 148, 174
Calabria, 15, 28
Calcagnini, Celio (Caelius Calcagninus), 86, 127
Calcagnini, Tomaso, 127
Calco, Bartolomeo, 27, 80
Calderini, Domizio, 109
Calecas, Manuel, *6-7, 8, 9
Calenzio, Elisio, 85, 204
Calfurnio, Giovanni, 7, 10, 20, 59, 60, 83, 86, 98, 165, 167, 188, 191, 200, 215
Callierges, Zacharias, 59, 60, 104, 109, 110, 158, 185, 191, 220, 226, 227
Callimachus of Cyrene, 64, 194, 225
Callistratus, 142
Callistus, Andronicus, 4, 13, 15, 16, 17, 18, 19, 35, 58, 64-65, 78, 82, 85, 92, 94, 101, 102, 103, 104, 106, 108, 109, 110, 113, 164, 170, 171, 172, 194, 197, 202, 210, 212, 220, 221, 223, 224, 225, 227, 230
Calofrenas, George, 56, 59, 187, 189
Calpurnius Siculus, 218
Camariotes, Matthaeus, *13-14, 169
Cambridge, 20, 23, 59, 83, 86, 110, 175
Camerarius, Joachim, 52, 99, 154, 213, 216
Cammelli, Giuseppe, 7
Campano, Giovanni Antonio, 34, 103, 179, 219
Canale, Nicholas, 210
Candido, Pier, 107, 171, 196
Canstatt, Baltasar von, 128
Canterbury, 171
Capriolo, Elia, 58, 157, 189
Caradasius, Matthaeus, 49, 145
Carbone, Lodovico, 106
Carteromachus. *See* Forteguerri
Casaubon, Meric, 171
Cassarino, Antonio, 214, 215, 217
Cassiano, Jacopo, 221
Castellus, Petrus, 82, 201, 208, 219
Castelnau de Clermont-Ludève, François Guillaume de (Cardinal), 51, 150
Castiglione, Baldassare, 35

Castreno, Demetrio, 26, 176, 213
Castrifrancanus, Albertus, 36, 180
Cataneus, Joannes Maria, 156
Celtis, Conrad, *33-34, 73, 79, 84, 123, 199, 202, 203
Ceporinus, Jacobus, *49-50, 51, 53, 102, 109, 146, 147, 152, 154, 185, 225
Ceratinus, Jacobus, 70, 119, 161
Cerdano, Antonio (Cardinal), 199
Cesarini, Giuliano (Cardinal), 76
Ceva, Niccolò, 216
Chalcondyles, Basilio, 83
Chalcondyles, Demetrius, 1, 2, 9, 10, 15, 16, 18, 25, 31, *34-36, 37, 56, 57, 71, 78, 82, 83, 85, 95, 96, 101, 102, 105, 107, 109, 113, 121, 128, 132, 133, 138, 139, 146, 151, 156, 167, 168, 170, 172, 177, 179, 180, 198, 202, 204, 212, 213, 218, 219, 224, 228
Chalcondyles, Ptolemy, 35
Chalcondyles, Theophilus-Tryphon, 18
Chambellan, David, 196
Chelius, Joannes, 42
Chéradame, Jean, 10, *48-49, 95, 145, 148, 150, 152, 160, 161, 162, 186, 212
Chesserius (Keserü), Michael, 213
Chigi, Agostino, 225
Chios, 104, 106
Choeroboscos, Georgios, 28, 69, 122, 160, 161, 162, 166, 181
Chrysococces, George, 78, 92, 197, 210, 211, 213
Chrysoloras, John, 109, 217
Chrysoloras, Manuel, xii, 2, 6, *7-12, 13, 14, 15, 16, 17, 18, 20, 21, 22, 26, 27, 28, 29, 31, 32, 33, 34, 35, 36, 37, 41, 42, 43, 45, 47, 48, 49, 50, 55, 68, 71, 75, 76, 77, 78, 81, 82, 85, 86, 88, 89, 92, 94, 97, 99, 100, 116, 120, 121, 122, 123, 125, 126, 127, 128, 129, 132, 133, 136, 137, 138, 139, 146, 149, 150, 153, 158, 165, 166, 167, 168, 180, 182, 192, 205, 206, 211, 214, 216, 220
Chrysostom, John, 75
Ciati, Lorenzo, 110, 228
Cicero, Marcus Tullius, 76, 77, 92, 94, 196, 211, 228
Cincio Romano, 100, 215, 216, 217
Città di Castello, 56
Clario, Daniel, 20, 58, 95
Claudius (Roman Emperor), 80
Clénard, Nicolas, xii, 116, 150, 232
Clermont, François de. *See* Castelnau
Codro. *See* Urceo

262   Index

Colluthus, 1
Colet, John, 143
Colocci, Angelo, 2, 84, 163, 228
Cologne, 22, 49, 91, 174
Commodus (Roman Emperor), 58
Comparini, Bartolomeo, 173, 191
Constance, 100, 217
Constantinople, 1, 4, 5, 6, 7, 8, 12, 13, 14, 15, 26, 55, 56, 58, 63, 76, 86, 88, 92, 94, 104, 106, 108, 110, 164, 165, 169, 180, 208, 210, 211, 230
Contarini, Gasparo, 36
Contoblacas, Andronicus, 31, 32, 172, 178, 179
Contrario, Andrea, 76
Cop, Guillaume, 24
Coppola, Francesco, 75, 115
Corbinelli, Antonio, 8, 63, 94, 101, 104, 106, 108, 110, 209, 211, 225, 232
Corderius, Petrus, 126
Corfu, 170
Corigliano, 1, 59
Corpus Christi College, Oxford, 21, 174
Correr, Gregorio, 79, 199
Corsi, Giovanni, 215
Cosmas of Trebizond, 201
Cospo, Angelo, 194
Courthardy, Pierre de, 215
Crastoni, Giovanni, 30, 64, 65, 76, 120, 155, 194
Cratander, Andreas, 45, 62, 84, 142, 143, 145, 148, 153, 159, 204
Cremona, 18
Crete, 1, 56, 59, 110, 224
Crivelli, Leodrisio, 27, 64, 111, 193, 229
Croke, Richard, 6, 22, 23, 24, 32, 52, 53, 73, 91, 99, 136, 137, 143, 144, 146, 154, 174, 175, 195, 216
Cruceius, Jacobus, 64, 194
Cuno, Johann, 13, 20, 32, 68, 87, 91, 105, 107, 169, 207, 209
Curio, Valentine, 23, 24, 39, 49, 68, 69, 70, 87, 146, 147, 148, 154, 159, 160, 162
Cusanus, Nicolaus, 63
Cydones, Demetrius, 165, 209
Cyprus, 187
Cyriaco of Ancona, 106, 165, 223
Cyrus the Great, 92

D

Damilas, Demetrius, 59, 78, 120, 171, 190, 197, 220
Danès, Pierre, 36, 151
Dati, Agostino, 78
Debrillacus, Claudius, 130

Decembrio, Pier Candido, 8, 26, 77, 171
Decembrio, Uberto, 8, 100, 232
Deloinus, Franciscus, 145
Demetrius of Sparta, 10
Demosthenes, xii, 8, 72, *93–96, 99, 148, 157, 162, 166, 195, 202, 206, 211, 212, 213, 227, 228
Denglius, Johannes, 148
D'Étaples (Stapulensis), Faber, 215
Deventer, 2, 74, 195
Dictys Cretensis, 56, 111
Dieler, Stephan, 42, 182
Dietrich, Veit, 179
Dinhard, 49
Diogenes Laertius, 28, 177
Dionysius of Halicarnassus, 27
Dionysius Periegetes, 50, 223, 225
Dionysius Thrax, 5, 7, 8, 13, 165, 166
Disticha Catonis, 77, 78, 88, 130, 133, 137, 138, 139, 197, 219
Donà, Pietro, 205
Donato, Lodovico, 193, 196
Donatus, Aelius, 8, 214
Donos, Andreas, 78, 197
Doria, Bartolomeo, 129, 136
Ducas, Demetrius, 11, 35, 116, 133, 168, 216
Dürer, Albrecht, 57, 58, 59, 83, 86, 110, 209
Dursos, Alfonsus, 18, 171, 190

E

Edenberg, Lucas, 138, 141
Egkirch, Erasmus, 42
Egypt, 36
Emmanuel of Constantinople, 186
Emser, Hieronymus, 207
England, 19, 21, 76, 96, 107, 113
Epictetus, 85
Erasmus, 2, 11, 20, 21, 22, 23, 24, 36, 37, 38, 44, 51, 57, 58, 59, 61, 66, 68, 70, 74, 76, 77, 84, 85, 86, 87, 88, 91, 93, 94, 96, 97, 99, 105, 106, 115, 116, 128, 136, 137, 138, 140, 141, 143, 144, 146, 148, 149, 154, 161, 174, 180, 188, 189, 195, 203, 204, 206, 213, 214, 215, 222
Erfurt, 73, 74
Ergersheim, Martin, 42, 182
Ernestus, Johannes Augustus, 203
Estienne, Henri, 65
Eterno, J., 162
Eton, 116
Etten, 22, 87
Etymologicum magnum, 41, 55, *58–59, 64, 156, 189, 191
Etymologicum parvum, 189

Euridice, 228
Euripides (Euripidis), *104–6, 115, 116, 167, 217, 221, 222, 223, 224, 225, 228
Eustathius, 69, 83, 122, 203
Exeter College, Oxford, 19

F
Faber, Wolfgang, 139
Faccino, Pontico, 212, 227
Fanuccio, Angelo, 157
Faraone, Francesco, 56, 116, 187
Farley, John, 76
Fausto, Vettor, 83, 102, 109, 111, 129, 149
Federigo Duke of Urbino, 193
Fenolleda, Arnau, 199
Fera, 26, 208
Ferdinand of Aragon (Ferrante), 27
Ferdinand of Castile, Naples, Aragon and Sicily, 51
Ferrara, 10, 12, 14, 15, 16, 19, 33, 41, 57, 58, 63, 66, 67, 68, 74, 82, 89, 92, 94, 96, 100, 102, 104, 106, 112, 116, 169, 188, 200, 208, 219, 221, 230, 231
Ferrarius, Franciscus, 64, 155
Feruffini, Domenico, 176
Feruffini, Filippo, 27, 176
Feruffini, Giovanni, 176
Ficino, Marsilio, 14, 63, 82, 100, 101, 110, 116, 169, 190, 228
Filelfo, Francesco, 4, 15, 17, 26, 27, 56, 58, 59, 61, 64, 82, 92, 94, 101, 102, 104, 105, 106, 108, 109, 110, 111, 164, 167, 169, 170, 171, 176, 186, 188, 189, 190, 191, 193, 201, 209, 210, 211, 217, 218, 219, 221, 223, 225, 226, 228, 229
Filelfo, Gian Mario, 111
Filetico, Martino, 103, 213, 219, 220
Finus, Daniel, 157
Fisher, John, 140
Flaminio, Giovanni Antonio, 36
Florence, 3, 4, 5, 6, 7, 8, 9, 10, 12, 13, 14, 18, 26, 30, 32, 34, 35, 36, 55, 56, 58, 59, 60, 61, 63, 64, 77, 81, 82, 83, 85, 86, 89, 92, 94, 95, 96, 98, 99, 100, 101, 102, 103, 104, 105, 106, 107, 108, 109, 110, 111, 113, 115, 172, 175, 177, 179, 191, 211, 213, 217, 220, 223, 224, 227
Fonzio, Bartolomeo, 18, 79, 82, 108, 109–10, 198, 227
Forstmaister, Gaspar, 128
Forteguerri, Scipione, 1, 2, 19, 20, 36, 57, 60, 84, 86, 95, 102, 107, 110, 122, 124, 127, 129, 135, 149, 156, 157, 159, 160, 163, 173, 188, 206, 219, 228
Fox, Richard, 21

Fracantius. *See* Bodianus
France, 5, 10, 18, 57, 69, 73, 76, 84, 85, 86, 90, 106, 108, 113, 218
Francesco da Castiglione, 63, 82, 175, 228
Francinus, Antonius, 152, 159
François of Valois, 105, 106, 126, 160
Frankfurt, 226
Free, John, 104, 107, 221
Froben, Johann, 44, 66, 68, 88, 91, 119, 135, 138, 140, 141, 143, 146, 174, 195
Froschauer, Christopher, 50, 152
Fuscus, Thomas, 127

G
Gabrieli, Angelo, 30, 56, 121, 124, 130, 135
Gaeta, 79
Galateo of Lecce, 1
Gale, Thomas, 171
Galiziotes, Andronicus, 13, 101, 201
Gallus, A., 148
Gallus, Jodocus, 32
Ganay, Germain de, 215
Garatone, Cristoforo, 5, 56
Gast, Robertus du, 174
Gaza, Theodore, 2, 4, 10, 11, *14–25, 30, 31, 32, 33, 35, 36, 37, 39, 41, 42, 43, 46, 47, 49, 50, 52, 53, 58, 59, 67, 68, 74, 77, 80, 82, 84, 86, 87, 88, 89, 90, 91, 92, 94, 96, 97, 100, 104, 106, 113, 119, 122, 127, 128, 131, 132, 133, 136, 137, 138, 139, 140, 141, 142, 143, 144, 145, 146, 147, 148, 149, 150, 151, 152, 153, 154, 157, 162, 165, 169, 170, 171, 172, 173, 174, 178, 180, 181, 183, 190, 191, 194, 196, 200, 201, 210, 221
Gebweiler, Hieronymus, 42, 139, 182
Gellius, Aulus, 98
George Alexandrou, 227
Georgenthal, 58, 59
George of Trebizond, 94, 108, 212
Georges d'Amboise, 57
Geraeander, Paulus, 142
Gerardo of Patras, 192, 200, 210, 213
Gerasinus of Byzantium, 175
Gerbel, Nicolaus, 128, 154, 228
Germany, 5, 11, 34, 40, 43, 46, 69, 73, 76, 80, 84, 87, 90, 102, 107, 109
Gesner, Conrad, 185
Gian Pietro da Lucca, 102, 164, 200, 207, 213, 217, 221, 226
Giovanelli, Francesco, 113
Giovanni of Ragusa (Cardinal), 63, 165, 192
Giovanni Stefano da Castiglione, 80
Giovio, Benedetto, 2

Girlando, Ercole, 25, 97, 153
Giunta (Junta), Bernardo, 134
Giunta (Junta), Filippo, 214
Giustiniani, Agostino, 24
Glareanus, Henricus, 22, 24, 39, 84, 149, 203
Gonzaga, Cecilia, 76
Gonzaga, Gian Francesco, 199
Gonzaga, Gian Lucido, 226
Gouda, 104
Gourmont, Gilles de, 10, 20, 21, 22, 31, 48, 49, 51, 67, 68, 69, 70, 73, 74, 88, 95, 97, 98–99, 103, 106, 119, 125, 126, 128, 129, 130, 131, 135, 136, 139, 140, 148, 158, 161, 194, 204, 206, 220
Grapheus, Joannes, 85
Gregoropoulos, Georgios, 56, 164, 187
Gregoropoulos, Joannes, 91, 156
Griffolini, Francesco, 205
Gritti, Andrea, 162, 180
Grocyn, William, 18, 19, 55, 172, 186
Grolierius, Joannes, 135
Grosseteste, Robert, 55, 76, 186
Grottaferrata, 15
Guarino, Battista, 9, 10, 15, 34, 62, 63, 75, 82, 167, 169, 214, 227
Guarino, Esopo, 79, 199
Guarino of Favera, 3, 59, 60, 70, 71–72, 83, 89, 122, 160, 191, 202
Guarino of Verona, 5, 7, 9, 10, 12, 18, 29, 32, 37, 41, 47, 55, 58, 79, 82, 86, 88, 89, 92, 96, 97, 98, 101, 104, 108, 109, 116, 120, 121, 127, 128, 139, 149, 165, 166, 167, 186, 192, 193, 199, 200, 205, 207, 209, 211, 213, 217, 219, 221, 226, 232
Guazzelli, Demetrio, 89
Guida, Johann, 42, 182
Guillard, Louis, 48, 145
Guillaume (abbot), 49, 150
Gupalatinus, Nicolaus, 170

H
Hachenborg, Paul, 124
Hadrian VI (pope), 51, 150, 185
Hagenau, 45, 52, 61, 87, 91, 93, 95, 109
Haliaenetus, Johannes, 128
Hallwiler, Hartmann, 45, 142, 143, 145, 146, 148, 153, 183
Hallwiler, Johann Rudolf, 183
Harpocration, Valerius, 55, *59–60, 157, 162, 190
Hedius, Caspar, 204
Hegius, Alexander, 74
Heidelberg, 32, 44, 45, 109, 226
Hephaestion, 152, 224

Heresbach, Conrad, 23, 24, 154
Hermann (count of Neuenahr), 22, 110
Hermogenes of Tarsus, 14, 169, 227
Hermonymus, George, 5, 18, 19, 31, 32, 65, 75, 76, 77, 78, 80, 86, 95, 98, 104, 108, 113, 170, 172, 175, 179, 194, 198, 212, 215, 216, 222, 229, 231
Herodian, Aelius, 3, 4, 5, 19, 28, 37, 69, 122, 122, 128, 133, 137, 138, 139, 160, 161, 162, 164
Hesiod, 49, 71, *100–102, 109, 147, 152, 167, 197, 198, 217, 218, 219, 221, 223, 225
Hesychius of Alexandria, 55, *61, 68–69, 158, 159, 160, 191
Hierocles, 79, 198
Hilarion of Verona, 59, 190
Hiltebrant, Johann, 128
Hody, Humphrey, 16
Homer, 26, 30, 39, 51, 52, 55, 58, 59, 76, *80–85, 89, 104, 109, 111, 134, 141, 144, 145, 147, 150, 151, 152, 153, 161, 175, 187, 189, 200, 201, 202, 203, 212, 217, 220, 225, 230, 231
Hopylius, Georgius, 49, 145
Horman, William, 232
Hummelberg, Michael, 33, 92, 93, 168, 207, 220, 228
Humphrey, Duke of Gloucester, 107
Hungary, 171
Hyperides, 190
Hypselas, Petrus, 78, 197
Hythlodaeus, Raphael, 31

I
Ialinas, Michael, 63
Ilias latina, 80, 81, 200
Ingolstadt, 34, 49, 79, 199
Isidore of Kiev, 106, 205, 209
Isocrates, 35, 42, 77, *96–97, 121, 126, 128, 158, 173, 206, 213, 214, 222
Italy, 6, 7, 8, 11, 13, 14, 16, 19, 33, 34, 38, 43, 55, 58, 69, 78, 82, 86, 98, 101, 102, 104, 108, 110, 218

J
Joannes, scribe, 187
Joannes de Pisnicze, 34
Joannes de Romano, 56
Joannes Philoponus, 5, 69, 122, 130, 145, 146, 159, 160, 161, 162, 194
John of Orléans, 10, 125
John XXIII (pope), 216
Junta. *See* Giunta

K

Karabelos, Phanourios, 63
Kierher, 220
Knoblouch, Johann, 42, 149, 219
Koroni, 187
Kracow, 31
Kress, Anton, 209, 228
Kuchel, Johann, 146

L

Labeo, Attius, 80
Lamparter, Gregory, 128, 179
Lapo da Castiglionchio, 205
Lascaris, Constantine, 1, 2, 3, 4, 5, 9, 10, 11, 15, 16, 20, 21, 23, 24, *26–31, 34, 35, 36, 37, 38, 41, 45, 56, 58, 59, 64, 65, 68, 74, 77, 78, 79, 80, 82, 84, 86, 89, 101, 102, 103, 104, 108, 109, 110, 111, 112, 113, 120, 121, 123, 130, 134, 135, 145, 146, 160, 162, 163, 164, 165, 167, 170, 172, 175, 176, 177, 178, 180, 181, 187, 193, 195, 198, 201, 208, 218, 219, 225, 229, 230, 231
Lascaris, Janus, 1, 57, 59, 60, 81, 83, 84, 94, 97, 105, 107, 108, 110, 173, 186, 188, 191, 203, 206, 216, 224, 228, 229
Lazarus, scribe, 178
Lecapenus, Georgius, 134, 143, 151, 152, 171
Lefèvre, Denys, 20, 174
Legrand, Émile, xii
Leipzig, 22, 32, 73, 91, 99, 109
Lemp, Andreas, 128
Lemp, Jakob, 128
Leo X (pope), 36, 43, 104, 158, 160, 183, 185, 220
Libanius, 228
Liège, 51, 52
Ligarius, Antonius, 49, 145
Ligarius, Joannes, 49, 145
Lily, William, 143
Linacre, Thomas, 18, 19, 159, 172
Lippi, Lorenzo, 101, 205, 218, 223
Locher, Jacob, 79
Löffelholtz, Johann, 167, 204
Lombardy, 8
London, 18, 65, 113, 231
Lonicer, Joannes, 109
Lorenzi, Giovanni, 214, 215
Loschi, Antonio, 81
Louber, Jacob, 179
Louis XII of France, 57, 187
Louvain, 11, 19, 21, 22, 23, 47, 87, 91, 93, 95, 97, 100, 104, 106, 195, 211
Lucanus, Marcus Annaeus, 191
Lucian of Samosata, 42, 44, *85–88, 91, 99, 127, 147, 148, 150, 152, 153, 154, 173, 182, 205, 206, 207, 228
Lucius, Claudius, 150
Luphdich, Johann, 128
Luscinius. *See* Nachtgall
Luther, Martin, 221
Lycophron, 223, 225
Lygizos, Michael, 56, 64, 78, 187, 193, 197, 209

M

Maciochus (Mazochius), Joannes, 127, 157
Madrid, 5, 26, 28
Magdalen College, Oxford, 172
Magister, Thomas, 158, 159, 161, 162, 185, 190
Main, Guillaume du, 70, 160
Mainente, Scipione, 205
Mainerius, Alvisius, 166
Malatesta, Federico, 153
Malatesta Novello, Domenico, 210
Malpaghini, Giovanni, 81
Manetti, Giannozzo, 64, 82, 92, 100, 101, 108, 109, 110, 193, 201, 209, 217, 220, 225, 226
Mangio, Benedetto, 189
Manius, L., 156
Mantua, 5, 14, 55, 82, 88, 89, 109, 226, 230
Manuel, pupil of C. Lascaris, 111, 229
Manutius, Aldus, 1, 2, 10, 11, 12, 19, 20, 23, 30, 31, *33, 34, 36, 37, 38, 41, 57, 58, 59, 60, 61, 65, 66, 67, 68, 73, 74, 83, 90, 95, 103, 105, 107, 110, 115, 116, 119, 121, 122, 123, 124, 126, 128, 129, 130, 131, 133, 134, 135, 137, 138, 139, 140, 142, 143, 146, 148, 150, 156, 157, 158, 160, 173, 178, 181, 188, 191, 206, 208, 212, 219, 224, 228
Maraschi, Giovanni Francesco, 89
Marcello, Pietro, 205
Marck, Antoine de la, 47, 51, 144, 153
Marinus, Jacobus, 213
Marrasio, Giovanni, 204
Marsiboius, Guilelmo, 159
Marsuppini, Carlo, 58, 64, 85, 201, 204
Martellus, Ludovicus, 134
Martens, Thierry, 11, 21, 47, 85, 87, 91, 95, 100, 104, 106, 140, 174, 204, 207
Martínez-Manzano, Teresa, 28
Martinozzi, Niccolò, 211
Marullus, Michael, 77
Matius, Gnaeus, 80
Maurus, Bernhard, 45, 141, 184
Medici, Giovanni de', 36
Medici, Giulio de' (Cardinal), 160

Medici, Lorenzo de', 18, 109, 202, 212
Medici, Lorenzo di Piero de', 167
Medici, Piero de', 18, 80, 82, 83, 89, 96, 122, 208
Mela, Philippus, 142
Melanchthon, Philip, 32, 37, 42, 44, *45–47, 51, 72, 74, 84, 85, 87, 91, 95, 96, 98, 99, 102, 104, 109, 141, 143, 145, 147, 150, 151, 152, 153, 154, 195, 197, 203, 205, 207, 213, 214
Melissopolitanus, Conrad, 42
Menander, 91
Merula, Giorgio, 17, 58, 63, 101, 107, 112, 113, 171, 172, 188, 217, 220, 223, 230
Messina, 1, 5, 13, 26, 27, 28, 29, 30, 35, 36, 56, 58, 59, 64, 77, 82, 101, 103, 111, 112, 113, 177, 178, 180, 201, 208, 218, 219, 225, 230, 231
Metrodorus, 130
Metzler, Johann, *52–53, 98, 154
Miani, Pietro, 63, 209
Michael the Notary, 63, 192, 199
Michelozzi, Niccolò, 208
Milan, 1, 4, 5, 9, 10, 14, 16, 18, 19, 26, 27, 28, 29, 35, 56, 57, 58, 59, 64, 73, 76, 78, 80, 81, 82, 83, 96, 100, 101, 102, 103, 107, 108, 109, 110, 111, 112, 113, 164, 172, 176, 177, 179, 187, 189, 213, 214, 218, 225, 230
Modena, 66
Molther, Menrad, 109, 226
Mombrizio, Bonino, 27, 102, 218
More, Thomas, 23, 31, 61, 86
Morrhius, Gerardus, 48
Moschopoulos, Manuel, 5, 7, 8, 13, 14, 28, 34, 35, 78, 101, 102, 108, 121, 134, 151, 152, 161, 164, 165, 171, 181, 190, 218
Moschus, Demetrius, 60, 78, 110, 167, 191, 198, 227
Moschus, George, 60
Moschus of Syracuse, 103, 120, 219
Mosellanus, Petrus, 22, 91, 97, 174
Motta, Antonius, 156, 187
Muriel, Jacobo Ximenes, 5
Musurus, Jacques, 203
Musurus, Marcus, 11, 19, 20, 33, 36, 60, 61, 90, 96, 98, 103, 107, 129, 135, 156, 158, 173, 190, 191, 203, 208, 220, 224

N
Nachtgall, Ottomar, 11, *42–44, 51, 87, 97, 102, 116, 133, 139, 144, 145, 147, 182, 183, 197, 207, 213, 219
Naples, 15, 27, 28, 29, 58, 113, 177, 218, 226

Navagero, Andrea, 109
Negri, Stefano, 78, 109
Nepos, Cornelius, 214
Nepos, Jacobus, 204
Nerli, Bernardo, 18, 172
Nervet, Jean, 161
New Testament, 50, 57, 58, 61, 62, *75–76, 105, 115, 116, 119, 132, 158, 189, 190, 196
Nicander of Colophon, 228
Niccoli, Niccolò, 5, 58, 94, 101, 104, 106, 109, 188, 211, 216, 223, 227
Niccolò della Luna, 63, 64, 193
Nicholas, John, 51, 151
Nicholas V (pope), 15, 16, 56, 79, 107
Nicolaus of 's-Hertogenbosch (Buschoducensis), 47, 184
Niger, Antonius, 53
Nonnus of Panopolis, 188, 217, 218, 226
Nountallius, Andreas, 149
Novara, 57
Novenianus, Philippus, 146
Nuñez de Guzman, Hernan, 20, 35, 57, 59, 110, 173, 180, 188, 190
Nuremberg, 16, 45, 87

O
Occo, Adolf, 77, 78, 80, 84, 87, 107, 108, 113, 197, 198, 201, 203, 209, 224, 231
Odasio, Lodovico, 98, 214, 215
Odoard, Jean, 49, 161
Oecolampadius, Joannes, *44–45, 46, 51, 62, 84, 142, 143, 145, 146, 148, 153, 183, 204
Ofterdingen, Johann, 128
Ognibene da Lonigo, 79, 191, 199
Oliverius of Lyons, 125
Oppian of Cilicia, 101, 201
Orbicius (Urbicius), 159, 161, 162
Orléans, 22, 32, 80, 194
Orsini, Fulvio, 211
Otranto, 1, 112
Ovid (Publius Ovdius Naso), 228
Oxford, 14, 19, 21, 76, 172, 174

P
Pace, Richard, 4, 19, 215
Padua, 5, 7, 9, 10, 13, 15, 16, 17, 18, 19, 20, 33, 34, 35, 36, 59, 64, 71, 81, 83, 85, 86, 89, 94, 96, 98, 101, 103, 107, 163, 167, 171, 173, 177, 180, 216, 221, 228
Paffraet, Richard, 74, 195
Paganinis, Paganinus de, 181
Pagninus, Sanctes, *50–51, 62, 151, 161, 185

Palazzolo, Antonio, 96, 213
Palmieri, Matteo, 9
Palmieri, Nardo, 58, 112, 230
Paludanus, J., 137
Pandolfini, Pandolfo, 9
Pandolfini, Pier Filippo, 79, 100, 107, 198
Pandolfino, Filippo di Alessandro, 220
Pannonius, Janus, 63, 192, 214
Panormita, Antonio, 15, 16, 198
Papias, 218
Pardus of Corinth, Gregory, 35, 69, 121, 122, 129, 130, 146, 149, 159, 160, 161, 162, 166, 173, 190
Paris, 4, 6, 10, 11, 19, 20, 21, 22, 31, 35, 38, 42, 45, 47, 48, 50, 51, 59, 67, 68, 69, 70, 74, 77, 78, 85, 86, 90, 95, 97, 98, 102, 103, 104, 105, 106, 108, 113, 119, 172, 174, 179, 182, 194, 203, 222
Parma, 90, 105
Parrhasius, Janus, 228
Passio, Francesco, 90, 208
Patrizio, Giovanni, 108
Paulus Aegineta, 56
Pavia, 14, 17, 18, 81, 90, 100, 216, 231
Pazzi, Alessandro de', 108
Pellegrino degli Agli, 214
Perleone, Pietro, 164, 219
Perreonus, Joannes, 151
Persius Flaccus, Aulus, 191
Persona, Cristoforo, 10, 63, 192
Pertusi, Agostino, 7
Perugia, 34, 219
Peter of Crete, 5, 55, 79, 209, 217, 226
Petit, Guillaume, 160
Petrarca, Francesco, 55, 81, 99, 106, 203, 216
Peutinger, Conrad, 42, 182, 226
Peutinger, Johann, 209
Pforzheim, 45
Phalaris, Letters of, 189
Pherecydes, 109
Philolaus of Croton, 77, 127, 197
Philostratus, Lucius Flavius, 177, 189, 205, 206
Philymnus, Thilonius, 85
Photius (Patriarch), 60
Phrynichus Arabius, 55, *60, 159, 161, 162, 173, 190
Piacenza, 64
Piccolomini, Enea Silvio, 75, 207
Pico della Mirandola, Giovanni Francesco, 36, 123, 129
Pierleoni, Pietro, 4
Piero Egineta, 188
Pierre d'Angleberme, 203
Pietro da Montagnana, 7, 9, 13, 64, 82, 89, 103, 104, 106, 155, 165, 208
Pilato, Leonzio, xii, 81, 104, 106, 201, 202, 221
Pimpinella, Vicenzo, 228
Pincianus, Joannes, 226
Pindar, 50, 102, *108–9, 113, 185, 217, 218, 220, 225
Pindar 'Thebanus', 80
Pio, Alberto, 33, 156, 223, 227
Pio, Leonello, 33
Pirckheimer, Willibald, 11, 45, 57, 58, 59, 61, 83, 86, 87, 90, 91, 110, 181, 183, 202, 203, 206, 207, 209, 213, 217, 228
Pirondolo, Nicola, 166
Pisa, 14
Piso, Battista, 127, 157
Pius, Baptista, 228
Pius II (pope), 218
Planudes, Maximus, 17, 77, 133, 137, 138, 139, 196, 197, 199, 206, 219
Platina, Bartolomeo, 89, 98, 208, 215
Plato, 4, 27, 33, 55, 77, *99–100, 101, 113, 115, 216, 217, 231
Plautus, Titus Maccius, 228
Pliny the Elder, 196
Plutarch of Chaeronea, 27, 28, 81, 94, 97, 99, 113, 158, 194, 206, 210, 216
Pluyette, Adam, 49, 148
Poggio Bracciolini, 92, 99, 193, 232
Poitiers, 32
Poland, 31, 34
Policastro, 15, 170
Poliziano, Angelo, 4, 5, 17, 18, 30, 56, 58, 59, 77, 78, 80, 82, 83, 89, 96, 97, 102, 103, 109, 110, 122, 160, 165, 172, 178, 189, 197, 198, 204, 208, 217, 218, 219, 220, 224, 227, 230, 231
Pollio, Symphorian, 42
Pollux, Julius, 55, *58, 157, 159, 188, 189
Pomponio Leto, Giulio, 120, 227
Poncher, François, 160
Pontano, Giovanni, 15
Portinari, Pier Francesco (Portinarius), 159
Posidippus, 130
Potken, Joannes, 141
Priscian (Priscianus Caesariensis), 8, 31
Proclus, philosopher, 14, 50, 169, 201
Proclus, saint, 179
Procopius of Caesarea, 59
Prousinouscus, J., 149
Psalter, 62, 64, *75–76, 96, 115, 119, 127, 141, 151, 182, 193, 196, 200
pseudo-Basil, 134

pseudo-Cebes, 124, 127, 130, 134, 145, 146, 197, 210
pseudo-Cyril, 41, 63, 65, 66, 67, 79, 155, 156, 157, 159, 160, 161, 162, 192
pseudo-Herodotus, 152, 154, 200, 214
pseudo-Libanius, 123
pseudo-Orpheus, 27, *110–11, 201, 202, 227, 228, 229
pseudo-Phocylides, 74, *77–79, 85, 121, 123, 124, 125, 126, 127, 129, 130, 131, 134, 140, 142, 145, 151, 197, 198, 219, 224
pseudo-Plutarch, 130, 134, 145, 146, 159, 160, 161, 162, 175
pseudo-Pythagoras. See *Aurea verba*
pseudo-Tryphon, 120, 121, 124, 129, 130, 134, 145, 149, 162
pseudo-Zonaras, 56, 192, 194
Ptolemaeus of Siena, Lactantius, 158
Publilius Syrus, 77

Q
Questenberg, Jacobus, 79
Quintilianus, Marcus Fabius, 2, 79, 80, 90, 91, 94, 96, 163, 211
Quintus of Smyrna, 1, *111–13, 199–200, 202, 229, 230, 231
Quirini, Lauro, 56, 59, 190

R
Ravanis, Petrus de, 145, 162
Reading, 19
Regensburg, 11
Reggio, 10, 80
Regiomontanus, Johannes, 16, 76, 171
Renier, Daniel, 36, 40
Renouard, Antoine Auguste, xii
Reschius, Conrad, 146
Rescius, Rutger, 21, 23, 91, 93, 137, 211
Reuchlin, Johann, 1, 5, 11, 13, 18, 19, 23, *31–33, 40, 41, 44, 45, 49, 57, 58, 59, 80, 85, 91, 92, 93, 95, 107, 110, 113, 128, 136, 157, 165, 167, 169, 172, 179, 182, 188, 194, 197, 199, 204, 207, 210, 212, 224, 228
Rhaxes, Nicolaus, 193
Rhenanus, Beatus, 22, 23, 59, 138, 141, 174, 182, 204, 209
Rheningen, Johann, 128
Rhodes, 26, 58, 101, 186, 225
Rhosos, Joannes, 10, 16, 58, 60, 78, 82, 107, 170, 171, 188, 191, 197, 202, 220
Rhusotas, Immanuel, 16, 64, 171, 193
Rianus, Christopher, 22, 87

Riccio, Bernardo, 187
Rinuccini, Alamanno, 97
Rinuccio Aretino, 79, 80, 88, 99–100, 199, 217
Rithaimer, Georg, 49, 149
Robert of Siciliy, 219
Rome, 15, 16, 18, 32, 34, 43, 56, 58, 60, 89, 92, 97, 98, 100, 104, 105, 107, 108, 109, 110, 116, 169, 170, 171, 172, 176, 179, 191, 218, 221, 222, 223, 224, 226, 228
Rosenperger, Johann, 34, 179
Rossetus, Petrus, 85
Rossi, Roberto de', 7, 94, 99, 232
Rousseus, Carolus, 125
Rovere, Giovanni Francesco della, 39
Rudolfinger, Johann, 42
Ruellius, Joannes, 186
Ruffus, Bartolomaeus, 151
Rullus, Joannes, 52, 154

S
Sabellico, Marcantonio, 36
Sabio, Stefano da, 63, 162
Saccano, Ludovico, 13, 64, 101, 201
Sacco, Cato, 221
Sainte Geneviève, monastery of, 49
Saint Magloire, monastery of, 49
Salandus, Joannes, 156
Salutati, Coluccio, 6, 7, 55, 81, 86, 98, 100, 165, 166, 200, 205, 213, 215, 232
San Giovanni a Piro, monastery of, 15
San Giovanni in Verdara, monastery of, 7, 13, 59, 64, 208
San Ildefonso, college of, 78
San Marco, monastery of, 59, 197, 223
Sannazaro, Jacopo, 108
San Niccolò di Casole, monastery of, 1
San Salvatore, monastery of, 5, 27, 56
Santa Justina, monastery of, 5
Santa Maria degli Angeli, monastery of, 107
Sassuolo da Prato, 73, 120, 190, 209
Savevsius, Humbert, 160
Scala, Alessandra di Bartolomeo, 107
Schedel, Hartmann, 34, 71, 101, 167, 180
Schlecta, Johann, 34
Scholarios, George, *12–13, 14, 15, 30, 32, 89, 169
Schott, Johann, 133, 207, 232
Schumann, Valentine, 73
Schurer, Lazarus, 143
Schurer, Matthias, 128, 132, 134, 138
Scinzenzeler, Joannes Angelus, 57

Scotti, Girolamo, 108
Scutariota, Joannes, 10, 64, 78, 82, 110, 167, 197, 201, 217, 225, 227
Scybenardus, Petrus, 45, 183
Sebastopoulos, Manuel, 13
Secer, Johann, 91, 141, 210
Secundinus, Nicolaus, 94, 212
Selling, William, 17, 171, 201
Senile, Cipriano, 202
Serbopoulos, Joannes, 19, 76, 96, 173, 186
Sernisius, Christophorus, 134
Sessa, Melchior, 145, 162
Sforza, Francesco, 26
Sforza, Gian Galeazzo, 177
Sforza, Ippolyta, 27
Sforza, Ludovico, 57, 187
Sgouropoulos, Demetrius, 11, 168
Shirwood, John, 16, 171
Siberch, John, 86
Sicily, 1, 5, 13, 14, 28, 30
Siena, 74, 108
Sigeros, Nicolaus, 203
Silva, Miguel, 158
Simler, Georg, xi, 11, 32, 33, *40–42, 45, 46, 128, 129, 182
Sixtus IV (pope), 186
Smyrna, 231
Soissons, 47
Solomon, 93
Soncino, Gershom, 57
Sophianos, Nicolaus, 31
Sophianos, Theodore, 13
Sophocles, xi, 57, 104, 105, *106–8, 188, 217, 218, 221, 223, 224
Souliardos, Michael, 60, 78, 191, 197
Sozomeno. *See* Zomino
Spain, 11, 35, 87, 92, 97, 116
Spiegel, Jacobus, 128
Sponheim, 34
Stapulensis. *See* D'Étaples
Stephanus of Byzantium, 55, *60–61, 156, 157, 159, 191
Stobaeus, Joannes, 191
Strabo, 227
Strasbourg, 11, 12, 42, 43, 44, 77, 87, 97, 102, 116, 182
Strategos, Caesar, 59, 186, 189, 191
Strazelius, Jean, 87
Strozzi, Alessandro, 66
Strozzi, Bartolomeo, 9
Strozzi, Palla, 4, 5, 8, 13, 15, 17, 76, 81, 94, 99, 100, 101, 102, 106, 108, 164, 165, 168, 196, 216, 225, 232

Strozzi, Piero degli, 196
Stuttgart, 33, 44
Suda lexicon, 4, 28, 35, *55–57, 59, 64, 69, 77, 116, 156, 158, 159, 164, 175, 177, 186, 187, 188, 224, 229
Sylvius, Dominicus, 10, 168
Syncellus, Michael, 17, 134, 143, 151, 152, 167, 171
Synesius of Cyrene, 182

T

Taberio, Giovanni, 61, 156, 191
Tedaldo della Casa, 81, 200, 205
Terentianus Maurus, 64, 194
Tertullianus, Quintus Septimius Florens, 121
Theocritus, 77, *102–4, 113, 125, 133, 198, 201, 212, 217, 219, 220, 221
Theodoricus, Matthias, 80, 199
Theodosius of Alexandria, 5, 8, 28, 164
Theognis of Megara, 77, 130, 197, 219
Theophrastus, 67, 68, 157
Thesaurus cornucopiae, 41, 68, 83, 122
Thessalonica, 13
Thorer (Torinus), Alban, 12, 153, 226
Thucydides, 32, 36, 179, 206, 224
Thytes, Angelo, 221, 223
Tifernas, Gregorio, 27, 31, 56, 101, 176, 178, 217, 218, 230
Tissard, François, 10, 85, 102, 103, 105, 106, 125, 126, 167
Tomeo, Niccolò Leonico, 35, 36, 86, 206
Torinus. *See* Thorer
Tornabuoni, Lorenzo, 202
Torre (Turrianus), Giovanni Francesco della, 18, 64, 80, 155, 156
Tortelli, Giovanni, 5, 13, 15, 63, 76, 88, 106, 207
Toussain, Jacques, 19, 23, 49, 154, 172, 196, 222
Traversari, Ambrogio, 58, 61, 64, 75, 76, 79, 92, 115, 163, 188, 193, 196, 200, 209, 210, 214, 216, 217, 223, 228
Trebelius Notianus, Hermannus, 127
Tricaelius, Joannes Maria, 66, 127, 157
Trino, Giovanni da, 40
Triphiodorus, 217, 226
Trissino, Giangiorgio, 202, 212
Trithemius, Johannes, 34, 76, 80
Trivizias, Georgius, 18, 58, 60, 109, 171, 188, 190, 191, 223, 226
Trivolis, Demetrius, 170, 190, 229
Tröster, Johannes, 11
Tübingen, 11, 32, 40, 44, 45, 74, 95

Tudor, Henry, later Henry VIII of England, 86
Tunstall, Cuthbert, 20, 59, 83, 110
Tutor, James, 37
Tzetzes, Joannes, 217

U
Ugoleto, Taddeo, 56, 90, 208
Ulpian of Ascalon, 157, 162
Urbanus, Henricus, 58, 59
Urbicius. *See* Orbicius
Urbino, 219
Urceo, Antonio Codro, 65, 78, 82, 102, 169, 194, 198, 208, 218, 219

V
Vadius, Angelus, 187
Valagussa, Giorgio, 89, 96, 208, 213
Valdo, Agosto, 110, 228
Valeriano, Pierio, 36, 38, 129, 215
Valerianus, Philippus, 42
Valerius Flaccus Setinus Balbus, Gaius, 110, 111, 227
Valla, Giorgio, 10, 13, 18, 27, 78, 101, 107, 110, 167, 169, 172, 176, 194, 198, 210, 216, 218, 223, 227, 229
Valla, Lorenzo, 79, 92, 94, 176, 199, 212
Valle, Niccolò della, 101-2, 201, 218
Variscus, Joannes, 181
Vatable, François, 10, 129, 136
Vatel, Jean, 23, 24, 145, 147, 149, 154
Vatican Library, 13, 19, 56, 59, 60, 70, 89, 104, 107, 108, 163, 165, 170, 186, 205
Velareus, Jodocus, 231
Venice, 1, 2, 7, 11, 12, 19, 20, 25, 30, 31, 33, 34, 36, 38, 39, 40, 41, 57, 58, 59, 60, 80, 85, 86, 91, 92, 95, 96, 98, 102, 103, 105, 107, 108, 109, 110, 111, 119, 171, 173, 178, 201, 210, 218, 230
Vergara, Francisco, 87, 92, 95, 97
Vergara, Juan, 78
Vergerio, Pier Paolo, 8, 81, 98, 99, 100, 216, 232
Vergil, (Publius Vergilius Maro), 47, 65, 76, 218, 228
Vespasiano da Bisticci, 9, 63, 193
Vespucci, Amerigo, 167
Vespucci, Giorgio Antonio, 167
Vettori, Francesco, 9
Vicens, Antonius, 20, 173
Vicenza, 30, 78, 163
Victorius, Petrus, 134
Vidovaeus, Petrus, 68, 69, 146, 159

Vienna, 34, 42, 49, 84, 199
Vigrammius, Gregorius, 42
Vincent, Augustine, 84
Virgilio, Marcello, 214
Virunio, Pontico, 10, 37, 57, 66, 86, 116, 123, 127, 188
Vitali, Francesco, 16, 78, 198
Vitelli, Cornelio, 19
Vittorino da Feltre, 5, 14, 56, 76, 79, 82, 88, 90, 92, 96, 101, 102, 104, 109, 164, 192, 195, 196, 200, 207, 209, 210, 212, 213, 217, 221, 226
Vives, Ludovicus, 25, 213
Volmar, Melchior, 12, 25, 31, 36, 85, 151
Volta, Giovanni, 215
Vratislava, 52, 98
Vuinshemius, Vitus, 96, 213

W
Walder, Johann, 14, 15
Warham William, 143
Wechel, Chrestien, 150
Widersdorf, Stephan, 42
Wiesendanger. *See* Ceporinus
Winckler, Andreas, 52, 154
Winther, Johann, 12, *51-51, 85, 152-53
Winther, Thomas, 186
Wittenberg, 46, 73, 84, 87, 91, 95, 98, 102, 104, 221
Wolfgang of Bavaria, 157
Wurmser, Nicolaus, 182

X
Xanthopoulos, Demetrius, 56, 201, 202, 230
Xenophon, 77, *91-93, 195, 196, 209, 210, 213, 228
Ximenes (Jimenez), Francisco (Cardinal), 51, 185
Xylotectus, Petrus, 151

Z
Zabarellis, Franciscus de, 200
Zacharides, Emmanuel, 194
Zambeccari, Pellegrino, 86, 205
Zamberti, Bartolomeo, 78, 107, 198, 213
Zanetellis (Zenoteles), Thomas Didymus Feltrinus de, 60, 191
Zeno, Antonio, 220
Zenoteles. *See* Zanetellis
Zomino (Sozomeno) of Pistoia, 9, 63, 100, 101, 166, 193, 217
Zurich, 50, 102, 185
Zwingli, Ulrich, 50, 109, 147

www.ingramcontent.com/pod-product-compliance
Lightning Source LLC
Chambersburg PA
CBHW050740110426
42814CB00006B/311